CHILDBIRTH AND THE LAW

CRIME, REASON AND HISTORY

Childbirth and the Law

JOHN SEYMOUR

With a Foreword by
The Honourable Madam Justice Lynn Smith
Supreme Court of British Columbia

OXFORD
UNIVERSITY PRESS

OXFORD
UNIVERSITY PRESS

Great Clarendon Street, Oxford OX2 6DP

Oxford University Press is a department of the University of Oxford.
It furthers the University's objective of excellence in research, scholarship,
and education by publishing worldwide in

Oxford New York

Athens Auckland Bangkok Bogotá Buenos Aires Calcutta
Cape Town Chennai Dar es Salaam Delhi Florence Hong Kong Istanbul
Karachi Kuala Lumpur Madrid Melbourne Mexico City Mumbai
Nairobi Paris São Paulo Singapore Taipei Tokyo Toronto Warsaw

and associated companies in Berlin Ibadan

Oxford is a registered trade mark of Oxford University Press
in the UK and certain other countries

Published in the United States
by Oxford University Press Inc., New York

British Library Cataloguing in Publication Data

Data available

Library of Congress Cataloging in Publication Data

Data available

Seymour, John (John A.)
Childbirth and the law / John Seymour.
p. cm.
Includes bibliographical references and index.
1. Obstetrics—Law and legislation. 2. Fetus—Legal status, laws, etc. 3. Pregnant
women—Legal status, laws, etc. 4. Obstetricians—Malpractice. 5. Childbirth. I. Title.
K4366 .S47 2000
342'.085—dc21 00–037460

ISBN 0–19–826468–2

1 3 5 7 9 10 8 6 4 2

Typeset in Times
by Jayvee, Trivandrum, India
Printed in Great Britain
on acid-free paper by
T. J. International Ltd., Padstow, Cornwall

For Heather

Foreword

Lawyers, judges, legal academics, medical practitioners and ethicists, health care providers, and policy makers, are all deeply in the debt of Professor John Seymour. In producing *Childbirth and the Law* he has accomplished several objectives, each of which on its own constitutes a feat of scholarship.

First, he has thoroughly researched and described the judge-made and statutory law relating to childbirth in four common-law jurisdictions: Australia, Canada, the United Kingdom, and the United States. Second, he has analysed existing approaches to the extremely difficult issues that arise in this area: for example, should there be a 'balancing of interests' between a pregnant woman and her fetus in connection with attempts to impose medical treatment against her consent or to restrict her substance abuse? Should an obstetrician or midwife view herself as having one patient or two? Third, Professor Seymour has advanced a model that has roots in some aspects of existing case law and theory but that greatly advances the discussion, a model of the woman and fetus as 'not-one-but-not-two' and of the woman as entitled to full human autonomy. Finally, and very impressively, he has stepped outside the legal frame. Particularly in his concluding chapter but indeed throughout the book, Professor Seymour has recognized and delineated limitations of the law as a means of resolving some of these issues.

This book will not only provide a valuable resource for those who want to know that the law *is* (it is meticulously researched, clearly written and scrupulously referenced) but also will provide insight and inspiration for those who want to continue to think through what the law *should be* (it is comprehensive and fair in its description of existing positions and forcefully eloquent in its delineation of the author's suggested approach).

To say that this book has filled a gap is like saying that childbirth is an important event — a serious understatement.

The Honourable Madam Justice Lynn Smith
Supreme Court of British Columbia

Preface and Acknowledgements

My research in the field of childbirth and the law began as a result of a request by the Australian Medical Association to inquire into the legal position of a doctor responsible for the care of a pregnant woman who declines medical intervention. The resulting inquiry required an examination of a number of other legal questions of concern to those who practise obstetrics and mid-wifery. The outcome of the inquiry was a report, *Fetal Welfare and the Law*, published in Canberra in 1995. The focus of this report was necessarily limited and I was conscious of the need for a more comprehensive study of the legal problems arising in the context of childbirth. This book attempts to fill this need.

No work of this kind can be completed without the assistance, advice, and support of numerous friends and colleagues. I am grateful to all those who helped me. These include: Susan Bewley, Peter Birks, Peter Cane, Kathleen Daly, Katrine Del Villar, John Devereux, Gillian Douglas, John Eekelaar, Jane Fortin, David Feldman, Andrew Grubb, Arthur Herbst, John Keown, Bartha Knoppers, Ian Kennedy, Edward Keyserlingk, John McLaren, Derek Morgan, Niki Lacey, Helen Newnham, Ngaire Naffine, Michael Peek, Margaret Vennell, and Alison Harvison Young. I offer them my thanks. Special thanks are due to Keith Barnes, who originally suggested that I undertake work in this field, and to Jim Davis who read draft chapters and dealt most patiently with my numerous requests for information on matters of tort law.

I was particularly fortunate to have Ben McGuire assisting me in the final stages of the preparation of the book. He has a keen eye for stylistic clumsi-ness and made many valuable suggestions as to the style and shape of the book. He also offered many astute comments on its substance. I am most grateful for his contribution.

I frequently needed assistance on the technical aspects of word processing and on the formatting of the manuscript. I am grateful to Rado Faletic, Ron Middleton, and Wendy Forster for providing this. I also offer my thanks to Richard Hart for his advice on the submission of the proposal for the book and to Mick Belson and Sally McCann for their editorial help.

Finally, I gratefully acknowledge the assistance of my wife, Heather. She read the manuscript, advised on medical details, prepared the Glossary of Medical Terms, and assisted with the preparation of the Table of Cases and the Index. More important, she provided encouragement and support during the four years that I spent working on the book.

The legal analysis offered in this book is based on material available to me prior to 31 October 1999. Since that date, there has been at least one major judicial decision. In *McFarlane v Tayside Health Board* [1999] 3 WLR 1301, the House of Lords re-examined the law relating to the assessment of damages following the unwanted birth of a normal child. As well as being authoritative in the United Kingdom, this decision may prove influential in Canada and Australia.

Contents

Table of Cases

1

Introduction

This book explores the law's impact on pregnant women, their fetuses, and the doctors and midwives who care for them. This impact might be felt during pregnancy or after a child's birth. During a pregnancy, the law might seek to protect the fetus. After the birth, if negligent antenatal or perinatal care has caused harm, the legal system might be called on to respond to a claim for damages by the parents and child.

Chapter 2 reviews the significant body of case law in which courts have been asked—and have occasionally agreed—to sanction intervention designed to protect the fetus. Such proceedings have most commonly been taken when a pregnant woman's use of an illegal drug threatens to harm the fetus or her decision not to consent to medical treatment (such as a caesarean section) poses a risk that the fetus will be stillborn or born with disabilities. The law's scope for antenatal intervention is limited in comparison with its role when medical negligence has caused harm for which parents and children seek damages. The operation of the law of negligence in the fields of obstetrics and midwifery is the subject of Chapters 3 to 7. The most obvious forms of harm that can be caused by negligent care during pregnancy or at the time of delivery are the birth of an injured or disabled child or a stillbirth or perinatal death. There are other circumstances in which damages claims can arise. Although the child is normal and healthy, the birth may be unwanted and if it can be ascribed, for example, to a negligently performed tubal ligation, the parents may sue. Further, if the child is born suffering from a genetic abnormality, damages can be sought on the ground that the doctor or midwife should have warned the parents of the risk and so allowed them to avoid the birth.

An examination of the desirability of legal intervention in the situations discussed in Chapter 2 raises a number of interrelated issues. First, there is the question of the legal status of the fetus; in particular, whether it has rights that the law will protect. This subject is dealt with in Chapter 8. Secondly, if a fetus has rights, it must be asked whether there are any circumstances in which these rights may override those of the woman. Contemplation of this possibility requires a discussion of the autonomy of a pregnant woman. If this is absolute, there can be no grounds for legal action to control or coerce her. Thirdly, whatever the conclusions reached on these theoretical issues, it is necessary to scrutinize the techniques and resources available to the law. Although there might be many who support the view that society should do its best to protect the fetus and to ensure the safe delivery of a healthy child, they might also conclude that coercive intervention does not offer an appropriate method of pursuing this goal. The subjects of the autonomy of a pregnant woman and the role of the law during pregnancy and at the time of delivery are examined in Chapter 9.

The remainder of the book focuses on the operation of negligence law. The legal problems brought before the courts in medical malpractice actions following childbirth are varied and complex. These actions raise questions about the way in which the principles of negligence law are applied. In particular, it is difficult to define the nature of the duty of care a doctor or midwife owes to a pregnant woman. To what extent does this duty include an obligation to take account of the welfare of her fetus? Attention must also be given to the fact that the climate in which obstetrics and midwifery are being practised is changing. Many pregnant women are now reluctant to rely on medical advice. Indeed, some see medical intervention as unnecessary in the context of the natural process of childbirth. This attitude has important implications. If women accept greater responsibility for the management of their own deliveries, their opportunities for suing those who provide antenatal and perinatal care may diminish. Alternatively, negligence actions may still be brought, but they might increasingly rest on the claim that the woman's choice was made on the basis of inadequate information. The woman's argument will be that, if she had been better informed, she would have followed the medical advice. We therefore encounter another facet of a pregnant woman's exercise of her autonomy: autonomy can be effectively exercised only if the actor has the information necessary to make informed choices.

Negligence claims resulting from obstetric misadventures thus raise difficult issues of principle. These are examined in Chapter 10. A further problem arises from analysis of negligence that harms a fetus. If a woman's conduct during pregnancy results in her child being born with injuries or disabilities, might she be liable to a damages claim by that child? To ask this question is to probe another of the implications of a woman's exercise of her autonomy during pregnancy. Should she be immune from legal intervention not only during pregnancy, but also after the birth of her child? This issue is discussed in Chapter 11.

While of considerable theoretical interest, the subject of maternal liability to damages claims is of less importance than the practicalities of actions against doctors and midwives. They are naturally concerned about the application of the law to their day-to-day practices. They need to know what is expected of them and what they must do to avoid liability to damages claims. These practical matters are the subject of Chapter 12. To put this discussion into context, it is necessary to consider policy questions about the efficiency, effectiveness, and appropriateness of the use of the law of negligence to compensate parents and children when they suffer harm as a result of poor antenatal or perinatal care. Some of these questions are considered in Chapter 13. This analysis reinforces the view that there is reason for scepticism as to the capacity of the law satisfactorily to resolve many of the problems that arise in the context of pregnancy and childbirth. This theme is explored in the concluding chapter.

Two qualifications must be added regarding the scope of this book. It does not set out to contribute to the debate on abortion. While it is obviously impossible to discuss the legal status of the fetus without referring to abortion (the topic is discussed in Chapter 8), this study is primarily concerned with the fetus that a pregnant woman carries to full term. Readers with an interest in the arguments for and against abortion should look elsewhere. A similar point must be made about the rapidly expanding field of medically assisted reproduction. No attempt has been made to deal with the legal questions arising in this field.

Since this book focuses on the law's impact on pregnancy and childbirth and it is written by a lawyer, it is necessary to acknowledge the incompleteness of lawyers' accounts of medical matters. A large number of court cases will be discussed. The way these are presented and analysed will irritate many readers who practise obstetrics and midwifery. These practitioners may feel that the accounts of these cases do not capture the reality of the events that gave rise to the proceedings. This is because the evidence on which court judgments are based is shaped for a particular purpose. Reports of medical malpractice matters, in particular, tend to provide selective accounts of what happened. This is an inevitable product of the adversarial system. At a trial, expert witnesses on one side will emphasize certain aspects of the case and those on the other side will emphasize different aspects. Plaintiffs and defendants will seek to present themselves in the best light. At the end of this process, a court must make findings of fact and it should not be forgotten that such findings are at best the court's 'belief or opinion about someone else's belief or opinion'.[1] In addition, many of the matters discussed in this book are reports of appellate court proceedings and hence reflect the operation of another process of selection; by its nature, an appeal focuses on certain aspects of a trial and ignores others. Finally, the way the cases have been summarized in this book may further distort the accounts of what happened. The result is a series of narratives that may provide only a partial indication of what occurred.

Part I of the book is purely descriptive; it seeks to identify the more important features of the current law in England, the United States, Canada, and Australia. Part II is analytical; it examines the broader implications of the law's intervention in the life of a pregnant woman and her newborn child.

---

[1] J. Frank, *Courts on Trial* (Princeton, 1949) 22.

Part I

The Current Law

2

Legal Intervention when a Fetus is Threatened or Harmed

This chapter examines how the law in the United States, Canada, and England has responded to parental behaviour which threatens the welfare of a fetus or causes it harm.[1] The aim of the various legal procedures discussed is to protect the fetus. This aim can be pursued in different ways and at different stages of the antenatal and perinatal period. During a woman's pregnancy, the law may be invoked in an attempt to prevent threatened harm. The same purpose may be pursued at the time of delivery. Alternatively, legal action might be taken immediately after the birth of an impaired child. At first sight, it may seem odd to regard postnatal intervention as a means of protecting the fetus, but it is possible for the law to take action after the event in order to express society's disapproval of certain conduct and so to seek to deter its repetition. In dealing with this aspect, the chapter will not consider the law relating to any damages claim that may be brought in respect of *in utero* harm. This subject will be discussed in Chapters 3 to 7.

MATERNAL CONDUCT OCCURRING DURING PREGNANCY

The law has frequently been used in an effort to prevent a pregnant woman engaging in conduct that threatens to harm her fetus. Particular attention has been paid to conduct such as ingesting alcohol or an illicit drug. Less common are cases in which women have declined antenatal care or have failed to observe the need for an adequate diet.

Child Protection Proceedings — Before Birth

Most of the cases in which action has been taken against pregnant women have been brought to court by way of neglect, dependency, or care proceedings. The nature of these actions (referred to as 'child protection proceedings') requires explanation. In all the countries examined, it is open to welfare authorities to take legal action designed to safeguard children from abuse or neglect. If successful, the action can result in state intervention, such as parental counselling and supervision, or a child's removal from home. Proceedings in which such actions have been taken against pregnant women

---

[1] There are no reported Australian cases.

have been based on the argument that the operation of child welfare laws should extend to the unborn and that conduct which puts the fetus at risk should be treated as child abuse or neglect.

In the United States such arguments have generally not been accepted. In *Cox v Court of Common Pleas*,[2] the woman, who was seven months pregnant, was a known drug user and had taken cocaine and opiates throughout her pregnancy. She had failed numerous drug screening tests during this time. She had also refused antenatal care. Her partner was a drug user and did not encourage her to seek proper care. Their four children were with foster parents, pending a decision as to their custody. Juvenile court proceedings were taken; the court exercised its neglect jurisdiction and ordered the woman not to use illegal drugs and to submit to a medical examination to determine the health of the fetus. When she failed to obey the order, the welfare authorities sought to have her committed to a secure drug treatment facility. The woman successfully challenged the juvenile court's order. The sole question was whether this court could exercise control over a pregnant woman for the benefit of her fetus. The majority of the Ohio Court of Appeals held that it could not.

Similar results have been reached in Michigan and California. *Re Dittrick*[3] involved a woman who, together with her partner, was suspected of having physically and sexually abused their first child. When she again became pregnant, court proceedings were taken and these resulted in an order granting a welfare agency temporary custody of the 'child'. The order was challenged and the Michigan Court of Appeals accepted the argument that the relevant child welfare statute did not apply to a fetus. The woman in *Re Steven S*[4] suffered from a psychiatric condition and her behaviour during her pregnancy was thought to be threatening the fetus. A juvenile court had accepted that the fetus was a child in need of care and had ordered the woman's detention in hospital until after the birth. On appeal it was held that the child welfare legislation did not apply to a fetus and could not provide a basis for detaining a pregnant woman to protect it.

The decisions reached in such cases reflect the view that a reference in a child protection statute to a 'child' does not apply to a fetus.[5] This does not mean, however, that a statute cannot be drafted to apply to a fetus. This course has been taken in Minnesota, for example, where legislation was enacted to authorize intervention to prevent drug use during pregnancy. Under the Act, health care professionals are required to advise a child welfare agency if they suspect that a woman is using illegal drugs during

---

[2] 537 NE 2d 721 (Ohio App, 1988).
[3] 263 NW 2d 37 (1977).   [4] 178 Cal Rptr 525 (1981).
[5] *Re Ruiz* 500 NE 2d 935 (Ohio Com Pl, 1986) — a case involving proceedings brought *after* the child's birth — adopted the contrary view, ruling that a viable fetus affected by the mother's heroin use was 'an abused child' for the purposes of Ohio's child abuse statute.

pregnancy. The agency must assess the situation and offer help; if this is refused, the agency can seek the woman's admission to a treatment facility.[6] The New Jersey legislation is expressed in broader terms. In setting out the procedure to be followed when a child is endangered, the Act states that the procedure can be used 'on behalf of an unborn child'.[7]

The contribution of the Canadian courts in this area is illustrated by three cases, of which the first was decided in 1987. The proceedings occurred in two stages. An application in respect of a pregnant woman was made under Ontario's child protection legislation on the ground that the woman had refused to submit to a full medical examination to determine the health of her fetus. It was held that a fetus could be found to be in need of protection; on the facts of the case, however, it was decided that there was insufficient evidence to establish the need at the time of the hearing.[8] A second application—reported as *Re Children's Aid Society and T*—was made two days later. The woman's condition was continuing to cause concern; it was suspected that the fetus was suffering from a potentially fatal infection and the woman still declined to seek medical care. In addition, she was described as behaving in an 'erratic' fashion. The Children's Aid Society was successful in its application for an order declaring that the 'unborn child' was a child in need of protection under Ontario's Child and Family Services Act 1984. The judge concluded that there was 'a possibility that this child will not be born alive, or that the child, although born alive, would be born with certain health defects'.[9] It was ordered that the fetus be made a ward of the Society for three months (this brought it under the Society's protection).

A different result was reached in *Re A (in utero)*.[10] The woman in this case was in an advanced stage of pregnancy. The family's situation was most unsatisfactory. All four children were state wards and proceedings had been taken to terminate their parents' access to them. The father, who was described as 'a very violent man', had a substantial criminal record and had threatened a member of the Children's Aid Society when she visited. The home was in a filthy condition. The parents would not co-operate with arrangements that had been made for the woman to receive antenatal care. Her condition was causing concern as she was suffering from moderately severe toxaemia with the attendant risk of eclampsia. Having had its offers of assistance rejected, the Children's Aid Society took court proceedings seeking an order that the 'unborn child' be placed under the supervision of the Society, that the mother be required to attend regularly for antenatal

---

[6] Minn Stat § 626.5561 (1998).   [7] NJ Stat § 30:4C–11 (1999).

[8] These proceedings are unreported. For an account of them, see S. Tateishi, 'Apprehending the Fetus *En Ventre Sa Mere*: a Study in Judicial Sleight of Hand' (1989) 53 Saskatchewan Law Review 113, 120–3 and S. Martin and M. Coleman, 'Judicial Intervention in Pregnancy' (1995) 40 McGill Law Journal 947, 959.

[9] (1987) 59 OR (2d) 204, 205.   [10] (1990) 72 DLR (4th) 722.

care, and that she make arrangements to go to a hospital for delivery. Alternatively, the Society sought an order that if the woman failed to accept supervision the 'unborn child' be made a ward of the Society and the woman be 'detained in hospital until the birth of the child and to undergo all necessary medical procedures for the well-being of the unborn child'.

The Ontario Family Court heard the case. The question was whether the court had authority to intervene to protect the fetus. First, the relevant child welfare legislation (Ontario's Child and Family Services Act 1984) was considered. The court ruled that this statute did not give it the power to intervene: 'I . . . cannot find anything in the definition of "child" . . . [or in] any other provision in the Act which would accord to the foetus any status as a person or right to protection under the Act.'[11] This did not end the matter. By the time of the hearing, the mother was virtually at full term and this fact caused the court concern. It was pointed out that there was still the question 'whether the court must remain passive in light of the apparent facts of this case which indicate that unless the mother obtains proper pre-natal care and proper medical care on the delivery of the foetus, there may be irreparable harm visited upon it'.[12] The judge later observed:

[The fetus has] developed virtually all the attributes of a person in law, without in fact being one. As such, the foetus in this case may truly be likened to a person under a disability, and perhaps deserving of some protection. It also seems to me that the mother, having opted to give life to the foetus, and having raised it to full term, has a duty to ensure that the balance of her pre-natal care and the child's birth be effected in a proper manner having regard to her apparent medical problems. This is simply a reflection of the mother's natural duty in such circumstances.[13]

The significance of this analysis requires explanation. The judge was considering the possibility of invoking powers other than those available in statutory child protection proceedings. He was contemplating the exercise of the *parens patriae* jurisdiction. This is an ancient jurisdiction which can be utilized in the interests of persons (such as children and the mentally disabled) who are unable to protect themselves; hence the reference to the fetus in this case as being similar to 'a person under a disability'. The Children's Aid Society had argued that the fetus should be regarded in this way and therefore asked the court to exercise its *parens patriae* powers. It was urged that these powers could be used in respect of a fetus 'in the advanced stages of pregnancy'. This argument was not accepted. Although the judge was tempted to intervene, he reluctantly concluded that he could not do so:

[H]ere the child is actually inside of the mother. It is, therefore, impossible in this case to take steps to protect the child without ultimately forcing the mother, under restraint if necessary, to undergo medical treatment and other processes, against her

---

[11] (1990) 72 DLR (4th) 722, 728.   [12] Ibid. 729.   [13] Ibid. 730.

will. I believe that the *parens patriae* jurisdiction is just not broad enough to envisage the forceable [*sic*] confinement of a parent as a necessary incident of its exercise. Even if it were, however, the court should be very wary about using its powers in such instances, as its routine exercise could possibly lead to some abuse of pregnant mothers.[14]

Thus the court expressly rejected the dual arguments that a fetus could be protected by treating it as a 'child' for the purposes of child protection legislation or by invoking the broad protective jurisdiction conferred by the *parens patriae* power.

The possibility of state intervention against a pregnant woman was more fully examined in *Winnipeg Child and Family Services (Northwest Area) v G.*[15] The case arose following a court order that a woman who was five months pregnant with her fourth child be placed in the custody of the Winnipeg Director of Child and Family Services and be detained at a health centre until the birth of her child. The purpose of the order was to protect the fetus, which was at risk of damage from the woman's glue sniffing. Previously, two of her children had been born seriously affected by the woman's addiction to glue sniffing; the proceedings had been taken in an attempt to prevent a repetition of this outcome. When the trial court's order was set aside on appeal, the welfare agency in turn appealed to the Supreme Court of Canada. For the purposes of this chapter, the major issue was whether the trial court had the power—under its *parens patriae* jurisdiction—to make an order designed to protect the fetus.[16] The Supreme Court ruled that it did not. It adopted the analysis employed in *Re A (in utero)* and held that: 'The law as it stands is clear: the courts do not have *parens patriae* or wardship jurisdiction over unborn children.'[17] It followed that 'the common law does not clothe the courts with power to order the detention of a pregnant woman for the purpose of preventing harm to her unborn child'.[18]

As in some parts of the United States, the relevant law in Canada is not to be found only in the decisions of the courts. In two Provinces, the legislatures have taken action to protect the fetus. In New Brunswick, the Child and Family Services and Family Relations Act 1980 defines 'child' as including an 'unborn child'. The effect of this is to allow child protection proceedings to be taken in an effort to safeguard a fetus. This occurred in one case involving a

---

[14] Ibid. 731–2.   [15] (1997) 152 DLR (4th) 193.

[16] In addition to proceedings under the *parens patriae* jurisdiction, the welfare agency sought an injunction to restrain the woman from breaching her duty of care to the fetus. The Supreme Court refused to accept the existence of such a duty. This aspect of the case is more fully discussed below, 285–6.

[17] (1997) 152 DLR (4th) 193, 215. The court also relied on the decision in *Re F (in utero)* [1988] 2 WLR 1288.

[18] (1997) 152 DLR (4th) 193, 219. Note, however, the dissenting judgment in which it was accepted that 'the state has an enforceable interest in ensuring, to the extent practicable, the well-being of the unborn child' (ibid. 220).

pregnant woman whose children were subject to custody or supervision orders and who was thought to be unable to care for them adequately. The welfare authorities obtained a six-month supervisory order with respect to the woman. This required her to be attended by a public health nurse, to consult a physician on a regular basis, to discuss with a social worker her plans for the child, and to give birth at a hospital.[19]

A different approach was taken in the Yukon. Section 133 of the Children's Act 1986 provides:

Where the director [of Family and Children's Services] has reasonable and probable grounds to believe and does believe that a foetus is being subjected to serious risk of being subjected to foetal alcohol syndrome or other congenital injury attributable to a pregnant woman subjecting herself during pregnancy to addictive or intoxicating substances, the director may apply to a judge for an order requiring the woman to participate in such reasonable supervision or counselling as the order specifies in respect of her use of addictive or intoxicating substances.

This section is designed to protect a fetus that is imperilled when a pregnant woman is taking alcohol or any addictive or intoxicating drug. There is at least one reported instance of its use.[20] Unlike the approach adopted in New Brunswick, the law in the Yukon does not provide for the taking of child protection proceedings: s 133 is a free-standing provision designed to deal with a particular type of maternal behaviour. Its drafting is loose; it is not clear what types of obligations and controls may be imposed on a pregnant woman pursuant to an order to participate in 'reasonable supervision or counselling'.

There has been no legislative intervention in England to protect the fetus and there are no reported cases in which it has been argued that the statute governing care proceedings (The Children Act 1989 (UK)) should apply to fetuses. In the light of the decision in *Re F (in utero)*,[21] it is unlikely that such an argument would succeed. The case concerned a pregnant woman who had suffered from severe mental disturbance for about ten years, accompanied by sporadic drug use. She had lived a nomadic existence in several European countries and had no means of support other than social security. The welfare department was concerned about the condition of the fetus and brought an application to have it made a ward (and so brought under the court's protection). The Court of Appeal decided that a fetus could not be the subject of wardship proceedings:

---

[19] *Minister of Health and Community Services v AD* (1990) 109 NBR (2d) 192.

[20] *Joe v Director of Family and Children's Services (Yukon)* (1986) 1 YR 169. The case is of little relevance, as it was confined to the issue of whether the absence of an accepted definition of 'foetal alcohol syndrome' meant that the section violated s 7 of the Charter of Rights and Freedoms.

[21] [1988] 2 WLR 1288.

In wardship proceedings the court is exercising a parental jurisdiction in which the paramount consideration is the child's welfare. But in the case of an unborn child the only orders to protect him or her which the court could make would be with regard to the mother herself. Thus in the first place there would have to be an order authorising [a court official] to find the mother. Then perhaps an order that she should live in a certain place and probably attend a certain hospital. All of these would be restrictive of the mother's liberty. Further, there could well be medical problems which would have to be solved: the mother might wish one course of action to be taken; it might be in the interests of the child that an alternative procedure should be followed. Until the child is actually born there must necessarily be an inherent incompatibility between any projected exercise of wardship jurisdiction and the rights and welfare of the mother.

The judgment also underlined other practical problems:

I think that there would be insuperable difficulties if one sought to enforce any order in respect of an unborn child against its mother, if that mother failed to comply with the order. I cannot contemplate the court ordering that this should be done by force, nor indeed is it possible to consider with any equanimity that the court should seek to enforce an order by committal.[22]

Child Protection Proceedings — After Birth

While the courts have been reluctant to permit child protection proceedings to be taken against a pregnant woman in an attempt to prevent a fetus from suffering harm, there has been no such reluctance to use these proceedings after a child has been born showing the ill-effects of antenatal behaviour. There have been several cases in the United States, Canada, and England in which evidence of antenatal harm has been admitted by a juvenile or family court faced with the task of deciding whether a child's situation required protective intervention. It is important to understand the concerns of a court acting in this way. The harm to the fetus has already occurred; a court taking this fact into account does so in order to assess the possibility of future harm to the child. The purpose is to determine whether the child needs protection in the form of support and supervision or, in extreme cases, removal from home.

The reported cases have usually concerned children born suffering the effects of maternal drug or alcohol abuse during pregnancy. In some, the details of the woman's conduct and its impact on the fetus have formed no more than a part of the evidence put before a court to support a claim that the child's parent or parents were unable to provide adequate care. In others, the evidence of substance abuse was the foundation on which the allegation rested. An example of a case in the first category was *Re 'Male' R*.[23] The

---

[22] Ibid. 1298 and 1301.   [23] 422 NYS 2d 819 (1979).

mother had taken barbiturates, cocaine, and alcohol during her pregnancy. The baby was born suffering from mild withdrawal symptoms and neglect proceedings were instituted. While there was some discussion of the fact that the child had been born with an impairment as a result of his mother's drug use, other factors were also emphasized. The mother refused to remain in a drug treatment programme and it was suggested that she was incapable of caring for the child while under the influence of drugs. The antenatal drug abuse was part of a pattern that indicated that the child would be in imminent danger of harm if allowed to remain with his mother. All the evidence therefore supported the conclusion that the child was a 'neglected child'.

In contrast, several cases have sought to determine the significance of antenatal drug taking when examined in isolation. *Re Baby X* involved neglect proceedings relating to a baby who began showing symptoms of drug withdrawal within twenty-four hours of birth. The mother's antenatal drug use was regarded by the Court of Appeals of Michigan as establishing neglect: 'We hold that a newborn suffering narcotics withdrawal symptoms as a consequence of prenatal maternal drug addiction may properly be considered a neglected child...'.[24] The court therefore affirmed the decision of the lower court to take the baby into temporary custody. Similarly, in *Re Troy D* (where the child was born suffering from the effects of amphetamines and opiates), the Californian Court of Appeal stated that: 'The fact that [the child] was diagnosed as being born under the influence of a dangerous drug is legally sufficient for the juvenile court to exercise jurisdiction.' The drug use indicated that the child was at risk and that protective intervention was needed: 'To enable juvenile courts to protect drug-exposed infants and to compel parents to undergo drug rehabilitation therapy and to afford child protection services to the family, courts must be able to assert jurisdiction over infants born at risk because of prenatal exposure to dangerous drugs.'[25] The juvenile court's order placing the child in foster care was approved. This course has not been adopted in all such cases. Some courts have refused to accept that evidence of antenatal drug use necessarily establishes that a child is neglected. In a New York decision relating to a child who was born affected by cocaine, the evidence of the mother's use of the drug was regarded as insufficient to show that the child was in such danger as to be a 'neglected child'.[26]

A different situation arose in *Re Smith*.[27] Unlike the cases in which children were born suffering drug withdrawal symptoms, here there was no clear evidence that the fetus had been harmed. During the course of the pregnancy the mother had drunk heavily; she had been advised to seek treatment for her

---

[24] Mich App, 293 NW 2d 736, 739 (1980).
[25] 263 Cal Rptr 869, 872 and 873 (Cal App 4 Dist, 1989).
[26] *Re Fletcher* 533 NYS 2d 241 (Fam Ct, 1988).   [27] 492 NYS 2d 331 (Fam Ct, 1985).

alcohol abuse, but had failed to do so. Also, she had not obtained antenatal care, other than arranging one appointment two days before the child's birth. When the child was born, there was no more than a possibility that the drinking had caused harm. The question was thus whether the child could be found to be neglected solely on the basis of the mother's antenatal conduct. It was held that the evidence of alcohol abuse and of the failure to obtain antenatal care was sufficient to support that conclusion. As in so many of these proceedings, the ruling was in fact a prediction: in this case, that the child of a confirmed alcoholic was unlikely to receive adequate care and was therefore in need of protective intervention.[28]

A Canadian case that also dealt with alcohol abuse was *Re Children's Aid Society for the District of Kenora and JL.*[29] The child was born with fetal alcohol syndrome; the mother had failed to seek help for her alcohol problem during pregnancy. It was held that her antenatal drinking could be taken into account in assessing the likelihood that the child would receive proper care. There were also other factors. The family had no permanent home, both parents had a long history of alcohol abuse, and there was no prospect of improvement. As it was clear that the parents could not provide adequate care for the child, she was made a ward of the Children's Aid Society. Another Canadian decision, *Re Superintendent of Family and Child Service and McDonald,*[30] was notable for the judge's emphatic statements on the subject of drug abuse. The mother had been a heroin addict since the age of 12. Between the ages of 23 and 25, she had intermittently participated in a methadone replacement programme, but had also taken other drugs. At 25 she gave birth to a drug-addicted child. Proudfoot J stated: 'From the evidence before me of the physical problems that a baby born drug-addicted has to endure, it would be incredible to come to any other conclusion than that a drug-addicted baby is born abused. That abuse has occurred during the gestation period.' It was therefore held that the child fell within the definition of 'a child in need of protection'.[31] Such a child could be in need of protection from the time of birth. The judge ordered that the child remain with the mother, but under the close supervision of the Superintendent of Family and Child Service, and that the mother should receive daily homemaker services, daily visits by a social worker, and three visits per week by a community health nurse.

In some parts of the United States, the view that antenatal drug use that affects the child is itself indicative of abuse or neglect has been legislatively endorsed. This is seen in a number of child protection statutes. For example, in Oklahoma, a child born dependent on a controlled substance can be dealt

---

[28] See also *Re Stefanel Tyesha C; Re Sebastian M* 556 NYS 2d 280 (AD 1 Dept, 1990); *Re Valerie D* 595 A 2d 922 (Conn App, 1991).

[29] (1981) 134 DLR (3d) 249.   [30] (1982) 135 DLR (3d) 330.   [31] Ibid. 335.

with as a 'deprived child'. In Illinois, a newborn infant whose blood, urine, or meconium contains any amount of a controlled substance can be considered a 'neglected' child.[32] The Indiana law goes further and includes in the definition of a 'child in need of services' a child born with fetal alcohol syndrome or with any amount of a controlled substance in his or her body, or one who is 'at a substantial risk of a life threatening condition' arising from the mother's use of alcohol or a controlled substance during pregnancy.[33]

D (a minor) v Berkshire CC[34] provided an example of an English court ordering intervention in respect of a child whose mother's drug abuse during pregnancy caused the child to be born drug dependent. The child was taken from the mother at birth and placed in hospital. The House of Lords ruled that when considering whether a child is in need of care, a juvenile court may take account of the period before birth to determine whether at the time the proceedings began the child's health or development was being avoidably impaired. It was held that the court's task is to assess the child's present and future situation. When this task is undertaken, evidence of maternal drug abuse—though not decisive—is relevant. This approach differs from that adopted in a number of the United States and Canadian cases discussed above, in which the courts were willing to accept that the antenatal drug use was sufficient to establish that the children were in need of protective intervention.

Criminal Proceedings—Before Birth

It is possible, although uncommon, for the criminal law to be utilized against a pregnant woman to control her and so safeguard her fetus. For example, it is open to a court sentencing a pregnant drug user to make a probation order and to include a condition that she enrol in a drug rehabilitation programme. Alternatively, a sentence of imprisonment may be imposed with a view to ensuring that the woman ceases to take drugs and receives medical care. This course was adopted in Washington, DC, in a case in which the defendant was convicted of cheque forgery.[35] She was a pregnant cocaine user. The judge sentenced her to a jail term to expire after she had given birth. He was reported as saying: 'She's apparently an addictive personality, and I'll be darned if I'm going to have a baby born that way.'[36]

Rather different was *People v Pointer*,[37] in which the Californian Court of Appeal dealt with a woman convicted of child endangerment. The charge had arisen as a result of the serious harm caused to her two children by her

---

[32] 10 Okl St § 7001–1.3 (1998); 325 ILCS 5/3 (1999).
[33] Burns Ind Code Ann § 31-34-1-10 and 31-34-1-11 (1999).   [34] [1987] 1 AC 317.
[35] The case is discussed in K. Jost, 'Mother Versus Child' 75 American Bar Association Journal (April 1989) 84, 88.
[36] Ibid.   [37] 199 Cal Rptr 357 (Cal App 1 Dist, 1984).

adherence to a macrobiotic diet. As she had made it clear that she would continue to adhere to her diet, it was feared that should she again conceive, her fetus would be at serious risk. She was sentenced to a five-year term of probation and one of the conditions of the order was that she should not conceive during the probationary period. On appeal, it was held that the condition, though reasonable, was 'over-broad' and that the protection of the fetus could be achieved by less restrictive means. The matter was remanded to the trial court for re-sentencing and it was suggested that a more appropriate condition would be a requirement to submit to pregnancy testing and to monitoring, should she be found to be pregnant. While the case does not illustrate the imposition of controls designed to protect a fetus (since the woman was not pregnant), it does indicate that the appellate court was prepared to use the criminal law in an attempt to prevent antenatal harm.

Criminal Proceedings — After Birth

More common than cases in which the criminal law has been used against pregnant women are those in which women have been prosecuted after the birth of children who have been affected by antenatal conduct. The majority of these cases have involved children who have been born drug-addicted. When the criminal law is invoked in this situation, the aim is not to protect the child from further harm — the damage has already been done *in utero* — but, by punishing the woman, to express society's condemnation of her antenatal behaviour and to deter her and other women from behaving similarly in future. The difficulty faced by those who believe that women who ingest drugs should be made criminally responsible for the harm done to the fetus is the identification of an appropriate charge. This has led to ingenious, but generally unsuccessful, attempts to extend the operation of the criminal law.

In a number of cases involving drug-addicted neonates, the mothers were charged with 'supplying' or 'delivering' drugs. In Georgia, a woman who had taken cocaine during her pregnancy was charged with delivering drugs to her daughter. The charge was dismissed on the ground that the purpose of the law was to punish the supply of drugs to another 'person' and that a fetus was not a 'person'.[38] This reflected the view that a fetus does not become a 'person' until it has been completely delivered from the body of its mother.[39] Accepting this interpretation of the law has led some prosecutors to lay charges based on the argument that the 'supply' or 'delivery' of the drugs occurred in the short period after birth (when the fetus had become a person), but before the umbilical cord was cut. This tactic was employed in *Johnson v State of Florida*.[40] The case dealt with an appeal by a woman who

---

[38] *State v Luster* 419 SE 2d 32 (Ga App, 1992).
[39] This aspect is discussed in Chapter 8.   [40] 602 So 2d 1288 (Fla, 1992).

had been convicted on two counts of delivering cocaine to her children; on each occasion the delivery of the drug was alleged to have occurred in the sixty to ninety seconds before the umbilical cord had been severed. The Supreme Court of Florida overturned the convictions on the ground that the law forbidding the supply of drugs was not intended for the prosecution of pregnant women. In the court's opinion, it had not been the intention of the legislature to criminalize the passing of a drug through the umbilical cord: '[T]he Legislature never intended for the general drug delivery statute to authorize prosecutions of those mothers who take illegal drugs close enough in time to childbirth that a doctor could testify that a tiny amount passed from mother to child in the few seconds before the umbilical cord was cut.'[41] A similar conclusion was reached in *People v Hardy*, where the Court of Appeals of Michigan described a charge formulated in this way as 'tenuous'.[42]

An alternative means of bringing a woman before a criminal court when her baby has been born addicted to drugs is to charge her with abusing, neglecting, or endangering a fetus. This tactic raises the question already encountered in the context of child protection proceedings: do laws designed to safeguard 'children' apply to fetuses? The Supreme Court of South Carolina has held that they do. In *Whitner v State of South Carolina*,[43] the court ruled that a woman who had taken cocaine during pregnancy, and whose child was born affected by the drug, had been properly charged under a statute that punished a person who endangered the life or health of a 'child'. This seems to be an isolated case; the court did not cite any other decisions in which such a statute had been interpreted in this manner. In other reported cases involving the antenatal ingestion of drugs, courts have held that a reference to a 'child' in a statute proscribing child abuse, neglect, or endangerment does not include a fetus. In *State of Ohio v Gray*, for example, a charge against a mother after she had given birth to a cocaine-affected baby was dismissed for this reason. The Supreme Court of Ohio held that the offence of creating a substantial risk to the health or safety of a 'child' cannot be committed by antenatal conduct. The fetus did not become a 'child' until she had been born.[44] The same result was reached in *Reyes v Superior Court*,[45] where a mother was charged with the felony of endangering her child by her conduct in continuing to take heroin during her pregnancy (despite being warned) and by her conduct in failing to seek antenatal care. She gave birth

[41] 578 So 2d 419, 424 (Fl App 5 Dist, 1991); adopted in 602 So 2d 1288, 1294 (Fla, 1992).
[42] 469 NW 2d 50, 52 (Mich App, 1991).   [43] 492 SE 2d 777 (SC, 1997).
[44] 584 NE 2d 710 (Ohio, 1992). See also *People v Morabito* 580 NYS 2d 843 (City Ct, 1992) (charge of child endangerment); *State of Florida v Gethers* 585 So 2d 1140 (Fla App 4 Dist, 1991) (charge of aggravated child abuse); and *Commonwealth of Kentucky v Welch* Ky, 864 SW 2d 280 (1993) (charge of child abuse).
[45] App, 141 Cal Rptr 912 (1977).

to twins addicted to heroin and suffering withdrawal symptoms. The court dismissed the charge, holding that the relevant section of the Penal Code did not apply to conduct endangering a fetus.

A more complex matter was *People v Stewart*.[46] There the woman was charged on the basis that her actions during pregnancy contributed to her child's death. A doctor had advised the defendant, who was in the eighth month of her pregnancy, that she had placenta praevia and that she should seek immediate medical assistance if she started bleeding. She was also advised to abstain from sexual intercourse. She allegedly had intercourse and took marijuana and amphetamines; she started bleeding twelve hours before she arrived at the hospital. She subsequently gave birth to a severely brain-damaged son, who died less than two months later. She was charged under s 270 of the California Penal Code with failing to provide medical care to a child. The prosecution specified three grounds for the charge: Stewart's alleged use of illegal drugs during her pregnancy, disregarding her doctor's instruction not to have sexual intercourse, and her alleged failure to go to the hospital promptly when bleeding began. The judge ruled that s 270 was not intended to impose a duty on a pregnant woman and the charge did not proceed.

In some parts of the United States, there have been proposals for legislation to extend the operation of the criminal law to cover a woman's behaviour during pregnancy. The Colorado Bill, for example, provided for a woman taking drugs during pregnancy to be charged with child abuse upon the birth of the child, while Bills introduced in Georgia, Louisiana, and Ohio sought to make it a felony to give birth to a drug-addicted child.[47] In Canada, too, the use of the criminal law has been contemplated. In 1989 the Law Reform Commission of Canada proposed the creation of new crimes against the fetus. One of the recommendations was that a woman who 'purposely causes . . . serious harm' to her fetus should be criminally liable.[48] This recommendation was not implemented.

CONDUCT BY A THIRD PARTY

In some of the cases discussed, the courts have referred to the conduct of the woman's partner; his alcoholism or drug taking, for example, can be taken into account in child protection proceedings initiated after the birth of an

---

[46] The case is described in L. A. Schott, 'The Pamela Rae Stewart Case and Fetal Harm: Prosecution or Prevention?' (1988) 11 Harvard Women's Law Journal 227.

[47] M. P. Spencer, 'Prosecutorial Immunity: The Response to Prenatal Drug Use' (1993) 25 Connecticut Law Review 393, 396.

[48] Law Reform Commission of Canada, *Crimes Against the Foetus* (Working Paper 58, 1989) 51.

impaired child. In this situation, the behaviour of the partner has obvious relevance in any decision as to whether protective intervention is required. In none of these matters, however, has the primary focus been on the antenatal conduct of the partner. Yet there are some circumstances in which legal action might be taken against him in an attempt to safeguard the fetus. This might be appropriate when he has assaulted his pregnant partner and caused or threatened harm to the fetus. Similarly, the criminal law can be invoked after an assault of this kind by a stranger. The problem with its use in this manner is that the laws punishing assault and homicide do not normally apply when the victim is a fetus. They are designed to punish those who harm a 'person' and a fetus does not become a 'person' until birth.[49]

There is nothing to prevent the enactment of legislation in an attempt to protect a fetus against attack by a third party. This has occurred in some parts of the United States and Australia. In Florida and Rhode Island, there are statutory provisions punishing the wilful killing of 'an unborn quick child', while in Indiana and Georgia feticide is a crime. The Californian law's definition of murder includes the unlawful killing of a fetus. A Minnesota Act has created a range of offences: murder or manslaughter of an 'unborn child' and assault on an 'unborn child'.[50] In Australia, Queensland has made it a crime unlawfully to assault a pregnant woman and to destroy the life of, or do grievous bodily harm or transmit a serious disease to, the 'child' before birth.[51] In Canada, another of the recommendations of the Law Reform Commission was that legislation be enacted to punish a person who 'recklessly or negligently causes destruction or serious harm' to a fetus.[52] The recommendation was not adopted.

WHEN MEDICAL INTERVENTION IS DECLINED

Before or at the time of delivery, a pregnant woman may decline to consent to recommended medical intervention. This may occur in a number of situations. A doctor might recommend antenatal screening or procedures to diagnose fetal abnormalities (such as amniocentesis, ultrasonography, chorionic villus sampling, or antibody screening). There are also circumstances in which the doctor may advise a blood transfusion, either for the mother or for the fetus (when it is rhesus sensitized). A further possibility is fetal surgery,

---

[49] This aspect of the law is more fully discussed in Chapter 8.

[50] Fla Stat § 782.09 (1998); RI Gen Laws § 11-23-5 (1998); Burns Ind Code Ann § 35-42-1-6 (1999); OCGA § 16-5-80 (1999); Cal Penal Code § 187 (1999); Minn Stat § 609.266, 609.2661-609.2665, 609.2671 (1998).

[51] Criminal Code (Qld), s 313(2).

[52] Law Reform Commission of Canada, *Crimes Against the Foetus* (Working Paper 58, 1989) 51.

such as bladder drainage. At any stage of the pregnancy, cervical cerclage may be thought advisable. At the time of the delivery, the doctor may recommend induction of labour, a forceps delivery, or a caesarean section. In some of these situations the effect of the woman's decision to withhold consent is impossible (or at least very difficult) to predict. There are others, however, in which a decision to decline intervention exposes the fetus to a well-recognized and statistically verifiable risk.[53] The question that such a decision poses is whether the law may be invoked to compel a competent woman to undergo recommended treatment which may maximize the chances of the safe delivery of a healthy baby. What is at issue here is the pregnant woman's express decision to decline a specific form of therapy; more is involved than an unwillingness to consult a doctor or to seek antenatal care.

In the United States the courts have, in the past, shown a willingness to override women's decisions. A 1987 survey of legal proceedings relating to obstetrical interventions indicated that court orders were granted in 17 of the 21 cases in which they were sought.[54] An early case concerned a pregnant woman, described as obese, angry, and uncooperative, who declined to consent to a caesarean section recommended for suggested fetal hypoxia. Her major reason for refusing was her fear of surgery. An emergency court hearing in the patient's room ended with an order that a caesarean section be performed.[55] The same result was reached in *Re Madyun*, despite the woman's desire for a natural delivery, based on religious beliefs, and her view that there was no danger to the baby or herself.[56] At the time the proceedings were begun, the woman had been dilated at 7 centimetres for 12 hours; her membranes had ruptured some 48 hours earlier. Her doctors thought there was a risk of fetal sepsis, which could result in brain damage or the death of the baby. The court ordered a caesarean section on the ground that the state had 'a compelling interest to intervene and protect the life and safety of the fetus'.[57] A healthy baby was delivered.

In some cases, the proposed intervention did not take the form of a caesarean section. In *Raleigh Fitkin-Paul Morgan Memorial Hospital v Anderson,*

[53] This aspect is discussed in Chapter 9.

[54] Fifteen of the twenty-one court orders sought were applications to perform caesarean sections (for various diagnoses, including fetal distress, previous caesarean, placenta praevia, Rh sensitization, and toxemia). Thirteen of these were obtained. In three cases, court orders for hospital detention were sought and two were obtained; both women were diabetic. In two cases, court orders were granted for intrauterine transfusions for Rh sensitization. See V. E. B. Kolder, J. Gallagher, and M. T. Parsons, 'Court-Ordered Obstetrical Interventions' (1987) 316 *New England Journal of Medicine* 1192.

[55] The case is discussed in W. A. Bowes and B. Selgestad, 'Fetal Versus Maternal Rights: Medical and Legal Perspectives' (1981) 58 *Obstetrics and Gynecology* 209, 209–211.

[56] *Re Madyun*; a report of the case appears as an appendix to *Re AC* 573 A 2d 1235, 1259 (DC App, 1990).

[57] Ibid. 1264.

the issue was whether a decision by a Jehovah's Witness to refuse a blood transfusion should be respected. The woman was thirty-two weeks pregnant and the medical testimony was as follows: 'The evidence establishes a probability that at some point in the pregnancy [the woman] will hemorrhage severely and that both she and the unborn child will die unless a blood transfusion is administered.' The trial court had refused to make an order requiring the woman to submit to a transfusion. The Supreme Court of New Jersey allowed an appeal against this decision: 'We are satisfied that the unborn child is entitled to the law's protection and that an appropriate order should be made to insure blood transfusions to the mother in the event that they are necessary in the opinion of the physician in charge at the time.'[58]

A similar approach was adopted in *Re Jamaica Hospital*, where it was held that intervention could be ordered in the case of a pregnant woman who had also refused a transfusion on religious grounds. At a bedside hearing, evidence was given that the woman (who was eighteen weeks pregnant) had suffered internal bleeding and needed a blood transfusion 'to stabilize her condition and to save the life of the unborn child'. There was testimony that the woman's condition was 'critical' and that the fetus was 'in mortal danger'. The trial judge ruled:

If her life were the only one involved here, the court would not interfere. . . . Her life, however, is not the only one at stake. The court must consider the life of the unborn fetus. . . . In this case, the state has a highly significant interest in protecting the life of a mid-term fetus, which outweighs the patient's right to refuse a blood transfusion on religious grounds.[59]

Crouse Irving Memorial Hospital Inc v Paddock [60] was a more complicated case involving a pregnant woman's need for a blood transfusion. She was anaemic and the placenta was on the anterior wall of the uterus. Her condition necessitated a caesarean section, to which she consented. Because of her religious beliefs, she was not willing to consent to a blood transfusion, should one have been needed. The hospital sought an order authorizing any necessary transfusion. Evidence was given that a caesarean section could entail blood loss and that excessive bleeding was especially likely because of the position of the placenta. The court authorized her doctors to give any necessary blood transfusions.

A different type of situation was considered in *Taft v Taft*.[61] There a woman in her fourth month of pregnancy had refused to undergo cervical cerclage because of her religious beliefs. The trial court had ordered that she submit to the procedure, in light of evidence that it was probable that she would miscarry if the operation were not performed. On appeal, the Supreme Judicial Court of Massachusetts refused to affirm the decision,

---

[58] 201 A 2d 537, 538 (1964).   [59] 491 NYS 2d 898, 899–900 (Sup, 1985).
[60] 485 NYS 2d 443 (Sup, 1985).   [61] 446 NE 2d 395 (Mass, 1983).

though it did not suggest that the court had lacked the power to make an order. Instead, it emphasized the insufficiency of the medical testimony. There was no expert evidence on the nature of the procedure, the risks that it posed for the woman and the fetus, or the risks that its non-performance posed for them. The court was left in doubt whether the procedure was 'merely desirable' or 'life-saving' and so the case for intervention had not been established.

In *Jefferson v Griffin Spalding County Hospital Authority*, the hospital sought an order authorizing the performance of a caesarean section. The procedure had been recommended because Mrs Jefferson had been diagnosed as having complete placenta praevia. Her doctors estimated that if a vaginal delivery was attempted, there was a 99 per cent chance that the fetus would die and a 50 per cent chance that the woman would die. Mrs Jefferson refused the caesarean section because of her religious beliefs. At an emergency hearing, the Georgia Superior Court authorized the use by the hospital of 'all medical procedures deemed necessary by the attending physician to preserve the life of the defendant's unborn child'.[62] The authorization envisaged the performance both of a sonogram (ultrasound) and a caesarean section. The woman and her husband appealed to the Supreme Court of Georgia and sought to have the trial court's order stayed. The application was refused. The court stated:

In denying the stay of the trial court's order and thereby clearing the way for immediate reexamination by sonogram and probably for surgery, we weighed the right of the mother to practice her religion and to refuse surgery on herself, against her unborn child's right to live. We found in favor of her child's right to live.[63]

A caesarean section was not performed and a healthy baby was delivered a few days after the hearing.[64]

A more comprehensive discussion of the issues is contained in the judgments of the District of Columbia Court of Appeals in *Re AC* (the Angela Carder case).[65] Angela Carder was first diagnosed as suffering from cancer at the age of 13. She underwent major surgery several times, together with multiple radiation treatments and chemotherapy. During a period of remission at the age of 27 she married and became pregnant. When she was approximately twenty-five weeks pregnant, she was admitted to hospital suffering from an inoperable tumour, which nearly filled her right lung. Two days later, when her condition had temporarily improved, she was asked if she really wanted to have her baby; she replied that she did. Her condition worsened and she was informed that her illness was terminal and that she would die

---

[62] Ga, 274 SE 2d 457, 458 (1981).　　[63] Ibid. 460.

[64] G. J. Annas, 'Forced Cesareans: The Most Unkindest Cut of All' (1982) 12(3) Hastings Center Report 16, 16.

[65] 573 A 2d 1235 (DC App, 1990).

within weeks. She agreed to palliative treatment designed to extend her life until at least her twenty-eighth week of pregnancy. She was told that her fetus would have a better chance of being born healthy if it survived until twenty-eight weeks. When again asked if she wanted to have the baby, she said 'something to the effect of "I don't know, I think so." '[66]

Her condition continued to deteriorate. The next morning a court was convened at the hospital in response to the hospital's request for an order relating to treatment. An obstetrician gave evidence as to the risks to the fetus if an immediate caesarean section was not performed. Another obstetrician testified that he would not feel comfortable intervening before twenty-eight weeks. Ms Carder was expected to die within twenty-four to forty-eight hours. She was heavily sedated and not able to carry on a meaningful conversation. There was no evidence before the court that she had consented to or even contemplated having a caesarean section before twenty-eight weeks. As she was unconscious, her wishes at the time of the hearing were not known and could not be ascertained. The court accepted that if an immediate caesarean section were performed, the chances of the fetus surviving were between 50 and 60 per cent. Citing the state's 'important and legitimate interest in protecting the potentiality of human life',[67] the court ordered the performance of a caesarean section. Ms Carder (who had regained consciousness) was informed by her doctors of the decision and initially agreed to the procedure. Later, she clearly mouthed several times, 'I don't want it done'. The court re-convened and heard evidence of the doctors' conversations with Ms Carder. After again finding that her wishes were not clear, the court once more ordered the caesarean section. An appeal was lodged, but the request for a stay was denied.[68] The caesarean was performed and the baby died a few hours afterwards. Angela Carder died two days later.

The hospital lodged an appeal in order to obtain a clarification of the law. Eight judges of the District of Columbia Court of Appeals heard detailed evidence from over one hundred interest groups, including health and women's rights lobbies. By a majority of seven to one, it was held that the trial court had erred. It had wrongly assumed that Ms Carder was incompetent. Further, if she had been incompetent, the judge should have done his best to ascertain what her wishes would have been, had she been able to express them. He should have made 'a substituted judgment on behalf of the patient, based on all the evidence'.[69] Only if there had been evidence as to her wishes should the question of overriding those wishes have been examined. In short, the trial court had been in too much of a hurry to consider the desirability of ordering the caesarean section; the importance of the preliminary inquiry to ascertain Ms Carder's wishes had been overlooked.

[66] 573 A 2d 1235, 1239.
[67] These words were quoted from *Roe v Wade* 410 US 113, 162; 35 L Ed 2d 147, 182 (1973).
[68] Reported as *Re A C* 533 A 2d 611 (DC, 1987).   [69] 573 A 2d 1235, 1249 (DC App, 1990).

Although this was the basis of the majority's judgment, the Court of Appeals offered some comments on compulsory intervention. These were made on the understanding that, because of Ms Carder's fluctuating condition, it was not possible to determine her views ('we simply cannot tell whether AC was ever competent, after being sedated, to make an informed decision one way or the other regarding the proposed caesarean section'[70]). Thus the case was not one in which there had been a competent refusal: '[T]here was no clear maternal–fetal conflict in this case arising from a competent decision by the mother to forgo a procedure for the benefit of the fetus.'[71]

The court favoured the view that normally a pregnant woman has the right to decide whether or not to consent to medical treatment: '[I]n virtually all cases the question of what is to be done is to be decided by the patient—the pregnant woman—on behalf of herself and the fetus.'[72] Further, it had reservations about invoking the law to override the decision of a competent woman. Nevertheless, it did not expressly state that a competent woman's refusal should never be overruled. The court noted, and did not express disapproval of, the decisions in *Raleigh, Jamaica Hospital, Crouse*, and *Jefferson*. The key word in the ruling is 'virtually'; it suggests that a woman's wishes should not prevail in all cases, but only in 'virtually all' cases. Later this was further explained: a court must abide by a patient's wishes 'unless there are truly extraordinary or compelling reasons to override them'. The court added: '[S]ome may doubt that there could ever be a situation extraordinary or compelling enough to justify a massive intrusion into a person's body, such as a caesarean section, against that person's will.'[73]

The dissenting judgment rejected this approach. It expressed disagreement with the 'very limited view' that the majority took as to the circumstances in which the rights of a pregnant woman could be overridden:

The state's interest in preserving human life and the viable unborn child's interest in survival are entitled . . . to more weight than I find them assigned by the majority when it states that 'in virtually all cases the decision of the patient . . . will control.' . . . I am concerned that the majority's emphasis on the 'extremely rare and truly exceptional' nature of the circumstances in which the unborn child's rights may prevail may move the law toward the extinguishment of the rights of unborn children in cases like *In re Madyun*.[74]

The difference is one of emphasis, for the majority judgment revealed some uncertainty. The importance of respecting the pregnant woman's rights was repeatedly stressed, but the court stopped short of absolutely rejecting compulsory intervention on behalf of a fetus. It did not 'quite foreclose the

---

[70] Ibid. 1247.   [71] Ibid. 1243.   [72] Ibid. 1237.
[73] Ibid. 1247 and 1252.   [74] Ibid. 1254 and 1257.

possibility that a conflicting state interest [here, the protection of the fetus] may be so compelling that the patient's wishes must yield'.[75]

The changed attitude signalled by the decision in *Re AC*—that normally a competent woman's decision to decline medical intervention should be respected—was also apparent in *Re Baby Boy Doe*.[76] The case involved a woman whose 36-week fetus was deteriorating as there was 'something wrong with the placenta' and the fetus was receiving insufficient oxygen. A caesarean section was recommended. Because of her religious beliefs, the woman declined to consent: 'given her abiding faith in God's healing powers, she chose to await natural childbirth'. The hospital sought a court order forcing the woman to undergo an immediate caesarean section. The application was refused and the refusal was affirmed on appeal. The woman later vaginally delivered 'an apparently normal and healthy, although somewhat underweight, baby boy'. Because of the importance of the issues raised, the Appellate Court of Illinois subsequently handed down a written judgment.

The court rejected the argument that the proper approach in a case of this kind was to balance the rights of the viable fetus against the right of a competent woman to choose the medical care which she deemed appropriate: 'We hold today that Illinois courts should not engage in such a balancing, and that a woman's competent choice in refusing medical treatment as invasive as a caesarean section during her pregnancy must be honored, even in circumstances where the choice may be harmful to her fetus.'[77] This ruling reflected the view that a caesarean section is so invasive that it should never be performed in the face of a competent refusal. In the court's opinion, it followed that *Jefferson* and *Madyun* had been wrongly decided. Such an analysis raises the question whether earlier decisions that had allowed less-invasive procedures to be performed without consent were also wrong. The court declined to answer this question. After noting that a blood transfusion had been ordered in *Raleigh*, the judgment stated: 'This and other similar blood transfusion cases are inapposite, because they involve a relatively non-invasive and risk-free procedure, as opposed to the massively invasive, risky, and painful caesarean section. Whether such non-invasive procedures are permissible in Illinois, we leave for another case.'[78]

The judgment in the leading Canadian case—which also arose following a woman's decision not to consent to a caesarean section—was primarily concerned with the correctness of the procedure employed. In *Re Baby R*, the physician had recommended a caesarean 'because of the likely complications with a natural birth and the real danger of injury to the child, or death,

---

[75] 573 A 2d 1235, 1252 (DC App, 1990).

[76] 632 NE 2d 326 (Ill App 1 Dist, 1994). Appeals to the United States Supreme Court were dismissed: 510 US 1032; 126 L Ed 2d 610 (1993) and 127 L Ed 2d 547 (1994). See also *Re Fetus Brown* 689 NE 2d 397 (Ill App 1 Dist, 1997).

[77] 632 NE 2d 326, 330 (Ill App 1 Dist, 1994).   [78] Ibid. 333.

with a normal birth.'[79] The Superintendent of the Department of Family and Child Services, relying on his powers under the British Columbia Family and Child Service Act 1980, had 'apprehended' the fetus; he thereby acquired the authority to consent to emergency medical treatment. It proved unnecessary to rely on the Superintendent's authorization, as the woman agreed to the performance of the caesarean and a healthy child was born. Subsequently, the intervention was reviewed, the issue being whether the fetus was a 'child' within the meaning of the Act. It was held that it was not and that the Superintendent therefore lacked the power to intervene. The British Columbia Supreme Court explained:

[T]he powers of the superintendent to apprehend are restricted to living children that have been delivered. Were it otherwise, then the state would be able to confine a mother to await her delivery of the child being apprehended. For the apprehension of a child to be effective there must be a measure of control over the body of the mother. Should it be lawful in this case to apprehend an unborn child hours before birth, then it would logically follow that an apprehension could take place a month or more before term.[80]

In 1992, the Family Division of the English High Court decided in favour of compulsory intervention. In *Re S (Adult: Refusal of Treatment)*,[81] a pregnant woman who had been admitted to hospital with ruptured membranes and who had been in labour for more than two days, was diagnosed as having a transverse lie; the elbow of the fetus was projecting through the cervix and the head was on the right side. Those responsible for the woman's treatment considered that the performance of a caesarean section was necessary. Because of her religious beliefs, the woman declined to consent to the caesarean. An application was made to the court for an order permitting the performance of the operation. Sir Stephen Brown, President of the Family Division, accepted the medical evidence that the woman's situation was 'desperately serious', as was that of the 'unborn child':

There is the gravest risk of a rupture of the uterus if the section is not carried out and the natural labour process is permitted to continue. The evidence of the surgeon is that we are concerned with 'minutes rather than hours' and that it is a 'life and death' situation. . . . The surgeon is emphatic. He says it is absolutely the case that the baby cannot be born alive if a Caesarean operation is not carried out.[82]

The court granted the application and made the necessary order. The operation was performed and the child was born dead. No principle can be extracted from the judgment, which was very brief. It was conceded that there was no English authority directly on the point. Reference was made to the decision of the District of Columbia Court of Appeals in *Re AC*. Reliance

---

[79] (1988) 53 DLR (4th) 69, 72.   [80] Ibid. 80.
[81] [1992] 3 WLR 806.   [82] Ibid. 807.

on this decision was plainly misconceived. As was explained earlier in the chapter, the majority expressed reservations about coercive intervention and explicitly stated that the case was not one in which there had been a competent refusal. Yet Sir Stephen Brown purported to rely on it in making the order.

That the ruling in *Re S* should not be regarded as authoritative in England was made clear by the Court of Appeal in *Re MB (Medical Treatment)*.[83] The court described it as 'a decision the correctness of which we must now call in doubt'.[84] Here a caesarean section was recommended because the fetus was in the breech position. The woman consented to the caesarean, but, because of her 'irrational fear of needles', declined to consent to the associated procedures. In particular, she refused to consent to an anaesthetizing injection. The hospital obtained a court order authorizing the performance of any necessary treatment. The woman appealed; the trial court's order was found to have been justified. On learning that her appeal had been dismissed, the woman co-operated and the caesarean section was successfully performed. In giving its reasons, the Court of Appeal found that, because of her 'needle phobia', the woman was incapable of making a decision; she was described as being 'temporarily incompetent'. On the basis of this finding, the court felt able to sanction the medical treatment that it considered to be in the woman's best interests. The finding of incompetence was crucial to the decision in *Re MB*. The court accepted that the decision of a competent woman should not be overridden:

A competent woman who has the capacity to decide may, for religious reasons, other reasons, for rational or irrational reasons or for no reason at all, choose not to have medical intervention, even though the consequence may be the death or serious handicap of the child she bears, or her own death. . . . If . . . the competent mother refuses to have the medical intervention, the doctors may not lawfully do more than attempt to persuade her. If that persuasion is unsuccessful, there are no further steps towards medical intervention to be taken.[85]

This conclusion was confirmed by the Court of Appeal in *St George's Healthcare NHS Trust v S*.[86] The case involved a 36-week pregnant woman who was diagnosed with pre-eclampsia and advised that she required immediate admission to hospital; she was told that her life and that of her fetus were in danger. The woman refused to go to hospital. She was articulate and intelligent; she understood the risks and was willing to run them. There seem to have been two reasons for her decision. She believed that pregnancy was a natural process and that any intervention should be avoided. She was also depressed: when one doctor pointed out that her baby might die, she responded that she was not interested in the pregnancy or the baby. Another doctor noted that the woman was 'profoundly indifferent to the fact that she

---

[83] [1997] 2 FLR 426.   [84] Ibid. 440.   [85] Ibid. 436–8.   [86] [1998] 3 WLR 936.

could die or be severely brain damaged if the pre-eclampsia [was] not treated'.[87] Her attitude led her doctors to suspect that she was suffering from a mental disorder and they therefore supported a social worker's application, made under the Mental Health Act 1983 (UK), that the woman be admitted to a mental hospital for assessment. This was granted and she was subsequently transferred to a general hospital, which then applied to the High Court for an order allowing it to undertake treatment. No evidence as to the woman's mental condition was offered to the court, which reached its decision on the basis that she was fully competent to decline treatment. An order was made dispensing with her consent. A caesarean section was perfomed. Though she did not physically resist, she made it clear, both orally and in writing, that she had not given consent to any medical treatment. The operation was successful and a healthy baby was delivered. Some time after her discharge from hospital, an appeal was lodged challenging the High Court's order authorizing the operation. The appeal was allowed:[88]

In our judgment while pregnancy increases the personal responsibilities of a woman it does not diminish her entitlement to decide whether or not to undergo medical treatment. Although human, and protected by the law in a number of different ways set out in the judgment in *In re M.B.* . . . an unborn child is not a separate person from its mother. Its need for medical assistance does not prevail over her rights. She is entitled not to be forced to submit to an invasion of her body against her will, whether her own life or that of her unborn child depends on it. Her right is not reduced or diminished merely because her decision to exercise it may appear morally repugnant. The [order] in this case involved the removal of the baby from within the body of her mother under physical compulsion. Unless lawfully justified this constituted an infringement of the mother's autonomy. Of themselves the perceived needs of the foetus did not provide the necessary justification.[89]

Later the court added: 'The caesarean section . . . (together with the accompanying medical procedures) amounted to trespass.'[90]

Thus there have been variations in the responses that the courts in the United States, Canada, and England have made to requests for the authorization of coercive intervention. There has also been uncertainty about the legal procedure to be employed when such requests are made. In a number of the United States cases, the applicants have invoked the court's *parens patriae* jurisdiction;[91] in some instances the court has directly authorized the

---

[87] Ibid. 945–6.

[88] Although lodged after the operation had been performed, the appeal was not fruitless. By allowing the appeal, the Court of Appeal opened the way to a damages claim against the hospital. It is interesting to speculate as to whether the hospital should have a defence to such a claim.

[89] Ibid. 957.   [90] Ibid. 967.

[91] See, for example, *Raleigh Fitkin-Paul Morgan Memorial Hospital v Anderson* 201 A 2d 537 (1964); *Taft v Taft* 446 NE 2d 395 (Mass, 1983); *Re Jamaica Hospital* 491 NYS 2d 898 (Sup, 1985); *Re Madyun* 573 A 2d 1235 (DC App, 1990); *Re Baby Boy Doe* 632 NE 2d 326 (Ill App 1 Dist, 1994).

medical intervention and in others the court has appointed a guardian (such as the doctor or a lawyer) for the fetus and empowered the guardian to give any necessary consent. On occasions, child protection proceedings have been taken in a juvenile court and temporary guardianship has been conferred on a welfare agency.[92] The leading Canadian case[93] was initiated by way of child protection proceedings. Sometimes the nature of the court's jurisdiction has not been made clear and the applicant has simply sought an order authorizing the performance of the procedure.[94] Alternatively, an application can be made for declaratory relief. This occurred in *Re A C*,[95] where the hospital sought a declaratory judgment. Similarly, in *Re S*,[96] *Re MB*,[97] and *St George's Healthcare NHS Trust v S*,[98] the courts were asked for declarations that the intervention was lawful. This recognized that any competent adult has the right to decline medical intervention. A doctor who treats such a person in the face of a refusal is liable for battery. An application for a declaration involves a request to a court to state that, in the special circumstances of the case, it will not be unlawful to proceed without consent. Finally, it should be noted that whatever procedure is employed, it is unusual for a court to *order* that intervention be undertaken. Normally, a court authorizes such intervention as is considered medically necessary. Whether the treatment is undertaken will depend on the clinical judgement of the doctor.[99]

ANTENATAL HARM: THE SCOPE OF THE LAW

One preliminary comment must be made before attempting to summarize the law's attitude to intervention designed to protect the fetus. This chapter has focused on the formal law, as developed in the higher courts. There may be many matters in which lower courts have sanctioned protective intervention. There may also be others that have not reached the courts and in which

---

[92] In *Jefferson v Griffin Spalding County Hospital Authority* Ga, 274 SE 2d 457 (1981), for example, the local welfare agency petitioned the juvenile court for temporary custody of the 'unborn child' on the ground that it was a deprived child without proper parental care. Temporary custody was granted to the agency, which was given authority to make all decisions and to give the necessary consent to a caesarean section.

[93] *Re Baby R* (1988) 53 DLR (4th) 69. There the trial court found the unborn child to be a child in need of protection (either because it was deprived of proper care or deprived of necessary medical attention); the Superintendent of Family and Child Services was given custody and guardianship of the unborn child and so was empowered to consent to the intervention.

[94] For example, *Crouse Irving Memorial Hospital Inc v Paddock* 485 NYS 2d 443 (Sup, 1985).

[95] 573 A 2d 1235 (DC App, 1990).   [96] [1992] 3 WLR 806.

[97] [1997] 2 FLR 426.   [98] [1998] 3 WLR 936.

[99] This approach is not invariably employed; the trial courts in *Re Madyun* and *Re A C* ordered that the caesarean sections be performed. It is interesting to speculate on the position of a doctor who, having been ordered by a court to undertake a specified procedure, decides not to proceed. It is unlikely that legal action would be undertaken against such a doctor.

the threat of legal intervention has been employed in order to impose controls designed to protect the fetus. One United States commentator has suggested that most cases of coercive medical treatment go unreported.[100] This is a field in which there may be a wide gulf between the formal law and day-to-day practices.

The great majority of the cases discussed have dealt with maternal conduct. Of these, many have been concerned with maternal alcohol or drug abuse. The courts have generally been unwilling to impose controls on pregnant women in an attempt to protect their fetuses against the adverse effects of alcohol or drugs. Whether the actions have taken the form of child protection or wardship proceedings, the courts except on rare occasions have ruled that a law designed to protect a 'child' from abuse or neglect does not confer protection on a fetus. The same conclusion is supported by the more authoritative decisions in proceedings in which the criminal law has been invoked after a child has been born suffering harm caused by antenatal conduct. These decisions suggest that prosecuting women who have used drugs or alcohol during pregnancy will fail; the better view is that a charge of abusing, endangering, or neglecting a 'child' is not appropriate when the victim is a fetus.

The fact that the courts have shown little willingness to intervene to protect the fetus from harmful conduct does not mean, however, that they have refused to respond when behaviour such as drug taking during pregnancy has caused harm. Account will be taken of such conduct in child protection proceedings brought after birth. Testimony as to drug abuse may be examined in isolation, but it is more likely to be viewed as part of the evidence which a court must consider in determining whether the child is in need of protective intervention. Either way, the information about past events will be used in an attempt to predict the likelihood of future harm.

The remaining category of cases in which legal action has been taken on behalf of the fetus is that in which women (often supported by their partners) have declined medical intervention during pregnancy or at the time of delivery. The courts have given varying answers when asked to sanction the use of compulsion. In a number of United States cases, judges have been willing to authorize treatment to which pregnant women have not consented. The significance of these decisions is uncertain. They have sometimes been based on questionable assumptions and the analysis employed has been perfunctory. It seems likely that in future the outcome of United States proceedings taken to allow the compulsory treatment of pregnant women will be determined on the basis of rulings in cases such as *Re AC* and *Re Baby Boy Doe*. While leaving the door open for some forms of compulsory intervention, the decisions

---

[100] L. C. Ikemoto, 'Furthering the Inquiry: Race, Class, and Culture in the Forced Medical Treatment of Pregnant Women' (1992) 59 Tennessee Law Review 487, 489.

in these cases indicate that normally the woman's decision must be respected. The leading English decisions have rejected the view that compulsion should be employed when a competent woman has declined intervention. In the most authoritative Canadian case, the court confined itself to an examination of the appropriateness of the procedure employed by the applicant.

The foregoing summary—which concentrates on judicial decisions—does not give a complete account of the relevant law. There is nothing to prevent the enactment of child protection statutes expressly designed to control behaviour that harms a fetus. Such legislation can include in the definition of child abuse or neglect the use of illegal drugs or alcohol during pregnancy. Laws of this kind have been enacted in some jurisdictions in the United States and Canada. Similarly, assault and homicide laws can be adapted to cover attacks in which the victim is a fetus. Statutes in some parts of the United States and Australia have done this.

The cases and legislation discussed in this chapter raise numerous questions, particularly with regard to the legal status of the fetus, the autonomy of pregnant women, and the proper role of the law in protecting fetuses. These issues will be discussed in Chapters 8 and 9. Before they are addressed, however, I shall examine the law relating to negligence actions against doctors and midwives.

3

Elements of a Negligence Action in Obstetrics and Midwifery

The previous chapter discussed the law's response when action was thought to be necessary to protect the fetus. In this and the following chapters, the focus shifts to the role of the law when antenatal or perinatal negligence has caused harm. This may occur in a number of situations. A woman may have suffered direct harm as a result of unsatisfactory care during pregnancy or at the time of delivery. In addition, she and her partner might be adversely affected by harm caused to the fetus. This harm might take the form of a still-birth or the baby's death soon after birth. A baby who survives might be in some way impaired. The impairment might be an *injury* (something from which it is possible to make a recovery) or a *disability* (involving long-term incapacitation).[1] Examples of injured children are those suffering from facial nerve palsy, forceps bruising, a fractured clavicle, or Erb palsy. A child born with cerebral palsy, brain damage, epilepsy, or paralysis suffers from a disability. Alternatively, the complaint might relate to the birth of an unwanted child, an outcome that might have been prevented if more adequate care or information had been provided.

In any of these circumstances, the parents or child might claim damages from a doctor or midwife on the ground that the harm has been caused by a failure to meet the required standard of care. Before dealing specifically with claims arising from antenatal or perinatal negligence, I shall outline the relevant principles that govern medical malpractice actions.

THE STANDARD OF CARE IN DIAGNOSIS AND TREATMENT

Setting the Standard

To bring a successful negligence action against a health care professional, a patient must prove that harm has been caused by a failure to provide the appropriate standard of care. It is for the court that hears the action to decide whether there has been such a failure. What criterion must it apply in reaching its decision? In one sense, the answer to this question is simple: the practitioner must display the standard of care expected of a competent member

---

[1] The distinction is discussed by J. Murphy, 'The Tortious Liability of Obstetricians for Injuries Sustained in Childbirth' (1994) 10 Professional Negligence 94.

of the relevant professional group. This, however, masks the fact that there is controversy as to the part that the members of the professional group should play in setting the standard. If, for example, doctors act in accordance with the practices approved by their peers, can it be assumed that they have met the required standard and are therefore protected against negligence claims? Or should the courts apply an independently formulated standard? What must be examined, therefore, is how the courts determine the levels of skill and expertise expected of those who undertake the tasks of diagnosis and treatment. Virtually all the cases to be discussed have involved doctors; the relevance of such cases to other health care professionals (such as midwives) will be examined later.

There is little variation in the way the required standard of care is defined by the courts in England, the United States, Canada, and Australia. Under the English law, the standard to be met is that of the ordinary skilled person exercising and professing to have that special skill.[2] This test has been adopted by the High Court of Australia.[3] Given the diversity in the United States jurisdictions, it is not possible to discover a principle universally accepted in that country. The situation is complicated by the fact that in many states there are legislative definitions of the standard of care which doctors must observe. Nevertheless, the following Kentucky Court of Appeals ruling is typical: '[A doctor is] under a duty to use that degree of care and skill which is expected of a reasonably competent practitioner in the same class to which he belongs, acting in the same or similar circumstances.'[4] The Canadian courts have used similar formulae. In the Ontario Court of Appeal, the standard was defined as follows: 'Every medical practitioner must bring to his task a reasonable degree of skill and knowledge and must exercise a reasonable degree of care. He is bound to exercise that degree of care and skill which could reasonably be expected of a normal, prudent practitioner of the same experience and standing.'[5] More briefly, in the words of the Supreme Court of Canada: '[Doctors] have a duty to conduct their practice in accordance with the conduct of a prudent and diligent doctor in the same circumstances.'[6] In some parts of the United States and Canada, the test has incorporated the 'locality rule', which requires that allowance be made for the type of community in which a doctor practises. It might be assumed, for example, that a country doctor should not be expected to provide the standard of care available in a large city. While it has not been universally

---

[2] *Bolam v Friern Hospital Management Committee* [1957] 1 WLR 582, 586. This formulation was accepted by the House of Lords in *Whitehouse v Jordan* [1981] 1 WLR 246, 258; *Maynard v West Midlands Regional Health Authority* [1984] 1 WLR 634, 638 and *Sidaway v Board of Governors of the Bethlem Royal Hospital* [1985] 1 AC 871, 897.

[3] *Rogers v Whitaker* (1992) 175 CLR 479, 487 (footnote omitted).

[4] *Blair v Eblen* Ky, 461 SW 2d 370, 373 (1970).

[5] *Crits v Sylvester* [1956] 1 DLR (2d) 502, 508.

[6] *Ter Neuzen v Korn* (1995) 127 DLR (4th) 577, 588.

abandoned, the rule has fallen into disfavour.[7] The tendency is to apply national standards, particularly in the case of specialists, whose accreditation is controlled by national bodies.

When considering how the law defines the standard of care applied in medical malpractice matters, it is important to appreciate the distinction between relying on customary practices and relying on acceptable practices.[8] There are obvious dangers in adopting the rule that the standard of care should be set by reference to doctors' usual practices; this could lead to the acceptance of substandard practices as the bench-mark. 'Negligence cannot be excused on the grounds that others practice the same kind of negligence.'[9] It is therefore preferable for the standard to be fixed on the basis of the level of competence reasonably expected of a doctor in the circumstances. Of the tests quoted above, those adopted in the United States and Canadian decisions reflect this view. This does not mean that the matter is free from doubt: there is still some support in the United States for the notion that a doctor who follows customary practices should be immune from liability.

Reference should also be made to a common misconception regarding the standard by which doctors should be judged. There are those who seek to distinguish between 'an error of judgement' of the kind which should not give rise to liability and an act or omission which can properly be regarded as negligent. That such a distinction is valueless was made clear by the House of Lords, in *Whitehouse v Jordan*, when it rejected a submission that a doctor facing a negligence claim had been guilty of no more than an 'error of judgement'.

[I]t is high time that the unacceptability of such an answer be finally exposed. To say that a surgeon committed an error of clinical judgment is wholly ambiguous, for, while some such errors may be completely consistent with the due exercise of professional skill, other acts or omissions in the course of exercising 'clinical judgment' may be so glaringly below proper standards as to make a finding of negligence inevitable.[10]

Merely to describe something as an error of judgment tells us nothing about whether it is negligent or not. The true position is that an error of judgment may, or may not, be negligent; it depends on the nature of the error. If it is one that would not have been made by a reasonably competent professional man professing to have the standard and type of skill that the defendant held himself out as having, and acting with

---

[7] See, for example, *Logan v Greenwich Hospital Association* 465 A 2d 294, 304–5 (Conn, 1983) and *Morrison v MacNamara* 407 A 2d 555, 561–5 (1979). For a Canadian case in which the locality rule was applied, see *Tiesmaki v Wilson* [1974] 4 WWR 19, 44; affirmed [1975] 6 WWR 639, 650.

[8] This distinction is discussed in J. H. King, 'In Search of a Standard of Care for the Medical Profession: The "Accepted Practice" Formula' (1975) 28 Vanderbilt Law Review 1213.

[9] *Vassos v Roussalis* Wyo, 625 P 2d 768, 772 (1981). See also *Anderson v Chasney* [1949] 4 DLR 71, 85–6: 'If a practitioner refuses to take an obvious precaution, he cannot exonerate himself by showing that others also neglect to take it.'

[10] [1981] 1 WLR 246, 257–8.

ordinary care, then it is negligent. If, on the other hand, it is an error that such a man, acting with ordinary care might have made, then it is not negligent.[11]

The Supreme Court of Minnesota has expressed a similar view:

[I]n professional malpractice cases the mostly subjective 'honest error in judgment' language is inappropriate in defining the scope of the professional's duty toward those the professional serves. . . . [I]n a medical negligence case, preferably the jury should be instructed as follows: A doctor is not negligent simply because his or her efforts prove unsuccessful. The fact a doctor may have chosen a method of treatment that later proves to be unsuccessful is not negligence if the treatment chosen was an accepted treatment on the basis of the information available to the doctor at the time a choice had to be made; a doctor must, however, use reasonable care to obtain the information needed to exercise his or her professional judgment, and an unsuccessful method of treatment chosen because of a failure to use such reasonable care would be negligence.[12]

The importance of the statement that doctors are not automatically liable if their efforts prove unsuccessful should be stressed. A finding of negligence can be made only if there has been a failure to foresee what a reasonably competent doctor, armed with the information available to him or her, should have foreseen:

[C]ourts should be careful not to rely upon the perfect vision afforded by hindsight. In order to evaluate a particular exercise of judgment fairly, the doctor's limited ability to foresee future events when determining a course of conduct must be borne in mind. Otherwise, the doctor will not be assessed according to the norms of the average doctor of reasonable ability in the same circumstances, but rather will be held accountable for mistakes that are apparent only after the fact.[13]

This principle has another aspect: a doctor must be judged on the basis of the medical knowledge available at the time, not on the basis of information which subsequently becomes available: ' "We must not look at the 1947 accident with 1954 spectacles." That is, courts must not, with the benefit of hindsight, judge too harshly doctors who act in accordance with prevailing standards of professional knowledge.'[14]

All persons who owe a duty of care to others must act prudently, but more than simple prudence is required. Like other professionals, doctors have special expertise that must be taken into account when assessing their actions. Doctors must exhibit a higher standard of skill and knowledge than those who lack medical expertise. A patient is entitled to be treated with the level of skill and knowledge expected of a doctor practising in the relevant field. This implies not only that the doctor has an obligation to have and employ

---

[11] [1981] 1 WLR 246, 263.   [12] *Ouellette v Subak* 391 NW 2d 810, 816 (Minn, 1986).
[13] *Lapointe v Hopital Le Gardeur* (1992) 90 DLR (4th) 7, 14.
[14] *Ter Neuzen v Korn* (1995) 127 DLR (4th) 577, 589. The quoted passage is from *Roe v Minister of Health* [1954] 2 QB 66, 84.

appropriate expertise, but also that there are differing levels of expertise. A patient who consults a general practitioner about a headache cannot expect the same level of knowledge and diagnostic skill as one who consults a neurosurgeon. Therefore, if any question of negligence arises the general practitioner's actions must be judged by reference to the standard of the competent general practitioner. Similarly, the patient who consults a specialist about a condition within that specialist's field can expect a higher level of skill and knowledge than a general practitioner could offer.[15]

Recognition of differing levels of expertise raises questions about the standard of care that must be provided by health care professionals other than doctors. This matter has been examined in the United States in proceedings involving chiropractors, podiatrists, and osteopaths. It has been held that these practitioners are entitled to have their conduct in the treatment of patients tested by the standards of the specialty to which they belong.[16] Similarly, the adequacy of a nurse's care is tested by reference to the performance of other nurses.[17] Thus, the same principle is applied as in malpractice claims involving doctors: the standard of care is assessed primarily on the basis of criteria established by competent members of the relevant professional group. This not only underlines the law's recognition of varying levels of skill and care, but also suggests that the patient has a part to play in determining the type of expertise which can be expected: '[A] person seeking treatment from a practitioner of a given school agrees to accept the curative practices and belief of that particular school, and if the practitioner treats the patient reasonably skilfully in accordance with the teachings of his school he incurs no liability.'[18]

The requirement that health care professionals provide the standard of care expected of competent members of their professional group applies while they are working within their areas of expertise. Practitioners who step outside their fields of expertise and undertake tasks that they are not qualified to perform will normally be judged by reference to standards applying to colleagues who are appropriately qualified. For example, a 'drugless healer' who continued to treat a patient when he should have known that the case was beyond his ability was held to have done so 'at his peril'.[19] Similarly, in a case against a chiropractor who claimed competence in the diagnosis of diabetes, it was held that if he claimed such competence, he should be held 'to the same degree of skill and care as medical doctors in the diagnostic

---

[15] *Sidaway v Board of Governors of the Bethlem Royal Hospital* [1985] 1 AC 871, 897; *Crits v Sylvester* (1956) 1 DLR (2d) 502, 508; *Roberts v Tardif* Me, 417 A 2d 444, 452 (1980); *McCormack v Lindberg* 352 NW 2d 30, 36 (Minn App, 1984); *Baker v Story* Tex App, 621 SW 2d 639, 642 (1981).

[16] *Creasey v Hogan* Or, 637 P 2d 114 (1981).

[17] *Fraijo v Hartland Hospital* App, 160 Cal Rptr 246, 252 (1979).

[18] *Sheppard v Firth* 334 P 2d 190, 192 (1959).

[19] *Kelly v Carroll* 219 P 2d 79, 88 (1950).

procedure'.[20] The practical problem raised by such a ruling is how the law should decide whether a health care professional has claimed competence outside his or her field of expertise. In any given case, it is necessary for a court to receive expert evidence as to the types of conditions that the practitioner is qualified to diagnose and treat. Once the evidence establishes that — except in an emergency — a practitioner has undertaken responsibilities which he or she is not trained to fulfil, a finding of negligence will result if the proper degree of care is not displayed. The negligence will lie in embarking on treatment that could not be competently offered. In such a situation, a duty to refer will arise; a nurse who fails to call on a doctor or a doctor who does not refer a patient to a specialist may be negligent.[21]

Expert Evidence

How do courts decide whether a doctor or other health care professional has exhibited the appropriate standard of skill and knowledge? This question makes it necessary to examine the role of expert medical evidence. It is best to begin this task by considering cases involving doctors. Normally a court must receive evidence from qualified medical practitioners before it will be in a position to decide whether a doctor has met the standards set by his or her colleagues. To test an allegation of negligence, a court must receive expert evidence on the nature of the patient's condition, alternative diagnoses, available treatments, and the practices employed by competent practitioners in similar situations. Only members of the relevant professional group are able to give evidence as to the practices which competent and experienced members of that group consider acceptable in a particular situation. Thus any court is heavily dependent on expert testimony.

This does not indicate how a court should proceed when evaluating such testimony. In a malpractice case that goes to trial there will normally be a conflict of medical testimony. Each side will have enlisted the aid of an expert or experts. Those testifying for the plaintiff will give evidence that the doctor's methods did not conform to the standards set by competent members of the relevant specialty. Experts testifying for the defendant practitioner will give evidence that these standards were met. It will be up to the court to resolve this conflict by assessing the credibility of the witnesses and the weight to be attached to their testimony. The complaint that because it relies on expert testimony, the law permits the medical profession to establish its own standards, overlooks the frequent need for a court to perform these tasks.

[20] *Dowell v Mossberg* 355 P 2d 624, 630 (1960).
[21] *King v Flamm* 442 SW 2d 679 (1969); *Wilsher v Essex Area Health Authority* [1987] 1 QB 730, 777; *MacDonald v York County Hospital* (1974) 1 OR (2d) 653, 682.

The important question, therefore, is how do the courts deal with medical evidence? The case law suggests that there are two possible courses of action. First, there is the approach adopted in the English decision in *Bolam*, which has been explained in the following manner:

The *Bolam* principle may be formulated as a rule that a doctor is not negligent if he acts in accordance with a practice accepted at the time as proper by a responsible body of medical opinion even though other doctors adopt a different practice. In short, the law imposes the duty of care: but the standard of care is a matter of medical judgment.[22]

The significance of this statement is that it indicates that a negligence claim against a doctor must fail once the court has received evidence that the standard of care provided was considered appropriate by a responsible group of doctors with expertise in the relevant field. Adopting this approach effectively relieves the court of the task of standard-setting. That task is delegated to the profession:

In matters of diagnosis and the carrying out of treatment the court is not tempted to put itself in the surgeon's shoes; it has to rely upon and evaluate expert evidence, remembering that it is no part of its task of evaluation to give effect to any preference it may have for one responsible body of professional opinion over another, provided it is satisfied by the expert evidence that both qualify as responsible bodies of medical opinion.[23]

In short, the *Bolam* approach employs 'an empirical rather than a normative test'.[24]

The practical effect of this approach is that a doctor who can adduce evidence of conformity to practices accepted by responsible colleagues will defeat a negligence claim. This does not mean, however, that English courts are precluded from assessing medical evidence. In *Bolitho v City and Hackney Health Authority*, the House of Lords stressed the significance of the *Bolam* test's reference to a 'responsible' body of opinion. It ruled that in some situations, it will be open to a court to decide that the views expressed by medical witnesses are not representative of those held by a 'responsible, reasonable or respectable' body of experts:

[T]he court has to be satisfied that the exponents of the body of opinion relied upon can demonstrate that such opinion has a logical basis. In particular in cases involving, as they so often do, the weighing of risks against benefits, the judge before accepting a body of opinion as being responsible, reasonable or respectable, will need to be satisfied that, in forming their views, the experts have directed their minds to the question of comparative risks and benefits and have reached a defensible conclusion on the matter.

[22] *Sidaway v Board of Governors of the Bethlem Royal Hospital* [1985] 1 AC 871, 881.
[23] Ibid. 895.
[24] J. A. Harrington, 'Privileging the Medical Norm: Liberalism, Self-Determination and Refusal of Treatment' (1996) 16 Legal Studies 348, 352.

The decision went on to emphasize that it will be rare for a court to conclude that an expert opinion is not 'logical' or 'defensible': '[I]t will very seldom be right for a judge to reach the conclusion that views genuinely held by a competent medical expert are unreasonable. The assessment of medical risks and benefits is a matter of clinical judgment which a judge would not normally be able to make without expert evidence.'[25]

Thus the English courts continue to apply the *Bolam* rule as explained in *Bolitho*: a doctor who adheres to standards set by responsible members of the profession will not be regarded as negligent. The alternative view is that which has been most clearly accepted in Australia. In the opinion of the High Court of Australia: '[The standard of care] is not determined solely or even primarily by reference to the practice followed or supported by a responsible body of opinion in the relevant profession . . .'. This represented an explicit rejection of the rule in *Bolam*: 'Even in the sphere of diagnosis and treatment, the heartland of the skilled medical practitioner, the *Bolam* principle has not always been applied [in Australia].'[26] This conclusion leaves a court free to decide that a practice sanctioned by a responsible body of medical opinion fails to meet the required standard, although the High Court conceded that the question whether a doctor has provided the appropriate standard of care is one 'in the resolution of which responsible professional opinion will have an influential, often a decisive, role to play . . .'.[27]

The law in the United States is unclear. A view similar to that adopted in *Bolam* is embodied in a number of decisions which have accepted that a doctor who has followed a practice endorsed by 'responsible' members of the relevant specialty should not be regarded as negligent. For example, it has been stated that:

Where two or more schools of thought exist among competent members of the medical profession concerning proper medical treatment for a given ailment, each of which is supported by responsible medical authority, it is not malpractice to be among the minority . . . who follow one of the accepted schools.[28]

Similarly, the Supreme Judicial Court of Maine observed: '[A] physician does not incur liability merely by electing to pursue one of several recognized courses of treatment.'[29]

There have been some cases, however, in which conformity to recognized medical practice did not allow the defendants to defeat negligence claims. The best known is *Helling v Carey*.[30] There it was alleged by the 32-year-old plaintiff that the defendant ophthalmologists had been negligent in failing to

---

[25] [1997] 3 WLR 1151, 1159, and 1160.
[26] *Rogers v Whitaker* (1992) 175 CLR 479, 487. Cp *Howarth v Adey* [1996] 2 VR 535, 547 for a contrary view.
[27] (1992) 175 CLR 479, 489.   [28] *Chumbler v McClure* 505 F 2d 489, 492 (1974).
[29] *Downer v Veilleux* Me, 322 A 2d 82, 87 (1974).   [30] Wash, 519 P 2d 981 (1974).

perform a test for glaucoma. It was established that it was not the practice for ophthalmologists to carry out routine glaucoma tests on patients under the age of 40. The defendants argued that their conformity with accepted medical practice should insulate them from liability. The Supreme Court of Washington rejected this argument. It was held that in the circumstances reasonable prudence required the test to be performed. Reference was made to a 1932 decision in which Justice Hand had stated: 'Courts must in the end say what is required; there are precautions so imperative that even their universal disregard will not excuse their omission.'[31] In *Helling*, one of the judges made the implications of this approach clear: 'I believe a greater duty of care could be imposed on the defendants than was established by their profession.'[32] It is difficult to estimate the significance of this decision. It was regarded by some as embodying a radical departure from the pre-existing law. While it has occasionally been followed,[33] it does not seem to have led to widespread changes in the law. As one commentator has remarked, the trend 'appears to be in the direction of affording greater weight, probably even conclusive weight, to professional standards'.[34]

In the Supreme Court of Canada it has been accepted that when a doctor 'acts in accordance with a recognized and respectable practice of the profession', he or she will not normally be found negligent.[35] The reason given is that courts do not have the expertise to assess complex medical evidence. This does not mean that conformity with standard practice inevitably allows a doctor to defeat a negligence claim. In some circumstances, such conformity may reveal negligence of a kind easily understood by the ordinary person. The court summarized its conclusions as follows:

[A]s a general rule, where a procedure involves difficult or uncertain questions of medical treatment or complex, scientific or highly technical matters that are beyond the ordinary experience and understanding of a judge or jury, it will not be open to find a standard medical practice negligent. On the other hand, as an exception to the general rule, if a standard practice fails to adopt obvious and reasonable precautions which are readily apparent to the ordinary finder of fact, then it is no excuse for a practitioner to claim that he or she was merely conforming to such a negligent common practice.[36]

Similarly, in an earlier decision the Manitoba Court of Appeal had emphasized that it is for the court, and not the expert witnesses, to decide whether the required standard has been met. It was suggested that the role of expert witnesses is 'to aid or guide the Court in reaching a sound decision'.[37]

---

[31] *The T. J. Hooper* 60 F 2d 737, 740 (1932).   [32] Wash, 519 P 2d 981, 984 (1974).

[33] For example, *Gates v Jensen* Wash, 595 P 2d 919 (1979) and *Harris v Groth* 663 P 2d 113 (Wash, 1983).

[34] J. H. King, *The Law of Medical Malpractice in a Nutshell* (St Paul, Minnesota, 2nd edn., 1986) 52.

[35] *Ter Neuzen v Korn* (1995) 127 DLR (4th) 577, 590.   [36] Ibid. 595.

[37] *Anderson v Chasney* [1949] 4 DLR 71, 92; affirmed [1950] 4 DLR 223.

Thus in the great majority of medical malpractice cases expert evidence is required if the issues are to be fully understood by a court. If a doctor can show conformity with approved practice, this is prima-facie evidence that the appropriate standard of care has been met. When a claim relates to allegedly negligent diagnosis or treatment, the chances are high that the court will not find a doctor negligent in the face of evidence establishing that a responsible body of expert opinion approved of the doctor's conduct. Nevertheless, a comparison of the law in the four countries discussed reveals different views as to the weight to be placed on medical evidence. In England, under the *Bolam* rule, a doctor who has adhered to practices approved by a responsible body of medical opinion will be immune from liability for negligence. In some parts of the United States, the same result will be reached, while in others the courts will scrutinize recognized practices and occasionally find them wanting. The High Court of Australia has ruled that a court must assert the power to decide that a practice accepted by competent doctors does not meet the required standard. The Supreme Court of Canada has expressed a similar view. In jurisdictions in which courts do not delegate their functions to medical witnesses, a good guide is as follows: 'Conformity with general practice . . . usually dispels negligence. . . . All the same, even a common practice may itself be condemned as negligent if fraught with obvious risks.'[38]

Similar conclusions can be drawn regarding the role of expert evidence when the conduct of a health care professional other than a doctor is under scrutiny. A court is likely to place great weight on evidence establishing that the professional has acted in accordance with practices approved by a responsible body of opinion in the relevant specialty. In jurisdictions in which the *Bolam* rule is not applied, conformity with such practices will not confer immunity. There are, however, special factors which must be considered when courts evaluate the conduct of health care professionals who are not doctors. Normally, reliance will be placed on the evidence of competent members of the relevant professional group. Thus, the testimony of a chiropractor will usually be regarded as the appropriate source of evidence as to the standard of care expected of a competent chiropractor. Relying on different sources would involve the risk of a member of one school of medical thought testifying against a member of another. Nevertheless, in some cases in the United States, this has occurred. For example, in Illinois, a physician who was sufficiently familiar with the standard of care to be expected of an osteopath was held to be competent to testify against an osteopath.[39]

Another difficulty is whether testimony from outside a specialty should be accepted as evidence that a member of that specialty has stepped outside his

[38] J. G. Fleming, *The Law of Torts* (Sydney, 9th edn., 1998) 133.

[39] *Bartimus v Paxton Community Hospital* 458 NE 2d 1072 (Ill App 4 Dist, 1983). See also *Creasey v Hogan* Or, 637 P 2d 114 (1981), but cp *Dolan v Galluzzo* 396 NE 2d 13 (1979), where a physician was not permitted to testify as to the standard of care of a podiatrist.

or her field of expertise. One view is that it is up to experienced members of the specialty to testify as to what is within the competence of a member of that specialty. The other is that it is appropriate for more highly qualified practitioners (who are likely to have a greater appreciation of the risk of unusual complications) to testify as to whether other health care professionals have sought to diagnose or treat a condition which they are not trained to manage. As was explained earlier, once it is clear that a health care professional *has* stepped outside his or her field of expertise, that professional — except in an emergency — will be required to display the standard of skill and knowledge expected of those trained to practise in the relevant field.

THE OBLIGATION TO PROVIDE APPROPRIATE INFORMATION

The foregoing discussion has considered how the law determines whether a doctor's diagnosis or treatment has been negligent. While the criterion employed (adherence to the standard expected of a competent practitioner) appears simple, different approaches can be taken to the task of determining how that standard should be set. A similar divergence of opinion emerges when attention is focused on a different form of negligence — that involving a failure to disclose information to a patient.

The law requires a doctor or other health care professional to provide a patient with the information necessary to make an informed choice about treatment. In spite of the view expressed by some courts that there is no need to distinguish between this duty and that imposed when diagnosis or treatment is undertaken,[40] it is clear that special considerations arise when a patient alleges a negligent failure to disclose. The law imposes a duty to provide information as to the patient's condition, the nature and purpose of a proposed medical procedure, the risks associated with it, possible alternatives, expected benefits, and the likely result if it is not undertaken. As with matters of diagnosis and treatment, the crucial question is whether the standard to be met should be set by members of the relevant professional group. When recommending an operation, is a doctor under a duty to provide the patient with only the information and advice which would be routinely given by a responsible practitioner in a similar situation? Or should a different obligation be imposed?

In England, in *Sidaway v Board of Governors of the Bethlem Royal Hospital*,[41] the House of Lords was divided as to whether the *Bolam* rule should govern the duty of disclosure. Only Lord Diplock was prepared to

---

[40] See, for example, *Sidaway v Board of Governors of the Bethlem Royal Hospital* [1985] 1 AC 871, 893 and *Rogers v Whitaker* (1992) 175 CLR 479, 489. In both decisions there is reference to a comprehensive obligation encompassing all aspects of the duty of care owed to a patient.
[41] [1985] 1 AC 871.

rule unequivocally that the doctor's conformity to accepted practice should insulate him from liability. At issue in this case was the surgeon's failure to volunteer unsought information as to the risk (less than 1 per cent) of damage to the spinal cord being caused by a laminectomy. Evidence was presented that when he omitted the warning, the surgeon had acted in accordance with a responsible body of specialist opinion. For Lord Diplock, this conclusively established compliance with the required standard. Two other members of the House were not prepared to go any further than to rule that the decision as to what should be disclosed to a patient was 'primarily' a matter of clinical judgement. Further, they also ruled that even when there had been conformity to accepted medical practice, it was open to a court to conclude that disclosure of a particular risk was so obviously necessary before a patient could make an informed decision that no reasonably prudent doctor could fail to make it.[42]

The judgments of the majority in *Sidaway* did not provide a clear statement of the principles that should apply when a patient alleges a negligent failure to disclose information. All that can be said is that though the applicability of the *Bolam* test was questioned, the rule survived. A similar rule applies to non-disclosure in many parts of the United States: in a number of States, the extent of a doctor's duty to disclose is determined by professional standards. The way the standard is commonly set is by reference to the type of disclosure which a reasonable and careful doctor would make under the same or similar circumstances.[43]

A different approach was adopted by Lord Scarman in his dissenting judgment in *Sidaway*. He refused to accept that the relevant standard should be set solely by reference to medical practice. In doing so, he adopted a position similar to that which had been taken in the Court of Appeal: '[T]he definition of the duty of care is not to be handed over to the medical or any other profession. The definition of the duty of care is a matter for the law and the courts. They cannot stand idly by if the profession, by an excess of paternalism, denies their patients a real choice.'[44] This echoed the assumptions underlying *Canterbury v Spence*.[45] Decided in 1972 by the United States Court of Appeals, District of Columbia Circuit, this case also involved a doctor's failure to warn of the risks associated with a laminectomy. The judgment noted the standard applied in a number of other decisions on failure to disclose: 'The majority of courts dealing with the problem have made the duty depend on whether it was the custom of physicians practicing in the community to make the particular disclosure to the patient.' The court rejected this approach: 'We do not agree that the patient's cause of action is dependent upon the existence and nonperformance of a relevant professional tradition.'[46]

[42] [1985] 1 AC 871, 900.   [43] See, for example, *Tatro v Lueken* Kan, 512 P 2d 529 (1973).
[44] [1984] 1 QB 493, 513.   [45] 464 F 2d 772 (1972).   [46] Ibid. 783 (footnotes omitted).

It was ruled that rather than employing the standard required by 'good medical practice', the criterion should be set by reference to the particular patient's needs:

The scope of the physician's communications to the patient . . . must be measured by the patient's need, and that need is the information material to the decision. Thus the test for determining whether a particular peril must be divulged is its materiality to the patient's decision: all risks potentially affecting the decision must be unmasked. And to safeguard the patient's interest in achieving his own determination on treatment, the law must itself set the standard for adequate disclosure.[47]

The court provided the following definition of materiality: '[W]e agree that "[a] risk is . . . material when a reasonable person, in what the physician knows or should know to be the patient's position, would be likely to attach significance to the risk or cluster of risks in deciding whether or not to undergo the proposed therapy." '[48]

The adoption of the criterion of patient need, rather than medical practice, reflected the law's respect for individual autonomy. As the court noted, every competent human being has the right to determine what shall be done to his or her own body. In the context of medical treatment, a person's exercise of this right depends on being in a position to make an informed choice. A person who makes an uninformed decision surrenders autonomy; he or she is dependent on the person who has greater knowledge. The ability to make an informed choice is thus vital to the exercise of full autonomy: 'True consent to what happens to one's self is the informed exercise of a choice, and that entails an opportunity to evaluate knowledgeably the options available and the risks attendant upon each.'[49] It is the patient's need that imposes the obligation on the doctor seeking to obtain consent to a medical procedure. This obligation is to facilitate informed decision-making. Such an analysis simultaneously identifies the source and nature of the doctor's duty.

The view expressed in *Canterbury v Spence*—that the standard by which to measure disclosure should be based on patient need—has been adopted in a number of United States jurisdictions.[50] This has had important ramifications for the law of medical malpractice. Some members of the medical profession felt that the new criterion imposed too onerous a burden on doctors and would generate excessive litigation. The result was that a number of States

[47] Ibid. 786–7 (footnotes omitted).
[48] Ibid. 787. This definition was adopted from that provided by J. R. Waltz and T. W. Scheuneman, 'Informed Consent to Therapy' (1970) 64 North Western University Law Review 628, 640.
[49] 464 F 2d 772, 780 (1972) (footnote omitted).
[50] For a useful review, see *Largey v Rothman* 540 A 2d 504 (NJ, 1988). For examples of cases in which *Canterbury v Spence* was followed, see *Harnish v Children's Hospital Medical Center* Mass, 439 NE 2d 240 (1982) and *Logan v Greenwich Hospital Association* 465 A 2d 294 (Conn, 1983).

passed legislation defining the standard by which a doctor's obligation to inform a patient should be measured.[51] Most of the Acts opted for one or other variant of the competent practitioner standard. The widespread legislative adoption of this standard, combined with the fact that a large number of judicial decisions has favoured the retention of the professional standard,[52] has meant that *Canterbury v Spence* still represents the minority view in the United States.

It is, however, the prevailing view in Canada and Australia. In *Reibl v Hughes*, the Supreme Court of Canada stated:

> To allow expert medical evidence to determine what risks are material and, hence, should be disclosed and, correlatively, what risks are not material is to hand over to the medical profession the entire question of the scope of the duty of disclosure, including the question whether there has been a breach of that duty.[53]

In Australia, the relevant decision was *Rogers v Whitaker*,[54] the facts of which vividly illustrate the nature of the duty which can be imposed on a doctor. The plaintiff, who had for many years been blind in her right eye, consulted the defendant, an ophthalmic surgeon, who advised an operation upon that eye. The plaintiff expressed her concerns about the health of her good eye, but did not ask specifically about the possibility of its being injured by the operation. She gave her consent to the procedure and underwent the surgery. There was no improvement to her right eye and she lost the sight in her left eye as the result of a condition known as sympathetic ophthalmia. She became almost totally blind. It was accepted that if the woman had been told of the risk of this complication, she would not have consented to the operation. While the defendant surgeon had performed the procedure with due care and skill, he was held to have breached his duty to inform the plaintiff of the risk of sympathetic ophthalmia. In reaching this conclusion, the court adopted the materiality test, expressing it in words very similar to those used in *Canterbury v Spence*.

A number of matters emerge from an examination of this decision. The risk of the occurrence of blindness was very remote: evidence was accepted that sympathetic ophthalmia occurs in approximately 1 in 14,000 operations of the kind performed. Yet it was held that there was a duty to disclose this very remote risk. In understanding this ruling, it is necessary to appreciate the importance that the court attached to the expressed concerns of the patient. Although she did not specifically ask about the statistical risks, she made it clear that she was very anxious about her 'good' eye. This highlights

---

[51] See A. Meisel and L. D. Kabnick, 'Informed Consent to Medical Treatment: an Analysis of Recent Legislation' (1980) 41 University of Pittsburgh Law Review 407.

[52] For example, *Ouellete v Mehalic* 534 A 2d 1331 (Me, 1988).

[53] (1980) 114 DLR (3d) 1, 13.

[54] (1992) 175 CLR 479. See also *Chappel v Hart* (1998) 156 ALR 517.

the doctor's obligation to respond to the needs of the particular patient. If specific questions are asked, these must be answered, no matter how remote the risk which is troubling the patient. If specific questions are not asked, there will still be situations—as in *Rogers v Whitaker*—in which it is clear that the patient has special concerns which the doctor must address.

This does not mean that a doctor is automatically liable for a failure to disclose all possible consequences, no matter how trivial or unlikely. The *Canterbury v Spence* definition of a material risk spoke of a risk to which a reasonable person in the patient's position would be likely to attach significance. Thus the test incorporates an objective element: the standard is set with regard to the needs of the reasonable patient. It would be wrong, therefore, to see the decision in *Rogers v Whitaker* as a response to the idiosyncratic anxieties of a particular patient. The High Court's ruling reflected the opinion that a reasonable patient in her position would attach significance to the possibility of blindness.

If this analysis is accepted, the doctor's obligation in *Rogers v Whitaker* was clear. More difficult to define is the obligation which arises when a patient asks no, or very few, questions. What type of information must be volunteered? Here the answer seems to be that the doctor must provide the information that a 'reasonable' or 'prudent' patient in a similar situation would regard as material to the decision to be made. A doctor who seeks to observe this requirement must exercise careful judgement. One factor is the probability of the occurrence of an adverse outcome; a doctor is not under an obligation to disclose all risks, however remote. It was accepted that liability does not arise for the non-disclosure of 'far-fetched or fanciful' risks; rather, the duty is to warn of 'real and foreseeable' risks.[55] Identifying the difference between these two categories of risks is not purely a matter of statistics. Although the probability of sympathetic ophthalmia was put at 1 in 14,000, the surgeon was liable for failing to refer to it. In this situation, what was significant was the seriousness of the harm suffered by the patient. This factor was also relevant in *Canterbury v Spence* and *Sidaway*, where the undisclosed risks were of paralysis and damage to the spinal cord. The obligation to warn is greater when the risk is highly specific, rather than general in nature.

There are some circumstances in which there is no obligation to provide material information.[56] The most obvious is a medical emergency, when there is no time for the doctor to give detailed explanations and information. If a patient is unconscious and the need for intervention is urgent, the doctor should make a decision on the basis of the patient's best interests. More

[55] (1992) 175 CLR 479, 494 (citations omitted).
[56] A good discussion of the exceptions to the rules on disclosure is contained in *Holt v Nelson* Wash App, 523 P 2d 211, 218–19 (1974).

difficult is the situation in which therapeutic privilege is invoked. This exception was recognized in *Canterbury v Spence*, where it was accepted that on some occasions disclosure will be detrimental to the interests of the patient. A patient might, for example, be emotionally distraught or physically debilitated and so be unable to reach a considered decision as to proposed treatment. In such circumstances, a doctor might be entitled to withhold information as to risks. Nevertheless, there are obvious dangers in the adoption of the therapeutic privilege exception:

The physician's privilege to withhold information for therapeutic reasons must be carefully circumscribed, however, for otherwise it might devour the disclosure rule itself. The privilege does not accept the paternalistic notion that the physician may remain silent simply because divulgence might prompt the patient to forego therapy the physician feels the patient really needs.[57]

Doubts about the dangers inherent in the therapeutic privilege exception led the Ontario Court of Justice to rule that it does not form part of Canadian law.[58] In *Reibl v Hughes*, however, Laskin CJC had conceded the possibility that a failure to provide full information might be appropriate in some circumstances: '[I]t may be the case that a particular patient may, because of emotional factors, be unable to cope with facts relevant to recommended surgery or treatment and the doctor may, in such a case, be justified in withholding or generalizing information as to which he would otherwise be required to be more specific.'[59]

There are also evidential issues that arise when the obligation to disclose risks is considered. In any proceedings alleging negligent non-disclosure, expert medical evidence on the level and type of risk attending a particular treatment will normally be required. This evidence is likely to prove conclusive. Similarly, expert evidence is likely to be conclusive on the question of the extent of knowledge that a practitioner in a particular field should possess. If he or she was unaware of the existence of certain risks, negligence can be established only if it is shown that there has been a failure to disclose information that could be expected of a competent practitioner working in the relevant field. On this matter, medical evidence will also be required: it is for experts in the field to show that there has been a failure to advise of risks of which a competent practitioner *ought* to have been aware.[60] In determining whether such a failure has occurred, it is necessary to recognize that there

[57] 464 F 2d 772, 789 (1972) (footnote omitted).

[58] *Meyer Estate v Rogers* (1991) 78 DLR (4th) 307 (Gen Div).

[59] (1980) 114 DLR (3d) 1, 13.

[60] 'The information a physician reasonably should possess is that information possessed by the average qualified physician or, in the case of a specialty, by the average qualified physician practicing that specialty.... What the physician should know involves professional expertise and can ordinarily be proved only through the testimony of experts.' *Harnish v Children's Hospital Medical Center* Mass, 439 NE 2d 240, 243 (1982) (citations omitted).

are varying levels of expertise. The obligation to be aware of risks will be correspondingly greater in the case of a specialist in the field. Less can be expected of the general practitioner or other health care professional. The courts are likely to defer to responsible members of the relevant specialty in determining what level of knowledge a member of that specialty should possess.

Two further comments must be made on actions arising from negligent non-disclosure. It is common for plaintiffs to combine such actions with claims relating to negligent diagnosis or treatment. For example, in *Salis v United States*,[61] a plaintiff who suffered serious injuries following an angiogram sought damages on the dual grounds that the doctor's decision to undertake the procedure had been negligent and that no explanation had been given, either of the risks of the procedure or of the availability of a more conservative alternative technique. By combining separate claims in this manner, a plaintiff will normally increase the chances of success. Further, there are some circumstances in which a complaint of non-disclosure might be easier to sustain than a complaint relating to negligent care. Expert medical evidence will often play a decisive part in a court's decision as to whether the required standard of care has been met. In a case in which it is alleged that this standard has not been met, a plaintiff may find it difficult to succeed in the face of evidence that the medical procedures employed were those which could be expected of a responsible member of the relevant specialty. In contrast, when the action relates to non-disclosure, the plaintiff's task will be easier, at least in those jurisdictions that do not accept that a doctor's duty to disclose is determined by professional standards. In these jurisdictions, it will often not be difficult for an aggrieved patient to convince a court that material information was not provided.

Finally, it should be noted that United States courts have frequently approached the subject of non-disclosure by asking whether the information provided by the doctor was sufficient to permit the patient to give 'informed consent' to the procedure in question. This concept is a misleading one when the focus is on the liability of medical professionals for non-disclosure. When such liability is at issue, the primary aim is to determine whether the professional has been negligent, not whether he or she has undertaken a medical procedure to which the patient has not given effective consent. To speak of 'informed consent' is to imply that anything less does not amount to consent. If this were so, any doctor who undertook an operation in circumstances where the patient did not fully understand the nature of, and risks associated with, that operation would be liable to an action in battery. While such a cause of action is a theoretical possibility, it is of little practical importance and diverts attention from the central issue, which is whether a doctor

---

[61] 522 F Supp 989 (1981).

has been negligent in a particular situation. This was recognized in *Canterbury v Spence*:

[W]e caution that uncritical use of the 'informed consent' label can be misleading. . . . In duty-to-disclose cases, the focus of attention is more properly upon the nature and content of the physician's divulgence than the patient's understanding or consent. . . . [T]he vital inquiry on duty to disclose relates to the physician's performance of an obligation, while one of the difficulties with analysis in terms of 'informed consent' is its tendency to imply that what is decisive is the degree of the patient's comprehension. . . . [T]he physician discharges the duty when he makes a reasonable effort to convey sufficient information although the patient, without fault of the physician, may not fully grasp it.[62]

Other United States cases and decisions by English, Canadian, and Australian courts have expressed similar criticisms of the concept of 'informed consent'.[63] These emphasize that what is at issue is the enforcement of an appropriate standard of care. The question is not whether a patient can be described as having fully comprehended the risks associated with a particular procedure; rather, it is whether the practitioner has discharged his or her obligation by taking all reasonable steps to enable the patient to make informed decisions about his or her welfare.

HARM AND THE PROBLEM OF CAUSATION

In all medical malpractice claims, a plaintiff who establishes a breach of the duty of care has done no more than surmount the first hurdle. There still remains the need to prove the causal link between this breach and the harm suffered: 'The law takes no cognizance of carelessness in the abstract. It concerns itself with carelessness only where there is a duty to take care and where failure in that duty has caused damage.'[64] Normally the need for the plaintiff to prove that some form of harm has been suffered presents no difficulties. It may be much more difficult to show that negligent treatment *caused* that harm. The legal principle may be stated simply. To succeed in an action for negligence in England, Canada, and Australia, a plaintiff must prove on the balance of probabilities (it was 'more likely than not') that the doctor's breach of the duty of care caused the harm suffered by the patient. Sometimes the test has been expressed by requiring proof that the medical

---

[62]   464 F 2d 772, 780, n 15 (1972).

[63]   The doctrine of informed consent 'is essentially a negligence concept': *Largey v Rothman* 540 A 2d 504, 506 (NJ, 1988). See also *Rogers v Whitaker* (1992) 175 CLR 479, 490; *Reibl v Hughes* (1980) 114 DLR (3d) 1, 11; *Sidaway v Board of Governors of the Bethlem Royal Hospital* [1985] 1 AC 871, 894.

[64]   *Donoghue v Stevenson* [1932] AC 562, 618.

negligence 'materially' or 'substantially' contributed to the harm.[65] A corollary of the requirement that the contribution be 'material' is that liability cannot arise in respect of conduct which comes within the exception *de minimis non curat lex* (the law does not concern itself with trifling matters).[66] In the United States, it is usual simply to refer to the need to show that the defendant caused the harm, although an alternative requirement is proof that the defendant's conduct 'proximately caused' the harm or was a 'substantial factor' in bringing it about.[67] A 1986 case in the District of Columbia ruled that what must be established is 'a direct and substantial causal relationship between the defendant's breach of the standard of care and the plaintiff's injuries *and* that the injuries were foreseeable'.[68]

Both in England and Canada there was for a time doubt as to whether the plaintiff or the defendant bears the burden of proof. This doubt arose as a result of the decision in *McGhee v National Coal Board*, where Lord Wilberforce suggested: '[I]t is a sound principle that where a person has, by breach of a duty of care, created a risk, and injury occurs within the area of that risk, the loss should be borne by him unless he shows that it had some other cause.'[69] Adoption of this principle suggests that the burden of disproving the causal link should lie on a doctor who created a risk of harm. This approach was rejected by the House of Lords and by the Supreme Court of Canada.[70] These decisions made it clear that it is for the plaintiff to prove the causal connection between medical negligence and the harm suffered. In Canada, however, this conclusion must be read subject to the qualifications expressed in *Snell v Farrell*:

In many malpractice cases, the facts lie particularly within the knowledge of the defendant. In these circumstances, very little affirmative evidence on the part of the plaintiff will justify the drawing of an inference of causation in the absence of evidence to the contrary. . . . The legal or ultimate burden remains with the plaintiff, but in the absence of evidence to the contrary adduced by the defendant, an inference of causation may be drawn, although positive or scientific proof of causation has not been adduced.[71]

---

[65] *Bonnington Castings Ltd v Wardlaw* [1956] AC 613, 620; *McGhee v National Coal Board* [1973] 1 WLR 1, 6, 8, 11, 13; *Wilsher v Essex Area Health Authority* [1988] 1 AC 1074, 1090; *Cherry v Borsman* (1991) 75 DLR (4th) 668, 682.

[66] *Bonnington Castings Ltd v Wardlaw* [1956] AC 613, 621.

[67] *Fall v White* 449 NE 2d 628 (Ind App 4 Dist, 1983); *Restatement of the Law, Second, Torts 2d, Volume 2*, § 431 (St Paul, Minnesota, 1965). On the need for proof that it was more likely than not or more probable than not that the negligence caused the harm, see: *Miles v Edward O Tabor, MD, Inc* Mass, 443 NE 2d 1302 (1982) and *Harvey v Fridley Medical Center* PA Minn, 315 NW 2d 225 (1982).

[68] *Psychiatric Institute of Washington v Allen* 509 A 2d 619, 624 (DC App, 1986).

[69] [1973] 1 WLR 1, 6.

[70] *Wilsher v Essex Area Health Authority* [1988] 1 AC 1074 and *Snell v Farrell* (1990) 72 DLR (4th) 289.

[71] *Snell v Farrell* (1990) 72 DLR (4th) 289, 300–1.

In short, decisions as to causation may be based on inferences rather than on scientific proof.

While the legal principles are clear, their application in medical malpractice claims is frequently difficult. There are many circumstances in which the factual cause of an adverse outcome cannot be confidently identified. The harm suffered by the patient might have been the result of medical negligence or it might have been the result of the condition for which the treatment was provided. For example, there was an English case in which a child who had been admitted to hospital with meningitis was negligently given an overdose of penicillin. The child became completely deaf. The hospital was sued on the ground that the overdose had materially contributed to the deafness. The plaintiff did not succeed as the cause of the harm could not be established. The deafness could equally well have been the result of the meningitis.[72]

The problems of establishing the necessary causal link are of a different kind when the negligence takes the form of a failure to disclose information. It must be established that the harm suffered was caused by the breach of the obligation to inform; this requires proof that the patient would not have consented to the medical procedure (and so would have avoided the harm) had the information been provided. The difficulty is to determine whether an objective or a subjective approach should be taken to the task of deciding whether the non-disclosure caused the harm. Let us assume that a patient has consented to an operation and that the duty of disclosure has been breached, either by a failure to act in accordance with accepted medical practice or by a failure to provide material information. The undisclosed risk eventuates and the patient suffers harm. Is the question whether the non-disclosure caused the harm to be decided on the basis that if the necessary information had been provided, *that particular patient* would have declined to consent to the operation? Or should the question be whether *a reasonable person in the patient's position* would have refused to consent had the information been provided? It is the decisions which have adopted the materiality test which have most closely examined this matter, but the analysis offered is equally applicable to jurisdictions which define a doctor's duty by reference to accepted medical practice.

In *Canterbury v Spence*, the court considered, but rejected, the argument that the question to be asked was whether the particular patient would have decided differently had the information been provided. This approach was described as 'second-best': 'It places the physician in jeopardy of the patient's hindsight and bitterness. It places the factfinder in the position of deciding whether a speculative answer to a hypothetical question is to be credited.' Hence the court's conclusion:

[72] *Kay v Ayrshire and Arran Health Board* [1987] 2 All ER 417.

Better it is, we believe, to resolve the causality issue on an objective basis: in terms of what a prudent person in the patient's position would have decided if suitably informed of all perils bearing significance. If adequate disclosure could reasonably be expected to have caused that person to decline the treatment because of the revelation of the kind of risk or danger that resulted in harm, causation is shown, but otherwise not.[73]

This ruling has been followed in many parts of the United States.[74] It has not gone unchallenged. If a patient has expressly or impliedly made it clear that he or she has particular concerns about a procedure, the doctor has an obligation to provide information which is relevant to those concerns, although such information might not have affected the decision of 'the prudent person in the patient's position'. The dangers of a wholly objective approach have been highlighted in a judgment by the Supreme Court of North Carolina:

In determining liability by whether a reasonable person would have submitted to treatment had he known of the risk that the defendant failed to relate, no consideration is given to the peculiar quirks and idiosyncrasies of the individual. His supposedly inviolable right to decide for himself what is to be done with his body is made subject to a standard set by others. The right to base one's consent on proper information is effectively vitiated for those with fears, apprehensions, religious beliefs, or superstitions outside the mainstream of society.[75]

This indicates that the obligation borne by the health care professional is not to formulate advice for a hypothetical patient, but for the patient for whom he or she is responsible. Such an approach was adopted in Australia, where the High Court in *Rogers v Whitaker* suggested that the particular concerns of the patient must be recognized: 'Even if a court were satisfied that a reasonable person in the patient's position would be unlikely to attach significance to a particular risk, the fact that the patient asked questions revealing concern about the risk would make the doctor aware that *this patient* did in fact attach significance to the risk.'[76] In an earlier decision, the New South Wales Court of Appeal went further and urged the need for a subjective approach:

[T]he question to be asked is whether, in the particular circumstances, the risk was such that the particular patient should have been told and, if told, would not have accepted the treatment. It is not whether a hypothetical 'reasonable' patient or even the hybrid 'reasonable patient in the position of the particular patient' would have accepted or rejected the treatment if fully and properly informed of the risks involved in it.[77]

---

[73] 464 F 2d 772, 791 (1972) (footnotes omitted).
[74] See, for example, *Harnish v Children's Hospital Medical Center* Mass, 439 NE 2d 240, 244 (1982) and *Largey v Rothman* 540 A 2d 504, 510 (NJ, 1988).
[75] *McPherson v Ellis* NC, 287 SE 2d 892, 897 (1982).   [76] (1992) 175 CLR 479, 487.
[77] *Ellis v Wallsend District Hospital* (1989) 17 NSWLR 553, 559; see also 579–82.

In spite of these rulings, the better view is that a purely subjective approach is unsatisfactory. The 'hybrid' test which the New South Wales court rejected is the one most likely to be applied. The compromise that this embodies was recognized by the Supreme Court of Canada in *Reibl v Hughes*. The court, while noting the need to take account of any special considerations affecting the particular patient, suggested that the question to be asked is whether a reasonable person in the patient's position would have refused to consent had the information been disclosed.[78] While this ruling has been challenged, it was reaffirmed by the Canadian Supreme Court in *Arndt v Smith*. In rejecting a wholly subjective approach, the majority noted that this approach 'fails to take into account the inherent unreliability of the self-serving assertion of a plaintiff'.[79] On this view, more is required of a plaintiff than a statement of honest belief that consent would not have been given had the risks been disclosed. The danger of relying on such a statement was thought to be that a doctor would be liable for failing to anticipate 'idiosyncratic' (that is, 'unreasonable') concerns. Hence the need to retain the 'reasonable person' as the point of reference: '[T]he "reasonable person" who sets the standard for the objective test must be taken to possess the patient's reasonable beliefs, fears, desires and expectations.'[80] The majority in *Arndt v Smith* thus saw the *Reibl* test as striking the proper balance between patients and doctors:

A purely subjective test could serve as an incitement for a disappointed patient to bring an action. The plaintiff will invariably state with all the confidence of hindsight and with all the enthusiasm of one contemplating an award of damages that consent would never have been given if the disclosure required by an idiosyncratic belief had been made. This would create an unfairness that cannot be accepted. It would bring inequitable and unnecessary pressure to bear upon the overburdened medical profession. On the other hand, a purely objective test which would set the standard by a reasonable person without the reasonable fears, concerns and circumstances of the particular plaintiff would unduly favour the medical profession.[81]

Finally, there are some cases in which non-disclosure is irrelevant. These are those in which it is clear that the patient would have consented to the procedure even if the appropriate information had been provided. The procedure might have been clearly desired by the patient and no alternative might have been available. In such a case it can frequently be inferred that the patient (or a reasonable person in his or her position) would have gone ahead with the operation in spite of being advised of the risk which later materialized.[82] A similar inference may be drawn if the operation represented the patient's only chance of avoiding a devastating consequence.[83]

---

[78] (1980) 114 DLR (3d) 1, 17.   [79] (1997) 148 DLR (4th) 48, 53.   [80] Ibid. 53–5.
[81] Ibid. 56–7.
[82] *Meyer Estate v Rogers* (1991) 78 DLR (4th) 307 (Gen Div).
[83] See, for example, *Goorkani v Tayside Health Board* [1991] 3 Med LR 33.

The foregoing discussion does not pretend to offer a comprehensive analysis of the law of medical negligence. Rather, its purpose has been to identify the elements of negligence that are particularly relevant to damages claims in the field of obstetrics and midwifery and to explore some of the particular legal problems encountered in this field. These matters will be more fully examined in the following chapters.

4

Negligent Treatment in Obstetrics and Midwifery

I shall now consider the application of the principles discussed in the previous chapter to cases in which doctors or midwives have provided unsatisfactory care and the woman or her child has suffered harm. Before this task is undertaken, it is necessary to address an important preliminary matter. This is whether, after a child is born, the law will permit a damages claim for negligence occurring before birth.

ARE DAMAGES RECOVERABLE FOR ANTENATAL INJURY?

Harm *in Utero* or at Delivery

At one time it was believed that a successful negligence action depended on proof of the breach of a duty of care owed to an existing person. As a fetus is not a legal person,[1] it was thought that there could be no such duty of care. This view has now been rejected in the United States, Canada, England, and Australia. In Canada the leading authority was the 1933 decision in *Montreal Tramways v Leveille*.[2] This case, like many that have dealt with the legal outcome of antenatal injury, involved a traffic accident in which a pregnant woman was injured; as a result, her child was born with a disability. It was held that the child was able to bring an action for damages.[3]

In the United States, *Bonbrest v Kotz*[4] recognized the claim of a child who is born alive, suffering from an injury or disability resulting from antenatal negligence. Here, a District of Columbia court rejected the argument that the fetus was no more than a part of the woman's body and, following *Montreal Tramways v Leveille*, ruled that there was nothing to prevent a damages claim being brought on behalf of the injured child. This decision was widely followed and the principle that a child may sue in respect of antenatal harm

---

[1] See below 137–9 and 144–5.   [2] [1933] 4 DLR 337.
[3] A similar result was reached in *Duval v Seguin* (1972) 26 DLR (3d) 418, another road accident case in which a pregnant woman was injured and her child was born mentally retarded and physically handicapped.
[4] 65 F Supp 138 (1946). While this case is regularly cited as the first United States decision to allow a torts claim in respect of antenatal negligence, an earlier ruling to this effect was made in *Cooper v Blanck* 39 So 2d 352 (1923); the judgment was not published until 1949.

is firmly established in the United States.[5] This principle was reinforced in a series of cases in which children who had been harmed when their mothers had ingested drugs during pregnancy sued the drug manufacturers. One group of cases resulted from the taking of Benedictin (an anti-nausea drug)[6] and another arose from the use of DES (Diethylstilbestrol, a synthetic compound of the female hormone oestrogen, widely prescribed from the 1940s to the 1970s to prevent miscarriages).[7] Although some of the actions failed, in none of the cases were any doubts expressed about the ability of an affected child to sue in respect of *in utero* harm.

In Australia and England, acceptance of a child's right to sue in respect of antenatal harm was slower. The landmark decision in Australia was reached in 1972 by the Victorian Supreme Court in *Watt v Rama*.[8] The proceedings were taken on behalf of a 3-year-old girl who was born suffering from brain damage and epilepsy. Her mother, while pregnant, had been injured in a car accident as a result of the defendant's negligent driving; the accident caused the girl to be born with disabilities. The court accepted that the child had a right to sue the negligent driver.

Watt v Rama's analysis of the common law was adopted in England,[9] but this is of little practical significance in view of the fact that the law in that country is now in statutory form. The relevant provisions of the Congenital Disabilities (Civil Liability) Act 1976 (UK) are as follows:

1. (1) If a child is born disabled as the result of such an occurrence before its birth as is mentioned in subsection (2) below, and a person (other than the child's own mother) is under this section answerable to the child in respect of the occurrence,[10] the child's disabilities are to be regarded as damage resulting from the wrongful act of that person and actionable accordingly at the suit of the child.
2. An occurrence to which this section applies is one which —
   (a) affected either parent of the child in his or her ability to have a normal, healthy child; or
   (b) affected the mother during her pregnancy, or affected her or the child in the course of its birth, so that the child is born with disabilities which would not otherwise have been present.

---

[5] See, for example: *Williams v Marion Rapid Transit* 87 NE 2d 334 (1949); *Damasiewicz v Gorsuch* 79 A 2d 550 (1951); *Woods v Lancet* 102 NE 2d 691 (1951); *Kelly v Gregory* 125 NYS 2d 696 (1953); *Hornbuckle v Plantation Pipe Line Company* 93 SE 2d 727 (1956); *Smith v Brennan* 157 A 2d 497 (1960); *Keyes v Construction Service Inc* 165 NE 2d 912 (1960); *Douglas v Town of Hartford* Conn, 542 F Supp 1267 (1982).

[6] See, for example, *Thompson v Merrell Dow Pharmaceuticals Inc* 551 A 2d 177 (NJ Super AD, 1988).

[7] *Bichler v Eli Lilly and Co* NY, 436 NE 2d 182 (1982) and *Hymowitz v Eli Lilly and Co* 539 NE 2d 1069 (NY, 1989).

[8] [1972] VR 353.

[9] *Burton v Islington Health Authority* and *De Martell v Merton and Sutton Health Authority* [1993] QB 204.

[10] Under s 1(3) a person is answerable to the child if he or she was liable in tort to the parent. This subsection is discussed below 244–6.

These provisions make it clear that when a child is born disabled as a result of negligence affecting the mother during her pregnancy or at the time of delivery, that child may sue for damages. A child who is 'born disabled' is defined in s 4(1) as 'being born with any deformity, disease or abnormality, including predisposition (whether or not susceptible of immediate prognosis) to physical or mental defect in the future'. As a result, the child may seek damages in respect of a wide variety of harms. One aspect of the legislation should be noted at this stage, as it is of special relevance to the matters discussed in the previous chapter. Section 1(5) states that a defendant who causes antenatal harm is not answerable to the child for anything done or omitted in a professional capacity 'if he took reasonable care having due regard to then received professional opinion applicable to the particular class of case'. This makes it clear that doctors and midwives who have allegedly breached their duty of care will be judged by reference to the *Bolam* standard.

Pre-Conception Harm

The law's recognition of a child's right to sue in respect of antenatal harm may not be confined to situations in which a fetus has been negligently damaged. There are United States and Australian cases that have dealt with claims arising when a person has negligently harmed a woman before she has conceived a child and the result of the negligence has been the birth of an impaired child. Some of these cases have held that negligence before a child is conceived can result in a successful damages claim on behalf of the affected child.

Two similar cases that arose in the United States and Australia reached identical results. *Renslow v Mennonite Hospital*[11] and *Kosky v The Trustees of the Sisters of Charity*[12] considered claims by children whose mothers, many years before conceiving them, had been negligently given transfusions of Rh positive blood, although their blood grouping was Rh negative. When they became pregnant and their children were delivered, both were premature. In *Renslow*, the child was born suffering from jaundice and hyperbilirubinemia and permanent damage resulted. In *Kosky*, the child became extremely ill and almost died. In each case it was held that the child had a cause of action in respect of the negligent conduct which occurred before conception. The plaintiff in *Renslow* submitted that the defendants owed 'a contingent prospective duty to a child not yet conceived but foreseeably harmed by a breach of duty to the child's mother'.[13] The majority of the Superior Court of Illinois accepted this submission.

---

[11] 367 NE 2d 1250 (1977). See also *Yeager v Bloomington Obstetrics and Gynecology Inc* 585 NE 2d 696 (Ind App 1 Dist, 1992).
[12] [1982] VR 961.   [13] 367 NE 2d 1250, 1254 (1977).

The courts have not been unanimous when dealing with the subject of pre-conception negligence. In *Renslow*, Ryan J dissented from the majority's ruling in the child's favour and later cases have echoed his doubts. In *Albala v City of New York*,[14] the infant plaintiff alleged that the defendant's negligent performance of an abortion on his mother, prior to his conception, perforated his mother's uterus. He claimed that as a result he sustained brain damage at birth. The Court of Appeals of New York declined to recognize the child's cause of action. The majority judgment found the decisions in cases such as *Renslow* 'unpersuasive' and expressed concern about the 'staggering implications'[15] of allowing actions based on pre-conception negligence. It was feared that virtually limitless liability could arise if recognition were given to a cause of action that might not crystallize for several generations. It was this fear that caused the New York Court of Appeals in *Enright v Eli Lilly and Co*[16] to refuse to recognize a claim arising from pre-conception negligence. There the action had been brought by the granddaughter of a woman who had ingested DES. The girl alleged that her injuries had been caused by her premature birth and that this, in turn, had been caused by the damage to her mother's reproductive organs resulting from her mother's *in utero* exposure to DES. In support of the ruling that the granddaughter's action could not succeed, Wachtler CJ stated: 'It is our duty to confine liability within manageable limits . . . Limiting liability to those who ingested the drug or were exposed to it in utero serves this purpose.'[17] The court therefore concluded that 'an injury to a mother which results in injuries to a later-conceived child does not establish a cause of action in favor of the child against the original tortfeasor.'[18]

Thus there is some uncertainty on this matter. In Australia, the law has permitted children who have been injured or disabled as a result of pre-conception negligence to bring a damages claim against a doctor. In the United States, there are decisions both for and against the recognition of such a claim. In England, the possibility of actions in respect of pre-conception negligence has been statutorily recognized. Under s 1(2)(a) of the Congenital Disabilities (Civil Liability) Act 1976 (UK), the rights which this Act confers on a disabled child include a right to bring an action in respect of any occurrence which has affected either parent's 'ability to have a normal, healthy child'. This wording would encompass such actions as the negligent performance of a blood transfusion or surgery and the manufacture or supply of harmful drugs. An exception is made by s 3(5); if either or both of the parents knew of the risk of their child being born disabled, compensation is not

---

[14] NY, 429 NE 2d 786 (1981).   [15] Ibid. 788.   [16] 570 NE 2d 198 (NY, 1991).
[17] Ibid. 203 (citations omitted).
[18] Ibid. 204. The very strong dissent by Hancock J should be noted; he considered it unacceptable that the fear of a proliferation of claims should be used as a reason for denying the cause of action.

payable in respect of pre-conception harm. Further, the legislation takes a stand on the problem posed by negligence which produces harm in the second and later generations. The Act gives effect to the Law Commission Report's recommendation that 'there should be no claim for pre-natal injury otherwise than at the suit of the first generation'.[19] This result is achieved by s 1(3), which provides that an injured child may sue only a person who owed a duty of care to his or her parents. This precludes any action by the grandchild of a person whose reproductive capacities were negligently harmed.

NEGLIGENT DIAGNOSIS OR TREATMENT

Chapter 3's analysis of the legal principles governing medical negligence included a discussion of the problems of establishing a failure to meet the required standard of care and of proving that the failure caused harm. These matters must be re-examined in the context of the provision of antenatal care and the management of childbirth. In order to avoid introducing unnecessary complexity into the discussion, attention will be focused on the liability of individual practitioners, whether doctors or midwives. In practice, damages claims are often brought not only against individuals, but also against the hospitals or health care authorities employing them. Analysis of this aspect of the law, which would require a discussion of the doctrine of vicarious liability, is beyond the scope of this book.[20]

A small number of the cases which will be discussed have dealt with claims that the medical treatment given to women before conception caused them to give birth to injured or disabled children. Far more numerous are the matters involving allegations that pregnant women have received negligent care, either antenatally or at the time of delivery. There are a wide variety of situations in which a damages claim can be made against a doctor or midwife when the care of a pregnant woman falls short of the standard expected and an adverse outcome results. Liability might arise from a diagnostic failure or unskilful treatment which causes harm to the mother, the birth of an injured or disabled child, or a stillbirth or perinatal death. A doctor or midwife who neglects to perform routine antenatal testing, such as checking the woman's blood pressure to diagnose hypertension, taking blood tests to diagnose

---

[19] Law Commission, *Report on Injuries to Unborn Children* (Law Com No 60, 1974) para 80.

[20] Examples of cases in which the vicarious liability of a hospital is discussed are: *Wilsher v Essex Area Health Authority* [1987] 1 QB 730; *City of Somerset v Hart* Ky, 549 SW 2d 814 (1977); *Piehl v Dalles General Hospital* Or, 571 P 2d 149 (1977); *Ellis v Wallsend District Hospital* (1989) 17 NSWLR 553. It should be noted that a distinction can be made between a hospital's vicarious liability and its direct liability for a 'systems failure' (a failure to put in place a safe system of care): *Bull v Devon Area Hospital Authority* [1993] 4 Med LR 117. For a discussion, in the context of an obstetrician's negligence, of whether a staff doctor is an independent contractor, see *Albain v Flower Hospital* 553 NE 2d 1038 (Ohio, 1990).

anaemia or syphilis, and generally monitoring the growth and health of the fetus will be liable to a damages claim if the mother or child is harmed by this failure. Alternatively, when a diagnosis has been made, there might be an omission to offer treatment (for example, when rhesus sensitization has been identified, but the necessary further investigations have not been undertaken). Liability can also arise in respect of the management of a delivery. There may, for example, be an omission to diagnose a breech presentation, malpresentation, disproportion, or fetal distress. Equally, when a problem has been diagnosed, liability might arise from a failure to intervene (by way, for instance, of inducing labour, caesarean section, or forceps delivery). When appropriate intervention is undertaken, the negligence might consist of a failure to display the necessary degree of skill and care. Further, in the case of the midwife, the negligence might take the form of an omission to refer the woman to a doctor when the situation is one which he or she is not trained to manage. A general practitioner might similarly be liable for a failure to refer to a consultant.

The following discussion examines a variety of cases in which damages have been sought by parents or children as a result of harm allegedly caused by pre-conception, antenatal, or perinatal negligence. When considering the cases outlined, it should be borne in mind that obstetric practices that were acceptable only a few years ago might now be rejected. The fact that some of the cases examined involved techniques now regarded as out of date does not diminish their legal relevance.

Harm Caused to Mother or Child

Pre-Conception Negligence

There have been some obstetric cases in which doctors have been successfully sued following the birth of children whose injuries or disabilities were caused by negligence that occurred before they were conceived. *Bergstreser v Mitchell*[21] is a United States decision that allowed such a claim to proceed. It was alleged that the negligent performance of a caesarean section had affected a subsequent pregnancy, which ended with the woman's uterus rupturing and the performance of a premature emergency caesarean section. The child suffered hypoxia and/or anoxia, leading to brain damage. The United States Court of Appeals allowed the child to bring an action for pre-conception negligence. Rather different was the decision by the New South Wales Court of Appeal in *X and Y (By Her Tutor X) v Pal and Others*.[22] Here a woman and her daughter took proceedings against three doctors; the

---

[21] 577 F 2d 22 (1978). See also *Jorgensen v Meade Johnson Laboratories Inc* 483 F 2d 237 (1973).
[22] (1991) 23 NSWLR 26.

alleged negligence (which was not contested) was that they had failed to test the woman for syphilis, which was later diagnosed. The girl was born with congenital syphilis and it was clear that this had been contracted from the mother; the child's condition was therefore caused by the failure to test the mother for the disease. The court was in no doubt about the negligence of the two doctors who had been involved in the management of the pregnancy. The third defendant (Dr Pal) had been responsible for the woman's care before she conceived the child. An obstetrician and gynaecologist, he had cared for the woman during an earlier pregnancy; when doing so he had neglected to have her screened for syphilis. The court held that he owed a duty of care to the child who had not been conceived at the time he was responsible for the mother's care.

Negligent Antenatal or Perinatal Care

Allegations that pregnant women have received negligent antenatal or perinatal care are common. A small proportion of these matters result from harm suffered by the mother alone. A maternal claim might be made, for example, after a negligent failure to diagnose a pregnancy. One such claim arose when the misdiagnosis was followed by the performance of laser ablation surgery on the woman's cervix and another when a pregnancy was misdiagnosed as a uterine tumour and an exploratory laparotomy was undertaken.[23] In each of these matters, the woman miscarried and, while there was doubt whether the operation had caused the miscarriage, it was held that damages could still be awarded for any harm (such as pain and discomfort and medical expenses) directly suffered by the woman. In another case, a woman, having had a normal delivery, suffered a ruptured uterus and a hysterectomy was performed. The woman succeeded in her claim that the rupture had been caused by a negligent failure to monitor the administration of the oxytocin used to induce labour.[24] A different form of negligence—failure to attend—was established in a Louisiana matter in which the child was stillborn.[25] While it was clear that the doctor should have gone to the hospital earlier, there was nothing to indicate that the failure to do so had caused the child's death. This did not, however, relieve the doctor of liability to the woman. She had remained in hospital for three hours without pain relief. The hospital's organization was such that she could not be given this without the doctor's written consent. His delay in going to the hospital to provide this consent was held to have caused

---

[23] *Rechenbach v Haftkowycz* 654 NE 2d 374 (Ohio App 8 Dist, 1995) and *Jarboe v Harting* Ky, 397 SW 2d 775 (1965).

[24] *Stack v Wapner* Pa Super, 368 A 2d 292 (1976). See also *Le Page v Kingston and Richmond Health Authority* [1997] 8 Med LR 229. This case involved a negligent failure to control a postpartum haemorrhage after the successful delivery of twins; a hysterectomy became the only available treatment.

[25] *Coleman v Touro Infirmary of New Orleans* 506 So 2d 571 (La App 4 Cir, 1987).

the woman unnecessary pain, suffering, and mental anguish. She was accordingly entitled to damages. The case does not suggest that an obstetrician is under an obligation to go to the hospital as soon as a woman is admitted; here, however, the woman was in need of pain relief and only the doctor could have arranged this.

Occasionally negligence will cause harm to both the woman and child. In *Cignetti v Camel*, which arose in Missouri, the husband and wife sued for damages.[26] The woman had had one child previously, by caesarean section; there had been complications after the procedure. When she again became pregnant, she informed her obstetrician that she had been told that any subsequent delivery would have to be by caesarean section. The second pregnancy proceeded without incident. Two weeks before the due date, the woman was admitted to hospital in severe pain; a resident physician determined that, although she was having irregular contractions, she was not in labour. The next morning the obstetrician performed an amniocentesis to determine the maturity of the fetus's lungs. The consultant decided that the lungs were not fully matured and that the woman's pain was caused by a gallbladder attack and so was unrelated to the pregnancy. The pain continued and the following day she had two acute attacks. After the second of these, the fetal heart tones were found to be weak. The obstetrician was called, came immediately, and performed a caesarean section. The baby was dead and the uterus had split in the position of the old scar. A subtotal hysterectomy was performed. The plaintiffs' expert witness testified that the care provided did not meet the standard expected of a consultant obstetrician. There had been a failure to respond appropriately in view of the advanced stage of the pregnancy, the prior history of delivery by caesarean section, and the woman's complaints of pain. While there was disagreement as to the significance of the results of the amniocentesis, the testimony of the plaintiffs' expert was that any risks arising from the possibility of immaturity were outweighed by the virtual certainty of death in the event of a uterine rupture. The argument was that the risks involved in not undertaking a caesarean section outweighed those involved in performing it. The Missouri Court of Appeals affirmed the jury's finding of negligence.

Actions following maternal deaths are less common. The proceedings in *Katsetos v Nolan*[27] involved a woman who, soon after a normal delivery, experienced a sharp drop in blood pressure and a rapid pulse; she quickly went into a state of shock. The consultant obstetrician considered the possibility of internal bleeding, but thought a pulmonary or amniotic fluid embolism was more likely. He therefore called in a physician. The woman died some seven hours later. The cause of death was internal bleeding resulting from a ruptured uterine artery. Both the obstetrician and the physician

---

[26] 692 SW 2d 329 (Mo App, 1985).   [27] 368 A 2d 172 (1976).

were sued. Several types of negligence were alleged: failure to diagnose the condition, failure to provide accepted treatment for shock, and failure to remain in attendance. The last-mentioned related to the fact that at some time during the day the obstetrician had left the hospital to see patients in his rooms. While it was accepted that a doctor has a duty not to leave a patient at a critical stage, here there was doubt whether his absence contributed to the death. A further issue arose regarding the ability of the doctors to prevent the death. There was evidence by a pathologist that a rare medical condition had made the artery very weak; because of this weakness, it would not have been possible to stop the bleeding by suturing or clamping the artery. In spite of such doubts, the award of damages against both doctors was upheld.

Another example is provided by a case in which a woman died from an amniotic fluid embolism. Oxytocin had been used when it was contra-indicated and its administration had been inadequately monitored. The contractions had been too strong and the uterus had ruptured. Evidence was given that the rupture could have allowed amniotic fluid to escape and that this could have produced the embolism. While there was some doubt about the exact mechanism, it was held that there was a substantial probability that the negligent management had led to both the rupture and the embolism. The doctor was held liable.[28] A different approach was taken to the question of causation in another case dealing with death by amniotic fluid embolism. The action in *Falcon v Memorial Hospital* was brought on the basis that the use of an intravenous line would have reduced the chances of death from the embolism; evidence was given that there would have been a 37.5 per cent chance of survival if an intravenous line had been used. It was held that the woman had been deprived of a 'substantial opportunity' of survival and that the doctor was therefore liable. Other members of the court strongly dissented:

The lost chance of survival theory does more than merely lower the threshold of proof of causation; it fundamentally alters the meaning of causation. . . . The recovery of damages for the loss of a mere chance eviscerates the principles that underlie our tort law. . . . By definition, the recovery sanctioned today is based on the mere possibility that the acts of the defendants caused the death [of the woman]. . . . Rather than deter-ring undesirable conduct, the rule imposed only penalizes the medical profession for inevitable unfavorable results. The lost chance of survival theory presumes to know the unknowable.[29]

If the majority's decision were to be generally accepted, the result would be the imposition of a considerable burden on obstetricians; there are many situations in which, with hindsight, the chances of avoiding an adverse outcome could have been increased. The dissenting judgment drew attention to the

[28] *Vialva v City of New York* 499 NYS 2d 977 (AD 2 Dept, 1986).
[29] 462 NW 2d 44, 65 and 67–8 (Mich, 1990).

dangers inherent in the decision to hold a doctor liable for a lost chance. The majority view represented a departure from the generally accepted rule that the medical negligence must be a material or substantial cause of the harm suffered by the patient.

Negligent antenatal or perinatal care can result in children being born with injuries or disabilities. A Louisiana example of a claim arising from the provision of allegedly negligent antenatal care related to a 1982 delivery.[30] The birth was difficult. Fundal pressure was used and when the baby's head began to emerge, the obstetrician tried unsuccessfully to apply forceps. A very large episiotomy was cut and the baby's head was delivered by forceps; shoulder dystocia occurred and unsuccessful efforts were made to rotate the baby. Finally, after the application of suprapubic pressure, the baby, weighing 11 lb 10 ounces, was delivered. She had a fractured right clavicle and right rib cage. She had suffered damage to the right brachial plexus nerves; this resulted in Erb palsy and consequent difficulty in raising her right arm. The injury was permanent. The action brought on the girl's behalf alleged that both the doctor who delivered the child and a colleague who had assisted with antenatal care had been negligent in two respects. The expert who testified for the plaintiff stated that the obstetricians had been negligent in failing to use a glucose loading test to exclude gestational diabetes (although the woman had shown no symptoms of diabetes). He further stated that an ultrasound should have been used to determine the baby's size. In the view of the witness, had the weight of the fetus been known, most obstetricians would have performed a caesarean section. On appeal, the trial court's finding that the doctors had not been negligent was upheld. There was a good deal of evidence that the care provided had met the standard expected of a competent obstetrician in 1982. At that time it was not the practice routinely to use glucose loading tests or to employ an ultrasound to determine the baby's weight.

This matter can be contrasted with an action taken in Calgary after the birth in 1988 of a child with one arm damaged by shoulder dystocia.[31] The negligence alleged was the general practitioner's failure to diagnose gestational diabetes; it was argued that had this been diagnosed, the risk of the child developing as a macrosomic baby would have been reduced and this, in turn, would have reduced the risk of shoulder dystocia. Much of the testimony focused on whether negligence was established simply by proof of a failure to do routine screening for gestational diabetes. Published guidelines suggested that such screening was desirable. Further, universal screening was recommended by the Alberta Medical Association and by the Society of Obstetricians and Gynaecologists of Canada. At the trial, differences of

---

[30] *Stein v Insurance Corporation of America* 566 So 2d 1114 (La App 2 Cir, 1990).
[31] *Pierre (Next Friend of) v Marshall* [1994] 8 WWR 478. See also *Hallatt v North West Anglia Health Authority* [1998] Lloyd's Law Reports: Medical 197.

opinion were expressed; one view favoured routine screening and the other said tests should be done only if recognized risk factors were present.

The defendant doctor's practice was not to test blood sugar levels unless there was an indication to do so. Here the urine analysis had disclosed at least 2 per cent glucose in the urine and he had noted that the woman's weight gain had been 'a little excessive', but he did not consider it 'unusual'. He did not do an ultrasound, preferring to rely on his own estimate of the baby's size. He had considered and dismissed the possibility of gestational diabetes. The doctor was held to have been negligent. He knew of the guidelines relating to screening, but his failure to undertake routine testing was not the sole factor. There were warning signs to which he did not respond. He knew that sugar in the urine could be a symptom of diabetes and that excessive weight gain could be another. He should have done more to exclude the possibility of gestational diabetes. By omitting to do so he was found to have failed to meet the standard expected of a careful and prudent general practitioner practising in Calgary in 1988. The case demonstrates that obstetric practice is constantly changing. Management that was acceptable in Louisiana in 1982 was not necessarily appropriate in Calgary six years later.

Another Canadian example of an action arising from negligent antenatal care was *Wipfli v Britten*.[32] The British Columbia Court of Appeal accepted that a family physician had been negligent in failing to diagnose twins, one of whom was born with severe brain damage. While it was not suggested that the non-diagnosis of twins was inevitably negligent, the antenatal care was substandard in the circumstances. The number of antenatal visits had been limited, there had been an omission to perform an ultrasound, there had been no pelvic examination at or near term, no response to the woman's weight gain and size, and an omission to order an oestriol estimation. In combination, these factors were indicative of negligence; they resulted in the inappropriate management of the delivery and hence caused the twin to be born with severe disabilities.

Actions arising solely from negligence at the time of delivery are more common. In a small number of these matters the claims have related to temporary harm suffered by the child. An example was provided by a case in which a doctor induced labour, having miscalculated the delivery date. The premature child suffered Respiratory Distress Syndrome in respect of which damages were awarded.[33] There have been numerous cases in which permanent harm has been caused; actions have been brought on behalf of children who have suffered Erb palsy, nerve damage to the shoulder, or eye damage.[34] In some instances the harm has been caused by the negligent use of forceps. The negligence might consist of a failure to employ proper technique (either

---

[32] (1984) 13 DLR (4th) 169.   [33] *Fabianke v Weaver* 527 So 2d 1253 (Ala, 1988).
[34] For example, *Dumes v Genest* 568 NE 2d 1179 (Mass App Ct, 1991); *Spellman v Mount* 696 P 2d 510 (Okl App, 1984); *Gaughan v Bedfordshire Health Authority* [1997] 8 Med LR 182.

in the application of the forceps or using excessive force) or the claim might relate to the decision to employ forceps rather than to undertake a caesarean section. An illustration was provided by a case arising from an action on behalf of a child who had suffered permanent injury to the brachial plexus nerves of the right shoulder. The doctor had applied low forceps to deliver the head and had then realized that he was dealing with a case of shoulder dystocia. He used excessive traction to complete the delivery, causing the nerve damage. Given that the woman's labour had been slow and that the baby was large, it was claimed that the doctor should have anticipated the risk and performed a caesarean section. Although the expert evidence conflicted, the trial court's finding of negligence was upheld on appeal.[35]

Another example of harm caused during a vaginal delivery was provided by an Illinois case. Early on the morning on which the child was delivered, the defendant doctor (who had been advised by nursing staff that the fetus was in the vertex position) by telephone ordered the administration of oxytocin to augment labour. A few hours later he examined the woman, diagnosed the baby as being in the vertex position, and ruptured the membranes. Thereafter nursing staff monitored the woman and continued to record a vertex presentation. About half an hour before the delivery, the doctor was advised that she was making good progress. Soon after, however, another nurse found that the cervix was fully dilated, that the fetus was in a breech position, and that the heartbeat was decelerating. The doctor was called and arrived three minutes later. He decided it was too late to perform a caesarean section. There was difficulty delivering the head; it was testified that the doctor 'pulled and twisted the baby's torso for several minutes'. When delivered, the baby was 'blue and not breathing'; she had suffered extensive kidney damage. It became apparent that the child had a gestational age of thirty-five to thirty-six weeks. Evidence was also given that the woman did not come into labour until some hours after the oxytocin had been administered and the membranes had been ruptured. The negligence alleged against the doctor was that he had wrongly prescribed oxytocin for a preterm baby when the woman was not in active labour, had wrongly ruptured the membranes when the baby was preterm, had failed to diagnose the breech presentation in time to do a caesarean section, and had applied undue pressure during the delivery. The appellate court found no reason to disturb the jury's finding of negligence. While there was some doubt about causation, particular emphasis was placed on the doctor's failure to determine that the baby was in a breech position and on his use of excessive pressure during the delivery.[36]

---

[35] *Jackson v Huang* 514 So 2d 727 (La App 2 Cir, 1987). See also *Bunch v Mercy Hospital of New Orleans* La App, 404 So 2d 520 (1981) and *Wale v Barnes* Fla, 278 So 2d 601 (1973). A Canadian case involving a difficult forceps delivery which should have been abandoned in favour of a caesarean section was *Robinson v Dick* (1986) 6 BCLR (2d) 330.

[36] *Alvis v Henderson Obstetrics* 592 NE 2d 678 (Ill App 3 Dist, 1992).

Claims arising from injury allegedly caused by a negligent failure to undertake a caesarean section are common. Such cases frequently reveal differences of opinion among the medical witnesses. In *James v Woolley*,[37] the Supreme Court of Alabama heard an appeal relating to a child injured during delivery. The 38-year-old mother was 5 ft 4 in and weighed 316 lb. When admitted to hospital for delivery, she suffered from high blood pressure and gestational diabetes. The consultant decided in favour of a vaginal delivery. Shoulder dystocia was diagnosed. Various methods were used to overcome the problem, but the baby, weighing 11 lb and 6 oz, was born with a paralysed arm. The damages action rested on the allegation that the consultant had been negligent in failing to arrange a caesarean section. An expert witness for the plaintiff was emphatic that the decision to proceed by way of vaginal delivery revealed a departure from the standard of care expected of a consultant:

Q. Do you believe that every pregnant woman who presents, as Mrs James did in this case, should have a C-section without any consideration of seeing whether or not she could vaginally deliver prior to the C-section?

A. Anytime a woman, particularly a gestational diabetic . . . is estimated to have a baby in excess of 4,000 grams, a caesarean section should be done. Here, by the way, I am quoting from the technical bulletin of the American College of Obstetricians and Gynecologists.[38]

Other expert witnesses expressed a different view. The court decided that more was at issue than a doctor making a choice between two alternatives, each of which had the support of a respectable body of medical opinion. It was impressed by the quoted passage, which suggested that the consultant had fallen below the required standard of care. It therefore ruled that it was open to a jury to find that the consultant had been negligent.

There have been many cases in which substantial awards have been made to brain-damaged children. Almost invariably the negligence alleged is the failure to perform a caesarean section, although other factors may also be involved. In one case arising when a child was born (in 1973) with cerebral palsy and mental retardation, the evidence showed that the woman had been admitted twenty-one days after her due date. Although she was experiencing light contractions, she was sent home. That night she had a dark yellow mucous discharge. She was readmitted the next evening and in the early hours of the following morning the fetal heart rate caused concern. Later that morning a caesarean section was performed. The doctor was found to have been negligent in not undertaking the caesarean on the day of her first admission. The doctor's awareness that the fetus was post-mature, that there had been meconium staining, and an absence of amniotic fluid should have

---

[37] 523 So 2d 110 (Ala, 1988).			[38] Ibid. 112.

alerted him to the need to act earlier. Further, he had failed to undertake oestriol testing or to perform an amniocentesis.[39]

A delay in undertaking a caesarean section was also crucial in *Reilly v United States*.[40] The child was born with major disabilities, including profound brain damage, retardation, and blindness. Some six hours after the woman had been admitted in labour, the fetal heart rate dropped. She made slow progress and the fetus was large and occipito posterior. According to the evidence, 'All these signs screamed that the baby was being asphyxiated and that a caesarean section should have been performed without delay.' The obstetrician nevertheless persisted in the view that a vaginal delivery was possible. When the woman was taken to the operating theatre the electronic monitor was removed (and so the doctor was unaware of further deterioration in the condition of the fetus). He applied vacuum suction to deliver the baby. The problems were compounded by the trauma of delivery. The evidence indicated that there had never been any grounds for expecting a safe vaginal delivery and it was found that in failing to perform a caesarean section when the fetal heart rate dropped, the doctor had been in breach of the standard of care expected of a competent obstetrician.

A further illustration was provided by *Williams v Lallie Kemp Charity Hospital*,[41] a Louisiana case in which the trial court accepted that the doctors had been negligent. The woman had been admitted to hospital with the fetus in the breech position and the child was born profoundly retarded. Three types of negligence were established. The fetal heart rate was not adequately monitored. A decision was made to deliver the child vaginally rather than by way of caesarean section. Forceps were not used, with the result that the delivery of the head was slow. Although the defendants argued that the child's condition was genetic, the court relied on expert evidence to establish that the disability had been caused by medical negligence. This evidence indicated that the injury had been caused 'by neonatal asphyxia, probably secondary to prolonged delivery of the head; seizures disorder, probably secondary to hypoxic brain damage; spasticity, probably secondary to hypoxic brain damage'. Particular emphasis was placed on the 'woefully inadequate' monitoring; a witness testified that the fetal heart rate should be monitored every thirty minutes during Stage 1 of labour and every five minutes during Stage 2. These requirements were said to be supported by the standards set by the American College of Obstetricians and Gynecologists.

In *Holt v Nelson*,[42] the claim combined allegations of negligent antenatal and perinatal care with allegations of negligent non-disclosure. For present purposes, it is sufficient to deal with the allegedly negligent diagnosis and

[39] *Nemmers v United States* 612 F Supp 928 (DC Ill, 1985).
[40] 665 F Supp 976 (DRI, 1987).   [41] 428 So 2d 1000 (La App 1 Cir, 1983).
[42] Wash App, 523 P 2d 211 (1974).

treatment. The action arose from the birth of a child suffering from spastic quadriplegia, brain damage, and cerebral palsy. Five weeks before the expected delivery date, the woman experienced bleeding. Seven weeks later (two weeks after the baby was due) she was admitted to hospital with further bleeding. The following morning, a diagnosis of partial placenta praevia was made and the doctor attempted to induce labour. When the fetal heart tones were found to be poor, a caesarean section was performed. The child was limp at birth and diagnosed as suffering from fetal anoxia. The plaintiff claimed that prior to the woman's admission to hospital the doctor had been negligent in failing to diagnose the placenta praevia, failing to arrange her early admission for caesarean section, and, once she had been admitted, attempting to induce labour and being too slow in undertaking the caesarean section. Faced with conflicting medical evidence as to the appropriate standard of care, the jury returned a verdict in favour of the doctor.

This outcome can be contrasted with that in *Muenstermann by Muenstermann v United States*.[43] The case also concerned a child born with cerebral palsy. During the pregnancy, a sonogram (ultrasound) had revealed placenta praevia. An attempt was made to induce labour, but the doctor desisted after ten hours when brachycardia was diagnosed. The woman went into labour five days later and her membranes were ruptured. When the fetal heart rate dropped severely, an emergency caesarean section was performed. Although there were other factors that the doctor should have taken into account (the large size of the fetus and polyhydramnious), the court placed particular emphasis on the doctor's attempt to perform a vaginal delivery when the woman had placenta praevia. It had no doubt that 'the presence of a placenta praevia alone requires a caesarean section'.[44]

Lane by Lane v Skyline Family Medical Center[45] was an action arising from the conduct of a general practitioner. The doctor had cared for a woman pregnant with twins; she delivered prematurely and one of the twins was born with brain damage. It was argued that the doctor's antenatal care had been substandard and that better care would have prevented the child from being born with disabilities. In particular, it was alleged that steps should have been taken to prevent a premature delivery. The Court of Appeals of Minnesota accepted that a general practitioner in such a situation has a duty to refer to a specialist any case that is beyond his or her knowledge or technical skill. A practitioner who does not do this will be held to the standard of care of the specialist to whom the referral should have been made. The action failed, however, because it could not be established that the standard of the doctor's antenatal care had fallen below that of a specialist. This result was reached because of the difficulty of determining the cause of the child's disabilities.

[43] 787 F Supp 499 (D Md, 1992).   [44] Ibid. 512.
[45] 363 NW 2d 318 (Minn App, 1985).

The plaintiffs asserted that the child's premature delivery caused an intra-ventricular haemorrhage and that this resulted in the cerebral palsy and mental retardation. A complicating factor was that twin-to-twin transfusion syndrome was also diagnosed. This in its turn caused polyhydamnios, which may have contributed to the premature labour. Evidence was given that had the labour been delayed the twin-to-twin transfusion would have continued and the child might have suffered greater harm. Further, the second twin might have been seriously affected. Thus it was not clear that the doctor could or should have attempted to delay labour. Because differing views could properly have been held on the appropriate treatment, it could not be established that he had failed to meet the standard of a competent specialist.

A more complex situation arose in British Columbia in *Cherry v Borsman*,[46] where the allegations of negligence took a number of forms. The defendant doctor attempted to terminate a pregnancy. He erred in determining the age of the fetus and therefore used a curette that was too small. As a result, he was found not to have used adequate care to ensure that the fetal material was removed. The pathology report noted that the specimen contained 'immature placental material only'; the doctor did not himself examine the tissue. The patient subsequently consulted another doctor, who advised her that she might still be pregnant. She reported this to the defendant. For a number of reasons, therefore, the defendant should have been alert to the possibility that the woman was still pregnant. He did not undertake further tests to exclude this possibility. He had thus been negligent, not only in the performance of the termination procedure, but also in his post-operative care. When the pregnancy was confirmed, the doctor advised the woman that there was little chance that the fetus could have been damaged by the termination procedure. This proved to be negligent advice. The child was delivered nine weeks prematurely, suffering from oligohydramnios syndrome and arthrogryposis. Some days later, she contracted necrotizing enterocolitis, her blood pressure fell, and permanent brain damage resulted. She suffered from cerebral palsy and could not walk unaided.

These facts gave rise to several claims, both by the mother and on behalf of the child. At this stage, it is only the claims relating to the harm suffered by the child as a result of the negligent diagnosis and treatment that will be discussed. The court found that by damaging the amniotic sac, the failed termination procedure had affected the early development of the fetus and had also led to the premature birth; the latter set in motion a series of events which produced the child's severe physical and mental handicaps. Thus the necessary causal link was established: it was held that the combination of negligent diagnosis and a negligent technique had caused or materially

---

[46] (1991) 75 DLR (4th) 668.

contributed to the disabilities suffered by the child. The doctor was ordered to pay substantial damages.

Bowers v Harrow Health Authority[47] was an English decision relating to a grossly disabled child. The case involved the delivery of twins. The first twin was delivered without any problems. The second twin was born suffering from serious brain damage and died at the age of 6. It was alleged that the obstetrical registrar had been negligent in managing the delivery. The registrar had formed the view that the second twin was lying longitudinally with a foot presenting, although he recorded that he could also feel a hand. He grasped the foot, ruptured the membranes, and attempted to extract the baby. When this procedure failed, it became obvious that the head was also presenting and he sought a consultant's help. Approximately ten minutes later, the consultant used forceps to deliver the baby. It was alleged that the registrar had failed to recognize that the second twin was lying transversely and that by rupturing the membranes, he had unnecessarily put the fetus at risk. The expert evidence before the court was conflicting. Two witnesses for the plaintiff testified that the registrar should have recognized the possibility that the fetus was lying transversely and that it was not appropriate for him to intervene by rupturing the membranes. Two witnesses for the defendant testified that the palpation of a foot and a hand was consistent with a longitudinal lie and that even if the lie had been transverse, it was appropriate to rupture the membranes and to attempt a breech extraction of the baby. The court found in favour of the plaintiff. The significant feature of the decision was that although the court accepted the rule formulated in *Bolam*, it felt able to choose between the two conflicting views. Thus, in effect, it held that the evidence presented on behalf of the doctor did not reflect the views of a reasonable body of competent obstetricians.

In contrast, in *Whitehouse v Jordan*,[48] the doctor was found not to have been negligent. A claim was made on behalf of a 10-year-old boy born with severe brain damage. Because of the mother's small stature and the size of the baby, it was apparent that the birth would be difficult. A trial of labour was undertaken and Kiellands forceps applied. The obstetrician's notes recorded 'a very tight fit' and, after pulling during five or six contractions, he concluded that a vaginal delivery would be too traumatic. A caesarean section was immediately and competently performed. On delivery, the baby was found to be apnoeic and was made to breathe after thirty-five minutes. A negligence claim succeeded at trial and damages were awarded; on appeal the decision was reversed. When hearing the appeal against this decision, the House of Lords accepted that the forceps delivery had caused the brain damage. The appeal was confined to one issue: whether the obstetrician had, in the course of the trial of forceps, been negligent in pulling too long and too

---

[47] [1995] 6 Med LR 16.   [48] [1981] 1 WLR 246.

strongly on the child's head. It was held that the evidence did not establish that there had been a breach of the standard of care expected of the ordinary skilled obstetrician.

Finally, there are the cases arising from the delivery of a stillborn child or from a perinatal death. Although it is impossible to categorize these matters, there is one group in which the major allegation is of a negligent failure to perform a caesarean section. A simple illustration was provided by a North Dakota case in which a woman was admitted to hospital in the evening after her membranes had spontaneously ruptured. The defendant doctor saw her at 9 a.m. the next day and was advised of the membrane rupture and of the fact that there had been meconium staining in the liquor. At 11.30 a.m. there was concern about the fetal heart tones and by 12.30 p.m. they could no longer be heard. An hour later, the child was born dead. It was held that the doctor's failure to recognize the significance of the woman's symptoms and the delay in delivering the child amounted to negligence.[49] A similar failure to appreciate the seriousness of the situation led to an Illinois obstetrician being found liable for negligence. He was responsible for the antenatal care of an 18-year-old woman; she had a small pelvis and a pelvimetry examination indicated that a vaginal delivery would be risky. Neither a glucose tolerance test nor an ultrasound was performed. The woman was admitted to hospital four weeks after the expected delivery date. The baby was large. After examining her at 8.30 a.m., the doctor left for his rooms. He did not order fetal monitoring, although he several times telephoned to check the woman's progress. When he returned at noon, he noted a drop in the fetal heart tones. At 12.16 p.m. a cord prolapse was observed. An effort was made to push the baby back up the birth canal. When this failed, a forceps delivery was attempted. This also failed and the baby died *in utero* at 12.35 p.m. It was accepted that if a caesarean section had been performed when the doctor had first examined the woman, the baby would probably have survived.[50]

In a District of Columbia case, an obstetrician's failure to check on a patient resulted in his liability in respect of a stillbirth. The woman (who was thirty-two weeks pregnant) telephoned the doctor at 6 p.m. to advise that her membranes had ruptured. He told her to go to hospital; she did so and staff telephoned him (at approximately 8 p.m.) and confirmed the premature rupture of the membranes. He ordered that she be placed on a fetal heart monitor. During the night, the monitor revealed decelerations in the heart rate, but the doctor was not advised of this. The fetus died at 5 a.m. The doctor came to the hospital at 9 a.m. Both he and the hospital were held liable in respect of the death of the fetus. The District of Columbia Court of Appeals stated:

[49] *Hopkins v Mc Bane* 427 NW 2d 85 (ND, 1988).
[50] *Jones v Karraker* Ill App, 440 NE 2d 420 (1982).

The testimony established that Dr Crooks, as the attending physician, was under a duty to know the status and well-being of his patient. He was responsible for knowing when fetal abnormalities were occurring and to be with his patient as soon as possible after they began. He should have been in contact with the hospital, or at least have assured [*sic*] that hospital personnel would be in contact with him regarding the status of his patient. The fetal tracings showed a baby in distress which should have been delivered by Caesarean section by approximately 11.20 p.m. Dr Crooks' status made him the only person who could have surgically intervened to deliver the baby. This evidence is sufficient to allow a reasonable juror to conclude that Dr Crooks had a duty to report to the hospital, assess the mother and fetus in light of the monitor tracing, and safely deliver the baby via Caesarean section. The evidence is also sufficient to allow for the conclusion that Dr Crooks' failure to do so resulted in the death of the baby.[51]

The subject of a doctor's obligation to attend was discussed in another case in which a woman asked the doctor whether he would deliver her child at home. He refused. The woman therefore placed herself under the care of a midwife. When the woman came into labour and the midwife was called, she advised that a doctor should be called. When telephoned, the doctor indicated that the woman should go to hospital, which she did. The baby was found to be dead. The parents sued the doctor on the ground of his failure to go to the home when complications arose. Their action did not succeed. Reference was made to accepted standards of obstetric care; it was noted that doctors no longer routinely did home deliveries and that good practice required delivery in hospital where the appropriate facilities were available. Further, there were complications here—a hand presentation—which required hospitalization and thus the doctor had advised the safest course. It was therefore held that the doctor had not breached his duty of care. The doctor's position was made clear: a physician 'is not required to accept professional employment on terms determined by the patient . . .'.[52]

In the cases discussed above, the negligence alleged was that of doctors, whether consultant obstetricians or general practitioners. In other matters, the focus has been on the conduct of the midwives. An English illustration was provided by a case in which the child was born with cerebral palsy; it was accepted that this had been caused by anoxia. The woman, a multigravida, was admitted to hospital after being in labour for two hours. On vaginal examination, the cervix was noted to be 8 cm dilated and she was in strong labour. The midwife performed an artificial rupture of the membranes and released clear liquor. The patient was not re-examined vaginally for over three hours. At this stage there had been minimal progress and the obstetrics registrar was summoned. He ordered the administration of syntocinon and left the woman in labour. The fetal heart rate deteriorated soon afterwards

---

[51] *Crooks v Williams* 508 A 2d 912, 915 (DC App, 1986).
[52] *Vidrine v Mayes* 127 So 2d 809, 811 (1961).

and the doctor returned and delivered the baby twenty minutes later. The judge found that the midwives had been unreasonably slow in calling the doctor, given that the patient had made very rapid progress in the first two hours of her labour and then had failed to deliver within the normal predicted time. The doctor was not found to have been negligent; he had reacted appropriately when called.[53] In a case of this kind, a midwife can be found negligent on the ground that she has not appreciated the need to summon assistance; she is liable in just the same way as a general practitioner who fails to refer a patient to a specialist. This point was vividly made in another English case in which the judge was extremely critical of the conduct of a midwife. The judge expressed the view that the midwife 'was overconfident in her own abilities and not in any way qualified to make the clinical judgment' which was required when decelerations in the fetal heart rate were observed.[54] This does not mean, however, that a midwife will be judged by standards applicable to a medical practitioner. This was demonstrated by a Californian case that also dealt with fetal monitoring. There a nurse had undertaken Doppler monitoring. She admitted that she had listened *after* rather than during the contractions and that, at times, she had listened for only fifteen seconds. The baby was delivered in poor condition and suffered seizures. The nurse was found to have failed to provide the required standard of care. The court pointed out that her conduct 'must not be measured by the standard of care required of a physician or surgeon, but by that of other nurses in the same or similar locality and under similar circumstances'.[55]

Unwanted Pregnancy or the Birth of an Unwanted Child

The birth of a child injured or disabled by medical negligence does not provide the only basis on which a damages claim can arise in the fields of obstetrics. The conception or birth of a child can be an unwanted result for which the parents may seek damages. The terminology used to describe such actions varies; the terms 'wrongful conception' and 'wrongful birth' are frequently employed. Such terms are misleading, for there is nothing 'wrongful' about the conception or birth. The descriptions 'unwanted pregnancy' and 'the birth of an unwanted child' are preferable, for they clearly indicate the nature of the complaint.

There are several situations in which medical negligence can result in an unwanted pregnancy or the birth of an unwanted child. A termination procedure might be inexpertly performed and the pregnancy might continue. Alternatively, a tubal ligation might be negligently undertaken and the

---

[53] *Murphy v Wirral Health Authority* [1996] 7 Med LR 99.
[54] *Wiszniewski v Central Manchester Health Authority* [1996] 7 Med LR 248, 256; decision affirmed by the Court of Appeal: [1998] Lloyd's Law Reports: Medical 223.
[55] *Alef v Alta Bates Hospital* 6 Cal Rptr 2d 900, 904 (Cal App 1 Dist, 1992).

woman become pregnant. In each of these situations, courts in the United
States, Canada, and England have accepted that the parents may sue the doctor who performed the procedure.[56] To allow such an action is to do no more
than apply the basic principles of negligence:

[A] physician who performs an abortion or sterilization procedure owes a legal duty
to the patient. Where the patient can establish failure to perform the procedure with
reasonable care and damages proximately resulting from breach of the duty, she is
entitled to recover as in any other medical malpractice action.[57]

Claims made in respect of pregnancies occurring after the negligent insertion
of an intra-uterine contraceptive device or the failure to replace such a device
are less common.[58] In practice, most of the reported cases relate to claims
made following the birth of unwanted children; reports of proceedings to
obtain damages solely for unwanted pregnancies (which are then terminated) are rare. The following discussion, therefore, will concentrate on
unwanted birth matters.

Identifying the Harm

Actions of this kind are not straightforward. As has been explained in the
previous chapter, to succeed in a medical negligence claim, a plaintiff must
establish not only a failure to take appropriate care, but also that this failure
caused harm of a kind which entitles a plaintiff to damages. When the action
is for an unwanted birth, a fundamental problem is the identification of the
harm suffered by the plaintiff. One view is that since all life is precious, it is
contrary to public policy for the law to recognize a claim that parents have
suffered injury as the result of the birth of a child. When this view is considered, a distinction can be made between the birth of a healthy, normal
child and the birth of a disabled child. Those who adhere unequivocally to a
belief in the sanctity of life would not accept such a distinction. Some courts,
however, have recognized that there is a difference between a claim made by
parents who, for economic or personal reasons, regard the birth of a normal

---

[56] Examples of cases in which pregnancies continued following the negligent performance of
termination procedures were: *Wilczynski v Goodman* 391 NE 2d 479 (1979); *Miller v Johnson*
343 SE 2d 301 (Va, 1986); *Nanke v Napier* 346 NW 2d 520 (Iowa, 1984); *Cherry v Borsman* (1991)
75 DLR (4th) 668, (1992) 94 DLR (4th) 487. Examples of cases in which tubal ligations were
negligently performed and pregnancies ensued were: *Boone v Mullendore* Ala, 416 So 2d 718
(1982); *McKernan v Aasheim* 687 P 2d 850 (Wash, 1984); *Fulton-DeKalb Hospital Authority v
Graves* 314 SE 2d 653 (Ga, 1984); *Morris v Sanchez, Stout v United States* 746 P 2d 184 (Okl,
1987); *Marciniak v Lundborg* 450 NW 2d 243 (Wis, 1990); *Girdley v Coats* 825 SW 2d 295
(Mo banc, 1992); *Cataford v Moreau* (1978) 114 DLR (3d) 585; *Udale v Bloomsbury Area Health
Authority* [1983] 1 WLR 1098; *Emeh v Kensington and Chelsea and Westminster Area Health
Authority* [1985] 1 QB 1012; *Walkin v South Manchester Health Authority* [1995] 1 WLR 1543.
[57] *Miller v Johnson* 343 SE 2d 301, 304 (Va, 1986).
[58] *Yasar v Cohen* 483 So 2d 1099 (La App 4 Cir, 1986) and *Jackson v Bumgardner* 347 SE 2d
743 (NC, 1986).

child as a calamity and a claim made by parents who react against the birth of a child solely because that child is disabled. Recognition of this difference has made some judges more reluctant to allow unwanted birth claims when the child is normal and healthy. On occasions, the courts' reaction has been hostile when the essence of the parents' claim is that they have been forced to accept the burden of caring for a normal child. A dissenting judge in an Australian case provided an example. He described an unwanted birth claim as 'improper to the point of obscenity' and quoted with approval the view that: 'Such a claim seems utterly offensive; there should be rejoicing that the ... mistake bestowed the gift of life upon the child.'[59] Similarly, in an Illinois judgment, it was remarked that to treat the birth of a normal child as an injury to the parents, 'offends fundamental values attached to human life'.[60] An acceptance of such views led the Court of Appeals of New York to rule that 'the birth of a healthy child does not constitute a cognizable legal harm for which an action in tort will lie'.[61]

To invoke a belief in the preciousness of human life in order to resist unwanted birth actions is, however, to adopt a perspective that is increasingly likely to be rejected. Recent changes in the social climate have led to a questioning of the view that places all the emphasis on the value of life. One manifestation of this more sceptical attitude is opposition to laws restricting access to abortion. Those who oppose laws preventing abortion do so on the basis that a woman should be free to decide all matters relating to childbearing. Where one stands on this issue is relevant to one's attitude to actions for unwanted births. A commitment to freedom of choice is incompatible with the belief that the birth of a child is invariably a blessing. A corollary of the view that a woman should be free to control her fertility is that she can legitimately claim to have suffered harm if her efforts to exercise that freedom (by way of a termination or sterilization procedure) have been thwarted by medical negligence. The growing recognition of women's freedom of choice—particularly in the United States (*Roe v Wade*[62] and *Planned Parenthood of South Eastern Pennsylvania v Casey*[63]) and in Canada (*R v Morgentaler*[64])—has fostered a climate which is much more favourable to the success of unwanted birth actions. Indeed, many of the United States decisions in unwanted birth cases have cited *Roe v Wade* as marking an important change

---

[59] *CES v Superclinics (Australia) Pty Ltd* (1995) 38 NSWLR 47, 86; the quoted passage was from *McKay v Essex Area Health Authority* [1982] 1 QB 1166, 1193.

[60] *Cockrum v Baumgartner* 447 NE 2d 385, 388 (Ill, 1983).

[61] *O'Toole v Greenberg* 477 NE 2d 445, 448 (NY, 1985). See also *Wilczynski v Goodman* 391 NE 2d 479, 487 (1979).

[62] 410 US 113; 35 L Ed 2d 147 (1973).

[63] 505 US 833; 120 L Ed 2d 674 (1992).

[64] (1988) 44 DLR (4th) 385. See also *Dobson (Litigation Guardian of) v Dobson* (1999) 174 DLR (4th) 1, 39, where it was accepted that there is an unrestricted legal right to abortion in Canada.

in the context within which these cases must be decided.[65] Some of these cases have explicitly made the point that a woman now has a legally recognized interest in limiting the size of her family.[66] While the law in England and Australia has not developed a presumption in favour of freedom of choice, the courts in these countries have been willing to respond to changing attitudes to the control of fertility.

Custodio v Bauer[67] provided a vivid illustration of a situation in which a Californian court had no difficulty in accepting that the birth of an unwanted child had placed a substantial burden on the parents. The plaintiffs had nine children and the woman suffered from bladder and kidney conditions. She underwent a tubal ligation, but this was negligently performed and she again became pregnant. She and her husband successfully sought damages. Cases of this kind support the view expressed in a dissenting judgment in *Flowers v District of Columbia*: '[I]t is naive—and often cruel—to say unequivocally that the birth of every child confers a benefit on every family that outweighs both the emotional and financial costs of supporting it.' Later the judgment added: 'It is facile and presumptuous to say that in every case an additional child is a family blessing, to the point that a family already under severe financial pressure should pay for a physician's negligence.'[68]

The courts in England, Canada, and Australia have reached similar conclusions. In *Emeh v Kensington and Chelsea and Westminster Area Health Authority*,[69] the English Court of Appeal held that there was no rule of public policy which prevented the recovery of damages for the birth of a child following a negligently performed sterilization. In so doing, it rejected the view, expressed in *Udale v Bloomsbury Area Health Authority*,[70] that the birth of a child was 'a blessing and an occasion for rejoicing'. The reasoning in *Emeh* was adopted by the Supreme Court of British Columbia in *Cherry v Borsman*.[71] Earlier, the Quebec Superior Court had had no difficulty in finding that the birth of a child was not invariably a happy event. This conclusion was not surprising, since the case before the court involved the birth of a child to a woman who already had ten children. The Chief Justice stated:

[T]he Court does not believe itself justified in concluding that the undesired birth of a healthy child, especially in a poor family consisting of 10 living children, constitutes

---

[65] See, for example, *McKernan v Aasheim* 687 P 2d 850 (Wash, 1984); *Speck v Finegold* Pa, 439 A 2d 110 (1981); *Lovelace Medical Center v Mendez* 805 P 2d 603 (NM, 1991); *Ochs v Borrelli* Conn, 445 A 2d 883 (1982). Further, *Griswold v Connecticut* 381 US 479; 14 L Ed 2d 510 (1965) is also cited in support of the proposition that there exists a constitutional right to use contraceptives to limit the size of one's family.

[66] *Fulton-DeKalb Hospital Authority v Graves* 314 SE 2d 653, 654 (Ga, 1984) and *Lovelace Medical Center v Mendez* 805 P 2d 603, 612 (NM, 1991).

[67] 59 Cal Rptr 463 (1967).

[68] 478 A 2d 1073, 1079 and 1082 (DC App, 1984).   [69] [1985] 1 QB 1012.

[70] [1983] 1 WLR 1098.

[71] (1991) 75 DLR (4th) 668, 691; affirmed (1992) 94 DLR (4th) 487.

such a happy and normal event that it would be offensive to the public order to have attached thereto pecuniary compensation in an appropriate case. [72]

The New South Wales Court of Appeal has expressed the same opinion.[73]

Thus there is now widespread agreement that the birth of an unwanted child can constitute a harm for which damages can be recovered in a negligence action. This does not mean that all traces of the ideological debate about the preciousness of human life have vanished from the law reports. Rather, the debate has taken a different form. It is now focused on the assessment of damages in cases involving unwanted births. When the arguments are examined, it becomes apparent that the discussion is simply another way of reopening the problem of identifying the nature of the harm suffered by the parents of an unwanted child. Having accepted that the parents of an unwanted child may claim to have suffered harm, the courts have generally had no difficulty in awarding damages to compensate for the expenses associated with the pregnancy and the delivery. There is, however, controversy over whether they should go further and award the parents damages to cover child-rearing expenses. It is in the context of this controversy that all the familiar arguments about the preciousness of human life are again marshalled. On the one hand is the view that it is unacceptable for parents who have the gift of a child to seek financial compensation for this gift. On the other is the belief that it is proper for the law to compensate parents for a financial burden which medical negligence has imposed on them. The courts have frequently shown themselves to be ambivalent as to the nature of the harm produced by the birth of an unwanted child. It is not uncommon for them to reach a compromise: unable to deny the existence of a cause of action, they have nevertheless expressed disapproval of the action by permitting the parents to recover no more than pregnancy-related expenses. In these cases the courts seem to have accepted that the *birth* of a child is a compensable harm, but have had much more difficulty accepting that the *consequence* of that event (liability to support the child) is a harm for which compensation can be awarded.

Causation

There are further problems to be considered with regard to a claim arising for an unwanted birth. To succeed in such a claim, a plaintiff must establish not only medical negligence, but also that this negligence *caused* harm. Once the harm (the birth of an unwanted child) has been identified, it is therefore necessary to examine causal issues. When the claim arises as a result of the continuation of a pregnancy following an inexpert termination procedure, the link between the negligence and the adverse outcome is clear. In contrast,

[72] *Cataford v Moreau* (1978) 114 DLR (3d) 585, 595.
[73] *CES v Superclinics (Australia) Pty Ltd* (1995) 38 NSWLR 47.

there is a possible causal argument when the claim relates to a negligently performed tubal ligation. It might be asserted that the subsequent unwanted pregnancy has been caused not by the negligence but by the intervening act of sexual intercourse and that this breaks the chain of causation. The courts have not accepted this argument. The medical negligence need not be the sole cause of the pregnancy, but only a proximate cause. An inexpertly performed tubal ligation fits this description. Further, the unwanted pregnancy cannot be dismissed as an unpredictable consequence of the procedure: 'It is difficult to conceive how the very act the consequences of which the operation [a tubal ligation] was designed to forestall, can be considered unforeseeable.'[74]

Another causal question can arise whether the action relates to a negligent termination or a negligent sterilization. A defendant doctor may assert that, once an unwanted pregnancy is diagnosed, it is for the woman to decide whether she will terminate it. If she elects not to do so, it can be argued that her decision, and not the doctor's conduct, has directly caused the unwanted birth. In addition, in all negligence actions, a plaintiff seeking damages has an obligation to mitigate the harm suffered; damages cannot be recovered for consequences that a claimant has had the opportunity to avoid. It would be open to a defendant doctor whose negligence has resulted in an unwanted pregnancy to concede liability to the extent of paying the expenses associated with a termination, but to argue that no further liability can be accepted if the pregnancy is allowed to proceed to full term.

No causal issue will arise if the stage at which the woman learns of the pregnancy is too late to permit her to obtain a safe termination. Similarly, no consideration need be given to the defence argument if the woman is unable to obtain a lawful abortion. The suggestion that the unwanted birth is the result of the woman's choice to allow the pregnancy to continue need be taken seriously only when there is nothing to prevent a woman who would otherwise have an abortion from doing so. The question to be addressed in this situation, therefore, is: does a decision to carry a pregnancy to full term break the causal link between the medical negligence and the unwanted birth? The English Court of Appeal examined the matter in *Emeh v Kensington and Chelsea and Westminster Area Health Authority*. There, following a failed tubal ligation, the woman had decided not to have the pregnancy terminated. The trial judge held that this decision broke the chain of causation. The Court of Appeal disagreed. It drew attention to a number of factors. The woman had discovered her pregnancy when she was between seventeen and twenty weeks pregnant. At this stage, the termination of the pregnancy would have involved three days in hospital and the procedure would not have been without risk. It would have caused considerable pain and discomfort. On the trial judge's ruling, the court commented:

[74] *Custodio v Bauer* 59 Cal Rptr 463, 472 (1967).

The judge, in saying that her failure to obtain an abortion was so unreasonable as to eclipse the defendants' wrongdoing, was . . . really saying that the defendants had the right to expect that, if they had not performed the operation properly, she would procure an abortion . . . I do not . . . think that the defendants had the right to expect any such thing. By their own negligence, they faced her with the very dilemma which she had sought to avoid by having herself sterilised. . . . Save in the most exceptional circumstances, I cannot think it right that the court should ever declare it unreasonable for a woman to decline to have an abortion in a case where there is no evidence that there were any medical or psychiatric grounds for terminating the particular pregnancy.[75]

A similar conclusion has been reached in the United States and Canada, where it has been held that a woman bringing an unwanted birth action has no duty to mitigate her damages by undergoing an abortion.[76] This conclusion has been reinforced by a suggestion that any inquiry as to why a woman plaintiff did not abort a pregnancy would be an invasion of privacy.[77] Such a ruling is consistent with the recognition of a woman's freedom of choice in matters affecting childbearing, a recognition that has proved central to the success of unwanted birth actions. It has been observed that: 'The right to have an abortion may not be automatically converted to an obligation to have one.'[78] This comment underlines the fact that there are obvious moral objections to the view that there can ever be a duty to abort a pregnancy. Here considerations as to the preciousness of the fetus are clearly relevant. A law that put pressure on a woman to abort would be repugnant. Another approach is to argue that the parents of an unwanted child can mitigate their damages by having the child adopted. This argument has also been rejected by the courts, on the ground that to require a woman to put her child up for adoption is an 'unreasonable' means of mitigating damage.[79]

Thus—however the causal argument is framed—a doctor who seeks to defeat an unwanted birth claim by asserting that the parents are under an obligation to minimize the harm caused by the birth of a child is likely to fail. What emerges, therefore, is that a doctor may be liable to pay damages if the use of a negligent technique has played a substantial part in the conception or birth of an unwanted child. Although relatively recently recognized, this form of liability is now well established; the only uncertainty relates to the proper assessment of damages. This aspect will be discussed in Chapter 7. First, it is necessary to consider a different form of negligence: the failure to provide appropriate information. This is the subject of the next chapter.

[75] [1985] 1 QB 1012, 1024.

[76] See, for example, *Morris v Frudenfeld* App, 185 Cal Rptr 76 (1982); *Jones v Malinowski* 473 A 2d 429 (Md, 1984); *Morris v Sanchez, Stout v United States* 746 P 2d 184 (Okl, 1987); *Marciniak v Lundborg* 450 NW 2d 243 (Wis, 1990); *Fredette v Wiebe* (1986) 29 DLR (4th) 534.

[77] *Flowers v District of Columbia* 478 A 2d 1073, 1081 (DC App, 1984).

[78] *Ziemba v Sternberg* 357 NYS 2d 265, 269 (1974).

[79] *Morris v Sanchez, Stout v United States* 746 P 2d 184, 189 (Okl, 1987); see also *Lovelace Medical Center v Mendez* 805 P 2d 603 (NM, 1991) and *Fredette v Wiebe* (1986) 29 DLR (4th) 534.

5

Negligent Failure to Provide Appropriate Information in Obstetrics and Midwifery

THE NATURE OF THE ACTION

All the obstetric cases so far discussed have involved allegations that medical techniques have been unsatisfactorily employed and that their unskilful use has caused an adverse or unwanted outcome. The claims have rested on the assertion that more competent diagnosis or treatment would have avoided that outcome. It is now necessary to consider cases arising from a different form of negligence: a failure to provide a pregnant woman with information to which she is entitled.

In Chapter 3, I outlined the principles governing a practitioner's obligation to advise a competent, conscious patient of the risks associated with treatment. The nature of this obligation varies; in some parts of the United States, and in Canada and Australia, there is a duty to provide a patient with information which she would consider material when being asked to consent to a medical procedure. In other parts of the United States and in England, the duty is to provide the information normally given by a responsible practitioner. Whichever criterion is employed, the failure to furnish appropriate information is no more than one element in a non-disclosure action. It must also be shown that if the information had been provided, the patient would have chosen a different course of action and so would have avoided the harm.

The circumstances in which allegations of negligent non-disclosure can be made against those responsible for the care and delivery of pregnant women are varied. In considering the relevant cases, I shall deal first with actions arising when the woman or her child suffered injury and then with those in which the alleged wrong consisted of the birth of an unwanted child.

HARM CAUSED TO MOTHER OR CHILD

In dealing with allegations that a woman or her child has been harmed by a failure to provide appropriate information, United States courts have sometimes applied the principles governing informed consent. An example of a situation in which this doctrine can be invoked in the field of obstetrics is when a doctor has failed to advise of the risks associated with an amniocentesis.[1] If miscarriage results, the woman will succeed in a damages action if she can establish that she would not have consented to the procedure had she been told of the risk. In contrast, *Roberts v Patel* illustrates a different application of the concept of informed consent. This case arose as a result of the birth of a baby with spastic quadriplegia. While in labour, the mother had questioned the decision to halt her labour and not to perform a caesarean section. She had asked about possible risks, but was assured that the decision would result in the delivery of a healthy baby. The United States District Court, Illinois, found that the doctors had breached the duty to advise the mother of the risks which the method of delivery posed for her and her child.[2] There have been other reported matters in which similar reasoning has been employed when a vaginal delivery has been performed and, in retrospect, it has become apparent that delivery by way of caesarean section would have been safer. In *Campbell v Pitt County Memorial Hospital*,[3] the woman was admitted to hospital for delivery and it was found that the baby was in the footling breech position. Neither the woman nor her husband was informed of this fact or of its significance. The baby girl was delivered vaginally and the cord became tangled around her legs, resulting in brain damage due to severe asphyxia and cerebral palsy. Both the doctor and the hospital were sued. The claim against the doctor was settled. As the jury found that the treatment provided by hospital staff was not negligent, the only way to make the hospital liable was by alleging lack of informed consent. This allegation succeeded. The steps in the argument were as follows. The nurses were responsible for ensuring that patients received adequate explanations of the risks they faced. They had failed to do this. Evidence was presented that, at the time of delivery (1979), the higher risks of a vaginal delivery of a baby in the footling breech position were well recognized. There was also testimony that parents who were informed of the risks of a vaginal delivery when the fetus was in this position would ordinarily opt for a caesarean section. Further, both Mr and Mrs Campbell testified that if they had been more fully informed, they would have chosen a caesarean section. Thus all the elements of a claim based on negligent non-disclosure were established: the judgment expressly recognized the existence of 'a legal duty to insure that plaintiffs' informed consent to a vaginal delivery of a footling breech baby had been obtained prior to delivery'.[4]

---

[1] See *Wheeldon v Madison* 374 NW 2d 367 (SD, 1985). Here the child was stillborn following an amniocentesis. It was accepted that the doctor was under a duty to advise the woman of the risk which the amniocentesis posed to the fetus.

[2] 620 F Supp 323, 326 (DC Ill, 1985).

[3] 352 SE 2d 902 (NC App, 1987). The decision of the Court of Appeals of North Carolina focused on the liability of the hospital for the negligence of the doctor and nurses; the doctor had conceded liability and had settled the claim against him. See also *Williams v Lallie Kemp Charity Hospital* 428 So 2d 1000 (La App 1 Cir, 1983).

[4] 352 SE 2d 902, 907 (NC App, 1987).

The Washington Court of Appeals provided a similar analysis in *Holt v Nelson*,[5] a case involving a child born with spastic quadriplegia, brain damage, and cerebral palsy. There were allegations of negligence in the form of failure to diagnose placenta praevia, an attempted vaginal delivery, and delay in the performance of a caesarean section. When the jury rejected these claims, an appeal was lodged solely on the ground that there had been a negligent failure to give the woman the opportunity to undergo an earlier caesarean section.[6] As in *Campbell*, the claim was that some time before the caesarean section was performed, the doctor was under an obligation to advise of the risks involved in proceeding with a natural birth and of the appropriateness of undertaking an immediate caesarean section. As counsel for the plaintiff put it, the complaint was that the doctor 'did not explain the risks involved in rupturing the membranes and attempting a vaginal delivery in the face of circumstances making a caesarean section the proper alternative'. The court offered a broad definition of the negligence to be proved. It was necessary for the plaintiffs to show that '[t]he defendant-doctor failed to inform the plaintiff-patient of alternative treatments, the reasonably foreseeable material risks of each alternative, and of no treatment at all'. Before proceeding, the doctor should have obtained the woman's informed consent; what was needed was, in the court's words, 'the patient's knowledgeable permission'.[7] A new trial was ordered. The plaintiffs bore the burden of establishing that the doctor was negligent in not telling the parents about a caesarean section as an alternative to a vaginal birth, that he did not tell the parents of the comparative risks, that a caesarean section would have been selected by the parents at an earlier time had they been informed, and that the injury to the child proximately resulted because the operation was performed too late.

In both *Campbell* and *Holt* it was accepted that the risks of a vaginal delivery were well recognized and that the performance of a caesarean section was the appropriate way of minimizing these risks. In contrast, in *Randall v United States*, medical opinion differed as to the preferred course of action. Prior to delivery, the mother of the plaintiff (a child born with Juvenile Laryngeal Papillomatosis (JLP)) was diagnosed as suffering from genital warts associated with Human Papilloma Virus (HPV). There was disagreement among the expert witnesses. The child had been born vaginally. One witness testified that the child should have been delivered by caesarean section, while another believed that a caesarean section was not indicated. The evidence established that there was no accepted standard as to the management of a pregnant woman suffering from HPV. The United States District

---

[5] Wash App, 523 P 2d 211 (1974). This case has been discussed above, see 69–70.

[6] The case illustrates how a plaintiff who is unable to establish that she received negligent treatment can also bring an action based on a failure to inform.

[7] Wash App, 523 P 2d 211, 215–17 (1974).

Court, District of Columbia, held that the absence of agreement as to the proper management of such a patient did not defeat the plaintiff's claim for damages:

The absence of a standard method of treatment or procedure . . . does not relieve [the hospital] of an obligation to counsel Ms. Randall [the plaintiff's mother] of the possible risks associated with HPV. . . . [P]laintiff has shown an obligation on behalf of [the hospital] to inform Ms. Randall as to the risks associated with a vaginal delivery.[8]

There are a number of obstetric cases illustrating differences of opinion as to the selection of the criterion by which allegations of non-disclosure should be judged. Earlier in the chapter it was explained that there are two views on this matter. One is that the standard should be set by reference to the practices of competent practitioners. The other is that the patient must be given the information which a reasonable person in her position would consider to be material. The former was adopted in *Charley v Cameron*. Here the action was brought because it was alleged that an indentation in the baby's head had been caused by a forceps delivery. No warning of the risk of such an outcome had been given. It was argued on the doctor's behalf that it was not the practice to inform a woman of the risk of a forceps delivery. This was accepted as a defence: the Supreme Court of Kansas held that the doctor's obligation to advise on the risks of a procedure must be assessed by reference to 'disclosures made by reasonable medical practitioners under the same or like circumstances'.[9] This decision should be contrasted with that in *Wheeldon v Madison*, a case dealing with a failure to advise of the risks associated with an amniocentesis. There it was ruled that: '[T]he right to know—to be informed—is a fundamental right personal to the patient and should not be subject to restriction by medical practices that may be at odds with the patient's informational needs.'[10] This ruling reflected the view that in such a situation, 'the patient's informational needs' were clear. This approach was also adopted in *Randall v United States*.[11] In examining the doctor's duty to disclose the risk of the child being born with JLP, the court applied the test developed in *Canterbury v Spence*. It was held that the doctor's obligation was to provide information that a reasonable person in the woman's position would consider material when deciding whether to have a vaginal or a caesarean delivery.

There are certain other aspects of the cases on non-disclosure that are relevant whichever criterion is adopted. In all these cases, there is a need to prove the causal link between the non-disclosure and the harm suffered. This has two aspects. First, it must be established that the procedure or technique caused the harm, the risks of which were not fully explained. In one case, a

---

[8] 859 F Supp 22, 32 (DDC, 1994).　　[9] Kan, 528 P 2d 1205, 1210 (1974).
[10] 374 NW 2d 367, 374 (SD, 1985).　　[11] 859 F Supp 22 (DDC, 1994).

doctor (like the defendant in *Charley v Cameron*) was sued for omitting to inform a woman of the risks involved in a forceps delivery.[12] It was alleged that the forceps had caused the child to suffer bruising, lacerations, and sub-dural haematomata. The claim initially failed because it was held that the child's injuries might have been the result of a difficult passage down the birth canal. The appellate court took a different view and ordered a retrial on the basis that there was prima-facie evidence that the injuries had been caused by the forceps. More clear cut was an action alleging a negligent omission to warn that induction of labour might result in a postpartum haemorrhage; this failed because there was no evidence that induction created an additional risk.[13]

The second element necessary to establish a causal link raises more diffi-cult questions. A successful non-disclosure action requires not only a failure to advise of risks which eventuated, but also a failure which causes the woman to choose (or not to choose) a particular course of action. This might be problematic. With hindsight, it may be too easy for a plaintiff to assert that had she been advised of a particular risk, she would have chosen differently. The dangers of self-serving testimony are obvious. These can be reduced by the application of a test with an objective element. If this approach is adopted, it is necessary to employ a two-stage process, as was done in *Randall*. First, there must be evidence that the plaintiff would have made a different choice had she been appropriately advised. Such evidence was before the court: Ms Randall had testified that had she been informed of the risk, she would have opted for a caesarean section. Secondly, the court must consider what a prudent person in the woman's position would have decided if suitably informed of the material risks. The court held: 'A reasonable pru-dent person, in Ms. Randall's position, having been made aware of the risk and severity of JLP in an infant, would have decided in favor of a Caesarean delivery.'[14] Thus the necessary causal link was established: there was credible evidence not only that the plaintiff would have opted to avoid the risks of a vaginal delivery had she been warned of those risks, but also that a prudent woman in her position would have reached this decision.

UNWANTED PREGNANCY OR THE BIRTH OF AN UNWANTED CHILD

The non-disclosure cases so far discussed have dealt with situations in which plaintiffs have complained that they would not have consented to a proced-ure or would have opted for a different procedure had they been properly

---

[12] *Wale v Barnes* Fla, 278 So 2d 601 (1973).
[13] *Parker v St Paul Fire & Marine Ins Co* La App, 335 So 2d 725 (1976).
[14] 859 F Supp 22, 32 (DDC, 1994).

advised. Complaints of this kind rest on the argument that a decision to have different medical treatment or to decline treatment would have avoided the harm suffered. There are other claims that do not depend on proof that the use of different medical techniques would have resulted in a better outcome. These arise when the harm complained of is not injury, disability, or death that more appropriate treatment could have prevented. Rather, such claims arise as a result of the conception or birth of an unwanted child, an outcome that the woman would have sought to avoid had she been better advised. It is the loss of the opportunity to escape the burdens imposed by conception or childbearing that forms the basis of actions of this kind. The illustrations to be discussed have something in common with the cases of unwanted births that have already been described; where they differ from those cases is that the allegations in the matters to be examined relate not to negligent technique but to a failure to provide information.

Tubal Ligation: Non-Disclosure of Risk of Failure

A woman who has undergone a tubal ligation and conceived an unwanted child can sue on the ground of the doctor's omission to warn her of the risk of failure of the procedure. The claim arises not because the operation has been negligently performed, but because the doctor has not advised the woman of the slight chance that re-canalization might occur and be followed by pregnancy. The woman's argument can take one of two forms. She might assert that had she been warned, she would not have had intercourse or would have taken other precautions to avoid pregnancy. Alternatively, she might claim that had she been advised of the risk of the failure of the tubal ligation, she would not have given her consent and she or her partner would have opted for a different (and more reliable) procedure. Either way, her claim will rest on the ground that had she been better informed she would have acted differently and would not have become pregnant. Thus she will assert that the unwanted pregnancy was caused by the negligent non-disclosure.

Claims resulting from an omission to advise of the risk of failure of a tubal ligation have produced differing results. In *Hartke v McKelway*,[15] a case arising in the District of Columbia, the defendant doctor who undertook a tubal cauterization not only failed to disclose the risk of re-canalization (between 0.1 per cent and 0.3 per cent), but he also told the patient that it was 'a 100 per cent sure operation'. When she subsequently became pregnant and gave birth, the woman sued on the ground of the non-disclosure of the risk of failure. The crucial question was whether the non-disclosure deprived the woman of information that she needed to avoid the unwanted birth. The court followed the decision in *Canterbury v Spence*[16] and accepted that

---

[15] 707 F 2d 1544 (1983).   [16] 464 F 2d 772 (1972); discussed above, 44–6.

the question to be asked was: what would a prudent person in the patient's position have decided if suitably informed? The doctor argued that he had no duty of disclosure because no reasonable person in the plaintiff's position would regard the relatively minor risk as significant. The rejection of this argument underlined the significance of taking account of a patient's particular circumstances. Here the doctor was aware that the plaintiff had a long history of gynaecological and pregnancy-related problems. She had suffered peritonitis after a caesarean section, had had an ectopic pregnancy, had been hospitalized numerous times for gynaecological procedures, and had told the doctor that she feared for her life if she again became pregnant. The court held that for such a patient information as to the risk of failure would have been highly significant: she had reason to be anxious about the effectiveness of the operation and, given the chance, might have opted for a hysterectomy or her partner might have had a vasectomy. The court therefore had no difficulty in concluding that a reasonable person in her position would have been influenced by information as to the failure rate. The omission to provide this information was negligent.

A similar approach had earlier been adopted in a Maryland case, *Sard v Hardy*,[17] in which the patient's special circumstances were again relevant. The woman's first pregnancy had ended with her developing eclampsia, having convulsions, and delivering a stillborn child. After two normal pregnancies and when pregnant with her third child, she arranged to have a tubal ligation; it was agreed that the procedure should be combined with the caesarean delivery of that child. Evidence was given that when a tubal ligation is performed at the same time as a caesarean section the failure rate is 2 per cent. The doctor did not explain this or describe alternative techniques and their failure rates. After the tubal ligation and the safe delivery of the third child, the woman again became pregnant and a further caesarean section was performed. She sued the doctor. An intermediate appellate court held that a reasonable person would not have considered a 2 per cent risk of failure to be material. This view was rejected by the Maryland Court of Appeals. It ruled that the question to be asked is: what information does a patient need to make an intelligent decision? Again, the test laid down in *Canterbury v Spence* was applied. The court held that, given her previous obstetric history and her concern about her health, the information as to the failure rate was material. Special importance was attached to the fact that the 2 per cent failure rate was associated with the combined procedure. The woman was not told that the risk of failure would be reduced if the sterilization were undertaken at a later time. As in *Hartke*, therefore, the case was decided in the plaintiff's favour on the ground that she had special reason to be concerned about the effectiveness of the procedure.

[17] 379 A 2d 1014 (1977).

These decisions can be contrasted with the approach adopted by the Australian and Canadian courts. In Australia, there has been a reluctance to allow claims based on an omission to explain the risk of failure of a tubal ligation. A Victorian case held that the omission was not causally linked to the pregnancy, because the patient would have proceeded with the operation even if she had been warned. In the judge's view, it was not possible to conclude that any reference to the 'infinitesimal or slight prospect of the failure of a tubal ligation' would have influenced the plaintiff or an ordinary person in her position in making the decision.[18] Similarly, in a South Australian matter, all the judges emphasized the remoteness of the risk of failure.[19] Canadian decisions have also focused on causation, although the conclusions reached have differed. In one, it was held that the failure to inform had not been causative, while in another it was decided that had the woman been warned, she would have sought alternative means of contraception. In a third, in which a woman had a laparoscopic tubal ligation, it was found that she would have opted for an abdominal procedure if she had been told of the risk of failure.[20]

English authority on liability for an omission to warn of the risk of failure of a tubal ligation is also mixed. In *Gold v Haringey Health Authority*,[21] despite the fact that the parents were 'delighted' with the birth (in 1979) of a child following a failed tubal ligation, the mother sued on the ground that there had been a negligent omission both to warn of the risk of the failure and to advise of the availability of a vasectomy as an alternative. The parents gave evidence that had they received the warning and advice, the woman would not have consented to the procedure and the husband would have undergone a vasectomy. The Court of Appeal applied the *Bolam* rule and held that as a substantial body of responsible doctors would not, in 1979, have warned of the risk of failure, the omission was not negligent.

By contrast, in *Lybert v Warrington Health Authority*,[22] the Court of Appeal made no reference to the *Bolam* test and accepted that the doctor had a duty to warn of the risk of failure. In this case, as in *Sard*, the tubal ligation (performed in 1989) was combined with a caesarean section to deliver the woman's third child. Again, notice was taken of the fact that the risk of failure was greater when the procedure was combined with a caesarean. When the woman became pregnant for the fourth time and sued for damages, the case focused on whether a warning had been given and, if it had, whether the couple would have used alternative means of contraception and so avoided conceiving an unwanted child. As so often occurs in cases of this

---

[18] *Petrunic v Barnes* (1988) Australian Torts Reports 80–147.

[19] *F v R* (1983) 33 SASR 189.

[20] *Grey v Webster* (1984) 14 DLR (4th) 706; *Joshi v Woolley* (1995) 4 BCLR (3d) 208; *Dendaas (Tyler) v Yackel* (1980) 109 DLR (3d) 455.

[21] [1988] 1 QB 481.   [22] [1996] 7 Med LR 71.

kind, there was disagreement about what the woman had been told about the tubal ligation. She stated that she had been told that the procedure was irreversible but had not been informed of the risk of failure. The consultant who had visited her after the operation had only 'a hazy recollection' of the conversation, but had recorded in his notes, 'Told re TL again, permanent, not 100%.' The court concluded that this was no more than a 'formula' and ruled that, whatever had been said, the woman had not been given a sufficiently clear and emphatic warning of the risk of failure. It also ruled that had a warning been given, there was an 'inherent likelihood' that the couple would have heeded it. Again, mention was made of the special circumstances; her three previous children had been delivered by way of caesarean section and she was therefore especially anxious to avoid a fourth pregnancy. This made it likely that if an adequate warning had been given, the couple would have used contraceptive measures and she would have undergone a hysterectomy as soon as possible. Thus it was held that the failure to warn was directly related to the conception of the fourth child.

It is not possible to reconcile *Gold* and *Lybert*. One explanation of the different results is that by the time the action arose in the latter case (1989), attitudes had changed and the obligation to advise of the risks of failure of a tubal ligation was recognized by the medical profession and thus there was no basis for contesting the allegation of negligence. If this explanation is accepted, the only issues which can arise in English cases relating to failed tubal ligations are factual ones: whether the warning was omitted and whether the omission was causally related to the unwanted pregnancy.

Thus there is some uncertainty about the law governing a doctor's liability for omitting to inform a woman of the risk of failure of a tubal ligation. In England there have been conflicting decisions, but it seems unlikely that in the future doctors will be able to defeat claims by arguing that providing a warning is not normal practice. The courts will probably look closely at the woman's circumstances and at the likelihood of her heeding a warning. Similarly, in the United States, the courts have imposed liability when there have been special reasons for concluding that a doctor should have provided information as to failure rates. A plaintiff's success may depend on her ability to convince a court that her circumstances were such that an omission to warn deprived her of information which was crucial to the decision which she was required to make. In the absence of such testimony, a court might be inclined to assume that the risk of the failure of a tubal ligation is so slight that an omission to discuss it would be unlikely to influence a woman's decision to undergo the procedure.

Once a woman has conceived an unwanted child, two possible outcomes must be considered. She may undergo a termination of pregnancy. She will then seek damages to compensate her for the pain and suffering, medical expenses, and lost wages associated with the pregnancy and its termination.

She will succeed if she can establish that had she been given the necessary information, she would have taken more effective contraceptive precautions and would thus have avoided the pregnancy. Alternatively, the child will be born, either because a termination was not an option or because the woman has chosen to allow the pregnancy to continue. She may then sue in respect of the unwanted birth. When this occurs, as has been explained in Chapter 4,[23] her decision will not be regarded as breaking the causal link between the non-disclosure and the birth.

Failure to Diagnose Pregnancy

Another form of action following non-disclosure arises when a woman asserts that she has given birth to an unwanted child as a result of a negligent failure to diagnose her pregnancy. While cases of this kind frequently also involve an element of medical negligence (as the failure is normally indicative of lack of diagnostic skill), they are best dealt with here as the woman's complaint relates primarily to the doctor's omission to provide information. In these matters there is no question of the non-disclosure being associated with the conception, since the woman is already pregnant when she consults her doctor. It is therefore only the unwanted birth in respect of which the woman can sue. Her claim will rest on the assertion that she did not learn of her pregnancy until it was too late to obtain an abortion.

Claims arising from the birth of unwanted children following the non-diagnosis of pregnancy are not common. Normally women will realize that they are pregnant and will not be able to assert that it was the doctor's failure to diagnose the pregnancy that deprived them of the opportunity to arrange a termination. An unusual combination of circumstances is required before this type of unwanted birth claim can succeed. In particular, it is only at a late stage of pregnancy that a woman who would have obtained a termination will find herself prevented from doing so and hence be in a position to bring an action. A simple example was provided by a 1974 New York case.[24] There the woman had consulted her doctor; in spite of various symptoms, he negligently failed to diagnose the pregnancy and the woman did not have it confirmed until she was four and a half months pregnant. She succeeded in her claim against the doctor. Similar results have been reached in England[25] and Australia. In the Australian case, *CES v Superclinics (Australia) Pty Ltd*,[26] an action was brought by a woman who, suspecting that she might be pregnant,

[23] See above 80–1.
[24] *Ziemba v Sternberg* 357 NYS 2d 265 (1974). See also *Fredette v Wiebe* (1986) 29 DLR (4th) 534.
[25] *Allen v Bloomsbury Health Authority* [1993] 1 All ER 651; *Gardiner v Mounfield and Lincolnshire Area Health Authority* [1990] 1 Med LR 205.
[26] (1995) 38 NSWLR 47.

several times consulted a clinic, and was told that she was not pregnant. On one of her visits, the advice was based on a test result that showed a false negative; on another occasion, the test was positive, but she was wrongly advised that it was negative. Finally, the woman visited her general practitioner, who found her to be nineteen weeks pregnant. It was then too late for her to have a safe termination and a normal, healthy child was delivered. The New South Wales Court of Appeal agreed that the clinic had been negligent in not diagnosing the pregnancy and hence being unable to inform her of it.

A second category of cases in which pregnancies have not been diagnosed is that in which attempted terminations have failed. In the Canadian case of *Cherry v Borsman*,[27] the defendant doctor was found not only to have negligently performed a dilatation and curettage, but also to have been negligent in his post-operative care. As a result of the latter, and in spite of the woman telling him that she thought she was still pregnant, the doctor had 'persisted in his opinion that the abortion had been successful'.[28] The result was that the pregnancy continued beyond the stage when the woman could have obtained a lawful termination. The child was delivered nine weeks prematurely, suffering from severe disabilities. The failure to diagnose the pregnancy was held to provide a second basis for liability and the doctor was ordered to pay substantial damages.

In cases arising from the non-diagnosis of a pregnancy, the claim rests on the assertion that the birth of the child could have been avoided if the woman had been told in time. The distinctive feature of such a claim is that the non-disclosure deprived her of the opportunity to choose to terminate the pregnancy. As in Chapter 4, we again encounter an assertion of the desirability of freedom of choice, but in a different context. The woman's action against the doctor rests on the argument that had the diagnosis been made in time, she would have obtained an abortion. Thus, proof of the non-diagnosis and consequent non-disclosure must be supplemented by evidence on the basis of which a court must speculate as to what would have occurred had the information been provided. The woman must establish that she could and would have obtained a termination if she had received timely information. To achieve this, she must show that the termination would have been lawful and that she would have gained access to the services of a doctor who would have performed the procedure. An action arising from the non-diagnosis of a pregnancy therefore has special features. The reason for taking such an action is, however, the same as that prompting proceedings when a child is born following an omission to warn of the risk of failure of a tubal ligation: the complaint is that the parent or parents have been forced to accept the unwanted burden of caring for the child.

---

[27] (1991) 75 DLR (4th) 668; affirmed on appeal (1992) 94 DLR (4th) 487.
[28] (1991) 75 DLR (4th) 668, 691.

When the Child is Disabled

Claims arising from unwanted births (whether the result of the non-diagnosis of a pregnancy or of a failed tubal ligation) must be distinguished from those made when the child was initially wanted, but becomes unwanted because he or she is born suffering from genetic abnormalities or a condition such as congenital rubella syndrome. In the cases already discussed, the parents had no desire to have a child, healthy or otherwise. When a wanted child is born abnormal, the parents' complaint relates not to the birth, but rather to the special burdens which the abnormality imposes. While the disabilities cannot be ascribed to poor medical technique—the defects are genetic or caused by disease and the child never had a chance of being normal—it is still open to the parents to show that the birth of the disabled child was negligently caused if they can prove an omission to advise of a foreseeable risk that the child would be abnormal. As with the cases already discussed, the essence of the claim is that the woman and her partner have been deprived of the opportunity to make an informed choice as to the continuance of the pregnancy.

Liability for non-disclosure can occur in two types of situations when children are born with abnormalities. Genetic counselling may be sought before a couple makes a decision to conceive a child. If the child is born disabled, the action will rest on the argument that had adequate information been provided, the couple would have decided not to conceive. The second situation is that in which a pregnant woman consults her doctor and later asserts that had the necessary information been provided, she would have terminated the pregnancy. In this type of case, the success of the claim depends on the woman's ability to establish that the opportunity to undergo a termination would have been available to her.[29]

In the cases to be discussed, the complaint was that had adequate information been provided, the parents would have taken action to avoid the special burdens and distress associated with bringing up a disabled child. Most of the courts before which unwanted birth actions have been brought have accepted that these burdens constitute a distinctive form of harm. On rare occasions, however, this has not been the case. Rejecting a claim in respect of a child with Down syndrome, a North Carolina court stated: '[W]e are unwilling to say that life, even life with severe defects, may ever amount to a legal

---

[29] It should be noted that it is only in some jurisdictions that a woman can obtain an abortion if it is likely that her child will be born with serious disabilities. The right to do so depends on the existence of provisions specifically conferring the right to abort a seriously deformed fetus. In the absence of such provisions, reliance must be placed on more general laws governing abortions; this will frequently mean that the woman must show that the continuance of the pregnancy would injure her health. Either way, the woman faces the task of establishing that, had she been properly informed, she would have been able to bring herself within the relevant law.

injury.'[30] As will be seen, the opposite view has been adopted in the great majority of matters.

The various cases can be categorized on the basis of the abnormalities suffered. Numerous actions have arisen from failure to provide information that would have allowed the women to avoid giving birth to children with Down syndrome. Here the negligence alleged has typically been the failure (in view of the woman's age or family history) to warn of the risk of giving birth to such a child. Such a failure has frequently been coupled with an omission to advise of the availability of a diagnostic test such as an amniocentesis, chorionic villus sampling, a triple test, or an ultrasound. In one case, a 37-year-old pregnant woman who later gave birth to a child with Down syndrome was not warned of the increased risk of genetic abnormalities in children born of women over 35 and it was not suggested that she might have an amniocentesis.[31] Sometimes there are additional factors indicative of negligence when such a child is born. In one matter, a 34-year-old woman had asked about genetic testing and about the desirability of an amniocentesis, but had been assured that an amniocentesis was unnecessary.[32] In another, the woman had several times informed the hospital staff that she had a sister with Down syndrome, but she received no genetic counselling and was not told of the availability of an amniocentesis.[33] In a third, an amniocentesis had been performed on a 39-year-old woman, but transmission of the result (showing the presence of a chromosomal abnormality) had been delayed until she was in the third trimester of her pregnancy, when it was too late to obtain a termination.[34]

In all these cases it was open to the courts to find the doctors negligent. The important feature in matters of this kind was the availability of a test offering a high chance of identifying the presence of the syndrome. In contrast was *Simmons v West Covina Medical Clinic*,[35] in which a woman (whose age was not given) sued for damages after delivering a child with Down syndrome. The negligence alleged was a general failure to provide genetic testing and counselling and, in particular, a failure to advise of the availability of the Alpha Feto Protein (AFP) test. It was accepted that the test provided only a 20 per cent chance of detecting Down syndrome in the fetus of a woman in the plaintiff's age group. The defendant doctors were successful in their argument that as the test offered only a 'mere possibility' of detecting the condition, their failure to advise it could not be shown to have deprived the woman of a substantial chance of avoiding the birth of the abnormal child.

[30] *Azzolino v Dingfelder* 337 SE 2d 528, 534 (NC, 1985).

[31] *Becker v Schwartz* 413 NYS 2d 895 (1978); see also *Berman v Allan* 404 A 2d 8 (1979).

[32] *Haymon v Wilkerson* 535 A 2d 880 (DC App, 1987).

[33] *Phillips v United States* 566 F Supp 1 (DSC, 1981). See also *Karlsons v Guerinot* 394 NYS 2d 933 (1977), where the 37-year-old woman had told the doctor that she had previously given birth to a deformed child.

[34] *Garrison v Medical Center of Delaware Inc* Del Supr, 581 A 2d 288 (1989).

[35] 260 Cal Rptr 772 (Cal App 2 Dist, 1989).

The defendants' success in this case arose from the plaintiff's inability to show that the omission had substantially caused the adverse outcome. A similar result was reached in an English case. In *Gregory v Pembrokeshire Health Authority*,[36] a woman who was concerned about the possibility of having a child with Down syndrome underwent an amniocentesis. This did not produce sufficient cultures to allow effective testing. Her obstetricians were informed of this fact, but decided that by the time a second amniocentesis had been performed and the results had been received, it would have been too late to obtain a termination. For reasons that were not clear (perhaps because each consultant had thought the other had undertaken the task) the woman was not told of the failure of the amniocentesis to produce a result. It was held that while the omission to inform her that the amniocentesis had been inconclusive was negligent, it could not be shown that this negligence caused the birth of the affected child. The trial court concluded that if the woman had been told that the amniocentesis had been inconclusive and had discussed the situation with the consultant, he would have advised her not to undergo a second amniocentesis. On the basis of what it knew of her attitudes and conduct, the court also concluded that had she received this advice, she would have followed it and hence the child would not have been aborted. On appeal it was held that there were no grounds for interfering with this analysis. What is noteworthy about this decision is the amount of speculation in which the trial court had to engage. As one of the appellate judges observed, the case turned on an assessment of the woman's hypothetical response to hypothetical advice at a hypothetical consultation.

Proceedings arising from the birth of children with congenital rubella are also common. A typical case was *Smith v Cote*.[37] There a woman, suspecting she might be pregnant, consulted the defendants, who were specialist obstetricians. Among other symptoms, she complained of nausea and pain; an antibiotic was prescribed and a pregnancy test recommended. Two days later she again visited the practice, complaining of an itchy rash and a slight fever. This was diagnosed as an allergic reaction to the antibiotic. Soon afterwards, her pregnancy was confirmed. Four months later, a rubella titre test indicated that she had been exposed to rubella. The child was born with multiple defects consistent with congenital rubella syndrome, including heart defects, blindness, deafness, and motor retardation. Court proceedings were taken; it was alleged that the defendants had negligently failed to perform a timely test for, and diagnosis of, rubella and had negligently failed to advise of the risks which rubella posed to the fetus. If these risks had been explained, the woman would have undergone a termination of pregnancy. It was held that it was open to a jury (after hearing evidence of what could be expected of a competent specialist) to find that the required standard of care had not been

[36] [1989] 1 Med LR 81.   [37] 513 A 2d 341 (NH, 1986).

provided and that the woman would have obtained a termination had she been advised of the risks. There have been many cases of this kind, not only in the United States but also in England and Australia.[38]

A different type of negligence in a case involving rubella was illustrated by *Procanik by Procanik v Cillo*.[39] There a woman consulted her doctor during the first trimester of pregnancy and told him that she had recently been diagnosed as having measles; she did not know if it was German measles. The doctor ordered a rubella titre test. The results were indicative of 'past infection of rubella'. The doctor negligently interpreted this finding and told the woman that she should not worry, as she had become immune to German measles as a child. In fact, the 'past infection' was the one about which she had consulted the doctor. When her child was born with the multiple defects of congenital rubella syndrome, the doctor was held to be liable to pay damages for the negligent misdiagnosis and his consequent failure to advise her of the risk to her fetus. While in this matter an important factor was the doctor's knowledge of the woman's pregnancy, a claim might succeed even in the absence of such knowledge. In one case, where a doctor diagnosed a woman's rubella rash as an allergic reaction and she gave birth to an abnormal child, the doctor was held to have been negligent for failing to inquire whether she was pregnant.[40]

There has also been a series of cases arising from the birth of children suffering from Tay Sachs disease. The disease afflicts children whose parents are Ashkenazic (that is, of eastern European Jewish origin). In *Goldberg v Ruskin*,[41] following the birth of a child with Tay Sachs disease, the doctor was found to have been negligent in failing to inform the parents of the risk, of failing to advise them of the availability of a simple test to determine whether they were carriers, and of failing to undertake the test. Similar cases have accepted that doctors are expected to be aware that Jews from eastern Europe are prone to the disease and that there are tests available to determine whether they are carriers.[42] What level of knowledge can be expected of a competent doctor is a matter to be established by expert testimony. The significance of this was demonstrated in *Munro v Regents of University of California*.[43] There the woman had been given genetic counselling; the doctor who provided this took a family history that indicated that neither parent was of eastern European origin. As the doctor's practice was to advise testing only if one or both parents were known to be Ashkenazic, he did not recommend

---

[38] For example, *Robak v United States* 658 F 2d 471 (1981); *Blake v Cruz* 698 P 2d 315 (Idaho, 1984); *Veivers v Connolly* [1995] 2 Qd R 326; *Salih v Enfield Health Authority* [1991] 3 All ER 400.

[39] 478 A 2d 755 (NJ, 1984).   [40] *Dumer v St Michael's Hospital* 233 NW 2d 372 (1975).

[41] 471 NE 2d 530 (Ill App 1 Dist, 1984).

[42] For example, *Howard v Lecher* 386 NYS 2d 460 (1976).

[43] 263 Cal Rptr 878 (Cal App 2 Dist, 1989).

a test. When the child was born with Tay Sachs disease, inquiries were made and it was found that the great-grandparents had been members of a French-Canadian community which had a slightly higher than normal prevalence of the disease. Expert testimony was heard to determine whether the failure to discover this fact breached the required standard of care. It was held that it did not. There had been nothing to indicate that the parents were in a high-risk group and it was accepted that there was an obligation to perform the relevant test only if the parents possessed characteristics that should have alerted the doctor to the risk. The court therefore rejected the plaintiff's argument that the doctor had a general duty to provide any information that might be relevant to the decision as to whether or not to take the test for Tay Sachs. The doctor was therefore not liable.

There are numerous other situations in which doctors have an obligation to disclose risks. Practitioners who provide negligent pre-conception counselling have been found liable in respect of the birth of children suffering from a wide variety of conditions. In one Massachusetts matter, a couple who wished to have children consulted a specialist in genetics as to the risk that the woman was a carrier of ectodermal dysplasia. The doctor advised them that she was not a carrier. The woman then conceived. The first child was normal; the second was born with anhidrotic ectodermal dysplasia. It was held that the parents could recover damages.[44] A similar basis for a damages claim was recognized in a North Carolina case in which parents sought counselling following the death of their first child soon after birth. Hospital staff (relying on a post mortem report by a cytogeneticist) advised them that the first child had displayed no genetic abnormality and that their risk of having an abnormal child was no higher than that faced by other couples. They therefore decided to have another child, who was born with a chromosome abnormality, Trisomy 9. The pathology slides relating to the first child were then re-examined, and a similar abnormality was found. It was held that it was open to a jury to find that the cytogeneticist and the hospital staff had been negligent.[45] A third example of a case in which a woman was able to sue her doctor in respect of inadequate pre-conception counselling involved a woman with sickle cell anaemia. The child was born suffering from this condition and the doctor was found to have been negligent for not advising the woman of the risk of this outcome.[46] In another case, the action was taken following the birth of a child suffering from polycystic kidney disease. The child died before the age of 3. The mother had had a previous child who died from the disease; before conceiving again she had sought advice. She was told that the chances of the second child being born with the disease were 'practically nil'.

[44] *Viccaro v Milunsky* 551 NE 2d 8 (Mass, 1990).
[45] *Gallagher v Duke University* 638 F Supp 979 (MDNC, 1986).
[46] *Dorlin v Providence Hospital* Mich App, 325 NW 2d 600 (1982).

She was also told that the condition was not hereditary, no tests were performed on the mother or father, and no research or investigation was undertaken before the reassurance was given. It was held that the advice provided did not meet the standard expected of a competent obstetrician.[47]

The cases in which consultations have occurred after the women have become pregnant have also involved a range of unusual conditions. In one, the child was born with severe genetic abnormalities (including the right leg missing, hydrocephaly, and menginomyelocele) and died at the age of 6. The doctor had performed an ultrasound at nineteen weeks gestation, but had not noted any abnormalities. The failure properly to interpret the ultrasound was the ground on which the parents sought to establish negligence.[48] Similar disabilities, but a different type of negligence, led to the proceedings in *Basten v United States*.[49] There, too, the child was born with meningomyelocele and hydrocephaly. The hospital was sued on the basis that a midwife had failed to offer the woman AFP testing. The woman was aware of the test (it had been mentioned in a talk given to a group of pregnant women), but she had not been told of its significance. The midwife's practice was not to offer the test unless the woman raised the matter. It was held that this did not discharge the duty of care; there was an obligation specifically to advise the woman at an appropriate stage of the pregnancy of the availability of the test. The onus should not have been placed on the woman. The outcome in this case can be contrasted with that in *Rance v Mid-Downes Health Authority*,[50] in which the child's abnormality was spina bifida. The negligence consisted of a failure to detect the problem on an ultrasound scan. The action failed, however, as the diagnosis was made too late to allow a lawful termination to be undertaken.

The facts were more complicated in *Siemieniec v Lutheran General Hospital*.[51] During the first trimester of her pregnancy, the plaintiff sought counselling regarding the likelihood of her child being born with haemophilia; she was concerned because two of her cousins had suffered from the disease. She was advised to take diagnostic tests, on the strength of which the doctor told her that the risk of her being a carrier was 'very low'. A decision was made to proceed with the pregnancy and the child was born with haemophilia B. It was found that the advice given was negligent in several respects: there had been a failure to advise that there were various types of haemophilia and that there was no reliable test for the variety suffered by the child; there had been no proper inquiry into the woman's health and medical background; and the death certificate of the cousin (who had suffered from the same type of haemophilia) had not been obtained.

---

[47] *Park v Chessin* 387 NYS 2d 204 (1976); 413 NYS 2d 895 (1978).
[48] *Keel v Banach* 624 So 2d 1022 (Ala, 1993).   [49] 848 F Supp 962 (MD Ala, 1994).
[50] [1991] 1 QB 587.   [51] 512 NE 2d 691 (Ill, 1987).

A rare example of ill-effects caused by maternal infection was seen in the Canadian case of *Arndt v Smith*. This was an action by the mother of a child born with congenital varicella syndrome; the child suffered brain damage which resulted in decreased oesophageal motility and made it necessary for her to be fed by tube. The mother had been infected with chicken pox during the twelfth or thirteenth week of pregnancy. The defendant doctor knew of her condition and of the risks that it posed to the fetus. The doctor had warned the woman of the risk of limb and skin abnormalities, but did not inform her of the much lesser risk (put at 0.23 per cent) of brain abnormalities. In the doctor's opinion it had not been medically advisable to do so. It was found that the child's abnormalities were the result of her mother's chicken pox and that the doctor had been negligent in failing to disclose the material risks posed by chicken pox during pregnancy. When the matter was reviewed by the Supreme Court of Canada, the focus was on causation. The majority agreed with the trial court's finding that the failure to disclose some of the risks did not affect the plaintiff's decision to continue the pregnancy to full term. Her claim for damages therefore failed. The decision is of special interest because of the court's analysis and application of the 'modified objective test' developed in *Reibl v Hughes*.[52] Under this test, the question asked is whether a reasonable person in the woman's position would have acted differently had all the risks been disclosed. On this matter, the majority ruled as follows:

[I]t is appropriate to infer from the evidence that a reasonable person in the plaintiff's position would not have decided to terminate her pregnancy in the face of the very small increased risk to the fetus posed by her exposure to the virus which causes chickenpox. Ms. Arndt did make a very general inquiry concerning the risks associated with maternal chickenpox. However, it should not be forgotten that the risk was indeed very small. In the absence of a specific and clearly expressed concern, there was nothing to indicate to the doctor that she had a particular concern in this regard. It follows that there was nothing disclosed by Ms. Arndt's question which could be used by the trier of fact as an indication of a particular fear regarding the possibility of giving birth to a disabled child which should be attributed to the hypothetical reasonable person in the patient's situation.[53]

This statement underlines the fact that a woman who claims that she was given inadequate information bears the burden of proving that she would have made a different choice had the appropriate information been provided.

Duffey v Fear[54] had unusual facts. The child's premature birth led to the administration of oxygen, which caused retrolental fibroplasia (RLF). It was accepted that the prematurity might have been caused by an infection arising

---

[52] (1980) 114 DLR (3d) 1: see above 54.   [53] (1997) 148 DLR (4th) 48, 57.
[54] 505 NYS 2d 136 (AD 1 Dept, 1986).

from an intra-uterine device (IUD) which had not been removed when the woman became pregnant. The doctor had told the woman that the presence of the IUD was not a cause for concern; he also thought that its removal might produce a miscarriage. There was disagreement whether, at the time of the child's birth (1970), it was known that the presence of an IUD increased the risk of prematurity. At that time there had been no published reports of a link between prematurity and the presence of an IUD. Thus there was no evidence that the failure to remove it represented a breach of the standard of care expected at the time. It followed that the advice that the IUD posed no risk to the fetus (advice which led the woman to decide to continue with the pregnancy) could not be shown to be negligent.

A different situation in which a failure to inform of risks can result in liability to a damages claim was illustrated by *Harbeson v Park-Davis Inc.*[55] The woman plaintiff (an epileptic) had taken Dilantin during one pregnancy and had given birth to a normal child. Before becoming pregnant for the second and third times, she had asked about the risks that the drug posed for a fetus. She was told these were minor (cleft palate and hirsuitism) and she therefore continued to take the drug. She delivered two children suffering from fetal hydantoin syndrome. She succeeded in her unwanted birth claim; the doctors were held to have had an obligation to advise her of 'grave risks' of the kind that eventuated. Their negligence was compounded by a failure to conduct an adequate literature search on the possible effects of the drug.

Finally, two rather different examples of non-disclosure should be noted. In the cases so far discussed, the claims have arisen from omissions to advise of the risk of the birth of an abnormal child. Occasionally, an action is taken even though it is not open to the plaintiff to assert that the doctor should have foreseen the risk of abnormality. An example was provided by a case in which the negligence consisted of a failure to diagnose the woman's pregnancy and an abnormal child was delivered. She learned of the pregnancy too late to undergo a safe termination and sued on the ground that she would have had an abortion because of her fear of giving birth to a defective child (this fear was based on her age and history of diabetes).[56] The second unusual case involved a claim made following an abortion. In *Lynch v Bay Ridge Obstetrical and Gynecological Associates,*[57] the plaintiff, thinking she was pregnant, had consulted a specialist. Without conducting blood or urine tests, he told her she was not pregnant. He then prescribed Provera, but did not explain the risks that this drug posed to a fetus. The woman later discovered her pregnancy and became aware of the risks. Being unwilling to run these risks, she had a termination. She sought damages for physical and

---

[55] Wash, 656 P 2d 483 (1983).
[56] *Comras v Lewin* NJ Super AD, 443 A 2d 229 (1982).
[57] 532 NE 2d 1239 (NY, 1988).

emotional injuries. The defendant doctor's argument that the decision to have a termination broke the causal link between the negligence and the harm suffered was rejected: it was held that the abortion, being a reasonable attempt to avoid the danger created by the defendant's negligence, was a foreseeable outcome.

This chapter has illustrated some of the situations in which a failure to provide a woman with information can result in a doctor or midwife being liable to a damages claim. The essential feature of such a claim is that the woman has been deprived of the opportunity to make a choice about the course of her pregnancy or treatment. A fuller analysis of the issues raised by such a claim will be offered in Chapters 10 and 12. First, it is necessary to consider two more unusual types of negligence action.

6

Other Actions in Obstetrics and Midwifery

There are two remaining—and more questionable—actions for negligence in obstetrics and midwifery: wrongful death and wrongful life. When unsatisfactory care has led to a stillbirth, there have been cases in which courts, in addition to allowing the parents to claim compensation under the common law, have allowed them to take action under wrongful death statutes. Further, when the negligence has taken the form of a failure to advise parents of the risk that their child would be abnormal, some courts have been willing to entertain a wrongful life action in which the disabled child claims damages in respect of the dreadful life which he or she must endure.

A WRONGFUL DEATH OR SURVIVAL ACTION FOLLOWING A STILLBIRTH

The statutes dealing with the compensation payable following a negligently caused death are of two types. First, there are those modelled on a nineteenth-century English Act, known as Lord Campbell's Act.[1] These are referred to as Wrongful Death Acts in the United States, and as Fatal Accidents Acts in England, Canada, and Australia. They provide that if the death of a person has been caused by the wrongful act of another and the deceased would have been able to bring an action if death had not ensued, an action for damages can be brought by the deceased's beneficiaries. The primary purpose of the legislation is to give compensation to the members of the family who might have expected to receive support from the deceased had he or she lived. Statutes in the second category are known as Survival Acts. These allow for the survival of certain types of damages claims that the deceased could have made had he or she lived. It is important to appreciate the different purposes embodied in the two classes of legislation. The basis on which a claim is made under a Wrongful Death/Fatal Accidents Act is that the *family members* have suffered loss as a result of being deprived of support. In contrast, the damages that can be recovered under a Survival Act are those to which the *deceased* would have been entitled had he or she survived.

The essential prerequisite for a successful action under a Wrongful Death/Fatal Accidents Act or under a Survival Act is the death of a person who would have had a right to seek damages had death not ensued. This

[1] 9 & 10 Vict, c 93 (1846).

requirement raises obvious difficulties when there has been a stillbirth. As has been explained in Chapter 4, it is now well established that a child born suffering the ill effects of antenatal negligence may sue. What the relevant decisions establish, however, is that a cause of action arises only if there has been a live birth: the child's right does not crystallize until birth. To recognize a stillborn fetus as an entity with a right to sue for damages would clearly be a significant departure from the principle accepted in the cases so far examined. In England and Canada, the courts have indicated that they will not sanction such a departure,[2] and in Australia, although the issue has not arisen, the courts would be likely to adopt the same view.

Thus it is only in the United States that it is necessary to consider the possible application of Wrongful Death Acts and Survival Acts following a stillbirth. Analysis of the relevant decisions is made difficult by the courts' frequent failure to pay sufficient attention to the important differences between the two types of Acts. The problems are compounded by the fact that sometimes the claims were made both under Wrongful Death Acts and Survival Acts. The situation is further complicated by the extension of some United States Survival Acts to permit the recovery of damages of the kind payable under Lord Campbell's Act. It is therefore not surprising that the distinction between the two types of actions can become blurred. What emerges is a number of unsatisfactory decisions in which the actions have sometimes been disallowed and sometimes allowed.

The Action Disallowed[3]

A typical wrongful death statute provides that if the death of a person is caused by a wrongful or negligent act, the wrongdoer is liable to pay damages if the circumstances were such that (had death not ensued) the person injured would have been able to maintain an action. The argument that a fetus is not a 'person' for the purposes of such an Act has frequently prevailed. While it is an argument which can equally be advanced with regard to a Survival Act (which also presupposes the existence of a 'person' whose

---

[2] See *Paton v British Pregnancy Advisory Service Trustees* [1979] 1 QB 276, 279; *Dehler v Ottawa Civic Hospital* (1979) 101 DLR (3d) 686, 695; and *Dobson (Litigation Guardian of) v Dobson* (1999) 174 DLR (4th) 1, 38. Further, in England, s 4 (2)(a) of the Congenital Disabilities (Civil Liability) Act 1976 (UK) makes it clear that the right of action which the Act confers in respect of antenatal injury may be exercised only by a child who is born alive. This precludes recovery for injuries causing a stillbirth.

[3] Examples of cases in which the action has been disallowed are: *Graf v Taggert* 204 A 2d 140 (1964); *Henry v Jones* 306 F Supp 726 (1969); *Toth v Goree* 237 NW 2d 297 (1975); *Smith v Columbus Community Hospital Inc* 387 NW 2d 490 (Neb, 1986); *Abdelaziz v AMISUB of Florida* 515 So 2d 269 (Fla App 3 Dist, 1987); *Giardina v Bennett* 545 A 2d 139 (NJ, 1988); *Milton v Cary Medical Center* 538 A 2d 252 (Me, 1988); *Rambo v Lawson* 799 SW 2d 62 (Mo banc, 1990); *Gentry v Gilmore* 613 So 2d 1241 (Ala, 1993).

right to sue survives after death), in practice judicial analysis has tended to concentrate on the meaning of the wording used in Wrongful Death Acts. In many cases, the result of this analysis has been to uphold the view that a child must be born alive before becoming a 'person' and so being entitled to sue for damages. This view has been explained as follows: '[T]here must be *life* before a cause of action, however limited, may accrue on anyone's behalf.'[4] This provides the most fundamental and most commonly expressed reason for denying parents a cause of action under a Wrongful Death statute when the outcome is a stillbirth: at the time of the injury, the fetus was not an entity possessing the right to bring an action for damages and nor could any such right subsequently arise, as the fetus never became a 'person'.

The courts that have disallowed wrongful death actions have advanced a number of other reasons. It has been questioned whether it is appropriate for the parents of a stillborn child to claim pecuniary compensation of the kind the legislation was designed to provide. For example, in one decision in which the action was disallowed, the court referred to the purpose of the legislation: 'Our determination is based on our perception that a fetus was not intended to be included in the statute as a being whose death can give rise to a claim for pecuniary loss by next-of-kin . . .'.[5] In another judgment, a different purpose was stressed: 'Damages given [in respect of a stillbirth] would not be for compensation purposes, but rather to punish the wrongdoer. This is not the type of recovery . . . the Wrongful Death Act . . . intended to provide.'[6] Further, it is common for judges to object that the assessment of damages in respect of a stillbirth would be impossibly speculative. They assert that it is unreasonable for a court to be required to predict what benefit the parents would have derived had the child survived. Resort to wrongful death proceedings can also be seen as misconceived: in reality, parents who bring such proceedings are primarily seeking damages for the distress occasioned by their loss. While there are differences of opinion as to whether such damages should be payable (an issue which will be discussed in Chapter 7), it can be argued that the parental claim should be seen for what it is and not be brought under the guise of a wrongful death action. On this analysis, while the parents should be permitted to sue in their own right, they should not also be permitted to bring an action on the basis that they are potential beneficiaries who have suffered an additional loss. Were they to be allowed to do so, the argument runs, 'double dipping' would result; in the words of one judge, the parents would receive 'an unmerited bounty'.[7]

---

[4] *McBride v Brookdale Hospital Medical Center* 498 NYS 2d 256, 259 (Sup, 1986) (emphasis in original).

[5] *Giardina v Bennett* 545 A 2d 139, 147 (NJ, 1988).

[6] *Carroll v Skloff* 202 A 2d 9, 11 (1964).

[7] *Endresz v Friedberg* 301 NYS 2d 65, 69 (1969).

The Action Allowed

It is only in a minority of United States jurisdictions that wrongful death claims following stillbirths have been denied. Several reasons have been given for allowing such claims.[8] As has been seen, to permit such a claim, it was first necessary to determine whether the various statutory references to the death of a 'person' could include a stillborn fetus. In many decisions, the courts had no difficulty concluding that it could. Further, this conclusion has sometimes been supported by the argument that the status of the fetus at the time of the injury is not relevant. What needs to be asked is whether, if death had not ensued, the child would have been able to maintain an action. On this interpretation, there is nothing to prevent a wrongful death claim following a stillbirth, since injury *in utero* can give rise to a subsequent cause of action. Courts that have reached this conclusion have offered a number of reasons for allowing the claim. They have asserted that it is illogical and arbitrary to insist that recovery for antenatal injury be possible only if the child is born alive: '[T]here is no perceptible reason why there should be a legally recognized difference between a death that occurs immediately before birth and one that occurs immediately after.'[9] This reflects the view that the loss suffered by the parents is substantially the same whether the child is stillborn or lives a few minutes. Further, it is a loss of the kind that can properly trigger the operation of the wrongful death legislation. As one court saw it, this legislation embodies a recognition of 'the legal right of the *survivors* to be compensated for *their* loss resulting from the victim's death': 'So far as compensation is concerned, there may be a quantitative but not a qualitative difference between the damage caused by the death of a newborn and that of a viable fetus; the damages reflect the same right of the parents—to recover the loss due to the death of their child.'[10]

This opinion has frequently been reinforced by reference to the dangers which would arise from the retention of the established rule requiring the birth of a child: '[I]t makes poor sense to sanction a legal doctrine that enables the tortfeasor whose deed brings about a stillbirth to escape liability but that renders one whose wrongdoing is less severe answerable in a

[8] The analysis which follows reflects the more important points made in such cases as: *Rainey v Horn* 72 So 2d 434 (1954); *White v Yup* 458 P 2d 617 (1969); *Chrisafogeorgis v Brandenberg* 304 NE 2d 88 (1973); *Presley v Newport Hospital* 365 A 2d 748 (1976); *Vaillancourt v Medical Center Hospital of Vermont, Inc* Vt, 425 A 2d 92 (1980); *O'Grady v Brown* 654 SW 2d 904 (Mo banc, 1983); *Hopkins v McBane* 359 NW 2d 862 (ND, 1984); *Greater Southeast Community Hospital v Williams* 482 A 2d 394 (DC App, 1984); *Amadio v Levin* 501 A 2d 1085 (Pa, 1985); *Summerfield v Superior Court, Maricopa Cty* 698 P 2d 712 (Ariz, 1985); *Werling v Sandy* 476 NE 2d 1053 (Ohio, 1985); *Wade v United States* 745 F Supp 1573 (D Hawaii, 1990); *Connor v Monkem Company, Inc* 898 SW 2d 89 (Mo banc, 1995).

[9] *Presley v Newport Hospital* 365 A 2d 748, 753 (1976).

[10] *Summerfield v Superior Court, Maricopa Cty* 698 P 2d 712, 721 (Ariz, 1985) (emphasis in original).

wrongful death or other negligence action merely because his victim survives birth.'[11] In some decisions, courts have emphasized this objection by suggesting that denial of a claim under a Wrongful Death Act would provide an incentive for a negligent medical practitioner to ensure that a child is stillborn:

[A] doctor or a midwife whose negligent acts in delivering a baby produced the baby's death would be legally immune from a lawsuit. However, if they badly injured the child they would be exposed to liability. Such a legal rule would produce the absurd result that an unborn child who was badly injured by the tortious acts of another, but who was born alive, could recover while an unborn child, who was more severely injured and died as a result of the tortious acts of another, could recover nothing.[12]

A broad policy argument has also been frequently adopted, namely that if the rule requiring live birth were to be retained, the legal system would be compelled to accept the existence of a wrong without a remedy. This reasoning was unashamedly based on the view that previously established principles should yield if they prevented the parents of a stillborn child from recovering compensation under a Wrongful Death Act. On occasions, this analysis was reinforced by reference to the need to avoid a narrow construction of such an Act: as a remedial statute, it should be liberally construed.

In a number of the cases which have allowed wrongful death actions following stillbirths, the courts have emphasized the importance of the viability of the fetus at the time when the negligent injury occurred. Sometimes, when the fetus was clearly viable, courts have made it clear that this fact facilitated a decision to allow the action (perhaps because it was easier to regard a viable fetus as a 'person'). Sometimes courts have expressly stated that a wrongful death action was possible only if the fetus was viable when injured. Occasionally this requirement has been abandoned and it has been held that proceedings may be taken under a Wrongful Death Act even though the fetus was not viable when injured. This aspect of the case law is more fully discussed in Chapter 8, in which the significance of viability is examined.

WRONGFUL LIFE

In the previous chapter I discussed cases in which parents of abnormal children recovered damages on the ground of a negligent failure to advise them of a foreseeable risk that their children would be born with genetic or other disabilities. In these matters, the success of the claims depended on the plaintiffs being able to establish that had the information been provided, they would have avoided conception or would have terminated the pregnancy.

---

[11] *Presley v Newport Hospital* 365 A 2d 748, 753 (1976).
[12] *Kwaterski v State Farm Mutual Automobile Ins Co* 148 NW 2d 107, 110 (1967).

There is another way in which a damages claim may be framed following the birth of an abnormal child. The action might be brought on behalf of the child, the claim being that he or she should not have been allowed to be born. An action of this kind can be contemplated only on behalf of a child who is born suffering substantial disabilities. Examples of congenital conditions in which it has been argued that the child would have been better off not being born are Tay Sachs disease, hydrocephalus, spina bifida, rubella syndrome, Down syndrome, and polycystic kidney disease. When a child is born with a condition of this kind, the argument is that the doctor's negligence (the failure to tell the parents of the risk of the condition and so give them the opportunity to avoid conception or to terminate the pregnancy) has caused the child to be born into a life of suffering.

The Action Disallowed

Most United States courts have refused to recognize wrongful life claims. Two main reasons—expressed by the New York Court of Appeals in *Becker v Schwartz* and *Park v Chessin*—have been given:

[T]here are two flaws in plaintiffs' claims on behalf of their infants for wrongful life. The first ... is that it does not appear that the infants suffered any legally cognizable injury.... Whether it is better never to have been born at all than to have been born with even gross deficiencies is a mystery more properly to be left to the philosophers and the theologians. Surely the law can assert no competence to resolve the issue, particularly in view of the very nearly uniform high value which the law and mankind has placed on human life, rather than its absence.... There is also a second flaw. The remedy afforded an injured party in negligence is designed to place that party in the position he would have occupied but for the negligence of the defendant.... Thus, the damages recoverable on behalf of an infant for wrongful life are limited to that which is necessary to restore the infant to the position he or she would have occupied were it not for the failure of the defendant to render advice to the infant's parents in a non-negligent manner. The theoretical hurdle to an assertion of damages on behalf of an infant accruing from a defendant's negligence in such a case becomes at once apparent.... Simply put, a cause of action brought on behalf of an infant seeking recovery for wrongful life demands a calculation of damages dependent upon a comparison between the Hobson's choice of life in an impaired state and nonexistence. This comparison the law is not equipped to make.[13]

There are numerous other United States decisions in which reliance has been placed on these two arguments—the absence of a legally cognizable injury and the impossibility of assessing damages—in order to disallow a wrongful life claim.[14] Similar reasoning has been adopted by the English

[13] 413 NYS 2d 895, 900 (1978).
[14] For example, *Gleitman v Cosgrove* 227 A 2d 689 (1967); *Dumer v St Michael's Hospital* 233 NW 2d 372 (1975); *Blake v Cruz* 698 P 2d 315 (Idaho, 1984); *Goldberg v Ruskin* 471 NE 2d 530

Court of Appeal in *McKay v Essex Area Health Authority*. Rejecting the claim (made on behalf of a child born suffering from the effects of antenatal rubella), Ackner LJ explained the decision as follows:

> The disabilities were caused by the rubella and not by the doctor . . . What then are [the child's] injuries, which the doctor's negligence has caused? The answer must be that there are none in any accepted sense. Her complaint is that she was allowed to be born at all, given the existence of her pre-natal injuries. How then are her damages to be assessed? . . . What the doctor is blamed for is causing or permitting her to be born at all. Thus, the compensation must be based on a comparison between the value of non-existence (the doctor's alleged negligence having deprived her of this) and the value of her existence in a disabled state. But how can a court begin to evaluate non-existence . . .? No comparison is possible and therefore no damage can be established which a court could recognise. This goes to the root of the whole cause of action.[15]

McKay has been followed in Australia.[16] In Canada, the question of the recognition of wrongful life actions has yet to be resolved.[17]

The Action Allowed

Of the small number of United States' decisions allowing the action, some have sought to address the problem of identifying the child's injury by asserting that it arises not from the fact of being alive but from the pain and suffering consequent upon being born disabled. The common factor in successful wrongful life actions appears to be a willingness to compensate a child for suffering and for the medical expenses associated with that suffering. Thus the

(Ill App 1 Dist, 1984); *James G v Caserta, Jennifer S v Kirdnual* 332 SE 2d 872 (W Va, 1985); *Smith v Cote* 513 A 2d 341 (NH, 1986); *Ellis v Sherman* 515 A 2d 1327 (Pa, 1986); *Bruggeman v Schimke* 718 P 2d 635 (Kan, 1986); *Siemieniec v Lutheran General Hospital* 512 NE 2d 691 (Ill, 1987); *Proffitt v Bartolo* 412 NW 2d 232 (Mich App, 1987); *Walker by Pizano v Mart* 790 P 2d 735 (Ariz, 1990).

[15] [1982] 1 QB 1166, 1189. Although the case was decided under the common law, the court expressed its opinion on the likely effect of the Congenital Disabilities (Civil Liability) Act 1976 (UK) (which came into force after the child had been born). The court suggested that the Act had enacted the recommendation of the Law Reform Commission, *Report on Injuries to Unborn Children* (Law Com No 60, 1974) para 89, that an action for wrongful life should not be permitted. On this analysis, a wrongful life action is precluded by s 1(2)(b) of the Act. An explanatory note (ibid. 47) states that: 'Subsection (2)(b) is so worded as to import the assumption that, but for the occurrence giving rise to a disabled birth, the child would have been born normal and healthy (not that it would not have been born at all).' Whether the Act has had this effect has been questioned: see J. E. S. Fortin, 'Is the "Wrongful Life" Action Really Dead?' [1987] Journal of Social Welfare Law 306, 312 and I. Kennedy and A. Grubb, *Medical Law: Text with Materials* (London, 2nd edn., 1994) 975–7.

[16] *Bannerman v Mills* (1991) Australian Torts Reports 81–079.

[17] *Cataford v Moreau* (1978) 114 DLR (3d) 585 rejected wrongful life as a cause of action in respect of the birth of a normal child and *Cherry v Borsman* (1991) 75 DLR (4th) 668 dealt inconclusively with the matter. In the latter case, the court allowed what it described as a 'wrongful life' claim, but also made it clear that the child in that case was not submitting that she would have been better off dead (ibid. 679).

crux of such actions is not so much a recognition of wrongful life but of wrongful suffering.

In *Curlender v Bio-Science Laboratories*, there had been a negligent failure to detect that the parents were the carriers of Tay Sachs disease and the child died of the disease at the age of 4. The Californian Court of Appeal remarked:

The reality of the 'wrongful-life' concept is that such a plaintiff both *exists* and *suffers*, due to the negligence of others. It is neither necessary nor just to retreat into meditation on the mysteries of life. We need not be concerned with the fact that had defendants not been negligent, the plaintiff might not have come into existence at all.[18]

On this basis, the child's cause of action was allowed and damages were awarded for the pain and suffering experienced during her four years of life; compensation was also given for the costs of providing special care.

In *Turpin v Sortini*, the pre-conception negligence had taken the form of a failure (by the defendant paediatrician and other medical staff) to recognize that the deafness suffered by the couple's first child was possibly the result of a hereditary condition. The parents claimed that had they been advised of this fact, they would not have conceived their second child, who was also born deaf. This case was obviously different from those previously discussed: it would be difficult to argue that a child whose only affliction was deafness would have been better off not being born. Nevertheless, the Supreme Court of California discussed the law on wrongful life claims and accepted that it is impossible to award general damages to a severely disabled child on the ground that it would have been better had he or she not been born. The court then criticized the reasoning employed in *Curlender*, pointing out that it paid insufficient attention to the fact that the child's claim was based on the assertion that had the defendants not been negligent, she would not have been born. The court explained:

Because nothing defendants could have done would have given plaintiff an unimpaired life, it appears inconsistent with basic tort principles to view the injury for which defendants are legally responsible solely by reference to plaintiff's present condition without taking into consideration the fact that if defendants had not been negligent she would not have been born at all.[19]

Having made this criticism, however, the court awarded special damages to the child for the expenses incurred in treating the hereditary ailment. This outcome was justified on the ground that a distinction could properly be made between general damages (which were not payable) and special damages (which were). An attempt was made to reinforce this conclusion by asserting that it would be 'illogical and anomalous'[20] to permit the parents of

[18] App, 165 Cal Rptr 477, 488 (1980) (emphasis in original).
[19] Cal 643 P 2d 954, 961 (1982).   [20] Ibid. 965.

an abnormal child to recover damages in a wrongful birth action, while denying the child the right to recover in a wrongful life action.

The approach adopted in *Turpin* has been followed in *Harbeson v Parke-
Davis Inc* and *Procanik by Procanik v Cillo*, in both of which impaired children, while being denied general damages, were able to recover special
damages when their parents had not been advised of the risk of congenital
deformities. The facts of *Harbeson v Parke-Davis Inc* have already been discussed;[21] the two children were held to be entitled to damages in respect of
the extraordinary medical expenses occasioned by the treatment of fetal
hydantoin syndrome. In *Procanik* (a case involving a child affected by
rubella[22]), there was also an award to the child of the costs of medical care. In
this case, as in *Turpin*, the question posed was whether, if parents can recover
damages for wrongful birth when their child is born with disabilities, there is
any reason for denying the child's right to recover for wrongful life. The
Supreme Court of New Jersey ruled that there was not: 'Whatever logic
inheres in permitting parents to recover for the cost of extraordinary medical
care incurred by a birth-defective child, but in denying the child's own right
to recover those expenses, must yield to the injustice of that result.' In contrast with the decision in *Curlender*, the court found it impossible to assess
damages for the child's pain and suffering. Further, it also rejected a claim for
damages for 'diminished childhood'; the court commented on how problematic and speculative it would be to try to calculate damages of this kind.[23]

Turpin, *Harbeson*, and *Procanik* have been strongly criticized in other
decisions. 'The essence of the *Turpin* rule is that logic should not defeat the
claim of a severely impaired child in need of help.'[24] A dissenting judgment in
Procanik further underlined this weakness. It noted that it is 'unfair and
unjust' to accept that a child has no claim for general damages for wrongful
life, while at the same time charging the doctors with the child's medical
expenses; it was seen as inconsistent to award special damages while simultaneously denying the child a cause of action.[25] This comment echoed the
doubts expressed by the dissenting judge in *Turpin*:

An order is internally inconsistent which permits a child to recover special damages
for a so-called wrongful life action, but denies all general damages for the very same
tort. While the modest compassion of the majority may be commendable, they suggest no principle of law that justifies so neatly circumscribing the nature of damages
suffered as a result of a defendant's negligence.[26]

More pointed were the comments in *Walker by Pizano v Mart*:

---

[21] See above 100.   [22] See above 96.
[23] 478 A 2d 755, 762–3 (NJ, 1984). Note, however, the dissent of Handler J with regard to the
claim for damages for 'impaired childhood'.
[24] *Smith v Cote* 513 A 2d 341, 354 (NH, 1986).
[25] 478 A 2d 755, 772 (NJ, 1984) (per Schreiber J).
[26] Cal, 643 P 2d 954, 966 (1982).

We believe . . . the limited recovery allowed by the courts recognizing the tort of wrongful life exhibits a fundamental casuistry in their reasoning. The conclusion that the child is impaired does not ineluctably imply that the child has suffered a legally congnizable [*sic*] injury. Principles of tort law require that the existence of injury be ascertained first; courts should allow the injury caused by defendant's negligence to define the damages recoverable, rather than allow impairment/damage the defendant did not cause to define the nature of the injury.[27]

The purpose of this chapter has been to identify two questionable types of claim, both of which have been recognized only in the United States. The problem with the decisions that have allowed a wrongful death or survival action following a stillbirth is that they depend on the view that a fetus is a 'person' for the purposes of the relevant legislation. This involves rejecting the widely accepted principle that it is only at birth that enforceable rights crystallize. Many courts have refused to take this step. Although actions for wrongful life have been permitted by a small number of United States courts, they have more frequently been disallowed in that country and the weight of authority is at present against the recognition of this cause of action.

A pervasive problem raised by wrongful death and wrongful life actions is the difficulty — perhaps the impossibility — of assessing damages. Indeed, the assessment of damages is a particularly troublesome and controversial aspect of any negligence action in the field of obstetrics or midwifery. It is to this subject that I turn in the next chapter.

[27] 790 P 2d 735, 740 (Ariz, 1990).

7

The Assessment of Damages

The range of harms in respect of which damages may be sought from negligent doctors and midwives is vast. The negligence may cause harm to the mother; alternatively, or in addition, it may result in the child being born injured or disabled. This latter outcome may lead to a claim for damages on behalf of the child and a claim by either or both parents. Similarly, parents may seek recompense when medical negligence has led to a stillbirth or a perinatal death. Quite different are the claims that arise when a child is unwanted; here, damages may be sought whether the child is normal or abnormal. In many of the situations described, difficult problems can arise as to the proper assessment of damages. It is beyond the scope of this chapter to offer a comprehensive review of the operation of the law of damages in this field. Nevertheless, an attempt will be made to identify the more important considerations that arise in the calculation of the damages to which parents and children are entitled when antenatal or perinatal negligence has been proved.

DAMAGES FOR INJURY OR DISABILITY

When a woman is negligently harmed in the course of delivering a child, she may recover damages for her own physical pain and suffering, for any additional medical and hospital expenses, and, where subsequent treatment prevents her from working, for loss of wages. Equally, when a child is born with a negligently caused injury or disability, damages are recoverable, in an action brought either by the parents or on the child's behalf. The damages can provide reimbursement of medical and hospital expenses and recompense for the child's pain and suffering. *Randall v United States*[1] provided a good illustration: the child was awarded damages for pain and suffering and for past and future medical expenses as her condition (Juvenile Laryngeal Papillomatosis) required surgery every two months. Whether compensation should be paid for the pain and suffering experienced by a very young baby is difficult to determine. In *Friel v Vineland Obstetrical and Gynecological Assn*,[2] the proceedings arose from a child's premature birth; she was cyanotic, and suffered from apnoea, intracranial haemorrhaging, central nervous difficulties, and respiratory failure. The defendants argued

---

[1] 859 F Supp 22 (DDC, 1994).   [2] 400 A 2d 147 (1979).

that if it could be shown that the child had fully recovered, no damages were payable. This argument was rejected. The Supreme Court of New Jersey ruled that a damages claim could be made on the child's behalf for the pain and suffering experienced during the lengthy hospitalizations following her birth.

If the child suffers from a disability, the need to provide special care may result in extra costs. Should the disability be a major one—such as cerebral palsy accompanied by brain damage—the total damages can be substantial. The Canadian case of *Cherry v Borsman*[3] illustrated this. The child suffered severe physical and mental disabilities. Damages were awarded not only for medical expenses and the cost of past care, but also for future care. She needed constant attention and had a life expectancy estimated at sixty years. The Supreme Court of British Columbia considered how the appropriate care could best be provided. The options were care in an institution, in a group home, or in her own home (initially living with her mother and later living independently). The court decided in favour of a normal home; as a result the award of damages covered the costs of a wheelchair, continuing therapy, the salary of a caregiver, respite care, transport, special furniture and equipment, medication, and attendance at summer camps. In addition, damages were awarded for the child's loss of future earning capacity, loss of the opportunity to enter into a marriage-like relationship, and loss of enjoyment of life. Further, it was ruled that some compensation should be offered to the girl for the lifelong distress that would be caused by her awareness of her disabilities and deformities.[4] Similarly, in an English case involving a child born with cerebral palsy, damages were awarded under a number of headings: pain and suffering, loss of amenities of life, past care, household alterations, special expenses, lost earning capacity, cost of care at home, and medical expenses.[5]

When a child is born with an injury or disability, it is not clear whether the parents can also recover damages for the impact that the birth has had on them. In the past, courts have been unwilling to award damages for non-physical harm and, as a result, damages are not normally payable for grief and distress. In England, Australia, and Canada, however, damages may be awarded for 'nervous shock'. This term refers to certain mental consequences arising directly from a physical injury or a fear of injury. Alternatively, a

---

[3] (1991) 75 DLR (4th) 668; affirmed on appeal (1992) 94 DLR (4th) 487. For a United States example, see *Muenstermann by Muenstermann v United States* 787 F Supp 499 (D Md, 1992).

[4] See also *Wipfli v Britten* (1984) 13 DLR (4th) 169, in which the British Columbia Court of Appeal allowed a brain-damaged child damages designed to ameliorate his sad lot in life and damages for the loss of earning capacity. Similarly, a substantial sum for 'non-pecuniary' damages was awarded in *Muenstermann by Muenstermann v United States* 787 F Supp 499 (D Md, 1992).

[5] *Nash v Southmead Health Authority* [1994] 5 Med LR 74.

person who is affected by witnessing or learning of harm suffered by another may be entitled to damages for nervous shock. The success of such a claim frequently depends on showing that the plaintiff was in close physical proximity to a distressing event; this requirement is sometimes expressed as a need to be in 'the impact zone'. It is not any form of distress which will be regarded as a compensable harm; to establish nervous shock, it must be shown that, as a direct result of a physical injury, the fear of such injury, or witnessing or hearing of another's injury, the plaintiff has suffered harm which has resulted in physical or psychiatric symptoms. Although there is some uncertainty as to the circumstances in which claims may be made for nervous shock, it is probably correct to say that liability can arise only for the reasonably foreseeable consequences of negligence. In the United States, similar principles have been developed; the courts' starting-point has been that damages are payable for mental distress only if it directly results from fear, from a physical injury or from the immediate impact of witnessing or hearing of some peril or harm to another. In many cases dealing with the latter type of claim, the need for the plaintiff to have been in the 'zone of danger' has been stressed.

Courts have sometimes awarded damages in response to claims by parents who have suffered severe distress as a result of the birth of an injured or disabled child. The extent to which this result can be achieved within the established rules is unclear. For example, when a woman and her fetus are injured by the negligent performance of a forceps delivery, she might seek damages for the nervous shock occasioned by the injury suffered by the child. For a claim of this kind to succeed, it would be necessary for her to demonstrate more than distress; she would have to show that she had suffered a recognizable psychiatric condition. If there is doubt whether the shock is a direct result of the injury which mother and child have suffered, it might be asserted that the mother is in the 'impact' or 'danger' zone and that she can claim to have experienced shock caused by witnessing the harm to her child. Similarly, a father who is present at a delivery might argue that he was also affected in this way.

While a number of judgments have referred to the 'shock' experienced by a mother who had given birth to an injured or disabled child, it is not clear that the term was used to refer to nervous shock of the kind previously identified by the courts. In England, in *S v Distillers Co (Biochemicals) Ltd*, the Court of Queen's Bench dealt with two cases in which children had been born with severe deformities as a result of their mothers taking thalidomide during pregnancy. In assessing the damages payable to one of the mothers, who was described as 'anxious, depressed and dependent on drugs to relieve her symptoms', Hinchcliffe J noted that she was 'grievously shocked at the birth of [the child]'. She was awarded damages in respect of the shock, the judge commenting:

For a happily married woman, it is difficult to comprehend any greater shock than seeing your child born misshapen and deformed. The fun and joy of motherhood is partially destroyed. Instead of enjoying and being able to show off the baby to your friends there is a natural reluctance to do so. This has not been the sort of shock which has worn off like so many cases of shock that come before the courts; this is permanent. Ever since the birth Mrs S has been depressed, anxious and worried. She is daily reminded of her handicap. There is always a cloud over her happiness. [6]

Similarly, in *Cherry v Borsman*, the mother was held to be entitled to damages for the emotional suffering caused by the birth of a child with severe disabilities. It was noted that: '[She] suffered a severe traumatic experience upon her learning of the physical and mental injuries sustained by her daughter. She will have many years of pain and emotional distress and she will have to cope with the burden of bringing up [the child] and giving her companionship throughout her life.'[7] In neither of these judgments was the precise basis for the damages award made clear; no attempt was made to determine whether the women suffered from nervous shock as it had previously been defined. Perhaps the courts, consciously or unconsciously, extended the operation of the law to permit recompense for the women's grief and disappointment.

The United States courts have occasionally shown a similar willingness to recognize a woman's entitlement to damages for the distress occasioned by giving birth to an injured or disabled child. This issue was discussed in *Friel v Vineland Obstetrical and Gynecological Assn*. At the time the action was begun it was not clear whether the child had suffered permanent damage; this was not going to be known until between the ages of 3 and 5. It was held that there was nothing to prevent the mother claiming damages for the continuing anxiety and distress caused by not knowing whether the child had suffered brain damage. In the court's words, '[A]nxiety and mental distress, when appropriately proven, are elements of damage in cases of injuries negligently inflicted on a child, at least where inflicted prenatally or at birth.'[8] It was stressed that the award of damages on this ground was a recognition of the direct impact of the medical negligence on the mother; the damages were not intended to compensate the child for the injuries suffered, for which the child had her own right of action.

Whether a father can also claim damages for distress is uncertain. In *Campbell v Pitt County Memorial Hospital*,[9] a father's action for damages to compensate him for the distress he experienced on the birth of a child with cerebral palsy was disallowed. It was held that damages for emotional distress were not recoverable unless the distress was the direct result of physical harm suffered by the plaintiff. As will be shown, however, there have been

[6] [1970] 1 WLR 114, 119, and 127.   [7] (1991) 75 DLR (4th) 668, 719.
[8] 400 A 2d 147, 153 (1979).   [9] 352 SE 2d 902 (NC App, 1987).

cases in which fathers have been able to recover damages in respect of the
anguish experienced in witnessing the birth of a stillborn child. The approach
adopted in *Campbell* may not, therefore, preclude the award of damages for
paternal distress.

Claims by a spouse or partner can also result in other categories of damages being awarded. He may incur medical and hospital expenses arising
from the further treatment of his partner. More controversially, recompense
may be sought for the loss of consortium, the loss of the partner's 'services,
society and comfort'.[10] Claims of this kind have succeeded in the United
States, on the basis that it was foreseeable that a husband's well-being could
be affected by harm negligently caused to his wife.

DAMAGES FOR STILLBIRTH OR PERINATAL DEATH

When medical negligence results in the death of a child soon after birth, special damages can be claimed; these include medical, hospital, and funeral
expenses. Damages of this kind are sometimes recovered by parents in
actions brought on their own behalf and sometimes in actions brought on
behalf of the child's estate under Survival Acts. As was explained in Chapter 6,
these statutes allow for the survival of certain types of damages claims which
the deceased could have made had he or she lived. There are differences in
the laws governing the damages that are recoverable under Survival Acts. In
addition to allowing compensation for medical, hospital, and funeral
expenses, damages for the child's pain and suffering can be awarded in some
United States and Canadian jurisdictions. Damages of this kind can also be
awarded in England, but not in Australia. In England and some Canadian
provinces, a nominal sum is payable for the child's loss of expectation of life.[11]

More difficult is the question of the damages payable to the parents to
compensate them for the harm that they have suffered. Following a stillbirth
or perinatal death, one or both parents may seek damages under the common
law. The principles applied in cases in which parents have claimed damages
for the distress occasioned by the birth of an impaired child (discussed
above) are again the starting-point when parents seek damages following a
stillbirth or perinatal death. In some United States cases, the courts have
adhered to established rules. In one it was held that when a stillbirth had been
caused by a delay in performing a caesarean section, the woman could

---

[10] *Friel v Vineland Obstetrical and Gynecological Assn* 400 A 2d 147, 151 (1979); see also
Simon v United States 438 F Supp 759, 763 (1977). But cp *Seef v Sutkus* 562 NE 2d 606 (Ill App 1
Dist, 1990).

[11] For an English example, see *Kralj v McGrath* [1986] 1 All ER 54, a case involving a child
who died after eight weeks; there the award of damages included sums for pain and suffering and
loss of expectation of life.

recover damages for the fear for her own personal safety, but not for the emotional distress caused by the stillbirth.[12] In another matter in which a negligently performed amniocentesis caused a stillbirth one month later, it was ruled that damages for emotional distress (including severe disappointment and bitterness) could not be recovered as the distress was not suffered at the time of the negligent act.[13] This decision reflected a strict application of the rule that damages are recoverable for distress only if it is suffered as a result of an injury sustained by the parent. Another illustration was provided by *District of Columbia v McNeill*.[14] There, a stillbirth followed a negligent estimation of the gestation of the fetus. The poor management had a direct effect on the woman at the time; she suffered fever and pain and was held to be entitled to recover damages for the resulting emotional distress. It was emphasized that no damages could be awarded to the woman for her grief.

In addition to stressing the requirement of direct injury, courts have sometimes approached the problem on the basis of the 'zone of danger' rule. In one case in which inadequate monitoring led to a stillbirth,[15] the Supreme Court of Vermont relied on this rule, concluding that since the woman was within this zone at the time of delivery, she had reason to fear for her own safety and hence could recover damages for emotional distress. In contrast, in *Seef v Sutkus*, an Illinois decision that also involved negligent monitoring resulting in a stillbirth, it was held that neither the woman nor her husband could claim to have suffered emotional distress caused by an injury or presence in the 'zone of danger'.[16] Different analyses have been offered in other cases. In *Khan v Hip Hospital*,[17] the 'zone of danger' principle was applied to allow a woman to recover damages for emotional distress after a stillbirth. Following the delivery, she recovered consciousness and at once became aware of the stillbirth; the court saw this as analogous to the situation of a person who had witnessed the death of a member of her immediate family. It was explained that not only was the woman located near the scene of the 'accident', but that she was also 'in some sense the scene itself'.[18]

In *Edinburg Hospital Authority v Trevino*, the woman suffered a haemorrhage during labour and an emergency caesarean section was performed; the child was stillborn. The Texas Court of Appeals rejected the defendant hospital's argument that the woman could claim damages for emotional distress only if this distress arose directly from injury to her:

---

[12] *Prado v Catholic Medical Center* 536 NYS 2d 474 (AD 2 Dept, 1988).
[13] *Tebbutt v Virostek* 483 NE 2d 1142 (NY, 1985).   [14] 613 A 2d 940 (DC App, 1992).
[15] *Vaillancourt v Medical Center Hospital of Vermont, Inc* Vt, 425 A 2d 92 (1980).
[16] *Seef v Sutkus* 562 NE 2d 606 (Ill App 1 Dist, 1990). See also *Littleton v Ob-Gyn Associates of Albany* 403 SE 2d 837 (Ga App, 1991); *Booth v Cathey* 893 SW 2d 715 (Tex App—Texarkana, 1995).
[17] 487 NYS 2d 700 (Sup, 1985).   [18] Citing *Haught v Maceluch* 681 F 2d 291, 299 (1982).

In this case, negligence during the delivery of a child which results in death of that child foreseeably causes mental anguish to the mother. The mental anguish includes the grief for loss of the child. [The mother] is entitled to recover for the mental distress that was a natural consequence of the hospital's negligence.[19]

The father's claim also succeeded, on the basis that it was appropriate to employ the 'zone of danger' rule:

[The father] was present immediately before the doctor ordered emergency surgery and witnessed his wife's hemorrhaging. He heard the doctor call for a surgical team and observed the delay in taking his wife to surgery. [The father] saw her immediately after the caesarean section and held their dead child in his arms. We hold that under these facts [the father] may recover as a bystander to his wife's injuries; that is, the risk of harm to [the father] was reasonably foreseeable under the circumstances.[20]

Damages following a stillbirth were also awarded in *Modaber v Kelley*.[21] The woman suffered from toxaemia and high blood pressure and there was a risk that she would experience convulsions and die; the doctor was not present at the birth. Emphasis was placed on the fact that the experience that she underwent was particularly distressing. The Supreme Court of Virginia not only approved the award of damages for the pain and suffering directly caused to the woman by the negligent management of the delivery, but it also accepted that damages could be awarded for the distress caused by the loss of the child. A similar result was reached in *Giardina v Bennett*. In awarding damages to parents after a stillbirth, the Supreme Court of New Jersey described the loss of their 'eagerly expected healthy baby' as 'serious and devastating' and said that it was one which 'predictably, engenders emotional distress and mental anguish'.[22]

In England, s 1A of the Fatal Accidents Act 1976 (UK) provides for the payment of a fixed sum for 'bereavement'. When a child is negligently injured *in utero* or at the time of delivery, is born alive and subsequently dies as a result of the negligence, the parents can invoke this provision and recover damages for bereavement. The operation of s 1A was noted in *Kerby v Redbridge Health Authority*.[23] The child lived only three days on a life-support machine. The mother received damages for her pain and suffering at the time of the delivery, for the 'immediate trauma' caused by learning that the baby was seriously disabled and was unlikely to survive, for the anguish experienced when she was asked to authorize the doctors to turn off the life-support machine, and for the distress which led her to develop a depressive illness. Her claim for damages for her 'dashed hopes' was, however, disallowed. The court reasoned that this was simply a claim for the s 1A bereavement

---

[19] 904 SW 2d 831, 836 (Tex App—Corpus Christi, 1995).   [20] Ibid. 837.

[21] 348 SE 2d 233 (Va, 1986). See also *Simon v United States* 438 F Supp 759 (1977).

[22] 545 A 2d 139, 141 (NJ, 1988).

[23] [1993] 4 Med LR 178. See also *Bowers v Harrow Health Authority* [1995] 6 Med LR 16.

expenses under another name and that she should not be permitted to recover these expenses twice. In both this case and an earlier one,[24] it was confirmed that damages were not payable to parents for the grief occasioned by the death of a child.

Kerby was a case involving a child who was born alive but lived only briefly. When a stillbirth has occurred, there is some authority for the view that damages *are* payable to the woman for emotional distress and for 'dashed hopes'. English courts have occasionally awarded damages for the loss of the satisfaction of bringing the pregnancy to a successful conclusion and for the psychological harm suffered by the woman.[25] While it is clear that the availability of bereavement expenses under s 1A of the Fatal Accidents Act is not a bar to such a claim (since these are payable only after a live birth), the award of damages for 'dashed hopes' may be open to attack on the ground that it is in fact an award to compensate for the grief occasioned by a stillbirth and so is not permitted by the common law.

Neither in Canada nor in Australia has the subject of the assessment of damages following a stillbirth or a perinatal death been fully examined. It is probable that when the issue comes before the courts in these countries, damages will be awarded under the headings recognized by the common law: pain and suffering experienced by the woman, and nervous shock. It is unlikely that a claim for damages for grief and disappointment will be allowed.[26]

Finally, the possibility of parents seeking damages under a Wrongful Death or Fatal Accidents Act must be examined. The purpose of this legislation is to compensate family members for the loss of financial support that they have suffered as a result of a death. In England, Canada, and Australia, a parental claim for compensation of this kind would probably not succeed, whether it arises from a stillbirth or a perinatal death. As has been explained in Chapter 6, a stillbirth cannot give rise to an action under a Fatal Accidents Act in any of these countries. Further, while it would theoretically be possible for parents to bring such an action following a perinatal death, the English, Canadian, and Australian courts would almost certainly disallow it.[27] This is because they would probably adopt the view that parents cannot

[24] *Kralj v McGrath* [1986] 1 All ER 54.

[25] *Grieve v Salford Health Authority* [1991] 2 Med LR 295.

[26] In two Australian jurisdictions (South Australia and the Northern Territory), there are special statutory provisions (Wrongs Act 1936 (SA), s 23A and Compensation (Fatal Injuries) Act (NT), s 10(3)(f)) allowing the payment of damages by way of *solatium* (a sum of money paid as a solace) to a parent whose child has died as a result of negligence. It is not clear how these provisions would be interpreted in the context of a perinatal death; they do not seem to be designed to apply to a death caused by actions taken before or at the time of birth.

[27] Further, with regard to the English law, the restriction imposed by s 4(4) of the Congenital Disabilities (Civil Liability) Act 1976 (UK) should be noted; this prevents any damages claim on behalf of a child who does not survive for at least forty-eight hours.

assert that the death of a child soon after birth has deprived them of an expected financial benefit.[28]

This view has not been universally adopted in the United States and it is therefore necessary to examine the case law on wrongful death actions arising from perinatal deaths and stillbirths. With regard to the former, a judge of the Supreme Court of Illinois confidently stated: 'It is unquestioned that there can be a recovery for the wrongful death of a child who lives but a moment after birth.'[29] In cases of this kind, the courts' task is to assess the pecuniary loss that the parents have suffered.[30] The approach adopted has frequently been rather slipshod. In *Simmons v University of Chicago Hospitals and Clinics*, in which the child died soon after birth, the Appellate Court of Illinois accepted that there was a rebuttable presumption as to substantial pecuniary loss arising from the death of a child. The jury had awarded the parents substantial damages and the Appellate Court saw no reason to overturn this verdict. An unsatisfactory feature of the case was that the damages were awarded for the loss of the child's society, yet this attracted no criticism on appeal.[31]

The subject of the assessment of damages under wrongful death legislation has been more fully discussed in the cases relating to stillborn children. The Supreme Court of Missouri saw the award of damages following a stillbirth as being consistent with the purposes of this legislation:

[The objectives of the wrongful death statute are] to provide compensation to bereaved plaintiffs for their loss, to ensure that tortfeasors pay for the consequences of their actions, and generally to deter harmful conduct which might lead to death. It should be clear that these reasons apply with equal force whether the deceased is born or unborn. Parents clearly have an interest in being protected against or compensated for the loss of a child they wish to have. The fetus itself has an interest in being protected from injury before birth . . . It follows logically that it should be protected against fatal injuries as well.[32]

A comment such as this ignores the difficulty of calculating the loss suffered by the parents of a stillborn child. Occasionally this difficulty has been recognized and the task has been labelled an impossible one: 'To allow recovery by the parents with respect to the unknown quantity of the financial value to the parents of the life of such a child is . . . to speculate beyond reason

---

[28] Support for this conclusion is provided by *Barnett v Cohen* [1921] 2 KB 461, in which it was held that the parent of a 3-year-old child has no cause of action under Lord Campbell's Act 1846 (UK). It was held that a claim under the Act must fail if there was 'a mere speculative possibility of benefit'; what was needed was 'a reasonable probability of pecuniary advantage' (ibid. 471).

[29] *Chrisafogeorgis v Brandenberg* 304 NE 2d 88, 90 (1973).

[30] It should be noted that, in some States, Wrongful Death Acts also expressly allow for the award of damages for non-pecuniary loss: see *White v Yupp* 458 P 2d 617 (1969).

[31] 617 NE 2d 278 (Ill App 1 Dist, 1993).

[32] *O'Grady v Brown* 654 SW 2d 904, 909 (Mo banc, 1983).

concerning its loss, for it is obviously impractical for anyone to know the potential of a child that never breathed.'[33] Underlying this statement was the concern that there was no way of knowing whether the child would have been born with an impairment. Yet in another case an Illinois court was not troubled by this uncertainty. As in *Simmons*, reliance was placed on a rebuttable presumption as to the pecuniary loss suffered by the parents. The calculation of damages therefore proceeded on the basis that there was 'nothing to indicate that the deceased baby ... would have been anything but a healthy, average, well-behaved child, with his entire life ahead of him'.[34]

Some United States courts have adopted a broad interpretation of the scope of Wrongful Death Acts and so have avoided facing up to the problem of calculating the damages that the parents of a stillborn child can claim under those Acts. An example of this has already been seen in the willingness of the Appellate Court of Illinois in *Simmons* to sanction a damages award for the loss of the child's society. Another illustration was provided by *Hopkins v McBane*.[35] There, in an action by a mother following a stillbirth, the Supreme Court of North Dakota recognized that damages payable under a Wrongful Death Act were originally designed to compensate the statutory beneficiaries for their pecuniary loss. It also recognized that it was no longer appropriate to regard the parents of a child who had died as suffering financial loss by being deprived of the wages that the child would have earned. Nevertheless, the court was unwilling to deny damages. It therefore adopted 'an expansive view' of the kinds of losses for which compensation could be paid under the Act and ruled that damages were recoverable for the loss of society, comfort, and companionship suffered by the mother as a result of the stillbirth of her child. It also awarded her damages for the grief and anguish caused by the loss. Similarly, in *Seef v Sutkus* (another case arising from a stillbirth), an award was made for loss of society, defined as the loss of the broad range of benefits family members receive, including love, care, companionship, and comfort. The court, while conceding the difficulty of assessing damages of this kind following a stillbirth, did not accept that to award compensation for loss of society was an indirect means of providing solace for grief.[36]

---

[33] *State v Sherman* 198 A 2d 71, 74 (1964).

[34] *Jones v Karraker* Ill App, 440 NE 2d 420, 426 (1982); affirmed on appeal: 457 NE 2d 23 (Ill, 1983).

[35] 427 NW 2d 85 (ND, 1988).

[36] 562 NE 2d 606 (Ill App 1 Dist, 1990). Other stillbirth cases where damages were awarded for loss of future society were *Smith v Mercy Hospital and Medical Center* 560 NE 2d 1164 (Ill App 1 Dist, 1990) and *Riley v Koneru* 593 NE 2d 788 (Ill App 1 Dist, 1992). In the former, a claim in respect of loss of services and future earnings was denied.

DAMAGES FOR UNWANTED PREGNANCY OR THE BIRTH OF
AN UNWANTED CHILD

A doctor's negligence can result in a woman being faced with an unwanted pregnancy. In such a situation, the pregnancy may be terminated, in which case the assessment of damages is not difficult. Damages can be recovered for the distress, anxiety, and discomfort occasioned by the pregnancy, for the woman's loss of wages, and for the medical and hospital expenses involved in the termination. Since actions of this kind are straightforward, they need not be further considered here.

Much more difficult is the assessment of damages for an unwanted birth. An unwanted birth may occur in a variety of circumstances. It may follow a negligently performed tubal ligation or a failure to diagnose a pregnancy. In such cases, the basis of the parents' claim is that they had not wanted to bear the burden of caring for the child. Alternatively, the child might have been wanted, but be born with a disability. Here the negligence complained of will be the non-disclosure of the foreseeable risk of the child being born with a disability. If the risk eventuates, the parents can sue on the ground that they were deprived of the opportunity to terminate the pregnancy. Thus two types of damages claims must be considered and a distinction made between damages claimed because a child, though normal, is unwanted and damages claimed because the child, although initially wanted, became unwanted when born with a disability.

A Normal Child

Arguably, the value of life is such that the birth of a normal child can never be a compensable harm. However, the majority of United States decisions in which this issue has been examined have rejected this argument.[37] No difficulties have arisen with the award of damages to compensate for pregnancy-related expenses. There have been numerous cases in which such damages have been allowed. Compensation has been given for the woman's loss of the amenities of life during the pregnancy and the perinatal period, her emotional distress as a result of the pregnancy, her distress and discomfort during

---

[37] Examples of United States cases which have examined the problem of the assessment of damages following the birth of an unwanted, normal child are: *Custodio v Bauer* 59 Cal Rptr 463 (1967); *Rieck v Medical Protective Company of Fort Wayne Indiana* 219 NW 2d 242 (1974); *Coleman v Garrison* Del Supr, 349 A 2d 8 (1975); *Ochs v Borrelli* Conn, 445 A 2d 883 (1982); *Boone v Mullendore* Ala, 416 So 2d 718 (1982); *University of Arizona Health Services Center v Superior Court* 667 P 2d 1294 (Ariz, 1983); *Cockrum v Baumgartner, Raja v Tulsky* 447 NE 2d 385 (Ill, 1983); *Fulton-De Kalb Hospital Authority v Graves* 314 SE 2d 653 (Ga, 1984); *Jones v Malinowski* 473 A 2d 429 (Md, 1984); *McKernan v Aasheim* 687 P 2d 850 (Wash, 1984); *Flowers v District of Columbia* 478 A 2d 1073 (DC App, 1984); *Morris v Sanchez, Stout v United States* 746 P 2d 184 (Okl, 1987); *Burke v Rivo* 551 NE 2d 1 (Mass, 1990); *Marciniak v Lundborg* 450 NW 2d 243 (Wis, 1990); *Lovelace Medical Center v Mendez* 805 P 2d 603 (NM, 1991).

the delivery, her loss of wages during pregnancy and until her return to work, and medical and hospital expenses associated with the antenatal care of the woman, the delivery, and postnatal care. In some cases, her partner has also received damages for loss of consortium.

More controversial is the question whether damages should be restricted to pregnancy-related expenses or whether they should also cover the costs of the child's upbringing. In many United States jurisdictions, the courts have held that the cost of rearing a normal child may not be recovered in an unwanted birth case. Several reasons have been advanced. The most fundamental objection is no more than a restatement of the reservations which initially greeted unwanted birth actions: since the presence of a normal child is a blessing, it is unacceptable for parents to seek compensation for the cost of caring for such a child. This objection is frequently expressed in the statement that the joy and companionship provided by a healthy child inevitably outweigh the costs of bringing up that child. When the argument is put in these terms, it is common for courts to express their disapproval of a claim for child-rearing expenses: 'A child is more than an economic liability. A child may provide its parents with love, companionship, a sense of achievement, and a limited form of immortality.'[38] From this viewpoint, to allow damages to cover child-rearing costs would be to bestow a 'windfall' on the parents. Courts adopting this view have, however, generally had no difficulty in awarding damages for pregnancy-related expenses. In doing so, they have reached something of a compromise. By denying child-rearing expenses, they signalled that it is not appropriate to treat the task of bringing up a healthy child as no more than an economic liability. At the same time their award of expenses related to the pregnancy indicated that a doctor does not have immunity in respect of the negligence which caused the unwanted birth.[39]

Other reasons advanced for disallowing claims for damages for child-rearing expenses have been that the calculation of these damages would be speculative and conjectural and that even if a satisfactory calculation could be made, the resulting awards would place an unreasonable burden on the medical profession. Finally, there is the view that actions in which parents sue for the recovery of the cost of children's upkeep can have a harmful effect on the children. When they later learn of the proceedings, they will realize that they were unwanted and that their parents were reluctant to bear the cost of caring for them.

Arguments of this kind have proven unpersuasive in a small number of United States courts. Predictably, the major reason for allowing the award of child-rearing expenses was disagreement with the view that the benefits of

---

[38] *McKernan v Aasheim* 687 P 2d 850, 854 (Wash, 1984).
[39] See, for example, *Smith v Gore* 728 SW 2d 738 (Tenn, 1987).

raising a healthy child are such that parents cannot claim that they have suffered harm. In some cases, the rejection of this view depended on the drawing of distinctions based on the differing circumstances in which unwanted births occur. In *Burke v Rivo*, in which the birth followed a failed tubal ligation, it was pointed out that when a woman has undergone a procedure specifically to avoid pregnancy, it cannot be asserted that the joy and pride in raising a child outweigh any economic loss: 'The very fact that a person has sought medical intervention to prevent him or her from having a child demonstrates that, for that person, the benefits of parenthood did not outweigh the burdens, economic and otherwise, of having a child.'[40] A distinction can be drawn between this situation and that arising when the parents' desire to avoid the birth of a child was founded on a fear that the child would be affected by a genetic defect. If their fears prove unfounded and a healthy child is born, it might be hard for them to deny that the birth was a blessing. As was noted in *University of Arizona Health Services Center v Superior Court*: '[W]here the parent sought sterilization in order to avoid the danger of genetic defect, the jury could easily find that the uneventful birth of a healthy, non-defective child was a blessing rather than a "damage".'[41]

Once it can be established that in the parents' particular circumstances, the unwanted birth is not a blessing, the major barrier to a claim for child-rearing expenses is removed. It can then be asserted that allowing a claim for such expenses is consistent with the basic principles of negligence law: if medical negligence causes the birth of an unwanted child, to make the defendant liable for child-rearing expenses is to do no more than impose liability for the reasonably foreseeable consequences of the negligence. To reach this conclusion it is also necessary to overcome the objection that children will be adversely affected by learning that they had been unwanted. One judge has asserted that the knowledge that someone else was contributing to his or her upkeep 'may in fact alleviate the child's distress at the knowledge of having been once unwanted'. He added, 'In any event, it is for the parents, not the courts, to decide whether a lawsuit would adversely affect the child and should not be maintained.'[42] In another case, it was observed that: '[I]t is not to disparage the value of human life and the societal need for harmonious family units to protect the parents' choice not to have children by recognizing child-rearing costs as a compensable element of damages in negligent sterilization cases.'[43]

Finally, a decision in favour of the award of child-rearing costs requires a denial of the argument that the calculation of these costs is too speculative; a typical reason for rejecting this argument is as follows:

[40] 551 NE 2d 1, 4 (Mass, 1990).
[41] 667 P 2d 1294, 1300 (Ariz, 1983). See also *Hartke v McKelway* 707 F 2d 1544 (1983).
[42] *Burke v Rivo* 551 NE 2d 1, 5 (Mass, 1990).
[43] *Jones v Malinowski* 473 A 2d 429, 435 (Md, 1984).

The determination of the anticipated costs of child-rearing is no more complicated or fanciful than many calculations of future losses made every day in tort cases. If a physician is negligent in caring for a new-born child, damage calculations would be made concerning the newborn's earning capacity and expected medical expenses over an entire lifetime. The expenses of rearing a child are far more easily determined. If there is any justification for denying recovery of normal tort damages in a case of this character, it is not that the cost of rearing a child is incapable of reasonable calculation . . .[44]

If the objection as to the assessment of damages is overcome, there remains the possibility that the award of child-rearing expenses would place an unreasonable burden on the medical profession. The courts have generally not regarded this argument as a strong one: if the elements of a negligence claim are established, the award of damages cannot be disallowed simply because of the nature of the burden which will fall on a defendant.

The number of United States cases that have used the above analysis to justify the award of full child-rearing expenses for a healthy child has been small. The adoption of a compromise involving the application of the 'benefits rule' has been more common. This takes the calculation of full compensation as its starting-point, but requires a deduction on the basis of an assessment of the benefits accruing to the family from the birth of the child. The benefits of parenthood are offset against its burdens. Making such a calculation is obviously difficult and some courts have suggested that the task is impossible. In *McKernan v Aasheim*, the court, having concluded that application of the established principles governing the assessment of damages required an offset to be allowed, concluded that the benefits rule could not be satisfactorily applied:

We believe that it is impossible to establish with reasonable certainty whether the birth of a particular healthy, normal child damaged its parents. Perhaps the costs of rearing and educating the child could be determined through use of actuarial tables or similar economic information. But whether these costs are outweighed by the emotional benefits which will be conferred by that child cannot be calculated. The child may turn out to be loving, obedient and attentive, or hostile, unruly and callous. . . . [I]t is impossible to tell, at an early stage in the child's life, whether its parents have sustained a net loss or net gain.[45]

The same point was put rhetorically in another judgment: 'Who . . . can strike a pecuniary balance between the triumphs, the failures, the ambitions, the disappointments, the joys, the sorrows, the pride, the shame, the redeeming hope that the child may bring to those who love him?'[46]

Further, the court in *McKernan v Aasheim* saw the adoption of the benefits rule as providing a motive for parents to disparage their child: to maximize

---

[44] *Burke v Rivo* 551 NE 2d 1, 5 (Mass, 1990).   [45] 687 P 2d 850, 855 (Wash, 1984).
[46] *Miller v Johnson* 343 SE 2d 301, 307 (Va, 1986).

the award of damages, they would seek to show that the birth of the child had conferred little benefit on them. In the court's view, it was unacceptable to put parents in the position of having to prove that 'their child was more trouble than it was worth':

[A]n unhandsome, colicky or otherwise 'undesirable' child would provide fewer offsetting benefits, and would therefore presumably be worth more monetarily. . . . The adoption of that rule would thus engender the unseemly spectacle of parents disparaging the 'value' of their children or the degree of their affection for them in open court. It is obvious, whether the conclusion is phrased in terms of 'public policy' . . . or otherwise, that such a result cannot be countenanced.[47]

In spite of such arguments, some courts have applied the rule and carried out calculations designed to offset the benefits derived from a healthy child against the financial burden of providing care and education. In *Ochs v Borrelli*, for example, the Supreme Court of Connecticut approved a reduction of damages on the basis of 'the satisfaction, the fun, the joy, the companionship, and the like' derived from bringing up a child. While conceding that these were 'noneconomic factors', the court rejected the argument that calculating the value of such factors was 'impermissibly speculative'.[48] Similarly, while providing no guidance as to how the task should be performed, an Arizona court has ruled that the pecuniary and non-pecuniary benefits derived by the parents from their relationship with the child should be offset against the costs of child-rearing.[49]

The subject of the assessment of damages following the birth of an unwanted but healthy child has received less attention in the English, Canadian, and Australian courts. In England, the courts initially adopted differing views on damages in unwanted birth cases. A number of considerations were noted: whether or not the birth of a healthy child should be regarded as a blessing, the difficulty of seeking to balance the benefits derived from the birth of such a child against the costs incurred, the risk that parents might denigrate the child in order to downplay these benefits and so maximize the sum awarded; the danger that parents who express love for the child and make the best of the situation would receive little, whereas those who are bitter and rejecting would receive more (and thus that 'virtue would go unrewarded'), and the possible effect on the child of learning that he or she was unwanted. One case concluded that the costs of bringing up a normal child were not recoverable and another concluded that they were.[50] The issue was re-examined by the Court of Appeal in *Emeh v Kensington and Chelsea and*

---

[47] 687 P 2d 850, 855 (Wash, 1984), citing *Public Health Trust v Brown* Fla App, 388 So 2d 1084, 1086 n 4 (1980).

[48] Conn, 445 A 2d 883, 886 (1982).

[49] *University of Arizona Health Sciences Center v Superior Court* 667 P 2d 1294 (Ariz, 1983).

[50] *Udale v Bloomsbury Area Health Authority* [1983] 1 WLR 1098; *Thake v Maurice* [1986] 1 QB 644.

Westminster Area Health Authority,[51] a case arising from a failed tubal ligation. In deciding in favour of the award of reasonable child-rearing costs, the
court indicated that it was not appropriate for it to take account of public policy arguments against such an award; instead, it saw its task as being to apply
established principles of tort law. Under these principles, compensation is
provided for the reasonably foreseeable consequences of negligence. In the
case of negligence leading to the birth of an unwanted child, it was foreseeable that the parents would incur child-rearing expenses. Thus the award of
these expenses was approved, together with damages for expenditure associated with the pregnancy, the mother's discomfort, pain and suffering, her loss
of future earnings, and loss of amenities of life. The principles laid down in
Emeh have been followed in a number of later cases.[52]

In Canada, in *Cataford v Moreau*,[53] the Quebec Superior Court awarded
damages to parents (who already had ten children) in respect of the birth of
an eleventh child, following a negligently performed tubal ligation. The
mother was held to be entitled to damages for loss of enjoyment of life, the
inconvenience of the unwanted pregnancy, anxiety, the suffering and inconvenience caused by the confinement, and the need to undergo a second tubal
ligation. The father received damages for the expenses of the confinement
and the second operation, as well as for loss of consortium. The court was,
however, reluctant to permit the parents to 'cash in' on their healthy child.[54]
While accepting that child-rearing expenses were recoverable, it took
account of the social security benefits which were payable as a result of the
birth of the child. In the court's view, these were almost sufficient to cover the
cost of bringing up the child and it therefore declined to make an award, ruling that any shortfall was more than offset by the benefits, both financial and
personal, of raising the child. In a later case, *Fredette v Wiebe*,[55] damages were
awarded to a woman who, as a single 17-year-old, had given birth to twins,
one of whom had a heart defect. The negligence had consisted of a failure
(after an unsuccessful termination of pregnancy) to diagnose her pregnancy
in time for her to have a further termination procedure. The case was not,
however, a typical unwanted birth case. By the time the twins were 18 months
old, the mother had entered into a new relationship and subsequently married. It was held that the harm suffered by her ceased at the time of the marriage, and she was therefore entitled only to non-pecuniary damages for the
anxiety, inconvenience, suffering, and loss of enjoyment of life experienced
by her as an impecunious single parent. Further, she had herself been negligent in not attending for a check-up after the failed termination procedure;

---

[51] [1985] 1 QB 1012.
[52] *Gardiner v Mounfield and Lincolnshire Area Health Authority* [1990] 1 Med LR 205;
Allen v Bloomsbury Health Authority [1993] 1 All ER 651.
[53] (1978) 114 DLR (3d) 585. See also *Kealey v Berezowski* (1996) 136 DLR (4th) 708.
[54] Ibid. 598. [55] (1986) 29 DLR (4th) 534.

she had therefore been contributorily negligent and the damages awarded to her were halved. Mention must also be made of *Cherry v Borsman*, which has been discussed in earlier chapters. This case involved the birth of a seriously disabled child and hence the approach adopted to the award of damages is not strictly relevant here. The Supreme Court of British Columbia did, however, review the law on the assessment of damages in unwanted birth cases. Adopting the reasoning of the English Court of Appeal in *Emeh*, it ruled that all costs resulting from the birth were recoverable.

In Australia, the only reported case dealing with the birth of an unwanted but healthy child is *CES v Superclinics (Australia) Pty Ltd*.[56] This decision provides little guidance on the assessment of damages. One of the three members of the New South Wales Court of Appeal would have disallowed the action on the ground that the birth of the child was a blessing. Of the remaining two judges, one was in favour of allowing the payment of pregnancy-related expenses and of full child-rearing costs. The other was in favour of allowing only expenses incurred up to the time when the mother could have surrendered the child for adoption; in his view, the mother, having chosen to keep the child, was not entitled to damages for the financial consequences of that choice. The law on this matter in Australia awaits further clarification.

A Disabled Child

When a child is unwanted because he or she has been born with a genetic disability or a condition such as congenital rubella syndrome, it is difficult to argue that the birth is a blessing. A common situation in which a damages claim is made in respect of the birth of a disabled child is when a doctor has failed to advise a pregnant woman of the risk that her child would be born with a disability and she asserts that had the risk been disclosed, she would have terminated the pregnancy. Another is when a tubal ligation is negligently performed and an abnormal child is born. In both types of case, the complaint is that harm has been suffered as the result of the birth of a child whose disabilities make him or her unwanted. When such a child has been born, two aspects of the resulting damages claim are problematic. First, it must be determined whether the extraordinary expenses associated with the abnormality are recoverable and, secondly, there is the question whether damages are payable to compensate the parents for their distress.

Many of the situations discussed earlier in the chapter have resulted in the births of children who, because of their serious abnormalities, require expensive special care. The assessment of the enormous costs of the care and treatment of severely disabled children does not present particular difficulties. Examples of the way in which the courts have dealt with this task have been

[56] (1995) 38 NSWLR 47.

given earlier in this chapter, as part of the discussion of cases involving the birth of children whose disabilities were caused by medical negligence before or at the time of delivery. When the negligence does not directly cause the harm to the child, however, a distinction must be made between negligence which results in the birth of a child who happens to be disabled and negligence which is causally related to the birth of a disabled child. The most common example of the first type of situation is that which arises when a tubal ligation has been negligently performed and a child is born disabled. Here the negligence is unconnected with the child's abnormality; while the doctor's failure to take care has led to the *birth* of an unwanted child, it is not causally related to the birth of a *disabled* child. The fact that the child is disabled is the result of chance. In contrast, in the second type of situation the negligence is of such a kind as to make it foreseeable that the child would be born with a specific disability. A case of this kind arises when the negligence takes the form of a failure to warn of the risk of the birth of a child with an abnormality (for example, a failure to advise a pregnant woman who has been in contact with rubella that her child might be born with congenital rubella syndrome). If the risk eventuates, the action against the doctor will allege that the negligence directly caused the birth of a child with an abnormality that should have been foreseen.

If the abnormality occurs by chance, the question to be determined is whether the doctor is liable not only for the cost of bringing up a normal child, but also for the extraordinary expenses associated with the abnormality. In England, it has been decided that the doctor may be liable to pay the full costs in such a situation. The Court of Appeal, in *Emeh v Kensington and Chelsea and Westminster Area Health Authority*,[57] dealt with the birth of a child with genetic abnormalities; the birth was the result of a negligent sterilization. It was held that there was nothing to prevent the mother from recovering in full for financial damage suffered, whether the child was normal or abnormal. As a result, she was awarded the reasonable costs of child-rearing, including the extra costs resulting from the abnormality. This award was made on the basis that the risk of the abnormality was foreseeable (Waller LJ quoted the incidence of the child's condition as being between 1:200 and 1:400).[58] This decision can be contrasted with two United States decisions, both of which disallowed claims for compensation for extraordinary expenses. In one, the child was born with a cleft lip and palate[59] and in the other[60] the child had an umbilical hernia. In both cases the claims for the costs of treating the defects were brought following negligently performed sterilization procedures. In

[57] [1985] 1 QB 1012.
[58] Ibid. 1019. See also *Allen v Bloomsbury Health Authority* [1993] 1 All ER 651.
[59] *Garrison v Foy* 486 NE 2d 5 (Ind App 3 Dist, 1985).
[60] *La Point v Shirley* 409 F Supp 118 (1976).

both, the courts stressed that the particular defects were not foreseeable: the only foreseeable consequence of the failure of the procedure was an unwanted birth, not the birth of an abnormal child.

In the second category of cases—where there has been a failure to advise of a risk that eventuated—liability is imposed on the basis that the child's disabilities were foreseeable. The principal question then becomes whether the damages should be limited to the extraordinary expenses associated with the care of a disabled child or whether full child-rearing costs (including those extraordinary expenses) should be payable. While full child-rearing costs have occasionally been awarded,[61] many courts have preferred to allow only extraordinary expenses. This has been done on the basis that typically parents who seek damages following the birth of an abnormal child wanted a child; it is only the abnormality that makes the child unwanted. They had expected to bear ordinary child-rearing costs: as was noted in *Smith v Cote* (a case involving a child born with congenital rubella syndrome), these costs were a price that they were willing to pay. On this ground, the Supreme Court of New Hampshire ruled: '[A] plaintiff in a wrongful birth case may recover the extraordinary medical and educational costs attributable to the child's deformities, but may not recover ordinary child-raising costs.' The judgment approved the payment not only of damages for the special expenses arising from the child's condition, but also recompense for 'the burdens imposed on a parent who must devote extraordinary time and effort to caring for a child with birth defects'.[62]

The 'extraordinary expenses' rule has been adopted in a number of other cases.[63] In *Phillips v United States* (which related to a child with Down syndrome), the task of calculating damages was approached on the basis that the special costs of home and institutional care should first be calculated and the cost of raising a 'normal' child be deducted.[64] The award in this case was made on the assumption that the child had a life expectancy of forty years. When such a period is specified, it is necessary to distinguish between claims brought by parents and those brought on behalf of the child. If the claim is made by the parents, they may receive only damages sufficient to meet their expenses during the child's minority. If the aim is to provide funds throughout the life of a disabled child, provision must be made for a payment in respect of the period after the parents' responsibility ends. In *Procanik by*

[61] For example, in *Robak v United States* 658 F 2d 471 (1981). Full expenses were also awarded in the only reported Australian decision dealing with the assessment of damages following the birth of an abnormal child: *Veivers v Connolly* [1995] 2 Qd R 326.

[62] 513 A 2d 341, 350 (NH, 1986).

[63] For example, *Phillips v United States* 575 F Supp 1309 (1983); *Procanik by Procanik v Cillo* 478 A 2d 755 (NJ, 1984); *Siemieniec v Lutheran General Hospital* 512 NE 2d 691 (Ill, 1987); *Viccaro v Milunsky* 551 NE 2d 8 (Mass, 1990). See also the decision of the English Court of Appeal in *Salih v Enfield Health Authority* [1991] 3 All ER 400.

[64] 575 F Supp 1309, 1317 (1983).

Procanik v Cillo (another case arising from the birth of a child with congenital rubella syndrome), a combined order was made: 'We hold that a child or his parents may recover special damages for extraordinary medical expenses incurred during infancy, and that the infant may recover those expenses during his majority.'[65]

A subsidiary question raised in cases of this kind is whether the 'benefits rule' should be applied. This rule has been discussed in the context of cases in which damages were claimed following the birth of normal children. At first sight, it might be thought that the parents of a disabled child do not derive a benefit that should be used as an offset in the calculation of damages. This view was rejected in *Phillips v United States*: 'The court finds that the "benefits" flowing from the child's birth despite his condition [Down syndrome] amount to fifty per cent of the damages for plaintiffs' mental anguish and emotional distress.'[66] It is possible that courts might make distinctions on the basis of the seriousness of the child's disabilities. A child born with Down syndrome might give his or her parents considerable pleasure, but there might be no offsetting benefit in the case of a child born with gross abnormalities.

There is one further aspect of the assessment of damages requiring comment. A parent whose child is born with a major disability will experience great distress and suffering. Earlier in the chapter, it was noted that when antenatal negligence causes a child to be born with an injury or disability, parents may seek damages for the anguish which they feel. Similarly, if they have not received information that would have resulted in a termination, they may claim damages following the birth of a child suffering from a genetic disability or a condition such as congenital rubella syndrome. As in the cases already discussed, the courts have reached different conclusions about parents' entitlement to damages for distress in these circumstances. Damages for emotional distress have been awarded in some unwanted birth matters: for example, parents have received damages of this kind following the birth of children with Down syndrome, Tay Sachs disease, and congenital rubella syndrome.[67] In *Schroeder v Perkel*,[68] damages were awarded to parents to compensate for the anguish caused by watching a child die of cystic fibrosis. As it was put in one case involving the birth of a Down syndrome child: '[The parents] are entitled to be recompensed for the mental and emotional anguish they have suffered and will continue to suffer on account of [their child's] condition.'[69] This ruling was later explained as follows: '[T]he shock

---

[65] 478 A 2d 755, 762 (NJ, 1984). [66] 575 F Supp 1309, 1320 (1983).
[67] See *Phillips v United States* 575 F Supp 1309 (1983); *Naccash v Burger* Va, 290 SE 2d 825 (1982); *Procanik by Procanik v Cillo* 478 A 2d 755 (NJ, 1984). For Australian authority, see *Veivers v Connolly* [1995] 2 Qd R 326.
[68] NJ, 432 A 2d 834 (1981). [69] *Berman v Allen* 404 A 2d 8, 15 (1979).

and bitterness of parents in having been deprived of any choice concerning the birth of their child provided a basis for emotional distress damages.'[70]

Some courts have adopted a different view. In *Siemieniec v Lutheran General Hospital*, the parents' claim for damages for emotional distress following the birth of a child with haemophilia was disallowed. The court saw no reason to expand the right to recover for negligently inflicted emotional distress; it regarded that right as being limited to those whose distress had been caused by a direct injury or threat.[71] Similarly, in *Smith v Cote* (where the child was born with rubella syndrome), the court rejected the argument that the parents were entitled to damages for their distress. The main reason was a desire to establish limits to the scope of negligence liability in this field: 'Every injury has ramifying consequences, like the ripplings of the waters, without end. The problem for the law is to limit the legal consequences of wrongs to a controllable degree.'[72] The English Court of Appeal has also indicated that damages are not payable for the grief occasioned by the birth of a disabled child.[73]

The cases reviewed in this chapter have demonstrated certain problems arising from the assessment of damages in obstetric cases. In some instances, these problems are simply illustrations of those which are regularly encountered by courts hearing medical malpractice claims. Thus, for example, when substandard care results in the birth of a severely disabled child, decisions must be made as to the sums payable for pain and suffering, medical expenses, the cost of special care, loss of amenities of life, and lost earning capacity. More difficult in a case such as this (or one involving a stillbirth) is whether damages should be paid to the parents for their distress and dashed hopes. The question of how to compensate parents is far more contentious in unwanted birth cases. It is uncertain whether the parents of a normal child born after a failed tubal ligation should receive the full cost of the child's upbringing or whether some deduction should be made in recognition of the fact that the child will bring the parents pleasure and satisfaction. A case of this kind highlights the distinctive problems associated with damages claims in obstetrics and midwifery.

Problems of this kind—like those discussed in Chapters 3 to 6—illustrate the difficulties arising from the use of tort law to compensate parents and children who have suffered harm as a result of childbirth. The appropriateness of employing negligence law for this purpose will be critically examined in Chapter 10, in which the focus shifts from a descriptive account of the operation of the law to an analysis of the conceptual complexities associated with legal intervention after childbirth.

[70] *Giardina v Bennett* 545 A 2d 139, 141 (NJ, 1988).

[71] 512 NE 2d 691, 707 (Ill, 1987). A similar result was reached in *Cauman v George Washington University* 630 A 2d 1104 (DC App, 1993).

[72] 513 A 2d 341, 351 (NH, 1986), quoting *Tobin v Grossman* 249 NE 2d 419, 424 (1969).

[73] *Salih v Enfield Health Authority* [1991] 3 All ER 400.

Part II

Assessing the Impact of the Law

Part II

Assessing the Impact of the Law

8

The Legal Status of the Fetus

The analysis contained in Part I revealed that the legal status of the fetus is uncertain. That the law recognizes its existence is clear. What is less clear is whether the law's concern is with the fetus itself or with what it will become after birth. When confronted with claims made on behalf of the fetus, the law has exhibited two different approaches. Sometimes it has regarded the fetus as a distinctive entity: the essential feature of this approach is an acknowledgement that the fetus exists and that its existence can trigger legal action. Alternatively, the law might elect to pay little attention to the fetus itself and, instead, view it as no more than an inchoate being, to be the object of legal notice only upon live birth. The contrast between these two models—actuality and potentiality—is central to the following discussion.

This discussion concentrates on legal analysis. It does not explore the ethical and philosophical questions raised by the claims with which the law has sought to deal. Further, the title of the chapter should not be taken as an indication that the fetus should be regarded as a separate entity. As will be seen in this and the succeeding chapter, my view is that its special nature can be understood only by taking account of the relationship between a pregnant woman and her fetus. The use of the term 'fetus' also requires comment. I have not addressed the problem of the proper definition of this term. While in some circumstances a distinction must be made between an embryo ('the developing organism from one week after conception to the end of the second month') and a fetus ('the developing young . . . after the end of the second month'[1]), reference to this distinction is not necessary here. Many of the cases discussed in this book have been concerned with full-term fetuses at the point of delivery and many have dealt with fetuses at a much earlier stage of development. The word 'fetus' will be used in a general sense to describe both embryos and fetuses, whatever their gestation. This usage has not been uniformly adopted by the courts. In addition, many of the judgments that will be cited employ the term 'unborn child' and, in so doing, add to the difficulties attending the debate about the legal status of the fetus.

This chapter examines some assumptions underlying the law's attempts to deal with claims advanced on behalf of the fetus. My purpose is to determine how the lawmakers view the fetus and whether it is recognized as a distinctive entity with interests deserving protection. As was seen in earlier chapters, the interests of fetuses have been scrutinized in the context of criminal,

---

[1] *Dorland's Illustrated Medical Dictionary* (Philadelphia and London, 24th edn., 1965).

child protection, and negligence proceedings, as well as in actions taken to impose medical treatment on unwilling women. The lessons to be learned from a re-examination of these proceedings are the principal subject of this chapter.

Before these lessons are identified, it is helpful to consider one aspect of inheritance law, since it was in this field of law that the earliest attempts were made to come to terms with the special nature of the fetus. These attempts provided a foundation on which later legal developments were built. Inheritance law has long acknowledged the need to take account of the existence of a fetus for the purpose of the transmission of property. There are many cases in which it has been accepted that references to 'children' in a will included 'unborn children'.[2] In one of these a court observed: '[T]hey [unborn children] are to be considered in being, in all cases, where it is for their benefit to be so considered.'[3] Similarly, it has been held that a child born after her father's death was entitled to share in his estate when he died intestate.[4] Whether or not there was a will, the significant point is that while the law recognized the claim, it did so only following birth: the right to the property vests once the child has been born alive. The law on the inheritance rights of the unborn did not, however, necessarily reflect a desire to protect the welfare of the fetus: '[I]t was the testator's intent, not the personhood of the fetus, that was the common law's primary concern.'[5] For the purposes of this chapter the important issue is whether inheritance law reflected a recognition of the fetus as an existing entity or only as a potential person. In an eighteenth-century case, Lord Hardwicke seemed to adopt the former approach: '[T]he plaintiff was *in* [sic] *ventre sa mere* [at the relevant time], and consequently a person *in rerum natura*, so that both by the rules of common law and civil law she was, to all intents and purposes, a child, as much as if born in the father's life-time.'[6] By contrast, in an early nineteenth-century case dealing with the inheritance of land, the House of Lords expressly refused to regard the fetus as having a legal existence before birth:

But his [the unborn child's] title to enter upon the estate after his birth is not a consequence of his supposed existence during the time he was *en ventre sa mere*, but because in the case of his taking by descent the law at the instant of his birth invests him, though a posthumous child, with the character of heir . . . If the law considered him to exist before his birth, the freehold, during the time of his being *en ventre sa*

---

   [2] *Re Holthausen's Will* 26 NYS 2d 140, 143 (1941). See also *Doe v Clarke* (1795) 2 H Bl 399; 126 ER 617; *Thellusson v Woodford* (1799) 4 Ves Jun 227; 31 ER 117; *Elliot v Joicey* [1935] AC 209.

   [3] *Thellusson v Woodford* (1799) 4 Ves Jun 227, 294; 31 ER 117, 150.

   [4] *Wallis v Hodson* (1740) 2 Atk 115, 117; 26 ER 472, 473. There it was held that, under the statute governing intestacy, a child born after her father's death was entitled to a share in his estate 'as much as if she had existed in his lifetime'.

   [5] A. E. Doudera, 'Fetal Rights? It Depends' (1982) 18 Trial 38, 39.

   [6] *Wallis v Hodson* (1740) 2 Atk 115, 117; 26 ER 472, 473.

mere would be vested in him in the eye of the law, and for the purposes of the law; but that is clearly not the case . . .[7]

This became the accepted view. The common law regarded the fetus as possessing interests which crystallize at birth; it has interests contingent on its being born alive. As Coke noted in the sixteenth century: '[T]he law in many cases hath consideration of [the fetus] in respect of the apparent expectation of his birth.'[8] A more recent Canadian explanation saw the law governing the inheritance rights of the unborn as being consistent with the adoption of 'a legal fiction' rather than with 'the recognition of the rights of the foetus *qua foetus*, as endowed with the status of personhood'.[9]

CRIMINAL PROCEEDINGS

Homicide and Assault

The 'Born Alive' Rule

A preoccupation with the question whether a fetus has the status of a person is apparent in other fields of law. For the criminal lawyer, the debate about the nature of a fetus is largely a debate about whether it is entitled to the protection conferred by the laws punishing homicide and assault. The courts of England, the United States, Canada, and Australia have generally held that an assailant who injures a fetus (with the result that it is stillborn) cannot, under the common law, be guilty of murder or manslaughter. This reflects an adherence to the 'born alive' rule. Only a 'person', an 'individual', or a 'human being' can be the victim of homicide and to fit any of these descriptions a child must be born alive. There have been numerous cases in which this principle has been adopted when an attack on a pregnant woman has resulted in a stillbirth. For example, in *Keeler v Superior Court of Amador County*, the Supreme Court of California ruled that a man who had deliberately caused a stillbirth by driving his knee into a woman's abdomen was not guilty of murder.[10] Sometimes, when an attack has killed both the pregnant woman and her fetus, prosecutors have sought two convictions of murder, but the application of the 'born alive' rule has prevented a murder conviction in respect of the fetus.[11] Similarly, a charge of vehicular homicide (arising

---

[7] *Thellusson v Woodford* (1805) 11 Ves Jun 112, 119–20; 32 ER 1030, 1033.
[8] *The Earl of Bedford's case* (1586) 7 Co Rep 7b, 8b–9a; 77 ER 421, 424.
[9] *Borowski v Attorney-General for Canada* (1987) 39 DLR (4th) 731, 743.
[10] 470 P 2d 617 (1970). See also *State v Wickstrom* 405 NW 2d 1 (Minn App, 1987). In England, the House of Lords has accepted that, in the absence of a specific statutory provision, a fetus cannot be the victim of a crime of violence if death is caused *in utero*: *Attorney-General's Reference (No 3 of 1994)* [1998] AC 245, 254.
[11] *People v Greer* 402 NE 2d 203 (1980). See also *State v Brewer* 826 P 2d 783 (Ariz, 1992).

from careless or drunken driving) will normally fail when a pregnant woman's injuries have led to a stillbirth.[12] The same result has been reached in cases of non-fatal violence. One involved a pregnant woman who was shot and the bullet lodged in the head of the fetus. The fetus survived. The assailant was held not to be guilty of committing the offence of battery on the fetus because it was not a 'person'.[13] An illustration of the operation of the 'born alive' rule in the field of midwifery was provided by the Canadian case of *R v Sullivan*.[14] Here the negligence of two midwives allegedly caused the fetus to die during the delivery. One of the charges they faced was causing the death of a person by criminal negligence. The Supreme Court of Canada held that the fetus was not a 'person' and that therefore the midwives could not be convicted of the charge.

Another corollary of adhering to the 'born alive' rule is that an assailant who inflicts injury on a fetus which survives and then dies as a result of the attack can be guilty of homicide. In England, the House of Lords accepted this view in *Attorney-General's Reference (No 3 of 1994)*.[15] That case dealt with a man who stabbed a woman who was approximately twenty-four weeks pregnant; the wound penetrated her uterus and injured the fetus. The woman went into premature labour two weeks later and a child was born. The child died after seventeen weeks; her death was caused by her gross prematurity, rather than the stab wound. The House of Lords held that it was possible for the defendant to be convicted of manslaughter in respect of the death of the child. A similar result was reached in a Western Australian case, also involving a stabbing, after which the child survived for seven months.[16]

United States cases have adopted the same approach in cases in which injury to the woman or fetus has been followed by the death of a child soon after birth.[17] Occasionally, however, difficulties have arisen as to whether the criterion of live birth has been satisfied. An illustration was provided by *People v Bolar*.[18] Here a woman who was eight months pregnant was injured in a car accident; she suffered an abruption of the placenta and an emergency caesarean section was performed. When delivered, the child was flaccid and not breathing, but had 'regular and faint' heartbeats. Attempts at resuscitation failed and the child's heart continued to beat for two to three minutes. The child was then declared dead. On the basis of the period during which the heart had been beating, the trial court was able to find that there had been a

---

[12] *People v Guthrie* Mich App, 293 NW 2d 775 (1980); *State v Soto* 378 NW 2d 625 (Minn, 1985); *State v McCall* 458 So 2d 875 (Fla App 2 Dist, 1984); *People v Flores* 4 Cal Rptr 2d 120 (Cal App 2 Dist, 1992).
[13] *Love v State* 450 So 2d 1191 (Fla App 4 Dist, 1984). For English authority, see *R v Tait* [1989] 3 WLR 891.
[14] (1991) 63 CCC (3d) 97.   [15] [1998] AC 245.
[16] *Martin v R (No 2)* (1996) 86 A Crim R 133. See also *R v F* (1996) 40 NSWLR 245.
[17] For example, *State v Anderson* 343 A 2d 505 (1975).
[18] Ill App, 440 NE 2d 639 (1982).

'live birth' and that therefore the driver who had caused the accident was guilty of reckless homicide. The Appellate Court of Illinois upheld this ruling. Other than identifying the need for 'the presence of some mechanical bodily function as an indicator of life', the court gave no guidance on the test to be applied. It discussed and rejected the use of a brain function test, but seemed to regard proof of breathing, of an independent circulation, or of a heartbeat as useful indicators.[19] The courts in England and Australia have not been confronted with such difficult factual situations; in the *Attorney-General's Reference* case and the corresponding Western Australian matter, the children lived for some months and thus there was no need to discuss the meaning of live birth. In England, however, it has been held that a child is born alive if 'it exists as a live child, that is to say, breathing and living by reason of its breathing through its own lungs alone, without deriving any of its living or power of living by or through any connection with its mother'.[20] In some jurisdictions, the legislatures have provided guidance on when a fetus is to be regarded as having been born alive. In Canada, for example, s 206 of the Criminal Code states that a child becomes a human being 'when it has completely proceeded in a living state from the body of its mother'. Similar formulas are used in a number of Australian statutes.[21]

On occasions, judges have felt uncomfortable about engaging in the line-drawing of the kind seen in *People v Bolar*. An illustration was *People v Chavez*, where the court, while applying the common law rule, expressed reservations about the conclusion that the woman's conviction for manslaughter of her newborn child depended on proof that the child had been born alive:

Beyond question, it is a difficult thing to draw a line and lay down a fixed general rule as to the precise time at which an unborn infant, or one in the process of being born, becomes a human being in the technical sense. There is not much change in the child itself between a moment before and a moment after its expulsion from the body of its mother, and normally, while still dependent on its mother, the child, for some time before it is born, has not only the possibility but a strong probability of an ability to live an independent life. It is well known that a baby may live and grow when removed from the body of its dead mother by a Caesarian [*sic*] operation. The mere removal of the baby in such a case or its birth in a normal case does not, of itself and alone, create a human being. While before birth or removal it is in a sense dependent upon its mother for life, there is another sense in which it has started an independent existence after it has reached a state of development where it is capable of living and where it will, in the normal course of nature and with ordinary care, continue to live and grow as a separate being. .... There is no sound reason why an infant should not be considered a human being when born or removed from the body of its mother, when it has

---

[19] Cp *People v Flores* 4 Cal Rptr 2d 120, 125–6 (Cal App 2 Dist, 1992).
[20] *Rance v Mid-Downs Health Authority* [1991] 1 QB 587, 621.
[21] For example, Crimes Act 1900 (NSW), s 20 and Criminal Code (Qld), s 292.

reached that stage of development where it is capable of living an independent life as a separate being, and where in the natural course of events it will so live if given normal and reasonable care. It should equally be held that a viable child in the process of being born is a human being within the meaning of the homicide statutes, whether or not the process has been fully completed. It should at least be considered a human being where it is a living baby and where in the natural course of events a birth which is already started would naturally be successfully completed.[22]

Underlying this view is the assumption that as there is so little difference between a full-term fetus (at least one in the process of being born) and a newborn child, it is artificial to deny the former the protection of the law of homicide. Occasionally this argument has been adopted and the common law's 'born alive' rule has been rejected. This occurred in *Commonwealth v Cass*,[23] a case involving a charge of vehicular homicide in which a woman pedestrian was injured and her eight-month fetus was stillborn as a result. The majority ruled that the law of homicide should be expanded to cover the killing of a viable fetus; it was held that such a fetus was a 'person' for the purposes of the vehicular homicide statute. The reason given for departing from the well-established rule was that the basis for maintaining it had disappeared. It was said that the early common law took the form it did because of the difficulty in deciding whether the fetus was alive at the time of an attack on a pregnant woman. The 'born alive' rule gave certainty at a time when medical science was undeveloped. In the view of the majority in *Cass*, this justification had vanished. As it was now possible for medical evidence to establish that the fetus was alive at the time of an attack, the difficulty of proving that the attack killed it was no longer a consideration. Hence the conclusion: 'We think that the better rule is that infliction of prenatal injuries resulting in the death of a viable fetus, before or after it is born, is homicide.'[24] This view, however, has gained little judicial support. While a small number of United States courts have accepted that a viable fetus is a 'person' for the purposes of homicide law,[25] the 'born alive' rule remains part of the criminal law in the majority of American States and in England, Australia, and Canada.

Legislative Intervention

In some of the cases which have considered and rejected the view that the 'born alive' rule should be abandoned and the law of homicide broadened, the debate, rather than being about the nature of the fetus, has been about the proper function of a court.[26] Here the reason given for refusing to extend the definition of homicide has been that it is not for a court to create new

   [22] 176 P 2d 92, 94 (1947).   [23] 467 NE 2d 1324 (Mass, 1984).   [24] Ibid. 1329.
   [25] For example, *Commonwealth v Lawrence* 536 NE 2d 571 (Mass, 1989); *State v Horne* 319 SE 2d 703 (SC, 1984); *Hughes v State* 868 P 2d 730 (Okl Cr, 1994).
   [26] For example, *State ex rel Atkinson v Wilson* 332 SE 2d 807 (W Va, 1984) and *State v Beale* 376 SE 2d 1 (NC, 1989).

crimes. If there is a gap in the criminal law, it is for the legislature to fill it. Several United States legislatures have taken the hint, sometimes in the wake of much publicized and brutal attacks on pregnant women. The resulting legislation reflects the policy that an attacker who causes a stillbirth should be punished for the destruction of the fetus in the same way as one who fatally attacks a person. Different approaches have been adopted. In some States, the definition of homicide has been expanded to encompass the killing of a fetus. In others, rather than stripping homicide of the 'born alive' rule, legislatures have created new crimes.

In California, following the decision in *Keeler*, the legislature amended s 187 of the Penal Code to define murder as 'the unlawful killing of a human being, or a fetus, with malice aforethought'. 'Fetus' was not defined. The effect of the amendment was clarified in *People v Smith*, a case involving a charge of murder against a man who severely beat his pregnant wife; he made it clear that he did not want the fetus to live. Two and a half weeks after the attack, the woman, who was then twelve to fifteen weeks pregnant, suffered a miscarriage. It was held that while the defendant was guilty of the crime of abortion, the charge of murder should be dismissed. Emphasis was placed on the importance of 'the capability for independent existence'; the court noted that until that is attained 'there is only the expectancy and potentiality for human life': 'We, therefore, construe section 187 as making its protection coextensive with the capability for independent human life, a concept embraced within the term *viability*.'[27] Thus, because the crime charged was homicide, the court fell back on concepts with which it was familiar. The essence of this crime is the destruction of an existing human life and therefore the court demanded proof that this had occurred.

A similar emphasis on the destruction of life was reflected in the legislation passed in other States. In Florida and Rhode Island, for example, the wilful killing of 'an unborn quick child' is manslaughter;[28] in the latter State the definition of 'quick child' is precise and makes it clear that the fetus must be viable.[29] In Georgia, the crime of feticide is the wilful killing of 'an unborn child so far developed as to be ordinarily called "quick"'.[30] As will be shown, the term 'quick' was employed in the early abortion statutes and the wording used in the provision is taken from a 1904 decision interpreting such a statute.[31] It was accepted at that time that the distinction between a woman being pregnant and being quick with child was well recognized; the woman

---

[27] App, 129 Cal Rptr 498, 502 (1976).

[28] Fla Stat § 782.09 (1998) and RI Gen Laws § 11–23–5 (1998).

[29] 'Quick child' means 'an unborn child whose heart is beating, who is experiencing electronically-measurable brain waves, who is discernibly moving, and who is so far developed and matured as to be capable of surviving the trauma of birth with the aid of usual medical care and facilities available in [the] state.' RI Gen Laws § 11–23–5(c) (1998).

[30] OCGA § 16–5–80 (1999).   [31] *Sullivan v State* 48 SE 949 (1904).

was 'quick' when she felt the child alive and quick within her.[32] The modern application of this archaic concept was considered in *Brinkley v State*, a 1984 case dealing with a man charged with feticide following the shooting of a pregnant woman during a robbery. Her sixteen-week fetus was stillborn. The defendant was held to have been properly convicted of feticide on the ground that the fetus had been found to be capable of movement.[33]

While some statutory provisions apply to persons who kill 'quick' fetuses, others apply more broadly. An example is provided by a Minnesota Act which created a range of offences: murder or manslaughter of an 'unborn child', and assault on an 'unborn child'. 'Unborn child' was defined as 'the unborn offspring of a human being conceived, but not yet born'.[34] The operation of the relevant provisions was discussed in *State v Merrill*.[35] The defendant had shot and killed a pregnant woman. He was charged with the murder of both the woman and her 'unborn child'. The evidence showed that the woman was twenty-seven or twenty-eight days pregnant at the time of the killing. At this stage, the fetus (referred to as the embryo) was 4–5 millimetres long. The defendant sought to have the charge in respect of the fetus dismissed. The foundation of his argument was that a distinction should be made between a non-viable and a viable fetus and that liability under the statute should arise only for the killing of a viable fetus. In particular, he claimed that it was unfair that he should be exposed to a criminal penalty in respect of the death of a fetus at such an early stage of development. To punish him for this result would be to penalize him for conduct at a time when he (and the woman) might not know that she was pregnant.[36] The Supreme Court of Minnesota rejected these arguments. It held that the statutory definition was sufficiently broad and clear to allow him to be found guilty of the murder of the 'unborn child': 'An embryo or nonviable fetus when it is within the mother's womb is "the unborn offspring of a human being."'[37] Two judges, however, expressed strong dissent. They found the statutory provisions to be unacceptably broad and vague. As one remarked, '[A]n unborn child can be a fertilized egg, an embryo, a nonviable fetus or a viable fetus.'[38] In their view, the reach of the statute should have been limited to viable fetuses. Laws as broadly drafted as that passed in Minnesota are unusual.[39]

---

[32] For a discussion of the early law, see *Brinkley v State* 322 SE 2d 49 (Ga, 1984).

[33] 322 SE 2d 49 (Ga, 1984); affirmed in *Smith v Newsome* 815 F 2d 1386 (11th Cir, 1987).

[34] Minn Stat § 609.266, 609.2661–609.2665, 609.2671 (1998).

[35] 450 NW 2d 318 (Minn, 1990).

[36] This argument raises obvious questions about the proof of the necessary *mens rea*.

[37] 450 NW 2d 318, 324 (Minn, 1990).   [38] Ibid. 326.

[39] Other examples of States with broadly drafted laws are Arizona (manslaughter includes '[k]nowingly or recklessly causing the death of an unborn child at any stage of its development by any physical injury to the mother of such child which would be murder if the death of the mother had occurred': A R S § 13–1103(A)(5) (1999)) and Indiana (feticide is 'knowingly or intentionally' terminating a human pregnancy 'with an intention other than to produce a live

The objective that they embody can, however, be pursued more obliquely. This is illustrated by the approach adopted by the Missouri legislature. Instead of creating the specific crime of killing an 'unborn child', the relevant statute provides: 'The life of each human being begins at conception.' This has been interpreted as amending the definition of 'person' and so allowing a manslaughter conviction of a drunken driver who collided with a car driven by a pregnant woman, killing her viable fetus.[40]

Neither England nor Canada has enacted legislation specifically designed to punish criminal attacks resulting in stillbirths. One Australian State has taken this step. In Queensland, it is a crime unlawfully to assault a woman 'pregnant with child' and to destroy the life of, or do grievous bodily harm or transmit a serious disease to, 'the child' before its birth.[41] By employing this wording, the provision seems to apply regardless of the stage of development attained by the fetus.

Drug Use during Pregnancy

An unwillingness to employ the criminal law against pregnant women who had taken illicit drugs was a feature of a number of the United States cases discussed in Chapter 2. The cases merit brief re-examination in order further to explore the response of the criminal law in situations in which the fetus is exposed to harm. The decisions reveal the same preoccupation with the question whether a fetus is entitled to the protection provided for a 'person'. In some matters, women who have taken drugs during pregnancy have been charged with 'supplying' or 'delivering' drugs to their fetuses. In Georgia, for example, a woman cocaine user who was charged with delivering drugs to her unborn daughter was acquitted on the ground that the purpose of the law was to punish the supply of drugs to another 'person' and that a fetus was not a 'person'.[42] Again we see the application of the rule that personhood is achieved only after live birth. An alternative procedure, when a baby is born affected by drugs, is to charge the woman with abusing, neglecting, or endangering a fetus. Predictably, in the majority of cases involving the antenatal ingestion of drugs, the courts have ruled that a reference to a 'child' in a statute proscribing child abuse, neglect, or endangerment does not include a fetus.[43]

---

birth or to remove a dead fetus': Burns Ind Code Ann § 35–42–1–6 (1999)). The Indiana section does not apply to lawful abortions.

[40] *State v Knapp* 843 SW 2d 345 (Mo banc, 1992). The statutory provision was § 1.205 RSMo (1986).

[41] Criminal Code (Qld), s 313 (2).

[42] *State v Luster* 419 SE 2d 32 (Ga App, 1992). See also *Johnson v State of Florida* 602 So 2d 1288 (Fla, 1992) and *People v Hardy* 469 NW 2d 50 (Mich App, 1991). These cases are discussed above, 17–18.

[43] See, for example, *Reyes v Superior Court* App, 141 Cal Rptr 912 (1977) and *State v Gray* 584 NE 2d 710 (Ohio, 1992). These cases are discussed above, 18.

An exception was *Whitner v State*,[44] which dealt with a woman charged with child abuse as a result of her ingestion of cocaine at a late stage in her pregnancy. The relevant Act defined a 'child' as a 'person under eighteen'. The Supreme Court of South Carolina ruled that a viable fetus was a 'person' for the purposes of the legislation and upheld the woman's conviction.

Abortion

One possible response to the conclusion that the criminal law does not normally regard a fetus as a 'person'—and therefore denies fetuses the protection offered by laws proscribing homicide, assault, the supply of drugs, and child abuse—is to assert that this conclusion is of little practical importance. It can be argued that laws prohibiting abortion fill any gap identified in these laws. It is therefore necessary to consider some features of these laws. The following brief discussion is not intended as a contribution to the debate on the controversial subject of abortion. Rather, it is offered as a background to the discussion of an issue central to this book: the role of the law in protecting the fetus. What follows, therefore, is primarily directed at determining whether abortion laws reflect a recognition of the existence of an entity that is entitled to protection. In addition, the analysis will seek to determine what the operation of these laws reveals about the legal status of the fetus.

The first point to note about the interpretation of the abortion laws is that the courts have adopted a familiar starting-point. In the United States, the best known authority is *Roe v Wade*. At issue in that case was a woman's right to an abortion. No such right could be asserted if the fetus was a 'person' who could not, by virtue of the Fourteenth Amendment to the United States Constitution, be deprived of life without due process of law. After reviewing the various constitutional provisions that used the word 'person', the Supreme Court of the United States concluded, 'None indicates, with any assurance, that it has any possible prenatal application.' It therefore ruled: '[T]he word "person", as used in the Fourteenth Amendment, does not include the unborn.'[45] In Canada the issue arose in a similar manner: in *Borowski v Attorney-General for Canada*, provisions allowing abortions were challenged on the basis of inconsistency with s 7 of the Canadian Charter of Rights and Freedoms, which states that 'everyone' has a right to life. The question was whether the word 'everyone' included a fetus. The Saskatchewan Court of Appeal held that it did not. It ruled that the guarantees under s 7 were not intended to extend to the unborn and that it could not therefore be argued that the section conferred on a fetus the right to life.[46] In an earlier decision,

---

[44]   492 SE 2d 777 (SC, 1997).
[45]   410 US 113, 157 and 158; 35 L Ed 2d 147, 179, and 180 (1973).
[46]   (1987) 39 DLR (4th) 731, 752, and 754.

Dehler v Ottawa Civic Hospital, the Ontario High Court had set out the position under the common law. After asking: 'What then is the legal position of an unborn child? Is it regarded in the eyes of the law as a person in the full legal sense?', it provided the following answers:

[T]he law does not regard an unborn child as an independent legal entity prior to birth.... A foetus, whatever its stage of development, is recognized as a person in the full sense only after birth.... [T]he law has set birth as the line of demarcation at which personhood is realized, at which full and independent legal rights attach, and until a child *en ventre sa mere* sees the light of day it does not have the rights of those already born.[47]

The Supreme Court of Canada approved this ruling in *Tremblay v Daigle*.[48]

The proceedings in *Dehler* arose following a general action taken to prevent the defendant hospital from performing abortions. In England and Australia, the question of the status of the fetus was raised in a similar context; in both countries, courts were faced with applications for injunctions to prevent women from terminating pregnancies. The courts refused these applications. Thus they explicitly rejected the argument that a fetus is an entity which has a right to life that the law should protect. In *Paton v British Pregnancy Advisory Service Trustees*, the law was stated in much the same way as in *Dehler*: 'The foetus cannot, in English law ... have a right of its own at least until it is born and has a separate existence from its mother.'[49] This view has been accepted in Australia.[50]

The question which this adherence to the 'born alive' rule poses is whether the fetus is a legal non-entity. The existence of a body of law prohibiting the performance of abortions would seem to preclude such a conclusion. It might be thought that such a prohibition implies the recognition of a fetus's right to protection. An examination of this hypothesis requires a discussion of the development of Anglo-American abortion laws. There is some uncertainty about the way the early common law viewed conduct that destroyed a fetus.[51]

---

[47] (1979) 101 DLR (3d) 686, 695. The decision was affirmed on appeal: (1980) 117 DLR (3d) 512. See also *Medhurst v Medhurst* (1984) 9 DLR (4th) 252.

[48] (1989) 62 DLR (4th) 634. See also *Winnipeg Child and Family Services (Northwest Area) v G* (1997) 152 DLR (4th) 193, 202–3.

[49] [1979] 1 QB 276, 279. See also *Paton v United Kingdom* [1980] 3 EHRR 408; *C v S* [1988] QB 135.

[50] *Attorney-General (Qld)(Ex rel Kerr) v T* (1983) 46 ALR 275 and *In the Marriage of F and F* (1989) FLC 92–031.

[51] For a discussion of the early common law, see: B. M. Dickens, *Abortion and the Law* (London, 1966); P. H. Winfield, 'The Unborn Child' (1942) 8 Cambridge Law Journal 76; C. Means, 'The Law of New York Concerning Abortion and the Status of the Foetus, 1664–1968: a Case of Cessation of Constitutionality (1968) 14 New York Law Forum 411; C. Means, 'The Phoenix of Abortion Freedom: is a Penumbral or Ninth Amendment Right About to Arise from the Nineteenth-Century Legislative Ashes of a Fourteenth-Century Common Law Liberty?' (1971) 17 New York Law Forum 335; J. Keown, *Abortion, Doctors and the Law: Some Aspects of the Legal Regulation of Abortion in England from 1803–1982* (Cambridge, 1988).

By the thirteenth century, emphasis was placed on the significance of 'quickening', a stage of development determined on the basis of whether the pregnant woman had felt movement. It was widely believed that 'quickening' marked the beginning of life and the law (which sought to prevent the destruction of life) therefore took no interest in conduct occurring before this stage had been reached. It followed that the destruction of a fetus before 'quickening' was not punishable. Whether an abortion performed after this stage was an offence is the subject of debate. It was not regarded as homicide, but it seems likely that it was punished as a less serious crime. It is not clear whether the aim was to protect an entity with identifiable characteristics (that is, a fetus which had 'quickened'). One seventeenth-century case dealt with a woman charged with having an abortion; the indictment stated that she had 'spoiled and destroyed then and there the infant in her womb'. A commentator has cited this case in support of the view that 'the predominant rationale of the law against abortion was the preservation of fetal life'.[52] This interpretation has, however, been questioned.[53] The arguments will not be pursued here. For present purposes it is sufficient to note that an examination of the common law governing abortion does not provide clear answers to questions about its underlying assumptions and objectives.

The scope of the relevant laws—though not the purposes which they were designed to fulfil—became clearer in the nineteenth century with the enactment, in England, of a series of statutes which also laid the foundations of the current law in the United States, Canada, and Australia. Section 1 of the first statute (passed in 1803)[54] created the offence of unlawfully administering 'any deadly poison, or other noxious and destructive substance or thing, with intent . . . thereby to cause and procure the miscarriage of any woman then being quick with child'. Section 2 created the offence of administering any such abortifacient or using any means 'with intent thereby to cause or procure the miscarriage of any woman not being, or not being proved to be, quick with child . . .'. The penalty under s 1 was death; under s 2 the maximum penalty was fourteen years' imprisonment.

The need to draw a distinction between a woman 'quick with child' and one who was not proved a source of difficulty. The words 'quick with child' could be taken as meaning no more than 'pregnant'. If this interpretation were adopted, the purpose of s 1 was to punish conduct aimed at destroying a fetus, while s 2 was directed at those who used drugs or instruments in order to perform an abortion upon a woman who was not (or who could not be proved to

---

[52] J. Keown, *Abortion, Doctors and the Law: Some Aspects of the Legal Regulation of Abortion in England from 1803–1982* (Cambridge, 1988) 7–8. The case (cited ibid.) was *R v Webb* (1602).

[53] See A. H. Young, 'John Keown's *Abortion, Doctors, and the Law* and the Relevance of British Abortion Regulation for Canada' (1990) 35 McGill Law Journal 976, 978.

[54] 43 Geo 3, c 58 (1803).

be) pregnant. Alternatively, the words 'quick with child' could be given their common law meaning and be interpreted as referring to a woman whose pregnancy had reached the stage at which the child had 'quickened'. This interpretation would support the view that s 1 was enacted to deal with conduct designed to procure a miscarriage after 'quickening', while s 2 was concerned with criminal behaviour at an earlier stage of pregnancy. In spite of this uncertainty, the 1828 Act,[55] which repealed the 1803 statute, retained the terminology of its predecessor.

An Act passed in 1837[56] simplified the law. This not only abandoned the distinction between a fetus which had 'quickened' and one which had not, but it also made it clear that it was not necessary to establish that the woman was pregnant in order to prove that the offence had been committed. Section 6 simply stated: 'That whosoever, with intent to procure the miscarriage of any woman, shall unlawfully administer to her or cause to be taken by her any poison or other noxious thing, or shall unlawfully use any instrument or other means whatsoever with the like intent, shall be guilty of felony.' Similar words were reproduced in s 58 of the Offences Against the Person Act 1861;[57] this further clarified the law by stating that the offence could be committed 'whether [the woman] be or be not with child'.

Several aspects of these early statutes are worthy of comment. The fact that the 1803 and 1828 Acts referred to conduct affecting a woman 'quick with child' might at first sight suggest that these statutes were concerned with the protection of the fetus, but a careful reading reveals that the statutes punished acts performed with the intention of procuring a miscarriage. The destruction of a fetus—whether 'quick' or otherwise—was not the conduct that the law proscribed. This was made clearer in the 1837 and 1861 versions, which omitted all reference to pregnancy, however described. Nevertheless, two interpretations of the wording of the statutes are possible. One is that the abortion laws were primarily concerned with the protection of pregnant women and that the targets of the legislation were criminal abortionists whose crude techniques threatened the life and health of vulnerable women. On this view, the law could properly focus on undesirable *conduct* (the use of drugs or instruments with intent to procure a miscarriage), rather than on the *result* of that conduct (the destruction of the fetus). The alternative explanation is that the law's concern was to protect the fetus, but that this aim could most effectively be achieved by proscribing certain conduct. On this analysis, what emerged was pragmatism. Proof of the destruction of a fetus would not always be easy. The prosecutor had to demonstrate that the fetus was alive at the time of the relevant conduct and that this conduct killed it. Removal of the need to establish these elements of the offence facilitated the obtaining of

[55] 9 Geo 4, c 31 (1828).   [56] 7 Will IV & 1 Vict, c 85 (1837).
[57] 24 & 25 Vict, c 100 (1861).

convictions. The adoption of this approach, far from indicating a lack of concern with the protection of the fetus, arguably offered the most efficient means of achieving that aim.

It is unnecessary to assert that one explanation rather than the other must be accepted. Both may be valid. The law might simultaneously seek to protect women from abortionists and to safeguard fetuses. Before this combination of aims is further discussed, it is necessary to examine another feature of the early statutes. The removal of the need to distinguish between a fetus which had 'quickened' and one which had not made law enforcement easier. It obviated the need to prove the stage of development attained by the fetus and thus assisted the prosecution. But the amendment had more important implications. It reflected a changed perception of the fetus. By the eighteenth century there was widespread support for the view that life began immediately after conception and consequently the significance attached to 'quickening' was criticized. The law was slow to adapt. The 1803 and 1828 Acts retained the old terminology, but responded to advances in medical knowledge by accepting that it was arbitrary and unscientific to punish conduct after 'quickening' but not before. The next step, taken in 1837, was to remove any need to consider whether the fetus was 'quick' or not. For present purposes, the significance of the redrafting lies not in the gradual simplification of the statutory provisions, but in what the changes said about the attitude of the law to the fetus. These changes were not necessarily indicative of a reduced interest in the nature of the fetus and the need to protect it. Further, it is important not to read too much into the fact that all acknowledgement of the existence of the fetus and its stage of development disappeared from the legislation. One interpretation of the changes was that the removal of the reference to the 'quick' fetus allowed the law to intervene to punish conduct occurring at an early stage of gestation and so embodied an expanded commitment to fetal protection. Certainly this is how some nineteenth-century doctors saw their campaign to remove from the legislation what they regarded as archaic references to 'quickening': the result of their agitation was that after the 1837 Act, conduct aimed at the destruction of a fetus at any stage of gestation was punishable.[58]

The next phase in the development of the law of abortion was marked by changes making it lawful for pregnancies to be terminated in certain circumstances. In England and Australia, these changes were the product of twentieth-century court decisions permitting the performance of an abortion when the continuance of the pregnancy would pose a serious threat to the

---

[58] See J. Keown, *Abortion, Doctors, and the Law: Some Aspects of the Legal Regulation of Abortion in England from 1803–1982* (Cambridge, 1988) 31–2. See also the views expressed in the 1859 report of the American Medical Association, discussed in *Roe v Wade* 410 US 113, 141–2; 35 L Ed 2d 147, 170–1 (1973).

woman's life or health.[59] These decisions were reached in a climate quite different from that prevailing in the previous century: medical advances had meant that, at least in the early stages of pregnancy, abortions had become much safer. The need to protect the woman against the criminal abortionist had begun to yield to a policy of permitting therapeutic abortions carried out by medical practitioners. Acceptance of this policy was further signalled by the enactment of legislation in England and three Australian States.[60] While the details of the various Acts are not relevant here, certain features of the statutes deserve comment. They all provide that a termination of a pregnancy may lawfully be performed when its continuance would pose a serious or disproportionate risk to the woman's life or health. The legislatures thus modified the principles that the courts had fashioned to mitigate the operation of the laws punishing abortion. In addition, provision was made for a termination when there was a substantial risk that the child would be born seriously handicapped. Further, all the Acts place restrictions on the abortion of a fetus which has attained a certain stage of development. In England the crucial stage is twenty-four weeks, in South Australia it is twenty-eight weeks, and in Western Australia it is twenty weeks. The selection of these time limits probably reflects the parliaments' view of the developmental stage at which a fetus is capable of surviving.[61]

In the United States and Canada, the development of the law's recognition of therapeutic abortions took a different course. Legislation allowing abortions in certain circumstances was in force in many parts of the United States by the middle of the twentieth century. In some States, the laws were stringent and allowed abortions only to preserve the life of the woman, while in others it was enough if the woman's health was at risk. Any legislation restricting access to abortion must be read subject to the decisions in *Roe v Wade*[62] and *Planned Parenthood of Southeastern Pennsylvania v Casey*.[63] *Roe v Wade* dealt with a constitutional challenge to a Texas statute restricting access to abortion. The Supreme Court of the United States ruled that by virtue of her constitutional right to privacy, a pregnant woman was entitled to undergo an abortion, although her freedom to do so was not absolute. In defining the circumstances in which the right to choose could be exercised, the court referred to the medical advances which had occurred in the twentieth century and described abortions performed in early pregnancy (that is, in the first trimester) as 'relatively safe'. This led the court to adopt a framework

---

[59] *R v Bourne* [1939] 1 KB 687; *R v Davidson* [1969] VR 667; *R v Wald* (1971) 3 NSW DCR 25.
[60] Abortion Act 1967 (UK), s 1; Criminal Law Consolidation Act 1935 (SA), s 82A; Criminal Code Act (NT), s 174; Health Act 1911 (WA), s 334.
[61] For a discussion of the United Kingdom Parliament's selection of the 24-week limit, and of the meaning of this limitation, see I. Kennedy and A. Grubb, *Medical Law: Text with Materials* (London, 2nd edn., 1994) 872–3.
[62] 410 US 113; 35 L Ed 2d 147 (1973).   [63] 505 US 833; 120 L Ed 2d 674 (1992).

permitting the state to pursue different approaches to the regulation of abortion, depending on the maturity of the fetus. Employing this framework, the court made a series of rulings. During the first trimester, when little risk to the woman is involved, there should be no restrictions on her freedom to decide to terminate her pregnancy. During the second trimester, when the risk was somewhat greater, the state could properly regulate abortion procedures (for example, by requiring abortions to be performed in licensed hospitals and by specifying the qualifications of those who perform them). During the third trimester (when the risk to the woman is substantial), the state could regulate, and even proscribe, abortion except where necessary to preserve the life or health of the woman.

The adoption of the trimester framework reflected the state's dual concerns: to protect both the woman and her fetus. A policy aimed at safeguarding a pregnant woman must take note of the stage of pregnancy at which an abortion can be safely performed. Yet to take account of gestation is also to acknowledge that the more mature a fetus is, the more deserving it is of protection. The court expressly recognized this and stressed the importance of viability (achieved at roughly the end of the second trimester); it ruled that once viability is attained, the state acquires a 'compelling' interest in protecting the fetus:

With respect to the State's important and legitimate interest in potential life, the 'compelling' point is at viability. This is so because the fetus then presumably has the capability of meaningful life outside the mother's womb. State regulation protective of fetal life after viability thus has both logical and biological justifications. If the State is interested in protecting fetal life after viability, it may go so far as to proscribe abortion during that period, except when it is necessary to preserve the life or health of the mother.[64]

In reaching this conclusion, the court acknowledged that there comes a stage in the development of a fetus at which it acquires characteristics entitling it to special protection. Thus the opinion in *Roe v Wade* supports the view that at least when viability is achieved, one function of laws regulating abortion is the protection of fetal life.

This view was reiterated by the Supreme Court of the United States in *Planned Parenthood of Southeastern Pennsylvania v Casey*. The majority of the court reaffirmed the 'essential holding' of *Roe v Wade*, including 'a recognition of the right of the woman to choose to have an abortion before viability' and 'the principle that the State has legitimate interests from the outset of the pregnancy in protecting the health of the woman and the life of the fetus that may become a child'.[65] The court's acceptance that the state has an interest in the life of the fetus *from the outset of the pregnancy* should be noted.

---

[64] 410 US 113, 163–4; 35 L Ed 2d 147, 183 (1973).
[65] 505 US 833, 846; 120 L Ed 2d 674, 694 (1992).

Roe's reference to the state's 'important and legitimate interest in potential life' was emphasized: 'That portion of the decision in *Roe* has been given too little acknowledgment and implementation by the Court in its subsequent cases.'[66] In the view of three of the justices, part of the reason for this was the adoption of the trimester framework. They therefore rejected it, explaining that 'in practice it undervalues the State's interest in potential life . . .'.[67] This is because the application of this rigid framework can lead to the conclusion that in the first trimester a fetus has no interests worthy of protection by the law. Such a conclusion would be 'incompatible with the recognition that there is a substantial state interest in potential life throughout pregnancy'.[68] To stress this aspect, however, is not to assert that line drawing is unnecessary. Rather, to reject lines drawn by reference to trimesters is to seek a more appropriate basis for drawing them. The court endorsed the significance of viability: 'The woman's right to terminate her pregnancy before viability is the most central principle of *Roe v Wade*.'[69] *Casey* thus echoes *Roe*'s recognition of the importance of a pregnant woman not being subjected to unwarranted controls, but qualifies this by placing additional emphasis on the obligation of the state to protect the interests of the fetus, particularly after viability.

In Canada, clarification of the law was also the result of a challenge to the provision governing abortions. In *R v Morgentaler*,[70] s 251 of the Criminal Code was attacked on the basis that it unjustifiably infringed a woman's right to security of the person guaranteed by s 7 of the Canadian Charter of Rights and Freedoms. The Supreme Court of Canada upheld the challenge. It indicated that the task of designing any new law restricting abortion should be left to the legislature.[71] One judge, however, suggested the adoption of a framework similar to that outlined in *Roe v Wade*. Citing this decision, Wilson J accepted 'a permissive approach to abortion in the early stages of pregnancy and a restrictive approach in the later stages'. This reflected the view that greater weight should be given to the state's interest in protecting the fetus 'in the later stages of pregnancy than in the earlier': 'The undeveloped foetus starts out as a newly-fertilized ovum; the fully developed foetus emerges ultimately as an infant. A developmental progression takes place in between these two extremes and . . . this progression has a direct bearing on the value of the foetus as potential life.' Wilson J adopted the language used

---

[66] Ibid. 871, 711.

[67] Ibid. 873, 712. See also *Webster v Reproductive Health Services* 492 US 490; 106 L Ed 2d 410 (1989) where three justices expressed the view that the trimester framework should be abandoned.

[68] 505 US 833, 876; 120 L Ed 2d 674, 714 (1992).   [69] Ibid. 871, 710.

[70] (1988) 44 DLR (4th) 385.

[71] Following the decision in *Morgentaler*, a Bill was introduced (Bill C 43, An Act Respecting Abortion, 1989), but this was not enacted.

in *Roe* and tentatively suggested that the state might acquire a 'compelling' interest in fetal protection 'somewhere in the second trimester'.[72]

CHILD PROTECTION PROCEEDINGS

As was seen in Chapter 2, there have been a number of cases in which courts have been asked to exercise either their child protection or *parens patriae* powers when maternal behaviour was endangering the fetus. The reported United States decisions have generally refused to accept that neglect or abuse proceedings can be used to impose controls on a pregnant woman in order to protect her fetus. In some judgments the reasoning has echoed that adopted in cases in which an attempt was made to employ the law of homicide: it was held that just as the homicide laws come into operation only when a 'person' has been killed, the child protection laws operate only when a 'child' or 'person' is threatened and neither term applies to a fetus.[73] A different result was reached in *Re Ruiz*, in which the issue was whether a baby born suffering the effects of the mother's antenatal heroin use was an 'abused child' under Ohio's child abuse statute. The heroin had been taken in the two weeks prior to delivery. The court posed the question whether the fetus was a 'child' for the purpose of this statute. After citing *Roe v Wade* as authority for the proposition that the state acquires a compelling interest in potential life once a fetus becomes viable, the court ruled: 'The essence of *Roe*, the state's interest in the potential human life at the time of viability, . . . compels a holding that a viable unborn fetus is to be considered a child under the provisions of [the statute].'[74] This decision represents a departure from the more widely accepted view that child protection laws do not apply to fetuses.[75] Since the baby had been born, this conclusion may have been reached because no awkward questions were posed about the use of child protection laws to control a pregnant woman. The decision should not be taken as raising significant doubts about the United States courts' willingness to employ child protection laws in an attempt to safeguard fetuses.

Nor are these laws likely to be employed to sanction antenatal intervention in Canada or England. While there was one Canadian case in which a fetus was made a ward of a welfare agency,[76] it is unlikely that this decision

---

[72] (1988) 44 DLR (4th) 385, 499.

[73] See, for example, *Re Dittrick* 263 NW 2d 37 (1977) and *Re Steven S* App, 178 Cal Rptr 525 (1981). These cases are discussed above, 8.

[74] 500 NE 2d 935 (Ohio Com Pl, 1986).

[75] Other cases in which courts dealing with children born drug-addicted have discussed the status of the fetus include *Re Troy D* 263 Cal Rptr 869 (Cal App 4 Dist, 1989) and *Re Valerie D* 595 A 2d 922 (Conn App, 1991).

[76] *Re Children's Aid Society and T* (1987) 59 OR (2d) 204; this case is discussed above 9.

will be regarded as correct in future. It was not followed in *Re A (in utero)*, a case that considered not only the operation of the relevant child welfare legislation (Ontario's Child and Family Services Act 1984) but also the possible exercise of the *parens patriae* jurisdiction. With regard to the statute, a familiar analysis was employed. It was ruled that this Act did not give the court the power to intervene: 'I . . . cannot find anything in the definition of "child" . . . [or in] any other provision in the Act which would accord to the foetus any status as a person or right to protection under the Act.'[77] The discussion of the use of the *parens patriae* power focused on the fact that, by the time of the hearing, the mother was virtually at full term. The judge observed: '[The fetus had] developed virtually all the attributes of a person in law, without in fact being one. As such, the foetus in this case may truly be likened to a person under a disability, and perhaps deserving of some protection.'[78] This takes note of gestation; the court recognized how much a mature fetus has in common with a 'person'. The analysis revealed the judge's dilemma: the fetus was not a 'person', but it could 'truly be likened' to one. The court therefore listened sympathetically to the argument that the similarity between a mature fetus and a 'person' would justify the extension of laws designed to protect children. Ultimately, the court rejected this argument. That this decision should be regarded as authoritative was made clear by the Supreme Court of Canada in *Winnipeg Child and Family Services (Northwest Area) v G*. There it was reiterated that a fetus is not a 'person'.[79] The English Court of Appeal had earlier reached a similar conclusion in *Re F (in utero)*. The court approved the ruling in *Paton* that a fetus cannot have any rights until it is born and has a separate existence; it therefore held that the wardship power over a 'minor' is exercisable only in respect of one who has become a person.[80]

It is always open to a legislature to draft a child protection statute in such a way as to apply to a fetus. As was explained in Chapter 2, in some parts of the United States and Canada, child protection provisions allow action to be taken on behalf of fetuses.[81] In some jurisdictions, the aim is to ensure the treatment of pregnant women who use illegal drugs or who expose their fetuses to the risk of being born with fetal alcohol syndrome. In others, the aim is less specific and the legislation permits child protection proceedings to be taken against a pregnant woman in order to compel her to accept welfare services.

---

[77] (1990) 72 DLR (4th) 722, 728.   [78] Ibid. 730.

[79] (1997) 152 DLR (4th) 193, 202–3 and 218. Note, however, the dissenting judgment's repudiation of the 'born alive' rule: 'it no longer makes sense to retain the rule where its application would be perverse' (ibid. 234).

[80] [1988] 2 WLR 1288, 1301.

[81] See above 8–9 and 11–12, for a discussion of the provisions enacted in Minnesota, New Jersey, New Brunswick, and the Yukon.

Another aspect of the operation of child protection laws is their application once a child has been born alive. As was shown in Chapter 2, courts have had no difficulty accepting that evidence of a pregnant woman's drug taking can be taken into account in determining whether intervention is desirable after the child has been born. When this course is adopted, there is no need to speculate about the law's attitude to the fetus: it is the child who is the focus of concern and the law takes notice of antenatal conduct in order to protect that child's interests. Such an approach reflects well-established practices in such areas as inheritance law, the criminal law, and the law of negligence.

PROCEEDINGS TO IMPOSE MEDICAL TREATMENT

In a number of cases, United States courts have authorized compulsory medical intervention in an effort to ensure the safe delivery of a healthy baby. Several of these cases recognized the existence of the fetus and accepted that it could be brought under the protection of a court. In *Raleigh Fitkin-Paul Morgan Memorial Hospital v Anderson*, the Supreme Court of New Jersey allowed an appeal against the trial court's decision not to order a pregnant woman to undergo a blood transfusion. The court commented: 'We are satisfied that the unborn child is entitled to the law's protection . . .'.[82] *Re Jamaica Hospital* was also concerned with the refusal of a transfusion, this time by a woman who was eighteen weeks pregnant. The trial judge ruled:

If her life were the only one involved here, the court would not interfere. . . . Her life, however, is not the only one at stake. The court must consider the life of the unborn fetus. . . . In this case, the state has a highly significant interest in protecting the life of a mid-term fetus, which outweighs the patient's right to refuse a blood transfusion on religious grounds.[83]

In *Jefferson v Griffin Spalding County Hospital Authority*, the performance of a caesarean section was authorized. In rejecting the appeal against the order, the Supreme Court of Georgia expressly invoked the 'unborn child's right to live'.[84] When doing so, it referred to the recognition, in *Roe v Wade*, of the state's interest in protecting the lives of viable fetuses. Similarly, in *Re Madyun*[85] (another case in which a caesarean section was ordered), the court relied on *Roe*'s identification of the state's 'important and legitimate interest in protecting the potentiality of human life' and noted that this interest becomes 'compelling' at viability. This language was echoed in the

---

[82] 201 A 2d 537, 538 (1964).   [83] 491 NYS 2d 898, 899–900 (Sup, 1985).
[84] Ga, 274 SE 2d 457, 460 (1981).
[85] *Re Madyun*; a report of the case appears as an appendix to *Re AC* 573 A 2d 1235, 1259 (DC App, 1990).

Madyun court's ruling that the state had 'a compelling interest to intervene and protect the life and safety of the fetus'.[86]

In all these cases the fetus was recognized as being entitled to immediate protection, either under the courts' *parens patriae* or neglect and dependency jurisdictions. This approach was adopted without doubts being expressed about the legal status of the fetus. In this respect, the medical treatment cases stand in sharp contrast to the criminal and child protection matters discussed earlier in this chapter. These matters revealed a preoccupation with problems of definition: the question posed was whether a fetus is an entity that can properly be brought within the operation of criminal or child protection laws. Such concerns are largely absent from the cases relating to medical intervention; the courts seem to have regarded them as being in a class of their own. They considered themselves free to focus on one question: whether the plight of the fetus justified compulsory medical intervention. This attitude may have been the product of deference to medical evidence. When testimony was received suggesting the existence of a 'medical emergency', it may have seemed inappropriate to scrutinize definitional issues of the kind which have figured so prominently in criminal and child protection matters.

There seems to be only one case in which the decision to authorize intervention was expressly based on a ruling as to the legal status of the fetus. This was *Re Jamaica Hospital*, where it was remarked: 'For the purposes of this proceeding ... the fetus can be regarded as a human being, to whom the court stands in parens patriae, and whom the court has an obligation to protect.'[87] In the other cases in which the matter of fetal status has been addressed, a different conclusion has usually been reached. An example was provided by the Canadian case *Re Baby R*.[88] There the patient's decision not to consent to a caesarean section was thought to be putting the fetus at risk. The Superintendent of the Department of Family and Child Services, relying on his powers under the British Columbia Family and Child Service Act 1980, had 'apprehended' the fetus; he thereby acquired the authority to consent to emergency medical treatment. Subsequently, the intervention was reviewed, the issue being whether the fetus was a 'child' within the meaning of the Act. It was held that it was not and that the Superintendent therefore lacked the power to intervene. The British Columbia Supreme Court noted: '[T]he powers of the superintendent to apprehend are restricted to living children that have been delivered.'[89]

---

[86] Ibid. 1264.   [87] 491 NYS 2d 898, 900 (Sup, 1985).   [88] (1988) 53 DLR (4th) 69.
[89] Ibid. 80. See also *Re Baby Boy Doe* 632 NE 2d 326 (Ill App 1 Dist, 1994); there proceedings were brought both under the Illinois Juvenile Court Act and under the *parens patriae* jurisdiction. While the Appellate Court of Illinois raised no objections to the use of the *parens patriae* jurisdiction, it seemed to agree with the trial court's ruling that the Juvenile Court Act could not apply to a fetus, as it was not a 'minor' for the purposes of the Act.

As was explained in Chapter 2, in the 1990s courts in the United States and England appear to have changed their attitude to medical intervention and rejected the argument that the interests of the fetus can justify resort to invasive medical procedures to which the woman has not consented. In reaching these decisions, the courts took as their starting-point the right of a pregnant woman—as a competent adult—to decline medical treatment. In so doing, they shifted the focus from questions about the interests of the fetus to questions about maternal autonomy. This aspect will be discussed in Chapter 9. At this stage, what must be considered is the contribution that the more recent cases have made to an understanding of the legal status of the fetus. In *Re MB (Medical Treatment)*, the English Court of Appeal dealt with an application for the authorization of a caesarean section. The court expressly held that a fetus is not an entity having rights that the law will protect in such a situation. It ruled: 'The foetus up to the moment of birth does not have any separate interests capable of being taken into account when a court has to consider an application for a declaration in respect of a caesarian [*sic*] section operation.'[90] In contrast, in *St George's Healthcare NHS Trust v S*, the same court refused to accept that the interests of the fetus could be disregarded purely on the basis that it was a non-entity.[91]

NEGLIGENCE ACTIONS

Differing Approaches

Examination of the cases in which damages claims have been made following antenatal or perinatal negligence reveals a great deal of ambivalence about the legal status of the fetus. These cases exhibit two different approaches to the task of determining whether such claims will be allowed. On the one hand are those matters in which liability is regarded as being dependent on the existence of an entity to which a duty of care is owed. On the other are those in which the existence of the fetus is viewed as being irrelevant.

In the United States cases particular emphasis has been placed on the existence of an entity which can be regarded as the potential beneficiary of the law's protection. The adoption of this perspective may have been the result of an historical accident, for the earliest decision set the scene for analyses preoccupied with the nature of the fetus. Decided in 1884, *Dietrich v Northampton*[92] was not a case in which the court was asked to rule on a living child's claim for damages for antenatal injury. Rather, it was a claim brought by the administrator of the estate of a child who had lived for ten or fifteen

---

[90] [1997] 2 FLR 426, 444. This statement was based on rulings made in *Paton v British Pregnancy Advisory Service Trustees* [1979] 1 QB 276 and *C v S* [1988] QB 135.
[91] [1998] 3 WLR 936, 952.   [92] 52 Am Rep 242 (1884).

minutes after a premature birth. The birth had been brought on by the mother's fall when she was four or five months pregnant; the fall was allegedly caused by the poor state of the highway. It was claimed that the local authority had negligently failed to maintain the highway. The major difficulty that Holmes J identified was 'whether an infant dying before it was able to live separated from its mother could be said to have become a person, recognized by the law as capable of having a *locus standi* in court, or of being represented there by an administrator'.[93] The answer offered was that it was not a 'person' as 'the unborn child was a part of the mother at the time of the injury'.[94] The claim was therefore disallowed. The decision was thus reached by way of a discussion of the nature of the fetus and not by way of posing the general question of whether a child could sue in respect of antenatal negligence.

Although the judgment was primarily concerned with a narrow question of statutory interpretation, it was seen in subsequent cases as establishing a principle to be taken into account in claims arising when children who survived had suffered antenatal harm. Sixteen years after the decision, another way of dealing with the problem was offered in a dissenting judgment by Boggs J in *Allaire v St Luke's Hospital*.[95] The case arose when a child was born with disabilities caused by injuries negligently inflicted on a pregnant woman when she was at full term. The judgment stressed the fact of viability and, while conceding that at an early stage of a pregnancy a fetus might be regarded as a part of the mother, ruled that a viable fetus is a life: 'it is but to deny a palpable fact to argue that there is but one life'.[96] Later the judge made it clear that he rejected the 'mere theory—known to be false—that the injury was not to [the child's] person, but to the person of the mother'.[97] Thus *Dietrich* was distinguished.

In spite of this dissent, the view expressed in *Dietrich* was to dominate in the United States until 1946, when *Bonbrest v Kotz*[98] ruled that at common law prenatal injury afforded a basis for a negligence action. Even when this view was finally adopted, however, the pattern of analysis established in *Dietrich* was perpetuated. As in the judgment of Boggs J, *Dietrich* was distinguished on the basis that the injury had occurred after viability:

Here ... we have a viable child—one capable of living outside the womb—and which has demonstrated its capacity to survive by *surviving*—are we to say *now* it has no locus standi in court or elsewhere? As to a viable child being 'part' of its mother—this argument seems to me to be a contradiction in terms. True, it is in the womb, but it is capable now of extra-uterine life—and while dependent for its continued development on sustenance derived from its peculiar relationship to its mother, it is not a 'part' of the mother in the sense of a constituent element—as that term is generally

---

[93] Ibid. 244.   [94] Ibid. 245.   [95] 56 NE 638 (1900).   [96] Ibid. 641.
[97] Ibid. 642.   [98] 65 F Supp 138 (1946).

understood. Modern medicine is replete with cases of living children being taken from dead mothers. Indeed, apart from viability, a non-viable foetus is not a part of its mother.[99]

Notwithstanding the final aside about a non-viable fetus, the court returned to the importance of viability: '[The fetus] has, if viable, its own bodily form and members, manifests all of the anatomical characteristics of individuality, possesses its own circulatory, vascular and excretory systems and is capable *now* of being ushered into the visible world.'[100] Other courts adopted the same approach. A 1949 judgment made a point of rejecting the 'time-worn' fiction embodied in *Dietrich* and refused to rule that 'as a matter of law the infant is a part of the mother until birth and has no existence in law until that time'.[101] In 1942, a dissenting judgment anticipating *Bonbrest* stated that: 'While it is a fact that there is a close dependence by the unborn child on the organism of the mother, it is not disputed today that the mother and the child are two separate and distinct entities.'[102]

The question as to the stage at which the existence of the fetus could be recognized for the purposes of negligence actions soon attracted further attention. The legal significance of viability was explained when it was noted that, by permitting a cause of action for prenatal injuries, 'the Courts have recognized not only the medical fact that a viable fetus is an individual capable of independent life apart from its mother, but also have accorded to the viable fetus the status of a distinct being capable of sustaining a legal wrong'.[103] Predictably, it was not long before this emphasis on the significance of viability was challenged. The challenges had the effect of further concentrating attention on the nature of the fetus. The decision in *Smith v Brennan* was typical. After noting that many cases had recognized that a fetus capable of separate existence is 'a distinct juridical entity', the court observed: '[N]o jurisdiction which has approved recovery for injury to a viable fetus has later denied recovery to a child who survived an injury suffered before it was viable.' It continued:

We see no reason for denying recovery for a prenatal injury because it occurred before the infant was capable of separate existence. In the first place, age is not the sole measure of viability, and there is no real way of determining in a borderline case whether or not a fetus was viable at the time of the injury, unless it was immediately born. Therefore, the viability rule is impossible of practical application.... In addition ... an unborn child is a distinct biological entity from the time of conception, and many branches of the law afford the unborn child protection throughout the period of gestation. The most important consideration, however, is that the viability distinction

---

[99] 65 F Supp 138, 140 (1946).
[100] Ibid. 141 (emphasis in original). See also *Woods v Lancet* 102 NE 2d 691 (1951).
[101] *Williams v Marion Rapid Transit* 87 NE 2d 334, 340 (1949).
[102] *Stemmer v Kline* 26 A 2d 684, 687 (1942).
[103] *Panagopoulous v Martin* 295 F Supp 220, 225 (1969).

has no relevance to the injustice of denying recovery for harm which can be proved to have resulted from the wrongful act of another. Whether viable or not at the time of the injury, the child sustains the same harm after birth, and therefore should be given the same opportunity for redress. [104]

The reference to the 'injustice' of denying recovery was a consideration reflected in other judgments. Having accepted the cause of action, United States courts were quick to emphasize their desire to provide recompense to all children injured by antenatal negligence. Again and again, judges asked rhetorically whether the law should accept the existence of a wrong without a remedy. By posing the question in this way, the courts allowed themselves to abandon distinctions between viable and non-viable fetuses. The rejection of this distinction, in its turn, had implications that the quoted passage made explicit: a fetus was recognized as 'a distinct biological entity from the time of conception'.

Although accepted in a number of other decisions,[105] this conclusion did not go unquestioned. In *Hornbuckle v Plantation Pipe Line Company*, Almand J expressed his reservations about the award of damages in respect of an injury caused before viability (here the negligence had occurred when the fetus was of about six weeks gestation). His argument drew on the criminal law; in his view, the distinction that the abortion laws made between a fetus that is 'quick' and one that is not should be embodied in the law of torts. As the plaintiff in the case before him could not show that the fetus was 'quick', the judge ruled that the damages claim must fail. He was concerned about the uncertainty that would result from the recognition of a cause of action that could arise immediately following conception. In addition, he was influenced by the fact that the relevant statutory provision governing actions in tort allowed any 'person' to recover damages for injury suffered. Predictably, he indicated that an immature fetus lacked legal personality, expressing this conclusion in homespun terms: 'Assuredly, we could not call an acorn a tree.'[106] A fellow judge had similar concerns: 'The cell is not the person of anyone, and whether it becomes such is dependent upon the processes of nature which raises it from a mere cell to a human being.'[107] Comments such as these highlight the way in which the debate about antenatal negligence was conducted in the United States. It was the identification of the *nature* of the fetus that was at issue. The assumption was that unless it was a distinctive entity, it could not possess rights. If it did not possess rights before birth, there could be no basis on which it was owed a duty of care and hence no basis on which damages could be sought on its behalf.

---

[104] 157 A 2d 497, 504 (1960).
[105] For example, *Hornbuckle v Plantation Pipe Line Company* 93 SE 2d 727 (1956); *Damasiewicz v Gorsuch* 79 A 2d 550 (1951); *Kelly v Gregory* 125 NYS 2d 696 (1953).
[106] 93 SE 2d 727, 730 (1956).   [107] Ibid. 729.

The contrast between analyses of this kind and the approach adopted by the English, Australian, and Canadian courts is striking. When dealing with actions arising from antenatal negligence, these courts have seen little need to discuss the nature and characteristics of the fetus. In Australia, the influential decision in *Watt v Rama* provided a good illustration of the formulation of an alternative theory. There the Victorian Supreme Court rejected the argument that the defendant (a motorist whose negligence had injured a pregnant woman causing antenatal injury) owed no duty of care to the fetus, since it was not an existing person and merely part of the mother. It did not, however, reach this position by asserting that the fetus was an entity to which a duty of care could be owed. Instead, the court relied on the basic principles of the law of negligence:

[The tort of negligence] . . . consists essentially of a breach by the defendant of a duty to take reasonable care which causes damage to the plaintiff. The foundation is the duty to take care, and whether such a duty exists depends upon a relationship existing, or coming into existence, between the parties which is capable in the particular circumstances of the case of imposing a duty on the one in relation to the other.[108]

To provide an answer to the question as to when a duty of care arises, the court referred to *Donoghue v Stevenson*, in which Lord Atkin held:

You must take reasonable care to avoid acts or omissions which you can reasonably foresee would be likely to injure your neighbour. Who, then, in law is my neighbour? The answer seems to be — persons who are so closely and directly affected by my act that I ought reasonably to have them in contemplation as being so affected when I am directing my mind to the acts or omissions which are called in question.[109]

The application of these principles provided a simple answer to the question of the motorist's liability to the injured child: it was reasonably foreseeable that the negligent driving could cause harm to a pregnant woman and it was also foreseeable that this harm would result in the child being born with injuries. The disabled child, when born, was a 'neighbour' of the kind envisaged by Lord Atkin.

Further, if it is accepted that a duty of care is owed to anyone who might foreseeably be harmed by negligent conduct, it follows that the duty need not necessarily be owed to a specific person. It is sufficient if the plaintiff is a member of a category of persons who might foreseeably be harmed by the negligent conduct. More important, if injury is caused, it does not matter whether the person injured was in existence at the time when the negligent act occurred: '[I]t would be immaterial whether at the time of fault the victim was in existence or not, so long as the victim was a member of a class which might reasonably and probably be affected by the act of carelessness.'[110] The

---

[108] [1972] VR 353, 359.   [109] [1932] AC 562, 580.   [110] [1972] VR 353, 373.

court made this point clear by referring to cases in which negligent manufacturers have been held liable for harm which their defective products caused to persons who had not been born when the products were made. The users of the products were members of a category of persons who could, at some future time, foreseeably suffer harm as a result of the manufacturers' negligence. The adoption of this approach was also consistent with the emphasis that the law has traditionally placed on the importance of live birth. The right to sue for damages arose, not when the injury was caused, but when the child was born suffering the effects of the injury. It was thus unnecessary to regard the fetus as possessing rights and a consequent capacity to sue for their breach: the relevant rights crystallized at birth.

While the court unanimously based its decision on the foregoing analysis, Gillard J acknowledged the existence of the fetus. In his view:

[I]t must be accepted that there is a rule of law which recognizes that an unborn child may possess rights. This implies there are correlative duties imposed on others in favour of the unborn child. It also implies that an unborn child is deemed to be a 'person' where the right is for his benefit, so that if he survives his birth and obtains the requisite capacity to institute proceedings for an infringement of his right, he may do so and obtain a remedy for the infringement when he was *en ventre sa mere*.

Later, he said that he was 'inclined to the view' that the child plaintiff 'was deemed to be a person in being at the time of the collision'.[111] In reaching this tentative conclusion, he was influenced by United States decisions (including some of those discussed above) and noted the recognition given to the existence of the fetus by inheritance law, the criminal law, and the Workers Compensation Act. In commenting on the operation of this statute, he cited 'the peculiar fiction of law by which a non-existent person is to be taken as existing'.[112] Ultimately, however, he did not express an opinion on whether that fiction should be adopted and was content to reach his decision by way of basic principles of negligence law.

There are a number of significant features of the *Watt v Rama* analysis of the imposition of liability for antenatal negligence. It allows for liability to be imposed even though there is no existing person to whom a duty of care is owed. Further, whether the negligence occurred at an early or late stage of pregnancy is irrelevant. What matters is that the child was born suffering from the foreseeable effects of this negligence. This approach makes it unnecessary to speculate about the nature and legal status of the fetus and whether it is an entity of the kind to which a duty of care can be owed. It is sufficient if the fetus, when born, is one of a category of persons who could foreseeably be harmed by the negligence. In the words of the court: '[There was] a potential relationship capable of imposing a duty on the defendant in

---

[111] Ibid. 376 and 377. [112] *Schofield v Orrell Colliery Co Ltd* [1909] 1 KB 178, 182.

relation to the child if and when born. On the birth the relationship crystal-lized and out of it arose a duty on the defendant in relation to the child.'[113]

The analysis offered in *Watt v Rama* was adopted by the English Court of Appeal in *Burton v Islington Health Authority* and *De Martell v Merton and Sutton Health Authority*.[114] The case dealt with two appeals in proceedings in which medical negligence had resulted in the birth of disabled children. The Court of Appeal (like its Australian counterpart) was faced with a submis-sion that since the harm had been suffered antenatally (and therefore before the plaintiffs had legal personality), no claim for damages could succeed. The court rejected this submission; as in the majority decision in *Watt v Rama*, reliance was placed on basic principles of negligence law. The views of Gillard J were noted, but not explicitly relied on. In passing, the court sug-gested that it would be open to the English courts to apply the maxim that an 'unborn child' shall be deemed to be born whenever its interests require it, and to treat the two plaintiffs in the case as lives in being at the time of the negligent conduct.[115] With the exception of these comments, the court saw little need to consider the legal status of the fetus.

Burton and *De Martell* dealt with claims on behalf of children born before the English law was put in statutory form. As has been explained in Chapter 4,[116] the current law on antenatal negligence claims is now embodied in the Congenital Disabilities (Civil Liability) Act 1976 (UK). This Act did not bring any change to the way English law regards the fetus. The Law Com-mission report on which the Act was based was content to rely on basic prin-ciples of tort law of the kind applied in *Watt v Rama*: 'The plaintiff [a child suing in respect of antenatal harm] has no legal existence at the time of his injury nor has he, prior to live birth, an existence separate from his mother. The fact of physical identification of mother and foetus is something which cannot be ignored . . .'. Although the report does not cite *Dietrich*, its refer-ence to the 'physical identification of mother and foetus' echoes the view of Holmes J that a fetus is a part of the mother's body. The report added that 'no rights should be given to the foetus'.[117] The Act was drafted in such a way as to ensure that this result was achieved. Under s 1(3), liability to the child in respect of antenatal harm can arise only if there has been a breach of a duty of care owed to a parent. This makes it clear that for the purposes of the Act, a fetus is not to be treated as an entity to which a duty of care is owed.

The Canadian courts have accepted the solution favoured in *Watt v Rama*. In *Duval v Seguin* (a case arising from a motor accident in which a child was born with injuries suffered *in utero*), the High Court of Ontario relied on the principles formulated in *Donoghue v Stevenson*. When a driver is driving

---

[113] [1972] VR 353, 360.   [114] [1993] QB 204.   [115] Ibid. 227.   [116] Above 57–8.
[117] Law Commission, *Report on Injuries to Unborn Children* (Law Com No 60, 1974) paras 33 and 75.

negligently: '[An unborn child] falls well within the area of potential danger which the driver is required to foresee and take reasonable care to avoid. In my opinion it is not necessary in the present case to consider whether the unborn child was a person in law or at which stage she became a person.'[118] The possibility that a fetus is a 'person' was more closely considered in *Cherry v Borsman*.[119] The action arose following the birth of a disabled child; her injuries had been caused by a negligently performed abortion procedure that had failed to terminate the pregnancy. In deciding that the child could sue for damages in respect of the negligent procedure, the Supreme Court of British Columbia also applied the *Donoghue v Stevenson* principle, commenting that, 'It is clearly foreseeable that a negligently performed abortion may affect a fetus.' The court was emphatic that this conclusion did not imply that the fetus was a 'person': 'A fetus does not become a person until it is born alive.'[120] On the facts of the case, such a ruling was crucial. If the fetus was a 'person' at the time of the procedure, the doctor's right to destroy it would have been challenged.[121] Only by denying that the fetus was a 'person' could the court simultaneously conclude that the procedure was lawful and that the child acquired a right to damages if the procedure failed:

[F]inding that there was a duty owed by the defendant doctor to the infant plaintiff is not conferring upon the fetus the status of legal personhood. It did not put the defendant in the impossible situation of owing a duty to one person to terminate the existence of another person. Had the abortion been successfully completed, the infant plaintiff would have had no rights. Her rights only arose when and because she was born alive. At that point she became an independent legal entity who could claim compensation for the injuries suffered *in utero*.[122]

It would be difficult to imagine a more vivid illustration of the problems that the courts experience when they seek to distinguish between actuality and potentiality. The success of the infant plaintiff's claim depended on acceptance of the argument that though the law took no notice of the existence of the fetus at the time of the failed termination procedure, the negligent performance of that procedure gave rise to rights which crystallized at birth. In this case, the fetus was found to be both a non-entity and a potential person. Although the defendant doctor appealed, the Court of Appeal of British Columbia affirmed the approach taken by the trial judge. The court adopted the *Duval v Seguin* view that a duty of care arose because the fetus fell within the area of potential danger that the doctor was required to foresee.[123] Major J of the Supreme Court of Canada offered further support for

---

[118] (1972) 26 DLR (3d) 418, 433.
[119] (1991) 75 DLR (4th) 668; affirmed (1992) 94 DLR (4th) 488.
[120] (1991) 75 DLR (4th) 668, 676.
[121] See the above discusssion (144–5) of *Dehler v Ottawa Civic Hospital*; this case was cited ibid. 677.
[122] (1991) 75 DLR (4th) 668, 677. [123] (1992) 94 DLR (4th) 488, 505.

this approach in *Dobson (Litigation Guardian of) v Dobson*, where he stated: 'There is no such thing as "liability for prenatal injuries".' In his opinion, under Canadian law, the fetus does not exist for purposes of civil action.[124]

Thus there is a significant difference between the analyses adopted by the Canadian, English, and Australian courts on the one hand, and, on the other, those offered by the United States courts. The preoccupation with the legal status and characteristics of the fetus which marks many United States decisions is absent in the decisions of the courts in the other three countries.

Pre-Conception Negligence

One further aspect of these differing approaches merits comment. In Chapter 4, it was seen that there have been some United States and Australian cases in which doctors have been liable to pay damages when children have been born suffering injuries caused by pre-conception negligence.[125] Obviously such a result can be reached only on the basis of the adoption of principles relating to foreseeability of harm. A simple example was seen in the Australian case, *X and Y (By Her Tutor X) v Pal and Others*. This case involved a successful action for damages by a child who was born with syphilis; the obstetrician who had been responsible for the mother's care before she conceived had negligently failed to test her for the disease. The New South Wales Court of Appeal was in no doubt about his liability: 'Dr Pal owed a duty of care to his patient and . . . it was foreseeable that if he did not exercise due care in treating her he may cause damage to children later born to her.'[126] In adopting this approach, the court echoed the view expressed in *Watt v Rama*: children not yet conceived but later born to the woman were members of a category of persons whom the doctor should have had in contemplation when he treated his patient. Once membership of such a category was established, it did not matter that the children were not in existence at the time of the negligent act or omission.

If, in contrast with the analysis employed in these Australian cases, the emphasis is placed on proof of the breach of a duty owed to a fetus, any action resulting from pre-conception negligence must automatically fail. It therefore seems reasonable to predict that claims relating to pre-conception negligence will be looked on less favourably by the United States courts, since these courts have tended to stress the importance of conduct which causes harm to an existing legal entity. In fact, the pattern is unclear. In some cases, United States courts have allowed claims in respect of pre-conception negligence and in others they have not. When they have not, the absence of an entity to which a duty is owed has sometimes been offered as an explanation.

---

[124] (1999) 174 DLR (4th) 1, 38.   [125] See above 58–60 and 61–2.
[126] (1991) 23 NSWLR 26, 44.

An illustration was *Albala v City of New York*. There the infant plaintiff alleged that the negligent performance of an abortion, prior to his conception, had perforated his mother's uterus and that this, in turn, had caused him to be born with brain damage. In addition to advancing policy reasons for disallowing the claim (a concern to keep tort actions within 'manageable bounds'), the Court of Appeals of New York distinguished the case before it from those in which damages claims arose from injury to a fetus during a pregnancy. In the latter type of case: '[A]t the time the tort is committed there are two identifiable beings within the zone of danger each of whom is owed a duty independent of the other and each of whom may be directly injured.'[127] It was held that, in pre-conception cases, it was 'inapposite' to rely on decisions dealing with injuries to fetuses.[128]

The court then considered the argument that 'at the time Ruth Albala underwent an abortion . . . it was foreseeable that she would again conceive and that the health of children born thereafter could be adversely affected by damage to her uterus'. It was not persuaded by this argument, observing that 'foreseeability alone is not the hallmark of legal duty'.[129] The reason offered was the need to limit the operation of negligence law. The court gave as an example a negligent motorist who collides with a woman and causes her injuries which affect her capacity to give birth to a normal child. In the court's view, it was unacceptable for such a motorist to be exposed to a damages claim on behalf of a subsequently conceived child who is born with disabilities resulting from the mother's condition. Thus separate threads were brought together. The earlier case law rejected the view that a fetus is merely part of the mother and consequently insisted on viewing it as a legal entity (the woman and her fetus are 'two identifiable beings'). Building on this, the decision in *Albala* saw the proof of the existence of an identifiable being (the fetus) as necessary for the maintenance of a 'reasonable and practical' response to claims on behalf of children who have suffered antenatal harm.[130]

Not all United States cases on pre-conception negligence have adopted this approach. In *Renslow v Mennonite Hospital*, the court noted that 'the plaintiff at the time of the conduct was in no sense a separate entity to whom the traditional duty of care could be owed'.[131] Nevertheless, it allowed the action arising from pre-conception negligence. In doing so, it did not rely solely on the foreseeability of the harm to the child. Instead, the judgment stressed the need for a breach of duty. After observing that the concept of

---

[127] NY, 429 NE 2d 786, 787 (1981).   [128] Ibid. 788.   [129] Ibid. 788.

[130] Ibid. 788. See also *Gallagher v Duke University* 638 F Supp 979 (MDNC, 1986) in which a child brought a wrongful life action after negligent pre-conception counselling had allegedly led to its birth with a chromosomal abnormality. It was held that the action could not succeed as the child was not in existence when the counselling was given and therefore could not be owed a duty of care.

[131] 367 NE 2d 1250, 1254 (1977).

legal duty was a flexible one, the court recognized that 'a duty may exist to one foreseeably harmed though he be unknown and remote in time and place'. Whether there was such a duty depended on the relationship between the parties (in this case, doctor and patient):

The cases allowing relief to an infant for injuries incurred in its previable state make it clear that a defendant may be held liable to a person whose existence was not apparent at the time of his act. We therefore find it illogical to bar relief for an act done prior to conception where the defendant would be liable for this same conduct had the child, unbeknownst to him, been conceived prior to his act.[132]

Thus the court argued by analogy and so side-stepped the problem of the non-existence of the fetus at the time of the negligence. It ruled that, if tortfeasors can be liable to entities of which they were unaware (pre-viable fetuses), they can also be liable to fetuses that have not yet been conceived.

Wrongful Death Actions

The damages actions so far discussed have arisen following the birth of children who have been harmed by antenatal negligence. In all these actions, it was accepted that live birth is a prerequisite to a successful claim: an injured child's right to sue crystallizes when he or she becomes a 'person' and so is in a position to seek recompense for the injuries or disabilities caused by the negligence. The law's object in such cases is to ease the burden the child will bear. This was explained in *Lecesse v McDonough*: 'If a foetus is born alive, it becomes a "person" with at least the theoretical possibility of survival and of enduring the consequences of prenatal injury throughout its life. A foetus not born alive seems . . . to incur no such risk of continuing injury . . .'.[133] On this analysis, there is no room for damages actions on behalf of children who die immediately after birth or who are stillborn. Yet, as has been seen in Chapter 6, there are numerous twentieth-century United States decisions in which the reasoning in *Dietrich* was not followed and stillbirths and perinatal deaths have resulted in successful wrongful death claims. The more important of these cases must be re-examined in order to determine what light they shed on the legal status of the fetus.

No theoretical difficulties arise in the case of a child who is born alive and dies moments after birth. Such a child has—however briefly—become a 'person' before dying and so the statutory beneficiaries may bring a wrongful death action on the basis that antenatal negligence has caused the death. While it is questionable whether such an action should succeed in the case of a perinatal death—given that the purpose of wrongful death proceedings is

---

[132] 367 NE 2d 1250, 1255 (1977). A similar result was reached in *Yeager v Bloomington Obstetrics and Gynecology* Inc 585 NE 2d 696 (Ind App 1 Dist, 1992).
[133] 279 NE 2d 339, 341 (1972).

to reimburse family members for the financial loss caused by a death—no violence is done to the 'born alive' rule by allowing the action. When a still-birth occurs, however, it is clear that the application of this rule would pre-clude a wrongful death action. In addition to *Lecesse*, there have been several United States decisions that have accepted this conclusion. In *Puhl v Mil-waukee Automobile Ins Co*, the well-established common law principle was reiterated. The fetus was described as having 'a potentiality of personality which is not realized until birth'. The judgment continued: 'Injuries suffered before birth impose a conditional liability on the tort-feasor. This liability becomes unconditional, or complete, upon the birth of the injured separate entity as a legal person. If such personality is not achieved, there would be no liability because of no damage to a legal person.'[134] Dixon CJ of the Supreme Court of Louisiana made the same point more tersely: 'The stillborn child has no rights, and can transmit none.'[135]

Yet in spite of the emphasis which has long been placed on the significance of live birth, some courts have allowed wrongful death actions to be brought following stillbirths. Typical of the arguments employed were those set out in *Presley v Newport Hospital*.[136] There the Supreme Court of Rhode Island addressed the question whether parents should have an action for wrongful death when their child had been stillborn. It therefore asked whether a still-born child was a 'person' for the purposes of the State's Wrongful Death Act. The court reviewed the leading cases on damages claims by children who had been born alive suffering the effects of antenatal negligence. *Dietrich*, the dissent in *Allaire*, and *Bonbrest* were noted. The court regarded *Bonbrest* as setting the stage for the recognition of wrongful death actions following still-births.[137] In discussing the cases in which such actions had been allowed, the court accepted that no distinction could properly be made between a child who dies just before birth and one who dies shortly afterwards. The rejection of this distinction was seen as being consistent with *Bonbrest*'s emphasis on the significance of viability; the court quoted the following statement with approval: 'It seems too plain for argument that where independent existence is possible and life is destroyed through a wrongful act a cause of action arises . . .'.[138] This analysis was echoed in a later decision by the Supreme Court of Ohio:

[A] cause of action may arise under the wrongful death statute when a viable fetus is stillborn since a life capable of independent existence has expired. It is logically

---

[134] 99 NW 2d 163, 170 (1959).
[135] *Danos v St Pierre* La, 402 So 2d 633, 636 (1981). See also *Modaber v Kelley* 348 SE 2d 233, 237 (Va, 1986).
[136] 365 A 2d 748 (1976).
[137] For a similar analysis of *Bonbrest*, see *Greater Southeast Community Hospital v Williams* 482 A 2d 394, 396–7 (DC App, 1984).
[138] *Verkennes v Corniea* 38 NW 2d 838, 841 (1949); cited 365 A 2d 748, 751 (1976).

indefensible as well as unjust to deny an action where the child is stillborn, and yet permit the action where the child survives birth but only for a short period of time.[139]

What was regarded as crucial here was the capacity for independent existence. Similarly, in *Chrisafogeorgis v Brandenberg*, the Supreme Court of Illinois ruled that this made the viable fetus sufficiently similar to a 'person' to allow the application of wrongful death legislation: '[V]iability is the appropriate line of demarcation. It is the time at which a child is capable of being delivered and remaining alive separate and independent of the mother. This can be said to be the critical stage of a "person" within the meaning of the [Illinois] Wrongful Death Act's language . . .'.[140] In *White v Yup*, the Supreme Court of Nevada went further, stating: 'A viable unborn child is, in fact, biologically speaking, a presently existing person and a living human being, because it has reached such a state of development that it can presently live outside the female body, as well as within it.'[141]

Presley's references to 'independent existence' and the destruction of 'life' reflected this view and also made it clear that the court regarded the fetus as separate. The judgment noted that, 'The myth, perpetuated by Mr. Justice Holmes in 1884 [in *Dietrich*], that the unborn fetus is but a part of its mother's body, has long since been laid to rest in both the law and medicine.'[142] The decision did not stop there. Having rejected 'the arbitrariness of birth as a demarcation line', the court went on to reject the distinction between viable and non-viable fetuses. It noted approvingly that a number of earlier decisions had 'cast the viability distinction aside as an anomaly owing its existence to long outmoded concepts of both science and law'. It concluded:

[V]iability is a concept bearing no relation to the attempts of the law to provide remedies for civil wrongs. If we profess allegiance to reason, it would be seditious to adopt so arbitrary and uncertain a concept as viability as a dividing line between those persons who shall enjoy the protection of our remedial laws and those who shall become, for most intents and purposes, nonentities. It seems that if live birth is to be characterized, as it so frequently has been, as an arbitrary line of demarcation, then viability, when enlisted to serve that same purpose, is a veritable *non sequitur*.[143]

As a result, the court had no hesitation in ruling that the stillborn child who was the subject of the proceedings, 'whether viable or nonviable', was a 'person' within the meaning of the Rhode Island Wrongful Death Act.[144]

There are, however, some limits to the United States courts' willingness to extend the operation of this legislation. It seems that at the time of the negligent conduct there must be some entity (however immature) which can

---

[139] *Werling v Sandy* 476 NE 2d 1053, 1055 (Ohio, 1985).   [140] 304 NE 2d 88, 92 (1973).

[141] 458 P 2d 617, 622 (1969). Similarly, in *Hall v Murphy* 113 SE 2d 790, 793 (SC, 1960), the Supreme Court of South Carolina ruled that a viable fetus is a 'person'. See also *Werling v Sandy* 476 NE 2d 1053, 1055 (Ohio, 1985).

[142] 365 A 2d 748, 753 (1976).   [143] Ibid. 753–4.   [144] Ibid. 754.

be regarded as a 'person' before a wrongful death statute can apply. This was made clear in *Carr v Wittingen*,[145] in which parents sought to bring a wrongful death action in respect of pre-conception negligence. Before becoming pregnant, the woman had undergone a laparotomy. She alleged that the negligent performance of the procedure had resulted in a uterine rupture that later caused the death of the fetus. The wrongful death action was disallowed on the ground that the fetus was not in existence at the time of the operation.

All the decisions that have recognized that stillbirths can result in wrongful death claims reveal a willingness to acknowledge that a fetus has a special legal status and that its destruction is analogous to the killing of a person. Some also exhibit a determination to stress that the woman and her fetus are separate. In cases such as *Amadio v Levin*, this approach seems to have been driven by a belief that only by emphasizing this will courts be able to award proper compensation for a negligently caused stillbirth. The majority judgment of the Supreme Court of Pennsylvania observed: '[A] child en ventre sa mere is an individual with the right to be free of pre-natal injury. If a child en ventre sa mere is an individual at the time of its injury, then, *a fortiori*, the child is also an individual when those injuries cause its death . . .'.[146] This emphasis on the existence of a separate individual was crucial to the decisions relating to stillbirths. In concurring with the majority, Zappala J quoted with approval from two judgments in which medical evidence was relied on to establish that the fetus was separate from its mother:[147]

While it is a fact that there is a close dependence by the unborn child on the organism of the mother, it is not disputed today that the mother and the child are two separate and distinct entities; that the unborn child has its own system of circulation of the blood separate and apart from the mother; that there is no communication between the two circulation systems; that the heart beat of the child is not in tune with that of the mother but is more rapid; that there is no dependence by the child on the mother except for sustenance. . . . It is not the fact that an unborn child is part of the mother, but that rather in the unborn state it lived with the mother, we might say, and from conception on developed its own distinct, separate personality.[148]

If the mother can die and the fetus live, or the fetus die and the mother live, how can it be said that there is only one life? If tortious conduct can injure one and not the other, how can it be said that there is not a duty owing to each?[149]

Comments such as these echo the assumption underlying the recognition of a wrongful death action following a stillbirth: the fetus has a separate existence and therefore possesses rights which the law will protect even when a

---

[145] 451 NW 2d 584 (Mich App, 1990).
[146] 501 A 2d 1085, 1087 (Pa, 1985). See also *Greater Southeast Community Hospital v Williams* 482 A 2d 394, 396 (DC App, 1984).
[147] 501 A 2d 1085, 1095 (Pa, 1985).   [148] *Stemmer v Kline* 26 A 2d 684, 687 (1942).
[149] *O'Neill v Morse* 188 NW 2d 785, 787 (1971).

live birth does not occur. While the decisions embodying this assumption offer interesting perspectives on the status of the fetus, it is nevertheless important not to over-emphasize their significance. As has already been noted, there is United States authority for the view that until there has been a live birth, no claim can arise in respect of antenatal injury. This view also prevails in Canada, England, and Australia.

SOME IMPLICATIONS

Criminal Proceedings

The foregoing discussion reveals that different perspectives can be adopted when the legal system is asked to protect a fetus. When the operation of the law relating to homicide is examined it is apparent that reliance has regularly been placed on the notion that since a fetus is not a 'person', its destruction cannot result in a murder or manslaughter charge. This preoccupation with problems of definition requires the identification of a decisive criterion: this is embodied in the 'born alive' rule. The retention of this rule has been questioned. Some judges have speculated about the meaning of 'born alive'. Some have asked whether the rule embodies a valid test. They have been troubled by what they see as the artificiality of denying a mature fetus the protection of the law of homicide, particularly if this protection is available to a child who does no more than display feeble and brief signs of life before dying. The law prohibiting homicide exists to punish those who take human life and it can be argued that life is present before birth and that the destruction of a fetus amounts to the destruction of human life. A number of courts and legislatures have accepted this argument and so have shown themselves willing to recognize the fetus as an entity deserving protection. Others have been tempted to do so. Sometimes reliance has been placed on criteria such as 'quickening' or viability as indicators of life. To emphasize 'life' is to stress the *similarities* between a fetus and a newborn child instead of stressing the *differences*. Once such reasoning is adopted, the way is paved for extension of the law of homicide (or the creation of an analogous offence) to cover situations in which an assailant's conduct against a pregnant woman (such as beating, kicking, stabbing, or shooting) is behaviour of the kind frequently associated with homicide charges.

This response, which reflects criticism of the limits imposed on the law of homicide, has not attracted much support in the United States, Canada, England, and Australia. The view that the 'born alive rule' should be retained predominates. Similarly, there have been few challenges to the rule in cases in which the criminal law has been invoked against a pregnant woman whose conduct (such as drug taking) has harmed her fetus. In these matters — as with the majority of homicide cases—the focus has been on the meaning of the statutory language and decisions have been reached on the basis that Acts prohibiting the supply of drugs to 'minors' or the abuse or endangerment of 'children' can have no application to fetuses.

Analysis of the assumptions embodied in the abortion laws is more difficult. In all four countries discussed in this book, courts interpreting these laws have been emphatic in rejecting the argument that a fetus is a 'person'. They have thus adopted a familiar starting-point, but—unlike some courts reviewing the operation of homicide laws—they have not expressed any doubts about their conclusion. This, however, does not throw any light on the purpose of the laws controlling abortion. The ruling that a fetus is not a 'person' leaves open the question whether it is an entity of a kind that abortion laws seek to protect. It can be argued that these laws exist to offer the protection that homicide laws fail to provide. This argument draws attention to the uncertainties inherent in abortion laws. As recognized in *Roe v Wade* and *Planned Parenthood of Southeastern Pennsylvania v Casey*, abortion laws exist both to protect women and to protect 'potential life'. It is necessary, however, to go beyond the relatively simple conclusion that abortion laws pursue dual purposes. In more recent times, these laws have reflected a growing acceptance that the law should not normally impede a woman seeking a termination. As a result, the various laws regulating abortion allow the pursuit of conflicting objectives. By sanctioning terminations in certain circumstances, they permit the destruction of fetuses. By imposing restrictions, they seek to protect them. The legal position is thus that abortions should be discouraged but permitted.[150] The state's mandate is thus a qualified one: while the fetus is recognized as a distinctive entity, it is not an entity the nature of which invariably entitles it to the protection of the law in the way that the law of homicide protects a person. For the purposes of this chapter, the important point is that whatever other functions they may perform, one of the purposes of the laws regulating abortion is the protection of the fetus. To the extent that they pursue this objective, they reflect a recognition of its special qualities. It is wrong, therefore, to assert that any inquiry into the status of the fetus is irrelevant to an understanding of the problem of abortion.[151] The clearest and most authoritative acknowledgements of these propositions are contained in *Roe v Wade* and *Casey*. In *Roe v Wade*, the Supreme Court of the United States referred to the state's 'important and legitimate interest in protecting the potentiality of human life'.[152] In *Casey*, the court emphasized this aspect of the decision and stressed that this interest exists from the

---

[150] J. A. Robertson, *Children of Choice: Freedom and the New Reproductive Technologies* (Princeton, 1994) 46.
[151] B. Steinbock, *Life before Birth: the Moral and Legal Status of Embryos and Fetuses* (New York, 1992) 44–5.
[152] 410 US 113, 162; 35 L Ed 2d 147, 182 (1973).

outset of the pregnancy.[153] These two decisions lend powerful support to the view that because it represents potential life, a fetus has intrinsic value and therefore the law can, in some circumstances, legitimately seek to protect it.

Offering United States authority for the recognition of the fetus's need for protection raises the question whether there is any support for it in Canadian, English, or Australian law. In Canada, the question is of theoretical interest only, since *R v Morgentaler* allowed a challenge to the provision governing abortion (s 251 of the Criminal Code).[154] Nevertheless, though this section was found to be unconstitutional, none of the judgments suggested that the protection of the fetus was not a valid objective for a legislature to pursue. Three members of the court were untroubled by the notion that the 'primary objective' of s 251 was to protect the fetus.[155] Neither English nor Australian courts have expressly dealt with the possibility that laws restricting abortion embody the assumption that the state has an interest in the protection of the fetus. The leading English decision on the law's willingness to recognize the existence of the fetus is *Attorney-General's Reference (No 3 of 1994)*. While it deals with the interpretation of homicide law and not abortion law, it contains suggestions that the fetus is a distinctive entity. In the words of Lord Mustill: 'I would . . . reject the reasoning which assumes that since (in the eyes of English law) the foetus does not have the attributes which make it a "person" it must be an adjunct of the mother. . . . [T]he foetus is neither. It is a unique organism.'[156] Lord Hope was more forthright: '[A]n embryo is in reality a separate organism from the mother from the moment of its conception.'[157]

It would be dangerous, however, to assume that these statements reveal the adoption of a perspective similar to that in *Roe* and *Casey*: while the two judges recognized the special nature of the fetus, their words contained no suggestion of a state interest in its protection. Indeed, Lord Mustill added: 'To apply to such an organism the principles of a law evolved in relation to autonomous beings is bound to mislead.'[158] Later in his judgment, he commented: '[T]he child en ventre sa mere does not have a distinct human personality, whose extinguishment gives rise to any penalties or liabilities at common law.'[159] Rather than seeking specific English references to the approach adopted by the United States Supreme Court, it is best to rely on general principles. The opinion in *Roe* drew on concepts long embodied in the law and these concepts have influenced the development of English and Australian abortion laws. The history of the English and United States laws has too much in common to allow the analysis offered in *Roe v Wade* to be

---

[153] 505 US 833, 846; 120 L Ed 2d 674, 694 (1992).

[154] In *Dobson (Litigation Guardian of) v Dobson* (1999) 174 DLR (4th) 1, 39, it was accepted that there is now an unrestricted legal right to abortion in Canada.

[155] (1988) 44 DLR (4th) 385, 452–3 and 499.   [156] [1998] AC 245, 256.

[157] Ibid. 267.   [158] Ibid. 256.   [159] Ibid. 261.

interpreted as relevant only to the United States. Given the nature and origins of English and Australian abortion statutes, it would be unconvincing to assert that these laws do not rest on a recognition of the special status of the fetus and an acceptance of the view that the state has an interest in protecting it. It is impossible to say whether this view forms part of Canadian law. There are echoes of *Roe v Wade* in *R v Morgentaler*. Perhaps these indicate that, were new legislation to be enacted in Canada, it could validly embody the assumption that the state has an interest in protecting fetal life. A statement by Major J in *Dobson (Litigation Guardian of) v Dobson* suggests otherwise. He noted: 'Under existing Canadian law the foetus does not exist for purposes of state protection . . .'.[160] This comment, however, was not made in the context of a discussion of abortion laws.

One additional feature of these laws requires comment. *Roe v Wade* and *Casey* not only identified the existence of a state interest in protecting potential life, but they also suggested that this interest is substantially increased when the fetus attains viability. As has been seen in many of the judgments discussed earlier in this chapter, an emphasis on the significance of viability is a feature of United States cases. This preoccupation with fetal development can be seen as having its origins in the early common law's recognition of 'quickening'. It is well established that the greater the maturity of the fetus, the more likely it is to attract the protection of the law.

This is important for two reasons. First, it is logically impossible for a legal system that takes account of the characteristics of the fetus to deny that the law is taking an interest in the fetus itself. The object of the system's concern is an existing entity; not simply the entity that it will become after live birth. This perspective reveals an attempt to take account of verifiable facts rather than a concern with abstract concepts such as personhood: the issue is no longer whether the law elects to bestow or withhold a certain status, but whether it will take account of 'the biological reality of progressive fetal development'.[161] The second reason is that to emphasize viability is to provide a strong justification for protective intervention once that stage is reached. While one must take some notice of *Casey*'s identification of a state interest in the fetus from conception, much more attention must be paid to the strength of this interest once the fetus is viable. At this stage, according to *Roe*, the interest becomes 'compelling'. *Roe* and *Casey* both support the proposition that a viable fetus has a special value and therefore a special status. Whether or not an immature fetus is a legal non-entity, these decisions make it difficult to deny that a viable fetus is an entity that the law will seek to protect.

---

[160] (1999) 174 DLR (4th) 1, 38.
[161] J. A. Robertson, *Children of Choice: Freedom and the New Reproductive Technologies* (Princeton, 1994) 53.

Again, the question must be asked whether the *Roe/Casey* view that a viable fetus has greater legal status has any relevance in Canada, England, or Australia. As was explained earlier in the chapter, one member of the Supreme Court of Canada in *Morgentaler*—following *Roe*—tentatively suggested that the state might acquire a 'compelling' interest in fetal protection 'somewhere in the second trimester'.[162] The question of the significance of viability has not been explicitly addressed in English or Australian decisions on abortion law. However, some support for the notion that the developmental stage of a fetus is important is provided by the fact that the legislation in England, South Australia, and Western Australia identifies gestational stages after which a legal abortion is more difficult to obtain.

Child Protection Proceedings

The response of courts when asked to use child protection laws to safeguard fetuses has normally been much the same as that adopted by courts asked to employ homicide laws for the same purpose. The focus has been on definitional problems and the result has been that juvenile and family courts have regularly ruled that a fetus is not an entity whose existence can be recognized before birth. There is another parallel. Reliance on the 'born alive' rule has not precluded the reception, after the child's birth, of evidence of harm caused antenatally. Just as evidence of antenatal criminal conduct can be taken into account for the purposes of a homicide charge after a child has been born alive, so can evidence of harmful antenatal conduct (such as maternal drug taking) be taken into account by a court undertaking the task of deciding whether the child is likely to receive adequate care in the future.

In the same way that the limits embodied in most homicide laws have led courts to express concern about the need to protect the fetus, there have occasionally been decisions in which courts have been willing to extend the operation of child protection laws to fetuses. As in the field of homicide law, these decisions have occasionally led to legislative action in the form of amendments to child protection statutes making it clear that they apply to fetuses. In the jurisdictions in which this legislative activity has occurred, and in those in which the courts have extended the reach of the child protection laws, there has thus been a recognition of the fetus as a distinctive entity entitled to protection. It must be emphasized that such developments have been rare. A review of the operation of child protection laws provides only limited support for the view that a fetus has legal status.

---

[162] (1988) 44 DLR (4th) 385, 499.

Proceedings to Impose Medical Treatment

The picture that emerges from a reconsideration of the matters involving medical treatment is confusing. In many of the cases in which the coercive treatment of a pregnant woman was authorized the courts did not regard the status of the fetus as problematic. One decision explicitly recognized the fetus as an entity entitled to the law's protection; one referred to a 'life' which should be safeguarded; one spoke of the fetus's right to life; and one expressly described the fetus as a human being. Although these comments are inconsistent with many of the principles accepted in other fields of law, only rarely have attempts been made to reconcile the analysis with those principles. In two cases, the courts' authorization of intervention was explictly linked to *Roe v Wade*'s identification of the state's interest in protecting viable fetuses. In one of these matters, reliance was placed on the ruling that this interest becomes 'compelling' at viability. It is probably no accident that this emphasis on fetal maturity is found in two cases in which caesarean sections were ordered. In these and other proceedings involving caesareans, the assumption may have been that a fetus ready to be delivered had so much in common with a child who had been born that it could properly be regarded as possessing rights which should be given immediate protection. In *Re Madyun*, reasoning of this kind was made explicit. The court underlined the fact that the fetus was more than simply viable. It was ready to be born: 'All that stood between the Madyun fetus and its independent existence, separate from its mother, was . . . a doctor's scalpel. In these circumstances, the life of the infant inside its mother's womb was entitled to be protected.'[163] This represents an emphatic recognition of the status of the fetus; significantly, it was achieved by describing the fetus as an 'infant'.

As has been explained earlier in the chapter, more recent decisions in the United States and England have expressed disapproval of coercive medical treatment designed to protect the fetus. In these decisions, the primary focus has been on the interests of the woman, rather than on the nature of the fetus. Thus, a reconsideration of these cases would contribute little to the analysis offered here. There are, however, two highly significant—and possibly conflicting—statements by the English Court of Appeal. Both statements related to applications for the authorization of caesarean sections. In *Re MB*, the court—invoking *Paton* and *C v S*—accepted that a fetus is not a 'person' and that it cannot have interests of its own until it is born and has a separate existence from its mother.[164] In *St George's Healthcare NHS Trust v S*, the court made a significant statement indicating a recognition of the distinctiveness of the fetus: 'Whatever else it may be a 36-week foetus is not nothing: if viable it is not lifeless and it is certainly human.'[165]

---

[163] 573 A 2d 1235, 1262 (DC App, 1990).   [164] [1997] 2 FLR 426, 440 and 444.

[165] [1998] 3 WLR 936, 952.

Negligence Actions

There are two different approaches in actions arising from antenatal negligence. In England, Canada, and Australia, courts dealing with such actions have generally confined themselves to asking whether a child born suffering the effects of negligent antenatal injury should be permitted to recover damages. When the question is posed this way, there is no need to speculate about the nature of the fetus. The question can be answered in the broader context of the operation of the law of torts. All that must be asked is whether the child was a member of a class of persons who would foreseeably suffer harm as a result of the negligence. Its legal status while a fetus is of no interest. Although such an approach does not necessarily deny the existence of the fetus, the result is that it is viewed solely as an inchoate being, capable of attracting the attention of the law only after live birth.

By contrast, in the United States courts the focus in negligence actions arising from antenatal injury has been primarily on whether the fetus is an entity of a kind that can possess rights and to which a duty of care can be owed. In the words of the Supreme Court of Illinois, '*Dietrich* and its progeny indicate this duty could be owed only to one with a legally identifiable existence.'[166] Once the courts adopted this approach, they became immersed in the type of analysis already seen in the discussion of other areas of the law. It was necessary to reach conclusions about the nature of the fetus. Emphasis was placed on the significance of viability and even (in a small number of cases) on 'quickening'. A preoccupation with the implications of viability—defined as a capacity for independent life—became an important feature of the negligence cases. A further consideration was added. Many of the judgments accepted that the pregnant woman and her fetus were two separate and distinct entities. This aspect was underlined in *Smith v Brennan*, where it was stated that it is clear that 'before birth an infant is a distinct entity, and that the law recognizes that rights which he will enjoy when born can be violated before his birth'.[167]

Another feature of the analysis was the courts' willingness to establish significant criteria and then to reject them. This is a further illustration of the tendency—encountered in the discussion of homicide laws—to abandon classifications and to seek out similarities. Once this is done, the way is paved for the conclusion that there are no relevant differences between a new-born child and a fully mature fetus, between a fully mature fetus and a viable fetus, or between a viable fetus and one that is not viable. The view that, at viability, a fetus became sufficiently distinctive to be the object of a duty of care gave way to an acceptance of the notion that a non-viable fetus has the

---

[166] *Renslow v Mennonite Hospital* 367 NE 2d 1250, 1254 (1977).
[167] 157 A 2d 497, 502 (1960).

necessary qualities to attract the protection of the law of negligence. This, in turn, led to the abandonment of all attempts to make distinctions on the basis of gestational development. Some courts accepted that because a fetus is a distinct biological entity from the time of conception, any harm to it could result in a damages action after the child's birth.

Many of the United States courts failed to recognize that this emphasis on the nature of the fetus might have been unnecessary, so fixed were they in their belief that it was imperative to establish the existence of an entity at the time the harm was done. This course was pursued even though these courts accepted that a live birth was the normal prerequisite for a successful damages claim. As has been seen, the English, Canadian, and Australian courts were able — without engaging in analysis of the nature of the fetus — to reach the conclusion that a child could properly make a damages claim in respect of antenatal negligence. In most situations involving an action arising from such negligence, the contrast between the two techniques is therefore of theoretical interest only. It can rightly be objected that all that emerges is that the same result can be reached by different routes. There is, however, one context in which the adoption of one method rather than the other has important practical consequences. The method used by some United States courts allows a stillbirth to result in a successful claim under a Wrongful Death Act. The method used in the other three countries does not.

The United States decisions relating to stillbirths focused on familiar concepts. Sometimes they were interpreted in a way consistent with established principles and sometimes they were not. For the purposes of the application of the wrongful death legislation, the key question was whether the action arose from the death of a 'person'. Some courts had no doubt that the 'born alive' rule should determine the answer in the case of a stillbirth: in their view, no liability could arise under the legislation until the potential of the fetus had been realized. The courts that rejected this view reached their conclusion by employing the techniques outlined. Questioning the validity of distinguishing between a viable fetus and one that survives for only a short period led to the view that a viable but stillborn fetus was sufficiently similar to a 'person' to allow the application of wrongful death legislation. In some cases the argument was taken further and it was suggested that more than similarities could be identified. One court, for example, declared a viable fetus to be 'biologically speaking, a presently existing person and a living human being, because it has reached such a state of development that it can presently live outside the female body . . .'.[168] As in other negligence matters, the rejection of one line of demarcation led to the abandonment of another. For some judges, viability, like birth, was an unacceptable dividing line; they

---

[168] *White v Yup* 458 P 2d 617, 622 (1969). See also *Greater Southeast Community Hospital v Williams* 482 A 2d 394, 397 (DC App, 1984) ('a viable fetus is an independent person').

felt able to conclude that a stillborn fetus, whether viable or non-viable, was entitled to the protection conferred by wrongful death legislation. The process of identifying the essential character of the fetus without reference to previously accepted criteria was seen in a dissenting judgment in the Supreme Court of Alabama: '[V]iability is an arbitrary, artificial, and varying standard that is illogical when considered against this Court's recognition . . . of the biological separateness of mother and child from the moment of conception.'[169] The justification offered for this position was that the law must recognize and protect 'potential life'. The judgment quoted with approval the view of a commentator: 'Potential life is no less potential during the first weeks of pregnancy than in the last weeks and a fetus is entitled to develop without outside interference.'[170] The decisions in which this view was adopted represented the high water mark of judicial personification of the fetus.

The Shadow of *Roe v Wade*

It is common for courts dealing with the problem of the status of the fetus in one legal context to look for assistance in other fields of law. This was seen, for example, in *Whitner v State*, which dealt with a woman charged with child abuse as a result of taking cocaine during pregnancy. There the court noted that 'it would be absurd to recognize the viable fetus as a person for purposes of homicide laws and wrongful death statutes but not for purposes of statutes proscribing child abuse'.[171] The same process operated in *Bonbrest v Kotz*[172] and other negligence cases,[173] in which judges observed that since the laws governing inheritance and abortion reflected a recognition of the existence of the fetus, they saw no reason why the law of negligence should not do likewise.

When United States cases are reviewed, there is one body of law that inevitably casts a far-reaching shadow: that dealing with abortion, and particularly the law derived from *Roe v Wade*. Many of the cases discussed in this chapter have cited this decision. Two important propositions emerge from the analysis that it offered. One is that the law will not prevent a woman from obtaining a termination of pregnancy in certain circumstances. In particular, the law will recognize the right of a woman to choose to abort a non-viable fetus. The second is that the state has an interest in protecting 'the potentiality of human life', an interest coexisting with the interest in safeguarding a pregnant woman's health. The seeming conflict between these propositions

---

[169] *Gentry v Gilmore* 613 So 2d 1241, 1249 (Ala, 1993).

[170] M. P. McCready, 'Recovery for the Wrongful Death of a Fetus' (1991) 25 University of Richmond Law Review 391, 405 (footnotes omitted).

[171] 492 SE 2d 777, 780 (SC, 1997).   [172] 65 F Supp 138 (1946).

[173] For example, *Smith v Brennan* 157 A 2d 497, 502 (1960).

has sometimes been drawn to the courts' attention. The argument in criminal proceedings has been that it is inconsistent for the state to assert an interest in protecting the fetus while at the same time permitting women who terminate their pregnancies to escape punishment. In *People v Smith*, the charge (in respect of the destruction by the father of a non-viable fetus) was laid under s 187 of the Californian Penal Code, which defined murder as including the unlawful killing of a fetus. The Californian Court of Appeal regarded it as impossible for homicide to be proved unless it could be shown that a human life had been taken. It therefore asked whether the destruction of a non-viable fetus represented the taking of life. In concluding that it did not, the court offered the following analysis:

If destruction of a non-viable fetus were susceptible to classification as the taking of human life and therefore murder, then the mother no more than the father would have the right to take human life. Yet we know from *Roe v Wade* . . . that the mother has an absolute right to destroy the fetus during the first trimester of gestation, and, under some of the language of that opinion, a right that is almost absolute to destroy the fetus during the second trimester . . . We do not believe the court intended to suggest that the mother has a constitutional right to destroy a fetus after it has become viable, but rather that the court assumed the commencement of viability at the end of the second trimester. The compelling point, said the court, is viability . . . and until viability has been reached the state has no interest in the fetus that it is entitled to protect against the wishes of the mother. The underlying rationale of *Wade*, therefore, is that until viability is reached, human life in the legal sense has not come into existence. Implicit in *Wade* is the conclusion that as a matter of constitutional law the destruction of a non-viable fetus is not a taking of human life. It follows that such destruction cannot constitute murder or other form of homicide, whether committed by a mother, a father (as here), or a third person.[174]

This was the court's way of acknowledging the principles articulated in *Roe v Wade* and simultaneously confining the operation of the law of homicide. While in some circumstances the state has an interest in protecting a non-viable fetus (which the court characterized as embodying 'only the expectancy and potentiality for human life'), such a fetus did not represent 'human life' and therefore its destruction did not amount to murder. In *State v Merrill*, the Supreme Court of Minnesota took a different view of the implications of *Roe v Wade*. The case involved an appeal against a conviction, under the State's fetal homicide statute, for the murder of an 'unborn child'. The defendant had argued that it was unacceptable for him to be exposed to a conviction for the murder of a non-viable fetus when a woman and her doctor who intentionally destroyed such a fetus would escape liability. Unlike the court in *People v Smith*, the majority held that the analysis offered in *Roe v Wade* had no relevance to the issue of an assailant's liability for the murder of a fetus:

---

[174] App, 129 Cal Rptr 498, 502 (1976) (citations omitted).

The situations are not similar. The defendant who assaults a pregnant woman causing the death of the fetus she is carrying destroys the fetus without the consent of the woman. This is not the same as the woman who elects to have her pregnancy terminated by one legally authorized to perform the act. In the case of abortion, the woman's choice and the doctor's actions are based on the woman's constitutionally protected right to privacy. This right encompasses the woman's decision whether to terminate or continue the pregnancy without interference from the state, at least until such time as the state's important interest in protecting the potentiality of human life predominates over the right to privacy which is usually at viability. . . . *Roe v Wade* protects the woman's right of choice, it does not protect, much less confer on an assailant, a third-party unilateral right to destroy the fetus.[175]

The court explained the relevance of this analysis to the charge before it:

[T]he fetal homicide statutes seek to protect the 'potentiality of human life', and they do so without impinging directly or indirectly on a pregnant woman's privacy rights. . . . The state's interest in protecting the 'potentiality of human life' includes protection of the unborn child, whether an embryo or a nonviable or viable fetus, and it protects, too, the woman's interest in her unborn child and her right to decide whether it shall be carried *in utero*. The interest of a criminal assailant in terminating a woman's pregnancy does not outweigh the woman's right to continue the pregnancy. In this context, the viability of the fetus is 'simply immaterial'.[176]

Maddox J succinctly made the same point in his dissenting judgment in the Alabama case of *Gentry v Gilmore*: '*Roe* is not implicated when . . . *both the State and the mother have congruent interests in preserving life and punishing its wrongful destruction.*'[177] Further, as was pointed out in *Brinkley v State*, the state has an interest in protecting not only the fetus, but also the woman, against the wrongdoing of a third party who can claim no right for his or her actions.[178]

Analysis of the kind seen in *Merrill* and *Gentry v Gilmore* avoids the difficulties involved in relying on *Roe* to define the nature of the fetus and the rights that the law recognizes it as possessing. It allows distinctions to be made on the basis of contextual differences and differences in the scope and purpose of the relevant laws. By focusing on these differences it is possible to accept the inconsistency of which the defendants in *Smith* and *Merrill* complained: namely, that between laws which punished a third party's destruction of a fetus and those which permitted abortion.

Similar issues arise in respect of claims arising from antenatal negligence. Some of the relevant cases have dealt with actions under Wrongful Death Acts following stillbirths. While the results reached may be questionable, the

---

[175] 450 NW 2d 318, 321–2 (Minn, 1990) (citations omitted).
[176] Ibid. 322. The quoted words are from *Smith v Newsome* 815 F 2d 1386, 1388 (11th Cir, 1987).
[177] 613 So 2d 1241, 1247 (Ala, 1993) (emphasis in original).
[178] 322 SE 2d 49, 53 (Ga, 1984).

analysis offered by a number of the judges is illuminating. In *Summerfield v Superior Court, Maricopa Cty*, the Supreme Court of Arizona addressed the submission that *Roe*'s ruling that a fetus is not a 'person' must prevent such proceedings under a Wrongful Death Act, since the legislation comes into operation only following the death of a 'person'. The submission was rejected on the ground that 'person' can mean different things in different contexts.[179] Alternatively, the argument can be put in the form that if *Roe* means that a woman is lawfully able to terminate her pregnancy in some circumstances, it is inconsistent to recognize the rights of a fetus in a wrongful death action. Occasionally this argument has succeeded. For example, in *Toth v Goree* (a case arising from the destruction of a three-month-old fetus), it was stated that:

If the mother can intentionally terminate the pregnancy at three months, without regard to the rights of the fetus, it becomes increasingly difficult to justify holding a third person liable to the fetus for unknowingly and unintentionally, but negligently, causing the pregnancy to end at that same stage. There would be an inherent conflict in giving the mother the right to terminate the pregnancy yet holding that an action may be brought on behalf of the same fetus under the wrongful death act.[180]

More commonly, this view has been rejected on the basis that the law relating to a woman's right to terminate her pregnancy has no relevance to the determination of the liability of a third party whose negligence destroys a fetus.[181] On this analysis, abortion law is concerned with the resolution of the conflict between the woman's rights and those of her fetus, while the law of negligence is concerned with the assessment of compensation when the interests of parents and their fetus have been harmed. This perspective was also well expressed by Maddox J in *Gentry v Gilmore*. His view was that *Roe* and other United States Supreme Court judgments on abortion 'do not involve the question whether the State can protect the potentiality of human life when the mother is not seeking to claim a constitutional right of privacy, but, on the contrary, is seeking to recover damages for the alleged wrongful termination of potential human life'.[182]

In the judge's view, once this distinction is made, the state's interest in protecting the potentiality of human life could properly be recognized for the

---

[179] 698 P 2d 712, 723 (Ariz, 1985).

[180] 237 NW 2d 297, 301 (1975). See also *Wallace v Wallace* NH, 421 A 2d 134, 137 (1980), which noted the seeming conflict between a law allowing a woman a right deliberately to destroy a non-viable fetus and one which makes a third party liable to a fetus for unintended negligent acts.

[181] For example, *O'Grady v Brown* 654 SW 2d 904 (Mo banc, 1983).

[182] 613 So 2d 1241, 1246–7 (Ala, 1993). Steinbock has made the same point as follows: 'Acknowledging the woman's right to have an abortion, stemming from her right to privacy, is entirely consistent with recognizing her right to be compensated when a wanted pregnancy is negligently terminated. Indeed, both prenatal wrongful-death actions and legal abortion can be seen as aspects of reproductive liberty.' See B. Steinbock, *Life before Birth: the Moral and Legal Status of Embryos and Fetuses* (New York, 1992) 102–3.

purposes of a wrongful death claim following a stillbirth. Again the judge stressed the congruence of maternal and state interests in this situation: '[T]he legislature has a right to protect nonviable fetal life when its interest is congruent with that of the mother'.[183] Although this was a dissenting opinion, it is one that has been adopted by other courts.[184] For the majority in *Gentry v Gilmore*, however, *Roe v Wade* was accepted as determining the outcome in a wrongful death case. The majority noted the importance that the Supreme Court of the United States had attached to viability. On the basis that it is only at viability that the state's interest in the protection of potential life becomes 'compelling', the majority in *Gentry v Gilmore* refused to accept that a wrongful death action could arise in respect of the destruction of a non-viable fetus. The majority thus interpreted *Roe v Wade*'s emphasis on the significance of viability as having relevance in contexts other than abortion law.

Hence there is disagreement as to the broader implications of *Roe v Wade*. Further, whatever view is adopted when a pregnant woman is not seeking to claim a right to privacy, the opinion raises difficulties in some of the situations examined in this chapter. While it indicates that the state has no business interfering in a woman's decision to terminate a pregnancy when the fetus is non-viable, it further suggests not only that the state has an interest in protecting the potentiality of human life, but also that this interest becomes 'compelling' when viability is attained. It is important not to oversimplify these rulings. Although the Supreme Court made it clear that the state has an interest in fetal protection, it did not suggest that there are circumstances in which the law may intervene to protect the viable fetus regardless of the rights of the woman. Nevertheless, even when the caution of the court's ruling is appreciated, it is apparent that there are some situations in which it might be argued that the state's interest in fetal protection justifies legal intervention against a pregnant woman, and hence an overriding of her right to privacy.

It is not intended to suggest that this analysis provides a conclusive argument in support of the view that such intervention may sometimes be justified. This subject will be further discussed in Chapter 9. At this stage, the aim is to draw attention to the possible application of the principles expressed in *Roe v Wade*. For present purposes, the question to be considered is whether it is legitimate to interpret the decision in the manner suggested. One way to escape this interpretation is to assert that *Roe v Wade* has no implications beyond the law of abortion. This view found some support in *Re Baby Boy Doe* (a case which arose from a woman's decision to decline a caesarean section). There the Appellate Court of Illinois made the following comments

---

[183] 613 So 2d 1241, 1247 (Ala, 1993).
[184] For example, *O'Grady v Brown* 654 SW 2d 904 (Mo banc, 1983).

on the submission that *Roe* implied that a viable fetus has rights which could be protected by the authorization of medical treatment:

Roe . . . merely stated that, in the context of abortion, the state's interest in the potential life of the fetus becomes compelling at the point of viability, and therefore the state is permitted to prohibit post-viability abortions, except where necessary to preserve the life or health of the woman. The fact that the state may prohibit post-viability pregnancy terminations does not translate into the proposition that the state may intrude upon the woman's right to remain free from unwanted physical invasion of her person when she chooses to carry her pregnancy to term. *Roe* and its progeny . . . make it clear that, even in the context of abortion, the state's compelling interest in the potential life of the fetus is insufficient to override the woman's interest in preserving her health.[185]

This statement is incomplete. While it is correct to say that *Roe* would not allow intervention that would threaten the woman's health, it does not necessarily follow that the state has no interest in protecting a viable fetus if this can be achieved without risk to the woman's health. To deny that the state has such an interest would be to pay insufficient attention to *Roe*'s recognition of the importance of 'protecting the potentiality of human life'. To dismiss this aspect of the decision as no more than an incidental comment made in the context of a discussion of the abortion laws is to adopt too narrow a view. It is artificial simply to ignore the possible implications of *Roe*'s recognition of the intrinsic value of the fetus. The method used in such cases as *Smith, Merrill, Gentry v Gilmore*, and *Toth v Goree* is to be preferred: these decisions attempted to come to terms with the broader ramifications of *Roe*.

CONCLUSION

When asking how the law views the fetus, the courts' starting-point has frequently been to determine whether a fetus is a 'person'. The most widely accepted view is that it is not. This conclusion, however, is unhelpful. While the law is adept at indicating what the fetus is *not*, it throws little light on what the fetus *is*. It is clear that it is not a non-entity. Whatever it is, in the words of the English Court of Appeal, it is 'not nothing'. Because they draw attention to this fact, a valuable function is performed by the United States cases that have explored the nature of the fetus and wrestled with questions relating to its personhood, the significance of viability, and the distinctive qualities of a non-viable fetus. The fact that the English, Canadian, and Australian courts have generally avoided asking such questions does not invalidate the speculation in which the United States courts have engaged. While it is possible to disagree

---

[185] 632 NE 2d 326, 334 (Ill App 1 Dist, 1994).

with many of the conclusions reached, such speculation provides a reminder that the law must take note of the existence of the fetus. The law responds to the fetus in a way that recognizes its distinctiveness and intrinsic value.

Support for this proposition is to be found in the laws restricting access to abortion. One of the functions of these laws is to protect the fetus. Reference can also be made to judicial and legislative extensions to the law of homicide: these embody the proposition that when an assailant attacks a pregnant woman and causes a stillbirth, that assailant has done more than injure a part of the woman. Further, while the operation of traditional homicide and child protection laws, and of laws imposing liability for antenatal negligence, rests on the 'born alive' rule, it is unconvincing to explain this on the basis that the fetus which suffered harm was a non-entity at the time the harm occurred. The fact that it was not a 'person' at the time is unimportant. When a murder charge is laid as a result of an antenatal attack which is followed by the live birth and death of the child, the charge rests on the assumption that, before the child's delivery, injury was caused to a specific, identifiable entity. Similarly, when a negligent doctor is held liable to pay a child damages in respect of poor antenatal or perinatal care, the basis of the action will be the doctor's failure to take proper account of the risks faced by a specific, identifiable entity. The success of the murder charge or the damages claim depends on the acceptance of a continuity: what was done to the fetus was done to a particular entity that in time becomes the person who is the subject of the proceedings. The fact that the character of the fetus changes at birth does not mean that before birth it is legally invisible. While the application of the 'born alive' rule precludes courts from asserting jurisdiction over the fetus, the rule nevertheless requires an acknowledgement of its existence. This assumption was explained by Lord Hope in *Attorney-General's Reference (No 3 of 1994)*: 'For the foetus, life lies in the future, not in the past. It is not sensible to say that it cannot ever be harmed, or that nothing can be done to it which can ever be dangerous.'[186]

A review of the case and statute law therefore suggests that the fetus is 'something', a distinct entity whose existence the law must take into account and whose claims to legal recognition become more pressing as it develops. For the purposes of this book, how the fetus is characterized is less important than the question whether this 'something' is the type of entity deserving the protection of the law.

Choosing Between Two Perspectives

Two perspectives emerge from the analysis in this chapter. Many courts (particularly those in the United States) that have heard proceedings relating to

---

[186] [1998] AC 245, 271.

fetal harm have confronted the question of the nature of the fetus. They have attempted to identify its essential characteristics, asking whether a fetus is a 'person', a 'body part', a 'potential life', or a 'life'. In answering these questions, they have frequently drawn and then discarded distinctions. If a fetus lacks personhood, does it have a good deal in common with a person? Is the similarity significant only if the fetus has the capacity for independent existence (that is, only if the fetus is viable)? Is viability unimportant, since both the viable and the non-viable fetus possess life (which begins at conception)? Posing such questions complicates the problem of identifying the nature of the fetus, since its nature may change as it develops.

In adopting this approach the courts have sought to categorize the fetus and have thus employed a *definitional* approach. The assumption seems to be that once the nature of the fetus has been identified, certain conclusions will inevitably follow as to the legal recognition to which it is entitled. A particularly clear example of the operation of this process is seen in the United States cases dealing with claims under wrongful death statutes in respect of stillbirths. These have frequently been decided on the basis that, since the relevant statutes refer to 'persons', they must be applied in the case of a stillbirth if the fetus can be categorized as a 'person'.

The alternative approach is to avoid definitional questions and to inquire about the nature and purpose of a particular law and the consequences of applying it. This method can be described as the *relational* approach. It focuses not upon the characteristics of the fetus, but upon the relationship between the woman, her fetus, and, in some situations, a third party. While this approach accepts that a fetus is a distinctive entity with intrinsic value, it recognizes that in some contexts it is appropriate for the law to intervene to protect fetal interests, but not in others. Crucial to making this distinction is an examination of the relationships between the parties to proceedings involving fetal harm. For example, a doctor or midwife caring for a pregnant woman is in a particular relationship to that woman and her fetus. The practitioner can be seen as owing a duty of care to both[187] and it is in the interests of both for there to be a possibility of a damages claim if the duty is breached. Similarly, when an assailant attacks a pregnant woman and causes a stillbirth, there is (as some courts and legislatures have recognized) no reason why that assailant should not be found guilty of an offence in respect of the destruction of the fetus. In each of these illustrations, there is a particular relationship between the woman, her fetus, and a third party. From this perspective, it is a consideration of the nature of that *relationship*, rather than of the nature and characteristics of the *fetus*, which determines whether it is appropriate for the law to acknowledge the existence of the fetus and the harm done to it.

---

[187] Whether this is so is more fully examined in Chapter 10.

This is the approach employed in cases such as *Merrill* and *Gentry v Gilmore*. These, while taking account of *Roe*'s recognition of a state interest in protecting potential life, went on to make distinctions on the basis of context and the nature of the relationships involved. In *Merrill*, the court implied that the fact that the state permits the destruction of potential life in one context (abortion) does not mean that it will permit in another (an attack on a pregnant woman). It pointed out that an assailant who destroys a fetus without the woman's consent cannot rely on principles applicable in the wholly different context arising when a woman chooses to have a lawful abortion. In one situation, the state's interest is in protecting both the woman and her fetus against the wrongdoing of a third party: their interests are 'congruent'. In the other, the state's concern is either with the regulation or the facilitation of the woman's exercise of her power of choice. Similarly, in *Gentry v Gilmore*, the dissenting judgment emphasized that the issue in a wrongful death action—whether damages were recoverable on behalf of a fetus—is quite different from that with which the law must deal in determining when a woman should be free to choose an abortion. Both cases suggest that it is appropriate for the state to pursue its interest in protecting potential life in one situation but not in another. This result is not possible if the debate is conducted on the basis of a definitional approach, focusing solely on whether the fetus is or is not potential life or is or is not a 'person'.

To adopt the relational perspective is to redefine the nature of the problem. The goal is no longer agreement as to the essential characteristics of the fetus and consequent agreement as to the rights possessed by an entity with those characteristics. There are two reasons for abandoning this goal. Consensus on the categorization of the fetus is unlikely. Further, to pursue consensus is to misunderstand the dilemma faced by the law. In *Tremblay v Daigle*, the Supreme Court of Canada made this point clear in commenting on the commonest of the definitional approaches: 'Ascribing personhood to a foetus in law is a fundamentally normative task. It results in the recognition of rights and duties—a matter which falls outside the concerns of scientific classification.'[188]

The reference to 'scientific classification' identifies the deficiencies of the definitional perspective. A system of classification aims to produce certainty. Given the normative character of the law, certainty is unattainable. The relational approach recognizes this and thus accommodates the inconsistencies in the law's perception of the legal status of the fetus. This approach does not seek consistency. It acknowledges that lawmakers will respond differently to claims made on behalf of the fetus, depending on the context, the actors involved, their relationships, and the techniques and purposes embodied in the particular law invoked. Some observers will regard the law's lack of

---

[188] (1989) 62 DLR (4th) 634, 650.

consistency as a strength. It allows for flexibility of response when there is the possibility of legal intervention to protect the fetus or to provide recompense for harm done to it. It allows questions to be asked about the proper role and limits of the law. To others, this flexibility will be seen as manifesting an unprincipled refusal to acknowledge the true nature of the fetus. It is beyond the scope of this chapter to explore the deeper moral and ethical issues raised by this debate. My purpose has been to examine the operation of the law in an attempt to discover how courts and legislatures have viewed the fetus. This examination suggests that it is fruitless to seek a once-and-for-all definition of the nature of the fetus and that therefore the relational perspective is to be preferred.

This perspective accepts the conclusion that in some circumstances the law will permit a woman intentionally to destroy her fetus, while in others it will award damages against a person who negligently injures a fetus. Any attempt to avoid such inconsistency is unlikely to succeed. The only course that can realistically be adopted is to seek principles explaining the law's varying responses to claims made on behalf of the fetus. In the context of abortion law, reliance can be placed on concepts such as a woman's right to privacy and, consequently, on her right to control her own fertility. In the context of the criminal law, the debate can focus on the propriety of extending the operation of the laws prohibiting homicide and assault in an attempt to protect the fetus. In the context of the law of torts, the issue is whether compensation is properly payable by those who cause antenatal harm. In all these situations, the question is not what the fetus is or is not, but whether the law can appropriately recognize and protect its interests. The point was cogently made by a New Hampshire judge in a wrongful death action:

The real question is not when life begins but rather, whether our death statute should be construed to allow a cause of action on behalf of a fetus that has not drawn a breath of air, seen the light of day, or possessed the capacity to survive in the world outside its mother ... To deny a nonviable fetus a cause of action is not to deny that life begins with conception. It is simply a policy determination that the law will not extend civil liability by giving a nonviable fetus a cause of action for negligence before it becomes a person ... [L]ife may begin with conception but causes of action do not.[189]

Thus it is necessary to go beyond the conclusion that the fetus is not a legal nonentity and, because it represents potential life, has intrinsic value. It must also be recognized that the fetus does not have a uniform value in the eyes of the law. The law makes choices as to the situations in which it will take account of actual or threatened antenatal harm. This raises an obvious question. In what circumstances—and against whom—should the law protect the fetus? This is one of the most important questions posed in this book. In particular—given the suggested relational perspective—it must be asked

[189] *Wallace v Wallace* NH, 421 A 2d 134, 136–7 (1980).

whether the nature of the relationship between a pregnant woman and her fetus means that the law should refuse to accept that she can ever owe a legal obligation to her fetus. This question will initially be addressed in Chapter 9, where I ask whether criminal or child protection laws should be used against a pregnant woman in an attempt to protect her fetus and whether the same aim should be pursued by allowing courts to order medical treatment. In Chapter 11, I ask whether the nature of the maternal/fetal relationship is such as to preclude a child from bringing a damages action against his or her mother on the basis of negligently caused antenatal harm.

9

A Question of Autonomy?

Chapter 2 discussed various situations in which the conduct of a pregnant woman might pose a risk to the fetus. The chapter showed how the law responded to requests for legal intervention to protect the fetus when, for example, the woman had taken drugs or alcohol or had declined to accept recommended medical treatment. Some of the issues raised by proceedings of this kind were considered in Chapter 8, which analysed the legal status of the fetus. Judges and legislators have given differing answers to the question whether it is entitled to legal protection. These answers have been partly determined by the context in which the law has been invoked. The purpose of the present chapter is further to explore the significance of context, particularly that created by the relationship between a pregnant woman and her fetus. The aim is to determine whether a pregnant woman should be immune from legal intervention when her conduct threatens or has harmed her fetus. Thus this chapter complements Chapter 8, where I argued that it is unsatisfactory to answer all questions relating to the appropriateness of legal intervention to protect a fetus by denying that it exists and has intrinsic value. This conclusion was the first step in the analysis. This chapter—adopting the relational perspective—seeks to complete the picture by addressing the legal implications of the special bond between a pregnant woman and her fetus.

THE PREGNANT WOMAN AND HER FETUS: ONE ENTITY OR TWO?

Three Models

One way of illuminating the nature of the maternal/fetal relationship is to consider three models of that relationship. A pregnant woman and her fetus can be seen as one entity. On this analysis the fetus is simply a part of the woman's body. Alternatively, the woman and her fetus can be regarded as separate entities. Between these two extremes is the view that the woman and her fetus are separate, but indivisibly linked.

Although much of the feminist literature discusses the body-part model, it is difficult to find many commentators who have unequivocally adopted it. Rothman has done so, referring to 'the baby not planted within the mother, but flesh of her flesh, part of her'.[1] While such a statement may seem

[1] B. K. Rothman, *Recreating Motherhood: Ideology and Technology in a Patriarchal Society* (New York, 1989) 161.

straightforward, semantic problems arise when we scrutinize it. In one sense, the assertion is incontrovertible: clearly a fetus is a part of a woman's body, since it is contained within her body. This use of language is the same as that employed when a room is described as part of a house. If this is what is meant by the body-part model, it does no more than state the obvious, that a fetus does not have a separate, independent existence. Yet the model might imply more than this and reflect the view that a fetus is merely a body part, with the result that woman and fetus are one entity. This is to deny the distinctiveness of the fetus.

The second model—that woman and fetus are separate entities—has been adopted by many obstetricians. It has been said, for example, that: 'When an obstetrician agrees to take on a pregnant woman as a patient, he actually acquires two patients: mother and baby.'[2] The medical perception of the relationship between a woman and her fetus may have been reinforced by recent developments in medicine. The growth of ultrasound imaging, amniocentesis, fetal heart monitoring, and *in utero* therapy and surgery can all be seen as contributing to the notion of the fetus as a separate entity:

The technological limitations of medicine once dictated the treatment of the pregnant woman and her unborn child as a single medical entity. The increasing ability to diagnose and treat the fetus and the greater awareness of the effects of maternal conduct on fetal health, however, have led doctors to perceive the fetus as an individual patient with needs distinct from those of its mother.[3]

The third model—referred to as 'not-one-but-not-two'[4]—emerges directly from the analysis of the first two. Its key feature is its emphasis on the shared needs and interdependence of the woman and her fetus, whose relationship is seen as characterized by '[c]onnectedness, mutuality, and reciprocity'.[5] There is no simple way of explaining the resulting model: 'Even to speak of the pre-birth period as one of mother–child "interdependence" does not begin to do justice to the experiential reality of pregnancy as a state of being that is neither unitary nor dual, exactly; a state to which we can apply no number known to us.'[6] This stresses the uniqueness of pregnancy: while the woman and her fetus are intimately connected, the fetus embodies potential life and will have a separate existence. In Dworkin's words: 'Her fetus is not merely "in her" as an inanimate object might be, or something alive but alien

---

[2] *Ledford v Martin* 359 SE 2d 505, 507 (NC App, 1987).

[3] 'Developments in the Law, Medical Technology and the Law' (1990) 103 Harvard Law Review 1519, 1556.

[4] I. Karpin, 'Legislating the Female Body: Reproductive Technology and the Reconstructed Woman' (1992) 3 Columbia Journal of Gender and Law 325, 329.

[5] K. De Gama, 'A Brave New World? Rights Discourse and the Politics of Reproductive Autonomy' (1993) 20 Journal of Law and Society 114, 115.

[6] M. Ashe, 'Law-Language of Maternity: Discourse Holding Nature in Contempt' (1988) 22 New England Law Review 521, 551.

that has been transplanted into her body. It is "of her and is hers more than anyone's" because it is, more than anyone else's, her creation and her responsibility; it is alive because *she* has made it come alive.'[7]

Assessing the Three Models

Part of the Woman's Body

The view that a fetus is no more than part of the woman's body cannot be reconciled with the physiological facts. As MacKinnon has noted, unlike a body part, the fetus is the result of a sexual relationship. She writes:

Physically, no body part takes as much and contributes as little. The fetus does not exist to serve the woman as her body parts do. The relation is more the other way around; on the biological level, the fetus is more like a parasite than a part. The woman's physical relation to her fetus is expected to end and does; when it does, her body still has all of its parts. She is whole with it or without it . . . Fetal dependence upon the pregnant woman does not make the fetus a part of her any more than fully dependent adults are parts of those on whom they are dependent. The fetus is a unique kind of whole that, after a certain point, can live or die without the mother. Whatever credibility the body part analogy has evaporates at the moment of viability. . . . No other body part gets up and walks away on its own eventually.[8]

Further, as Kluge has observed: '[T]he fetus, inclusive of its supportive placenta, is not a biological part of the mother. It is both physiologically and genetically a distinct organism, having its own physiological integrity, genetic code, etc.'[9] A similar point was made by King, who states that the fetus 'is *genetically* a separate entity from a point at or near conception'.[10]

The courts do not now adopt the body-part model. As was seen in Chapter 8, United States courts initially followed Holmes J's ruling in *Dietrich* that a fetus was no more than a part of the mother. In time this view was rejected and the distinctiveness of the fetus was acknowledged.[11] In England, the body-part analysis proved more enduring. In 1974, the Law Commission accepted 'the fact of physical identification of mother and foetus'.[12] A challenge to this assumption came in the decision of the House of Lords in *Attorney-General's Reference (No 3 of 1994)*,[13] a case arising from an attack

---

[7] R. Dworkin, *Life's Dominion. An Argument About Abortion and Euthanasia* (New York, 1993) 55 (emphasis in original). The quoted words are taken from C. A. MacKinnon, 'Reflections on Sex Equality under Law' (1991) 100 Yale Law Journal 1281, 1316.

[8] C. A. MacKinnon, ibid. 1314–15.

[9] E-H. W. Kluge, 'When Caesarian Section Operations Imposed by a Court are Justified' (1988) 14 Journal of Medical Ethics 206, 208.

[10] P. A. King, 'The Juridical Status of the Fetus: a Proposal for Legal Protection of the Unborn' (1979) 77 Michigan Law Review 1647, 1660 (emphasis in original).

[11] See above 156–8.

[12] Law Commission, *Report on Injuries to Unborn Children* (Law Com No 60, 1974) para 33.

[13] [1998] AC 245.

on a pregnant woman. In reaching its decision, the House considered the following ruling by the Court of Appeal:

In the eyes of the law the foetus is taken to be a part of the mother until it has an existence independent of the mother. Thus an intention to cause serious bodily injury to the foetus is an intention to cause serious bodily injury to a part of the mother just as an intention to injure her arm or leg would be so viewed.[14]

Lord Mustill rejected this:

[The baby] and her mother were closely related but, even apart from differing environmental influences, they were not, had not been, and in the future never would be 'the same'. There was, of course, an intimate bond between the foetus and the mother, created by the total dependence of the foetus on the protective physical environment furnished by the mother.... But the relationship was one of bond, not of identity. The mother and the foetus were two distinct organisms living symbiotically, not a single organism with two aspects. The mother's leg was part of the mother; the foetus was not.[15]

Similarly, Lord Hope stated:

The Court of Appeal ... held that a foetus before birth must be taken to be an integral part of the mother, in the same way as her arm or leg. . . . I am not satisfied that this is the correct approach. The creation of an embryo from which a foetus is developed requires the bringing together of genetic material from the father as well as from the mother. The science of human fertilisation and embryology has now been developed to the point where the embryo may be created outside the mother and then placed inside her as a live embryo. This practice ... serves to remind us that an embryo is in reality a separate organism from the mother from the moment of its conception. This individuality is retained by it throughout its development until it achieves an independent existence on being born. So the foetus cannot be regarded as an integral part of the mother in the sense indicated by the Court of Appeal, notwithstanding its dependence upon the mother for its survival until birth.[16]

This view was echoed in the ruling by the Court of Appeal, in *St George's Healthcare NHS Trust v S*, that 'the interests of the foetus cannot be disregarded on the basis that in refusing treatment that would benefit the foetus a mother is simply refusing treatment for herself'.[17]

In Canada, however, the body-part model has received some support. In *Winnipeg Child and Family Services (Northwest Area) v G*, the majority of the Supreme Court of Canada had no doubt that 'the law has always treated the mother and unborn child as one'.[18] The court was dealing with the question whether a pregnant woman could be guilty of tortious conduct towards her fetus.[19] In ruling that she could not, the majority expressly adopted the body-part model: 'To sue a pregnant woman on behalf of her unborn foetus

---

[14] [1996] 2 WLR 412, 422.   [15] [1998] AC 245, 255.   [16] Ibid. 267.
[17] [1998] 3 WLR 936, 953.   [18] (1997) 152 DLR (4th) 193, 207.   [19] See below 285.

therefore posits the anomaly of one part of a legal and physical entity suing itself.'[20] It is not clear whether this statement should be interpreted as applying only to the particular context in which it was made. If not, it suggests that the body-part model is likely to continue to be a feature of Canadian law.

Some would argue that this model should be retained. Their concern is that any questioning of it will undermine the autonomy of a pregnant woman. If the first priority is the preservation of a pregnant woman's freedom of choice, the attractions of regarding a fetus as a part of her body are obvious. Once a fetus is defined in this way, no question arises of its having interests which the law might safeguard. The woman's freedom is absolute, because any decisions which she makes, and any conduct in which she engages, cannot have effects which extend beyond her own body. This conclusion provides a complete answer to any attempts by the law to interfere with a pregnant woman's right to self-determination.

This analysis is flawed, since it employs too narrow a focus. Its deficiency is that it regards the adoption of an artificial definition of the fetus as being necessary to preserve maternal autonomy. As has been shown in Chapter 8, this approach should be avoided. There it was suggested that the law's response to the fetus can be determined on the basis of the context in which the law is being invoked rather than on the basis of a definitive characterization of the nature of the fetus. One of the illustrations used was the problem posed by a criminal assault causing the destruction of a pregnant woman's fetus. If the fetus is regarded as no more than a body part (and its destruction treated as no more than an assault on her), it is impossible for the law to respond to the real nature of the harm caused. It was the realization of the artificiality of such an approach that led the House of Lords to reject the view that an intention to cause serious bodily injury to a fetus is an intention to cause serious bodily injury to a part of the mother and so is indistinguishable from an intention to injure her arm or leg. Similarly, the body-part fiction cannot prevail in the face of the case law (reviewed in Chapters 4 and 5) which recognizes the right of a child to claim damages in respect of negligent antenatal injury. It is impossible to view the fetus as an entity that develops into a person who can assert an independent cause of action, while at the same time claiming that the negligence has done no more than harm a part of the woman's body.

To shackle the law by adhering to the body-part model is to pay an unnecessary price for the preservation of maternal autonomy. To adopt the analysis employed in *Gentry v Gilmore*,[21] when a criminal attack on a pregnant woman has led to a miscarriage, the law can respond to the destruction of the fetus on the basis that the woman's interests and those of the fetus are

---

[20] (1997) 152 DLR (4th) 193, 207. See also *Dobson (Litigation Guardian of) v Dobson* (1999) 174 DLR (4th) 1, where it was held that a child could not sue his mother in respect of injuries caused by her negligent driving before he was born.

[21] See above 180.

congruent. Equally, it is in the woman's interests for a child negligently injured *in utero* to be able to sue for damages. In situations in which the claims of the woman and the fetus might be in conflict (such as when medical treatment is refused), a different approach can be adopted and the interests of the fetus given little or no weight. This does not make it any easier to decide whether the woman's interests should always prevail over those of the fetus in such a situation, but it leaves the question to be answered on its merits rather than being determined on the basis of an artificial characterization of the nature of a fetus. If the fetus is acknowledged as having inchoate interests that the law can protect in some circumstances but not in others, the resolution of the problem posed by a possible conflict between those interests and the pregnant woman's autonomy interests will be explicitly addressed. If the fetus is dismissed as a body part, the problem will be ignored.

The body-part model must therefore be rejected, not only because it is inherently unsatisfactory, but also because it relies on a fiction that precludes (or severely hinders) the fashioning of appropriate legal responses when harm is caused to a fetus. A preoccupation with the pregnant woman's autonomy should not be allowed to stand in the way of legal intervention against persons other than the woman. Far from ignoring the woman's interests, laws permitting actions against third parties foster those interests. A legal system that acknowledges the distinctiveness of the fetus can in some circumstances confer benefits on the woman.

Separate Entities

One response to criticism of the body-part model is to concede its artificiality and to assert that to recognize the distinctive nature of the fetus it is necessary to view a pregnant woman and her fetus as separate entities, each with a range of rights. Such an analysis could, for example, be employed in the context of a pregnant woman's decision to decline medical intervention. Here, the fetus could be regarded as an individual patient with needs distinct from those of its mother. The same analysis could be applied to justify child protection proceedings in a case involving illicit drug use by a pregnant woman: the fetus could be seen as an entity entitled to the law's protection against the threat posed by the drug taking.

In both situations, the dilemma created by adopting the separate entities model is immediately apparent. As will be shown, the woman has certain autonomy rights. If the fetus is envisaged as a separate entity—also with rights—the potential for conflict is clear. In some circumstances, a choice must be made between the woman's rights and those of the fetus. Those who focus on the woman stress that any recognition of fetal rights will diminish her autonomy. One set of rights must be pitted or, at least, weighed against the other. In MacKinnon's words: '[T]he only point of recognizing fetal personhood, or a separate fetal entity, is to assert the interests of the fetus *against* the pregnant woman.'[22] While this is an overstatement—since there is nothing to prevent the recognition of fetal interests which may be asserted against all persons *except* the pregnant woman—the comment does identify possible implications of the separate entities model. If the rights of the fetus and those of the pregnant woman are seen as being opposed, one must 'win' and the other must 'lose'. If the rights of the fetus prevail, this will inevitably lead to the diminution of some of the woman's rights. The more the individuality of the fetus is stressed, the less the individuality of the woman is recognized: 'As the characteristics of personhood are increasingly attributed to the fetus, so the characteristics of personhood belonging to the mother are correspondingly devalued.'[23]

On this analysis, adopting the separate entities model reduces the woman to a 'container' or 'incubator', with the result that she is devalued and her interests disregarded.[24] The use of ultrasound imaging reinforces this perception and so affects the way the pregnant woman is viewed: 'Feminist critics emphasise the degrading impact fetal-imaging techniques have on the pregnant woman. She now becomes the "maternal environment", the "site" of the fetus, a passive spectator in her own pregnancy.'[25] This, in its turn, can lead to the perception of the fetus as an entity requiring protection, an attitude that will encourage the exercise of control over the woman. This process has been identified as: 'wresting control of the "endangered" fetus from the woman and removing it to a place of masculine scrutiny and control—the clinic, the laboratory, and, if need be, the courtroom.'[26] The assertion of such control is thus seen as a direct result of ascribing rights to the fetus. The consequence can be the overriding of the woman's rights: 'That fetal rights threaten and in fact supersede women's autonomy is most clearly shown in the occurrence of coerced caesarean section where women have been legally constrained to have the operation on the grounds that the fetus required it.'[27] This underlines the political implications of the debate about the way in which the relationship between a woman and her fetus is defined. The issue is whether control should ever be exercised over pregnant women. To exercise control is to deny autonomy: '[S]o long as pregnant woman and foetus are constructed as separate, and rights remain the foundation of legal

---

[22] C. A. MacKinnon, 'Reflections on Sex Equality Under Law' (1991) 100 Yale Law Journal 1281, 1315 (emphasis in original).

[23] B. Bennett, 'Pregnant Women and the Duty to Rescue: a Feminist Response to the Fetal Rights Debate' (1991) 9 Law in Context 70, 85.

[24] G. J. Annas, 'Pregnant Women as Fetal Containers' (1986) 16(6) Hastings Center Report 13, 14.

[25] R. P. Petchesky, 'Fetal Images: the Power of Visual Culture in the Politics of Reproduction' (1987) 13 Feminist Studies 263, 277.

[26] I. Karpin, 'Legislating the Female Body: Reproductive Technology and the Reconstructed Woman' (1992) 3 Columbia Journal of Gender and Law 325, 333–4.

[27] R. Rowland, *Living Laboratories: Women and Reproductive Technologies* (Bloomington, 1992) 123.

protection, the door remains open for foetal rights arguments, which speak in the language of child protection, but sound more loudly in the language of controlling women.'[28] From this perspective, 'The real question posed by the "fetal rights" phenomenon has much less to do with the status of the fetus than with the status of women.'[29]

For some commentators, a tendency to control pregnant women is characteristic of a male-dominated medical profession. This perspective is inseparable from a concern about the 'medicalization' of childbirth.[30] Many regard control over the care of pregnant women as having passed into the hands of a medical profession dominated by male attitudes. These attitudes, it is argued, predispose doctors to support intervention and intervention is more readily justified if the fetus can be viewed as a separate entity, possessing rights which need to be safeguarded. Providing the necessary protection demands the imposition of controls over pregnant women; adopting such a position can be seen as characteristic of a patriarchy.[31] On this analysis, patriarchal values, medicalization, and the separate entities model form part of a single pattern of thought: 'The medical model of pregnancy . . . encourages the physician to view the fetus and mother as two separate patients, and to see pregnancy as inherently a conflict of interests between the two.'[32]

Some might argue that the fact that the separate entities model sets the scene for a conflict between a pregnant woman and her fetus is a sufficient ground for rejecting it: a competent woman's autonomy must be preserved, the recognition of the separate existence of the fetus (with the consequent ascription of rights to it) endangers this autonomy and so must be avoided if the woman's interests are not to be devalued. While concern about this conflict is valid, the implication is that any legal intervention designed to exert control over a pregnant woman is *ex hypothesi* unacceptable. This line of reasoning is unsatisfactory. As will be shown later in the chapter, the problem requires a more sophisticated analysis.

Those who accept the separate entities model concede that its adoption would open up the possibility of conflict between the pregnant woman and her fetus. They see this conflict as unavoidable and assert that in some circumstances it should be resolved in favour of the fetus. They thus urge the acknowledgement of fetal rights that the law can protect, even at the expense of the woman's rights. One commentator has suggested that a fetus should

[28] A. Diduck, 'Child Protection and Foetal Rights in Canada' (1993) 5 Journal of Child Law 133, 136.

[29] J. Gallagher, 'Fetal Personhood and Women's Policy', in V. Sapiro (ed.), *Women, Biology, and Public Policy* (Beverly Hills, 1985) 91, 110–11.

[30] See below 304–6.

[31] B. K. Rothman, *Recreating Motherhood: Ideology and Technology in a Patriarchal Society* (New York, 1989) 158.

[32] B. K. Rothman, 'Commentary' (1986) 16(1) Hastings Center Report 25.

be entitled to rights and legal protection 'analogous' to those conferred on a child:

Since the unborn child has health needs and vulnerabilities analogous to those of children, and since between the child when unborn and after birth there is continuity in all essential respects, then it would seem logical and just to assign to parents duties to their unborn children analogous (when applicable) to those they have to their children, and to recognize in unborn children analogous rights (when applicable) to those already granted to children.[33]

The difficulty with this approach is its assumption that the rights of a fetus can be identified by reference to those possessed by a legal person. This assumption is inconsistent with the rulings made in many of the cases discussed in Chapter 8. These denied that a fetus can be equated with a person. Thus the problem becomes the definition of fetal rights in such a way as to take account of the special nature of the fetus. United States courts have occasionally accepted that a child has 'a legal right to begin life with a sound mind and body'.[34] The significance of this is difficult to determine. A right of this kind has been recognized in actions in which third parties have been sued for antenatal negligence which caused harm to a fetus subsequently born alive. The statements identifying a right to be born 'with a sound mind and body' may represent no more than an attempt to underline the fact that it is not only the pregnant woman who may be harmed by negligent conduct, but also the fetus whose injuries become apparent at birth.[35] On this analysis, such statements are relevant in one context only and cannot be interpreted as recognizing a fetal right that the law will endeavour to protect in all situations.

Nevertheless, recognizing a right to be born unaffected by wrongfully caused injury—and, perhaps, a consequent recognition of the separate entities model—is sometimes implicit in the cases discussed earlier in this book. The actions in which the compulsory treatment of pregnant women has been authorized can be interpreted as recognizing, if not a right to be born healthy, at least a right not to be harmed by maternal conduct. In some of these matters, the fetus was treated as representing 'life' and having 'a right to live'; one judgment went so far as to state that the fetus could be regarded as a human being for the purposes of the proceedings.[36] These illustrations of courts employing the separate entities model have, however, been challenged. In England, in *Re MB (Medical Treatment)*,[37] the Court of

---

[33] E. W. Keyserlingk, *The Unborn Child's Right to Prenatal Care. A Comparative Law Perspective* (Montreal, 1984) 103.

[34] *Smith v Brennan* 157 A 2d 497, 503 (1960); *Womack v Buchhorn* 187 NW 2d 218, 222 (1971).

[35] *Stallman v Youngquist* 531 NE 2d 355, 359 (Ill, 1988); this view was also adopted in *Re Baby Boy Doe* 632 NE 2d 326, 332 (Ill App 1 Dist, 1994).

[36] See above 154–5.   [37] [1997] 2 FLR 426.

Appeal ruled that a fetus does not have interests which must be taken into account in determining whether a caesarean section should be performed. Similarly, in *Re Baby Boy Doe*, the Appellate Court of Illinois, while conceding that 'a fetus is not treated as only a part of its mother', refused to accept that it was an entity whose interests should be balanced against those of the pregnant woman in order to determine whether a caesarean section should be authorized.[38]

In the context of criminal or child protection proceedings, the courts have shown little willingness to treat a pregnant woman and her fetus as separate entities. The decisions discussed in Chapter 2 indicate that the argument that a fetus should be treated in either of these contexts as being entitled to separate protection has generally failed. While a small number of legislatures have enacted criminal and child protection statutes which apply to fetuses (most notably, Acts extending the definition of the crime of homicide or creating new crimes such as feticide or the killing of an 'unborn child'), it would be unwise to conclude that this represents a significant trend towards the adoption of the separate entities model.

The cases dealing with damages claims in respect of antenatal negligence present a more complex picture. As was seen in Chapter 8, many of the relevant United States decisions have expressly stated that the mother and fetus are two entities and that a duty of care is owed to each. English courts have not found it necessary to treat the fetus as a separate entity in order to award damages for *in utero* injury. The Congenital Disabilities (Civil Liability) Act 1976 (UK) is consistent with this approach. By refusing to recognize the possibility of a breach of a duty of care owed to the fetus, the Act rejected the separate entities model. The Canadian and Australian courts have also seen no need to adopt the model, although the unusual case of *Cherry v Borsman* may contain a hint of its acceptance. There, in dealing with a case arising from injury caused to a child by a failed termination procedure, the British Columbia Court of Appeal seemed to recognize that the fetus is separate: 'We think that a surgeon on performing an abortion in a case such as this owes a duty of care to the mother to perform his task properly but at the same time owes a duty of care to the foetus not to harm it if he should fail in meeting the duty of care he owes to the mother.'[39] The more recent decision in *Winnipeg Child and Family Services (Northwest Area) v G*[40] may, however, indicate that analysis of this kind has no place in Canadian law.

The conclusions to be drawn from a review of the law's willingness to accept the separate entities model are, therefore, unclear. In the context of negligence actions, United States courts have regularly recognized the model. They have also occasionally done so in the context of medical treatment

---

[38] 632 NE 2d 326, 330, 332 (Ill App 1 Dist, 1994). [39] (1992) 94 DLR (4th) 487, 504.
[40] (1997) 152 DLR (4th) 193: see above 192.

cases. Decisions in cases in which the criminal law or child protection law has been invoked have generally refused to employ the separate entities model. There is no English authority for the recognition of the separateness of the fetus, although the rulings in the *Attorney-General's Reference* case and *St George's Healthcare NHS Trust v S* that it is not a part of the mother's body may represent a move in that direction. *Re MB* refused to recognize the fetus as an entity whose interests could be taken into account. The separate entities model finds little or no support in Canadian and Australian decisions. In the United States, Australia, and Canada, there has been limited statutory recognition of the model in child protection and criminal legislation. The analysis will not be taken further at this stage. All that can be said is that the model has found uncertain support from some courts and legislatures.

'Not-One-But-Not-Two'

The strength of the third model lies in its recognition of the nature of the maternal/fetal relationship and hence in its ability to accommodate the conclusion that a fetus has inchoate interests, but that these interests should be promoted in such a way as to acknowledge the rights of the woman. It thus seeks to avoid the oversimplifications implicit in both the single entity and the separate entities models. In particular, it replaces the latter's emphasis on separateness and conflict with the identification of the importance of the interdependence of a woman and her fetus. This can be seen as the adoption of a characteristically female view of the relationship. Underlying this analysis is an acceptance of the distinction that some feminist theorists make between female and male patterns of thought.[41] Those who make the distinction highlight women's tendency to stress their intimate connection with others: 'This "sense of connection" is the source of different women's values, different ways of "knowing", and different moral reasoning.'[42] The validity of this theory will not be explored. It has been referred to here because it suggests an underlying difference between the 'not-one-but-not-two' model and the separate entities model. For those who accept the existence of distinctively male and female perceptions, the separate entities model reveals a male view, which sees the world in terms of separateness, autonomy, and individuality. Commitment to this perspective leads to a preoccupation with rights and so creates the possibility of a conflict between the rights of the woman and those of her fetus. A different model emerges

---

[41] C. Gilligan, *In a Different Voice: Psychological Theory and Women's Development* (Cambridge, Mass, 1982); R. West, 'Jurisprudence and Gender' (1988) 55 University of Chicago Law Review 1; S. Noonan, 'Theorizing Connection' (1992) 30 Alberta Law Review 719.

[42] L. Close, *Doctor Knows Best? A Critique of Court-Ordered Caesarean Section* (Research Paper, Australian National University Law Faculty, 1993) 15.

from a world-view taking connectedness and interdependence as its starting-point.

While the single entity model forecloses the possibility of intervention on behalf of the fetus, and the separate entities model invites it, the 'not-one-but-not-two' model does neither. It permits the recognition of the fetus as a distinctive entity, but it also embodies a reminder of the relationship existing between the pregnant woman and her fetus. In so doing, it can accommodate the view (outlined in Chapter 8) that one way of determining whether the law should intervene to protect the fetus is to appreciate the context in which the intervention is being considered. It might, for example, be appropriate for the law to punish a third party for an attack on a pregnant woman that destroys her fetus, but for it to take a different view of a woman's decision to terminate her pregnancy. The strength of the 'not-one-but-not-two' model therefore lies in its reminder that the interests of the woman and her fetus cannot be viewed in isolation. It allows the recognition of fetal interests, while at the same time providing a basis on which to make discriminating decisions as to the circumstances in which the law should intervene to protect those interests.

There is some implicit judicial support for the 'not-one-but-not-two' model. The relevant cases have been discussed in Chapter 8. In a number of these, courts have rejected the argument that laws permitting abortions are incompatible with other laws punishing third parties who injure or harm fetuses. In doing so, they have indirectly acknowledged that the relationship between a woman and her fetus compels the conclusion that in certain circumstances her decision to terminate a pregnancy is none of the law's business. On this view, such a decision must be accepted as a manifestation of a right to privacy, a right that becomes relevant only because the woman's connection with her fetus is so close. More obliquely, there was a recognition of the relationship in the cases in which courts refused to allow child protection laws to be used to impose controls on a pregnant woman in an attempt to protect her fetus. These decisions reflected the opinion that the imposition of such controls would impinge too greatly on the rights of the pregnant woman. In these circumstances, therefore, the courts have suggested that the interests of the fetus could not be examined in isolation.

Nevertheless, it is rare for the courts explicitly to adopt something resembling the 'not-one-but-not-two' model. One illustration was provided by the judgment in *Stallman v Youngquist*, where the Supreme Court of Illinois rejected the argument that a child born suffering the ill-effects of her mother's antenatal negligence could sue her for damages:

It would be a legal fiction to treat the fetus as a separate legal person with rights hostile to and assertable against its mother. The relationship between a pregnant woman and her fetus is unlike the relationship between any other plaintiff and defendant. No other plaintiff depends exclusively on any other defendant for everything necessary for life itself. No other defendant must go through biological changes of the most profound type, possibly at the risk of her own life, in order to bring forth an adversary into the world.[43]

Another example was seen in *Attorney-General's Reference (No 3 of 1994)*, where Lord Mustill suggested that a fetus is 'an organism sui generis lacking . . . the entire range of characteristics both of the mother to which it is physically linked and of the complete human being which it will later become'. He added: 'I would . . . reject the reasoning which assumes that since (in the eyes of English law) the foetus does not have the attributes which make it a "person" it must be an adjunct of the mother. . . . [T]he foetus is neither. It is a unique organism.'[44]

That the fetus is a 'unique organism'—a potential human life, although not an entity possessing rights—has been most clearly recognized in the cases involving damages claims for antenatal negligence by third parties. While some United States courts have postulated the existence of separate entities in order to allow such claims, courts in England, Canada, and Australia have not done so. Instead, they have treated the fetus as a special sort of entity with contingent interests that crystallize on live birth. This is consistent with the 'not-one-but-not-two' model: the fetus has the potential to acquire rights (and so the pregnant woman and her fetus are not 'one'), but it does not actually possess rights (and so the pregnant woman and her fetus are not 'two'). Similarly, while the law is reluctant to take action against a pregnant drug user in order to protect the fetus, it is equally unwilling to treat her drug taking as behaviour affecting her alone. The harm done to the fetus can be taken into account in care proceedings initiated after the child is born. Legal responses of this kind suggest that a pregnant woman and her fetus are something more than 'one', but not yet 'two'. Because the fetus has a special status, account can be taken of actions which will have consequences after its birth, but this is not done in order to suggest its separateness. Thus much of the law reflects the uncertainty expressed in the formula 'not-one-but-not-two': a pregnant woman and her fetus represent two sets of overlapping interests possessed by two peculiarly interdependent entities.

This model has the virtue of flexibility. It recognizes the existence and value of the fetus, but does so in a way that denies its separateness and so makes it unnecessary to assume that pregnancy involves a conflict between two competing entities. It also enables the woman's interests to be taken into account. The model's recognition of the relationship between a pregnant woman and her fetus sets the scene for the protection of fetal interests when these are threatened or harmed by a third party, but may produce a different

---

[43]   531 NE 2d 355, 360 (Ill, 1988).
[44]   [1998] AC 245, 255–6. See also the discussion of the implications of *Stallman v Youngquist* 531 NE 2d 355 (Ill, 1988) in *Re Baby Boy Doe* 632 NE 2d 326, 331–2 (Ill App 1 Dist, 1994).

result when they are threatened or harmed by the woman. The model thus offers a middle ground. It avoids the rigidity and oversimplification implicit in the single-entity and separate-entities models. It provides a framework within which a discriminating approach can be taken to questions relating to the protection of the fetus.

It does no more than this, however. To suggest that a distinction can be made between the legal position of a pregnant woman and that of other persons whose conduct affects a fetus does not inevitably lead to the conclusion that in all circumstances she should be immune from legal intervention. To decide whether she should enjoy such immunity, it is necessary to examine a number of other considerations. Foremost among these is the weight that should be given to a pregnant woman's autonomy. The following discussion of this issue is concerned solely with the question of the respect to be given to the informed decision of a competent woman. The questions arising when there is doubt about the basis on which a decision has been made, or about the competence of the woman to reach a considered decision, will be discussed in Chapter 12.

AUTONOMY: SOME BASIC PRINCIPLES

The concept of autonomy is a protean one and has been the subject of much academic analysis; an extended discussion of the topic is beyond the scope of this book.[45] For present purposes, it is sufficient to identify a distinction relevant to the types of situations considered in this chapter. When the possibility of compulsory medical intervention (such as a caesarean section) is raised, the question is whether a pregnant woman is *immune from interference* with her bodily integrity. In this context, she is viewed as a passive individual and it must be decided whether it is lawful for surgery to be performed on her without her consent. In another context (such as when she is taking drugs or alcohol), a different aspect of autonomy is at issue. Here she is adopting an active role and the question is whether she is *free to engage in certain conduct*. When she is cast in the role of an active individual asserting the right to behave in a certain manner, she wants the law to leave her alone. In contrast, the woman who asserts the right to decline surgery is seeking to use the law as a shield to resist a positive infringement of her rights.[46]

---

[45] See, for example, G. Dworkin, *The Theory and Practice of Autonomy* (New York, 1988); R. H. Fallon, 'Two Senses of Autonomy' (1994) 46 Stanford Law Review 875; J. E. Fleming, 'Securing Deliberative Autonomy' (1995) 48 Stanford Law Review 1.

[46] The distinction suggested here is similar to that between negative and positive liberty; it is outlined by Fallon, who states that it was originated by Isaiah Berlin in 'Two Concepts of Liberty', in *Four Essays on Liberty* (Oxford, 1969) 118. See R. H. Fallon, 'Two Senses of Autonomy' (1994) 46 Stanford Law Review 875.

A pregnant woman, like any other competent adult, has certain basic rights. She has the right (for any or no reason) to decline medical treatment. This has long been recognized by the common law in the United States, Canada, England, and Australia. In *Schloendorff v Society of New York Hospital*, for example, Justice Cardozo stated: 'Every human being of adult years and sound mind has a right to determine what shall be done with his own body; and a surgeon who performs an operation without his patient's consent commits an assault, for which he is liable in damages.'[47] The Ontario Court of Appeal provided a fuller explanation in *Malette v Shulman*:

The right of a person to control his or her own body is a concept that has long been recognized at common law. The tort of battery has traditionally protected the interest in bodily security from unwanted physical interference. Basically, any intentional non-consensual touching which is harmful or offensive to a person's reasonable sense of dignity is actionable. Of course, a person may choose to waive this protection and consent to the intentional invasion of this interest, in which case an action for battery will not be maintainable. No special exceptions are made for medical care, other than in emergency situations, and the general rules governing actions for battery are applicable to the doctor–patient relationship. Thus, as a matter of common law, a medical intervention in which a doctor touches the body of a patient would constitute a battery if the patient did not consent to the intervention. Patients have the decisive role in the medical decision-making process.

Later, the court added: 'The right to determine what shall be done with one's own body is a fundamental right in our society. The concepts inherent in this right are the bedrock upon which the principles of self-determination and individual autonomy are based.'[48]

Similarly, in *Re T (Adult: Refusal of Treatment)*, the English Court of Appeal made it plain that medical treatment cannot be imposed even when its refusal will result in the likely or certain death of the patient. In this case, Lord Donaldson acknowledged that a patient suffering no mental incapacity has 'an absolute right to choose whether to consent to medical treatment, to refuse it or to choose one rather than another of the treatments being offered'. He added: 'This right of choice is not limited to decisions which others might regard as sensible. It exists notwithstanding that the reasons for making the choice are rational, irrational, unknown or even non-existent.'[49] Though the matter has yet to be fully explored in Australia, the same principles apply.[50]

In the United States and Canada, the common law principles relating to medical treatment are supplemented by constitutional protections. The Fifth and Fourteenth Amendments to the United States Constitution protect the

---

[47] 105 NE 92, 93 (1914).   [48] (1990) 67 DLR (4th) 321, 327, and 336.
[49] [1992] 3 WLR 782, 786 (citation omitted).
[50] *Secretary, Department of Health and Community Services v JWB and SMB* (1992) 175 CLR 218, 309.

right to liberty, and in Canada s 7 of the Charter of Rights and Freedoms acknowledges both the right to liberty and to security of the person. The right to liberty provides a basis for asserting a right to decline medical treatment. In *Cruzan v Director, Missouri Department of Health*, the Supreme Court of the United States accepted that 'a competent person has a constitutionally protected liberty interest in refusing unwanted medical treatment'. This is because 'our notions of liberty are inextricably entwined with our idea of physical freedom and self-determination'.[51] Similarly, in *R v Morgentaler*, Justice Wilson concluded: '[T]he right to liberty contained in s 7 [of the Charter] guarantees to every individual a degree of personal autonomy over important decisions intimately affecting their private lives.'[52] In emphasizing the importance of this right, however, she adopted a different approach from that taken by the other members of the majority. They preferred to treat any infringement of the power to make decisions in matters affecting health as an infringement of the Charter's guarantee of the security of the person.

The right to privacy is another source of the right to decline treatment. While this right is not explicitly protected in the United States Constitution, it exists 'in the penumbra' of the guarantees embodied in the Bill of Rights.[53] *Morgentaler*'s description of the right to liberty guaranteeing 'a degree of personal autonomy over important decisions' may hint at the recognition of a right to privacy. Alternatively, this formula may suggest an acknowledgement—of the kind made in *Cruzan*—of the importance of self-determination. Mention should also be made of United States cases in which treatment has been declined on religious grounds. In these cases, courts have occasionally referred to the right of patients to practise their religions without interference:

Even though we may consider [the patient's] beliefs unwise, foolish or ridiculous, in the absence of an overriding danger to society we may not permit interference therewith . . . for the sole purpose of compelling her to accept medical treatment forbidden by her religious principles, and previously refused by her with full knowledge of the probable consequences.[54]

In matters involving medical treatment, however, the recognition of a right to religious freedom may have little significance in itself; while religious beliefs *explain* a patient's decision to decline treatment, the right to make such a decision is grounded on other rights (such as the right to liberty or bodily integrity).

The breadth—or otherwise—of the rights which have been identified should be noted. A number of expressions were used: a right to determine

---

[51] 497 US 261, 278 and 287; 111 L Ed 2d 224, 241, and 248 (1990).

[52] (1988) 44 DLR (4th) 385, 490.

[53] *Griswold v Connecticut* 381 US 479, 484; 14 L Ed 2d 510, 514 (1965); see also *Roe v Wade* 410 US 113; 35 L Ed 2d 147 (1973).

[54] *Re Estate of Brooks* 205 NE 2d 435, 442 (1965).

what shall be done with one's own body (*Schloendorff*), a right to control one's own body (*Malette*), a right to self-determination (*Malette* and *Cruzan*), a right to refuse medical treatment (*Re T*), a right to liberty (United States Constitution and Canadian Charter of Rights and Freedoms), a right to security of the person (Canadian Charter of Rights and Freedoms), and a right to privacy (*Griswold* and *Roe*). Some of these formulations encompass a much broader right than the right to decline treatment (an immunity from interference) and are thus relevant to the second and problematic aspect of autonomy: the right to engage in certain conduct. Its acknowledgement demands an acceptance of the existence of one or other of the broader formulations quoted: the right to self-determination, to liberty, or to privacy. A pregnant woman who withholds consent to invasive treatment can confidently rely on a well-established body of law recognizing her right to do so. There are few circumstances in which the law can curtail so fundamental a right. It is only if her competence is in doubt that her decision can be overridden. In contrast, the position of a pregnant woman who takes drugs or alcohol and who claims that the law should not intervene is less clear. She must establish a broad right to engage in conduct that is potentially harmful to the fetus. If she cannot do so, the opportunities for legal intervention may be greater. To determine whether such intervention should be allowed, the question to be answered is whether she should be able to exercise freedom of choice in all circumstances.

No attempt will be made to offer an answer at this stage. The point to be noted is that asserting 'autonomy' can involve relying on a variety of different rights. Appreciating this fact is an essential prerequisite to a discussion of the central question addressed in this chapter: whether the woman's rights (however defined) should ever be overridden when her conduct threatens her fetus. When considering this question it is necessary to recall the nature of the maternal/fetal relationship, a relationship that involves 'not-one-but-not-two'. To adopt this model is to recognize that maternal autonomy—although important—is not the sole consideration. It is unsatisfactory to rely solely on assertions about the woman's autonomy when examining arguments relating to legal intervention against a pregnant woman. To do this is to oversimplify the analysis and to ignore the fact that the woman's decision may subsequently have an effect on another human being. The Canadian Royal Commission on New Reproductive Technologies made this mistake when it observed: 'A woman has the right to make her own choices, whether they are good or bad, because it is the woman whose body and health are affected, the woman who must live with her decision, and the woman who must bear the consequences of that decision for the rest of her life.'[55] While this statement is correct, it is incomplete. In some circumstances, the 'body

---

[55] Canada, *Proceed with Care: Final Report of the Royal Commission on New Reproductive Technologies, Volume 2* (1993) 956.

and health' of the child, after birth, will be affected. If the focus is exclusively on the woman and her autonomy, this fact will be overlooked.

The need to recognize the claims of the fetus was emphasized in *Roe v Wade*. While being careful to stress the importance of a pregnant woman's right to privacy and self-determination, the United States Supreme Court also made it clear that a fetus has value in the eyes of the law. It therefore ruled that the state has an 'important and legitimate interest in protecting the potentiality of human life'.[56] Whether this statement should be interpreted as being relevant only to the understanding of the law in the United States is problematic. In Chapter 8, I suggested that it would be difficult to sustain the argument that the laws in England, Canada, and Australia do not in some circumstances acknowledge the existence and value of fetal life. Nevertheless, such an acknowledgement is not the equivalent of a recognition of a state obligation to protect the fetus. Thus the proposition advanced in *Roe v Wade* cannot be regarded as forming part of the law in England, Canada, or Australia. The implications of the proposition are worth exploring, however, for it offers a possible basis for legal action against a pregnant woman and so illuminates some of the issues discussed in this chapter.

Before considering these implications, it is necessary to examine the nature of the state's interest in protecting potential human life. This interest can be seen as arising from an obligation to protect the vulnerable.[57] While this rationale was not made explicit in *Roe v Wade*, it was implicit in the decisions in which the *parens patriae* jurisdiction was invoked to allow intervention. A second explanation of the state's interest relates to the cost of caring for disabled children. There are substantial costs involved in providing medical, educational, and welfare services for children born with major disabilities and it can be argued that the state has a legitimate interest in avoiding or minimizing these costs.[58] If this view is accepted, it is proper for the state to take what steps it can to ensure the birth of healthy children.

Whether or not these concerns justify a state interest in protecting potential life, the decision in *Roe v Wade* identifies the existence of such an interest and so provides a rationale for intervention against a pregnant woman. It thus clarifies the problem with which this chapter deals. Can pursuit of this interest ever justify overriding the autonomy interests of a pregnant woman? As was seen in Chapter 2, the courts have addressed this issue in two different contexts in which fetuses were thought to be at risk of harm: when the risk arose from a decision to decline medical intervention and when it was posed by the woman's conduct during pregnancy. Each of these situations will be considered in turn.

[56] 410 US 113, 162; 35 L Ed 2d 147, 182 (1973).
[57] See generally R. E. Goodin, *Protecting the Vulnerable — a Reanalysis of Our Social Responsibilities* (London, 1985).
[58] S. Balisy, 'Maternal Substance Abuse: the Need to Provide Legal Protection for the Fetus' (1987) 60 Southern California Law Review 1209, 1223.

LEGAL INTERVENTION TO IMPOSE TREATMENT

Some Assumptions

That a pregnant woman has certain autonomy rights is indisputable. These, however, are not absolute. Like any other citizen, she may have her rights curtailed by the state, provided it employs proper procedures and has a sufficiently compelling reason to do so. The question is whether a desire to protect the fetus can provide this compelling reason and so justify legal action that can result in compulsory intervention.

Before offering an answer, I should make clear one of the assumptions underlying the analysis. This is that there are some circumstances in which medical evidence clearly establishes that there are risks associated with childbirth and that medical intervention can reduce those risks. It is conceded that there are some who would dispute this proposition and who would assert either that childbirth is a natural process, free of risks, or that any risks which may arise cannot be reduced by resort to medical intervention. In rejecting these assertions, I do not propose to enter the debate about levels of intervention or to deny the validity of the complaints made by those who deplore the 'medicalization' of childbirth. Instead, I argue that there are certain conditions in pregnancy and at the time of delivery which pose well-documented risks to the woman and her fetus,[59] including maternal diabetes or hypertension, rhesus sensitization, fetal distress, a major degree of placenta praevia or abruptio placentae, retained placenta, cord prolapse, multiple pregnancy, obstructed or prolonged labour, transverse lie, and severe post-partum haemorrhage. There is good evidence that appropriate intervention can reduce the risks posed by these conditions. For example, treatment of

[59] A full review of this evidence is beyond the scope of this book. Among the most relevant discussions of this evidence are: D. R. Hollingsworth and T. R. Moore, 'Diabetes and Pregnancy', in R. K. Creasy and R. Resnik (eds.), *Maternal-Fetal Medicine: Principles and Practice* (Philadelphia, 2nd edn., 1989) 925; M. J. Peek *et al.*, 'Maternal and Neonatal Outcome of Patients Classified According to the Australasian Society for the Study of Hypertension in Pregnancy Consensus Statement' (1995) 162 *Medical Journal of Australia* 186; J. M. Bowman, 'Hemolytic Disease (Erythroblastosis Fetalis)', in R. K. Creasy and R. Resnik (eds.), *Maternal-Fetal Medicine: Principles and Practice* (Philadelphia, 2nd edn., 1989) 613; P. J. Steer, 'Intrapartum Care Including the Detection and Management of Fetal Dysfunction' and D. M. F. Gibb, 'Operative Delivery', in R. V. Clements (ed.), *Safe Practice in Obstetrics and Gynaecology* (Edinburgh, 1994) 191 and 223; M. C. Frederiksen *et al.*, 'Placenta Previa: A 22-Year Analysis' (1999) 180 *American Journal of Obstetrics and Gynecology* 1432; J. M. Crane *et al.*, 'Neonatal Outcomes with Placenta Previa' (1999) 93 *Obstetrics and Gynecology* 541; A. Tandberg *et al.*, 'Manual Removal of the Placenta. Incidence and Clinical Significance' (1999) 78 Acta Obstetrica et Gynecologica Scandinavica 33; A. M. Prabulos and E. H. Philipson, 'Umbilical Cord Prolapse. Is the Time from Diagnosis to Delivery Critical?' (1998) 43 *Journal of Reproductive Medicine* 129; J. D. Seffah, 'Maternal and Perinatal Mortality and Morbidity Associated with Transverse Lie' (1999) 65 *International Journal of Gynaecology and Obstetrics* 11; G. Chamberlain, 'Antenatal Care and the Identification of High-Risk Women', in R. V. Clements (ed.), *Safe Practice in Obstetrics and Gynaecology* (Edinburgh, 1994) 169.

maternal diabetes or hypertension can reduce the risks to both mother and baby and an intra-uterine transfusion can prevent severe haemolytic disease of the newborn child. A caesarean section may be essential to save the life of both mother and child in the case of major placental pathology. A cord prolapse poses an immediate threat to the baby and death or brain damage may result unless the baby is delivered within ten minutes. Usually this will necessitate the performance of a caesarean section. Similarly, a forceps delivery or a caesarean section may reduce the risk of fetal death or injury in cases of fetal distress or reduce the risk of fetal or maternal death or injury (for example, urinary and rectal fistulae) in cases of obstructed labour. When identifying the possible benefits of intervention it is, of course, necessary also to acknowledge the risks associated with that intervention. In particular, it is clear that a caesarean section poses a number of risks for the woman.

What is being asserted, therefore, is that there exist well-recognized obstetric risks, which may or may not eventuate and may or may not be reduced or avoided by medical intervention. It is only in rare obstetric situations that it can be asserted with certainty that harm will occur if intervention is not undertaken. It can never be asserted that medical intervention will inevitably prevent it. What can be demonstrated in a particular situation is the existence of a *statistically verifiable risk* to the woman or her fetus. The fact that it does not occur in this situation does not mean that it will never do so. The fact that medical advice is not always correct does not mean that it is never correct. Overlooking these obvious propositions can lead to the misuse of anecdotal evidence. In the field of obstetrics, it is not uncommon for a woman to decline to follow medical advice and to deliver a healthy child. Such an outcome is sometimes incorrectly relied on as evidence that the doctor was 'wrong' and the patient was 'right'. This is to misinterpret the outcome. When harm does not eventuate, it is fallacious to assert that no risks existed. All that a competent doctor can do is to identify and explain the risks presented in a particular situation. A properly informed woman may elect to accept those risks.

The analysis which follows is thus based on the assumption that while the limitations of medical knowledge must be recognized, there is sound evidence that in some situations a woman's decision not to follow a doctor's advice can put her and her fetus at serious risk. Sometimes the risk will eventuate. To claim that intervention in childbirth is never justified and is never potentially beneficial is to ignore the medical evidence. It cannot therefore be asserted that a pregnant woman's decision to decline intervention is an unproblematic exercise of her autonomy.

This conclusion is reinforced by the attitude displayed by the courts in cases involving obstetric malpractice. In Chapter 4, it was seen that it is well established that when a woman or her fetus has suffered harm, doctors and midwives can be liable in negligence for their failure to undertake antenatal or perinatal intervention. When harm results from non-intervention they can also be liable for a failure to advise of the risk of that harm. The cases in which liability of either kind has been imposed rest on the view that in certain circumstances childbirth carries risks, that a competent doctor or midwife will recognize these risks, and can be held liable for failing to intervene to reduce them. While it is theoretically possible to reject the case law embodying this view, its existence cannot be ignored. It is logically impossible for a legal system to deny the presence of risks that medical intervention can reduce while at the same time treating as negligent a doctor who does not respond when these risks are or should be apparent. It is also logically impossible for a legal system to hold a doctor liable for the non-disclosure of the risks that a pregnant woman is facing, while simultaneously refusing to accept the validity of medical evidence as to the reality of those risks. Either medical technology has something to offer in some circumstances or it does not. If it does not, the basis for a damages action—either for non-intervention or for non-disclosure—will disappear. The current operation of negligence law in the context of obstetric malpractice suggests that this is unlikely to occur.

A Balancing of Interests?

It is against this background that I consider the question whether a desire to protect a fetus (or, more accurately, to reduce the risks to which it is exposed) can ever justify legal action to permit intervention to which a competent woman has declined to give consent. Before this is done, it should be noted that, given that woman and fetus are 'not-one-but-not-two', intervention might also be undertaken to protect the woman. There are some situations at the time of delivery in which a woman can, in the absence of intervention, face a serious risk of injury or death. Coercive treatment to avert such a risk cannot be justified. The law on this is clear: a competent patient may decline treatment for any reason or no reason, regardless of the danger and notwithstanding that death or serious harm is virtually certain to follow. This principle, however, applies to situations in which the only person affected is the patient. Before considering whether it is equally applicable to a decision made by a pregnant woman, it is helpful to examine the law's attitude when the treatment might benefit another person.

Medical Treatment for the Benefit of Another Person

There have been a number of cases in which courts have been asked to authorize medical treatment for the benefit of third parties. The most relevant are those in which intervention has been sought against parents to protect children. Parents have obligations to their children—such as to provide food and clothing, medical care, and education—and these obligations are legally enforceable. The question is whether duties of this kind can be used as a foundation on which to base the more demanding obligation to submit to unwanted medical treatment.

United States courts have occasionally had to rule on the argument that the state's interest in child protection justifies the compulsory medical treatment of a parent. The way the argument has been framed is that the state has an obligation to ensure the survival of a parent in order to prevent the abandonment of the child. An example was provided by *Re President and Directors of Georgetown College Inc*, in which a Jehovah's Witness who had a 7-month-old child refused a blood transfusion after bleeding heavily from a ruptured ulcer. A court-ordered transfusion was performed as it was thought that she would die without it. The judge asserted that the state's interest in preventing the abandonment of the child could be a sufficient basis for imposing medical treatment on the mother: 'The state, as *parens patriae*, will not allow a parent to abandon a child, and so it should not allow this most ultimate of voluntary abandonments. The patient has a responsibility to the community to care for her infant. Thus the people had an interest in preserving the life of this mother.'[60]

A similar result was initially reached in *Re Dubreuil*, an obstetric case. The woman, a Jehovah's Witness, was admitted to hospital for the delivery of her fourth child. She gave her consent to a caesarean section, but indicated that she would not consent to a blood transfusion, should one be necessary. During the caesarean section, she lost a significant amount of blood because of a clotting disorder. When she maintained her refusal to consent to a blood transfusion, the hospital obtained an order allowing one. Again the trial court relied on the state's interest in protecting the children: '[T]his court believes that the demands of the state (and society) outweigh the wishes of Patricia Dubreuil and that every medical effort should be made to prolong her life so that she can care for her four minor children until their respective majorities.'[61]

The decision was overruled by the Supreme Court of Florida, which stressed the importance of respecting the woman's wishes regarding medical treatment. Nevertheless, the argument relating to the protection of the children was not completely rejected. The court noted that had the woman died, her husband would have become the children's guardian. It was therefore unnecessary to make a stark choice between medical intervention and abandonment. This persuaded the court that the state interest in intervention was not sufficient in this case. The court explicitly declined to 'rule out

---

[60] 331 F 2d 1000, 1008 (1964).

[61] 629 So 2d 819, 821 (Fla, 1993). See also *Re Jamaica Hospital* 491 NYS 2d 898 (Sup, 1985), a case in which a pregnant woman was ordered to have a blood transfusion; the court, in addition to stressing the state's interest in preserving the life of the fetus, considered that the state had an interest in preserving the woman's life for the benefit of her other children.

the possibility that some case not yet before us may present a compelling interest to prevent abandonment'.[62]

In both decisions there was a recognition not only of a possible state interest in protecting children, but also of the significance of the parent–child (or, more specifically, the mother–child) relationship. This relationship was seen as creating obligations that the state had an interest in enforcing on the child's behalf. Such an analysis was rejected in *Fosmire v Nicoleau*. The case also involved a refusal, by a Jehovah's Witness, of a blood transfusion following a caesarean section. The New York Court of Appeals declined to attach significance to the parent–child relationship, emphasizing instead the right of citizens 'to make their own medical care choices without regard to their . . . status as parents'. The woman's right to refuse the transfusion was 'not conditioned on [her] being without minor children . . .'.[63]

While some of these cases support the view that the state's interest in the welfare of children justifies the overriding of a parental decision to decline medical treatment, they do not constitute a convincing body of law. The conclusion reached in *Fosmire v Nicoleau* seems more consistent with the current emphasis (in the United States, Canada, England, and Australia) on the importance of recognizing the right to self-determination in medical matters.[64] Further, the approach adopted in this case is also consistent with the attitude courts have displayed to situations in which one person is in a position to save another. The law will not compel a sacrifice for the benefit of another, whether that other be a child or not. In particular, it will not compel a person to accept medical treatment to save the life of another. This proposition is illustrated by the decision in *McFall v Shimp*. There a court refused to order a man to donate bone marrow to save the life of his cousin who was dying of aplastic anaemia. Although the judge considered the man's refusal to be morally indefensible, he declined to order the operation, saying:

The common law has consistently held to a rule which provides that one human being is under no legal compulsion to give aid or to take action to save another human being or to rescue. . . . For our law to *compel* defendant to submit to an intrusion of his body would change every concept and principle upon which our society is founded. To do so would defeat the sanctity of the individual, and would impose a rule which would know no limits, and one could not imagine where the line would be drawn.[65]

Enough has been said to indicate that it is difficult to sustain the proposition that the law does or should allow one person to be compelled to undergo medical treatment to benefit another. While the proposition might be more

---

[62] 629 So 2d 819, 827 (Fla, 1993).   [63] 551 NE 2d 77, 84 and 83 (NY, 1990).

[64] See also *Norwood Hospital v Munoz* 564 NE 2d 1017 (Mass, 1991).

[65] 10 Pa D & C 3d 90, 91 (1978) (emphasis in original). See also *Re Pescinski* 226 NW 2d 180 (1975) and *Curran v Bosze* 566 NE 2d 1319 (Ill, 1990), which held that a sibling cannot be forced to make a life-saving donation of bone marrow or a kidney.

strongly urged when there is a parent–child relationship, the same answer is given: the right to self-determination will prevail. Even when a child's life or health is threatened, the argument that the state has a sufficiently compelling interest to justify overriding a parental decision to decline medical treatment is unlikely to succeed.

Medical Treatment for the Benefit of a Fetus

The purpose of the proceedings in cases such as *Dubreuil* and *Fosmire v Nicoleau* was to ensure that the mother would survive to fulfil her obligations to her children. In contrast, in the cases in which legal intervention before a child's delivery was considered, the aims were to protect the fetus and to facilitate the safe delivery of a healthy child. These cases have been discussed in Chapter 2. It is necessary to reconsider them in order to determine how the courts dealt with questions relating to fetal interests and maternal autonomy.

In some decisions, courts have cited *Roe v Wade*[66] in support of the view that the state has an interest in protecting potential human life. The court in *Jefferson v Griffin Spalding County Hospital Authority* relied on this proposition in performing a balancing exercise in order to justify a caesarean section: 'The Court finds that the intrusion involved into the life of [the woman and her husband] is outweighed by the duty of the State to protect a living, unborn human being from meeting his or her death before being given the opportunity to live.'[67] A mathematical approach to weighing fetal and maternal interests was adopted in *Re Madyun*. There the woman's decision not to consent to a caesarean section was estimated to have posed a risk of fetal sepsis (which could have resulted in brain damage or the death of the baby) of between 50 and 75 per cent. The risk to the mother of undergoing the operation was put at 0.25 per cent. The court explicitly balanced these risks in reaching a decision to order the procedure: 'Given the significant risks to the fetus versus the minimal risks to the mother, the Court concludes that there is a compelling interest to intervene and protect the life and safety of the fetus.'[68] The reference to the 'compelling' nature of the interest was a further echo of *Roe v Wade*: the *Madyun* fetus was viable and this fact was seen as increasing the state's obligation to protect it.

While seizing on *Roe v Wade*'s identification of a state interest in fetal protection, such decisions failed to examine the interests of the woman. This aspect was considered in *Re AC*,[69] a case in which the court was asked to authorize a caesarean section. The judgment described the woman's right to forgo medical treatment as 'of constitutional magnitude' and later referred generally to the need for the court to defend the woman's 'liberty and privacy

---

[66] 410 US 113; 35 L Ed 2d 147 (1973).   [67] Ga, 274 SE 2d 457, 460 (1981).
[68] 573 A 2d 1235, 1264 (DC App, 1990).   [69] 573 A 2d 1235 (DC App, 1990).

interests and bodily integrity'.[70] The reference to privacy interests has special significance in the context of a woman's power to make decisions about the management of her pregnancy.[71] The importance of the right to privacy in this context was recognized in *Roe v Wade*, although the court added the qualification that: 'The pregnant woman cannot be isolated in her privacy.'[72] This suggests that the right to privacy might not confer absolute protection on a pregnant woman. Surprisingly, the courts dealing with medical treatment matters have not relied on this statement.

Re AC did not consider the full implications of acknowledging the woman's constitutionally protected interests. These were explored by the Appellate Court of Illinois in *Re Baby Boy Doe*. The judgment criticized the *Jefferson* and *Madyun* courts for failing to recognize 'the constitutional dimension of the woman's right to refuse treatment, or the magnitude of that right'.[73] The court therefore rejected the argument that a conflict over the performance of a caesarean section should be resolved by balancing the rights of the viable fetus against the right of a competent woman to decline medical intervention: 'We hold today that Illinois courts should not engage in such a balancing, and that a woman's competent choice in refusing medical treatment as invasive as a cesarean section during her pregnancy must be honored, even in circumstances where the choice may be harmful to her fetus.'[74] The court relied on *Stallman v Youngquist*[75] to support the following conclusion:

[A] woman's right to refuse invasive medical treatment, derived from her rights to privacy, bodily integrity, and religious liberty, is not diminished during pregnancy. The woman retains the same right to refuse invasive treatment, even of lifesaving or other beneficial nature, that she can exercise when she is not pregnant. The potential impact upon the fetus is not legally relevant; to the contrary, the *Stallman* court explicitly rejected the view that the woman's rights can be subordinated to fetal rights.[76]

The question posed by this ruling is whether the *Roe v Wade* principle — that in some circumstances, the state has an interest in protecting potential human life — has no application in medical treatment cases. The Illinois court rejected the view that the state's power to regulate abortions translates 'into the proposition that the state may intrude upon the woman's right to remain

---

[70] Ibid. 1244 and 1248. Similarly, *Re Baby Boy Doe* referred to the woman's right to privacy and bodily integrity: 632 NE 2d 326, 332 (Ill App 1, Dist 1994).

[71] See also *Taft v Taft* 446 NE 2d 395 (Mass, 1983), where the court recognized the woman's right to privacy in proceedings relating to the appropriateness of ordering her to undergo cervical cerclage.

[72] 410 US 113, 159; 35 L Ed 2d 147, 180 (1973). See also *Griswold v Connecticut* 381 US 479; 14 L Ed 2d 510 (1965) for a recognition of the right to privacy in this context.

[73] 632 NE 2d 326, 333 (Ill App 1 Dist, 1994).   [74] Ibid. 330.

[75] 531 NE 2d 355 (Ill, 1988).   [76] 632 NE 2d 326, 332 (Ill App 1 Dist, 1994).

free from unwanted physical invasion of her person when she chooses to carry her pregnancy to term'. It added: '*Roe* and its progeny . . . make it clear that, even in the context of abortion, the state's compelling interest in the potential life of the fetus is insufficient to override the woman's interest in preserving her health.'[77]

The significance of this is difficult to assess. On one view, *Roe* dealt solely with the law of abortion and has no relevance to the decision a court must make when it is asked to authorize medical treatment designed to safeguard the fetus. Alternatively, *Roe* can be accepted as authority for the proposition that while the state has an interest in protecting potential human life, that interest cannot be allowed to override the woman's interest in matters relating to her health. Support for the latter interpretation was provided by *Baby Boy Doe*'s citation of *Thornburgh v American College of Obstetricians and Gynecologists*.[78] This decision was seen as indicating that it was improper to require a 'trade-off' between the woman's health and fetal survival and as stressing that 'the woman's health is always the paramount consideration; any degree of increased risk to the woman's health is unacceptable'.[79] This analysis allows the decision in *Baby Boy Doe* to be seen as consistent with the ruling in *Roe v Wade*. Both recognize that a fetus has interests that a court will protect, but not at the expense of the woman's interest in her health. That this is the correct way of interpreting the judgment in *Baby Boy Doe* was suggested by its reference to the purpose of the medical intervention:

The proposed cesarean section was never suggested as necessary, or even useful, to the preservation of [the mother's] life or health. To the contrary, it would pose greater risk to her. Further, even in cases where the rejected treatment is clearly necessary to sustain life, these factors alone are not sufficiently compelling to outweigh an individual's right to refuse treatment.[80]

This can be interpreted as a direct application of the principles enunciated in *Roe v Wade*. When a woman is pregnant, the law should not intrude in a manner that threatens her life or health. When an abortion is being considered, the threat may lie in intervention to prevent the termination. When a child is about to be delivered, the threat may lie in intervention to facilitate the birth. *Roe v Wade* indicates that in neither situation should a woman be compelled to face such a threat.

Such an analysis answers some questions but raises others. *Re Baby Boy Doe* expressly recognized a pregnant woman's right to withhold consent to 'medical treatment as invasive as a cesarean section'. The court's ruling was that whatever the risk to the fetus, 'invasive' treatment could never be justified in the face of a competent refusal. In *Re AC*, the District of Columbia Court of Appeals came close to saying the same thing: '[S]ome may doubt

---

[77] 632 NE 2d 326, 334 (Ill App 1 Dist, 1994). [78] 476 US 747; 90 L Ed 2d 779 (1986).
[79] 632 NE 2d 326, 333 (Ill App 1 Dist, 1994). [80] Ibid. 334.

that there could ever be a situation extraordinary or compelling enough to justify a massive intrusion into a person's body, such as a caesarean section, against that person's will.'[81] To emphasize the intrusiveness of a procedure such as a caesarean is, however, implicitly to suggest a balancing approach: if some forms of intervention involve too drastic a violation of a woman's rights, perhaps there are other less intrusive forms that might be acceptable? The decision in *Re Baby Boy Doe* did not preclude this possibility. The court was aware that its reference to the invasiveness of a caesarean section raised the question whether less invasive procedures could be ordered in some circumstances. It declined to answer this question. After mentioning a decision in which a blood transfusion had been authorized, the judgment continued: 'This and other similar blood transfusion cases are inapposite, because they involve a relatively non-invasive and risk-free procedure, as opposed to the massively invasive, risky, and painful cesarean section. Whether such non-invasive procedures are permissible in Illinois, we leave for another case.'[82] While this comment opens the door to a case-by-case approach, it is difficult to know how much significance to attach to it. The statement may be no more than a manifestation of the well-recognized judicial habit of cautiously refusing to rule on an issue not directly raised by the facts of a case. Nevertheless, a similar uncertainty had earlier been revealed in *Re AC*, where the court, while stating that in 'virtually all cases' the decision must be the woman's, did not 'quite foreclose the possibility that a conflicting state interest [in the protection of the fetus] may be so compelling that the patient's wishes must yield . . .'.[83]

The second question raised by the analysis adopted in *Re Baby Boy Doe* is whether it supports the conclusion that intervention to protect the fetus is justified when it poses no threat to the woman's life or health. The situation that arose in *Re S*[84] underlines this point. There the transverse lie posed a grave risk to the fetus and to the mother.[85] If the court-ordered caesarean section had not been performed, there would have been a substantial possibility that the woman's uterus would have ruptured and that she would have died. Here it could be argued that legal intervention was appropriate: in contrast with the situation in *Baby Boy Doe*, intervention—far from exposing the woman to risk—was likely to benefit her. It would be difficult to argue that the performance of a caesarean section to treat a transverse lie would not

[81] 573 A 2d 1235, 1252 (DC App 1990).
[82] 632 NE 2d 326, 333 (Ill App 1 Dist, 1994). Cp *Re Fetus Brown* 689 NE 2d 397 (Ill App 1 Dist, 1997).
[83] 573 A 2d 1235, 1252 (DC App, 1990).   [84] [1992] 3 WLR 806: see above 27.
[85] The fetus was already dead when the caesarean section was performed and so there was no basis on which to argue that a state interest in the preservation of fetal life justified the performance of the procedure. Once the fetus was dead, the only possible ground for the performance of unwanted surgery on a competent patient would have been that this was necessary to save her life. As has been made clear, this ground cannot justify treatment to which a patient has declined to consent. The analysis offered in the text poses the question whether intervention would have been justified if the fetus had been alive.

diminish the risk that the woman faces. If the woman's right to decline treatment is absolute, this fact is immaterial. If the analysis suggested by *Roe v Wade* is applied, however, a different conclusion may be reached in a case involving unwanted medical treatment. As has been seen, *Re Baby Boy Doe* can be interpreted as rejecting any 'trade-off' exposing a woman to increased risk. The Illinois court took care to stress that on the facts before it, the proposed caesarean section was not only unnecessary to the preservation of the mother's life or health, but also that it would have posed greater risks to her. To emphasize this aspect is to suggest the possibility that the state's interest in protecting the potentiality of human life might justify coercive intervention provided it does not expose the woman to increased risk.

Thus an exploration of the broader implications of *Roe v Wade* reveals a number of complexities. If the decision is regarded as relevant for the purposes of this chapter, the recognition of the value of potential human life must be accommodated within any attempt to answer questions about legal intervention. Further, relying on the Supreme Court's opinion invites speculation as to whether treatment would pose a threat to the life or health of the mother. If no such threat is apparent, a commitment to protecting the fetus may justify the use of compulsion. This opens the door to court-ordered intervention in some situations. Similarly, the door to non-invasive intervention was left open by the decision in *Baby Boy Doe*. Qualifications such as these must, however, be rejected if a pregnant woman is seen as having an absolute right to decline treatment. To accept this view is to regard *Roe v Wade* as having no application in medical treatment cases. It is logically impossible to assert that a competent adult has, in all circumstances, the right to decline treatment and at the same time to urge that the protection of fetal interests justifies state intervention, provided that the intervention is neither 'invasive' nor a threat to the life or health of the pregnant woman.

The foregoing analysis applies to the law in the United States. In England, the decision of the Court of Appeal in *Re MB (Medical Treatment)* left no room for doubt on the matter. The court refused to undertake *any* balancing of maternal and fetal interests. To take this position is to indicate that a woman's right to determine what is done to her and her fetus is absolute and that no fetal interest, however clear and pressing, can justify any coercive medical intervention, however minor. The court ruled as follows: '[A] competent woman who has the capacity to decide may, for religious reasons, other reasons, or for no reasons at all, choose not to have medical intervention, even though . . . the consequence may be the death or serious handicap of the child she bears or her own death.'[86] A similar conclusion was reached, also by the Court of Appeal, in *St George's Healthcare NHS v S*. The court emphasized the importance of preserving a patient's autonomy:

---

[86] [1997] 2 FLR 426, 444.

[H]ow can a forced invasion of a competent adult's body against her will even for the most laudable of motives (the preservation of life) be ordered without irremediably damaging the principle of self-determination? When human life is at stake the pressure to provide an affirmative answer authorising unwanted medical intervention is very powerful. Nevertheless, the autonomy of each individual requires continuing protection even, perhaps particularly, when the motive for interfering with it is readily understandable, and indeed to many would appear commendable . . .[87]

The court therefore ruled that a fetus's need for medical assistance could not prevail over the woman's rights. 'In our judgment while pregnancy increases the personal responsibilities of a woman it does not diminish her entitlement to decide whether or not to undergo medical treatment. . . . She is entitled not to be forced to submit to an invasion of her body against her will, whether her own life or that of her unborn child depends on it.'[88] These rulings indicate that there is no basis on which an English court can accept the argument that the state has an obligation to protect fetal interests when these interests seem to be threatened by a pregnant woman's decision to decline treatment. Thus they echo the conclusion reached in the earlier discussion of the law's attitude to attempts to compel a person to undergo medical treatment for the benefit of another. Indeed, as was pointed out in *Re AC*, the view that no such sacrifice should be required can be more strongly urged when the intended beneficiary is a fetus: 'Surely . . . a fetus cannot have rights in this respect superior to those of a person who has already been born.'[89]

Thus the English courts have produced an unqualified answer to the question whether, when a pregnant woman has declined medical treatment, legal action should ever be taken in the interests of fetal protection. The analysis offered by these courts is preferable to that which emerges from an examination of the United States law. While *Roe v Wade*'s recognition of a state interest in protecting the fetus cannot be ignored, the identification of such an interest is no more than the first step in dealing with the problem of coercive medical intervention. The real issue is whether the woman's exercise of her autonomy should ever be limited in order to allow such intervention. Ultimately, *Roe v Wade* offers no basis on which to answer this question. If the matter is to be decided solely by reference to abstract principles, it is apparent that the English decisions offer a clearer answer: in matters of medical treatment, the woman's autonomy must be respected. Two comments must, however, be made on this conclusion. First, the cases discussed have involved the possibility of seriously invasive procedures, the coercive performance of which would represent an extreme violation of a woman's autonomy. Perhaps the possibility of resort to non-invasive procedures cannot so easily be rejected on the basis of a desire to respect maternal autonomy. Secondly,

---

[87] [1998] 3 WLR 936, 953.   [88] Ibid. 957.   [89] 573 A 2d 1235, 1244 (DC App, 1990).

while they raise fundamental questions, arguments about autonomy are not the only ones demanding consideration. These matters will now be explored.

The Nature of the Legal Process

The value of moving beyond abstract questions relating to fetal and maternal interests is demonstrated by adopting a perspective drawing attention to the nature of the legal process typically employed to allow coercive treatment. Many of the cases discussed in Chapter 2 were decided very quickly. In *Re S*, the matter was brought to the notice of court officials at 1.30 p.m., the hearing began at 2 p.m., and the declaration was made at 2.18 p.m. The judgment was one page long. There was no time for the case to be fully argued and no opportunity for the court to reflect on the judgment that it delivered. The problems would have been compounded had the emergency arisen in the middle of the night. Similar difficulties have been identified in the United States. One study reported that in fourteen out of sixteen cases surveyed it took six hours or less to obtain a court order, and in three of these cases 'the court orders were actually obtained in an hour or less'.[90] The procedure was emphatically condemned in *Re AC*:

[A]ny judicial proceeding in a case such as this will ordinarily take place—like the one before us here—under time constraints so pressing that it is difficult or impossible for the mother to communicate adequately with counsel, or for counsel to organize an effective factual and legal presentation in defense of her liberty and privacy interests and bodily integrity. Any intrusion implicating such basic values ought not to be lightly undertaken when the mother not only is precluded from conducting pre-trial discovery . . . but also is in no position to prepare meaningfully for trial.[91]

The court went on to quote the following criticisms:

The procedural shortcomings rampant in these cases are not mere technical deficiencies. They undermine the authority of the decisions themselves, posing serious questions as to whether judges can, in the absence of genuine notice, adequate representation, explicit standards of proof, and right of appeal, realistically frame principled and useful legal responses to the dilemmas with which they are being confronted.[92]

Another criticism is that the cases are frequently heard without the woman being present or represented.[93] As a result:

[90] V. E. B. Kolder *et al.*, 'Court-Ordered Obstetrical Interventions' (1987) 316 *New England Journal of Medicine* 1192, 1193.

[91] *Re AC* 573 A 2d 1235, 1248 (DC App, 1990).

[92] J. Gallagher, 'Prenatal Invasions and Interventions: What's Wrong with Fetal Rights' (1987) 10 Harvard Women's Law Journal 9, 49.

[93] K. De Gama, 'A Brave New World? Rights Discourse and the Politics of Reproductive Autonomy' (1993) 20 Journal of Law and Society 114, 121. The woman who was the subject of the proceedings in *Re S* was not represented.

[J]udges who hear these cases will typically hear only the doctor's side and will learn little or nothing of the risks of surgical delivery or the ambiguity of many fetal diagnostic procedures. If they attempt to balance the maternal and fetal risks, judges will have no choice but to accept the physician's assessment and, therefore, to implement his or her recommendations.[94]

Further, if the woman is not present, the court will have no opportunity to hear her personal reasons for reaching a decision to decline intervention. *St George's Healthcare NHS v S* illustrated this and other procedural deficiencies. The Court of Appeal was critical of the trial process: the order authorizing the caesarean section had not only been made without the woman being represented, but it had also been made without her knowledge and without any attempt to inform her or her solicitor of the application. No provision was made for her to apply to vary the order.[95] Further, the trial judge had been told 'some things which were not true' and had not been told 'some other things which would have been highly material'.[96]

Not only must the nature of the legal process be considered, but attention must also be given to the reality of court-ordered medical treatment. There would be something distasteful about using the law to compel a patient to receive treatment: 'Do we really want to restrain, forcibly medicate, and operate on a competent, refusing adult? Such a procedure . . . is certainly brutish and not what one generally associates with medical care.'[97] This aspect troubled the court in *Re A C*. The implications of ordering the performance of a caesarean section were made plain:

Enforcement could be accomplished only through physical force or its equivalent. AC would have to be fastened with restraints to the operating table, or perhaps involuntarily rendered unconscious by forcibly injecting her with an anesthetic, and then subjected to unwanted major surgery. Such actions would surely give one pause in a civilized society.[98]

This passage was quoted with approval in *Re Baby Boy Doe*. An interesting aspect of the proceedings in this case was an attempt to avoid addressing concerns of this kind. Counsel for the Public Guardian (who had argued for compulsory intervention) was 'opposed to any effort to use force', but reserved the right to bring proceedings requiring the woman to show cause why she should not be held in contempt had she refused to consent and the baby had been stillborn or born severely retarded.[99] What contempt proceedings would have achieved is not clear.

---

[94] N. Rhoden, 'The Judge in the Delivery Room: the Emergence of Court-ordered Cesareans' (1986) 74 California Law Review 1951, 2025 (footnote omitted).

[95] [1998] 3 WLR 936, 967.   [96] Ibid. 966.

[97] S. Elias and G. J. Annas, *Reproductive Genetics and the Law* (Chicago, 1987) 259.

[98] 573 A 2d 1235, 1244 (DC App, 1990).

[99] 632 NE 2d 326, 330 (Ill App 1 Dist, 1994).

Differing Perspectives

There are other factors to be taken into account in considering the appropriateness of resorting to the law when a competent pregnant woman has declined medical intervention. In this situation there is a possible conflict not only between the woman's interests and those of her fetus, but also between the woman and her doctor or midwife.[100] This represents a collision between two different perspectives. Doctors are trained to anticipate and minimize risk. They will frequently take the view that it is good medicine to seek to avoid a known risk, even a statistically remote one; their instinct will therefore be to err on the side of intervention. Experienced doctors will have seen the disastrous consequences that occur when the risk eventuates. They will also be aware that a failure to intervene when a recognized risk is present might be regarded as a failure to provide an appropriate standard of care and so expose them to damages claims.[101] The woman's perspective may be quite different. If she declines to follow medical advice, she may do so on the basis that her right to bodily autonomy entitles her to decide what is best for herself and her fetus. She may take this course because of a belief in natural childbirth, or for religious reasons, or because she believes that the risk is worth running. Whatever her reasons, she is asserting that the decision is hers. '[A] patient's assessment of the degree of risk she is willing to assume for the sake of predicted benefits is a wholly subjective matter.'[102]

The temptation to assess the 'reasonableness' of a woman's decision should be resisted. She may decide not to have a caesarean section following a diagnosis of fetal distress. Although there may be a risk to the fetus, other factors may affect her decision. She may be unwilling to accept the risks associated with surgery and anaesthesia. She may also be influenced by the fact that a caesarean 'can adversely affect her future reproductive life, making rupture of her uterus in future pregnancies more likely, and repeat cesarean section for each future delivery far more probable'.[103] In many circumstances it would be very difficult confidently to assert that a woman who is aware of these factors and who decides against a caesarean has elected to run an 'unreasonable' risk. This is not to suggest that there will not be situations in which a decision not to consent to a caesarean section will endanger the woman's life and that of the fetus. A case of obstructed labour would fit this description. Yet even in such an emergency—when it might be argued that the woman's decision was manifestly unreasonable—a procedure as

---

[100] B. Bennett, 'Pregnant Women and the Duty to Rescue: a Feminist Response to the Fetal Rights Debate' (1991) 9 Law in Context 70, 75.

[101] This possibility is discussed in Chapter 12.

[102] A. R. Fleischman, 'The Fetus is a Patient', in S. Cohen and N. Taub (eds.), *Reproductive Laws for the 1990s* (Clifton, NJ, 1989) 249, 252.

[103] Ibid. 255.

invasive as a caesarean section should not be performed in the face of a competent refusal.

The argument against compulsory intervention is reinforced if it is recognized that diagnoses are sometimes uncertain and that the outcome of intervention cannot always be guaranteed. Medical advice is not infallible. 'Doctors are sometimes wrong, and our increasingly sophisticated medical technology does not enable doctors to guarantee a particular outcome.'[104] In the words of the Ethics Committee of the Royal College of Obstetricians and Gynaecologists: 'There are limits to the accuracy and effectiveness of many diagnostic and therapeutic procedures during pregnancy and confinement. . . . For example, the methods for detecting fetal distress antenatally and during labour are not always reliable indicators of a poor outcome.'[105] This element of uncertainty should not be ignored when considering a woman's decision to decline to follow medical advice. While it is questionable to describe as 'unreasonable' a decision to run a risk that is virtually sure to eventuate, it is even more questionable to so describe a decision the outcome of which is uncertain.

Commentators have expressed fears about the possibility of special rules being formulated for pregnant women, stressing that a pregnant woman should not be treated differently from any other patient who has decided not to accept medical advice: 'It seems wrong to say that patients have the right to be wrong in all cases except pregnancy.'[106] Similarly: '[T]here is great danger in over-riding a competent individual's decision about treatment that affects her body. Society runs the risk of creating a new class—pregnant women—who are deemed incompetent to make decisions, while their peers, non-pregnant women and men, have the right to bodily integrity.'[107] Such a comment draws attention to the possible effect of gender on medical decision-making. Some commentators have suggested that decisions declining treatment are more likely to be labelled 'irrational' when the patient is a woman. It is therefore argued that the bodily integrity of women 'is systematically accorded less respect than that of men', with the result that women's wishes are more likely to be overridden.[108] If this tendency exists, it may be more prominent when a woman is pregnant: the temptation to conclude that the making of a decision that appears to be irrational indicates a lack of capacity will obviously be stronger when the aim of protecting the fetus is uppermost.

[104] S. Goldberg, 'Medical Choices During Pregnancy: Whose Decision Is It Anyway?' (1989) 41 Rutgers Law Review 591, 621.
[105] Royal College of Obstetricians and Gynaecologists, *A Consideration of the Law and Ethics in Relation to Court-Authorised Obstetric Intervention* (1994) 13.
[106] S. Elias and G. J. Annas, *Reproductive Genetics and the Law* (Chicago, 1987) 260.
[107] S. Goldberg, 'Medical Choices During Pregnancy: Whose Decision Is It Anyway?' (1989) 41 Rutgers Law Review 591, 623.
[108] J. E. Hanigsberg, 'Homologizing Pregnancy and Motherhood: a Consideration of Abortion' (1995) 94 Michigan Law Review 371, 384–5.

This is not to suggest that pregnant women will not sometimes make tragic mistakes. Occasionally women in labour who decline medical advice will die, as will their fetuses. Occasionally their decisions will result in their children being born with brain damage or other disabilities which intervention might have avoided. 'A policy of absolute deference to the medical decisions of the mother may produce tragedy in the individual case.'[109] Further, the conclusion that women's views should be respected should not be allowed to obscure the distressing position of conscientious doctors whose advice has been declined. It is not surprising that they will find it difficult to stand by and watch when they feel that they are able to help:

Physicians may have a low tolerance for many patients' often unstated fears concerning minor medical problems or low-risk invasive procedures, such as Cesarean section. When an apparently competent mother decides on a course of action that clearly places her infant's life at risk, the confusion and possible anger of those who otherwise would do everything possible to save that infant is understandable.[110]

Earlier in the chapter, I discussed the possibility of balancing fetal and maternal interests. What has emerged is the need to undertake a different form of balancing: given that there is no simple solution to the problem posed by a maternal decision putting a fetus at risk, should society permit intervention (with all its objectionable features) or defer to maternal autonomy (and so occasionally fail to prevent harm to the fetus)? One commentator has answered as follows: 'Mistakes will be made in pregnancy and birth as in every other human context. They may be made by doctors; they may be made by patients and their families. While the fetus is within the body of a woman, the power and responsibility to choose must rest with her.'[111] This accepts that the dangers posed by the authorization of compulsory intervention are too great: '[P]reventing . . . tragedies comes at the cost of embracing an unprecedented and problematic tyranny of medicine and technology, and a tyranny whose potential scope knows no bounds.'[112] Such a conclusion is based on principle rather than on any assumptions about the greater likelihood of women making the correct decisions: 'We defer to the decision making of those most directly involved, not out of naivete or a belief that people invariably will act in their own or one another's best interests, but out of recognition that licensing state intervention in such intimate areas exacts unacceptable social costs.'[113]

[109] 'Developments in the Law, Medical Technology and the Law' (1990) 103 Harvard Law Review 1519, 1572.

[110] L. J. Nelson *et al.*, 'Forced Medical Treatment of Pregnant Women: "Compelling Each to Live as Seems Good to the Rest"' (1986) 37 Hastings Law Journal 703, 713.

[111] J. Gallagher, 'Fetus as Patient', in S. Cohen and N. Taub (eds.), *Reproductive Laws for the 1990s* (Clifton, NJ, 1989) 185, 215.

[112] N. Rhoden, 'The Judge in the Delivery Room: the Emergence of Court-Ordered Cesareans' (1986) 74 California Law Review 1951, 2029–30.

[113] J. Gallagher, 'Prenatal Invasions and Interventions: What's Wrong with Fetal Rights' (1987) 10 Harvard Women's Law Journal 9, 57.

Risks Posed by Antenatal Conduct

When discussing the possibility of legal intervention to compel treatment, I made certain assumptions regarding the validity of the evidence establishing the existence of risks associated with childbirth. Similar assumptions can be made regarding the evidence as to the harm that certain forms of maternal antenatal conduct can do to the fetus.[114] Cigarette smoking during pregnancy can retard fetal growth, result in low birth weight or premature birth, and increase the risk of abruptio placentae, placenta praevia, premature rupture of the membranes, bleeding during pregnancy, stillbirth, and neonatal death. It may also be associated with deficits in growth and emotional and intellectual development and with an increased incidence of childhood cancer. Alcohol abuse produces a greater likelihood of intra-uterine growth retardation, perinatal mortality, abruptio placentae, premature rupture of the membranes, and premature birth. Further, heavy drinking can result in the birth of a child with fetal alcohol syndrome, characterized by congenital malformations, growth and mental retardation, central nervous system impairment, and proneness to learning and speech disabilities and severe behavioural problems. Taking drugs such as heroin and cocaine during pregnancy often causes fetal harm, although much of this is a product of associated health, nutritional, and social problems. The most common complications caused by these drugs are premature labour, intra-uterine growth retardation, abruptio placentae, premature rupture of the membranes, and perinatal death. The neonate may experience narcotic withdrawal and long-term developmental retardation. In addition, cocaine use can result in children being born suffering from physical abnormalities (such as atresias and limb reductions, neurological and gastrointestinal abnormalities, and brain damage). As well as causing direct harm to her fetus, a pregnant woman can also put her fetus at risk by failing to obtain antenatal care. Competent antenatal care can not only allow the woman's health and the development of the fetus to be monitored, but it can also ensure that potentially damaging infections are detected.

---

[114] Examples of research on these effects include: E. K. Adams and C. L. Melvin, 'Costs of Maternal Conditions Attributable to Smoking during Pregnancy' (1998) 15 *American Journal of Preventive Medicine* 212; P. P. Wong and A. Bauman, 'How Well Does Epidemiological Evidence Hold for the Relationship between Smoking and Adverse Obstetric Outcomes in New South Wales?' (1997) 37 *Australian and New Zealand Journal of Obstetrics and Gynaecology* 168; J. L. Johnson and M. Leff, 'Children of Substance Abusers: Overview of Research Findings' (1999) 103 *Pediatrics* 1085; C. L. Wagner *et al.*, 'The Impact of Prenatal Drug Exposure on the Neonate' (1998) 25 *Obstetrics and Gynecology Clinics of North America* 169.

A Balancing of Interests?

Once it is accepted that there is satisfactory medical evidence of the harm that can be caused to a fetus by a pregnant woman's cigarette smoking, alcohol or drug consumption, or failure to obtain antenatal care, the question to be considered is whether a desire to protect the fetus against this harm can justify intervention to impose controls on a pregnant woman. Thus we encounter, in a different context, a problem already discussed: whether a fetus possesses interests that the law might seek to protect and, if so, whether those interests can ever override those of the pregnant woman. Earlier in the chapter, I suggested that a special kind of autonomy interest is involved when a pregnant woman smokes or takes drugs or alcohol: by acting in this manner she is asserting a freedom to engage in certain conduct. As has been shown, a number of rights might be invoked to support such a claim. In particular, rights to self-determination, liberty, or privacy might be asserted. Can any of these support a claim that a pregnant woman has the right to act as she chooses, regardless of the risk to her fetus?

The argument that a woman can rely on a right to self-determination or liberty to justify such conduct can be questioned. Similarly, it is not clear that drug taking or smoking should be respected as a manifestation of the right to privacy. Following *Roe v Wade*, this right has been seen as conferring a broad right to procreative autonomy. To rely on a concept of this kind to confer immunity in respect of drug taking or smoking is dubious. The notion of privacy invoked in *Roe v Wade* was adopted in recognition of the deeply personal nature of the decision that a woman must make in determining whether to continue with a pregnancy. To deny a woman the opportunity to make this decision would represent a major intrusion into the way she lives her life. To view drug taking or smoking as raising comparable privacy issues would trivialize *Roe v Wade*. This point has been made with regard to drug and alcohol use:

Abortion rights grew out of a body of law that established privacy rights in activities related to marriage, contraception, family relationships, and child rearing and education. It is not clear that a woman's constitutional right to make reproductive and family choices should be extended to prevent a state from interfering with her choice to use drugs or alcohol during pregnancy.... [A] woman's right to reproductive choice in the abortion context is more compelling than any right she might have to engage in behavior that harms a child she intends to carry to term.[115]

More tersely, in a South Carolina case involving neglect proceedings against a woman who had taken cocaine during pregnancy, a judge remarked: 'It

---

[115] J. Wilton, 'Compelled Hospitalization and Treatment during Pregnancy: Mental Health Statutes as Models for Legislation to Protect Children from Prenatal Drug and Alcohol Exposure' (1991) 25 Family Law Quarterly 149, 156.

strains belief for [her] to argue that using crack cocaine during pregnancy is encompassed within the constitutionally recognized right of privacy.'[116]

While such a comment obviously embodies a value judgement, it should not be rejected out of hand. Although views will differ, it is not self-evident that drug taking or smoking by a pregnant woman represents an expression of autonomy that the state should necessarily respect.[117] Nor is it self-evident that a pregnant woman who ingests harmful substances is asserting a right of a kind that outweighs any possible state interest in fetal protection. The dangers of employing 'rights talk' in this context should be recognized: it is misleading to dress up personal preferences in the garb of fundamental rights.[118] This is not to reach a conclusion about the justification, or otherwise, for state intervention to control a pregnant woman's conduct. It is simply to suggest that it is questionable to object to such intervention solely on the ground that it would violate a right that the state is bound to honour.

This analysis, however, is confined to a scrutiny of rights in the abstract. If it is accepted that a pregnant woman's claim that she should be free to take illicit drugs does not provide a conclusive answer to the state's demand that action should be taken to protect the fetus, it is still necessary to examine the intervention that would be undertaken to prevent conduct of the kind discussed. The answer may be that the woman would be placed under surveillance or in protective custody until her child is delivered. If this were the outcome, obviously the fundamental right to liberty would be infringed. It is only when the reality of the intervention is appreciated that a proper balancing of interests can be undertaken. The question becomes whether the state's interest in protecting potential human life can justify a substantial interference with the pregnant woman's right to liberty. In *Dobson (Litigation Guardian of) v Dobson*, McLachlin J of the Supreme Court of Canada was in no doubt as to the answer. She regarded it as objectionable for the law to permit the scrutiny of a woman's conduct during pregnancy: this would have the potential to jeopardize the woman's 'fundamental right' to liberty and to 'control her body and make decisions in her own interest'. She also invoked an additional right—to equal treatment. She noted that, while Canadians generally enjoy full rights to decide personal matters, state scrutiny of the conduct of a pregnant woman would mean that she would not enjoy that right. If the law were to attempt to protect her fetus, she would be 'subject to a host of additional restrictions'.[119]

---

[116] *Whitner v State* 492 SE 2d 777, 786 (SC, 1997).

[117] Further, when the relevant conduct is taking a drug such as heroin or cocaine, there is no basis on which the woman can invoke a 'right', since the ingestion of such drugs is illegal.

[118] J. E. Fleming, 'Securing Deliberative Autonomy' (1995) 48 Stanford Law Review 1, 41. See also M. A. Glendon, *Rights Talk: the Impoverishment of Political Discourse* (New York, 1991).

[119] (1999) 174 DLR (4th) 1, 34.

In an earlier decision, *Winnipeg Child and Family Services (Northwest Area) v G*, the Supreme Court of Canada undertook a full examination of the issues raised by maternal drug use. The case arose because of concern that a pregnant woman's glue sniffing was threatening the welfare of her fetus. The proceedings before the Supreme Court dealt with the question whether the woman should have been placed in the custody of the Winnipeg welfare agency until the birth of her child. The agency argued that the woman should be regarded as being under an enforceable duty 'to refrain from activities that have no substantial value to a pregnant woman's well-being or right of self-determination and that have the potential to cause grave and irreparable harm to the child's life, health and ability to function after birth'.[120]

The majority judgment rejected the argument. Some of the reasons offered related to the fact that one of the causes of action depended on establishing that the mother owed a duty of care enforceable under tort law. This aspect of the case will be discussed in Chapter 11. For present purposes, the important point is that, while the majority conceded that solvent abuse 'may not be the type of self-determination that deserves protection'[121] (and so was unwilling to view the woman as exercising a right), it saw no way of distinguishing between conduct which has 'substantial value' for a pregnant woman's well-being and that which does not. Further, in the course of its discussion of the possible use of the *parens patriae* jurisdiction to protect a fetus, the judgment stressed the magnitude of the infringement of a woman's right to liberty that would result. It saw this infringement as different in kind from infringements resulting from the use of the *parens patriae* power in respect of children who have been born:

[T]he invasion of liberty involved in making court orders affecting the unborn child, is of a different order than the invasion of liberty involved in court orders relating to born children. The *parens patriae* power over born children permits the courts to override the liberty of the parents to make decisions on behalf of their children where a parental choice may result in harm to a child . . . The only liberty interest affected is the parent's interest in making decisions for *his or her child*. By contrast, extension of the *parens patriae* jurisdiction of the court to unborn children has the potential to affect a much broader range of liberty interests. The court cannot make decisions for the unborn child without inevitably making decisions for the mother herself. The intrusion is therefore far greater than simply limiting the mother's choices concerning her child. Any choice concerning her child inevitably affects her. For example, to sustain the order requested in the case at bar would interfere with the pregnant woman's ability to choose where to live and what medical treatment to undergo. . . . [This] would seriously intrude on the rights of women.[122]

Such a conclusion reflects the view that any interests the fetus might possess

---

[120] (1997) 152 DLR (4th) 193, 210.   [121] Ibid. 211.
[122] Ibid. 218–19 (citations omitted; emphasis in original).

cannot justify the overriding of an interest so fundamental as the woman's right to liberty.

Balancing fetal interests against the woman's autonomy interests may be unacceptable in this context. The discussion has proceeded on the basis that a woman's conduct during pregnancy can be viewed in the same way as her conduct at the time of delivery: the assumption has been that in each situation she makes choices and the problem is to determine whether the law should respect those choices. Yet it might be wrong to regard antenatal conduct such as taking alcohol or drugs or glue sniffing as the product of a considered choice. By engaging in such conduct, a woman may not be proclaiming her autonomy; she may be simply living her life. Any analysis that overlooks the fact that this life has been partly determined by social, economic, and cultural conditions is deficient.[123] The majority judgment in the *Winnipeg* case recognized this: '[L]ifestyle "choices" like alcohol consumption, drug abuse, and poor nutrition may be the products of circumstance and illness rather than free choice . . .'.[124] The judgment went on to quote the following comments:

[W]omen do not abuse drugs out of a lack of care for their fetuses. Drug abusing pregnant women, like other drug abusers, are addicts. People do not want to be drug addicts. . . . Treating pregnant substance abusers as fetal abusers ignores the range of conditions that contribute to problems like drug addiction and lack of nutrition, such as limited quality pre-natal care, lack of food for impoverished women, and lack of treatment for substance abusers.[125]

This suggests that it is unsatisfactory to view a woman who engages in potentially harmful conduct (such as drug abuse) as heedlessly asserting her interests at the expense of those of her fetus. Her conduct may not be the product of a freely made decision that the threat of legal action might persuade her to reconsider. Appreciating this perspective draws attention to the need to look critically at the role the law can be expected to perform in this difficult area.

The prospect of legal intervention against pregnant women also raises broad policy issues. It must be asked whether it would be acceptable for society to introduce a system of surveillance and control designed to protect the fetus. Those who have contemplated this possibility have shown how intrusive such a system could become:

[Women might] be prohibited from using alcohol or other substances harmful to the fetus during pregnancy, or be kept from the workplace because of toxic effects on the

---

[123] C. Wells, 'Patients, Consent and Criminal Law' [1994] Journal of Social Welfare and Family Law 65, 69.

[124] (1997) 152 DLR (4th) 193, 211.

[125] J. E. Hanigsberg, 'Power and Procreation: State Interference in Pregnancy' (1991) 23 Ottawa Law Review 35, 53.

fetus. They could be ordered to take drugs, such as insulin for diabetes, medications for fetal deficiencies, or intrauterine blood transfusions for Rh factor. Pregnant anorexic teenagers could be force-fed. Prenatal screening and diagnostic procedures, from amniocentesis to sonography or even fetoscopy, could be made mandatory.[126]

To this list of possible conduct which might attract the attention of the law could be added other examples, such as smoking, eating a poor diet, engaging in excessive exercise or in intercourse late in pregnancy, taking legally available drugs, and failing to heed medical advice. One report has warned of the danger of creating 'a society that [would] require monitoring of all pregnant and potentially fertile women to assure effective enforcement of . . . fetal rights . . .'. It added: 'Monitoring and enforcement problems could threaten to turn our society into a prototype of an Orwellian novel if fetal interests override maternal choice.'[127]

There is also the need to ensure that the evidence of risk to the fetus is sufficiently clear to warrant intervention. In the absence of such evidence, intervention may be based on speculation. While certain forms of maternal conduct pose clearly documented risks to the fetus, there may be doubt about the effects of others. This point troubled the court in the *Winnipeg* case, where the majority noted that determining what will cause grave harm to a fetus 'is a difficult endeavour with which medical researchers continually struggle'. The judgment added: 'The difference between confinement and freedom . . . may depend on a grasp of the latest research and its implications.'[128]

Again, therefore, a balancing exercise must be undertaken. Although intervention may occasionally benefit a fetus, this benefit would come at too high a price. The dangers of relying on coercive laws, which would permit broad-ranging and possibly speculative intervention in the lives of pregnant women, are too great.

The Nature of the Legal Process: Criminal Proceedings

In Chapter 2 it was seen that both criminal and child protection laws have been invoked in an attempt to protect fetuses against maternal conduct. The

---

[126] J. A. Robertson, 'The Right to Procreate and In Utero Fetal Therapy' (1982) 3 Journal of Legal Medicine 333, 358 (footnotes omitted).

[127] H. Brown *et al.* (eds.), 'Special Project: Legal Rights and Issues Surrounding Conception, Pregnancy, and Birth' (1986) 39 Vanderbilt Law Review 597, 849. Some commentators, while recognizing the dangers of intrusiveness, argue that intervention should be possible when a pregnant woman engages in substance abuse: by limiting liability in this manner, a clear line can be drawn between maternal conduct which can and cannot be prohibited. See S. B. Glink, 'The Prosecution of Maternal Fetal Abuse: is This the Answer?' [1991] University of Illinois Law Review 533, 570.

[128] (1997) 152 DLR (4th) 193, 211.

courts have generally refused to apply either body of law for this purpose. Were they right to take this course? Can a case be made for the imposition of legislative controls on pregnant women? To deal with these questions, it is necessary to re-examine the techniques available to the law and to assess their appropriateness and effectiveness.

Little need be said about the use of the criminal law during a woman's pregnancy. When a pregnant woman is found guilty of an offence, it is possible for a court to impose a penalty having the incidental effect of protecting the fetus. This may be acceptable when the penalty is a proper response to the offence committed. In a case of drug use, if the offence and the offender's circumstances warrant probation, there may be nothing objectionable about adding a condition requiring participation in a drug rehabilitation programme. Such a condition, while directed at the offender, might incidentally benefit the fetus. Although the use of the law in this way obviously raises questions about the role of the criminal law in dealing with drug abuse, in principle there is no basis for objecting to its use for the collateral purpose of protecting the fetus. This must be done within a sentencing framework that fixes the maximum sentence by reference to the offence of which the woman is guilty. It would be unacceptable if, in order to protect the fetus, a sentence were imposed different in kind from, or more severe than, that which would normally be employed. Injustice will result if a disproportionate sentence is imposed as an indirect means of conferring protection on the fetus. Imprisoning a pregnant woman for a minor theft, for example, in an attempt to ensure that she receives antenatal care would be unjust if such a sanction would not be imposed on the woman were she not pregnant. To use the law in this manner would distort the sentencing process.

An alternative is the post-natal use of the criminal law. On a number of occasions, women have been prosecuted for abusing, neglecting, or endangering their fetuses when their children have been born suffering the ill-effects of antenatal conduct. Such prosecutions have typically followed the birth of drug-affected children whose mothers have taken illicit drugs during pregnancy. An alternative charge in such a case has been that of supplying drugs. As was seen in Chapter 2, criminal charges in respect of abuse, neglect, or endangerment have generally failed on the ground that the reference in the relevant provisions to 'children' could not be interpreted as applying to fetuses. Attempts to defeat such rulings by charging women with supplying drugs to minors in the few seconds before the umbilical cord was cut have also failed. It must be asked whether such outcomes were correct and, therefore, whether the law should punish a woman for antenatal conduct harming her fetus. The argument that in some circumstances the criminal law should be used in this way has been put as follows: '[C]riminal prosecution for culpable prenatal conduct that causes severe impairment to offspring . . . may turn out to be an effective tool for demonstrating society's protection of children and deterring egregiously harmful prenatal conduct in certain cases.'[129]

To determine whether it is appropriate to employ the law to punish a woman whose antenatal conduct has harmed her child it is helpful to consider the hypothetical example of a woman who, in spite of warnings, has regularly taken heroin during her pregnancy and who has given birth to a drug-addicted child. Should she be found guilty of an offence (such as abuse of her fetus or giving birth to a drug-affected child) and so be liable to a criminal penalty? The arguments in favour of criminalizing her conduct are that by taking this course society expresses its condemnation of this conduct and deters other women from acting as she has acted. While the use of the criminal law would have a denunciatory effect, it seems most unlikely that it would act as a deterrent. Taking heroin is itself a criminal offence. Why should a woman who is not deterred by existing penalties be deterred by the imposition of a special penalty for drug use in pregnancy?[130] To assert that a pregnant woman is particularly likely to respond to the threat of a criminal sanction is to adopt an oversimplified view of human behaviour. Her drug use is likely to be the product of complex social and personal forces beyond the reach of the criminal law. Further, she has a special incentive to cease taking drugs: by doing so, she will increase her chances of delivering a healthy baby. If this powerful incentive does not influence her behaviour, it is unconvincing to argue that her conduct will be affected by the threat of a criminal penalty. It seems naive to assume that relying on the criminal law will produce obedient conformity among pregnant women who take illegal drugs.

In addition to arguments about the deterrent effect of the criminal law, attention must be paid to its methods. In particular, the clumsy and limited nature of its sanctions should be examined. What sanction should be imposed on a woman who has given birth to a drug-affected child? Even if she has the means to pay, imposing a fine would be inappropriate. A stronger case might be made for the use of detention or a probation order. In particular, it can be argued that a probation order could be employed to allow counselling and rehabilitation to be provided.[131] This argument is flawed: if the aim is to offer support and treatment, this is unlikely to be achieved within

---

[129] J. A. Robertson, 'Reconciling Offspring and Maternal Interests During Pregnancy', in S. Cohen and N. Taub (eds.), *Reproductive Laws for the 1990s* (Clifton, NJ, 1989) 259, 263. See also S. Balisy, 'Maternal Substance Abuse: the Need to Provide Legal Protection for the Fetus' (1987) 60 Southern California Law Review 1209, 1235.

[130] J. Denison, 'The Efficacy and Constitutionality of Criminal Punishment for Maternal Substance Abuse' (1991) 64 Southern California Law Review 1103, 1129–30.

[131] This view has been put forward by Glink, who argues for the use of the criminal law for rehabilitative purposes. The 'ideal sentence', in her opinion, is an extended period of probation (5 to 10 years) coupled with mandatory confinement for 12 to 18 months in a drug rehabilitation programme. See S. B. Glink, 'The Prosecution of Maternal Fetal Abuse: is This the Answer?' [1991] University of Illinois Law Review 533, 577.

the framework of a criminal sentence. Coerced change is difficult to accomplish; therapeutic programmes have more prospect of success if they are voluntarily undertaken.

The Nature of the Legal Process: Child Protection Proceedings

If it is agreed that a punitive approach would be ineffective, the use of benevolently intentioned child protection laws might provide a solution. Bringing a pregnant woman within the operation of these laws might result in the provision of welfare services that would ultimately benefit both the woman and her child.

As was seen in Chapter 2, the courts have generally refused to employ child protection proceedings to safeguard a fetus in the same way as they are utilized to safeguard a child who has been abused or neglected. The courts have been right to do so. Their rulings that legislation seeking to protect a 'child' against neglect or abuse cannot be applied to protect a fetus are more than exercises in statutory interpretation. They recognize that resorting to child protection laws is an artificial and inappropriate response to a threat to a fetus. The legal mechanisms on which these laws rely and the orders for which they provide are not adapted to the protection of the fetus. The notion of proceedings begun, for example, by 'apprehending' a fetus is manifestly absurd, as is the claim that a fetus can be taken into 'temporary custody' or made a ward of a welfare agency.[132] In addition, the types of orders necessary to ensure the protection of the fetus are not substantially different from those employed by the criminal law; they would involve placing the pregnant woman under supervision or in detention. As was seen earlier in the chapter, the Supreme Court of Canada in *Winnipeg Child and Family Services (Northwest Area) v G* drew attention to the invasion of liberty which would be involved in placing a glue-sniffing woman in custody, and in *Re Baby R* the British Columbia Supreme Court was clearly dismayed by the thought that the state should confine a pregnant woman until her delivery.[133] The fact that the intervention is benevolently intentioned does not alter its reality. Also— as was noted with regard to the possible use of the criminal law—coercive benevolence is most unlikely to achieve its aim; if society wishes to provide support and assistance to a pregnant woman whose behaviour might harm her fetus, it has little chance of succeeding within the alienating framework of a court order.

One qualification must be added to this discussion. In Chapter 2 it was seen that the courts have accepted that care proceedings may properly be taken

---

[132] These procedures were employed, respectively, in *Re Baby R* (1988) 53 DLR (4th) 69; *Re Dittrick Infant* 263 NW 2d 37 (1977) and *Children's Aid Society and T* (1987) 59 OR (2d) 204. See above 27, 8, and 9–10.

[133] (1988) 53 DLR (4th) 69, 80.

after a child has been born suffering the effects of maternal conduct. For example, evidence of the use of illegal drugs can be admitted in these proceedings to determine whether a child is, or is likely to be, abused or neglected. Such testimony can be received for the purpose of assessing the child's present and future situation and, in particular, the parents' ability to care for their child. This has implications for a pregnant woman's freedom of action. A woman who asserts her right to be free of controls during pregnancy cannot be entirely free if her conduct can have legal consequences after the child's birth. These consequences can include intervention in her life (and, in extreme cases, the loss of custody of her child). Thus the law can impose retrospective constraints. This is not improper. Child protection laws require that the welfare of the child should take precedence over parental interests. Nevertheless, the significance of laws operating in the manner described should not be overlooked. It is possible that a woman will be subject to pressure if she is aware that certain conduct during pregnancy will lead to welfare intervention after her child is born.[134]

THE BROADER PICTURE: BY-PRODUCTS OF LEGAL INTERVENTION

There are other factors to be taken into account when considering the appropriateness of legal intervention against a pregnant woman, whether during pregnancy or at the time of delivery. The trusting relationship between a practitioner and the woman could be distorted by resort to the law. If a doctor considers taking legal action to compel a woman to submit to treatment, there is a danger that the relationship will become an adversarial one. This will not be in the best interests of the woman or her fetus; these interests are much more likely to be advanced if the relationship is viewed as a partnership in pursuit of a common goal.[135] Doctors should advise, not coerce. There are many doctors who would feel uncomfortable about the idea of coerced treatment and who would regard it as unethical: 'The role of the doctor is to facilitate health, not to inflict it on the public. Medicine has no general right to enforce its diagnostic techniques, therapies or palliatives on an unconsenting or unwilling patient.'[136] This view was endorsed by committees established by the American College of Obstetricians and Gynecologists[137] and by the

---

[134] The possibility of postnatal legal intervention acting as a retrospective curb on a pregnant woman's exercise of her autonomy would be more marked in the case of a child's negligence claim against his or her mother. This subject is discussed in Chapter 11.

[135] L. J. Nelson and N. Milliken, 'Compelled Medical Treatment of Pregnant Women: Life, Liberty and Law in Conflict' (1988) 259 *Journal of the American Medical Association* 1060, 1065.

[136] S. McLean, 'The Right to Consent to Medical Treatment', in T. Campbell *et al.* (eds.), *Human Rights: from Rhetoric to Reality* (Oxford, 1986) 148, 161.

[137] American College of Obstetricians and Gynecologists, Committee on Ethics, *Patient Choice: Maternal–Fetal Conflict*, Opinion No 55 (1987).

Royal College of Obstetricians and Gynaecologists. Both opposed the coercive treatment of pregnant women. The guidelines laid down by the latter made the point as follows: '[I]t is inappropriate, and unlikely to be helpful or necessary, to invoke judicial intervention to overrule an informed and competent woman's refusal of a proposed medical treatment, even though her refusal might place her life and that of her fetus at risk.'[138]

This statement was approved by the English Court of Appeal in *Re MB*.[139] Similarly, in *Re Baby Boy Doe*, the Appellate Court of Illinois noted that the medical profession strongly supported upholding the pregnant woman's autonomy:

The American Medical Association's Board of Trustees cautions that the physician's duty is not to dictate the pregnant woman's decision, but to ensure that she is provided with the appropriate information to make an informed decision. If the woman rejects the doctor's recommendation, the appropriate response is not to attempt to force the recommended procedure upon her, but to urge her to seek consultation and counseling from a variety of sources.

Referring to the case before it, the court went on to describe the doctors' actions in seeking court authorization for a caesarean section as 'inconsistent with the ethical position taken by the profession'.[140] Whether this position is the one currently adopted by the majority of the profession is unclear. In a 1987 United States survey of senior practitioners, 46 per cent 'thought that mothers who refused medical advice and thereby endangered the life of the fetus should be detained in hospitals or other facilities so that compliance could be ensured'; 47 per cent 'thought that the precedent set by the courts in cases requiring emergency cesarean sections for the sake of the fetus should be extended to include other procedures that are potentially lifesaving for the fetus, such as intrauterine transfusion, as these procedures come to represent the standard of care'.[141]

In addition to ethical considerations, the effect that involvement in legal proceedings can have on the role of doctors and midwives should be noted. When a doctor takes legal action to compel a pregnant woman to accept treatment, that doctor becomes the woman's adversary rather than her care giver. Further, when a woman's conduct during pregnancy is threatening or has harmed her fetus, this is most likely to come to official notice as a result of information provided by a doctor or nurse. For example, if criminal proceedings were to be taken against a woman who has given birth to a drug-affected child, it would be a health care professional who would initiate the

---

[138] Royal College of Obstetricians and Gynaecologists, *A Consideration of the Law and Ethics in Relation to Court-Authorised Obstetric Intervention* (1994) 15.
[139] [1997] 2 FLR 426, 438.   [140] 632 NE 2d 326, 335 (Ill App 1 Dist, 1994).
[141] V. E. B. Kolder *et al.*, 'Court-Ordered Obstetrical Interventions' (1987) 316 *New England Journal of Medicine* 1192, 1193.

prosecution and provide the necessary evidence. This is not a role with which many doctors and nurses would feel comfortable. While involvement with the criminal law is likely to be particularly unappealing, those who are caring for a pregnant woman might also have reservations about participating in child protection proceedings. A doctor who reports a pregnant drug user to a welfare agency runs the risk of alienating her and making it impossible to continue providing medical care. Finally, there is the fact that any disclosure of information to officials would undermine the confidentiality attaching to all consultations. It would be disturbing for a woman to visit a doctor or midwife knowing that any information she gives could be employed in court proceedings. Worse, she might withhold important facts: 'The knowledge that personal records might be disclosed could destroy a woman's trust in her doctor and cause her to conceal facts which could be vital to both her health and the health of her fetus.'[142] In short, the task of coercing women — of functioning as 'pregnancy police'[143] — is one that would cause great difficulties for health care professionals; it is also a task that many of them would find uncongenial, if not repugnant.

There is another argument against allowing doctors and midwives to become involved in legal proceedings designed to control pregnant women. To invoke the law is to run the risk of driving women away from antenatal care and hospital delivery, thus perhaps endangering both the women and their fetuses.[144] There have been cases in the United States in which women have not returned to hospitals or have gone into hiding to avoid further contact with their medical advisers.[145] Further, the possibility of legal action could deter pregnant women from seeking medical care. If an antenatal visit could trigger a system of surveillance — with the possibility of exposure to criminal or child protection proceedings — women might be discouraged from consulting a midwife or doctor. This is particularly likely in the case of maternal drug abuse: 'There is some evidence . . . that a major effect of . . . highly publicized cases is to discourage other pregnant women from obtaining

[142] R. Manson and J. Marolt, 'A New Crime, Fetal Neglect: State Intervention to Protect the Unborn — Protection at What Cost?' (1988) 24 California Western Law Review 161, 172.

[143] S. Goldberg, 'Of Gametes and Guardians: the Impropriety of Appointing Guardians ad Litem for Fetuses and Embryos' (1991) 66 Washington Law Review 503, 541.

[144] D. E. Johnsen, 'The Creation of Fetal Rights: Conflicts with Women's Constitutional Rights to Liberty, Privacy, and Equal Protection' (1986) 95 Yale Law Journal 599, 612 and L. A. Schott, 'The Pamela Rae Stewart Case and Fetal Harm: Prosecution or Prevention?' (1988) 11 Harvard Women's Law Journal 227, 243–4.

[145] For example, in a 1982 Michigan case the police were instructed by a judge to apprehend a pregnant woman and escort her to the hospital to undergo a caesarean section. Rather than submit to a procedure against her religious beliefs, the woman fled into hiding. (See J. Gallagher, 'Prenatal Invasions and Interventions: What's Wrong with Fetal Rights?' (1987) 10 Harvard Women's Law Journal 9, 47.) Similarly, the woman who was the subject of the proceedings in *Raleigh Fitkin-Paul Morgan Memorial Hospital v Anderson* 201 A 2d 537 (1964) did not return to the hospital after the court order had been made authorizing a blood transfusion.

proper prenatal care out of fear of criminal prosecution, thus potentially exacerbating the problem.'[146] Women taking illegal drugs are particularly likely to be the targets of legal intervention and these women have high-risk pregnancies; the result might be that those with the greatest need for antenatal care would be most likely to be deterred from seeking medical help.[147]

These difficulties are the product of the law's methods, particularly its reliance on coercion. Other problems emerge from the concepts that it employs. As was seen in Chapter 8, judges and legislatures have paid special attention to the developmental stage attained by the fetus: the more mature the fetus, the greater is the pressure for legal intervention to protect it. This aspect of the law was most clearly reflected in the emphasis that *Roe v Wade* placed on viability. Yet laws embodying this approach will not be effective in protecting fetuses against the most common forms of harm. Maternal conduct such as drug and alcohol abuse and smoking can be particularly damaging at an early stage of gestation. If society is serious about employing the law to prevent fetal harm, intervention should occur early in pregnancy rather than late. Yet this would be inconsistent with a perspective that sees the state's interest in protecting the fetus as becoming more compelling during the later stages of gestation. '[T]he *Roe* Court's perception of a slowly accruing interest in protecting fetal life does not hold true in the fetal health context . . .'.[148]

There is another reason to be suspicious of resort to the law to coerce or control pregnant women. Laws that do so tend to be invoked against the poor, the disadvantaged, and members of minority groups. Research in the United States, for example, reveals that a woman who abuses alcohol or who takes illegal drugs during pregnancy is more likely to be made the subject of criminal or child protection proceedings if she is poor and black. Similarly, the majority of women in respect of whom compulsory treatment orders have been sought were members of minority ethnic groups.[149]

It is also necessary to question certain assumptions about the way the law might operate in this field. Central to the analysis offered in this and the preceding chapter is the view that the state in some contexts has an interest in protecting potential human life. This interest can be invoked by those advocating the use of criminal or child protection proceedings against a pregnant woman or proceedings to compel the provision of medical treatment. To

---

[146] R. H. Blank, *Mother and Fetus: Changing Notions of Maternal Responsibility* (New York, 1992) 170.

[147] D. E. Johnsen, 'A New Threat to Pregnant Women's Autonomy' (1987) 17(4) Hastings Center Report 33, 38.

[148] J. Wilton, 'Compelled Hospitalization and Treatment during Pregnancy: Mental Health Statutes as Models for Legislation to Protect Children from Prenatal Drug and Alcohol Exposure' (1991) 25 Family Law Quarterly 149, 156.

[149] V. E. B. Kolder *et al.*, 'Court-Ordered Obstetrical Interventions' (1987) 316 *New England Journal of Medicine* 1192, 1193.

focus on proceedings of this kind is to overlook the fact that the law might use other mechanisms in an attempt to protect fetal life. The state might fulfil its role without targeting pregnant women. Its obligation might be discharged by the enactment of laws requiring relevant agencies to provide educational, health, and welfare services for them. Such laws are more likely to provide a humane and effective response to the complex social problems giving rise to alcohol and drug abuse in pregnancy: '[T]he state could generously fund addiction prevention and voluntary treatment programs, with a special emphasis on averting gestational substance abuse. Before pursuing invasive solutions, the legislature should seriously consider making voluntary treatment more readily available.'[150] If this perspective is adopted, the law has a role to play, but it is a different one from that exemplified in the cases considered earlier in the chapter.

CONCLUSION

While respect for maternal autonomy provides the starting-point in any discussion of legal intervention designed to protect a fetus, a desire to maintain this autonomy cannot provide the sole basis on which decisions as to intervention are based. To assert that no action to protect a fetus against maternal conduct can be contemplated because this action will impinge on the rights of the woman is to oversimplify the problems with which this chapter has dealt. More is at issue than maternal autonomy. When a pregnancy is to be carried to full term, certain forms of antenatal conduct and certain maternal decisions at the time of delivery have the potential to harm the child that the fetus will become. A woman's conduct and decisions during pregnancy cannot be regarded as affecting her alone. A woman who harms her fetus harms more than herself. The law can justifiably restrict the autonomy of any person whose conduct threatens or harms another. It is not self-evident that a pregnant woman's autonomy should not be restricted in order to prevent harm to her fetus.

To accept this conclusion is to do no more than recognize that, while a pregnant woman—like any other competent adult—can insist that her rights be respected, her autonomy is not absolute. Analyses overlooking this fact fail to appreciate that autonomy is not a quality that a person does or does not possess. Rather, it is a capacity that may or may not be exercised in the context of a particular relationship.[151] To determine whether legal intervention

---

[150] K. R. Lichtenberg, 'Gestational Substance Abuse: a Call for a Thoughtful Legislative Response' (1990) 65 Washington Law Review 377, 387.

[151] For a similar analysis of autonomy, see J. Nedelsky, 'Reconceiving Autonomy: Sources, Thoughts and Possibilities' (1989) 1 Yale Journal of Law and Feminism 7 and 'Reconceiving Rights as Relationship' (1993) 1 Review of Constitutional Studies 1.

against a pregnant woman should be permitted to protect her fetus, there-fore, the focus should be on the nature of the relationship between them. The relationship is one of interdependence. It is the recognition of this interde-pendence that provides the most convincing basis on which to argue in favour of maternal immunity. If woman and fetus are 'not-one-but-not-two', it seems to follow that it is inappropriate for a pregnant woman to be placed under a legal obligation to her fetus. On this view, she cannot owe such an obligation to an entity that both is, and is not, a part of her. The 'not-one-but-not-two' model also hints at the indeterminate nature of the fetus, a factor used by some commentators to support the argument that intervention to protect the fetus cannot be justified to override maternal rights: '[I]t is rea-sonable to maintain that the interests of the individual who is indisputably a person should prevail.'[152] Similarly: 'Given the lack of consensus about the moral status of the fetus and the proper resolution of the maternal–fetal con-flict of interests, it is arbitrary to claim that the physician's decision to protect the fetus, rather than to honor the pregnant woman's decision to refuse treat-ment, is the morally correct choice.'[153]

These comments are a reminder of the special nature of the fetus. In Chap-ter 8, I argued that its intrinsic value should not be ignored. This argument echoed the analysis offered in *Roe v Wade*, from which two relevant propos-itions emerge. One is that the state has an interest in protecting the potential-ity of human life. The other is that this interest may not be pursued if to do so would threaten the life or health of the pregnant woman. In combination, these two propositions endorse the view that the autonomy of a pregnant woman is not absolute. The Supreme Court of the United States made this explicit when it noted that a pregnant woman 'cannot be isolated in her pri-vacy'.[154] It must be asked whether the court's analysis provides a basis for questioning the conclusion that the nature of the maternal/fetal relationship is of itself sufficient to defeat any argument in favour of coercive interven-tion. The Supreme Court's recognition of the need to protect a pregnant woman's life and health may leave the door open to intervention in some situ-ations. That a competent woman has the right not to have invasive surgical procedures imposed on her to protect the fetus seems undeniable. More debatable is whether her right to be free of non-invasive procedures—which pose no risk to her and which might benefit her and the fetus—should also receive the law's protection. On this analysis, it might be possible for courts to proceed on a case-by-case basis, seeking to determine whether the state's

---

[152] M. Mahowald, 'Beyond Abortion: Refusal of Caesarean Section' (1989) 3 Bioethics 106, 118.

[153] L. J. Nelson *et al.*, 'Forced Medical Treatment of Pregnant Women: "Compelling Each to Live as Seems Good to the Rest"' (1986) 37 Hastings Law Journal 703, 719.

[154] 410 US 113, 159; 35 L Ed 2d 147, 180 (1973).

interest in protecting fetal life, combined with the absence of risk to the woman, will tip the balance in favour of intervention.

There are dangers in adopting a case-by-case approach. It may be unwise to regard a particular form of intervention as carrying no, or minimal, risk to the woman. Procedures and treatments that in the past have been thought to be safe have sometimes been found not to be so. In addition, drawing a line between acceptable treatment involving low or minimal risk and unacceptable treatment involving significant risk would be difficult. What one doctor would represent as an uncontroversial example of safe intervention, another might regard as subjecting the woman to a degree of risk. A 'slippery slope' would quickly loom. If one type of treatment were to be accepted as safe — and therefore able to be employed without consent — pressure would build to extend the range of such treatments. It would, therefore, be unwise to pursue a policy that seeks to distinguish between acceptable and unacceptable intervention.

A number of other factors must be taken into account when proceedings to protect the fetus are being considered. The nature of the relevant legal procedures must be appreciated. In this chapter, I have suggested that court action against a pregnant woman is a clumsy and insensitive means of seeking to promote fetal welfare. The 'quick fix' which coercive intervention seems to offer is an illusion.[155] The techniques and mechanisms of the criminal law and child protection laws are ill suited to the pursuit of a policy of fetal protection. Court proceedings taken in order to compel women to accept medical treatment are likely to be hurried and slipshod. Further, court action will certainly diminish the trust that should exist between pregnant women and their care givers. This may deter women from seeking antenatal care. Resort to the courts is likely to be at best ineffective and at worst counterproductive.

Thus there is a need for scepticism about the role that legal coercion can play in a society seeking to promote the welfare of pregnant women and their fetuses: 'Our interest in helping future children by improving prenatal care would best be furthered by helping pregnant women to make informed, less constrained choices, not by punishing women or depriving them of choices altogether.'[156] This conclusion suggests that attention should be given to the development of programmes emphasizing education and promoting more effective communication between health care professionals and pregnant women. It also suggests persuasion, not coercion, should be used. Ultimately, it will be up to the individual woman to decide whether to accept advice. On

---

[155] T. B. Dawson, 'A Feminist Response to "Unborn Child Abuse: Contemplating Legal Solution"' (1991) 9 Canadian Journal of Family Law 157, 172.

[156] D. E. Johnsen, 'A New Threat to Pregnant Women's Autonomy' (1987) 17(4) Hastings Center Report 33, 33.

occasions the advice will be rejected, the fetus will be harmed and the child will suffer:

This view may seem callous to the rights of the fetuses, as some fetuses that might be salvaged may die or may be born defective. This is tragic, but it is likely to be rare. It is the price that society pays for protecting the rights of all competent adults and for preventing forcible physical violations of pregnant women by coercive obstetricians and judges. The choice between fetal health and maternal liberty is laced with moral and ethical dilemmas. The force of law cannot magically make them disappear.[157]

It is more acceptable to allow that pregnant women will occasionally harm their fetuses than to seek to create an elaborate system of surveillance and control. This view is informed by a realistic appreciation of the law's limitations. Instead of instituting court proceedings, every effort should be made to put women in a position in which they can make informed decisions in the best interests of themselves and their fetuses. This is a more principled approach and one likely to be more effective in promoting the welfare of the vast majority of fetuses.[158]

[157] S. Elias and G. J. Annas, *Reproductive Genetics and the Law* (Chicago, 1987) 262.
[158] G. J. Annas, 'Protecting the Liberty of Pregnant Patients' (1987) 316 *New England Journal of Medicine* 1213, 1214.

10

Applying the Law of Negligence

Chapters 4 to 7 examined a variety of situations in which doctors and midwives are liable to damages claims arising from antenatal or perinatal negligence. In dealing with these claims, courts have sought to resolve special problems associated with the application of negligence law in the field of obstetrics. This chapter examines some of these problems.

The most distinctive feature of this area of law is that the negligent treatment of a pregnant woman can result in liability not only to her, but also to her child. It is the liability to the child that is problematic. A doctor or midwife who cares for a pregnant woman is in a legal relationship with her, but a second legal relationship may also be present or later materialize. When providing care, a practitioner must therefore be aware of the existence of a potential plaintiff whose demand for compensation might subsequently have to be acknowledged. Further, the liability to this potential plaintiff will frequently be substantial. In a large number of the cases arising from antenatal negligence, the harm suffered by the woman has been insignificant compared with that suffered by the child.

TO WHOM IS A DUTY OF CARE OWED?

Negligent Diagnosis or Treatment

It is difficult to identify the basis of an action by a child who has suffered harm as a result of antenatal negligence. For such an action to succeed, it must be shown that a breach of a duty of care has occurred. As has been explained in Chapter 8, the Anglo-American legal systems have adopted two different approaches to the problem of establishing the source of that duty. On one view, the success of a damages claim made on behalf of a child depends on the proof of the breach of a duty of care specifically owed to the fetus. This rationale is a feature of many United States decisions and it can be understood only against the background of the development of the law in that country. In *Renslow v Mennonite Hospital*, the Supreme Court of Illinois offered the following explanation: 'Historically, negligence could not be founded upon the breach of a duty owed only to some person other than the plaintiff. . . . *Dietrich* and its progeny indicate this duty could be owed only to one with a legally identifiable existence.'[1] This view was widely adopted in the United

---

[1] 367 NE 2d 1250, 1254 (1977) (citations omitted). *Dietrich* is discussed above, 156–7.

States and there were many courts which accepted that when a child claimed damages for antenatal harm, the identification of the fetus as an entity to which a duty of care could be owed was a prerequisite for a successful action. In England, Canada, and Australia, this view has not prevailed. In these countries the courts have avoided discussion of the legal status of the fetus and have applied basic principles of negligence law in order to determine whether a child may sue in respect of antenatal harm. They have stated that the question to be asked is whether the child was a member of a class of persons who could foreseeably suffer harm as a result of the negligence. This question can be answered without speculation about the existence and status of the fetus.

In some respects, one approach is as satisfactory as the other. On either analysis, the fact that the harm occurred antenatally does not prevent the claim from succeeding. The injury or disability manifests itself after birth, when there is a living plaintiff who may bring the action. While this conclusion is not reassuring, it may be inescapable. The more closely the case law is examined, the more obvious it becomes that it is impossible to identify principles that can be satisfactorily applied. Nevertheless, it is instructive to scrutinize the different methods employed by the courts.

There are deficiencies in an explanation that relies on the concept of foreseeability, but ignores the existence of the fetus. The most important of these is its artificiality. This can be demonstrated by re-examining the analysis offered in *Watt v Rama*.[2] There the majority judges were troubled by the problem that a claim in respect of antenatal negligence is made on behalf of a person who did not exist at the time when the negligence occurred. They overcame this difficulty by stating that 'it would be immaterial whether at the time of fault the victim was in existence or not, so long as the victim was a member of a class which might reasonably and probably be affected by the act of carelessness'.[3] The court reinforced this by referring to cases in which negligent manufacturers have been held liable for harm that their defective products caused to persons who had not been born when the products were made. The users of the products were members of a category of persons who could foreseeably suffer harm at some future time as a result of the manufacturers' negligence. Thus an analogy was suggested: the fetus could be viewed in the same manner as an unborn consumer.

It is not wholly satisfactory to adopt this analysis to impose liability on a doctor or midwife whose negligent antenatal or perinatal care causes harm to a fetus. The practitioner who cares for a pregnant woman is in a direct and individual relationship with that woman and assumes responsibility for the welfare of her fetus. While the fetus may lack legal personality, it exists, has its own characteristics, and can be exposed to risks of which the practitioner

[2] See above 160–2.   [3] [1972] VR 353, 373.

is expected to be aware. Should the child be born injured or disabled, the practitioner's liability will depend on the nature of the care provided to the woman and her fetus. Relevant factors will be her health and the size and condition of the fetus during labour. The specificity of the practitioner's obligation cannot be ignored. The presence of the fetus imposes a distinctive duty, different from the generalized obligation that a manufacturer owes to all future consumers. The child suing in respect of antenatal negligence is in a different category from such consumers, who are members of a group of potential plaintiffs who were neither identifiable nor in existence at the time of the negligent conduct. By contrast, the fetus was an identifiable entity at the time of the negligence and the defendant was in a specific relationship with that entity and with the woman who gave birth. The child is not a being who comes from nowhere, suddenly appearing on the scene to lodge a claim. The presence of the pregnant woman is another distinctive feature. In the case of a manufacturer, there is no additional plaintiff to whom a duty of care is also owed.

There is another reason for questioning the analogy used in *Watt v Rama*. In the case of antenatal injury, the harm is suffered *before* birth, whereas in a case involving a careless manufacturer, the harm is suffered by a legal person. To overcome this problem, the decision adopted the notion that the rights of a child born suffering the ill-effects of antenatal negligence 'crystallize' at birth. This requires accepting the artificial view that while the harm was caused *in utero*, the wrong in respect of which proceedings can be taken does not manifest itself until birth. Unlike the victim of a careless manufacturer, a child born injured or disabled as a result of antenatal negligence suffers no injury as a legal person. The child was already injured when he or she became a person. As Phillips J remarked in *Burton v Islington Health Authority*: 'To say that the plaintiff suffered his injuries the moment after his birth rather than in the period leading up to his birth involves a legal fiction.'[4] Further, relying on this fiction depends on a process of working backwards from injury to duty.[5] The weakness in this approach is that it does not identify the duty breached by the negligent conduct. Rather, the existence of a duty at the time of this conduct is assumed and liability is imposed simply on the basis that foreseeable harm has been caused. Consequently, the approach throws no light on the nature of the duty owed to the 'not-one-but-not-two' entity for which the doctor or midwife is responsible.

Criticism of the analysis offered in cases such as *Watt v Rama* poses the question whether it is necessary to accept the *Renslow* analysis and so postulate the existence of a legally distinct entity on whose behalf a damages claim may be made. To take this course is to treat the fetus as an entity to which a

---

[4] [1993] QB 204, 219.
[5] P. F. Cane, 'Injuries to Unborn Children' (1977) 51 Australian Law Journal 704, 707.

duty of care is directly owed, an entity with a right to be free of tortious injury. One problem with this approach is that it confers legal personality on a fetus and (as has been explained in Chapter 8) is inconsistent with a well-established body of law relating to the fetus. More importantly, it opens up the possibility of conflict between a pregnant woman and her fetus. This possibility is implicit in the analysis in *Albala v City of New York*, where the New York Court of Appeals explained the grounds for a claim based on negligent *in utero* injury in the following manner: '[A]t the time the tort is committed there are two identifiable beings within the zone of danger each of whom is owed a duty independent of the other and each of whom may be directly injured.'[6] The crucial word in this passage is 'independent'. If the fetus is an entity to which a duty of care is owed, the discharge of this duty might in some circumstances require action inconsistent with the interests of the pregnant woman. This outcome has been rejected on the basis of the arguments set out in Chapter 9. It is an outcome which cannot be reconciled with the 'not-one-but-not-two' model of the maternal/fetal relationship. Practitioners caring for pregnant women are not responsible for the care of 'one', nor are they responsible for the care of 'two'. Adopting the 'not-one-but-not-two' model precludes the view that a duty of care is specifically owed to the fetus.

Thus neither an analysis that relies on broad principles of foreseeability, nor one that requires the existence of two entities and independent duties of care, provides an adequate explanation of the nature of the obligation owed to a pregnant woman by a doctor or midwife. Instead, it is more convincing to argue that while a practitioner owes a duty of care to the woman, this duty *includes* a duty in respect of her fetus. This conclusion can be adopted without seeing the fetus as a legal 'person'. It assumes no more than that the fetus is an existing entity whose welfare must be taken into account since it will become a human being. To echo *Roe v Wade*, doctors and midwives—like the state—can display a legitimate interest in the potentiality of human life. While there is only one patient—the woman—and while she is the only person who can be considered to be in a legal relationship with her practitioner, that practitioner has obligations that extend beyond her. Although concern for her well-being is the practitioner's primary concern, it is not the sole concern. To accept this view is to regard the woman as the representative of the fetus. She speaks for it and has a vital interest in its welfare. From this it follows that any act or omission which leads to the birth of an injured or disabled child reflects a failure to respect this interest and so amounts to a breach of the duty of care owed to her.[7]

---

[6] NY, 429 NE 2d 786, 787 (1981).

[7] '[T]he woman relies upon the doctor both for her own care and that of the unborn child. In a sense, there is reliance by the child through the agency of the mother': I. Kennedy and A. Grubb, *Medical Law: Text with Materials* (London, 2nd edn., 1994) 936.

As has been seen in Chapter 5, a breach of such a duty may take many forms. For the purposes of discussion, let us assume that a doctor's failure to perform a caesarean section has caused a child to be born with brain damage. No problems will arise in an action brought by the *mother* for the harm done to her by the birth of a disabled child. The mother can legitimately seek recompense for this wrong, including sums for pain and suffering and all the associated medical and childcare expenses. To explain the basis on which the *child* can also bring an action, I have suggested that the duty of care owed by a doctor or midwife to the woman encompasses a duty in respect of her fetus. On this view, the practitioner has a duty to take account of its welfare and thus bears an obligation that depends on the perception of a pregnant woman as 'not-one-but-not-two'. Harm caused by the breach of this composite duty will make the doctor accountable not only to the woman but also to her child. The crucial consequence of the adoption of this analysis is that it allows the child to claim that the breach caused harm *different* from that experienced by the mother. This aspect is of considerable practical importance. In addition to seeking damages for pain and suffering, a brain-damaged child with an individual cause of action will be permitted to seek damages for loss of future earning capacity, for loss of enjoyment of life, and for the lifelong cost of care. It is when damages of this kind are considered that the significance of allowing the child his or her own cause of action can be appreciated.

Identifying the nature of the duty borne by a doctor or midwife might give rise to special difficulties in England. As was explained in Chapter 4, the law on antenatal negligence in that country is governed by the Congenital Disabilities (Civil Liability) Act 1976 (UK). Under s 1(1) and (2), a person whose negligence has affected the mother during her pregnancy, or has affected her or the child in the course of birth, and who is 'answerable to the child', is liable in respect of any resulting disabilities. Section 1(3) states that such a person:

is answerable to the child if he was liable in tort to the [mother] or would, if sued in due time, have been so; and it is no answer that there could not have been such liability because the [mother] suffered no actionable injury, if there was a breach of legal duty which, accompanied by injury, would have given rise to the liability.[8]

The effect of this is that where antenatal or perinatal negligence has caused harm to a child, a doctor or midwife is liable to the child only if the practitioner breached a duty of care owed to the pregnant woman. The resulting cause of action is thus derivative. The latter part of the provision makes it clear that an injury to the woman is not a prerequisite to the child's action. It is failing to fulfil the obligation 'not to breach a duty owed to the mother in such a way as to cause injury to the child' which gives rise to a damages claim

---

[8] The provision allows for liability to either parent. For present purposes it is only the defendant's potential liability to the mother which is relevant and hence the amended wording.

by the child.[9] As was explained by the Law Commission Report on which the Act was based, this approach is consistent with the position adopted by the English common law. The report stated that a fetus has no legal existence and referred to the 'physical identification' of a pregnant woman and her fetus.[10] The point was reinforced in the Commission's note to the draft Bill: '[T]here is no nexus of legal duty, whether at common law or under statute, as between the defendant and the child *"in utero"*.'[11] The Act reflects this perspective. It thus precludes speculation about a parallel duty of care being owed in respect of the welfare of the fetus. It also represents a rejection of the common law principle that a child injured *in utero* may bring an action on the basis that he or she was a member of a category of persons who could foreseeably suffer harm as a result of negligence.[12]

On one view, the effect of this provision has been unintentionally to restrict the operation of the law. The argument is as follows. Since a prerequisite of liability to the child is potential liability in tort to the woman, the child's action will fail unless medical intervention or non-intervention has breached a duty to the woman. There may be situations in which a child, though injured by perinatal negligence, will not have a remedy because there has been no breach of an obligation owed directly to the woman: 'Inexpert manipulation of forceps, inadequate use of available monitoring equipment or a failure to make a Caesarean incision at an appropriate time all appear to be wrongs which primarily affect the child's well-being rather than the mother's and outside the scope of any duty to her.'[13] It is possible to take this analysis further and to imagine situations in which the antenatal conduct which harms the fetus—far from being a breach of the duty of care owed to the woman—benefits her. For example, a doctor might prescribe tetracycline to treat the woman's upper respiratory tract infection and this might subsequently damage the child's teeth.

On this interpretation, there will be circumstances in which a child born suffering the effects of antenatal negligence will be denied a remedy. This explanation of the effect of the English legislation may well be correct. If so, the Act embodies a rejection of the view that a doctor or midwife owes a composite duty. It accepts that the obligation owed to the woman does not include an obligation to her to safeguard the child's well-being. Such a result draws attention to the problems arising when the existence of the fetus is ignored and all attention is focused on the duty owed to the woman. If the

---

[9] P. F. Cane, 'Injuries to Unborn Children' (1977) 51 Australian Law Journal 704, 708.

[10] Law Commission, *Report on Injuries to Unborn Children* (Law Com No 60, 1974) para 33.

[11] Ibid. 47, explanatory note 4 to cl. 1.

[12] Section 4(5) of the Act makes it clear that the common law as to actions in respect of antenatal negligence no longer applies.

[13] J. M. Eekelaar and R. W. J. Dingwall, 'Some Legal Issues in Obstetric Practice' [1984] Journal of Social Welfare Law 258, 265.

suggested interpretation is right, the provision has failed to come to terms with the 'not-one-but-not-two' model of pregnancy.

Negligent Non-Disclosure

Analysis of the duty owed by a doctor or midwife raises special problems when the negligence takes the form of a failure to advise of risks of intervention or non-intervention. In this situation it can be argued that the obligation is owed only to the woman. It is she who should be advised, for example, of the risks to the fetus of not undertaking a caesarean section when there are signs of acute fetal distress. She must make the decision whether to consent to the procedure. Should she withhold consent and the child is born with brain damage, the basis on which a damages claim could be made is that she received insufficient information to make an informed assessment.

If the duty to provide information in this situation can be owed to the woman alone, can this duty encompass a duty in respect of the fetus? As was explained in Chapter 3, the cases in which the doctrine of informed consent was initially developed involved patients' complaints about the failure to advise of the risks of surgery (such as a spinal operation). The complaints rested on the assumption that the patients were entitled to be informed of the risks to which the procedures exposed *them*. The problem arising in obstetric matters is that the complaint frequently relates not to the failure to advise the woman of the risks to which *she* was exposed, but to a failure to explain to her the risks to which her *fetus* was exposed. If the duty to disclose can be owed only to the woman, it is not clear how a child may bring a non-disclosure action for harm suffered.[14]

The courts do not seem to have been troubled by this difficulty. It has generally been accepted that a child harmed as a result of the provision of inadequate antenatal information to the mother may sue on the basis of a duty owed to the mother. The issue was noted in *Roberts v Patel*, which arose as a result of the birth of a baby with spastic quadriplegia. While in labour, the mother had questioned the decision to halt her labour and not to perform a caesarean section. She had asked about possible risks, but was assured that the decision would result in the delivery of a healthy baby. The United States District Court, Illinois, held that: 'Joshua's mother's physicians owed a duty . . . not only to Joshua's mother, but to Joshua as well; in this situation the physician had two patients.' The court continued:

The physician must have a duty to disclose to his patient risks not only to the mother but to the child as well. In making an informed decision, Joshua's natural mother was concerned not only about risk of the treatment to her own safety but also to her

---

[14] The English legislation solves this problem by providing that the child's cause of action arises from the breach of the duty of care owed to the mother.

unborn child. Indeed, the risks to her child may have been paramount in her concerns. . . . In such situations the failure to inform the natural mother of risks inherent
in a procedure subjected *both* the mother and her unborn child to unwarranted risks
of unwanted treatment. [15]

It was therefore ruled that both Joshua and his mother could bring an action
based on the doctor's failure to obtain the mother's informed consent. There
is no difficulty with the court's conclusion about the nature of the duty which
the doctor owed to the mother: she had an interest in the safe delivery of a
healthy baby and the doctor's failure to protect that interest could result in
liability to pay her damages. More problematic is the court's acceptance that
the child had his own cause of action; it was in order to reach this result that
the court found it necessary to identify 'two patients'. In Chapter 9, I raised
doubts about the 'two patients' model. Yet rejection of this model makes it
difficult to explain how two causes of action can result from the breach of a
single duty of care. The Supreme Court of Arizona provided a possible solution. After noting that a doctor providing antenatal care has a duty to both
the mother and the developing fetus, the court described the obligation as
including a duty to inform parents about fetal problems and risks. It added
that 'the duty owed to the parent inures derivatively to the child'.[16] This
analysis is consistent with the hypothesis offered earlier: the duty owed to the
woman includes a duty in respect of the welfare of her fetus.

RELIANCE ON THE DOCTRINE OF INFORMED CONSENT

Identifying the Limits of the Doctrine

In addition to raising questions relating to the object of a doctor or midwife's
duty of care, an examination of the operation of the law on negligent non-
disclosure in the field of obstetrics reveals further problems. Reference has
been made to the fact that liability for this form of negligence developed from
the application of rules requiring practitioners to obtain patients' informed
consent before undertaking surgery. Relying on this concept to determine
the liability of those who provide antenatal or perinatal care will sometimes
be questionable. The application of the concept to the provision of such care
therefore requires closer analysis.

In Chapter 3, it was seen that the law recognizes a competent patient's
right to the information necessary to make an informed choice about treatment. The cases in which liability has been imposed for the breach of this
obligation have typically been those in which patients have consented to

---

[15] 620 F Supp 323, 326 (DC Ill, 1985) (emphasis in original).
[16] *Walker by Pizano v Mart* 790 P 2d 735, 739 (Ariz, 1990).

elective surgery and have sued their surgeons when complications have occurred. Their claims have rested on the allegation that the risk which even-tuated was not adequately explained and that had an explanation been pro-vided, consent would not have been given. Had consent been withheld, the harm would have been avoided.

Claims resting on the absence of informed consent have succeeded in a variety of cases arising from obstetric misadventures. Yet the principles gov-erning the duty to inform and advise are not always easy to apply in the con-text of obstetric care. The difficulties arising from the fact that the duty to provide information is owed to the woman have already been noted. In con-fronting this issue, *Roberts v Patel* also illustrated a further problem. The court assumed that the mother had been required to make a decision as to treatment and that she was entitled to receive information on the basis of which she could make an informed choice. This assumption may have been justified on the facts of the case. The woman had questioned the doctor's actions and had asked about a caesarean section. In this situation, she can perhaps be seen as having consented to a particular procedure—a vaginal delivery—on the basis of inadequate information.

It will often not be apparent that a pregnant woman has been required to make a choice of the kind made by a patient considering elective surgery. There have been some cases in which courts have not been troubled by this problem. In *Campbell v Pitt County Memorial Hospital*,[17] the woman was admitted to hospital and it was found that the baby was in the footling breech position. Neither the woman nor her husband was informed of this fact or of its significance. The baby girl was delivered vaginally and sustained brain damage as a result of the cord becoming tangled around her legs. Both the doctor who had performed the delivery and the hospital were sued. The claim against the doctor was settled and as the jury found that the treatment provided by hospital staff was not negligent, the only way to make the hos-pital liable was by alleging lack of informed consent. This allegation suc-ceeded. The steps in the argument were as follows. The court accepted that it was the responsibility of the nurses to ensure that patients had received adequate explanations of the risks they faced. They had failed to do this. Evi-dence was presented that the higher risks of a vaginal delivery of a baby in the footling breech position were well recognized in 1979. There was also testi-mony that parents who were informed of the risks of a vaginal delivery when the fetus was in this position would ordinarily opt for a caesarean section. Further, both Mr and Mrs Campbell testified that if they had been more fully informed, they would have chosen a caesarean section. Thus all the elements

[17] 352 SE 2d 902 (NC App, 1987). The decision of the Court of Appeals of North Carolina focused on the liability of the hospital for the negligence of the doctor and nurses; the doctor had conceded liability and had settled the claim against him. See also *Williams v Lallie Kemp Char-ity Hospital* 428 So 2d 1000 (La App 1 Cir, 1983).

of a claim based on negligent non-disclosure were found to be present: the judgment expressly recognized the existence of 'a legal duty to insure that plaintiffs' informed consent to a vaginal delivery of a footling breech baby had been obtained prior to delivery'.[18]

The Washington Court of Appeals adopted a similar approach in *Holt v Nelson*,[19] which arose following the birth of a child with spastic quadriplegia, brain damage, and cerebral palsy. The negligence alleged was a failure to diagnose placenta praevia, an attempted vaginal delivery, and delay in the performance of a caesarean section. When the jury rejected these allegations, an appeal was lodged solely on the ground that there had been a negligent failure to give the woman the opportunity to undergo an earlier caesarean section. As in *Campbell*, the claim was that some time before the caesarean section was performed, the doctor was under an obligation to advise of the risks of a vaginal delivery and of the appropriateness of undertaking an immediate caesarean section. As counsel for the plaintiff put it, the complaint was that the doctor 'did not explain the risks involved in rupturing the membranes and attempting a vaginal delivery in the face of circumstances making a caesarean section the proper alternative'.[20] The court offered a broad definition of the negligence to be proved. It was necessary for the plaintiffs to show that '[t]he defendant-doctor failed to inform the plaintiff-patient of alternative treatments, the reasonably foreseeable material risks of each alternative, and of no treatment at all'.[21] Before allowing the labour to continue, the doctor should have obtained the woman's informed consent.

These cases illustrate courts accepting the argument that a vaginal delivery can in some circumstances be viewed as a medical procedure to which informed consent must be given.[22] In the words used in *Holt*, the doctor should have obtained the woman's 'knowledgeable permission'[23] before allowing the labour to continue. As in *Campbell*, this implies that a choice had to be made and that a woman who has not been informed of the risks of a vaginal delivery (and who has not been advised of the possible advantages of a caesarean section) can be regarded in the same way as a patient who has consented to an eye or spinal operation in the absence of adequate information as to risks and alternatives. The cases also raise the possibility of viewing childbirth as involving a series of procedures to which consent must be given. If a vaginal delivery is a procedure to which 'knowledgeable' consent must be given, does the management of a delivery involve a series of separate procedures, every one of which must be explained and consented to so that the

---

[18] 352 SE 2d 902, 907 (NC App, 1987).   [19] Wash App, 523 P 2d 211 (1974).
[20] Ibid. 215.   [21] Ibid. 216.
[22] See also *Randall v United States* 859 F Supp 22 (DDC, 1994). This case has been discussed above, 84–5.
[23] Wash App, 523 P 2d 211, 216–17 (1974).

woman can make informed decisions? If so, is it open to a woman whose child has suffered harm to claim damages on the ground that though she consented to a particular procedure which caused the harm, no attempt was made to advise her of the risks?

There are many doctors and midwives who would question the suggestion that a pregnant woman can and should make a series of decisions during childbirth and that as a corollary they have a legal duty to obtain consent to every procedure after having explained the risks associated with it. Many practitioners would see it as their legal duty to practise 'good medicine': that is, to take all steps which they consider to be necessary to ensure the safe delivery of a healthy baby. Indeed, they would regard themselves as liable to a damages claim if they did not meet this standard, a standard set by reference to the practices of competent practitioners in the relevant specialty, whether consultant obstetrician, general practitioner, or midwife. This view was illustrated in *Charley v Cameron*,[24] a case arising from an injury allegedly caused to a child by a forceps delivery. The defendant doctor submitted that there had been no need for him to obtain consent to the use of forceps. In this he was supported by the testimony of his colleagues: the medical evidence favoured the view that forceps were used whenever good medical judgement suggested that this was appropriate; consent was never sought. This argument was accepted. Whether this decision should be followed today is uncertain. As will be seen in Chapter 12, other judges have expressed different views on the need for consent to the use of forceps. The important point at this stage is that the case illustrated one view of the practice of obstetrics and midwifery: that a pregnant woman puts herself in the practitioner's hands and relies on his or her judgement. On this view, the practitioner's obligation is to provide the type and standard of care approved by competent colleagues.

The approach taken in *Charley v Cameron* is consistent with the assertion of medical control over a delivery. It contrasts with the perception (discussed in Chapter 12) that childbirth is a process that the woman controls by way of a series of decisions, the effective making of which depends on doctors and midwives providing information about risks. For the purposes of this chapter, the question is whether the law should accommodate the latter perception by relying exclusively on the application of the doctrine of informed consent. In my opinion, it should not. The analysis offered in cases such as *Holt* and *Campbell* is unconvincing. It is artificial to regard a woman who has a vaginal delivery unaccompanied by any operative procedures as making a decision—informed or otherwise—about the way in which her child is to be delivered. If she is not required to make a choice, there is no decision-making process to which her doctor is obliged to contribute. In the words of the

---

[24] Kan, 528 P 2d 1205 (1974).

Supreme Court of Pennsylvania, 'because labor is inevitable and there is no choice to be made, the informed consent doctrine does not apply to the natural delivery process'.[25]

Reliance on the doctrine of informed consent should be confined within proper limits. There are some decisions that are helpful in defining those limits. They suggest that it is useful to think in terms of informed consent only when a choice must be made as to whether to undergo a particular procedure. An example was provided by *Karlsons v Guerinot*, in which the action was brought following the birth of a child with Down syndrome. The parents alleged that the woman should have been advised of the risk (which was said to arise from the fact that she had a thyroid condition and had previously given birth to a 'deformed child'). They claimed that the woman would have obtained an abortion had the information been provided. The argument was that there had been a failure to obtain informed consent to the continuation of the pregnancy. This argument was rejected and though limited damages were awarded, the Appellate Division of the Supreme Court of New York made it clear that the parents could not invoke the doctrine of informed consent:

[A] cause of action based upon [the doctrine of informed consent] exists only where the injury suffered arises from *an affirmative violation of the patient's physical integrity* and, where nondisclosure of risks is concerned, these risks are directly related to such affirmative treatment. Here, the resultant harm did not arise out of any affirmative violation of the mother's physical integrity. Furthermore, the alleged undisclosed risks did not relate to any affirmative treatment but rather to the condition of pregnancy itself.[26]

A similar analysis was adopted in *Reed v Campagnolo*.[27] The plaintiffs' child was born suffering from a number of genetic abnormalities. These included meningomyelocele, hydrocephaly, an imperforate anus, and one kidney. The parents alleged that the defendant doctors had been negligent in failing to inform them of the existence or need for Alpha Feto Protein (AFP) testing to detect serious birth defects. They further alleged that had they been informed of the existence of the test they would have requested it, it would have revealed elevated protein levels, and that this would have led them to request an amniocentesis. This, in turn, would have revealed the extent of the fetal defects and the parents would have terminated the pregnancy. One of the grounds on which they sought damages was that the continuation of the pregnancy represented a decision made without informed consent because of the failure to provide information about the availability of AFP testing.

---

[25] *Sinclair by Sinclair v Block* 633 A 2d 1137, 1141 (Pa, 1993).
[26] 394 NYS 2d 933, 939 (1977) (emphasis added). See also *Pratt v University of Minnesota Affiliated Hospitals and Clinics* 414 NW 2d 399 (Minn, 1987).
[27] 630 A 2d 1145 (Md, 1993).

The Court of Appeals of Maryland rejected this claim. It did not agree that there was something to which the parents had consented (to forgo AFP testing) in the absence of information as to risks. It did not accept the argument that the continuation of a pregnancy was a decision requiring informed consent. In reaching this conclusion, the court relied on the *Karlsons* view that an action on the basis of lack of informed consent can succeed only in the context of an affirmative act by a doctor. The same point was made in another decision in which there had been misplaced reliance on the doctrine of informed consent: 'The risk of harm must inhere in the treatment itself.'[28]

This represents a more satisfactory approach. The judgment in *Karlsons* avoided the artificiality inherent in cases such as *Holt* and *Campbell*. It recognized that it is appropriate to invoke the doctrine of informed consent only when it is necessary for a patient to make a choice to allow intervention. The doctrine has no place in cases in which a woman has not objected to the continuance of normal labour. Nor has it any place in cases in which the woman's only 'decision' (if it can be described as such) was to allow her pregnancy to continue. *Karlsons* may, however, be too restrictive in confining the application of the doctrine of informed consent to actions involving harm caused by 'an affirmative violation of the patient's physical integrity'. While such an approach is consistent with the origins of that doctrine, there are non-invasive forms of treatment carrying risks to a pregnant woman and/or her fetus. Prescribing a drug with the potential to harm the fetus is an obvious example. This suggests that liability should be imposed under the doctrine whenever there is affirmative treatment to which informed consent has not been obtained. A patient is entitled to be properly informed before making a choice that carries risks.

Thus it is necessary to limit the application of the doctrine of informed consent in cases arising from antenatal and perinatal negligence. When it is clear that a pregnant woman has made a choice and there is doubt about the adequacy of the information she received, it is appropriate to rely on the doctrine. In other situations in which there has been a failure to provide information, it is not appropriate to do so. This does not necessarily mean, however, that no duty to advise of risks will arise in these situations. A possible source of this duty will now be considered.

An Alternative Formulation: a General Duty to Inform?

The hypothesis offered is that all health care professionals have a general obligation to provide information to their patients. They are repositories of

---

[28] *Cauman v George Washington University* 630 A 2d 1104, 1108 (DC App, 1993), where the District of Columbia Court of Appeals refused to treat the negligent interpretation of antenatal tests (and a consequent failure to provide information that might have led the woman to abort a child born with abnormalities) as raising any question of 'informed consent'.

specialized information and patients are dependent on them.[29] In *Atlanta Obstetrics and Gynaecology Group v Abelson*, the Supreme Court of Georgia accepted the existence of 'a generalized duty to impart relevant information to a patient concerning his or her medical condition'.[30] This proposition was derived from *Goldberg v Ruskin*,[31] a case involving an unwanted birth action resulting from an allegation that the doctor had failed to advise the parents of the risk that they were carriers of Tay Sachs disease. *Karlsons v Guerinot* adopted a similar approach. Having ruled that the doctrine of informed consent could not be invoked in a claim arising from a failure to advise of the risk of the birth of a child with Down syndrome, the court stated: 'Allegations such as these have traditionally formed the basis of actions in medical malpractice . . . '.[32] While the judgment did not define the precise nature of the doctor's duty, this comment indicates that non-disclosure is best viewed as a form of professional negligence. A similar analysis was offered in *Smith v Cote*, a case dealing with a failure to advise of the risks posed by maternal rubella. The court accepted that the doctor had an obligation to facilitate the making of a choice by the woman. The duty borne by the doctor was viewed as arising from *Roe v Wade*'s recognition of a woman's freedom to choose whether to terminate a pregnancy. Recognition of this freedom was regarded as imposing 'a duty to exercise care in providing information that bears on that choice'.[33]

Many of the other decisions that have awarded damages for unwanted births reinforce this conclusion. While they frequently fail to address the question of the precise nature of the obligation owed by a practitioner to a pregnant woman, these cases can be understood only on the basis that they embody an implicit recognition of a duty to be alert to risks and to give information about them. Failure to do so is a failure to provide an appropriate standard of care. This analysis should not be limited to unwanted birth cases. The relationship between a pregnant woman and her doctor or midwife gives rise to expectations on the part of the woman. These expectations impose obligations on the practitioner, including an obligation to advise of risks. Further, this conclusion is consistent with the recognition of the need to respect a pregnant woman's autonomy. This subject was discussed in Chapter 9. To stress a woman's right to information is to respect her autonomy: 'True consent to what happens to one's self is the informed exercise of a choice, and that entails an opportunity to evaluate knowledgeably the options available and the risks attendant upon each.'[34] If a woman is to exercise autonomy in respect of her pregnancy and the manner of delivery of her child, she must be

---

[29] R. P. Balkin and J. L. R. Davis, *Law of Torts* (Sydney, 2nd edn., 1996) 214–15.

[30] 398 SE 2d 557, 561 (Ga, 1990).   [31] 471 NE 2d 530, 537 (Ill App 1 Dist, 1984).

[32] 394 NYS 2d 933, 939 (1977) (citation omitted).

[33] 513 A 2d 341, 344 (NH, 1986).

[34] *Canterbury v Spence* 464 F 2d 772, 780 (1972) (footnote omitted).

told of any risks and of the options open to her. The authentic exercise of autonomy demands that the woman be properly informed. The implications of this will be discussed in Chapter 12.

THE BIRTH OF AN UNWANTED CHILD

Speculation about the nature of an obstetrician's or midwife's obligations can be supplemented by asking who has suffered harm as a result of the negligence. If negligence has not caused a party harm, it is reasonable to suppose that no compensation can be claimed. Thus in the examples already discussed, it may do no violence to basic principles for a child to assert that he or she has suffered harm as a result of the doctor's failure to perform a caesarean section or omission to explain to the mother the risks to the fetus of not doing so. The application of this analysis is more troublesome, however, in some of the other types of proceedings arising from antenatal negligence.

A clear example of the operation of the principle that only a person who has suffered harm can sue for damages is provided by an unwanted birth case. When a healthy child has been born and the mother can establish that the birth was caused by medical negligence (such as a negligently performed tubal ligation), the resulting action is taken to allow the woman to obtain damages for the harm she has suffered. Her complaint is that she has been forced to accept the unwanted burden of bringing up a child born as the result of the negligence.[35] It is thus she who complains of a wrong caused by the breach of a duty owed to her. The cause of action is hers and is not one which can also give rise to a claim by the child that he or she has suffered harm because of the breach of the duty of care owed to the mother. While it was seen in Chapter 4 that there has been debate as to whether the birth of a normal child should be regarded as a wrong suffered by the mother, there is no basis on which a court would view the child as having suffered a compensable wrong by being born.

Analysis becomes more difficult when the unwanted birth claim relates to an abnormal child. As was seen in Chapter 5, a typical example is when a child is born disabled as a result of the woman contracting rubella during pregnancy. The mother's action will rest on the argument that the doctor should have diagnosed the condition and that had she been informed of the risks which it posed to the fetus, she would have terminated the pregnancy. Her claim is a personal one: that the doctor was under an obligation to provide her with appropriate information and that the negligent failure to do so deprived her of the power of choice. From this perspective, there is no way in

---

[35] Because this burden may be shared by her partner, he may also be a plaintiff. To simplify the analysis, this possibility is not considered here.

which the affected child could formulate a claim for damages. The child's disability has not been caused by medical negligence; it was the result of the mother's rubella. Unlike the child injured by a failure to undertake a timely caesarean section, this child cannot assert that the disability was the result of the breach of the duty which the doctor owed to the woman to provide appropriate information.

To view an action arising from the unwanted birth of a disabled child in this manner is to see the wrong as suffered by the mother. The negligence has imposed on her an unwanted and particularly onerous burden and it is for this reason that she seeks recompense. As in other cases involving antenatal negligence, the practical significance of this explanation of a non-disclosure claim is substantial. If the action is confined to proof of the wrong that the mother suffered, it will not be possible for a court to award damages to the child for pain and suffering, loss of future earning capacity, loss of enjoyment of life, or the costs of care during his or her entire lifetime. To accept this analysis is also to accept that it is not open to a child born with congenital rubella syndrome to assert that a duty owed to him or her has been breached. This conclusion is reinforced by many of the decisions dealing with wrongful life actions. The nature of these actions has been discussed in Chapter 6, where it was seen that courts have occasionally been asked to award disabled children damages on the basis that the doctors were negligent in allowing them to be born. Such claims have generally been disallowed. Much of the judicial analysis has concentrated on the impossibility of assessing damages, since a fair assessment would require the making of a comparison between existence and non-existence. In some cases, however, the courts have addressed the preliminary question whether the doctors could be regarded as having breached a duty owed to the fetus. An example of this approach was seen in *McKay v Essex Area Health Authority*. There the English Court of Appeal refused to accept that there could be any duty the breach of which could provide a basis for an action by a child born suffering the effects of antenatal rubella. In the words of Stephenson LJ, the defendants were not 'under any duty to the child to give the child's mother an opportunity to terminate the child's life'. He added: 'That duty may be owed to the mother, but it cannot be owed to the child.'[36]

Thus the argument is that, since there has been no breach of a duty of care owed to the child, the child born with congenital rubella syndrome has no cause of action. The difficulty with this conclusion is that it indicates that the torts system can offer only a partial response to the event giving rise to the action. At the centre of an unwanted birth claim is a child. When that child is grossly disabled, he or she is the real victim and will need lifelong support. Yet the child cannot be directly compensated. Perhaps this result is

[36] [1982] 1 QB 1166, 1180.

inescapable: negligence law is not designed to right all wrongs and the child's tragic condition might be regarded as a tragedy beyond the reach of the civil law of compensation. The problem with this conclusion is that the law will treat this tragedy as compensable if the parents bring a claim. The logic of a legal system that allows an unwanted birth action but not one for wrongful life must be questioned. It must be asked whether there is much difference between the damages payable in the former action and those that the courts have found impossible to calculate in the latter. The damages payable to the parents in an unwanted birth case are not designed to compensate them for the devastating impact of the birth of the child, an impact which will affect them and other members of the family for the rest of their lives. Although the parents' hopes have been dashed and they have been denied the pleasure of rearing a normal child, the courts do not normally see it as their task to award compensation for these losses. Instead, they focus on damages that can be calculated: the expenses associated with the care of the disabled child.

The same reasoning could be applied in a wrongful life case. While it may be self-evidently inappropriate for a court to seek to compensate a disabled child for a life of suffering, it is not self-evident that the child should be denied damages to cover the cost of care. If a court hearing an unwanted birth action recognizes that the child needs support, it is not obvious that it is unacceptable for a court hearing a wrongful life action to respond to the same need. This is not to suggest that a doctor should necessarily be made liable to a wrongful life action: the fact that the child's condition is not the result of medical negligence cannot be ignored. Rather, the difficulty is that an unwanted birth action can be seen as allowing a child to obtain indirectly benefits that are not available directly.

If it is agreed that the doctor's non-disclosure was the cause of the child's existence, it makes as much sense to award the *child* damages to provide financial support as it does to award the *parents* damages of that kind. This conclusion was adopted in *Procanik by Procanik v Cillo*. The case arose from the doctor's failure to diagnose that the woman had contracted rubella during her pregnancy; the child was born with congenital rubella syndrome and suffered multiple defects. The majority judges made it clear that they were unwilling to accept the distinction between a child's wrongful life action and the parents' unwanted birth action:

Law is more than an exercise in logic, and logical analysis, although essential to a system of ordered justice, should not become a [*sic*] instrument of injustice. Whatever logic inheres in permitting parents to recover for the cost of extraordinary medical care incurred by a birth-defective child, but in denying the child's own right to recover those expenses, must yield to the injustice of that result.[37]

---

[37] 478 A 2d 755, 762 (NJ, 1984). The judgment made it clear that, if damages were to be

On this basis, compensation was authorized for the medical expenses directly attributable to the birth defects, but not for the lifelong suffering which the child would have to endure as a result of those defects. The decision, therefore, was robustly practical: the majority found a way to award the child damages, but avoided the need to compare non-existence with the child's impaired existence.

A dissenting judgment reached a similar result by way of a different analysis. Handler J felt able to rule that the *child* had suffered a wrong for which damages are recoverable. He defined this wrong as an 'impaired childhood'. In his view, 'the wrongful deprivation of the individual choice either to bear or not to bear a handicapped child is a tort — *to the infant* as well as the parents . . .'.[38] He explained the nature of the wrong suffered by the child by citing his earlier judgment in *Berman v Allan*. That case dealt with a claim arising from the birth of a girl with Down syndrome; the negligence was a failure to inform the woman of the availability of an amniocentesis. It was accepted that had she been properly advised, she would have undergone the test and would have terminated the pregnancy if the condition had been revealed. While the majority held that a tort had not been committed on the girl, Handler J dissented on the following ground:

[T]he infant has come into this world and is here, encumbered by an injury attributable to the malpractice of the doctors. That injury does not consist of the child's afflicted condition; her affliction was not the doctor's doing. Rather, the injury consists of a diminished childhood in being born of parents kept ignorant of her defective state while unborn and who, on that account, were less fit to accept and assume their parental responsibilities. The frightful weight of the child's natural handicap has been made more burdensome by defendants' negligence because her parents' capacity had been impaired . . .[39]

This is a questionable argument. It does not assume that the child has suffered direct harm (such as occurs when brain damage has been caused by a negligent failure to perform a caesarean section). Rather, the analysis is based on an assumption that harm (an impaired childhood) has been indirectly caused to the child by the impact of the negligence on the parents. Thus it offers a way of permitting the child to claim damages on a basis consistent with the principle that compensation is payable only if negligently caused harm can be demonstrated. Whether a doctor or midwife should be held liable for producing a situation in which a child suffers an 'impaired childhood' is debatable. Decisions on this question will ultimately be made on policy grounds. A concern for policy was implicit in Handler J's argument in *Procanik*: he had no doubt that unsatisfactory genetic counselling of parents

payable, it was necessary to recognize the child's cause of action as the parents' claim was barred by the statute of limitations.

[38] Ibid. 765 (emphasis added).   [39] 404 A 2d 8, 19 (1979).

'can have a demonstrable adverse impact on the afflicted child',[40] and believed that the law should ensure 'a direct recovery for the unfortunate infant'.[41]

STILLBIRTHS

At first sight, characterization of the action that can be taken following a negligently caused stillbirth is simple. The would-be parents have been deprived of the joy of having a child and their hopes have been dashed. The wrong has been inflicted on them alone and the only difficulty is the assessment of damages. In particular, opinions will differ as to whether damages should be awarded for grief and distress. The majority of United States courts, however, have not accepted this approach and have been willing to entertain claims under wrongful death and survival Acts following stillbirths. As was explained in Chapter 6, these statutes provide that if the death of a person has been caused by the wrongful act of another and the deceased would have been able to bring an action if death had not ensued, an action for damages can be brought by the beneficiaries.

The crucial feature of decisions which have allowed claims in respect of stillbirths under these Acts is that they have refused to apply the 'born alive' rule. They have accepted that for the purposes of the legislation, a fetus is a 'person'. In *Amadio v Levin*, the majority of the Supreme Court of Pennsylvania held: '[A] child en ventre sa mere is an individual with the right to be free of pre-natal injury.'[42] This is to treat the fetus as an entity to which a duty of care is directly owed and therefore to regard it as possessing rights before birth. Earlier in this chapter, I raised doubts about this analysis and suggested that it is generally inappropriate to employ it in actions arising from antenatal negligence. I also suggested that it was unnecessary to do so as these actions could be understood by postulating a composite duty owed to the pregnant woman and her fetus. This duty encompasses an obligation to protect the welfare of the child that the fetus will become. This solution is not available to make sense of decisions allowing wrongful death and survival claims following stillbirths. These depend on the view that a fetus that never becomes a child has an independent cause of action for negligence.

The discussion in *Amadio v Levin* provides a convenient review of the issues. The court repeatedly stressed that the pregnant woman and her fetus are separate. By emphasizing this aspect, the majority was able to identify 'the deceased child's *independent* injuries or possible pain and suffering' and therefore to reject the argument that the parents were seeking double compensation for one injury. It regarded the 'double dipping' argument as

---

[40] 478 A 2d 755, 767 (NJ, 1984).   [41] Ibid. 765.   [42] 501 A 2d 1085, 1087 (Pa, 1985).

perpetuating the notion that the fetus was inseparable from the mother. Hence its conclusion: 'Once the child is recognized as a separate individual ... medical and funeral costs incurred as well as any economic losses are recoverable by the child's estate, not by the mother.'[43] Similarly, in a concurring judgment, Zappala J made it clear that he believed that the award of adequate compensation depended on allowing a separate cause of action on behalf of the estate of the fetus.[44] He supported this by noting that it was well recognized that a fetus 'is not merely a part of its mother's body but is in fact a distinct individual'.[45]

Although they did not cite the case, the majority judges were employing the type of analysis established in *Bonbrest v Kotz*.[46] The judgment in that case relied on conclusions reached about the qualities of a viable fetus in order to reject the *Dietrich* view that a fetus was no more than a part of a woman's body. This set the scene for accepting that a fetus is an 'individual' for the purposes of a wrongful death or survival Act. The confusion created by *Bonbrest* thus explains the analytical framework employed in *Amadio*. This link was made explicit in *Greater Southeast Community Hospital v Williams*, where the majority of the District of Columbia Court of Appeals reached its conclusion as to the applicability of the District's wrongful death and survival statutes by way of the analysis offered in *Bonbrest*. Anticipating the view expressed in *Amadio*, the court stated:

Inherent in our adoption of *Bonbrest* is the recognition that a viable fetus is an independent person with the right to be free of prenatal injury. The liability for prenatal injury recognised in *Bonbrest* arises at the time of the injury. If a viable fetus is a 'person injured' at the time of the injury, then perforce the fetus is a 'person' when he dies of those injuries, and it can make no difference in liability under the wrongful death and survival statutes whether the fetus dies of the injuries just prior to or just after birth.[47]

The flaw in analysis of this kind is that *Bonbrest* dealt with a different type of claim, one made on behalf of *a living child* who had been born suffering the ill-effects of antenatal negligence. The dissenting judge recognized this: 'I have no quarrel with the majority's decision to adopt the rule announced in *Bonbrest v Kotz* ... and I would join in that decision if *Bonbrest* had any bearing on the outcome of this appeal. But *Bonbrest* does not apply to this case.'[48]

Another manifestation of the techniques employed in cases allowing wrongful death and survival actions after stillbirths has been the way in which certain criteria have been manipulated. The starting-point has been that the legislation applies only following the death of a 'person', namely, one who has been born alive. Yet, as in *Williams*, the majority in *Amadio* could see no

---

[43] Ibid. 1088 (original emphasis).   [44] Ibid. 1091.   [45] Ibid. 1094.
[46] 65 F Supp 138 (1946). See above 157–8.
[47] 482 A 2d 394, 397 (DC App, 1984).   [48] Ibid. 398.

reason to distinguish between a fetus and a newborn child for the purposes of a wrongful death action: '[T]he recovery afforded the estate of a stillborn is no different than the recovery afforded the estate of a child that dies within seconds of its release from its mother's womb.'[49] Some decisions have asserted that viability is the essential feature of personhood, and hence a pre-requisite to a wrongful death claim. An ingenious application of this prin-ciple was seen in *Ferguson v District of Columbia*, which dealt with an action under the District's survival Act. It was alleged that medical negligence had caused the premature delivery of a non-viable fetus. The court disallowed the action:

Just as a viable fetus that is injured possesses rights under the survival statute whether death occurs prior to or subsequent to birth, likewise, the existence of rights *vel non* of a non-viable fetus under the survival statute cannot turn on that happenstance either. The concept underlying our survival statute is that the representative is merely bringing a lawsuit that decedent could have brought had he or she not died. Where the fetus emerges from the mother without the developmental capacity to survive, it would contradict the theory of a survival action to provide a cause of action to the rep-resentative of the fetus. Absent clear indication of contrary legislative intent, it would be anomalous to view an action as one that could have been brought by the fetus had the fetus not died when the fetus had never developed the capacity to survive in the first place.[50]

This ruling was reinforced by the suggestion that while there is the possi-bility of two causes of action arising for separate harms caused to the woman and her viable fetus, prior to viability any harm to a pregnant woman is an injury to the woman alone.[51] Such a ruling is absurd. It is clearly unsatisfac-tory for the law of negligence to operate on the basis that a duty of care can be owed to a fetus only when it is viable. Were this rule to be applied gener-ally, the result would be that a doctor or midwife caring for a pregnant woman would initially owe a duty of care only to her, but once the fetus was viable would owe an additional duty of care to the fetus.

The methods employed by courts in actions under wrongful death and sur-vival Acts reveal the deficiencies of relying on what is referred to in Chapter 8 as the definitional perspective. Drawing conclusions from abstract analyses of the nature of the fetus can distort the law. Further, this method itself is par-ticularly unhelpful in the context of wrongful death and survival actions. It diverts attention from the questions that should be asked about the purposes of such actions. The need to ask these questions was recognized by two of the dissenting judges in *Amadio v Levin*. Nix CJ examined the objectives of com-pensatory laws. He noted that the primary aim is to restore the victim to his

---

[49] 501 A 2d 1085, 1089 (Pa, 1985).   [50] 629 A 2d 15, 17 (DC App, 1993).
[51] The court cited *Jones v Howard University* 589 A 2d 419 (DC App, 1991) and *Coughlin v George Washington University Health Plan* 565 A 2d 67 (DC App, 1989).

or her prior state: 'Tort law was never intended to unjustly enrich, or to provide the occasion for the fulfillment of all fanciful aspirations.'[52] He quoted
with approval from an 1850 decision: 'The measure is the actual, not the speculative loss. The primary end of damages is compensation; and not of every
injurious consequence that may have been suffered.'[53] Flaherty J focused on
matters of statutory interpretation and on the nature of the harm caused by
the negligence:

[N]either the Wrongful Death Act nor the Survival Act was intended to provide a
recovery in cases where the person on whose behalf the suits are brought was never
alive. For purposes of monetary recovery, a stillborn child was never alive. Further,
the emotional distress injuries which the parents of the stillborn child allegedly suffered as a result of the stillbirth are recoverable in actions brought by the parents in
their own rights. . . . No one doubts the suffering and terrible disappointment which
most expectant parents would experience upon learning that their child was stillborn,
and if a wrong were committed which caused the stillbirth, the wrongdoer should be
liable in damages to the parents. *But not twice!*[54]

This analysis—which depends on considering the purposes which com-
pensatory laws can properly fulfil—is preferable to relying on abstract characterization of the nature of the fetus. The compensation which a Wrongful
Death Act is designed to provide (for the loss by the deceased's dependants
of actual or anticipated financial support) is not the type of recompense
which parents who have suffered a stillbirth should receive. The same comment can be made of the compensation that a Survival Act is designed to provide (for the harm suffered by the deceased). Neither Act was intended to
confer a right to compensation on family members or beneficiaries of an
entity that was never alive. Speculation on the 'personhood' of the fetus
obscures this fact. Nix CJ recognized this: 'When we cut through the seman-
tics, the essence of the issue presented is the right to transmit a property
interest after death, in this case a chose in action.'[55] He held that it is not for a
court to create a new right, that is, one vested in a fetus that has not been
born alive.

In addition, even if the definitional perspective were to be adopted, the
cases that have employed it to allow wrongful death and survival actions following stillbirths have frequently relied on unconvincing reasoning. The central feature of the analysis offered in such cases is its emphasis on the
existence of a separate entity to which a tortfeasor can be liable. The conclusion that such liability should be imposed does not necessarily follow from

---

[52] 501 A 2d 1085, 1101 (Pa, 1985).

[53] Ibid. 1102, citing *Forsyth v Palmer* 14 Pa 96, 97 (1850). Surprisingly, the judge did not go on
to rule that a wrongful death claim following a stillbirth was 'fanciful' or 'speculative'. Instead,
he fell back on the definitional approach and ruled that all elements of the resulting damages
claim were 'subsumed in the claim of the mother'. 501 A 2d 1085, 1102 (Pa, 1985.)

[54] Ibid. 1104–5 (emphasis in original).   [55] Ibid. 1104.

the rejection of the view that a fetus is merely part of the woman's body. This is because the rejection of this model does not inevitably mean that a fetus must be a 'person' on whose behalf an independent damages claim may be brought. It is unsatisfactory to rely on the assumption that a fetus must be either a body part or a person. To do so is to ignore the distinctive nature of the fetus and its relationship with the woman who bears it. The conclusion that it is a person postulates a separation of woman and fetus that is as unacceptable as the body-part model.

One response to the above analysis is that it simply confirms the wisdom of the 'born alive' rule. It demonstrates that courts that depart from it and seek to base their conclusions about legal intervention on a characterization of the nature of the fetus do so at their peril. This response is both correct and incorrect. The decisions that have allowed wrongful death and survival actions following stillbirths could have been avoided by adherence to the 'born alive' rule. Yet mechanical adherence to this rule can obscure the need for careful assessment of the purposes which wrongful death and survival actions are designed to fulfil. It is only on the basis of such an assessment that satisfying answers to questions about liability for antenatal negligence will be fashioned. Numerous United States courts have failed to appreciate this fact. They have failed to understand the 'not-one-but-not-two' model and have continued to view the fetus as a separate entity. Consequently, they have reached conclusions that have distorted the law by extending the scope of wrongful death and survival actions. Courts allowing wrongful death or survival actions after stillbirths have offered a solution to a non-existent problem: there are no family members or beneficiaries who can claim to have suffered financial loss as a result of a stillbirth. They have manipulated the legislation to allow parents to receive what the judges have regarded as appropriate compensation for their loss. The English and Canadian courts have rightly rejected such an approach.

CAUSATION

In addition to raising questions relating to the duty of care and the identification of harm, the field of obstetrics also poses special problems of causation. Whether an adverse outcome takes the form of a stillbirth, the immediate death of the child, or its delivery with an injury or a disability, success in a damages claim depends on the plaintiff establishing a causal link between the medical negligence and that outcome. Plaintiffs bear the burden of proving on the balance of probabilities that the negligence caused or materially contributed to the harm.[56] Sometimes proving the causal relationship will be

[56] See above 50–1.

difficult. When the allegation relates to stillbirth, death, or birth with a disability, the problem arises from the fact that it is often not easy to determine whether the outcome was the product of negligent antenatal or perinatal care or of some unidentified intra-uterine process which occurred at an earlier stage of the pregnancy.

The Problem of Cerebral Palsy

In the fields of obstetrics and midwifery, the problem is dramatically demonstrated by claims relating to the birth of children with cerebral palsy. These are among the most troubling of all obstetric malpractice matters. Not only is it frequently difficult to demonstrate the required causal connection, but also a great deal hangs on the outcome, for both the plaintiff and defendant. Often the damages claimed are massive. When the actions succeed, the allegation has commonly been that the doctor was too slow in performing the delivery, with the result that the child suffered intra-uterine anoxia. In such cases, it has been accepted that it was this delay which caused the child's cerebral palsy. This assumption about the connection between the quality of obstetric care and cerebral palsy can be questioned:

Research has now shown that a much smaller proportion of cerebral palsy is caused by birth asphyxia than was previously thought. Much of what is classified as birth asphyxia is actually the first sign of a severely affected child whose problem started long before labour. In most cases of cerebral palsy it is unlikely that different obstetric care would have resulted in a better outcome.[57]

Indeed, it has been estimated that approximately 92 per cent of cases of cerebral palsy are caused by events occurring at an early stage of pregnancy.[58] This estimate underlines the difficulty of making findings about the causes of cerebral palsy.

The practical problems were explored in two English cases. Each was concerned with the identification of the time at which the fetus suffered harm. This was at issue because the negligence alleged was a delay in performing a caesarean section. In *Robertson v Nottingham Health Authority*,[59] the Court of Appeal upheld the trial judge's finding that the child's cerebral palsy was not caused by any event that occurred in the twelve hours before birth. There

---

[57] F. J. Stanley, 'Cerebral Palsy: the Courts Catch up with Sad Realities' (1994) 161 *Medical Journal of Australia* 236 (references omitted). See also F. J. Stanley and L. Watson, 'Trends in Perinatal Mortality and Cerebral Palsy in Western Australia, 1967 to 1985' (1992) 304 *British Medical Journal* 1658.

[58] E. Blair and F. J. Stanley, 'Intrapartum Asphyxia: a Rare Cause of Cerebral Palsy' (1988) 112 *Journal of Pediatrics* 515, 518 (Table 2). See also K. B. Nelson and J. H. Ellenberg, 'Antecedents of Cerebral Palsy: Multivariate Analysis of Risk' (1986) 315 *New England Journal of Medicine* 81.

[59] [1997] 8 Med LR 1.

was evidence that before the woman was admitted to hospital, the fetus was compromised as a result of placental insufficiency. The Court of Appeal stressed the complexity of the medical evidence on which it had been necessary for the trial court to rule. It was noted that the trial was 'trespassing on the frontiers of medical knowledge and understanding' and that it was therefore not surprising that expert witnesses had put forward differing explanations of the cause of the child's condition. An indication of the difficulties was the fact that the initial diagnosis of perinatal hypoxia gave way (after a CT scan) to a diagnosis of hydrancephaly and finally (after a MRI scan) to a diagnosis of multicystic-leuco-encephalo-malacia.[60]

A different result was reached in *Hill v West Lancashire Health Authority*.[61] There, in spite of conflicting expert testimony and the absence of the cardiotocograph, the trial court determined that the child's cerebral palsy was caused by hypoxia suffered in the hour before his birth (although the possibility of an earlier period of hypoxia was conceded). The court ruled therefore that the delay in performing a caesarean section in the face of evidence of fetal distress was a material cause of the child's condition. A distinctive feature of this case was that the complications indicating fetal distress occurred before labour commenced, whereas most reported cases of obstetric cerebral palsy have involved intrapartum hypoxia.[62]

Claims Arising from Failure to Advise of Risks

As was seen earlier in the chapter, a damages claim against a doctor or midwife may rest on an alleged failure to provide information as to the risks facing a pregnant woman and her fetus. The risks may be those associated with intervention or with a vaginal delivery. Alternatively, the failure may take the form of an omission to warn of the risk of the birth of a child with a disability. Proof of a negligent failure to provide appropriate information is, however, no more than the first step in an action arising from non-disclosure. A plaintiff must also show that the failure caused the harm. Proof of this element requires evidence that had the woman received the information, she would have acted in such a way as to avoid the harm. In all categories of non-disclosure cases, therefore, a successful action depends on a prediction as to the course the woman would have adopted had the information been provided.

In making such a prediction, a court must place substantial reliance on the woman's testimony. To a large extent, proof of the necessary causal link depends on her. In many cases this will not be problematic. In some, there may be reason to doubt the woman's claim. It is common for those who have

---

[60] [1997] 8 Med LR 1, 9.   [61] [1997] 8 Med LR 196.
[62] Comment by Margaret Puxon QC, ibid. 215.

taken a risk and suffered adverse consequences to assert that had they under-stood the risk, they would have decided not to run it. The wisdom of hindsight will convince them that this was so. There is a second problem. Even when there is convincing evidence as to what the woman would have done if adequately advised, it will still be necessary to establish that had the advice been heeded, the harm would have been avoided.

To explore the implications of this analysis, it is useful to focus on two types of situation that can occur during labour. One involves harm arising from intervention and the other from non-intervention. In each, the claim will rest on the assertion that the woman would have sought or agreed to dif-ferent procedures had she been better informed. Two examples of interven-tion that might have adverse consequences are the use of forceps and the cutting of an episiotomy. The former might result in a child being born with bruising and the latter in the woman experiencing long-term pain and dis-comfort. In either case it is open to the woman subsequently to argue that she would not have given her consent to the procedure had the risk which even-tuated been explained to her. To succeed in her claim, the woman would have to show that there was an alternative that she would have chosen. This requirement may be difficult to satisfy in view of the special nature of child-birth. Further, if the woman asserts that she would have refused consent had the information as to risks been provided when she was in labour, she must demonstrate that avoidance of the procedure would have produced a satis-factory result. Had she declined to consent to a forceps delivery or an episiotomy, the outcome might have been worse than the one of which she complains. Thus she might be unable to sustain the argument that had the information been provided, the harm would have been avoided.

The problems take a different form when the complaint relates to non-intervention. A situation in which liability might arise for failure to inform of risks is when a practitioner, knowing that the woman is opposed to medical intervention, allows a vaginal delivery to occur and a disabled child is born. Should the woman or child wish to sue the practitioner, two causal problems would arise. The first is whether the woman would have sought intervention had she received adequate information as to the risks faced. A court would look closely at her claim as to the effect which the failure to provide this infor-mation had on her conduct. It might inquire into the strength of her commit-ment to natural childbirth and conclude that even if the information had been provided, she would have elected to run the risks involved. Or the court might employ an objective approach, accepting that any 'reasonable' woman would have agreed to intervention had she been told that a vaginal delivery posed a substantial risk to herself or the fetus. On this view it would be easy to establish the causal link between the adverse outcome and the failure to warn of the risks. The application of an objective standard would, however, be open to criticism. The woman might disagree with the practitioner's assessment. Alternatively, she might accept it, but nevertheless be willing to run the risks. All these considerations suggest that the task of predicting what the woman would have done had the information been provided might be difficult. In the situation described, a woman might not find it easy to convince a court that she would have sought intervention had the information been provided. Should she surmount this hurdle, a second causal problem must be overcome. If it is clear that the woman would have requested and obtained a caesarean section, it must also be established that the child would not have been born with a disability had the operation been performed. This aspect of the claim would depend on medical evidence as to the likelihood of intervention being beneficial.

Claims arising from an omission to warn of the risk of the birth of a child with a genetic disability or a condition such as congenital rubella syndrome present different causal issues. In some United States cases, actions of this kind have been disallowed on the basis that the doctors had not caused the harm suffered by the child. This view was explained in a dissenting judgment in *Becker v Schwartz* (a case arising from the birth of a child with Down syndrome):

Any attempt to find the physician responsible, even to a limited extent, for an injury which the child unquestionably inherited from his parents, requires a distortion or abandonment of fundamental legal principles . . . The heart of the problem in these cases is that the physician cannot be said to have caused the defect. The disorder is genetic and not the result of any injury negligently inflicted by the doctor. In addition it is incurable and was incurable from the moment of conception. Thus the doctor's alleged negligent failure to detect it during prenatal examination cannot be considered a cause of the condition by analogy to those cases in which the doctor has failed to make a timely diagnosis of a curable disease. The child's handicap is an inexorable result of conception and birth.[63]

A rejection of an unwanted birth claim on this ground is unusual. As was seen in Chapter 5, the majority of courts in the United States, Canada, England, and Australia have recognized a cause of action when a child is born with a genetic disability. They have done so by accepting that the failure to warn of the risk of the disability can cause the harm by depriving the woman of the opportunity of terminating the pregnancy. In adopting this explanation, these courts have paid little attention to the difficulties involved in establishing the necessary causal link.

The major problem is that the success of an action relating to an unwanted birth is peculiarly dependent on the woman's testimony that she would have sought and obtained a termination had the risk been explained to her. The

[63] 413 NYS 2d 895, 904 (1978). See also: *Wilson v Kuenzi* 751 SW 2d 741, 745 (Mo banc, 1988), where this judgment was adopted and the claim (relating to the birth of a child with Down syndrome) was disallowed; *Atlanta Obstetrics and Gynecology Group v Abelson* 398 SE 2d 557(Ga, 1990).

possibility of self-serving testimony is obvious, as is the danger of relying on hindsight. In *Wilson v Kuenzi*, the court was sceptical: 'In the wrongful birth action, the right to recovery is based solely on the woman testifying, long after the fact and when it is in her financial interest to do so, that she would have chosen to abort if the physician had but told her of the amniocentesis test.' After noting that the percentage of women who refuse to consider abortion, even under pressure, is 'sometimes astounding', the court added: 'It would seem that testimony either more verifiable based upon experience or more verifiable by some objective standard should be required as the basis for any action for substantial damages.'[64] The court's reference to the possibility of a woman resisting the idea of an abortion is particularly pertinent in the case of the birth of a child when the risk of an abnormality was very small. With the benefit of hindsight, the woman may be convinced that she would not have allowed the pregnancy to continue had the appropriate information been provided. If, however, she had been most anxious to have a child, she might have been willing to run a statistically remote risk.

One court went so far as to suggest that the success of a non-disclosure action of this kind depends on the way the plaintiff chooses to view the outcome.[65] The majority judgment in *Azzolino v Dingfelder*[66] echoed this concern. It quoted with approval the following comment:

[W]rongful birth is not an ordinary tort. It is one thing to compensate destruction; it is quite another to compensate creation. This so-called 'wrong' is unique: it is a new and on-going condition. As life, it necessarily interacts with other lives. Indeed, it draws its 'injurious' nature from the predilections of the other lives it touches. It is naïve to suggest that such a situation falls neatly into conventional tort principles . . .[67]

While this statement raises questions as to whether the birth of a child can ever be regarded as a 'wrong', this aspect need not be further addressed here. Instead, what is noteworthy is the suggestion that the birth was regarded as a harm because of 'the predilections of the other lives it touches':

[T]he tort of wrongful birth will be peculiarly subject to fraudulent claims. The wrongful birth claim will almost always hinge upon testimony given by the parents after the birth concerning their desire prior to the birth to terminate the fetus should it be defective. The temptation will be great for parents, if not to invent such a prior desire to abort, to at least deny the possibility that they might have changed their minds and allowed the child to be born even if they had known of the defects it would suffer.[68]

---

[64] 751 SW 2d 741, 745–6 (Mo banc, 1988).

[65] '[I]t is a cause based on an after-the-event contingency which plaintiffs make operable by the operation of their minds . . .': *Howard v Lecher* 386 NYS 2d 460, 463 (1976). The case dealt with an action arising from a doctor's failure to identify the parents as potential carriers of Tay-Sachs and his failure to offer tests to determine whether the fetus was affected.

[66] 337 SE 2d 528 (NC, 1985).

[67] D. A. Burgman, 'Wrongful Birth Damages: Mandate and Mishandling by Judicial Fiat' 13 Valparaiso University Law Review 127, 170 (1978); cited 337 SE 2d 528, 534–5 (NC, 1985).

[68] 337 SE 2d 528, 535 (NC, 1985).

The court identified a further difficulty:

Additionally, since the parents will decide which 'defects' would have led them to abort the fetus, other questions will rapidly arise in jurisdictions recognizing wrongful birth claims when determining whether such claims will be permitted in particular cases. When will parents in those jurisdictions be allowed to decide that their child is so 'defective' that given a chance they would have aborted it while still a fetus and, as a result, then be allowed to hold their physician civilly liable? When a fetus is only the carrier of a deliterious [*sic*] gene and not itself impaired? When the fetus is of one sex rather than the other? Should such issues be left exclusively to the parents with doctors being found liable for breaching their duty to inform parents of any fetal conditions to which they know or should know the parents may object?[69]

The essence of these concerns is that the outcome of the action will be determined by the wishes and attitudes of the parents. There are other considerations. A doctor's liability for non-disclosure leading to the birth of a disabled child depends on proof that this non-disclosure deprived the woman of the opportunity—which she would have taken—to terminate the pregnancy. She must therefore be able to assert that the law would have allowed an abortion in her situation. A woman who cannot do so is unable to seek damages. Further, even if the law confers a right to an abortion, the woman may be unable to exercise that right. Access to abortion services might be limited in her community. Thus, the more the causal problem is examined, the more apparent it becomes that the success of the action will be dependent on extraneous factors.

Pre-Conception Negligence

Claims arising from pre-conception negligence give rise to a different type of causal problem. In Chapter 4, I discussed the cases in which children claimed damages for harm suffered as a result of negligence which affected their mothers' capacity to give birth to healthy babies. These cases arose, for example, from the administration of a blood transfusion, damage to the uterus at the time of a prior termination of pregnancy or a caesarean section, the failure to diagnose syphilis, or the ingestion of Diethylstilbestrol (DES). In some of these matters, the allegation was that the pre-conception procedures performed on the women caused direct harm to their children. In the cases involving the use of DES, however, the allegation against the manufacturer of the drug was that the ingestion of the drug caused the women's daughters to suffer from reproductive tract abnormalities, including cancer. This, in turn, impaired their childbearing capacity and the children affected sued for damages. Thus the actions were brought by the grandchildren of the women who were prescribed DES.

[69] 337 SE 2d 528, 535 (NC, 1985).

Cases involving pre-conception negligence raise questions about the foreseeability of the harm suffered by the children. Obviously the only duty of care borne by the doctors who provided the treatment or by the drug manufacturers would be owed to the women. At the time of the relevant conduct, there was no fetus whose welfare had to be taken into account. The only basis for imposing liability would be that when women of childbearing age are treated or take drugs, it is foreseeable that they might become pregnant and that harm caused to them could in turn cause antenatal harm to their children or grandchildren.

Thus, in the context of pre-conception negligence, there will be problems not only with causation, but also with the extent to which it is foreseeable that the treatment of one person will have adverse effects on another. On the former matter, it is apparent that a child plaintiff may not always find it easy to prove that the pre-conception negligence caused the harm: '[T]he difficulty of establishing [the required causal] connection will increase the more removed in time is the wrongful act from the accrual of the cause of action. This problem will be particularly acute in the case of an act which is alleged to have occurred before conception.'[70] Proof of foreseeability is even more problematic. This was underlined in a dissenting judgment in *Renslow v Mennonite Hospital*. There the majority held that the child could maintain an action based on the allegation that she had suffered harm as a result of a negligent blood transfusion given to her mother several years before her conception. In his dissent, Ryan J stated: 'Though the majority decision pays lip service to the concepts of duty and foreseeability, the effect of the decision is to emasculate these principles whenever causation can be shown.'[71] Questions relating to foreseeability are obviously particularly troubling when a grandchild of the affected woman sues for damages. It must be asked whether liability should extend beyond the first generation. *Enright by Enright v Eli Lilly & Co*[72] provided an illustration of the difficulties. There the plaintiff alleged that her grandmother's use of DES while pregnant with her mother caused physical abnormalities in her mother's reproductive organs which prevented her mother from carrying her to term. As a result of the plaintiff's premature birth, she sustained severe physical disabilities, including cerebral palsy. The majority refused to allow the claim:

[T]he cause of action plaintiffs ask us to recognize here could not be confined without the drawing of artificial and arbitrary boundaries. For all we know, the rippling effects of DES exposure may extend for generations. It is our duty to confine liability within manageable limits. Limiting liability to those who ingested the drug or who were exposed to it in utero serves this purpose.[73]

---

[70] P. J. Pace, 'Civil Liability for Pre-Natal Injuries' (1977) 40 Modern Law Review 141, 144.
[71] 367 NE 2d 1250, 1262 (1977). The case is discussed above 58–9.
[72] 570 NE 2d 198 (NY, 1991).   [73] Ibid. 203 (1991) (citations omitted).

Analysis of this kind was rejected in the dissenting judgment of Hancock J:

[T]his sort of 'floodgates of litigation' alarum seems singularly unpersuasive in view of our Court's repeated admonitions that it is not 'a ground for denying a cause of action that there will be a proliferation of claims' and *'if a cognizable wrong has been committed that there must be a remedy, whatever the burden of* [*sic*] *the courts'*. Beyond that, however, when defendants' arguments are applied here to urge that although claims of DES daughters should be allowed the claims of granddaughters should not be, their forebodings strike a peculiarly ironic note: i.e. the very fact of the 'insidious nature' of DES which may make the defendants liable for injuries to a future generation is advanced as the reason why they should not be liable for injuries to that generation. Should we be saying to these defendants and other companies which manufacture drugs 'you must be careful to produce reasonably "safe" drugs and to warn of the risks of taking such drugs but in deciding whether a drug is "safe" you may completely ignore the havoc a particular drug may wreck [*sic*] on a future generation? I think not.[74]

To adopt this view is to accept the consequences of applying the foreseeability test. On this analysis, liability should be imposed once it is clear that harm to a member of a succeeding generation will foreseeably result from the negligence. In contrast with this view, as the majority made clear, is the belief that account should be taken of the policy implications of imposing seemingly limitless liability. It is, of course, open to a legislature to intervene on the basis of such policy considerations. This course was adopted in England, where the Congenital Disabilities (Civil Liability) Act 1976 (UK) makes it clear that claims for pre-conception negligence should not extend beyond the first generation.[75] In the absence of such a solution, however, the problem of the extent to which the effects of pre-conception negligence can fairly be regarded as foreseeable will continue to trouble the courts.

DAMAGES

No distinctive problems as to the calculation of damages are posed by the majority of cases involving obstetric misadventures. When negligent antenatal or perinatal care has harmed the woman or the fetus, resulting in the birth of an impaired child, the assessment of the compensation payable can normally be undertaken on the basis of conventional principles. There is one category of case, however, in which the approach adopted by the courts raises questions about the appropriateness of employing these principles.

---

[74] 570 NE 2d 198, 207 (NY, 1991) (citations omitted, emphasis in original).
[75] See above 60.

The Birth of an Unwanted Child

As has been explained in Chapters 4 and 5, there are a number of ways in which an action can arise from the birth of an unwanted child. The negligent performance of a tubal ligation might result in a woman giving birth or the non-disclosure of the risk of failure of the procedure may produce the same outcome. Alternatively, the negligence might take the form of a failure to advise of the risk of the birth of a child with a genetic abnormality or a condition such as congenital rubella syndrome. The two categories of cases give rise to different problems with regard to the assessment of damages.

A Normal Child

When a failed tubal ligation has resulted in the birth of a normal but unwanted child, courts have been unsure how to characterize the harm suffered by the parents.[76] No problems of principle arise if the harm is viewed as residing in the effects of an unwanted pregnancy and subsequent delivery. The difficulties emerge when the long-term consequences are considered. An obvious result of giving birth to a child is the ensuing obligation to support it. This involves parents in considerable expense, for which some courts have been unwilling to award damages. This reluctance stems from distaste for the notion that the burden of the upkeep of a healthy child can ever be a compensable harm. This distaste, in its turn, is frequently based on an unspoken adherence to the view that since life is precious, the birth of a child should be regarded as a blessing.

One way in which the difficulties in the assessment of damages have become apparent is in decisions that have adopted a compromise. *McKernan v Aasheim* (a case arising from a failed tubal ligation) provided an illustration. The court was loath to accept the parents' argument that the birth of a healthy child represented an injury to them. It stated that 'to permit recovery of child-rearing costs would violate the public policy of [the State of Washington]'.[77] Yet the court was also concerned to ensure that the defendant doctor was not immune from liability in respect of the failure of the tubal ligation. It therefore held that the parents could recover damages in respect of the pain and suffering and expense associated with the operation and with the pregnancy and delivery. The conclusion that the parents were entitled to damages of this kind, but not to those relating to the upbringing of the child, was inconsistent with the basic principles governing the calculation of damages. If the doctor's conduct was negligent and had caused harm for which the parents could seek damages, it is artificial for those damages to exclude compensation for the clearly foreseeable results of the negligence. The

---

[76] See above 76–9.   [77] 687 P 2d 850, 856 (Wash, 1984).

obvious consequence of a failed tubal ligation is the birth of a child. The obvious consequence of that outcome is liability for the child's upkeep.

Thus the court's uncertainty about the nature of the harm suffered by the parents of an unwanted but normal child was predictably reflected in uncertainty as to the assessment of the damages payable. A second problem with the application of the principles of negligence law is seen in the attempts, by some courts, to produce a fair result by applying the 'benefits rule'.[78] The application of this rule requires a finding that while the parents of an unwanted child are entitled to damages to compensate them for the expense of rearing the child, deductions must be made on the basis of the benefits the parents will receive from that child. The difficulty of undertaking such calculations is obvious. *McKernan v Aasheim* also illustrated this difficulty. One of the reasons that led the court to deny child-rearing costs was that while in any assessment of damages it is theoretically desirable to offset benefits against burdens, in practice the task was impossible in the case before it. While the court recognized that a child is more than an economic liability (and hence that an off-set should be allowed) it could not see how the benefits rule could be applied:

[W]hether [the costs of rearing and educating the child] are outweighed by the emotional benefits which will be conferred by that child cannot be calculated. The child may turn out to be loving, obedient and attentive, or hostile, unruly or callous. . . . [I]t is impossible to tell, at an early stage in the child's life, whether its parents have sustained a net loss or a net gain.[79]

Comments of this kind demonstrate the type of speculation in which courts dealing with unwanted birth matters have frequently engaged. Further, even if the benefits derived from a child can be assigned a monetary value, there is another objection to the application of the benefits rule. Its critics have expressed concern that relying on the rule encourages parents to disparage the value of their child: '[A]n unhandsome, colicky or otherwise "undesirable" child would provide fewer offsetting benefits, and would therefore presumably be worth more monetarily in a "wrongful birth" case.'[80] A corollary of this is the view that the institution of unwanted birth actions will have an adverse impact on the child as he or she will be labelled an 'emotional bastard'.[81] In answer to this, one judgment has asserted that it is for the parents to weigh the risk that psychological damage will be caused to the child who is the subject of the action.[82]

Some courts have encountered a further difficulty. They have gone beyond the problem of determining how a monetary sum can be placed on the harm

---

[78] See above 125–6.   [79] 687 P 2d 850, 855 (Wash, 1984).
[80] *Public Health Trust v Brown* Fla App, 388 So 2d 1084, 1086, n 4 (1980).
[81] *Boone v Mullendore* Ala, 416 So 2d 718, 722 (1982).
[82] *Hartke v McKelway* 707 F 2d 1544, 1552, n 8 (1983).

suffered by the parents and have questioned the fairness of making the doctor liable for the entire cost of the child's upkeep. In *Rieck v Medical Protective Co*, the Supreme Court of Wisconsin explained these doubts in a homely fashion:

To permit the parents to keep their child and shift the entire cost of its upbringing to a physician who failed to determine or inform them of the fact of pregnancy would be to create a new category of surrogate parent. Every child's smile, every bond of love and affection, every reason for parental pride in a child's achievements, every contribution by the child to the welfare and well-being of the family and parents, is to remain with the mother and father. For the most part, these are intangible benefits, but they are nonetheless real. On the other hand, every financial cost or detriment ... including the cost of food, clothing and education, would be shifted to the physician who allegedly failed to timely diagnose the fact of pregnancy. We hold that such result would be wholly out of proportion to the culpability involved, and that the allowance of recovery would place too unreasonable a burden upon physicians ...[83]

The rationale that it would be unjust to make the doctor liable for the full cost of the child's upkeep can be questioned. It may not be appropriate for a court to reach its conclusion in order to avoid placing an 'unreasonable burden' upon a doctor. This point was made in *McKernan v Aasheim*: 'It is not our place to deny recovery of certain damages merely in order to insulate health care providers from the shock of big tort judgments.'[84] Nevertheless, the argument that imposing liability for childcare expenses is 'wholly out of proportion to the culpability involved' cannot be ignored. To put it another way, liability of this kind can be seen as subjecting the doctor to 'a kind of medical paternity suit'.[85]

There is no need to take the analysis further. It is clear that the courts dealing with unwanted birth actions have encountered enormous difficulties in assessing damages on the basis of established principles of law. The tasks of fairly assigning culpability and placing a monetary value on the harm suffered by the parents of an unwanted healthy child are not ones which can be satisfactorily undertaken within the framework offered by negligence law.

A Disabled Child

The problem posed by the calculation of damages in respect of the birth of a child with a genetic or other congenital disability is also complex. The difficulty is whether the damages should cover the full cost of the care of the disabled child or only the difference between the costs of caring for a normal child and those of caring for a child with a disability. This difficulty arises

---

[83] 219 NW 2d 242, 244–5 (1974). See also *White v United States* 510 F Supp 146 (1981) and *Kingsbury v Smith* NH, 442 A 2d 1003 (1982) on refusal to award full child-rearing costs because of the unreasonable burden on the practitioner.

[84] 687 P 2d 850, 854 (Wash, 1984).   [85] *Becker v Schwartz* 413 NYS 2d 895, 907 (1978).

because it can be argued that although the parents did not want a *disabled* child, they cannot claim to be unwilling to bear the cost of raising a *normal* child. Their cause of action arises from the characteristics of the particular child, not from the fact that a child has been born. On this analysis, the costs of care of a normal child should be deducted from any damages awarded. These costs were expenses the parents expected and were willing to bear before they were deprived of the opportunity to terminate the pregnancy. The result would be that the damages awarded would be limited to the special costs payable in respect of the abnormality.

As has been seen in Chapter 7, there have been cases in which awards have been limited to damages specifically associated with the birth and rearing of an abnormal child. Major components are payments for medical expenses, for nursing care, and for full-time institutional care when the child has been born severely disabled. There are also cases in which the full costs of child-care have been awarded. When this occurs, there can be disagreement as to whether the parent of a disabled child can be said to derive some pleasure and benefit from bringing up the child. In *Phillips v United States*,[86] for example, the damages payable were reduced by 50 per cent to take account of the benefits flowing from the birth of a child with Down syndrome.

Once again, the case law demonstrates the difficulty of fairly assessing the compensation payable to the parents of an unwanted child. It can be argued that the damages should cover all expenses involved in the child's care. The primary reason is that it is artificial to seek to distinguish between costs arising from the disability and those that would have to be met were the child normal. If it is accepted that the doctor's negligence has caused the harm, it might be unsatisfactory to seek to divide up the burden on the basis that the parents had expected to bear part of it. In addition, reliance on the benefits rule might further distort the outcome: it is even more difficult to apply this rule in the case of a disabled child than in the case of an unwanted, but normal child. Finally, a robust conclusion in favour of the payment of full damages will result in a calculation based on well-established principles. When a child suffers brain damage as a result of a doctor's negligent management of the delivery, a court will have little difficulty calculating the cost of the child's upkeep. It will not speculate as to the possible benefits that the parents will derive from caring for the child.

The fact that some courts hearing unwanted birth claims in respect of disabled children have engaged in such speculation probably springs from their feeling that unwanted birth claims are suspect. Assumptions as to the preciousness of life still underpin some judgments in cases involving disabled children and the suspicion that parents will seek 'windfalls' following the birth of such children is occasionally expressed.[87] Such assumptions complicate

---

[86] 575 F Supp 1309 (1983).   [87] *Berman v Allan* 404 A 2d 8, 14 (1979).

the task of assessing damages following the birth of a child with genetic disabilities or a condition such as congenital rubella syndrome. Further, the fact that the disabilities are genetic or the result of a medical condition provides another reason for uncertainty: it is understandable that courts will occasionally be reluctant to order a doctor to pay full child-rearing expenses when the child's disabilities have not been caused by medical negligence.

CONCLUSION: POLICY DECISIONS?

This chapter has identified a number of ways in which the application of the principles governing negligence law has produced distinctive difficulties when obstetric misadventures have occurred. Sometimes these principles have been employed in a questionable manner. The cases reveal uncertainty about the nature of a doctor or midwife's duty of care. They also demonstrate special problems in the application of the doctrine of informed consent and in proof of causation. In addition, there is the difficulty of identifying the type of harm for which compensation should be paid. A corollary of this has frequently been disagreement as to the assessment of damages.

Of these matters, the most troubling are those generated by the courts' often unspoken assumptions about the nature of the duty of care which a practitioner owes to a pregnant woman. These are the product of the fact that a doctor or midwife who provides antenatal or perinatal care is responsible for 'not-one-but-not-two'. The chapter has drawn attention to the dangers of failing to appreciate the significance of this concept and, in particular, of treating the fetus as an entity to which a duty of care is directly owed. Even when these dangers are recognized, it is not easy to determine how and in what circumstances the breach of a duty owed primarily to the woman can result in an action not only by her but also by the affected child. I have suggested that it is necessary to view the duty as a composite one: the obligation to the woman includes a duty in respect of her fetus. This explanation is offered as a solution to some of the questions posed by actions in which children born with disabilities seek damages. When these disabilities are the result of poor medical techniques, analysis is comparatively straightforward. When, however, the disabilities are the product of a failure to provide information as to the risks of childbirth, analysis becomes more complex. The duty to provide such information can be discharged only by giving the necessary information to the woman, yet the child may wish to sue in respect of harm caused by the failure to fulfil that duty. More complex are cases arising from the birth of a child with a foreseeable genetic or other disability. Although some courts have been prepared to entertain wrongful life claims in such situations, there are insuperable difficulties regarding the nature of the breach of duty of care that the child can allege. It is more satisfactory to accept that the relevant duty—to make the woman aware of the risks—can be owed only to her. To adopt this conclusion, however, is to accept that the child who must bear the burdens arising from the disability cannot establish a cause of action.

Ultimately it is not possible to reach a satisfying conclusion about the basis on which damages may be awarded in respect of antenatal negligence. This result should be unsurprising in view of the conclusion reached in Chapter 8: if the legal status of the fetus is ambiguous, the law will be unable to give clear and consistent answers about the way in which the principles of the law of negligence should be applied when a fetus is harmed. In particular, since the law takes note of what the fetus will become rather than what it is, identifying the nature of the duty of care imposed on those who practise obstetrics or midwifery is controversial. The definition of this duty lends itself to judicial manipulation, depending on the result that is thought to be just. This is not peculiar to cases involving antenatal negligence. As Prosser has pointed out: ' "[D]uty" is not sacrosanct in itself, but is only an expression of the sum total of those considerations of policy which lead the law to say that the plaintiff is entitled to protection.'[88] A similar point has been made by Kennedy, commenting on *Burton v Islington Health Authority*: 'All attempts to manoeuvre the common law's building blocks of duty, breach and damage seem at best contrived and at worst flawed.'[89]

It follows that the courts will be influenced by policy considerations. Sometimes these are not made explicit. It is likely that an unspoken aim in many English decisions is to avoid the difficulties associated with assigning legal status to the fetus. Occasionally courts make it clear that a decision has been driven by a desire to produce a particular outcome. In *Montreal Tramways v Leveille*, for example, Lamont J embraced the view that it was only fair and just that a child should be able to sue in respect of antenatal injury and that if the existing law produced a different result, it should be changed:

If a child after birth has no right of action for pre-natal injuries, we have a wrong inflicted for which there is no remedy, for, although the father may be entitled to compensation for the loss he has incurred and the mother for what she has suffered, yet there is a residuum of injury for which compensation cannot be had save at the suit of the child. If a right of action be denied to the child it will be compelled, without any fault on its part, to go through life carrying the seal of another's fault and bearing a very heavy burden of infirmity and inconvenience without any compensation therefor. To my mind it is but natural justice that a child, if born alive and viable, should be allowed to maintain an action in the Courts for injuries wrongfully committed upon its person while in the womb of its mother.[90]

---

[88] *Prosser and Keeton on the Law of Torts* (St Paul, Minnesota, 5th edn., 1984) 358 (citations omitted).

[89] [1993] Medical Law Review 103, 105.   [90] [1933] 4 DLR 337, 345.

Such an approach is open to criticism. As Gillard J noted in *Watt v Rama*, relying on the tenets of natural justice points to what the law ought to be rather than to what it is.[91] Nevertheless, while offering no clear principles, this approach has the merit of recognizing that issues of policy must be openly addressed. Some of these will be discussed in Chapter 14.

[91] [1972] VR 353, 364.

11

After Birth: Maternal Liability for Antenatal Conduct?

In Chapter 9, I suggested that the law should not seek to coerce or control a pregnant woman in an attempt to protect her fetus. This conclusion would preclude all forms of legal intervention against the woman before her child is born. It leaves open the question whether a woman whose negligent conduct has resulted in her child being born with injuries or disabilities should be liable to a damages claim by the child. It is not difficult to envisage situations in which a woman's conduct during pregnancy might be considered negligent. Antenatal behaviour fitting this description includes smoking, taking illicit drugs, or excessive alcohol consumption.[1] Before considering the possibility of a woman being liable to her child for such conduct, it is necessary to review the law on parents' liability to damages claims by their children. If parents are in all circumstances immune to such claims, there can be no basis on which to suggest that a woman might be liable to her child in respect of antenatal behaviour.

DAMAGES CLAIMS AGAINST PARENTS

There was a time when United States courts regularly expressed the view that parents should be immune to damages claims brought by children for personal injuries.[2] A number of reasons were given, the most important being that it was contrary to public policy to allow actions that would disrupt the family unit or undermine parental authority.[3] The obvious practical question was also raised as to where parents would find the funds to meet a claim. In addition, if this difficulty were overcome, the effect that a successful action by a child might have on the financial welfare of other members of the family must be considered. It was not long, however, before the doctrine of parental immunity was challenged and its operation restricted. In *Schenk v Schenk*,[4]

---

[1] For a brief discussion of the effects which such maternal conduct can have on the fetus, see above 223.

[2] The doctrine of parental tort immunity was articulated in cases such as: *Hewellette v George* 9 So 885 (1891); *McKelvey v McKelvey* 77 SW 664 (1903); *Roller v Roller* 79 P 788 (1905).

[3] For a review and discussion of these reasons, see *Stallman v Youngquist* 504 NE 2d 920 (Ill App 1 Dist, 1987).

[4] 241 NE 2d 12 (1968).

for example, the immunity was limited to acts arising out of family relation-ships and directly connected with family purposes and objectives. In some States the doctrine was abolished. As a result, there are now very few, if any, jurisdictions in which parental immunity is preserved in absolute form. In the words of the Massachusetts Supreme Judicial Court: 'Children enjoy the same right to protection and to legal redress for wrongs done them as others enjoy. Only the strongest reasons, grounded in public policy, can justify limi-tation or abolition of those rights.'[5] One commentator has summarized the current position as follows:

[T]he courts acknowledge that the modern trend and proper approach in light of modern conditions and conceptions of public policy dictate a relaxation if not aboli-tion of the parental immunity doctrine. . . . These decisions show that the growing trend is to abolish the crude, blanket immunity with far greater concern given to just what acts, if any, the courts want to protect from state scrutiny.[6]

This approach allows United States courts generally to proceed on a case-by-case basis and to ask whether the situation before them is one in which parental immunity can be justified. A number of judgments have suggested that parents should not be liable to damages claims arising from acts per-formed as part of the parent–child relationship; these are acts requiring the exercise of ordinary parental discretion.[7] To impose liability for such conduct would involve the courts in the difficult task of setting standards to be met by parents in the course of raising children. A refusal to do so is consistent with the view that state interference with family life should be kept to a minimum. While this view has not been universally adopted,[8] it has received much sup-port in United States courts. Nevertheless, parents can be answerable to their children in situations that do not give rise to questions relating to the proper standard of day-to-day care. The clearest example is when a child sues in respect of injuries caused by a parent's negligent driving. Many courts have had little difficulty in deciding that parental immunity should not be allowed in such cases.[9]

There were obvious reasons for reaching this conclusion: the parent in such an action is no more than a nominal defendant, but one whose culpability

---

[5] *Sorensen v Sorensen* Mass, 339 NE 2d 907, 912 (1975).

[6] R. Beal, ' "Can I Sue Mommy?" An Analysis of a Woman's Tort Liability for Prenatal Injuries to her Child Born Alive' (1984) 21 San Diego Law Review 325, 342 (citations omitted).

[7] For example, *Goller v White* 122 NW 2d 193 (1963); *Felderhof v Felderhof* 473 SW 2d 928 (1971).

[8] Some judges have felt able to impose a duty on the basis of a 'reasonable parent' standard: see *Gibson v Gibson* Sup, 92 Cal Rptr 288 (1971); *Anderson v Stream* Minn, 295 NW 2d 595 (1980).

[9] For example, *Stallman v Youngquist* 504 NE 2d 920 (Ill App 1 Dist, 1987); *Black v Solmitz* Me, 409 A 2d 634 (1979); *Sorensen v Sorensen* Mass, 339 NE 2d 907, 912 (1975); *Nocktonick v Nocktonick* Kan, 611 P 2d 135 (1980).

must be established if the child is to receive the benefits of a parent's insurance policy. It would be unjust if the child were precluded from receiving these benefits: '[T]he child is not to be denied the benefit of insurance that would be available for a stranger.'[10] Further, allowing a damages claim is beneficial to the family rather than detrimental. As the Appellate Court of Illinois observed, the disruption to family life is not the lawsuit but the injury itself resulting from parental negligence. 'It can hardly aid family reconciliation to deny an injured child access to the courts and, through the courts, to deny access to any liability insurance that the family might maintain.'[11] The judgment continued:

Although insurance cannot create liability where no legal duty previously existed, it remains, nevertheless, a proper element in a discussion of the public policy behind abrogation of parental immunity. Where insurance exists, the domestic tranquillity argument is hollow; in reality, the sought after litigation is not between child and parent but between child and parent's insurance carrier. Far from being a potential source of disharmony, the action is more likely to preserve the family unit in pursuit of a common goal—the easing of family financial difficulties stemming from the child's injuries.[12]

The doctrine of parental immunity has never been generally adopted by courts in England, Canada, or Australia. Nevertheless, the conclusions reached have been similar to those of the majority of United States courts. There is little English authority on the matter. In *Surtees v Kingston-upon-Thames*,[13] the Court of Appeal held that there is no bar to an action by a child who has been injured by parental negligence. It stressed that any duty of care was not the product of the relationship between parent and child, but derived from the particular circumstances in which the claim arose. In *Hahn v Conley*, the High Court of Australia drew a distinction between a parent acting in his or her capacity as a parent and a parent acting in circumstances in which a stranger would owe a duty of care. Barwick CJ ruled: '[T]here is no general duty of care . . . imposed by the law upon a parent simply because of the blood relationship.'[14] He explained: 'In the case of the parent, as in the case of a stranger it seems to me that the duty of care springs out of the particular situation: the extent and nature of the steps which it may be necessary to take to discharge the duty may well be influenced by the fact of parenthood, though parenthood is not itself the source of the duty.'[15] The Canadian law is the same as that in England and Australia.[16]

[10] *Badigian v Badigian* 174 NE 2d 718, 722 (1961).
[11] *Stallman v Youngquist* 504 NE 2d 920, 925 (Ill App 1 Dist, 1987).   [12] Ibid. 926.
[13] [1991] 2 FLR 559.   [14] (1971) 126 CLR 276, 283–4.   [15] Ibid. 284.
[16] In *Dobson (Litigation Guardian of) v Dobson* (1997) 148 DLR (4th) 332, 335, the New Brunswick Court of Appeal (citing *Deziel v Deziel* [1953] 1 DLR 651) accepted that 'it is common ground' that a child may sue a parent in tort. The correctness of this decision was not doubted when the Supreme Court of Canada ruled on the appeal in *Dobson*.

Thus, in none of the countries discussed in this book is it likely that a claim of parental immunity will automatically defeat a damages action by a child. While the courts will take account of the nature of the parent/child relationship when hearing such an action, they will normally prefer to reach a decision on the basis of an assessment of the appropriateness of allowing the claim to proceed. Particular attention will be paid to considerations of public policy.

MATERNAL LIABILITY FOR CONDUCT DURING PREGNANCY?

Identifying the Problem

In some circumstances children may sue parents when their negligent conduct has caused harm. In Chapter 4, I showed that a third party may be liable to a child in respect of antenatal negligence. These propositions provide the background for considering the possible liability of a woman whose negligence during pregnancy has resulted in the birth of an injured or disabled child.

One way of addressing the problem is to employ the analysis offered in Chapter 9 and to assert that the answers are implicit in the adoption of the 'not-one-but-not-two' model of pregnancy. On this view, the fetus is not an entity of a kind to which the woman can owe a duty of care and therefore it is impossible for her to be liable to pay damages to her injured child. This might represent an oversimplified approach. The cases discussed in Chapters 4 and 5 show that a child may sue a doctor or midwife in respect of harm caused by antenatal negligence. As was seen in Chapter 10, the practitioner's liability in such an action is not dependent on identifying the fetus as a separate entity to which a duty of care is directly owed. Whether or not the fetus is separate is irrelevant to the assignment of liability for antenatal negligence: liability arises as a result of conduct that causes harm after the child is born. This poses the question whether a pregnant woman could be made liable for antenatal conduct in the same way as a doctor or midwife can be. The duty of care she would be required to discharge could be formulated in much the same way as that suggested for doctors and midwives in Chapter 12: to take all steps to avoid a reasonably foreseeable risk to the fetus. Is there any reason not to impose such an obligation on a pregnant woman when the law accepts that a third party such as a doctor or midwife must bear responsibility when antenatal negligence has caused a child to be born with an injury or disability?

English Law

The English law provides a clear answer to the question of a woman's liability to her child in respect of antenatal conduct. Section 1(1) of the Congenital

Disabilities (Civil Liability) Act 1976 (UK) makes it clear that the right of action for antenatal negligence that the Act confers on a child may be exercised against any person other than the child's mother.[17] The English Act was passed as a result of the recommendations made in the Law Commission's *Report on Injuries to Unborn Children*.[18] Its earlier Working Paper[19] proposed that a child injured as a result of the mother's antenatal negligence should be able to sue her. After consultation, it reached the opposite conclusion. It was particularly influenced by a submission by the Bar Council, which, while recognizing that 'logic and principle' dictate that a mother should be liable to her child for her negligent acts, urged that 'in any system of law there are areas in which logic and principle ought to yield to social acceptability and natural sentiment'. It supported this argument by pointing out that when a child is born with a disability the relationship with the mother will be stressful. Making her liable to pay compensation would exacerbate the situation. The Council also drew on one of the general criticisms made of a parent/child damages claim: that it is not apparent where a parent would find the funds to meet such a claim. Finally, concern was expressed about the problem of defining, and setting limits to, the maternal conduct that could be considered negligent.[20]

United States, Canadian, and Australian Law

In some parts of the United States, as in the United Kingdom, the issue of a mother's liability to her child for antenatal harm has been resolved by legislation. For example, a Missouri provision dealing with the protection of 'unborn children' states that nothing in the section 'shall be interpreted as creating a cause of action against a woman for indirectly harming her unborn child by failing to properly care for herself or by failing to follow any particular program of prenatal care'.[21] In other parts of the United States and in Canada and Australia, the relevant law is to be found in a series of judicial decisions. In the first of these — *Grodin v Grodin*[22] — the Court of Appeals of Michigan ruled on a claim by a child that his mother had negligently failed to seek proper antenatal care, had failed to ask her doctor to undertake a pregnancy test, and had not informed the doctor that she was taking tetracycline.

---

[17] The fact that the English legislation made mothers immune to damages claims but not fathers has been criticized as illogical and discriminatory, since many of the policy reasons for denying a child a right of action against the mother apply almost equally to the father: P. J. Pace, 'Civil Liability for Pre-Natal Injuries' (1977) 40 Modern Law Review 141, 154–5. See also Royal Commission on Civil Liability and Compensation for Personal Injury, *Report, Volume 1* (1978) para 1471. Discussion of this aspect is beyond the scope of this book.

[18] Law Commission, *Report on Injuries to Unborn Children* (Law Com No 60, 1974).

[19] Law Commission, *Injuries to Unborn Children* (Working Paper No 47, 1973).

[20] Law Commission, *Report on Injuries to Unborn Children* (Law Com No 60, 1974) para 55.

[21] § 1. 205. 4 RS Mo (1999).   [22] Mich App, 301 NW 2d 869 (1981).

The harm that he alleged was that the use of the drug during pregnancy had caused him to develop brown and discoloured teeth. Unlike many of the courts that have dealt with children's claims against parents, the court did not make a distinction between acts involving the exercise of ordinary parental discretion and duties owed to the world at large. Instead, it held that the mother could be liable if the use of the tetracycline was not 'a reasonable exercise of parental discretion'.[23] The court did not express an opinion on whether the woman's conduct was in fact unreasonable; the case was remanded for a jury to decide the question.

Grodin was an unusual decision. Most of the leading cases on maternal liability for antenatal conduct have arisen following road accidents. In these, the courts—like the English Law Commission—have recognized the difficulty of defining the type of maternal conduct that could be regarded as negligent. Two responses to this difficulty have emerged. One is to focus on the undesirable consequences of imposing on a pregnant woman any duty of care in respect of her fetus. The other is to acknowledge the existence of a duty but to seek to limit its definition in order to avoid these consequences.

In the United States, the fullest examination of the issues was provided in *Stallman v Youngquist*.[24] There the Supreme Court of Illinois decided that a woman whose negligent driving while pregnant had resulted in injury to her child should not bear the same liability as a third person who had caused prenatal injury. The court dismissed *Grodin* as 'unpersuasive' on the ground that the judgment had failed to appreciate the profound implications of holding the mother liable.[25] Addressing these implications, *Stallman* ruled in favour of immunity on the ground that the imposition of liability on the woman would create a burden that was both inappropriate and too demanding. The analysis was complicated by the assumption that imposing a duty of care on a pregnant woman would involve the recognition of a child's correlative right to begin life with a sound mind and body.[26] Nevertheless, the court's unwillingness to allow the imposition of a new and potentially limitless duty of care was made clear:

[T]he recognition of a legal right to begin life with a sound mind and body on the part of a fetus which is assertable after birth against its mother would have serious ramifications for all women and their families, and for the way in which society views women and women's reproductive abilities. The recognition of such a right by [*sic*] a fetus would necessitate the recognition of a legal duty on the part of the woman who is the mother; a legal duty, as opposed to a moral duty, to effectuate the best prenatal environment possible. . . . Since anything which a pregnant woman does or does not do may have an impact, either positive or negative, on her developing fetus, any act or

---

[23] Ibid. 871. The court's analysis of the law relating to parental immunity was subsequently held to be incorrect: *Mayberry v Pryor* 352 NW 2d 322 (Mich App, 1984).

[24] 531 NE 2d 355 (Ill, 1988).   [25] Ibid. 358.

[26] For a discussion of this right, see above 197.

omission on her part could render her liable to her subsequently born child. . . . A legal right of a fetus to begin life with a sound mind and body assertable against a mother would make a pregnant woman the guarantor of the mind and body of her child at birth. A legal duty to guarantee the mental and physical health of another has never before been recognized in law. . . . If a legally cognizable duty on the part of mothers were recognized, then a judicially defined standard of conduct would have to be met. It must be asked, By what judicially defined standard would a mother have her every act or omission while pregnant subjected to State scrutiny? By what objective standard could a jury be guided in determining whether a pregnant woman did all that was necessary in order not to breach a legal duty to not interfere with her fetus' separate and independent right to be born whole? In what way would prejudicial and stereotypical beliefs about the reproductive abilities of women be kept from interfering with a jury's determination of whether a particular woman was negligent at any point during her pregnancy?[27]

The court also pointed out that if attempts were made to set standards, it would be impossible for some women to meet them:

Pregnancy does not come only to those women who have within their means all that is necessary to effectuate the best possible prenatal environment: any female of child-bearing age may become pregnant. Within this pool of potential defendants are representatives of all socio-economic backgrounds: the well-educated and the ignorant; the rich and the poor; those women who have access to good health care and good prenatal care and those who, for an infinite number of reasons, have not had access to any health care services.[28]

In addition to these expressions of concern about the breadth of the duty of care that would have to be imposed to make a woman liable for her conduct during pregnancy, the court considered the nature of pregnancy:

The relationship between a pregnant woman and her fetus is unlike the relationship between any other plaintiff and defendant. No other plaintiff depends exclusively on any other defendant for everything necessary for life itself. No other defendant must go through biological changes of the most profound type, possibly at the risk of her own life, in order to bring forth an adversary into the world. It is, after all, the whole life of the pregnant woman which impacts on the development of the fetus. As opposed to the third-party defendant, it is the mother's every waking and sleeping moment which, for better or worse, shapes the prenatal environment which forms the world for the developing fetus.[29]

It was on this basis that the court concluded that the woman's situation was different from that of a third party: 'Logic does not demand that a pregnant woman be treated in a court of law as a stranger to her developing fetus.'[30] This view was reinforced by historical analysis. Earlier, the judgment had

---

[27] 531 NE 2d 355, 359–60 (Ill, 1988). The *Stallman* view that a woman is under no duty to guarantee the mental and physical health of her child at birth was also adopted in *Re Baby Boy Doe* 632 NE 2d 326, 332 (Ill App 1 Dist, 1994).
[28] 531 NE 2d 355, 360 (Ill, 1988).   [29] Ibid. 360.   [30] Ibid. 360.

traced the law's development to accommodate claims against third parties guilty of antenatal negligence. It concluded:

The error that a fetus cannot be harmed in a legally cognizable way when the woman who is its mother is injured has been corrected; the law will no longer treat the fetus as only a part of its mother. The law will not now make an error of a different sort, one with enormous implications for all women who have been, are, may be, or might become pregnant: the law will not treat a fetus as an entity which is entirely separate from its mother.[31]

The court's characterization of the relationship between a pregnant woman and her fetus is consistent with the 'not-one-but-not-two' model. In *Winnipeg Child and Family Services (Northwest Area) v G*, the Supreme Court of Canada, by adopting a different model, reached the same conclusion as that offered in *Stallman*. One reason advanced by the court for refusing to treat the fetus as possessing rights assertable against the woman was that the law 'has always treated the mother and unborn child as one'.[32] The judgment continued: 'To permit an unborn child to sue its pregnant mother-to-be would introduce a radically new conception into the law; the unborn child and its mother as separate juristic persons in a mutually separable and antagonistic relation.'[33]

In *Winnipeg*, the issue of a woman's potential liability for conduct during pregnancy arose in an unusual context. The proceedings leading to the appeal had included an application to invoke tort law against a pregnant woman whose glue sniffing was thought to be likely to harm her fetus. In addition to being asked to rule on the possible use of the *parens patriae* jurisdiction to protect the fetus, the Supreme Court of Canada was asked to determine whether an injunction could be obtained to detain her for the same purpose. The basis on which the injunction was sought was that it was necessary to restrain her tortious conduct. The action was taken on behalf of the fetus; it did not involve a child's damages claim against the mother. Therefore the judgment, though helpful, did not deal directly with the question of maternal liability for negligence.

In considering whether the woman owed her fetus a duty of care, the majority accepted that a fetus cannot possess legal rights as it is not a person under the common law. Rights are acquired only on live birth. The court then asked whether the law should be extended to allow a fetus to assert rights against the mother. In support of its ruling against such an extension, the court, in addition to invoking the one entity model, expressed concern about the ramifications of accepting that a woman could owe her fetus obligations enforceable by an injunction. The court was aware that recognizing such obligations could pave the way for damages claims arising from women's

---

[31] Ibid. 359.   [32] (1997) 152 DLR (4th) 193, 207.   [33] Ibid. 207–8.

antenatal conduct. The reason for the court's anxiety was the same as that which led it to refuse to extend the protection of the *parens patriae* jurisdiction to the fetus: a distaste for the imposition of legal controls on pregnant women.

The result was that the judgment provided broad support for the view expressed in *Stallman* rather than offering a close analysis of the reasons for allowing a child's damages claim against a third party, but not against his or her mother. In making it clear that the law should not set or enforce standards of conduct for pregnant women, the court raised doubts about the possibility of formulating a duty to which all pregnant women could be expected to adhere. It expressed concern about the law treating what the court described as 'lifestyle choices'[34] as breaches of a duty of care. This fear is reminiscent of that which has led courts to refuse to make parents liable to their children in respect of acts performed as part of the parent–child relationship. Indeed, the *Winnipeg* court expressly referred to the inappropriateness of the law setting standards for day-to-day child care. It asked rhetorically whether children should be permitted to sue for harm caused by second-hand smoke inhaled round the family dinner table or for 'poor grades due to alcoholism or a parent's undue fondness for the office or the golf course?' The court asked: 'If we permit lifestyle actions, where do we draw the line?' Further, it noted that the difficulties multiply 'when the lifestyle in question is that of a pregnant woman whose liberty is intimately and inescapably bound to her unborn child'.[35]

Thus the decisions in both *Stallman* and *Winnipeg* were primarily based on an unwillingness to allow the common law to expose pregnant women to intrusive legal intervention. One response to this analysis is that it is possible to fashion an appropriate definition of the duty that a pregnant woman must discharge. This is to argue that rather than attempting the task of setting standards relating to 'lifestyle', the law has the capacity to define a pregnant woman's duty of care in such a way as to confine her legal obligations within realistic limits. The majority of the Supreme Court of New Hampshire in *Bonte for Bonte v Bonte*[36] had earlier accepted this answer. Here the child's injuries had been caused by the mother's alleged negligence in crossing the road. In the court's view, the problem of her liability could be resolved solely by applying established principles of tort law. Since it was clear that a child may bring a damages action for antenatal negligence, the only problem was whether the doctrine of parental immunity should be invoked to shield parents from damages claims by their children. Having noted how the doctrine had been abandoned in New Hampshire, the majority ruled:

Because our cases hold that a child born alive may maintain a cause of action against another for injuries sustained while in utero, and a child may sue his or her mother in

---

[34] (1997) 152 DLR (4th) 193, 208.   [35] Ibid. 209.   [36] 616 A 2d 464 (NH, 1992).

tort for the mother's negligence, it follows that a child born alive has a cause of action against his or her mother for the mother's negligence that caused injury to the child when in utero.[37]

The court rejected the submission that the imposition of controls during pregnancy was unacceptable:

We disagree that our decision today deprives a mother of her right to control her life during pregnancy; rather, she is required to act with the appropriate duty of care, as we have consistently held other persons are required to act, with respect to the fetus. The mother will be held to the same standard of care as that required of her once the child is born. Whether her actions are negligent is a determination for the finder of fact, considering the facts and circumstances of the particular case.[38]

Thus the court had no doubt that a pregnant woman should be subject to an 'appropriate duty of care', a duty defined by reference to the standard of care 'required of her once the child is born'.[39] This view was not shared by the dissenting judges, Brock CJ and Batchelder J. Echoing *Stallman*, they questioned whether 'the nature and scope of the duty can be articulated with consistency and predictability by the courts'. They were concerned that 'a rule of law attempting to distinguish between acts of the mother that involve privacy interests and those that may be considered common torts would result in arbitrary line-drawing resulting in inconsistent verdicts.'[40]

The possibility of confining a pregnant woman's duty of care within manageable limits was also addressed in *Winnipeg*. The welfare agency that had sought intervention submitted: '[T]he duty of care should be to refrain from activities that have no substantial value to a pregnant woman's well-being or right of self-determination and that have the potential to cause grave and irreparable harm to the child's life, health and ability to function after birth.'[41] The majority of the court disagreed; the principal reason for rejecting this formulation was that it was too vague: 'What does substantial value to a woman's well-being mean? What does a woman's well-being include? What is involved in a woman's right of self determination—all her choices, or merely some of them? And if some only, what is the criterion of distinction?' The majority concluded: 'No bright lines emerge to distinguish tortious behaviour from non-tortious once the door is opened to suing a pregnant mother for lifestyle choices adversely affecting the foetus.'[42]

The Supreme Court of Canada reiterated this view in *Dobson (Litigation Guardian of) v Dobson*,[43] a case that directly raised the question of a

---

[37] Ibid. 466.   [38] Ibid. 466.   [39] Ibid. 466.   [40] Ibid. 468.

[41] (1997) 152 DLR (4th) 193, 210.

[42] Ibid. 210–11. The dissenting judgment by Major J (Sopinka J concurring) did not share these doubts. There it was stated that a court's ability to intervene should be limited to extreme cases 'where the conduct of the mother has a reasonable probability of causing serious irreparable harm to the unborn child': ibid. 238.

[43] (1999) 174 DLR (4th) 1.

woman's liability for antenatal conduct resulting in her child being born with disabilities. The claim arose from a car accident caused by a pregnant woman's allegedly negligent driving. Her fetus was injured and was delivered prematurely the same day. The child was born with mental and physical impairments, including cerebral palsy. In order to determine whether he could sue his mother, the court employed a two-stage test. It was accepted that before imposing a duty of care a court should be satisfied, first, that there is a sufficiently close relationship between the parties to give rise to a duty of care and, secondly, that there are no public policy considerations that ought to negate or limit the scope of the duty.[44] While having no difficulty with the first limb of the test, the court held that public policy considerations indicated that the law should not impose on a pregnant woman a duty of care towards her fetus or subsequently born child.[45] Two policy concerns were identified. These related to the privacy and autonomy rights of pregnant women and the difficulties inherent in articulating a standard of conduct for pregnant women.

With regard to the first concern, the court was unwilling to impose a duty of care on a pregnant woman because 'to do so would result in very extensive and unacceptable intrusions into the bodily integrity, privacy and autonomy rights of women'.[46] This was explained as follows:

The unique and special relationship between a mother-to-be and her foetus determines the outcome . . . There is no other relationship in the realm of human existence which can serve as a basis for comparison. It is for this reason that there can be no analogy between a child's action for prenatal negligence brought against some third-party tortfeasor, on the one hand, and against his or her mother, on the other. The inseparable unity between an expectant woman and her foetus distinguishes the situation of the mother-to-be from that of a negligent third party.[47]

The court then offered a familiar analysis:

Everything the pregnant woman does or fails to do may have a potentially detrimental impact on her foetus. Everything the pregnant woman eats or drinks, and every physical action she takes, may affect the foetus. Indeed, the foetus is entirely dependent upon its mother-to-be. Although the imposition of tort liability on a third party for prenatal negligence advances the interests of both mother and child, it does not significantly impair the right of third parties to control their own lives. In contrast to the third-party defendant, a pregnant woman's every waking and sleeping moment, in essence, her entire existence, is connected to the foetus she may potentially harm. If a mother were to be held liable for prenatal negligence, this could render the most mundane decision taken in the course of her daily life as a pregnant woman subject to the scrutiny of the courts.[48]

---

[44] This two-stage test was formulated in *City of Kamloops v Nielsen* [1984] 2 SCR 2.
[45] (1999) 174 DLR (4th) 1, 11.   [46] Ibid. 12.   [47] Ibid. 12.   [48] Ibid. 13.

As in *Winnipeg*, the court was required to consider the possibility that the duty of care could be defined in such a way as to avoid over-inclusiveness. One submission was that the required standard of care could be set by reference to the conduct of 'the reasonable pregnant woman'. Another was that a distinction could be drawn between situations in which a pregnant woman owes a general duty of care and those in which she is free to make 'lifestyle choices peculiar to parenthood'. Both solutions were rejected. The 'reasonable pregnant woman' test was rejected because it was not thought appropriate for a court to dictate how a woman should behave throughout a pregnancy. The court, echoing *Stallman*, also noted that any attempt to set an objective standard would be objectionable as such a standard would not take account of the individual woman's situation.[49] The possibility of conferring immunity only in respect of 'lifestyle' choices was rejected on the ground that a definition based on a distinction between duties owed to the world at large and those arising from parenthood was 'unworkable'. It was the court's view that 'many potential acts of negligence are inextricably intertwined with the lifestyle choices, the familial roles and the working lives of pregnant women'.[50] More specifically, it added: 'Driving is an integral part of parenting in a great many families.'[51] The judgment reinforced the point:

[A] rule of tort law attempting to distinguish between acts of a mother-to-be involving privacy interests and those constituting common torts would of necessity result in arbitrary line-drawing and inconsistent verdicts. Simply to state that a 'general duty of care' will not apply to 'lifestyle choices' is to leave open the possibility that many actions taken by pregnant women will not be considered lifestyle choices for the purposes of litigation.[52]

It is important to appreciate the basis of the court's reasoning here. Although the majority judgment did not use the term, it was the fear of the 'slippery slope' that underlay the ruling: 'to impose tort liability on mothers for prenatal negligence would have consequences which are impossible for the courts to assess adequately'.[53] The fear was that if the action were allowed, the law would impose a duty of care that could be enforced in a variety of other contexts. This would pave the way for unacceptably intrusive controls over pregnant women.

This analysis accepts that the common law cannot treat a pregnant woman's driving as a special form of activity. The New South Wales Court of Appeal expressed a contrary view in *Lynch v Lynch (By Her Tutor Lynch)*.[54] In holding that the child (who had been born with cerebral palsy) was entitled to maintain an action against her mother in respect of her careless driving while pregnant, the court limited its ruling to the context of the child's right

---

[49] Ibid. 23–4. [50] Ibid. 20. [51] Ibid. 25. [52] Ibid. 27.
[53] Ibid. 16–17. [54] (1991) 25 NSWLR 411.

to recover under a compulsory insurance scheme. The judge rejected the submission that if the claim succeeded, 'every act or omission of the mother between conception and birth would be subjected to scrutiny and analysis'.[55] His response was that 'the question with which this Court is concerned is a narrow one and does not, in my opinion, involve far reaching questions of policy'.[56] He went on to draw attention to the fact that the essential feature of the action was that in some respects it was an artificial one. The mother was a nominal defendant; only by suing her could the child gain access to the motor vehicle insurance fund.

The decision in *Lynch* thus employed different reasoning from that in *Stallman* and *Dobson*. The New South Wales court felt able to rule in favour of the infant plaintiff without considering the nature of the duty of care borne by a pregnant woman and without examining the possible ramifications of making her liable in respect of negligent driving. In contrast, the dissenting judge in *Dobson* reached a conclusion in favour of the child by way of an analysis that confronted the problem of the woman's duty of care. In the view of Major J, there were no clear and compelling policy reasons for barring the child's cause of action:

[The mother] was already under a legal obligation to drive carefully. She owed a duty of care to passengers in her car and to other users of the highway . . . In these circumstances, it would be unjustified to hold that [she] should not be liable to her born alive child on the grounds that such liability would restrict her freedom of action. Her freedom of action in respect of her driving was already restricted by her duty of care to users of the highway. Hence, to acknowledge that the suffering of her born alive child . . . was within the reasonably foreseeable ambit of the risk created by her negligent driving is hardly a limitation of her freedom of action. . . . [The mother's] freedom of action is not in issue, and the suggestion that her son's rights ought to be negatived so as to protect her freedom of action is misplaced.[57]

He reinforced his analysis by offering an example of circumstances in which the majority's ruling could give rise to difficulties. He imagined a situation in which another pregnant woman was a passenger in Cynthia Dobson's car. The judge pointed out that if, as a result of her negligent driving, the other pregnant woman gave birth to an injured child, there would be no doubt that the child would have a right to sue Cynthia Dobson: 'In those circumstances, policy reasons flowing from Cynthia Dobson's freedom of action capable of negativing [her son's] right to sue seem impossible to formulate. His mother's freedom of action in respect of her driving was already restricted by the duty of care she owed to, *inter alia*, another born alive child.'[58]

---

[55] (1991) 25 NSWLR 411, 414.   [56] Ibid. 415.
[57] (1999) 174 DLR (4th) 1, 40–1.   [58] Ibid. 42–3.

His view was that tort law is well equipped to distinguish between circumstances in which there is a duty of care and those in which there is not.[59] Unlike the majority, he identified a clear difference between situations in which a pregnant woman owes a duty of care to a third party and those in which she is free to make 'lifestyle' choices: 'The distinction is plain and is obscured only by slippery slope and flood-gate types of argument founded in an understandably emotional response to the question.'[60] He did not share the majority's fears about the broader implications of recognizing that the woman owed a duty of care:

[T]here is no need to beware that, in deciding this appeal on its own facts, we will have decided infinitely more difficult cases truly involving lifestyle choices and autonomy interests of pregnant women. On the contrary, the very depth, complexity and importance of such cases demands that they not be decided until they in fact arise before this Court.[61]

This comment reveals a rejection of another fundamental feature of the majority judgment. Central to the majority's ruling was the view that the *common law* could not accommodate the imposition of a duty in respect of a mother's antenatal conduct. Once the common law has recognized a duty in one context, it can be extended by analogy:

If [the] action were allowed, even in the narrow context of negligent driving, it would have to recognize a duty and articulate a standard of care for the conduct of pregnant women. As a matter of tort law, this carries the risk that the duty would be applied in other contexts where it would impose unreasonable obligations upon pregnant women.[62]

This is more than a repetition of the reasons for the court's unwillingness to allow intrusive intervention in the life of a pregnant woman. The majority drew attention to the nature of the common law. It stressed that while it would be possible for legislation to provide a carefully tailored exception to allow a child to receive the benefit of the mother's motor vehicle insurance cover, the courts cannot create such an exception. This aspect was clearly explained in the concurring judgment by McLachlin J: 'I am not persuaded that the common law can be narrowed to achieve the result here sought while staying true to its principles.'[63] When judges attempt to produce this result, they encounter a dilemma:

[E]ither they shape the common law in a way that has the potential to render pregnant women liable for a broad range of conduct and unjustifiably trammel liberty and rights to equal treatment; or they accept category-based restrictions antithetical to the common law method.[64]

---

[59] Ibid. 43. [60] Ibid. 42. [61] Ibid. 43. [62] Ibid. 28.
[63] Ibid. 35. [64] Ibid. 36.

Dobson thus reached the same conclusion as *Stallman* and *Winnipeg*. It also agreed with the dissenting judgment in *Bonte*. In addition, it drew support from the report of the Royal Commission on New Reproductive Technologies, which recommended that 'civil liability never be imposed upon a woman for harm done to her fetus during pregnancy'.[65]

Implicit in the analysis offered in cases such as *Stallman* and *Dobson* is an answer to the question why, when a child suffers harm as a result of antenatal injury, the mother should be immune from liability, while a third party enjoys no such immunity. This aspect was most directly addressed by Brock CJ and Batchelder J in their dissent in *Bonte*. Dismissing as 'a mechanical application of logic' the majority's willingness to extend a pregnant woman's liability on the ground that a third party can be liable in respect of antenatal negligence, they explained:

Holding a third party liable for negligently inflicted prenatal injuries furthers the child's legal right to begin life free of injuries caused by the negligence of others, but does not significantly restrict the behavior or actions of the defendant beyond the limitations already imposed by the duty owed to the world at large by long standing rules of tort law. Third parties, despite this recently imposed duty to the fetus, are able to continue to act much as they did before the cause of action was recognized. Imposing the same duty on the mother, however, will constrain her behavior and affirmatively mandate acts which have traditionally rested solely in the province of the individual free from judicial scrutiny, guided, until now, by the mother's sense of personal responsibility and moral, not legal, obligation to her fetus.[66]

On this view, the imposition of liability on the woman would necessitate the formulation of a duty of care different in kind from that borne by all other members of the community.

Analysis of the case law therefore suggests different answers to the question whether the common law should impose liability on a woman in respect of harm caused to her child by antenatal conduct. The better view is that offered in *Stallman* and *Dobson*. This view can be simply explained. The woman's immunity should be recognized because she could be made liable only by imposing on her a duty of care that would be impossibly broad and therefore an unduly onerous restriction on her autonomy. To make her liable in respect of her conduct before her child's birth would require proof of a failure to discharge a duty of a kind that it is not the business of the law of negligence to enforce. The setting of standards for antenatal conduct is not a role that negligence law can properly fulfil.

Finally, although a woman's liability to her child for negligent driving while pregnant is not central to the problem with which this chapter deals,

---

[65] Canada, *Proceed with Care: Final Report of the Royal Commission on New Reproductive Technologies, Volume 2* (1993) 964.
[66] 616 A 2d 464, 467 (NH, 1992).

some additional comments on this subject are necessary. The decision of the majority in *Dobson* was reached on the basis that the techniques of the common law could not appropriately be employed to impose liability on a woman in respect of her conduct during pregnancy. Once a court has recognized that a pregnant woman is under a duty of care in one context, there would be no way for that court to impose restrictions that would prevent a court imposing a duty in another. This analysis does not preclude the enactment of a statute to impose on a mother liability in respect of negligent driving. It is open to a legislature to create a limited exception to the rule of maternal immunity for antenatal negligence, an exception that would take account of the obvious benefit of allowing a child access to the proceeds of a mother's insurance policy. In *Dobson*, the majority raised no objection to the enactment of legislation to achieve this objective; it noted that such legislation, if carefully drafted, 'would not constitute an undue intrusion into the privacy and autonomy rights of pregnant women in Canada'.[67]

In making this comment, the court was aware that the United Kingdom had adopted a statutory solution. Section 2 of the Congenital Disabilities (Civil Liability) Act 1976 (UK) created a special exception to the rule that children may not sue their mothers in respect of antenatal harm. It provides as follows:

2. A woman driving a motor vehicle when she knows (or ought reasonably to know) herself to be pregnant is to be regarded as being under the same duty to take care for the safety of her unborn child as the law imposes on her with respect to the safety of other people; and if in consequence of her breach of that duty her child is born with disabilities which would not otherwise have been present, those disabilities are to be regarded as damage resulting from her wrongful act and actionable accordingly at the suit of the child.

This section reflects the view of the United Kingdom Law Commission that:

[T]he child suffering from pre-natal injury caused in a road accident should be in a similar position to the child, or any other person, injured in a road accident, and . . . the child whose pre-natal injury was caused by his own mother's negligence should not be singled out as the one class of blameless victims of negligent road accidents to be unentitled to compensation.[68]

Broader Implications: Fetal Status and Maternal Autonomy

If the analysis is confined to the applicability of the principles of the common law of negligence, the answer to questions relating to maternal liability for conduct during pregnancy is that it is impossible satisfactorily to define the

---

[67] (1999) 174 DLR (4th) 1, 30.
[68] Law Commission, *Report on Injuries to Unborn Children* (Law Com No 60, 1974) para 60.

duty of care that a pregnant woman can be required to discharge in order to escape liability to a damages claim by her child. In addition, there are difficulties arising from the fact that the duties imposed may vary, depending on the stage of pregnancy. Further, the potential liability of a woman who does not know that she is pregnant would be difficult to assess. It would be unsatisfactory to assert that such a woman could be made liable for antenatal conduct if she ought to have known that she was pregnant.

Related to these considerations are the practical objections to which reference was made in the general discussion of parental liability. If the problems of defining the duty were overcome and an award of damages made, any payment to the child would deplete the family finances and disadvantage other children. Further, making such an award would be likely to create disharmony in the family: 'To impose tort liability on a mother for an unreasonable lapse of prenatal care could have devastating consequences for the future relationship between the mother and her born alive child.'[69] Thus the conclusion on a woman's postnatal liability for negligence during pregnancy is ultimately reached on the same basis as that offered in Chapter 9. Like child protection and criminal laws, the law of negligence cannot resolve problems arising from maternal conduct during pregnancy. It cannot appropriately accommodate damages claims by children in respect of their mothers' antenatal conduct.

This analysis applies to maternal antenatal negligence in general. It can accommodate the making of a statutory exception with respect to negligent driving while pregnant. There are no legal or policy reasons for denying injured children the benefits to be derived from their mothers' insurance policies.[70] In addition, to recognize that an exception can be made in driving claims is consistent with the adoption of the relational perspective explained in Chapter 8. To allow such claims is to acknowledge that they arise in a context in which it is in the interests of both mother and child to permit legal intervention. Here, to echo *Gentry v Gilmore*, their interests are 'congruent'.[71] In this situation, the legal relationship between the child and the mother (plaintiff and nominal defendant) and between the mother and her insurer justifies legal intervention that recognizes the existence of the fetus. This is a situation in which it is appropriate for the law to respond when harm

[69] (1999) 174 DLR (4th) 1, 21.

[70] Difficult questions might, however, arise if the child dies as a result of the mother's negligent driving while pregnant. In *Chamness v Fairtrace* 511 NE 2d 839 (Ill App 5 Dist, 1987), a father, as administrator of the estate of a viable fetus, brought a wrongful death action against his wife whose negligence had resulted in a stillbirth. It was held that the doctrine of parental immunity prevented the action from succeeding. One factor in the court's decision was that if the action had been allowed, the woman would have benefited financially.

[71] 613 So 2d 1241, 1247 (Ala, 1993): see above 180. This consideration was recognized by the majority in *Dobson (Litigation Guardian of) v Dobson* (1999) 174 DLR (4th) 1, 31; the court noted that an insurance payment would benefit both and that the interests of mother and child were therefore aligned.

has been caused to a fetus. To accept this is not to imply that legal intervention will necessarily be desirable in other circumstances. Further, to argue that attention must be paid to the role the law can properly play is to reinforce the point—also made in Chapter 8—that decisions as to legal intervention to safeguard a fetus cannot be made on the basis of abstract analysis of its status. For example, it is superficial to conclude that a mother cannot be sued by a child in respect of antenatal conduct because allowing such an action would permit a woman to be sued for harm that she has caused to a part of herself.

In his dissenting judgment in *Dobson*, Major J underlined the need for rigorous analysis. He regarded the majority as failing to appreciate the legal difference between a fetus and a child. In his view, the case did not raise the question of maternal autonomy. He argued that policy concerns relating to the relationship between a woman and her fetus do not apply to mother and her born child: 'This action was brought on behalf of a legal person, not a foetus.' He added: '[I]n this appeal the pregnant woman's perspective is not the only legally recognized perspective. It competes with the recognized perspective of her born alive child.'[72] He saw the majority's approach as 'one-sided' and begging the question:

The bare assertion of social policy concerns expressly and unilaterally centred on a pregnant woman's rights are not a sufficient answer to the question whether a pregnant woman's rights should prevail over the equally recognized rights of her born alive child.[73]

Such comments reinforce the view that it is unsatisfactory to see the issue of maternal liability simply in terms of maternal autonomy. In Chapter 9, I suggested that it is unacceptable to base conclusions as to legal intervention to protect a fetus solely on arguments as to the absoluteness of a pregnant woman's autonomy. This is particularly true when the possibility of a damages action arising from conduct during pregnancy is being considered. While all competent adults may exercise autonomy, the law can properly place retrospective restraints on their conduct by imposing liability to pay damages for harm negligently caused to other persons. A woman who harms her fetus harms more than herself. It is fallacious to deny that a pregnant woman's conduct can injure an entity that will become a human being. It does not inevitably follow that because a pregnant woman is autonomous she should not be held accountable to her child.

Some commentators have drawn attention to the fact that a corollary of the law's respect for autonomy is an expectation that it will be responsibly exercised. A dissenting opinion in the report of the Canadian Royal Commission on New Reproductive Technologies stated:

---

[72] (1999) 174 DLR (4th) 1, 40.   [73] Ibid. 43–4.

Autonomy is a necessary good, but it is not an absolute. All of us have ... the right to make our own choices, but rights necessarily entail responsibilities; where our choices may or do harm others, our choices are, in fact, limited, and we are held accountable, whatever our gender. It is the suspension of that accountability with respect to pregnant women which would constitute the setting of a different (and lower) standard of behaviour.[74]

This statement was quoted with approval and the argument developed in the dissenting judgment in *Winnipeg Child and Family Services (Northwest Area) v G*. There the view that a pregnant woman should be accountable for her actions was based on the assumption that she had made a choice to carry her fetus to term:

Having chosen to bring a life into this world, [the] woman must accept some responsibility for its well-being. ... [T]hat responsibility entails, at the least, the requirement that the pregnant woman refrain from the abuse of substances that have, on proof to the civil standard, a reasonable probability of causing serious and irreparable damage to the foetus.[75]

Later the judge stated:

It is a fundamental precept of our society and justice system that society *can* restrict an individual's right to autonomy where the exercise of that right causes harm to others. Conversely, it would be unjust *not* to restrict one person's right of autonomy when the exercise of that right causes harm to others.[76]

The judgment made it clear that its conclusion applied to a woman who had had the option to obtain an abortion: hence the assumption that a 'choice' had been made to carry the pregnancy to term. Obviously there will be situations in which abortion is not freely available and even when it is an option, it is questionable to assume that a woman who does not obtain one has freely decided to continue her pregnancy. This assumption ignores the legal, emotional, and financial barriers that a woman must overcome to obtain an abortion. These considerations cast doubt on the assumptions underlying the judgment. Nevertheless, it does draw attention to the fact that arguments based on a preoccupation with maternal autonomy can be challenged.

None of these comments is offered as a reason for resiling from the conclusion that a woman should not, under the common law, be liable to a child's damages claim arising from conduct during pregnancy. Rather, the aim has been to clarify the basis on which this conclusion has been reached. Respect for maternal autonomy is one factor to be taken into account when considering

---

[74] Canada, *Proceed with Care: Final Report of the Royal Commission on New Reproductive Technologies, Volume 2* (1993) 1131.

[75] (1997) 152 DLR (4th) 193, 237. The conduct in question was glue sniffing: see above 11.

[76] Ibid. 240 (emphasis in original).

the applicability of the principles of negligence law. As has been seen, a belief in the importance of the autonomy of a pregnant woman and of her right to control her own life underlies the judgments in *Stallman* and *Winnipeg* and the dissent in *Bonte*. The point was explicitly made in *Stallman*: 'Holding a mother liable for the unintentional infliction of prenatal injuries subjects to State scrutiny all the decisions a woman must make in attempting to carry a pregnancy to term, and infringes on her right to privacy and bodily auton-omy.'[77] Nevertheless, it is not sufficient to explain a conclusion in favour of maternal immunity solely on the basis of the need to respect autonomy. The question of *why* a mother should not be accountable for antenatal conduct cannot be satisfactorily answered by reiterating the indisputable proposition that she is an autonomous being. Ultimately, the answer is the same as that reached in Chapter 9 regarding the inappropriateness of invoking the law when a woman is taking illicit drugs or has declined medical intervention: 'A woman is under no duty to guarantee the mental and physical health of her child at birth, and thus cannot be compelled to do or not do anything merely for the benefit of her unborn child.'[78] If this view is accepted, it would be inconsistent to reject direct control over a pregnant woman's behaviour, yet subsequently to allow indirect control by way of a damages action.

MATERNAL NEGLIGENCE AND JOINT LIABILITY?

Identifying the Problem

One further aspect of the operation of negligence law remains to be con-sidered. This is whether there are circumstances in which the damages paid by a doctor or midwife should be reduced on the ground that a woman's conduct during pregnancy has contributed to the harm suffered by her child. Two examples will make the problem clear.

A woman who is in labour and soon to deliver twins is examined by her obstetrician at 4 p.m. The first twin is presenting as a breech. The doctor explains to the woman the risks of a vaginal delivery and recommends an immediate caesarean section. The woman decides not to consent to the pro-cedure. Her labour continues and at 3 a.m. the next day the doctor again advises the woman to have a caesarean. The woman consents, but there is a substantial delay as it takes the hospital staff some time to assemble a team of theatre staff and to open a theatre. The first twin is born with brain damage. The child sues the hospital in respect of the disabilities. The hospital admits negligence, but argues that the situation would not have arisen had the

[77] 531 NE 2d 355, 360 (Ill, 1988).
[78] *Re Baby Boy Doe* 632 NE 2d 326, 332 (Ill App 1 Dist, 1994).

woman agreed to the caesarean section when it was first recommended. The hospital therefore submits that the damages that it must pay should be reduced on the ground that the woman's decision contributed to the adverse outcome.

The second example is of a planned homebirth managed by a midwife. Difficulties arise during the labour and the midwife explains that she is concerned about the welfare of the fetus and recommends that the woman be transferred to a hospital. The woman declines to accept this advice and the child is born with brain damage. The child sues the midwife on the basis that, with hindsight, it was apparent that the fetus was large and that the midwife had been negligent to agree to a homebirth. The midwife concedes this, but argues that the harm would have been avoided had the woman accepted the advice as to the need for hospitalization. The midwife therefore claims that the damages should be reduced to take account of the effect of the woman's decision.

A Question of Contributory Negligence?

In each of these situations, the proceedings might be brought by the mother and by the disabled child. One preliminary point can be made when considering the likely outcome. If the actions are to succeed, the plaintiff must establish that the medical negligence caused the adverse outcome. In each case, the defendant might deny this. The hospital that was unable to organize a speedy caesarean section will submit that the chain of events leading to the adverse outcome was initiated by the woman's decision to decline to consent to a caesarean section when it was first recommended. The midwife who managed the homebirth will submit that the adverse outcome would have been avoided had her advice as to hospitalization been accepted. In both cases, the defendants will argue that any negligence on their part was of little consequence compared with the conduct of the woman. Such an argument might succeed. The following analysis assumes that it will not and that the medical negligence will be found to be a causal factor. The issue therefore will be whether it can be argued that the damages payable should be reduced because the woman's conduct was also a causal factor.

In each case, the harm that has prompted the proceedings has been the birth of a brain-damaged child. The view that the damages payable by the hospital or the midwife should be reduced will rest on the argument that the woman's decisions significantly contributed to the outcome. The submission will therefore be that the woman was guilty of contributory negligence. As was seen in Chapter 10, the obligation of a person caring for a pregnant woman is owed to her. She is the patient with whom the practitioner deals. The woman has the power to play an active role and make choices that will affect the fetus. This suggests that her conduct should be relevant in assessing a practitioner's liability for negligence. This was the view adopted by the English Law Commission. The fact that it employed the body-part model as its starting-point does not invalidate its analysis:

[T]he physical fact of identification between mother and foetus during pregnancy ought to mean that the mother's own negligence should reduce the damages payable by a tortfeasor. The medical treatment and medication of a pregnant woman depends so much upon her co-operation and care for herself that the possibility of joint liability (perhaps with the mother herself most to blame) is one which cannot be ignored. In such circumstances we think it would be wrong if, perhaps for very slight carelessness in comparison with the mother's own negligence, a doctor . . . had to compensate the child in full for his disability.[79]

The Commission therefore recommended that 'a mother's negligence should be available as a partial defence to a tortfeasor where her fault has also contributed to her child's pre-natal injury'.[80] This recommendation was accepted and the result was s 1(7) of the Congenital Disabilities (Civil Liability) Act 1976, which provides:

If in the child's action under this section [which deals with disabilities resulting from antenatal injury] it is shown that the parent affected shared the responsibility for the child being born disabled, the damages are to be reduced to such extent as the court thinks just and equitable having regard to the extent of the parent's responsibility.

One way of viewing this provision is to see it as a logical outcome of the adoption, in s 1(3) of the Act,[81] of the rule that the success of a child's action in respect of antenatal negligence depends on proof of the breach of a duty owed to the mother. The subsection states that a person will be answerable to the child only if he or she was 'liable in tort' to the mother. Once this principle is established, the argument in favour of s 1(7) seems unanswerable. Proof of liability to the mother is a prerequisite to the child's action. Any liability to the mother is reduced by her contributory negligence. If that liability is reduced, the extent of the liability to the child is correspondingly reduced.

The intricacies of the United Kingdom legislation are not the primary focus of this chapter. Of greater concern are the questions of principle and policy raised by s 1(7). These questions must be addressed whether or not a statute such as the Congenital Disabilities (Civil Liability) Act 1976 is in force. A solution of the kind embodied in s 1(7) can be criticized on a number of grounds. The most obvious objection is that it is inconsistent with the view that women should not be liable to their children in respect of their conduct during pregnancy. In England, s 1(1) of the Act embodies this view. It has

---

[79] Law Commission, *Report on Injuries to Unborn Children* (Law Com No 60, 1974) para 65.
[80] Ibid. para 66.   [81] See above 244–5.

been adopted in Canada (in *Dobson*) and in the leading United States decision (*Stallman*). If a woman cannot be sued by her child for harm caused by her conduct during pregnancy, and therefore cannot be joined as a co-defendant in the child's negligence action against a doctor or midwife, it is logically difficult to see how her contribution to an adverse outcome can be taken into account. If she cannot be sued, she cannot owe an enforceable duty of care to her child. If she owes no such duty, on what basis can the doctor or midwife claim that the woman was partially at fault?

The argument can be reinforced by considering one of the major reasons for conferring immunity on a parent. This is that it would be destructive of family relationships to allow children to sue their parents. Permitting a reduction in damages on the basis of the mother's shared responsibility might produce the same result. The Report of the Royal Commission on Civil Liability expressed reservations about s 1(7) for this reason. It suggested that the provision would lead to a mother becoming involved in court proceedings and this could 'gravely damage family relations'.[82] The Report added: 'It would bring into open court matters with which the mother could be reproached by the child when he grew up. . . . A mother's conduct during pregnancy would have to be investigated.'[83] Further: 'In view of the social objections which we see to an action against the mother, it would seem strange to allow the same sort of situation to come in by a side door through contributory negligence.'[84] The same point was made by a commentator:

There is . . . a certain lack of logic [in the Act] in that, if a general cause of action against a mother is to be denied because of the bitterness this would engender, a similar argument ought to apply in relation to the bitterness which would probably ensue from a decision of the court that the mother's 'imputed negligence' and consequent 'responsibility' had reduced or obliterated the damages to which the child would otherwise have been entitled.[85]

On this view, it is inconsistent to reject the notion that the mother can be a defendant in an action brought by her child while accepting that her behaviour can be taken into account to reduce the damages that a child receives. The Royal Commission was convinced by arguments of this kind. While conceding the strength of the view that it is unfair that a doctor should bear all the responsibility when the woman's conduct has contributed to an adverse outcome, its report concluded as follows: 'We think . . . that the new concept of a parent's contributory negligence diminishing the extent of the defendant's

---

[82] Royal Commission on Civil Liability and Compensation for Personal Injury, *Report, Volume 1* (1978) para 1462.
[83] Ibid. para 1473.   [84] Ibid. para 1475.
[85] P. J. Pace, 'Civil Liability for Pre-Natal Injuries' (1977) 40 Modern Law Review 141, 157.

liability to the child is undesirable and we recommend that section 1(7) . . . should be repealed.'[86] This recommendation has not been followed.

There is a more fundamental objection to the application of the subsection to the two hypothetical situations discussed. It must be asked whether it is appropriate to think in terms of contributory negligence in these situations. The analysis offered in Chapter 9 suggests that there can be no basis for labelling as negligent a woman's decision to decline to consent to a caesarean section or to hospitalization. The woman may decline medical advice for any reason or no reason. If this conclusion is accepted, there can be no question that the woman in either situation has engaged in conduct that could give rise to problems of the kind discussed in *Dobson* and *Stallman*. There is no need to speculate as to whether she should be immune in respect of her negligence. There has been no negligence.

The conclusion that there is no room for analysis depending on the identification of contributory negligence may not, however, offer a complete answer to the problem. The policy questions raised by s 1(7) must still be addressed. It should be noted that, although the Law Commission used the concept of 'contributory negligence' as its starting-point, the subsection does not use this term. Instead, it refers to a parent who has 'shared the responsibility' for the child being born with a disability. In each of the examples that I have offered, it could be said that the woman has 'shared the responsibility' for the adverse outcome.

There is no satisfactory answer to the question whether account should be taken of this fact to reduce the damages payable by the hospital or the midwife. The crucial factor in the two illustrations is, of course, that if the damages are reduced, the disabled children will suffer financially. Yet it is unjust that the hospital and the midwife (or their insurance companies[87]) should bear the full burden of responsibility. In each case, the defendant's argument will be that the woman's decision exposed the child to risks that could have been avoided. More important, the defendant hospital and midwife will argue that it is unacceptable for them to bear liability for harm caused by factors beyond their control. Ultimately, therefore, we are faced with an unfair result whichever course is adopted. There is no way of resolving this dilemma. Those who are disturbed by the prospect of an innocent child suffering financially because of a pregnant woman's conduct might argue that society should concentrate on the goal of compensating disabled children, and should therefore accept the resulting injustice to the defendants. Yet

---

[86] Royal Commission on Civil Liability and Compensation for Personal Injury, *Report, Volume 1* (1978) para 1477.

[87] In some jurisdictions there are special rules relating to the ability of an insurance company to claim a contribution. An examination of the operation of insurance laws is beyond the scope of this book.

equally it can be urged that the torts system does not exist simply to compensate those who have suffered harm. It must also ensure the just imposition of liability. The damages payable by a defendant should depend on a proper assessment of responsibility, not on the extent of the plaintiff's need. While it is difficult to predict, it seems likely that the answer that the law will give to the hospital and to the midwife is that they must take their patients as they find them and provide the standard of care expected of a competent member of the relevant specialty.

CONCLUSION

This chapter has considered two problems. One is the possible liability of a mother to pay damages to a child whose injuries or disabilities have been caused by her conduct during pregnancy. The better view is that such liability should not be imposed. The common law of negligence cannot define the duty of care that a pregnant woman must discharge without intruding into areas of human activity that it cannot properly regulate. This conclusion is reinforced by a consideration of the broader question of a parent's general liability to pay damages to a child in respect of negligently caused harm. To allow a child to make a damages claim against a parent would normally be at best pointless, since the parent would have no funds to meet the claim, and at worst harmful, because of the effect on family life.

This answer, however, is incomplete. The problem posed by a pregnant woman whose negligent driving results in her child being born with injuries or disabilities remains a troubling one. Some lawyers might be satisfied with the answer that while the techniques of the common law cannot be adapted to allow such a child to obtain an insurance payment, there is nothing to prevent the enactment of a statute to permit this result. To concede this, however, is to accept that there are some circumstances in which a pregnant woman does owe a duty of care in respect of her fetus. The common law/statute distinction does not provide a basis for addressing the fundamental question of a pregnant woman's obligations. Nor can the matter be resolved by reiterating the importance of a pregnant woman's autonomy. This might prevail to the extent that the courts recognize that it is inappropriate to marshal the forces of negligence law against a mother whose conduct during pregnancy has resulted in the birth of a disabled child. Yet it is superficial to view the conclusion that legal liability should not be imposed on her as a proclamation of the inviolability of maternal autonomy.

The second problem examined in this chapter is that posed by cases in which a woman's decision relating to the manner of delivery of her child has contributed to an adverse outcome, such as brain damage. If a practitioner's negligence has also contributed to this outcome, the question to be resolved is whether the damages payable by that practitioner should be reduced. Neither the English legislation nor the application of common law principles relating to contributory negligence offers a convincing answer. This may be because the problem is insoluble. If the damages are reduced, the affected child will be disadvantaged. If they are not, a different type of injustice will occur, as the practitioner will be forced to bear the full burden of responsibility for harm caused by factors beyond his or her control.

12

The Duty of Care in
Obstetrics and Midwifery

In Chapter 10 it was seen that the application of the principles of tort law in cases of obstetric negligence has presented complex problems. In particular, while negligence law requires proof of a breach of a duty of care as the first step in a successful damages claim, defining the duty borne by those who provide antenatal and perinatal care is difficult. This chapter offers two definitions of this duty and explores some of the implications of adopting them. Before this task is undertaken, it is necessary to refer to the changing social climate in which doctors and midwives must discharge the obligations the law imposes on them. This climate is likely to affect the way in which the principles determining their liability will be applied.

A CHANGING CLIMATE: CHALLENGING MEDICALIZATION

The call for recognition of maternal autonomy is becoming more pressing in the context of the management of childbirth. This development has several facets. There is the view that a pregnant woman should exercise control over the delivery of her child. This view is frequently buttressed by a rejection of the 'medicalization' of childbirth.[1] A corollary of this is a rejection of intervention at the time of delivery. Many critics of current obstetric practice express concern about rates of intervention (particularly rates of caesarean sections). Childbirth, it is argued, is essentially a natural process and medical intervention should normally be avoided. There are some who go further and indicate strong scepticism about the value of any intervention.

Feminist analyses have introduced a further dimension into the discussion. Medical intervention in childbirth can be represented as a manifestation of male control over pregnant women. The argument is that when a member of the male-dominated medical profession intervenes to deliver a baby, the result is that the woman loses control over a process in respect of which she has a right to make decisions. This argument is sometimes supplemented by adopting an historical perspective: twentieth-century changes in childbirth practices can be seen as the product of the male medical profession's successful campaign to displace midwives. Those who accept such an analysis

[1] See, for example, A. Oakley, *The Captured Womb. A History of the Medical Care of Pregnant Women* (Oxford, 1986) 275–93.

urge that women should reassert control over childbirth. This has two implications. First, pregnant women should choose how their deliveries are managed. Secondly, this goal is most likely to be achieved if their antenatal and perinatal care is provided, not by a doctor who is trained to intervene, but by a midwife who will see the task as the facilitation of a natural process.

A woman's exercise of the power of choice—particularly when she has chosen to rely on a midwife specifically in order to achieve a natural delivery—can have important legal implications. There will frequently be situations in which a midwife may wish to retain responsibility for the management of a delivery because of her commitment to natural childbirth and because she knows that the woman shares this commitment. The question is whether such a midwife who perseveres with a delivery in the face of recognized risks is immune from liability for failing to seek assistance. The answer is that the midwife will not be liable if the delivery is managed in accordance with the wishes of a woman who is competent to make decisions as to the birth of her child and who has been adequately informed as to any risks she and her fetus are facing. There will, therefore, be certain legal consequences if the mode of delivery is determined by the woman's wishes. If the woman exercises control (for example, by making it clear that she wants the midwife to deliver her child vaginally), she can be seen as having chosen a certain type of care. She has chosen a practitioner who will practise in a certain manner. She cannot therefore complain if there is an adverse outcome as a result of complications that the midwife is not trained to manage. If a woman asserts the power to decide how her child is born, the opportunity for her (and for her child) to sue the midwife if something goes wrong may be reduced. To the extent that she takes control, the woman absolves her midwife of responsibility. This is an inescapable consequence of the assertion of autonomy: it is a double-edged sword.

Further, if we accept the argument that it is appropriate for a woman to decline intervention on the ground that birth is a natural process and that medical technology has nothing to offer, this will raise questions about many of the decisions discussed in Chapter 4. There it was shown that in numerous cases doctors have been found negligent for *failing* to intervene. These decisions were reached by relying on medical testimony as to the probable efficacy of intervention. The courts accepted that the medical evidence established that harm was caused to the fetus as a result of a failure to intervene and that this failure represented a breach of the standard of care to be expected of a competent practitioner. If, in contrast, a court were to adopt a different starting-point, to assume that intervention is undesirable and hence be sceptical of medical evidence which suggests otherwise, it would be very difficult for a negligence action arising from non-intervention to succeed. Such a result would be the inevitable outcome of judicial adoption of the view that the medical profession's perception of childbirth is self-serving and unsupported by the evidence. To reject the 'medicalization' of childbirth is, therefore, to diminish the scope for the operation of negligence law in the field of obstetrics.

While it is important not to overstate the extent to which the developments outlined will affect the application of negligence law, it is necessary to be aware that the changing climate might produce some situations in which courts will be required to adapt established principles in order to determine whether a doctor or midwife has breached the duty of care owed to a pregnant woman. Any definition of this duty must take this possibility into account.

DEFINING THE PRACTITIONER'S DUTY OF CARE

In Chapter 3, it was explained that a health care professional is obliged to exercise the degree of skill and care reasonably expected of a competent practitioner in the circumstances. In the fields of obstetrics and midwifery this requirement must be expressed in a manner which recognizes the fact, as noted in Chapter 10, that the duty of care is a composite one. Here I offer two ways in which such a duty can be formulated. The first is that a practitioner caring for a pregnant woman owes the woman a duty to do all that a competent practitioner would do to avoid a foreseeable risk of harm to her and to avoid a foreseeable risk of the child being born with an injury or disability. The second is that such a practitioner owes the woman a duty to take all reasonable steps to facilitate the safe delivery of a healthy child.

Either formulation provides an adequate starting-point for an exploration of the scope of the obligation borne by doctors and midwives. Both accept that a distinctive feature of this area of law is that a practitioner can be liable for an outcome that is judged on the basis of the condition of a person who was not directly owed a duty of care. This is different, for example, from the situation of an orthopaedic surgeon who undertakes a hip replacement. This practitioner is judged solely by reference to the discharge of the duty of care owed to the patient on whom the operation was performed. A doctor or midwife who manages a delivery is judged by reference not only to the effect on the woman, but also to the effect on the child.

Setting the Standard

Special Features of Obstetrics and Midwifery

A distinctive feature of obstetrics and midwifery is that the successful delivery of a healthy child may be accomplished with the assistance of a consultant obstetrician, a general practitioner, a midwife, or without any assistance at all.

The problem that this poses is that the level of skill and expertise required for the management of a particular delivery will not be clear in advance. To understand the relevance of this it is necessary to refer to the analysis offered in Chapter 3. There it was explained that the law of negligence recognizes that health care professionals possess different types of expertise and knowledge.[2] When it is alleged that a practitioner has been negligent, the question asked is whether in the circumstances the practitioner displayed the level of competence to be expected of a prudent member of the relevant specialty. Thus a general practitioner who undertakes surgery within his or her area of expertise will be required to display the skill and knowledge of a competent general practitioner. A neurosurgeon who undertakes spinal surgery will be required to display the skill and knowledge of a competent neurosurgeon. When non-specialists step outside their area of competence, however, and perform tasks requiring special expertise, they will (except in an emergency) be judged by reference to the standards expected of members of the relevant specialty. For example, if a general practitioner elects to undertake surgery of a kind normally performed only by a specialist surgeon, he or she will be judged on the basis of the standards expected of members of that specialty.

While applying these principles is not always easy, the basic assumption — that health care professionals should usually undertake only those tasks that they are qualified to perform — provides a clear starting-point for any inquiry into an allegation of medical negligence. In the field of obstetrics, however, the assumption that competent performance requires certain qualifications cannot always be made. It is not possible to identify particular fields of expertise within which members of the relevant specialties (midwifery, general practice, or obstetrics) may properly operate. The Supreme Court of British Columbia recognized this in *R v Sullivan and Lemay*:

The standard to be applied is that of a competent childbirth attendant, whether the title is midwife, general practitioner or obstetrician. . . . I see the various professions; that is, midwifery, general medical practice and the practice of specialty obstetrics as overlapping circles with a hard core of obstetrical skill common to all three circles.[3]

The management of a normal delivery is within the field of expertise of a midwife, a general practitioner, or a specialist obstetrician. At first sight this might suggest that a broad distinction can be drawn on the basis that midwives and general practitioners are qualified to manage normal deliveries, while consultant obstetricians are qualified to manage both normal deliveries and those requiring more specialized knowledge and intervention. The problem with this argument is that it is never possible to predict that a delivery will be normal. Unexpected complications can and do arise.

---

[2] See above 36–8.   [3] (1986) 31 CCC (3d) 62, 68.

The Standard Expected of Midwives

The difficulties can best be illustrated by comparing the potential liability for negligence of a consultant obstetrician with that of a midwife. If, for example, an obstetrician managing a vaginal delivery fails to recognize the risks to the fetus posed by its size or position, by fetal distress, or by the woman's hypertension or diabetes, and the baby is born injured or disabled as a result, the obstetrician may be liable to a damages claim. A court hearing such a claim will determine liability on the basis of whether the care provided was that to be expected of a competent specialist in the circumstances. Similarly, if a midwife fails to recognize risks of the kind listed, he or she may be sued and the management of the delivery will be assessed by reference to the standard of care expected of a competent midwife. In each case, expert evidence will be required as to the level of skill and knowledge required.

The question to be addressed is whether the *same* skill and knowledge can be required of a midwife as of an obstetrician. Both are performing the same task, the management of a delivery. Does it follow that the midwife must be judged by the same standards as are applied to the obstetrician? Two approaches are possible. On one view, midwives hold themselves out as competent to manage deliveries and should be regarded as negligent if (to adopt one of the tests suggested above) a child is born injured or disabled and the risk of this outcome was reasonably foreseeable. On this basis, the midwife should be liable for performing a procedure that, in retrospect, he or she was not competent to undertake. The midwife would be regarded in the same way as a general practitioner who performs a surgical procedure of a kind normally undertaken only by a consultant surgeon. The midwife would be judged by reference to the standards expected of a specialist.

The alternative view is that this sets too demanding a standard and that questions must be asked about the nature of the risk and whether it could reasonably have been foreseen by a competent midwife. Posing the question this way recognizes that the law does not expect midwives to possess the expertise of consultant obstetricians. This is the better view. It was accepted in a Californian decision in which a 'labor and delivery' nurse was found not to have provided the required standard of care; the negligence consisted of failing adequately to monitor the fetal heart rate and failing to appreciate that the labour was abnormal. The court ruled that her conduct 'must not be measured by the standard of care required of a physician or surgeon, but by that of other nurses in the same or similar locality and under similar circumstances'.[4]

Midwives should be judged by this standard when performing procedures that competent midwives can appropriately undertake. An illustration of

---

[4] *Alef v Alta Bates Hospital* 6 Cal Rptr 2d 900, 904 (Cal App 1 Dist, 1992). The locality rule is discussed above 34–5.

how liability can arise when midwives are acting within their field of expertise was provided by an English case, *Gaughan v Bedfordshire Health Authority*.[5] Here, despite the presence of shoulder dystocia, the delivery was held to be within the capacity of a competent midwife and the negligence lay in the midwife's decision to persist with traction and in not being aware of the alternative techniques of suprapubic pressure and rotation. Her failure to alert a doctor to the possibility of a problem was not regarded as negligent. The court did not challenge the view that 'experienced midwives are perfectly capable of running a labour room on their own and that there was no need to call on medical assistance unless a problem arose'.[6]

In contrast, there are some situations in which a failure to seek help will amount to negligence. Midwives may be liable to damages claims when they continue with a delivery in the face of complications that a competent midwife is not qualified to manage. In this situation the law will frequently impose an obligation to recognize that the delivery is one with which they cannot cope unaided. Here there is a duty to refer the case to a doctor. Liability will arise when a midwife has not acknowledged his or her limitations in a situation in which a competent midwife would have recognized the existence of risks. There is English authority to support this proposition. In *Wiszniewski v Central Manchester Health Authority* (a case arising from the birth of a child with cerebral palsy), an experienced midwife who failed to appreciate the significance of the deceleration in the fetal heart rate during labour and who did not call a doctor was described as 'seriously negligent'.[7] The judge said that the midwife 'was overconfident in her own abilities and not in any way qualified to make the clinical judgment' required in the case.[8]

A distinctive feature of the practice of midwifery is, therefore, that liability can arise from a failure to seek assistance. The English law expressly recognizes this in rules of special relevance to midwives who are responsible for deliveries in birthing centres and for homebirths. These articulate the legal duties of midwives in such a way as to underline their liability to damages claims if they fail to make appropriate referrals. Rule 40(3) of the Nurses, Midwives and Health Visitors Rules 1983[9] states: 'In an emergency, or where a deviation from the norm which is outside her current sphere of practice becomes apparent in the mother or baby during the antenatal, intranatal or postnatal periods, a practising midwife shall call a registered medical practitioner or such other qualified health professional who may reasonably be expected to have the requisite skills and experience to assist her.' For these purposes, an emergency means 'a situation in which a sudden, unexpected event occurs relating to the health or condition of the mother or baby which

---

[5] [1997] 8 Med LR 182.   [6] Ibid. 187.   [7] [1966] 7 Med LR 248, 263.
[8] Ibid. 256. This aspect of the decision was not questioned on appeal: [1998] Lloyd's Law Reports: Medical 223.
[9] SI 1983, No 873.

requires immediate attention'.[10] Rules of this kind probably do no more than indicate that a midwife attending a delivery has the same duty of care as any other health care professional: wherever possible, a practitioner has a duty to call in an appropriately qualified colleague when a patient's condition is one that he or she is not trained to manage.

There are four stages at which a midwife might be liable for failing to recognize that a pregnancy or delivery is one that he or she might not be able to manage without a doctor's assistance. At the first consultation, the midwife might not realize that the pregnancy involves complications with which he or she should not deal unaided. Examples include women with a past history of eclampsia or caesarean section, women who have had a renal transplant, and women suffering from diabetes, a known clotting disorder, severe hypertension, or gross obesity. In the course of antenatal care a midwife who diagnoses a multiple pregnancy, a breech presentation, or severe pre-eclampsia might be negligent for failing to appreciate the potential risks to the woman and her fetus. Similarly, during labour, if the labour is prolonged, or there is a breech or face presentation, a cord prolapse, disproportion, or severe fetal distress, a midwife who does not seek assistance might be considered negligent. After the delivery, there might be complications in the form of a retained placenta or severe haemorrhage. With all the complications described, the negligence might consist of failing to appreciate the risks of a diagnosed condition or of failing to make the diagnosis. An example of non-diagnosis was provided by an English case in which the midwife left the woman too long without performing a vaginal examination and so did not realize that the assistance of a doctor was needed.[11]

It is not intended to suggest that absolute standards can be established. Opinions will differ as to the appropriateness of a midwife assuming sole responsibility for the care of a woman in any of the situations listed. Whether assuming the care of a woman in a particular category is negligent will be determined on the basis of expert evidence as to the practices of competent midwives. What is indisputable is that there are some conditions in pregnancy that put the woman or her fetus at risk. A midwife who undertakes the care of a woman suffering from such a condition without having access to or without seeking assistance is liable to be regarded as negligent. A midwife supervising a homebirth is particularly vulnerable to a damages claim if he or she has agreed to manage a high-risk case and something goes wrong. The negligence might consist of accepting sole responsibility, accepting responsibility in circumstances in which help might not be available, or in failing to transfer a woman to hospital when complications occur. In the case of a midwife managing a difficult delivery in a hospital, the negligence would consist—as in *Wiszniewski*—of failing to seek help. Put in general terms,

---

[10] Rule 27.   [11] *Murphy v Wirral Health Authority* [1996] 7 Med LR 99.

therefore, a midwife's obligation is to recognize that a delivery may not be normal or, having recognized this possibility, to request assistance. This obligation is measured by the standards set by competent midwives.

The Standard Expected of General Practitioners and Specialists

Setting the standard of care required of general practitioners who provide antenatal and obstetric care also gives rise to difficult questions. In some respects, the care should be judged by reference to standards different from those applied to a midwife. A doctor's medical training equips him or her to recognize medical complications that may not have been covered in a midwife's course of study. Yet it can be argued that a midwife can be expected to provide more skilled antenatal and perinatal care than a general practitioner. On this view, the midwife conducts a specialized practice and should display a higher level of expertise (including a greater ability to identify risks) than a general practitioner who might perform far fewer deliveries.

There is another way of addressing the problem. General practitioners who provide obstetric care hold themselves out as being competent to do so. In a sense, they have elected to step into an area requiring special expertise. They might thus be in the same position as general practitioners who undertake surgery of a kind normally performed only by a consultant surgeon. The case law, however, does not suggest that this means that they should invariably be judged by reference to the standards applicable to a consultant obstetrician. In Chapter 4, mention was made of a Canadian decision, *Pierre (Next Friend of) v Marshall*,[12] in which the general practitioner's management of a delivery was judged by reference to the standard of care expected of a careful and prudent general practitioner. Presumably the delivery was one which a general practitioner was competent to manage. In contrast, in *Lane by Lane v Skyline Family Medical Center*,[13] the Court of Appeals of Minnesota held that the pregnancy was not one with which a general practitioner was trained to deal. The doctor was therefore under an obligation to refer the matter to a specialist. When he failed to do so, he was judged by reference to the standard of care expected of a consultant obstetrician.

The standard of care required of a general practitioner should probably be defined in the same way as that required of a midwife. A general practitioner who provides obstetric care should be judged by reference to the standard expected of a competent general practitioner in similar circumstances. The obligation such a practitioner bears includes a duty to recognize when the course of a pregnancy or delivery is, or is likely to be, abnormal. A failure to recognize abnormality, or to seek specialist assistance when an abnormality is present, would be regarded as negligent.

---

[12] [1994] 8 WWR 478: see above 65–6.
[13] 363 NW 2d 318 (Minn App, 1985): see above 70–1.

Little need be said about the obligation borne by a specialist obstetrician. The care provided by such a practitioner is judged by reference to that expected of a competent specialist. Chapter 4 includes numerous examples of cases in which it was alleged that this standard was not met. In general, these cases do not raise difficult theoretical questions as to the definition of the duty of care. There is, however, one distinctive problem. Consultants normally work at hospitals and midwives provide much of the perinatal care of their patients. This can give rise to questions as to where responsibility lies. Frequently a consultant will be dependent on telephone information provided by a midwife. If that information suggests that there might be complications, the consultant is under an obligation closely to question the midwife as to the condition of the woman and her fetus. Unless doubts are allayed, the consultant might be liable to a damages claim if he or she fails to attend and something goes wrong. The basis of the claim would be that the consultant was negligent in relying on a midwife who was subsequently shown to be unqualified to manage the delivery. The English Court of Appeal recognized this form of negligence in *Wiszniewski*. There the court accepted that after the midwife had reported on the patient, the failure of the doctor (a Senior House Officer) to attend was a cause of the brain damage suffered by the child. This conclusion depended on a certain amount of speculation: it was assumed that had he attended he would have examined the woman and would have ruptured her membranes. This, in turn, would have led him to recognize the need for an immediate caesarean section. The analysis accepted that such a response could be expected 'of a reasonably competent SHO'.[14]

LIABILITY FOR FAILURE TO ADVISE OF RISKS

The obligation of a health care professional to provide a patient with appropriate information is an onerous one. In the fields of obstetrics and midwifery, particularly difficult questions arise about the circumstances in which liability will be imposed for failing to provide information as to risks. In Chapter 10, I suggested that while a practitioner's liability for non-disclosure can sometimes be explained by reference to the law's insistence on informed consent, in others this concern does not assist in identifying the situations in which liability can arise. I shall first deal with medical procedures giving rise to questions relating to informed consent and will then deal with a practitioner's general duty to advise a pregnant woman of risks.

[14] [1998] Lloyd's Law Reports: Medical 223, 240. While identifying a possible form of negligence, the decision was unsatisfactory. The evidence as to precisely what the midwife told the doctor was unclear. It was not clear that the midwife provided information that should have alerted a competent SHO of the need to attend.

It is not always easy to distinguish between situations in which the doctrine of informed consent applies and those in which it does not. Childbirth is a process that can, but does not inevitably, involve the use of procedures that should be employed only with the subject's informed consent. The obvious example of an obstetric procedure that should not be performed on a competent woman without her informed consent is a caesarean section. This is a surgical procedure which, unless there are exceptional circumstances, should be undertaken only after the woman has consented, having been advised of the risks to herself and to the fetus. Should there be a failure to explain risks that eventuate, a damages claim could be made if the woman can prove that the harm was caused by the procedure and that she would not have consented to it had the information been made available. The same conclusion would follow when an epidural anaesthetic has caused harm and the risks associated with it have not been explained. It does no violence to the doctrine of informed consent to apply it in either of these situations: both a caesarean section and an epidural anaesthetic represent 'an affirmative violation' of the woman's physical integrity.[15]

There are other procedures that may or may not require informed consent. These include the use of forceps, the artificial rupture of the membranes, the administration of syntocinon, and the performance of an episiotomy. Forceps deliveries have been discussed in a number of United States decisions. In *Sinclair by Sinclair v Block*, the Supreme Court of Pennsylvania examined a claim on behalf of a child born with injuries caused by a forceps delivery. The parents had argued that the use of forceps was an operative procedure requiring specific consent. The defendant doctor challenged this, claiming that the application of forceps was included within the woman's general consent to the management of her delivery. The majority of the court accepted this argument:

We agree that the use of forceps to facilitate natural childbirth is not an operative procedure that implicates the doctrine of informed consent. . . . [T]he physician's use of forceps involved the application of a tool to assist in the natural delivery process, and as such, was merely an extension of the physician's hands. . . . Moreover, we find that the physician's attempt to use forceps is part of one event: the natural delivery process.[16]

The judgment continued: '[W]e hold that the natural delivery process does not require that the patient give specific informed consent for the procedure; rather, general consent is appropriate.'[17] One judge, however, dissented. In the view of Papadakos J, the majority's view of the informed consent issue 'defies both logic and common sense':

---

[15] See above 251–2.   [16] 633 A 2d 1137, 1140 (Pa, 1993).   [17] Ibid. 1141.

Medical intervention is frequently beneficial in cases of injury or illness just as it is in some cases of childbirth that have become problematic. It is the medical intervention itself that constitutes the procedure that a patient must give informed consent to, however, not the underlying physical condition. On this basis, it is absurd to claim that the use of forceps is part of the natural delivery process. It is not. It is a specific form of drastic medical intervention in the process and informed consent should be required just as it is for a caesarian [*sic*]. Use of forceps is an invasive procedure. It is well known that forceps can cause serious injury to, or serious disfiguration of, the child. A prospective mother could reasonably choose to avoid the use of forceps for the sake of the child's safety and elect to choose. Because the majority takes away that right, I vigorously dissent.[18]

This decision suggests that there are two ways of viewing the use of forceps: as part of 'the natural delivery process' or as a separate operative procedure. The latter view was adopted in *Villaneuva v Harrington*.[19] There a forceps delivery caused the baby to suffer a haematoma; he later died. The Court of Appeals of Washington upheld the claim that informed consent should have been obtained before the forceps were used. It is impossible to predict whether courts in other parts of the United States and elsewhere will adopt this view. More problematic is the likely attitude of the courts to the artificial rupture of the membranes. This can also be regarded as a specific procedure requiring consent or as part of the natural process of childbirth. It is not clear whether the same might be said of the administration of syntocinon. In *Bankert by Bankert v United States*,[20] the United States District Court considered a claim arising following the birth of a child with cerebral palsy. The mother had had a previous caesarean section and her uterus ruptured during the delivery. A hysterectomy was later performed. One of the grounds on which the claim for damages succeeded was that the doctor had failed to obtain the woman's informed consent to the use of pitocin. The court accepted that she should have been advised that administration of the drug increases the risk of uterine rupture. It rejected the argument that separate consent was not required to the use of the drug. Unlike the majority in *Sinclair*, the court did not agree that a general consent relating to the management of a vaginal delivery could be taken as consent to associated procedures. Finally, there is the cutting of an episiotomy. This is easier to characterize. It should, if possible, be treated as a specific procedure to which consent must be obtained.

Thus there are a range of procedures of varying degrees of risk and invasiveness that should normally be performed only after informed consent has been obtained. There are others where the law is unclear. The conclusion that a doctor might be liable for failing to obtain informed consent to the use of forceps, the administration of syntocinon, or the cutting of an episiotomy

---

[18] 633 A 2d 1137, 1142–3 (Pa, 1993).   [19] 906 P 2d 374 (Wash App Div 3, 1995).
[20] 937 F Supp 1169 (D Md, 1996).

raises obvious questions in the context of childbirth. There will be some circumstances during a delivery in which it might be artificial to require a practitioner managing a delivery to provide adequate information about a proposed procedure or to expect a woman to reach a considered decision. This aspect will be examined later in the chapter. For present purposes, the important point is that when the performance of certain procedures is under scrutiny, it is appropriate to adopt the doctrine of informed consent as a starting-point. In contrast, if no affirmative intervention is involved, it is unsatisfactory to invoke this doctrine. When this is the case, however, it cannot be assumed that a doctor or midwife is not under a duty to advise of risks. In Chapter 10, I suggested that those undertaking antenatal or perinatal care have a general duty to provide the pregnant woman with information as to the foreseeable risks that she and her fetus face. The implications of the recognition of such a duty must now be explored. This analysis must be considered against the background of the alternative formulations of the duty of care offered earlier in this chapter. The first was that a practitioner caring for a pregnant woman owes her a duty to do all that a competent practitioner would do to avoid a foreseeable risk of harm to her and to avoid a foreseeable risk of the child being born with an injury or disability. The second was that such a practitioner owes the woman a duty to take all reasonable steps to facilitate the safe delivery of a healthy child. Whichever definition of the duty is adopted, discharging it will in some circumstances require the provision of information as to risks. This information might be provided during antenatal care or at the time of delivery.

Antenatal Care

In Chapter 5, I reviewed a range of cases in which liability was imposed for non-disclosure. These included matters in which damages were awarded after a failure to advise a pregnant woman of the risk of giving birth to a child with abnormalities. In these cases, the duty to provide the information arose because the parents were in a recognized category of risk. For example, the woman had symptoms consistent with rubella, she was in an age group in which the chances of the birth of a child with Down syndrome were increased, or the parents were of eastern European Jewish (Ashkenazi) origin and therefore more likely to conceive a child with Tay Sachs disease.

This suggests one principle that can be used to define the circumstances in which there is a duty to provide information: the practitioner's obligation arises when there is a foreseeable risk of an adverse outcome. Support for this proposition is found in *Munro v Regents of the University of California*. The case arose following the birth of a child with Tay Sachs disease. The family history indicated that neither parent was of eastern European Jewish origin. The doctor therefore did not discuss or recommend a screening test for Tay Sachs disease. It was later learned that one of the child's ancestors was a member of a French-Canadian group with a slightly higher than normal incidence of the disease. The child's parents argued that the doctor had been in breach of a duty to provide information on the basis of which they could have decided whether to undertake the test. This argument was rejected. Citing one of its earlier decisions, the California Court of Appeal indicated that doctors are not under an obligation to provide all information necessary for a patient to evaluate his or her position. The court stressed the remoteness of the risk and the fact that there had been nothing to alert the doctor to the possibility that the parents were carriers of the disease.[21]

On this analysis, limits to the duty to inform may be set. It would be wrong to conclude that a doctor or midwife is liable to a damages claim whenever a pregnant woman has not been informed of a risk and that risk has materialized. The obligation should be imposed only in respect of a reasonably foreseeable risk. Normally, there must be a specific cue to which it would be negligent not to respond. What is required to enable a pregnant woman to make informed decisions about her own welfare and that of her fetus should therefore be determined by reference to the condition and circumstances of the particular woman. Whether there has been a failure to recognize a reasonably foreseeable risk will be determined on the basis of medical evidence as to the practices of competent doctors and midwives. This was illustrated by the United States decision in *Reed v Campagnolo*, where the parents of a disabled child alleged that the defendant doctors had been negligent in failing to inform them of the existence or need for Alpha Feto Protein (AFP) testing to detect serious birth defects. The court accepted that the allegation was in fact a complaint as to a failure to provide proper care. It therefore held that to decide whether the doctors were negligent in failing to offer a test that would have provided relevant information, it was necessary to hear expert evidence as to the appropriate standard of care. This required proof that it was the practice of competent doctors to offer AFP testing in such a situation. In the absence of such testimony, the court noted, the parents might assert an absolute right to all information that might be relevant to the continuance of the pregnancy. The unacceptability of such an outcome was made clear:

What the [parents] seek is a rule that the appropriate tests for predictive genetic counseling will be determined by what reasonable persons, similarly situated to the plaintiffs, would want to know. But the rule cannot focus exclusively on the plaintiff. A fair rule would have to look at all of the possible tests that might be given and evaluate the reasons for excluding some and perhaps recommending one or more others. That approach requires expert testimony.[22]

---

[21] 263 Cal Rptr 878, 884–5 (Cal App 2 Dist, 1989), citing *Scalere v Stenson* 260 Cal Rptr 152 (Cal App 2 Dist, 1989).
[22] 630 A 2d 1145, 1154 (Md 1993).

This analysis is correct. It would be inappropriate to impose an unqualified obligation to provide all information necessary to allow parents to make an informed decision as to whether to conceive a child or, if conception has already occurred, whether to allow the pregnancy to continue. It would be unjust to find a doctor or midwife negligent simply because of a failure to provide information that, in retrospect, the parents would have wanted.

There are numerous situations, however, in which it is clear that a pregnant woman is in a recognized category of risk and this fact might give rise to an obligation to provide information as to risks she and the fetus are facing. There is clear evidence, for instance, that diabetes and hypertension in pregnancy pose significant risks for the woman and her fetus. A woman with diabetes should be advised that if the condition is not controlled a stillbirth or the death of the child may result. Similarly, a woman with hypertension should be warned of the dangers of not taking her medication. Another situation where there might be an obligation to offer information is when the woman is known to be taking prescribed drugs that might harm the fetus. For example, an epileptic taking anticonvulsants should be warned that use of some of these drugs greatly increases the risk that her child will be born with spina bifida.

While a duty to provide information arises when a recognized risk exists, it is not clear whether there are some circumstances in which a heavier burden is borne. In some situations, there might be a general obligation to offer antenatal testing. Some of the cases dealing with this subject have implicitly accepted that a particular risk must be foreseeable before liability can arise for failure to offer a diagnostic test. For example, it has been held that it is negligent not to offer an amniocentesis to a woman over 35 in order to detect the presence of Down syndrome.[23] Here the woman's membership of an identified risk category gave rise to the duty. But if an obligation is to be imposed in this situation, might not one also be imposed in respect of a failure to employ a general diagnostic test that detects a range of deformities? One example is the performance of an ultrasound when the fetus has attained 18–20 weeks' gestation. This procedure can reveal major fetal abnormalities such as meningomyelocoele, diaphragmatic hernia, gastroschisis, and significant cardiac defects. Other procedures that can be offered are nuchal scanning, triple testing, screening for diabetes, cystic fibrosis, spina bifida, toxoplasmosis, and blood tests for rhesus antibodies, syphilis, hepatitis B and C, and HIV.

It cannot, of course, be suggested that there is medical consensus about the desirability of undertaking such tests. There will be differences of opinion as to the value of employing some of them. False positives will create unnecessary anxiety. The resource implications must be also considered: it might be unacceptably expensive and, given the small number of abnormalities

---

[23] See above 94.

detected, relatively inefficient to make some tests widely available. Some women with normal pregnancies will miscarry as a result of a diagnostic test. Thus utilitarian analysis might create doubt about the value of routine testing.[24] Nevertheless, the availability of certain tests raises the possibility that in some circumstances doctors and midwives providing antenatal care will be regarded as negligent if they fail routinely to explain and offer them to the women for whom they are caring. Whether, in a particular situation, a failure to do so will amount to negligence will depend—as *Reed v Campagnolo* suggested—on the practices adopted by competent members of the relevant specialty.

If my argument is accepted, a substantial burden is borne by doctors and midwives who provide antenatal care. The duty to provide specific information as to the foreseeable risks that a particular woman is running broadens into a general obligation to give access to information many parents would consider desirable. At this point, the issue is no longer what constitutes negligent non-disclosure, but what constitutes an appropriate standard of antenatal care. For example, the argument of a woman who complains of the lost opportunity to have an ultrasound and who has given birth to a child with meningomyelocoele would be as follows: 'A competent practitioner would have offered, and explained the benefits of, an ultrasound. If I had been offered the opportunity to undergo this procedure, I would have accepted. If I had done so, the meningomyelocoele would almost certainly have been diagnosed. Had I received this diagnosis, I would have terminated the pregnancy.'

The obligation to provide antenatal information may not be confined to the provision of advice about diagnostic procedures and the risks posed by the woman's medical condition. More general information might be required, such as that relating to diet, to the dangers of excessive exercise, smoking or drinking, or the ingestion of drugs. While the provision of advice on such matters is obviously good medicine, the question is whether liability for negligence can be established if it is not provided. Here the foreseeability principle can be appropriately applied. A doctor or midwife who is aware that a pregnant woman is smoking or drinking heavily or ingesting illegal drugs might be regarded as negligent for failing to warn of the recognized risks that these activities pose for the fetus. No liability should be imposed if the practitioner had no reason to suspect that the woman was behaving this way.

Perinatal Care

Examples of situations in which recognized intrapartum risks can arise have been noted in Chapter 10; in *Campbell v Pitt County Memorial Hospital* there

---

[24] J. G. Thornton, 'Should Obstetricians be Utilitarian?', in S. Bewley and R. H. Ward (eds.), *Ethics in Obstetrics and Gynaecology* (London, 1994) 53, 64.

was a breech presentation and *Holt v Nelson* was a case involving placenta praevia. While the courts' reliance on the doctrine of informed consent was unconvincing, the cases illustrated situations in which it would be reasonable to impose on the doctors an obligation to advise of the risks of a vaginal delivery, and of advantages and risks of a caesarean section. Other conditions in which it might be negligent not to provide such an explanation would be cord prolapse, antepartum haemorrhage, obstructed or prolonged labour, and a transverse lie.

In all these situations, what is at issue is the standard of care provided. When complications arise during a delivery it may be artificial to distinguish between negligence taking the form of failure to intervene and negligence taking the form of failure to advise of the risks of non-intervention. Usually the question will be whether the delivery was competently managed and whether intervention should have been undertaken. Should harm occur and the woman or her child wish to sue, the claim will generally rest on an allegation of negligent diagnosis or treatment. Typically, the woman will have put herself in the hands of the practitioner and will have relied on his or her skill and judgement.

In some cases, however, it will be appropriate for the claim to be framed in terms of a failure to volunteer information as to risks. These will arise when the woman is committed to natural childbirth and seeks out a midwife or doctor who shares this commitment. Frequently, the attitude of the woman and her practitioner will reflect an antipathy to the 'medicalization' of the process. If, as a result of this attitude, labour is permitted to continue in the face of risks that a competent practitioner would recognize, it may be open to the woman or her child to sue for damages if there is an adverse outcome. The claim will not rest on the quality of the care provided—since the practitioner would answer that the delivery was managed in accordance with the woman's wishes—but on the failure to advise her of the risks she was running. The woman's argument will be that although she initially elected to have an intervention-free delivery, she would have changed her mind had she been adequately informed of the risks.

Thus it is important for practitioners to appreciate that a commitment to non-intervention in childbirth does not preclude damages claims. The fact that a practitioner believes that intervention should normally be avoided does not relieve him or her of the obligation to recognize risks that a pregnant woman might be running and to advise her of those risks. If a woman is to make a choice as to the manner of delivery of her child, it should be an informed choice. It is not for a practitioner who adopts a non-interventionist philosophy to decide on the woman's behalf that she should run a risk which intervention might minimize. A practitioner who passively accedes to a woman's wishes without attempting to explain the risks faced by the woman and her fetus would be in breach of a duty to inform, and the woman and her child could complain that her acquiescence in the management of the delivery was based on insufficient information.

Similarly, liability can be incurred if a practitioner recommends some form of intervention and the woman does not agree. Here it is appropriate to speak of the need for an 'informed refusal'. The nature of this concept was explored in *Truman v Thomas*,[25] a case arising from a woman's decision not to follow a doctor's advice to have a pap smear. The woman later died of cancer of the cervix. In a wrongful death action, it was claimed that the doctor had been under a duty to do more than simply recommend the procedure and that he should have explained the risks of failing to undergo it. The claim succeeded. The Supreme Court of California relied on an earlier decision where it had noted: '[T]he patient, being unlearned in medical sciences, has an abject dependence upon and trust in his physician for the information upon which he relies during the decisional process . . .'.[26] The court in *Truman* therefore accepted that a patient must be told not only of risks inherent in a procedure, but also of risks inherent in a decision not to undergo it: 'If a patient indicates that he or she is going to *decline* the risk-free test or treatment, then the doctor has the additional duty of advising of all material risks of which a reasonable person would want to be informed before deciding not to undergo the procedure.'[27] While the court framed its ruling in terms of a 'risk-free test or treatment' (here a pap smear), the proposition that there is an obligation to advise of the risk of declining intervention would have general application.

The Standard of Care

The above analysis reveals some of the implications of accepting that a general obligation to provide information as to risks is part of the duty which a doctor or midwife must discharge when assuming responsibility for antenatal or perinatal care. There is also the question of the standard by which a practitioner who negligently fails to provide information is to be judged. A distinction must be made between a failure to recognize risks and a failure to explain those risks to a patient. The first requires a discussion of the knowledge a member of a specialty can be expected to possess. The second requires consideration of the obligation arising once risks have been recognized. With regard to the level of knowledge that a doctor or midwife must possess in order to fulfil a general duty to provide a pregnant woman with information relevant to her own welfare and that of her fetus, the professional standard is the one which should be adopted. This requires evidence as to the skill and

---

[25] Cal, 611 P 2d 902 (1980).
[26] *Cobbs v Grant* 502 P 2d 1, 9 (1972), cited Cal, 611 P 2d 902, 905 (1980).
[27] Cal, 611 P 2d 902, 906 (1980) (emphasis in original).

knowledge expected of a competent member of the medical or midwifery profession. If it is alleged that a doctor or midwife has failed to recognize a risk and has therefore been unable to warn a woman about it, liability can be fairly imposed only if it can be shown that a competent doctor or midwife would have had the knowledge necessary to appreciate the risk.

There are difficulties regarding the definition of the obligation to be discharged once risks have been recognized. In Chapter 3, it was seen that the courts have explored two views as to the type of information that a health care professional must provide. One is that a practitioner is obliged to give a patient the information that a competent member of the practitioner's specialty would provide. This is to regard conformity with accepted practice as discharging the duty of care. The other view is that the focus should be on patient need and that the information provided should be that which a reasonable patient in her position would consider material. The argument in favour of this criterion is that its adoption will ensure respect for the woman's autonomy; to leave it to a doctor or midwife to decide which risks should be explained and which should not is paternalistic. While there is significant judicial support for the latter analysis, the danger is that it might impose too heavy a burden on those who practise obstetrics and midwifery. The circumstances in which a duty to provide information might arise must therefore be explored. Particular attention will be paid to the level of knowledge to be expected of a practitioner. As in the earlier discussion, I shall first consider antenatal care.

Special problems arise in determining a midwife's liability for the provision of negligent antenatal care. A comparison can be made on the basis of decisions discussed earlier in the book. In Chapter 5, I reviewed cases in which doctors were held to have been negligent for failing to recognize the risk of the birth of a child with a genetic abnormality. It was seen that liability was imposed following the birth of children with a variety of conditions including Down syndrome and Tay Sachs disease. Is a midwife who assumes responsibility for the antenatal care of a pregnant woman to be liable for a failure to warn her of the risk of such an outcome? If so, the result will be that the obligation to provide information imposed on the midwife will be the same as that borne by a consultant obstetrician. One way in which this conclusion can be supported is by arguing that a midwife who provides antenatal care without the involvement of a doctor has stepped outside his or her field. This is to accept that a midwife's field of expertise is limited to the management of normal deliveries. Once outside this field, he or she will be judged by reference to the standards applied to consultants who undertake antenatal care. The midwife will therefore be regarded as negligent for failing to identify a risk that a competent obstetrician would recognize.

The alternative view is that the provision of full antenatal care is within the field of expertise of midwives and that when they undertake it they should be

judged on the basis of the level of knowledge and diagnostic skill which can
be expected of a competent midwife. This means that if an action is brought
against a midwife who has failed to warn a woman of the risk of giving birth
to a child with a genetic abnormality, the midwife's liability will be determined by reference to expert evidence as to whether the abnormality was
one with which a competent midwife would have been familiar. In such a situation, the courts will proceed on a case-by-case basis. It might be found, for
example, that while any competent midwife could be expected to recognize
the increased risk that a woman over 35 will give birth to a child with Down
syndrome, a midwife cannot be expected to recognize the risk that Ashkenazi parents will give birth to a child with Tay Sachs disease.

Nor do the difficulties end with liability to warn of genetic abnormalities. It
is not clear in what circumstances a midwife is under an obligation to provide
information about the risks posed by medical conditions or by drug reac-
tions. Perhaps a midwife can be expected to warn a pregnant woman of the
risk to the fetus of maternal rubella, but a court might one day be asked to
decide if it is negligent for a midwife to fail to recognize and explain to a
woman who has had chickenpox during pregnancy the risk that her child will
suffer from congenital varicella syndrome. Similarly, a court might be asked
to decide if it is negligent for a midwife to fail to explain to an epileptic
woman that taking anticonvulsants may result in her child being born with
spina bifida. Another illustration would be provided by a woman with a past
history of deep venous thrombosis. Such a woman might experience further
clotting problems during or immediately after the delivery. A midwife
responsible for her antenatal care might have an obligation to advise the
woman of this risk and offer prophylactic anticoagulants. In all these cases a
court would have to reach decisions as to the level of knowledge expected of
a competent midwife. Finally, there is the question of the obligation routinely to offer tests. Examples of tests which pregnant women might want to
undergo were discussed earlier in the chapter. These include ultrasounds at
18–20 weeks' gestation, nuchal scanning, triple testing, screening for diabetes
and blood tests for rhesus antibodies, syphilis, hepatitis B and C, and HIV.
Should it be assumed that any competent midwife will be familiar with these
tests? If so, a midwife who fails to offer and explain them will be regarded as
negligent.

Similar difficulties arise in the assessment of liability for failure to provide
information at the time of delivery. As was explained earlier in this chapter,
all practitioners who assume responsibility for the management of deliveries
can be regarded as negligent if they elect to persevere with vaginal deliveries
in the face of complications that they are not competent to manage. Normally, the liability imposed in this situation will arise because the care fell
below the standard expected in the circumstances. It is only in an unusual
situation that the complaint will take the form of an allegation of a failure

to provide information as to risks. Here the practitioner will be liable to a damages claim if he or she fails to recognize, and advise the woman of, the risks of allowing labour to continue, provided the risks are such as would have been recognized by a competent member of the practitioner's specialty. Liability for non-disclosure at the time of delivery is not, however, limited to that which arises from the non-disclosure of the risks of a vaginal delivery. The obligation to provide information includes an obligation to advise of the risks of intervention. All forms of intervention carry risks and the obligation of the doctor or midwife is to present a balanced view of the risks and benefits of non-intervention and intervention. Doubts and uncertainties must be explained; where the evidence is equivocal, this must be revealed.

When the special role of midwives is considered, questions emerge about the level of knowledge that can be expected. In Chapter 4, I reviewed a number of cases in which doctors were regarded as negligent for failing to intervene. Implicit in these cases was the view that, because of their knowledge and training, these doctors should have recognized the risks the women and their fetuses were facing. The problem posed by these cases is whether their findings can be applied to a midwife who, pursuant to a woman's wishes, allows labour to continue in spite of the risk of complications. Is a midwife to be treated as having the same level of knowledge as a consultant obstetrician and hence to be liable in any situation in which a consultant who does not identify a risk would be liable? The answer—suggested earlier—is that this level of knowledge should not be presumed. The standard of care provided by a midwife (and this includes the discharge of the duty to recognize risks) should be judged by reference to the standard set by competent midwives.

This conclusion, of course, makes it necessary to distinguish between the risks that competent midwives should recognize and those that their training has not equipped them to identify. Earlier in this chapter, I suggested that it would be difficult to argue that a midwife should not recognize the risks faced by a pregnant woman with a past history of eclampsia or caesarean section, women suffering from diabetes, a known clotting disorder, severe hypertension, or gross obesity. Equally, the risks involved in a multiple pregnancy or a breech presentation should be recognized, as should those posed by prolonged labour, disproportion, severe fetal distress, or a major post-partum haemorrhage. Although opinions will differ as to some of the conditions listed, my argument is that a midwife who respects a woman's desire for a natural delivery and allows labour to continue in spite of the existence of conditions of this kind can be expected to recognize the risks and, accordingly, has an obligation to inform the woman of those risks.

Thus any attempt to define the obligation of a midwife to provide a pregnant woman with information as to risks requires a decision as to whether there are only certain types of risks to which a competent midwife can be expected to alert a woman in the course of undertaking antenatal or perinatal care. If so, the task is to identify them by distinguishing between risks of which a competent midwife can be expected to be aware and risks which a midwife's training has not equipped him or her to detect. This conclusion is particularly important when viewed against the background of the natural childbirth movement and the consequent preference for excluding doctors and relying instead on midwives. Depending on the level of skill and training of the midwife, a woman who exercises her power of choice and opts for a natural delivery under the sole care of a midwife might be seen as opting for care that reduces her access to information as to possible risks. Should there be an adverse outcome, the chances of a successful action based on negligent non-disclosure will be diminished.

This analysis might be rejected on the ground that it depends on the view that the level of knowledge (and consequent ability to identify risks) that can be expected of a competent midwife is not as high as that to be expected of a consultant obstetrician. If it were accepted that midwives possess this higher level of expertise, the consequences would be substantial. It would be necessary to accept that a midwife's liability to a damages claim for non-disclosure would be the same as that of a consultant. This would involve abandoning the principle that a midwife, like a member of any other specialty, should be judged by reference to the level of skill and knowledge reasonably expected of a competent member of that specialty.

Finally, it is important to recognize that the potential liability of practitioners for failing to provide antenatal and perinatal information is to a large extent a product of technological developments. As the availability of sophisticated techniques increases, so does the obligation of doctors and midwives to be aware of them and to utilize them. In particular, those who provide antenatal care must confront the possibility that the increasing use of diagnostic procedures gives rise to a duty to undertake *routine* testing to detect genetic abnormalities. This, in turn, requires a decision as to the amount of information that a pregnant woman is entitled to expect. Occasionally, in the context of a doctor's failure to detect the risk of a congenital abnormality, courts have expressed concern about expanding practitioners' liability for failing to detect or warn of possible abnormalities. For example, in *Azzolino v Dingfelder*, the court gave the following warning:

As medical science advances in its capability to detect genetic imperfections in a fetus, physicians in jurisdictions recognizing claims for wrongful birth will be forced to carry an increasingly heavy burden in determining what information is important to parents when attempting to obtain their informed consent for the fetus to be carried to term.[28]

As technological advances continue, it is possible that a failure to perform certain routine antenatal tests will be regarded as negligent. In determining

[28] 337 SE 2d 528, 535 (NC, 1985).

whether the required standard has been met, courts will principally rely on testimony as to what level of knowledge can be required of a competent member of a specialty. The analysis is further complicated by the fact that it is not only the impact of technological developments that must be appreciated. Account must also be taken of changing attitudes and expectations. In England, the United States, Canada, and Australia, the community is now better informed about medical matters and more demanding. Therefore, a doctor or midwife should normally assume that a pregnant woman will want to know about a wide range of risks. Whether the natural childbirth movement's rejection of the 'medicalization' of childbirth suggests that the opposite assumption should occasionally be made is, however, difficult to determine. A woman who wishes to experience a natural delivery and who therefore chooses a midwife who shares her philosophy might be precluded from alleging a breach of the duty of care if there is doubt about the need for a midwife to possess the expertise necessary to utilize sophisticated diagnostic techniques. On the other hand, there might be doubt whether the choice of care giver can be taken as an indication that the woman was willing to forgo access to those techniques.

TWO PRACTICAL PROBLEMS

Fully Informed Choice in the Context of Childbirth

The discussion, earlier in the chapter, of a practitioner's obligation to advise a woman of the risks that she and her fetus face at the time of delivery suggested that the obligation can arise in two ways. It may be to provide information on the basis of which the woman can decide whether to consent to a specific intervention (such as an episiotomy) or it may be to provide information as to the risks of non-intervention. This analysis was offered in order to define the obligation owed to a woman who is capable of making considered decisions about the management of her delivery. There will be some situations, however, in which there might be doubt as to whether she has this capacity. When these arise, it might be unrealistic to expect a practitioner to provide, or a woman to absorb, the necessary information.

Many of the difficulties arise from the nature of childbirth. In the real world of a labour ward, judicial pronouncements about the importance of informed decision-making may sound unconvincing. At the time of a delivery, the woman might be exhausted, distressed, in pain, and affected by drugs. It might be inappropriate at this stage either to expect a practitioner to obtain consent to individual procedures or to expect the woman to reach a considered decision about each of these procedures. Equally, it might be inappropriate to expect a practitioner to explain, or the woman to assess, the risks of a vaginal delivery when complications have arisen. If the woman or her child were later to bring an action on the basis of the non-disclosure of a risk that eventuated, the defendant doctor or midwife might answer that the woman's pain and distress impaired her capacity for decision-making and therefore it was not feasible to embark on a careful explanation that would have enabled the woman to evaluate the risks and reach an informed decision.

Further, there is the difficulty caused by an emergency in which the doctor or midwife will want to deliver the baby quickly. While there are some risks that any competent practitioner should anticipate and explain—such as those posed by a breech presentation and placenta praevia—there are others that can arise unexpectedly. Not all complications can be anticipated in time to allow a calm discussion before labour begins. In some cases immediate intervention might be desirable. An example would be when acute severe fetal distress is diagnosed and the doctor concludes that a caesarean section should be performed to minimize the risk of brain damage to the baby. In such a case, the obligation to provide information as to the comparative risks of intervention and non-intervention might be difficult to discharge effectively, particularly after prolonged labour. The presence of what the doctor perceives to be an emergency might hinder the provision of a full explanation. While the law imposes an obligation to obtain consent before performing the caesarean—and hence an obligation to explain the risks associated with the procedure—the doctor may conclude that higher priority should be given to making the necessary arrangements (alerting the operating theatre, locating an anaesthetist and paediatrician) rather than to sitting down and talking to the woman. In short, concern for the welfare of the woman and her fetus might lead the doctor to want to act rather than to talk. This is not to suggest that there are circumstances in which the consent of a competent woman is unnecessary: it is normal practice for a consent form to be signed before a caesarean section is performed. Nevertheless, there will be situations where doubts can be raised about the feasibility of a doctor providing, and a woman absorbing, a full explanation of the risks of a vaginal delivery as compared with those of a caesarean section.

In noting such doubts, however, it is important for doctors to recognize the dangers of too readily assuming that it is impractical to involve a woman in the decision-making process. A commentator has noted that doctors' responses are so deeply engrained that they often do not consider the possibility of offering a pregnant woman any choice.[29] Instead, they act on the basis that there is only one course that is natural and right. Such an attitude prevents the sharing of information. It is also one that is difficult for the

---

[29] N. K. Rhoden, 'Informed Consent in Obstetrics: Some Special Problems' (1987) 9 Western New England Law Review 67, 69.

woman to challenge. She will be vulnerable to pressure, not only because of the physical effects of labour, but also because of her anxiety to do what is best for the future welfare of her child.[30] Thus, while the doctors' legitimate arguments about the practical impediments to achieving shared decision-making at the time of delivery must be taken into account, there must also be an acknowledgement that there are certain styles of practice that inhibit the creation of a partnership between the woman and her doctor.

The obvious solution to the problem of providing information would be for the doctor or midwife to do this beforehand. The woman could be informed, for example, that in some circumstances it is desirable artificially to rupture the membranes, to use forceps, or to perform an episiotomy. The risks associated with these procedures would be explained and any special considerations—such as those arising when the fetus is in the breech position or is very large—would be discussed. The circumstances in which a caesarean section might be appropriate, and the risks involved, would be outlined. The aim would be to give the woman any information she is likely to require so that decisions need not be made during the delivery. The advantages of an advance discussion of the options and the risks attending them are obvious. The woman will be given the opportunity to absorb the information and to question it. She will be able to reach a decision as to the procedures to which she will and will not consent. The doctor will be well placed to discharge the obligation to provide information. When these requirements are met, the result will be a shared decision. In these circumstances, the practice of good medicine and the avoidance of legal liability would coincide.

A woman who was willing to run the risks would give her consent to the use of the procedures. A woman who was unwilling to do so would decline to consent to the use of one or more of the procedures. It would then be up to the practitioner to decide whether to continue to provide care. The practitioner may conclude that it is unwise to do so in view of the conditions the woman wishes to impose. He or she may regard these conditions as an unacceptable impediment to the provision of the best care for the woman and her fetus. It is not open to a woman to impose restraints that a practitioner is unwilling to accept. As was remarked in a United States judgment, a doctor 'is not required to accept professional employment on terms determined by the patient . . .'.[31]

This solution envisages the provision of a full and comprehensible account of the risks of childbirth. Yet if it were performed as part of routine antenatal care, this task would have to be undertaken in an abstract fashion, without any reason to suppose that the risks discussed were relevant to the particular woman's situation. Further, questions would arise as to how full the information should be. Should every possible risk—even the most remote—be

---

[30] Ibid. 85–8.   [31] *Vidrine v Mayes* 127 So 2d 809, 811 (1961).

explained? If so, the experience might prove distressing to a woman who is statistically likely to have a pregnancy and delivery free of complications. Yet this outcome must be accepted if the information is to be provided ante-natally, in order to avoid the need to offer explanations when an unexpected emergency has arisen.

There are other difficulties with a solution relying on the antenatal provision of information in order to prepare a woman for a possible emergency. In areas without a properly funded public health system, poor women may not receive any antenatal care[32] and thus will not have the opportunity to learn of risks. For women who do receive antenatal care, the proposed solution is most likely to be practicable when one midwife or doctor looks after a woman throughout her pregnancy and attends the delivery. This practitioner is in a position to provide appropriate advice in the early stages of the pregnancy and to supplement it subsequently. Such an arrangement allows a relationship to be established and fosters trust between the woman and her care giver. It thus facilitates the continuous provision and reception of information. In practice, the management of a pregnancy will frequently not take this course. It requires one practitioner to be continuously available throughout the pregnancy. Most midwives and doctors are unwilling or unable to provide this service.

For a number of reasons, therefore, the ideal solution of advance provision of comprehensive information frequently cannot be achieved. Either there will be no antenatal care or, more commonly, the person who has provided this care will not be available for the delivery. This is likely to give rise to difficulties in the type of emergency necessitating a caesarean section. The following is an illustration. A woman receives her antenatal care from a variety of persons (her general practitioner and staff of a hospital clinic). She comes into labour at 2 a.m. and is admitted to a hospital. None of the practitioners whom she knows is on call and her admission is arranged by a junior doctor, who refers her case to the obstetrics registrar. The registrar has never met the woman. The registrar examines the woman and her labour continues. Some twenty-two hours later (at midnight) a cord prolapse is diagnosed and another obstetrics registrar (whom the woman has not met) is called. This registrar recommends a caesarean section, adding that the baby is at serious risk.

In such a situation, the woman must reach a considered decision as to whether to consent to the procedure. There may be doubts as to whether she is in a fit state to appreciate or assess the risks that the fetus faces and so may not be capable of making an informed choice. The woman may decline to

---

[32] In the United States, it has been noted that medical resources 'are apportioned by wealth' and that pregnant women who can afford it will obtain good antenatal care, while poor women may get no care at all. See L. A. Schott, 'The Pamela Rae Stewart Case and Fetal Harm: Prosecution or Prevention?' (1988) 11 Harvard Women's Law Journal 227, 237.

give consent and her child may be born seriously disabled as a result of anoxia. The woman may (on her child's behalf) sue the registrar and the hospital for damages on the ground that she had not been made properly aware of the risks she was running. She might assert that her condition should have made it obvious to the registrar that she lacked the competence to make an informed decision. It is no answer to suggest that the registrar should not have been put in this position and that one of the practitioners who undertook the antenatal care should have assumed responsibility for the provision of information about the possible need for a caesarean section. The woman's condition during her pregnancy may have given no indication that the need might arise. More importantly, even if a provider of antenatal care had offered a routine explanation of the circumstances in which an emergency caesarean might be desirable, this would not relieve the registrar of liability. It is the registrar who wishes to undertake the caesarean who bears the obligation of providing the information necessary to allow the woman to make an informed decision. The registrar cannot assume that someone else will have done so.

Thus the dilemma facing a practitioner who is unsure of a woman's capacity to reach a decision at the time of a delivery becomes clearer. The hypothetical, fully competent, appropriately informed woman who is in a position to make a considered decision may not always correspond with the woman for whom a doctor or midwife is responsible in the final stages of labour. To determine how the law might view such a woman, it is necessary to re-examine some of the case law on consent to medical treatment. In Chapter 9, it was seen that a competent patient may decline treatment for any reason or no reason and that this decision must be respected, regardless of the risk. If an emergency arises and the patient is incapable of giving consent, a doctor is not prevented from providing treatment when this is in the patient's best interests:

To the general rule that the patient's consent must be obtained before an operation can be carried out there is one well-recognised exception. . . . [I]f a patient is unconscious and therefore unable to give or to withhold his consent, emergency medical treatment which may include surgical procedures can be lawfully carried out. Indeed, once the care of the patient has been assumed . . . a failure to give necessary treatment may well be a ground for complaint. The treatment which can be so given, however, is, within broad limits, confined to such treatment as is necessary to meet the emergency and such as needs to be carried out at once and before the patient is likely to be in a position to make a decision for himself.[33]

One qualification must be added to the proposition that an emergency can permit non-consensual treatment. If a patient has given instructions in advance, the presence of an emergency cannot be used to override them.

---

[33] *Re F (Mental Patient: Sterilisation)* [1990] 2 AC 1, 30.

This principle was illustrated by *Malette v Schulman*,[34] which dealt with a claim by a patient who had been admitted to hospital unconscious. She carried a card stating that in no circumstances should she be given a blood transfusion. Although the defendant surgeon read the card, he administered a transfusion, believing it was necessary to save her life. The patient's damages claim (for battery) succeeded. Thus an emergency will not justify the provision of treatment in the face of a valid and operative refusal.

The application of the rules governing emergency treatment may not always be easy in the case of a pregnant woman. No problem will arise if it is her life that is in danger. If it is accepted that a pregnant woman should be treated in the same manner as any other patient, a pregnant woman who is brought into hospital unconscious after a road accident should be given the treatment necessary to save her life. However, it may be less clear that the emergency principle should be applied when there is a high risk of stillbirth, but the woman's life is not endangered. If the guiding principle is that in all circumstances the woman's autonomy is to be respected, a doctor would not be permitted to intervene solely to protect the fetus. This would require medical personnel to accept the risk of the child being stillborn rather than to undertake intervention to which the woman has not expressly consented. There is one way to avoid this dilemma. When it is impossible to secure the necessary consent, an attempt can be made to obtain information as to the views that the woman would be likely to express had she had the opportunity to do so. Family members might be able to give an indication of her attitudes. On the basis of this information, the doctor might make an informed guess as to what the woman would want.

To proceed in this manner is different from reaching a decision by assuming that a reasonable pregnant woman would consent to intervention that allows her the best chance of giving birth to a healthy child. No doubt there are many doctors who would wish to act on this assumption and to take whatever action they believe to be in the best interests of the child. Whether they should do so depends on the conclusion reached about the value attached to maternal autonomy. Accepting the view that medical intervention to protect a fetus is not justified in the face of an informed refusal by a competent woman may leave the way open for medical intervention which has *not* been expressly refused. Provided there is nothing to suggest that the woman has withheld consent, this would be to substitute the emphasis on consent for an emphasis on facilitating the birth of a healthy child. This conclusion has important implications for the autonomy of the pregnant woman. The assumption would be that the interests of the fetus should prevail in the absence of a clearly expressed decision by the woman.

---

[34] (1990) 67 DLR (4th) 321.

Yet to act on this assumption might result in an unacceptable diminution of maternal autonomy: 'beneficence requires respect for autonomy'.[35] The only solution to the dilemma presented by the unconscious pregnant woman whose fetus is in danger is to enquire about her likely wishes. The problem faced when there is doubt about a pregnant woman's wishes was explored in *Re AC* (the Angela Carder case).[36] Ms Carder, who was pregnant and dying of cancer, was heavily sedated and unable to communicate her wishes effectively. The doctors wished to perform a caesarean section. They sought and obtained a court order to authorize the procedure. When Ms Carder regained consciousness, she was informed by her doctors of the decision and initially gave consent. Later, she clearly mouthed several times, 'I don't want it done'. The court reconvened and heard evidence of the doctors' conversations with Ms Carder. After again finding that her wishes were not clear, the court confirmed the order to perform the caesarean section.

On appeal to the District of Columbia Court of Appeals, it was held that the trial court had erred by assuming that Ms Carder was incompetent. Further, even if this had been the case, the trial judge should have done his best to ascertain what her wishes would have been had she been able to express them. The trial court should have made 'a substituted judgment on behalf of the patient, based on all the evidence'.[37] Performing this task properly would have required a consideration of any previously expressed wishes, decisions made by her in similar contexts, and any general evidence relating to her attitudes and values.[38] The presence of the fetus would be a factor; on the evidence before it, the court might have concluded that Ms Carder was unlikely to be concerned solely with her own welfare and would have wanted to avoid harming the fetus. This case therefore illustrates one court's solution to the problem arising when a woman's wishes cannot be directly ascertained. A decision must be made as to what choice she would have made, had she been competent. Once this has been done, these wishes must be respected. An inability to communicate consent or refusal must not be taken as an indication that a doctor is free to undertake any procedures thought to be in the best interests of the fetus.

The facts of *Re AC* were unusual. Of greater practical importance is the problem posed by the woman who has clearly expressed her wishes and has declined intervention. If treatment against her will is to be contemplated, her competence must be assessed. Any evidence of incapacity must be derived from some source other than a scrutiny of the nature and consequences of the decision. In some proceedings, courts have accepted evidence of a psychiatric condition and have held that the condition made the woman incapable;

---

[35] A. Grubb, 'Treatment Decisions: Keeping it in the Family', in A. Grubb (ed.), *Choices and Decisions in Health Care* (Chichester, 1993) 37, 40.

[36] 573 A 2d 1235 (DC App, 1990). [37] Ibid. 1249.

[38] Her husband and mother were available and could have given evidence as to her wishes.

as a result, her decision was overridden.[39] There are obvious dangers in relying on mental health powers in order to impose treatment on a pregnant woman. It is all too easy to pay lip-service to the principle of bodily inviolability and simultaneously to cast doubt on the competence of a patient in order to provide the treatment that the patient is thought to need.[40] This problem was examined in *St George's Healthcare NHS Trust v S*, in which the English Court of Appeal made it clear that the powers conferred by the Mental Health Act 1983 (UK) had been improperly used to detain a woman who had declined to consent to a caesarean section. She had in fact been competent. The court stated: 'The Act cannot be deployed to achieve the detention of an individual against her will merely because her thinking process is unusual, even apparently bizarre and irrational, and contrary to the views of the overwhelming majority of the community at large.'[41]

This statement draws attention to the need for proof of incapacity before non-consensual treatment is undertaken. It cannot be assumed that a woman is incompetent because her decision seems irrational or because she is in the throes of labour: '[W]omen in labour are no longer presumed to be incompetent because of the accompanying pain and stress, but their competence will rather have to be assessed according to the same criteria applicable to all other patients who are in pain . . .'.[42] Nor should her decision to decline intervention be overridden on the basis that the delivery of a healthy baby will make her grateful that her wishes were disregarded. This rationale is paternalistic and provides a ready-made ground for coercive intervention. The doctor would have to do no more than assert that he or she had predicted that the woman was likely to change her mind and would regret her decision.[43]

Identifying situations in which incapacity cannot be assumed does not assist in establishing the criteria to be met before a patient can be declared to be competent. The relevant principles were discussed in *Re MB (Medical Treatment)*.[44] The proceedings arose because the fetus was in a footling breech position and the doctors had recommended a caesarean section. The woman understood the reasons for this recommendation and gave her consent. She was not willing to consent to anaesthesia by injection or by the use of a mask. The operation was twice cancelled, first when she refused to consent to the necessary injection and later when she pushed away the mask. A court order allowing the performance of any necessary treatment was obtained. Her appeal against this order was dismissed and the procedure was successfully performed.

---

[39] English examples were *Tameside and Glossop Acute Services Trust v CH* [1996] 1 FLR 762 and *Norfolk and Norwich Healthcare (NHS) Trust v W* [1996] 2 FLR 613.

[40] I. Kennedy and A. Grubb, *Medical Law: Text and Materials* (London, 2nd edn., 1994) 334.

[41] [1998] 3 WLR 936, 957.

[42] S. Michalowski, 'Court-Authorised Caesarean Sections—the End of a Trend?' (1999) 62 Modern Law Review 115, 118.

[43] Ibid. 120.   [44] [1997] 2 FLR 426.

When the Court of Appeal subsequently gave its reasons for its decision, it concluded that the woman had lacked the capacity to reach a considered decision to decline anaesthesia. The court paid particular attention to her refusal to consent to an injection. It found that she had 'an irrational fear of needles'. There was evidence that she panicked when she entered the operating theatre—'the needle or mask dominated her thinking'—and at this stage 'she was not capable of making a decision at all'.[45] After referring to the general principle that a mentally competent patient has an absolute right to refuse medical treatment for any or no reason, the court went on to examine the issue of competence. It adopted a two-part test: a patient has the capacity to refuse treatment if, first, she can comprehend and retain the necessary information (including information about the reasonably foreseeable consequences of a decision); and, secondly, if she is able to weigh up the information and reach a decision based on it. Applying this test, the court concluded that the woman was temporarily incompetent; her phobia and panic amounted to impairments that disabled her. This finding was the sole basis for the decision confirming the trial judge's authorization of the intervention: the court emphasized that there could be no basis for overriding the decision of a mentally competent woman, whatever the risk which that decision posed for her or her fetus.

While the court in *Re MB* stated the governing principles in a persuasive manner, their application in that case is questionable. The fact that the woman had an 'irrational' fear of needles need not necessarily have led to the conclusion that she lacked the capacity to reach a decision. In some situations, the fear of an operation might be a rational reason for refusing consent; why was this not so in *Re MB*? According to the judgment, the only criterion should be whether the woman's fear 'resulted in an inability to understand, retain, believe and weigh the treatment information'.[46] It has been suggested that the court failed to apply this criterion and thus displayed only nominal adherence to the principles that it articulated.[47] On this view, the court's approach allowed it to do indirectly what it was forbidden to do directly: to find a justification for intervention designed to protect the fetus. This aspect was also apparent in the way the court explained its reason for permitting intervention. Identifying a lack of capacity was not sufficient to justify compulsory intervention. It was also necessary to establish that the intervention was in the *woman*'s best interests. The court did this by way of a finding that the woman had wanted her child to be born healthy; it also found that 'she was likely to suffer significant long-term damage if there was no operation and the child was born handicapped or died'.[48] This analysis may also be

---

[45] Ibid. 431.
[46] S. Michalowski, 'Court-Authorised Caesarean Sections—The End of a Trend?' (1999) 62 Modern Law Review 115, 118.
[47] Ibid. 119.   [48] [1997] 2 FLR 426, 439.

suspect. It was assumed that any risk to the fetus could be interpreted as a risk to the woman's health and hence that intervention was in her best interests. Such reasoning could easily provide an indirect way of justifying non-consensual intervention in order to protect the fetus.

Although the problem was not raised by the facts of *Re MB*, the court made some comments on the law's approach when a woman's decision to decline treatment is made after many hours of labour. The court quoted with approval from *Re T (Adult: Refusal of Treatment)*, where it was accepted that patients may be deprived of capacity or have it reduced 'by reason of temporary factors, such as unconsciousness or confusion or other effects of shock, severe fatigue, pain or drugs being used in their treatment'.[49] When such factors are present, those responsible for a patient's care must be satisfied that they are 'operating to such a degree that the ability to decide is absent'.[50] Whether — and, if so, when — a woman in labour will lose her capacity and so be liable to intervention to which she has not consented will be difficult to determine. All that can be done is to apply the principles adopted in *Re MB* and to ask whether she no longer has the capacity to comprehend and retain the necessary information or to weigh that information and reach a considered decision.

Re T[51] suggests another approach to the problem arising when there is uncertainty as to whether consent has been refused. This English case involved a woman who had been brought up as a Jehovah's Witness, but did not practise the faith. She was thirty-four weeks pregnant and was admitted to hospital following a car accident. After a day in which she had been given three doses of pethidine and had talked with her mother, who was a practising Jehovah's Witness, the woman — 'out of the blue' — announced that she would not consent to a blood transfusion. At this stage, there had been no suggestion that one might be necessary. Later, a caesarean section was proposed. Members of the hospital staff told her that a blood transfusion was rarely required following a caesarean and that there were alternative procedures available. It was not explained that a transfusion might become necessary to save her life. She then signed a form indicating that she did not consent to a blood transfusion. She did not read the form before she signed it, nor was it read or explained to her. Complications arose during the procedure and the patient would have been given a blood transfusion but for her express refusal. She was transferred to intensive care, where her condition deteriorated. Her father and boyfriend took legal action and it was ruled that

[49] [1992] 3 WLR 782, 796.

[50] [1997] 2 FLR 426, 437. *Rochdale Healthcare (NHS) Trust v C* [1997] 1 FCR 274 was an example of a case in which a woman 'in the throes of labour' was held not to be 'capable of weighing-up the information that she was given'; the performance of a caesarean section was therefore authorized.

[51] [1992] 3 WLR 782.

in the circumstances it was lawful for the hospital to administer a blood transfusion to the woman.

The Court of Appeal dismissed an appeal brought on her behalf. After stressing the need to establish whether the patient had the capacity to consent to or refuse treatment, the court added two further principles. The first—that the patient must have made the decision without undue influence—warrants only brief comment. In *Re T*, the patient's refusal was held to have been vitiated because her mother had overborne her will. Such situations will not be common, but, when they do occur and it is therefore clear that the patient has not made an effective decision to decline treatment, there may be nothing to prevent a doctor from acting in the best interests of the patient. More important for present purposes is the second principle, that the patient's refusal must have been intended to apply in the circumstances that arose. On the facts of the case, it was found that in refusing a blood transfusion, the woman had not envisaged that particular emergency. It was therefore held not to be an effective refusal. The woman had been misled as to the availability and effectiveness of alternative procedures to blood transfusions and also as to the likelihood that she would require a transfusion. It followed that she did not adequately consider the possibility that a transfusion might be necessary to sustain her life.

Were this ruling to be unreservedly adopted, the implications for the practice of obstetrics would be significant. One feature of this field is the speed with which a woman's condition during delivery can change. Labour that appears to be progressing normally can quickly turn into an emergency in which the welfare of the woman or her fetus is threatened. This fact will sometimes make it necessary to determine (retrospectively) exactly what a patient had in mind when specifying the procedures to which she would and would not consent. The point can be illustrated by reference to the obligations of a doctor or midwife to a woman who is committed to natural childbirth. If a woman gives clear instructions that she wants such a delivery, is this to be taken as an indication that no matter how her labour progresses, consent has not been given to intervention? If so, the relevance of the ruling in *Re T* immediately becomes apparent. Are the woman's instructions to be interpreted on the basis that they do not apply to a situation that she had not envisaged? If so, they may not be binding on the doctor or midwife if an unexpected emergency arises. Alternatively, her instructions can be taken as embodying a competent, informed decision as to the management of the delivery and therefore inhibiting any intervention to which consent has not been given.

There would be obvious dangers in adopting principles that allow doctors to ignore a woman's instructions whenever it can be argued that she had not fully appreciated the risk to the fetus. Particularly when a woman has been in prolonged labour it might be all too easy for a doctor to assert that 'she did not really understand what was happening, so I did what I thought was best'. To accept such an argument would be to pave the way for practices paying insufficient attention to maternal autonomy. For this reason, it would be unwise to place much reliance on *Re T*. The circumstances in which it can be confidently concluded that a woman's specific instructions can be disregarded will be limited.

Liability for Non-Intervention?

The definitions, offered earlier in the chapter, of the duty of care owed by a doctor or midwife to a pregnant woman included an obligation to avoid foreseeable risk to the child or, alternatively, to facilitate the birth of a healthy child. If it is accepted that a duty is owed in respect of the outcome of a pregnancy, an important practical question arises as to the practitioner's liability for non-intervention when that non-intervention was the result of the woman's decision. If, for example, a woman declines to consent to a caesarean section and her child is born with brain damage, is any claim by the child against the doctor necessarily barred? For the issue to be properly raised it must be assumed that the woman reached her decision on the basis of adequate information as to the risks to herself and the fetus, that there is medical evidence that a competent doctor would have undertaken a caesarean section in the circumstances, and that its performance would probably have averted the harm. Can it be argued that in some situations the doctor's obligation in respect of the outcome gives rise to a duty to override the woman's wishes?

This is to return to the subject of maternal autonomy (discussed in Chapter 9), but it is to view it through the lens of negligence law. To sustain the argument that a doctor in this situation has an obligation to override the woman's wishes it is necessary to accept that a duty of care is directly owed to the fetus. In Chapter 10, I considered and rejected this possibility. If the doctor owes no duty independent of that owed to the pregnant woman, no liability to a damages claim can arise if respecting her wishes results in the birth of a disabled child. There can be no basis on which a child who has suffered antenatal harm as a result of the woman's decision as to the management of her delivery can sue in respect of a practitioner's failure to intervene in an attempt to protect the fetus.[52] This analysis is consistent with that offered in

---

[52] In England, the Congenital Disabilities (Civil Liability) Act 1976 (UK) seems to put the matter beyond doubt. This makes it clear that the only duty of care is that owed to the woman. This suggests that there can be no possibility of a doctor or midwife being liable to pay damages to a child if he or she follows the woman's wishes: it is difficult to see how a practitioner could be in breach of a legal duty towards the mother when doing what she demands. (J. M. Eekelaar and R. W. J. Dingwall, 'Some Legal Issues in Obstetric Practice' [1984] Journal of Social Welfare Law 258, 265.)

Chapter 9: the autonomy of a pregnant woman should be respected, even when the choices she makes may prove not to be in the best interests of the child. The law's recognition of this autonomy reinforces the conclusion that there can be no obligation to undertake treatment in defiance of a woman's wishes. Quite the reverse. A practitioner who did so would be guilty of battery.

It is important, however, not to oversimplify the analysis. It is not enough to state that a practitioner who respects a woman's decision to decline intervention will be immune from a damages claim. As has been seen, the woman must be competent to make the decision and the assessment of competence will sometimes be difficult. If, because of her condition, the woman is not competent to reach a decision as to treatment, the practitioner may be under an obligation to intervene. Breach of this obligation might expose him or her to a damages claim by the child. The claim would rest on the assertion that regardless of the views she expressed at the time, the woman lacked the capacity to reach a decision and that the practitioner should have realized this. The essence of the claim would be an allegation that the practitioner's election not to intervene amounted to a negligent failure to assess the woman's competence.

A further consideration arises in the case of a woman who is competent. In the situation discussed here, the doctor has an obligation to explain the risks that the woman and her fetus are facing. If this obligation is not discharged, an action may be brought on the basis of a failure to provide the information the woman needed to reach her decision not to consent to the caesarean section. In the case of a doctor (particularly an obstetrician who has been called to an emergency by a midwife), the task of providing information to a woman who has expressed her antipathy to medical intervention may prove difficult. The woman may reject the information. In such a situation, it may not be easy for the doctor to discharge the obligation to make the woman aware of the risks when she has made it clear that she has no trust in members of the medical profession.[53] The doctor's difficulties will be exacerbated when the woman has expressed a preference for natural childbirth, but is distressed after a long labour. It is not unknown for an anaesthetist to act on the basis of a woman's request for pain relief and afterwards to be told that this was not what she had really wanted.[54] What emerges here is the collision between two irreconcilable perceptions of the proper management of childbirth. On the one hand is the view that in some circumstances medical intervention has something to offer. On the other is the proclamation of the importance of maternal autonomy and a distrust of medical paternalism. There is also a

[53] Discussion, 'How Far Should Doctors Respect Rights and Autonomy?', in S. Bewley and R. H. Ward (eds.), *Ethics in Obstetrics and Gynaecology* (London, 1994) 103.

[54] Discussion, 'What Does Choice Mean?', in S. Bewley and R. H. Ward (eds.), *Ethics in Obstetrics and Gynaecology* (London, 1994) 74.

paradox here. Because of her views, the woman may have concluded that a doctor does not possess expertise that could contribute to the safe delivery of a healthy baby. Yet if she delivers a brain-damaged child, the child might succeed in a damages action against the doctor if it can be proved that the doctor was aware that she was running a risk that the doctor made insufficient efforts to explain.

CONCLUSION

Doctors and midwives who provide antenatal and perinatal care must do so in an uncertain and changing legal environment. They can be liable to damages claims if they fail to meet certain standards. The uncertainty lies in identifying those standards and defining the duty that they must discharge in order to meet them. In this chapter, I have offered two formulations of this duty. The first is that a practitioner caring for a pregnant woman owes the woman a duty to do all that a competent practitioner would do to avoid a foreseeable risk of harm to her and to avoid a foreseeable risk of the child being born with an injury or disability. The second is that such a practitioner owes the woman a duty to take all reasonable steps to facilitate the safe delivery of a healthy child.

To offer alternative formulations is to prompt the question whether one is preferable to the other. Adopting the facilitation of the safe delivery of a healthy child as the criterion would impose a heavier burden on doctors and midwives. This is because it could allow a finding of negligence whenever the birth of a healthy baby does not eventuate. It is unacceptable to expose practitioners to legal liability whenever there is a less than perfect result. There is another danger in the second formulation. If a practitioner bears an obligation to facilitate the safe delivery of a *healthy* child, this could have far-reaching implications whenever a child is born suffering from a genetic defect or a condition such as congenital rubella syndrome. The birth of such a child might in itself raise a presumption that the practitioner has breached the duty of care and so almost guarantee the success of an action for the unwanted birth of a disabled child.

While the law has a part to play in ensuring that appropriate standards of care are provided, it must be realistic in setting those standards. This realism can be achieved only by accepting that the obligation is to do all that a competent practitioner would do to avoid a foreseeable risk of harm to the woman and to avoid a foreseeable risk of the child being born with an injury or disability. It is for these reasons that the first formulation is preferable: the standard of care should be set by reference to the practices of a competent member of the relevant specialty—obstetrics, general practice, or midwifery.

The difficulty of the task of identifying the appropriate standard of care further underlines the problems arising from the composite nature of the duty that a practitioner owes to 'not-one-but-not-two'. The obligation is not only to provide non-negligent care, but also to do all that is reasonably possible to produce a particular outcome. Any duty owed in respect of the welfare of the fetus cannot, however, override the duty owed to the woman. The obligation as to the outcome also imposes a duty to provide information that will facilitate it. The task of defining the circumstances in which that obligation has been breached is complicated by technological advances and changes in attitudes to childbirth. In addition, the obligation includes not only a duty to obtain informed consent to any invasive intervention, but also to provide general information as to risks. While the proposition that a competent woman has a right to adequate information on the basis of which to make decisions about the management of her delivery can be easily stated, in practice it will sometimes be difficult to apply. If, during labour, there is doubt about her capacity to reach a considered decision, the nature of the practitioner's obligation may be unclear. Yet the dangers of assuming lack of capacity are obvious: a woman might be exposed to unwanted and paternalistic intervention on the questionable ground that she did not fully understand the ramifications of her decision.

13

The Reality of Negligence Actions and the Need for Reform

Chapter 10 discussed problems arising from the courts' application of the principles of negligence law in actions arising from obstetric misadventures. Chapter 12 sought to provide some answers to practitioners' questions as to how the interpretation of these principles will lead to the imposition of liability to damages claims. It is not satisfactory, however, to confine the analysis to a theoretical discussion of principles and the nature of the duty of care borne by a doctor or midwife. It is necessary also to examine the practicalities of the system in which the law of negligence operates. When this task is undertaken it becomes clear that there are major deficiencies in the way that the law meets the needs of plaintiffs and defendants in medical malpractice matters. The identification of these deficiencies suggests that a range of reforms should be considered.

THE REALITY OF MEDICAL MALPRACTICE ACTIONS

The System in Action

An extended discussion of the effectiveness of procedures for dealing with medical malpractice is beyond the scope of this book. The task has been undertaken in a number of studies.[1] I shall therefore do no more than briefly identify some doubts about the fairness and efficiency of the system.

A plaintiff seeking to prove that medical negligence caused an adverse outcome faces a daunting task. It may be difficult to find out exactly what happened. Given the tendency of professionals to close ranks, it may be even more difficult to obtain the services of a medical expert willing to testify against a colleague. Bringing a claim can be expensive. In the absence of a

---

[1] For example, Liability and Compensation in Health Care: a Report to the Conference of Deputy Ministers of Health of the Federal/Provincial/Territorial Review on Liability and Compensation Issues in Health Care (J. R. S. Prichard, Chairman), *Appendix A: Health Care Liability and Compensation Review—Working Paper* (Toronto, 1990); P. C. Weiler, *Medical Malpractice on Trial* (Cambridge, Mass, 1991) and P. C. Weiler *et al.*, *A Measure of Malpractice: Medical Injury, Malpractice Litigation, and Patient Compensation* (Cambridge, Mass, 1993); I. Kennedy and A. Grubb, *Medical Law: Text with Materials* (London, 2nd edn., 1994); Review of Professional Indemnity Arrangements for Health Care Professionals, *Compensation and Professional Indemnity in Health Care: an Interim Report* (Canberra, 1994); M. M. Rosenthal *et al.* (eds.), *Medical Mishaps: Pieces of the Puzzle* (Buckingham, 1999).

contingency fee system or effective arrangements to provide legal aid, only the wealthy can seek redress. A comment on the operation of the system in England underlines this point:

[F]inancial restrictions on eligibility for civil Legal Aid mean that in practice only the poorest individuals qualify for assistance, and only the rich or the foolhardy are willing to accept the financial risk which bringing an action entails. This severely curtails access to the legal system by injured patients who may have perfectly valid claims for compensation but are simply financially unwilling to put all their personal assets at risk if, ultimately, they are unable to prove fault or causation.[2]

Further, for those who overcome the hurdles and bring an action, there is frequently a substantial delay between the incident and the hearing. Proceedings are often distressing and lengthy.

Some of these problems are due to the fact that the system is adversarial and depends on proof of fault. Of two similar cases, one may succeed and the other may fail. The different results may not be an accurate reflection of the merits of the claims; rather, they may depend on the performance of the witnesses and the attitudes of judges and juries. In particular, doubts can be raised about the way that evidence is presented:

Faith in unqualified adversarialism is . . . eroded by the experts' own damning indictment of a system which, it is said, sets up the scientists themselves as adversaries, accentuates their disagreement whilst obscuring their common ground, implicates them in partisan interest which is antithetical to their commitment to scientific objectivity, and prevents them from explaining the true import of their evidence to the court.[3]

This concern about the way the system operates is fundamental: on one view, the court process is unsuited to the task of making reliable and authoritative determinations concerning the complex scientific and technical issues that often arise in medical malpractice matters.[4]

Further, the adversarial process is not designed to involve the parties in an open and shared search for information as to what went wrong. The system discourages the sort of interaction that would allow a frank explanation to be given. If there is the likelihood of a legal action, the potential defendant will be unwilling to make admissions. Adversarial procedures require the parties to act as hardheaded opponents who seek tactical advantages. In this process, a plaintiff is particularly likely to be disadvantaged. It is not difficult for a defendant's lawyer to delay and obstruct the progress of a claim. Often there

---

[2] M. Jones, 'Arbitration for Medical Negligence Claims in the NHS' (1992) 8 Professional Negligence 142, 144.

[3] P. Roberts, 'Forensic Science Evidence after Runciman' [1994] Criminal Law Review 780, 784.

[4] Liability and Compensation in Health Care, *Appendix A: Health Care Liability and Compensation Review — Working Paper* (Toronto, 1990) 4.

will be an imbalance of power: when doctors are sued, their insurance companies will normally manage the conduct of the case and they may be able to draw on experience and resources not available to the plaintiff's lawyers. A plaintiff needs determination and staying power. Without these qualities, he or she may be worn down and abandon the claim. Alternatively, an offer of settlement might be accepted. One United States study of medical malpractice actions has suggested that nine out of ten claims are resolved by negotiated settlements rather than court verdicts:

Usually both sides find it sensible to save time and money by voluntary compromise rather than by insisting upon having their day in court. The terms of these negotiated settlements are influenced not only by the formal legal rules of liability and damages that would be applied by a jury if the case were to go as far as a verdict, but also by the relative ability of each side to bear the costs of *not* settling, of waiting years for a trial.[5]

The important lesson to be learned from this analysis is that the law of negligence, at least when applied to medical cases, frequently does not operate in such a way as to promote principled findings on the basis of a careful assessment of the merits of a claim. Further, as the study also points out, the pressure to settle is particularly likely to be felt by the plaintiff. If his or her medical condition is serious, the greater is the immediate need for compensation and the greater the consequent pressure to 'sell' the tort claim to the defendant for a fraction of the amount that the claim might be worth if appraised on its merits.[6]

Statistical studies have confirmed that the system does not serve plaintiffs well. Only a small proportion of patients suffering medically related injuries obtain compensation. The Harvard Medical Practice Study revealed that there are a substantial number of patients who have suffered harm as a result of negligent treatment who do not make a claim for damages. The study found that 'slightly more than 7 patients suffered a negligent adverse event for every patient who filed a tort claim'.[7] A litigation gap has also been identified in Canada, where it has been estimated that 'at most one [medical malpractice] claim is filed for every 25 potentially valid claims'.[8] Further, when claims are made, the proportion that are successful is not high. In England it has been estimated that 'some payment' is made in 30–40 per cent of medical negligence claims.[9] The Harvard Medical Practice Study found that

---

[5] P. C. Weiler, *Medical Malpractice on Trial* (Cambridge, Mass, 1991) 53 (original emphasis).

[6] Ibid. 53.

[7] P. C. Weiler *et al., A Measure of Malpractice* (Cambridge, Mass, 1993) 69. This was in fact a substantial underestimate of the gap as many of the claims that were filed involved harm that could not be shown to have been negligently caused.

[8] D. Dewees *et al.*, 'Canadian Malpractice Liability: an Empirical Analysis of Recent Trends', in Liability and Compensation in Health Care, *Appendix B: Research Papers: Volume 1: Scope and Trends in Health Care Liability in Canada* (Toronto, 1990) ch. 8, 7.

[9] Royal Commission on Civil Liability and Compensation for Personal Injury, *Report, Volume 1* (London, 1978) para 1326.

approximately 50 per cent of the patients who brought malpractice claims received some payment.[10] Combining this figure and that relating to the litigation gap suggests that of the patients harmed by medical negligence, only one in fifteen received some financial compensation from the tort system.[11] Although comprehensive information is not available in Australia, the situation there seems to be similar: very few patients who have suffered adverse outcomes make damages claims and even fewer receive any payment.[12]

When a claim succeeds, it is clear that the torts system is not an efficient method of directing compensation to the plaintiff. Large parts of damages awards are received by the lawyers who run the cases. In addition, there are the costs of administering insurance schemes and operating the courts, and of the time lost by the parties. One analysis of the operation of medical insurance schemes in the United States estimated that 55–60 cents was spent to deliver 40–45 cents into the hands of an injured patient.[13]

When the defendants' perspective is considered, deficiencies in the system are also apparent. A Canadian report has pointed out that some very doubtful claims are made; these represent a serious irritant and expense.[14] The Harvard Medical Practice Study confirmed this when it noted that 'many innocent doctors are subjected to unwarranted tort suits'. The authors referred to 'the financial and emotional burdens imposed on innocent doctors as they seek ultimate vindication against a groundless malpractice suit'.[15] The reference to the emotional burdens is significant. A doctor who has been threatened with, or involved in, legal proceedings is likely to find it distressing to have his or her competence questioned. Even when a case is ultimately settled, the experience is a very upsetting one. Confidence can be undermined and the effect on morale can be severe. The result may be that the doctor starts to view his or her patients as potential adversaries rather than as persons with whom a relationship of trust can be established.[16] This in turn can reduce career satisfaction. The process can be self-perpetuating: the erosion of trust can be both a cause and a consequence of the increased level of litigation.[17]

---

[10] P. C. Weiler *et al.*, *A Measure of Malpractice* (Cambridge, Mass, 1993) 74.

[11] Ibid. 74–5.

[12] Review of Professional Indemnity Arrangements for Health Care Professionals, *Compensation and Professional Indemnity in Health Care: an Interim Report* (Canberra, 1994) 36.

[13] P. C. Weiler, *Medical Malpractice on Trial* (Cambridge, Mass, 1991) 53. In Canada, the figure is better; there it has been estimated that approximately 52 cents of every dollar spent on compensation goes to patients: Liability and Compensation in Health Care, *Appendix A: Health Care Liability and Compensation Review — Working Paper* (Toronto, 1990) 115.

[14] Liability and Compensation in Health Care, *Appendix A: Health Care Liability and Compensation Review — Working Paper* (Toronto, 1990) 228.

[15] P. C. Weiler *et al.*, *A Measure of Malpractice* (Cambridge, Mass, 1993) 75.

[16] Liability and Compensation in Health Care, *Appendix A: Health Care Liability and Compensation Review — Working Paper* (Toronto, 1990) 131.

[17] Committee to Study Medical Professional Liability and the Delivery of Obstetrical Care, *Medical Professional Liability and the Delivery of Obstetrical Care, Volume 1* (Washington, 1989) 87.

Reference has been made to the role of settlements. The pressure to settle may also be felt by a defendant doctor. This can occur if the practitioner, although reasonably confident that the allegation of negligence cannot be sustained, wishes to avoid the publicity attending a trial. Such publicity can damage or in some cases destroy a health care professional's capacity to continue in practice. This, in turn, identifies another disturbing feature of the system. A practitioner whose obvious negligence has caused a patient harm will settle a claim and avoid publicity. A competent and conscientious practitioner whose conduct may not have been negligent can be vindicated only by a trial accompanied by the risk of damaging publicity. Even if the claim does not succeed, the victory may be a pyrrhic one, since the public is likely to remember the practitioner as one who has been sued. An English report underlined the significance of this: the process exposes to publicity those doctors whose behaviour is on the face of it the least reprehensible.[18]

Fear of litigation is a factor in many doctors' lives. Further, it is common for doctors and their insurers to complain of a litigation 'crisis'. It is not clear whether this is justified.[19] While it is indisputable that the number of damages claims against doctors has risen and the sums awarded have increased, there are some who are sceptical of the view that such developments indicate a crisis. In answer to doctors who express concern about the prevalence of litigation, the sceptics point to the need to consider the legitimacy of the complaints of negligence. They also criticize doctors' unwillingness to recognize that times have changed and that the rise of the consumer movement has made patients more demanding and less forgiving. This will be reflected in a greater propensity to litigate. Occasionally the criticism goes further and doctors are characterized as a lobby group intent on minimizing their liability. In addition — at least in the United States — doubts have been raised about the motivation of insurance companies which have identified a litigation crisis: '[S]ome commentators have begun to speculate that the malpractice "crisis" is not the fault of plaintiffs, or even lawyers or doctors: — but a "non-crisis" manufactured by the insurance industry to protect its excessive profits.'[20] Finally, the so-called medical malpractice 'crisis' must be viewed against the background of recent developments in other fields of negligence law. Perhaps there is 'a general torts crisis'. Many organizations — from schools to government departments — are being forced to face the prospect of novel damages claims.[21]

---

[18] Royal Commission on Civil Liability and Compensation for Personal Injury, *Report, Volume 1* (London, 1978) para 1343.

[19] For a review suggesting the need to be cautious about accepting that a litigation 'crisis' faces doctors, see D. Dewees *et al.*, 'Canadian Malpractice Liability: an Empirical Analysis of Recent Trends', in Liability and Compensation in Health Care, *Appendix B: Research Papers: Volume 1: Scope and Trends in Health Care Liability in Canada* (Toronto, 1990).

[20] N. Terry, 'The Malpractice Crisis in the United States: a Dispatch from the Trenches' (1986) 2 Professional Negligence 145, 148.

[21] Ibid. 150.

Whether or not there is a litigation crisis, it is clear that the conduct of many doctors is affected by the operation of negligence law. One effect can be the practice of defensive medicine. This is the undertaking of clinically unnecessary tests and procedures in an attempt to avoid liability. This adds to the costs of providing medical services by wasting resources. One United States study estimated that in 1984 the price of defensive medical practice was over $US9 billion.[22] Like the talk of a litigation crisis, however, the belief that doctors engage in the practice of defensive medicine has been challenged. In contrast with the 1984 study are other analyses indicating that there is no consensus on the matter.[23] Further, it might be unwise to adopt a purely negative view of defensive medicine. In some circumstances it might forestall patient injuries. It will also be desirable if it results in doctors taking more time to explain procedures and the risks attached to them.[24]

One matter on which there is clear evidence is the cost of insurance. In many parts of the United States, Canada, and Australia, doctors must normally bear the expense of medical insurance; in some specialties premiums are very high and have increased substantially in the last decade or so.[25] Whatever adds to the costs of providing medical services will be passed on to patients.

The law governing actions for medical malpractice law is therefore open to the objection that it serves neither plaintiffs nor defendants well. It places substantial burdens on doctors and is perceived by them as frequently operating unfairly. Ultimately, however, it is the system's deficiencies in meeting patients' needs that should be stressed. It provides a slow, cumbersome, uneconomic, haphazard mechanism for compensating the victims of medical misadventure. The conclusion reached in the Harvard Medical Practice Study identifies the central consideration: 'the real tort crisis may consist in *too few* claims'.[26] This puts the operation of the system into perspective. While the concerns of practitioners cannot be ignored, the authors of the Harvard study point out that they found 'several times as many seriously disabled patients who received no legal redress for their injury as innocent doctors who bore the burden of defending against unwarranted malpractice claims'.[27]

---

[22] R. A. Reynolds *et al.*, 'The Cost of Medical Professional Liability' (1987) 257 *Journal of American Medical Association* 2776.

[23] P. C. Weiler, *Medical Malpractice on Trial* (Cambridge, Mass, 1991) 85.

[24] P. C. Weiler *et al.*, *A Measure of Malpractice* (Cambridge, Mass, 1993) 133–4.

[25] The situation in England is different as the National Health Service accepts liability for the actions of the doctors whom it employs. Also in some parts of the United States insurance cover is provided by the hospital with which the doctor is associated.

[26] P. C. Weiler *et al.*, *A Measure of Malpractice* (Cambridge, Mass, 1993) 62 (emphasis in original).

[27] Ibid. 76.

Standard Setting

The foregoing analysis is incomplete. There are many commentators who, while conceding the validity of many of the criticisms of the operation of negligence law, point to its role in enforcing and improving standards of care. They argue that the system's primary justification is that it fulfils a deterrent role and so prevents injuries to potential future victims. It is not easy to determine how well it does this. Once again, the Harvard Medical Practice Study offers the most illuminating conclusions. The key finding was that doctors do alter their behaviour in response to the threat of legal action. One of the authors of the study, commenting on this and other research, described himself as 'satisfied that tort law has had a substantial effect on the way physicians now practice in [the United States]'.[28] This is not the same, however, as saying that the operation of negligence law produces better patient care. On this matter, the results are less clear. Although describing it as 'statistically fragile', the Harvard Medical Practice Study found some evidence that malpractice litigation 'does have an injury prevention effect'.[29]

Questions can be raised about how well negligence law fulfils its standard-setting role. The fact that the litigation gap is so large means that in any given situation the probability that negligence will result in a damages claim is low. Further, in many cases factors other than the practitioner's culpability will influence the decision to take action. When proceedings are brought, the plaintiff's chances of obtaining damages are not high. If damages are awarded, the size of the award 'depends on the fortuitous occurrence and severity of the patient's injuries, rather than on the degree of the doctor's culpability'. Thus, a momentary slip by a normally meticulous surgeon can result in a massive judgment if serious harm to the patient results, but a doctor whose departure from the standard of care is 'deliberate and egregious' will escape with minor liability if the injury is less serious. Indeed, there may be no liability if the injury is such that there is little incentive for the plaintiff to take on the burden of a lawsuit.[30] Further, with regard to a momentary slip, it must be asked whether fallibility of this kind is the type of behaviour that the sanctions of negligence law are able to prevent. It might be thought that concern for the welfare of the patient would be a more effective inducement to take care than would the threat of a damages action some years later.[31]

There is also the fact that because a significant number of unfounded claims are brought, many innocent doctors are subjected to unwarranted tort suits. This, in the eyes of many doctors, gives the system a 'Kafkaesque'[32]

---

[28] P. C. Weiler, *Medical Malpractice on Trial* (Cambridge, Mass, 1991) 89.
[29] P. C. Weiler *et al.*, *A Measure of Malpractice* (Cambridge, Mass, 1993) 132.
[30] Ibid. 17–18.
[31] P. C. Weiler, *Medical Malpractice on Trial* (Cambridge, Mass, 1991) 81.
[32] Ibid. 81.

quality: 'Malpractice litigation appears . . . to be sending as confusing a signal as would our traffic laws if the police regularly gave out more tickets to drivers who go through green lights than to those who go through red lights.'[33] While this argument should not be over-emphasized—as has been noted, the system *does* send out signals of which most doctors are aware—it is probably safe to conclude that negligence law is a crude and haphazard method of regulating standards of care.

The tentativeness of this conclusion must, however, be emphasized. While it is possible empirically to assess the system's effectiveness in providing compensation to the victims of medical negligence, estimating its contribution to the maintenance of standards is more difficult. The view that tort law exerts a preventive influence 'rests on a logical inference that imposing liability on those at fault in prior accidents will induce similarly situated individuals to avoid such culpably risky behavior in the future'.[34] This assumption may be plausible, but it is difficult to prove or disprove.

Special Features of Obstetric Litigation

Procedures for dealing with obstetric misadventures share the characteristics of other medical malpractice actions. In addition, there are some special features of their operation. Frequently, doubts about the way the system distinguishes between those who are entitled to recompense and those who are not are particularly troubling in this field. Reference has been made to the fact that only a small minority of children born with cerebral palsy can establish that their condition was due to negligence; the great majority cannot obtain damages.[35] It would be a rash observer who would confidently assert that the legal system has the capacity accurately to distinguish between the two in all, or even most, cases. Further, if this reservation is ignored, it must be asked whether society can justify the expenditure of an enormous effort on a small minority of cerebral palsy children, while paying less attention to the plight of the great majority. The point was made by an English report. After referring to a study which had estimated that the number of children living at home with severe congenital disabilities was 90,000, it commented: 'Of these 90,000 severely handicapped children, probably no more than one half per cent have grounds for claiming tort compensation.'[36] Another example of the selective operation of the system was noted in Chapter 10. When an unwanted birth has occurred, a woman who does not believe in abortion will be unable to bring an action, whereas one who does not share her views will

[33] P. C. Weiler *et al.*, *A Measure of Malpractice* (Cambridge, Mass, 1993) 75.
[34] P. C. Weiler, *Medical Malpractice on Trial* (Cambridge, Mass, 1991) 73.
[35] See above 263–4.
[36] Royal Commission on Civil Liability and Compensation for Personal Injury, *Report, Volume 1* (London, 1978) para 1456.

be eligible for substantial compensation. As with the cerebral palsy cases, the law of negligence singles out certain cases for generous assistance, while failing to provide for others.

The problem of delay is a particularly noteworthy feature of obstetric actions. This is illustrated by many of the cases discussed in Chapter 4. Delays of ten years between the birth of a child and the court's decision are common. In some cases the delay was over twenty years. The prolonged process imposes strain on both plaintiffs and defendants and doubts can obviously be raised about their capacity and the capacity of others involved in the proceedings to recall precisely what happened.

The impact of malpractice litigation on the practice of obstetrics also requires special comment. Those who work in this specialty face a much higher risk of being sued than do members of most other specialties. The number of claims against obstetricians is increasing in all four countries discussed in this book. In the United States, 73 per cent of obstetrician/gynaecologists report that they have been sued at least once.[37] Actions on behalf of brain-damaged children are a source of particular concern; one United States study found that 31 per cent of the claims made against obstetricians in 1987 were made in respect of brain-damaged infants.[38] A successful claim in such a case can result in the award of a very substantial sum in damages.[39] This, in turn, means that doctors practising in the field pay high insurance premiums. Expressions of concern about a litigation 'crisis' are particularly insistent in this field. In this specialty as in others, however, there are some who criticize the received wisdom on the impact of the law. One United States study of court decisions in obstetric cases echoed the view that there is a substantial litigation gap: the study found that only a small proportion of the cases involving negligence lead to a claim and few of these result in a trial. Of these, 'physicians win most of the time'.[40]

While this finding is important, it does not address doctors' concerns about litigation. There is evidence that in each of the countries studied in this book

[37] O. R. Bowen, 'Keynote Address', in V. P. Rostow and R. J. Bulger (eds.), *Medical Professional Liability and the Delivery of Obstetrical Care, Volume 2, An Interdisciplinary Review* (Washington, 1989) 1.

[38] Committee to Study Medical Professional Liability and the Delivery of Obstetrical Care, *Medical Professional Liability and the Delivery of Obstetrical Care, Volume 1* (Washington, 1989) 76.

[39] Large damages awards are particularly likely to be made by United States courts: awards in the 'eight-figure range' are no longer considered remarkable (P. C. Weiler, *Medical Malpractice on Trial* (Cambridge, Mass, 1991) 48). He cites *Reilly v United States* 665 F Supp 976 (DRI, 1987), in which $US11m was awarded following the birth of a brain-damaged child.

[40] S. Daniels and L. Andrews, 'The Shadow of the Law: Jury Decisions in Obstetrics and Gynecology Cases', in V. P. Rostow and R. J. Bulger (eds.), *Medical Professional Liability and the Delivery of Obstetrical Care, Volume 2, An Interdisciplinary Review* (Washington, 1989) 161, 191. For Australian analysis of the 'crisis' in obstetrics, see Commonwealth of Australia, Senate Community Affairs Reference Committee, *Rocking the Cradle: a Report into Childbirth Procedures* (Canberra, 1999) 182–3.

the burden imposed by the high cost of maintaining insurance or a fear of litigation has led some doctors to retire early from the practice of obstetrics and has deterred others from entering the field. A United Kingdom report referred to the 'considerable' anxiety experienced by obstetricians as a result of the threat of litigation. The report also noted the possibility that the increasing levels of litigation had deterred some young doctors from specializing in obstetrics.[41] Concern about doctors' growing unwillingness to practise obstetrics has also been expressed in Australia[42] and in Canada, although the Canadian research pointed out that other factors also operate to make the specialty unattractive.[43]

It is in the United States, however, that the impact of insurance costs and the threat of litigation have been most closely studied. While the findings must be interpreted in the light of an understanding of the special features of medical practice in that country, they warrant close examination. A comprehensive review of the various surveys conducted among practitioners providing obstetric care concluded:

The data suggest that significant numbers of each of the provider groups studied are eliminating obstetrical practice, or limiting it earlier in their careers than they might otherwise have done, because of professional liability concerns. In addition, significant numbers of obstetrical providers report that they are cutting down on services to high-risk women because they fear being sued.[44]

Of particular interest are the findings regarding the willingness of general practitioners to practise obstetrics. There is evidence that the attrition rate among general practitioners is higher than among specialists. A 1987 study found that 23.3 per cent of members of the American Academy of Family Physicians had stopped practising obstetrics because of professional liability concerns.[45] One noteworthy feature is the effect of high insurance premiums on general practitioners who undertake a limited amount of obstetric work. It has been reported, for example, that in a rural North Carolina clinic, the annual malpractice premium was $28,000 so long as the doctors confined

---

[41] House of Commons, Health Committee, Second Report, *Maternity Services, Volume 1* (London, 1992) paras 160 and 161.

[42] P. Niselle and J. F. Murray, 'Obstetrics in Crisis?' (1993) 159 *Medical Journal of Australia* 219 and A. H. MacLennan, 'Who Will Deliver the Next Generation?' (1993) 159 *Medical Journal of Australia* 261.

[43] Liability and Compensation in Health Care, *Appendix A: Health Care Liability and Compensation Review—Working Paper* (Toronto, 1990) 139–41, 143. See also: W. Hannah *et al.*, 'Submission of Working Group on Obstetrics and Gynaecology', in *Appendix B: Research Papers, Volume 2, The Effects of Liability on Health Care Providers* 48.

[44] Committee to Study Medical Professional Liability and the Delivery of Obstetrical Care, *Medical Professional Liability and the Delivery of Obstetrical Care, Volume 1* (Washington, 1989) 6.

[45] Ibid. 46.

themselves to general practice. As soon as the clinic performed a single delivery, the premium increased to $140,000.[46]

Studies have also been undertaken of the impact on midwives of the changes in the environment in which they practise. Nurse-midwives have expressed concern about the difficulty of obtaining insurance cover and the high premiums that they must pay when insurance is available. This concern has led to changes in the organization of nurse-midwifery practice and has curtailed opportunities for nurse-midwives: 'The difficulties of obtaining professional liability insurance in many states have made it virtually impossible for nurse-midwives to practice other than as the employees of physicians.'[47] In addition, some companies that insure obstetricians have placed surcharges on premiums paid by obstetricians who employ or work with nurse-midwives. There is evidence that the non-availability of insurance cover or its increased cost has led some nurse-midwives to give up midwifery practice.[48] A commentary on a study of the legal liability of midwives concluded that 'the continued ability of nurse-midwives to furnish obstetrical care depends crucially on resolving the threat that medical professional liability issues pose for this group of obstetrical providers'.[49]

It has also been suggested that practitioners' unwillingness to provide obstetric care has had a disproportionate effect on the availability of services for low-income women, many of whom will fall into high-risk categories. Particularly disturbing are the findings of a survey of centres providing obstetric care for low-income women. This concluded:

The vast majority of centers surveyed felt the impact of malpractice costs on the health services they offered. Nearly every center furnishing maternity care experienced a reduction in its ability to provide or purchase necessary health services for pregnant women. Many centers with adequate staff to furnish at least low-risk maternity care have been forced to curtail or eliminate services because insurers refuse to provide delivery coverage except at exorbitant costs that clinics cannot afford. Still other health centers have seen the disintegration of their referral arrangements to specialists as more and more obstetricians either leave the practice of obstetrics altogether or else refuse to treat those they perceive to be high-risk patients.[50]

[46] P. C. Weiler, *Medical Malpractice on Trial* (Cambridge, Mass, 1991) 208–9.
[47] Committee to Study Medical Professional Liability and the Delivery of Obstetrical Care, *Medical Professional Liability and the Delivery of Obstetrical Care, Volume 1* (Washington, 1989) 51.
[48] Ibid. 52.
[49] V. P. Rostow and R. J. Bulger (eds.), Preface, *Medical Professional Liability and the Delivery of Obstetrical Care, Volume 2, an Interdisciplinary Review* (Washington, 1989) xii.
[50] D. Hughes *et al.*, 'Obstetrical Care for Low-Income Women: the Effects of Medical Malpractice on Community Health Centers', in V. P. Rostow and R. J. Bulger (eds.), *Medical Professional Liability and the Delivery of Obstetrical Care, Volume 2, An Interdisciplinary Review* (Washington, 1989) 59, 73.

The authors of the study commented 'the rapid escalation of medical malpractice premiums has taken a terrible toll on the number of medical care providers who are willing or able to serve low-income pregnant women'.[51]

Other findings emerged from the United States surveys. One was that the current medico-legal climate has eroded doctor–patient trust.[52] Another concerned the impact of this climate on teaching practices. A United States professor of obstetrics is reported as saying that while in the past he had always taught students that they should perform only medically indicated caesarean sections, uninfluenced by other considerations, he now felt that he could no longer teach in this manner.[53] A third set of findings concerned the practice of defensive medicine. A 1985 study by the American College of Obstetricians and Gynecologists found that 41 per cent of the obstetricians surveyed had altered the way they practised as a result of fear of litigation. The changes that they made included: increased use of testing and other diagnostic procedures, increased use of the practice of requiring that consent to the management of a delivery be in writing, increased frequency of consultations with other doctors, increased willingness to provide written or taped information to women, and more frequent explanations of potential risks of procedures.[54]

As a committee commenting on this report noted, for the most part these changes led to better patient care.[55] There are some changes in practice, however, that give grounds for concern. Of special interest is the impact of the fear of liability on the rate of caesarean sections. The most comprehensive United States review concluded that professional liability concerns are one of the many variables affecting the rate.[56] Other reasons given included the fact that the woman had previously had a caesarean section, dystocia, a diagnosis of fetal distress, delayed childbearing, unwillingness to deliver a breech vaginally, unwillingness to use forceps, low birth weight, and multiple pregnancy. The review concluded that there were no data indicating the number of caesareans that could be ascribed purely to defensive medicine; it added that 'there is a great deal of anecdotal data to suggest that this is a widespread phenomenon'.[57] The author of one of the studies cited was in no doubt: 'There is overwhelming evidence that part of the recent rise in the cesarean section rate [in the United States] is the result of the medical-legal environment. Given the current siege mentality among clinicians, one wonders why the cesarean section rate is not higher.'[58]

---

[51] Ibid. 73.
[52] Committee to Study Medical Professional Liability and the Delivery of Obstetrical Care, *Medical Professional Liability and the Delivery of Obstetrical Care, Volume 1* (Washington, 1989) 87.
[53] Ibid. 83.   [54] Ibid. 73–4.   [55] Ibid. 74.   [56] Ibid. 75.   [57] Ibid. 76.
[58] B. P. Sachs, 'Is the Rising Rate of Caesarean Sections a Result of More Defensive Medicine?,' in V. P. Rostow and R. J. Bulger (eds.), *Medical Professional Liability and the Delivery of Obstetrical Care, Volume 2, An Interdisciplinary Review* (Washington, 1989) 27, 37.

A practice related to the increase in the caesarean section rate—and one that is itself a manifestation of defensive medicine—is the use of electronic fetal monitoring (EFM). While initially EFM was thought to be useful in detecting asphyxia and is widely practised, clinical trials conducted in a number of countries have indicated that there is little or no benefit from the use of EFM: 'These studies suggest that EFM has simply not done what its proponents argued it would do: it has not reduced neonatal morbidity and death, and . . . it has not reduced the frequency of developmental disability.'[59] In spite of this evidence, however, fear of litigation seems to have resulted in the continuing use of EFM: 'The legal literature suggests that EFM has become the accepted standard of care in many [United States] jurisdictions. The allegation of failure to monitor is commonplace in plaintiffs' medical malpractice complaints.'[60] Thus a doctor who fails to employ the technique takes a risk; if something goes wrong, such a failure is 'the smoking gun' that the tort lawyer needs to make a case.[61] Equally, when an EFM is performed and there is an abnormal tracing, this can be a major factor leading to the initiation of a malpractice claim. Thus there is 'some truth' in the perception that fetal monitoring and a timely caesarean section can keep a doctor out of court.[62]

There is also some evidence supporting the view that fear of litigation promotes defensive medicine among those who practise obstetrics in Canada. This suggested that obstetric tests and investigations (such as ultrasounds and glucose testing) were being performed 'even though clinical judgment' did not indicate that they were necessary.[63] A comment on the finding that the number of diagnostic tests had increased indicated that litigation concerns were a major reason for the increase.[64] Other trends, also partly ascribed to a fear of litigation, have been the increasing number of antenatal transfers of women with uncomplicated pregnancies from small rural hospitals to large urban centres and the increased demand for expensive

[59] Committee to Study Medical Professional Liability and the Delivery of Obstetrical Care, *Medical Professional Liability and the Delivery of Obstetrical Care, Volume 1* (Washington, 1989) 79. See also S. B. Thacker, 'The Impact of Technology Assessment and Medical Malpractice on the Diffusion of Medical Technologies: the Case of Electronic Fetal Monitoring', in V. P. Rostow and R. J. Bulger (eds.), *Medical Professional Liability and the Delivery of Obstetrical Care, Volume 2, An Interdisciplinary Review* (Washington, 1989) 9.

[60] Committee to Study Medical Professional Liability and the Delivery of Obstetrical Care, *Medical Professional Liability and the Delivery of Obstetrical Care, Volume 1* (Washington, 1989) 81.

[61] P. C. Weiler, *Medical Malpractice on Trial* (Cambridge, Mass, 1991) 86.

[62] B. P. Sachs, 'Is the Rising Rate of Caesarean Sections a Result of More Defensive Medicine?', in V. P. Rostow and R. J. Bulger (eds.), *Medical Professional Liability and the Delivery of Obstetrical Care, Volume 2, An Interdisciplinary Review* (Washington, 1989) 27, 36.

[63] Liability and Compensation in Health Care, *Appendix A: Health Care Liability and Compensation Review—Working Paper* (Toronto, 1990) 137.

[64] W. Hannah *et al.*, 'Submission of Working Group on Obstetrics and Gynaecology', in *Appendix B: Research Papers, Volume 2, The Effects of Liability on Health Care Providers* (Toronto, 1990) 88.

equipment in rural hospitals. Like the United States surveys, the study also pointed to the increasing number of caesareans performed because the doctors felt that they were less likely to be sued if they took this course.[65]

The conclusions to be drawn about the rate of caesarean sections are, therefore, unclear. While fear of litigation is a variable, it is not possible to determine its significance. Further, it should not be overlooked that it is now more common for caesareans to be performed because the women have requested them. Finally, a warning of the danger of overestimating the effect of fear of litigation is provided by the fact that the rate of caesarean sections has also risen in the last two decades in countries with much lower levels of litigation than in the United States and in countries with no fault schemes.[66]

THE WAY FORWARD

The analysis has demonstrated that not only are there serious problems with the way that negligence law deals with allegations of medical malpractice, but also that these problems are particularly troubling when the allegations arise from adverse obstetric outcomes. To propose that negligence law should no longer apply to medical malpractice in general or to obstetric malpractice in particular would, however, be unrealistic. It would be unacceptable to argue that health care professionals, unlike any other members of the community, should be immune to allegations of negligence. Rather, the way forward lies in the adoption of two related policies, based on the view that both in theory and in practice, the application of negligence law to cases involving obstetric misadventure frequently fails to provide sensible, just, or efficient solutions. The policies that should be pursued are to confine and reform the operation of negligence law and to seek alternatives that will more effectively promote the aims of providing appropriate compensation and of setting and maintaining standards of care and punishing their breach.

Reform of Negligence Law

There are specific changes that can be made to confine the operation of the law of negligence in the field of obstetrics. For example, the law can make it clear that no child can bring a wrongful life action. This result seems to have been achieved in Canada, England, and Australia.[67] A statute enacted in Pennsylvania prevents wrongful life actions: 'There shall be no cause of action on behalf of any person based on a claim of that person that, but for an

---

[65] Liability and Compensation in Health Care, *Appendix A: Health Care Liability and Compensation Review—Working Paper* (Toronto, 1990) 138.

[66] P. C. Weiler, *Medical Malpractice on Trial* (Cambridge, Mass, 1991) 87.

[67] See above 107–8.

act or omission of the defendant, the person would not have been conceived or, once conceived, would or should have been aborted.'[68] In the United States there has also been legislation designed to prevent or regulate wrongful birth actions. The Pennsylvania Act forbids such actions: 'There shall be no cause of action or award of damages on behalf of any person based on a claim that, but for an act or omission of the defendant, a person once conceived would not or should not have been born.'[69] In other States, concern about the frequency with which cases are brought following the birth of unwanted children has also led to the enactment of legislation. In Maine, 'the birth of a normal, healthy child does not constitute a legally recognizable injury and . . . it is contrary to public policy to award damages for the birth or rearing of a healthy child.' The damages payable after a failed sterilization and birth of a healthy child are limited to medical and hospital expenses, pain and suffering connected with the pregnancy, and the mother's loss of earnings.[70] Finally, it is only in some States that a wrongful death action can be brought on behalf of a stillborn child. The Canadian and Australian courts are most unlikely to allow this form of action. In England, the Congenital Disabilities (Civil Liabilities) Act 1976 does not provide for a damages claim on behalf of a stillborn child and also indicates that, even when a child is born alive, there should be no cause of action for loss of expectation of life unless the child survives for forty-eight hours.[71]

Views on the desirability of restricting causes of action following adverse obstetric outcomes will differ. Some may consider it too radical to regulate the operation of negligence law in this manner. For those who hold this opinion, it will be preferable to concentrate on reforms improving the way that negligence law deals with all types of medical malpractice. In considering possible reforms, it is necessary to identify the motives of those who advocate them. Doctors might support reform to find 'some relief from an erratic and burdensome litigation system'. Lawyers, in contrast, might aim to make the system more accessible to patients and to impose stiffer sanctions on doctors.[72] Amidst these competing purposes, it is important not to lose sight of the fact that the system should be designed primarily to ensure that the needs of patients who have suffered harm are met as efficiently as possible and that just decisions are reached as to where responsibility should lie. Proposals for reform must be judged by reference to their potential to fulfil these aims.

One reform designed to ease the burden on medical practitioners is the creation of mechanisms to divert claims from the courts. Pre-trial panels were introduced in some parts of the United States to screen out unmeritorious claims and speed the settlement of those having merit. A decision that is

---

[68] 42 PaCS § 8305 (1999).   [69] 42 PaCS § 8305 (1999).   [70] 24 MRS § 2931 (1998).
[71] Congenital Disabilities (Civil Liabilities) Act 1976 (UK), s 4(4).
[72] P. C. Weiler *et al.*, *A Measure of Malpractice. Medical Injury, Malpractice Litigation, and Patient Compensation* (Cambridge, Mass, 1993) vii.

adverse to a patient does not prevent the filing of court proceedings, but this decision can be made admissible as evidence in these proceedings. Some criticisms have been made of screening panels and the results have been mixed.[73] Their use has lowered the insurance premiums paid by obstetricians and gynaecologists and has increased the number of settlements. They do not, however, seem to have reduced the frequency of claims and they can produce delays and added expense.

Another reform supported by doctors but often opposed by lawyers has been the statutory imposition of caps on damages. In some parts of the United States these have taken the form of limitations on damages for pain and suffering and in others ceilings have been placed on both economic and non-economic compensation.[74] A different approach to the fixing of damages is to replace single lump sum payments with structured settlements providing a combination of periodic payments and occasional lump sum payments. This reform can benefit both plaintiffs and defendants. A problem with lump sum awards is that they offer no means of revising incorrect assessments. If the patient recovers or dies earlier than expected, the sum awarded will be a windfall for the victim or his or her heirs. Equally, the patient might live longer than expected or the disability might worsen, making the award inadequate. Laws allowing periodic payments can provide flexibility and so offer both sides protection against future contingencies.[75] In spite of this, for some plaintiffs the award of a large lump sum is considered preferable; it can be seen as a symbolic victory and a vindication.

Alternative Procedures

There are limits as to what can be achieved by reforming negligence law. In addition to pursuing this course, therefore, attention must be given to the development of alternative methods of responding to obstetric misadventures. These can take a number of forms.

Arbitration or an Administrative Tribunal

Tribunals other than courts can be used as the setting for dealing with allegations of unsatisfactory care. One model relies on voluntary arbitration. This has had some success in reducing the number of claims requiring court adjudication. It also produces results more quickly and at lower cost. Further, the use of informal dispute resolution procedures has the advantage of allowing patients to receive an explanation, a sympathetic response, and an apology.

---

[73] P. C. Weiler, *Medical Malpractice on Trial* (Cambridge, Mass, 1991) 29.

[74] Ibid. 32. Such a change has special significance in the United States; there it has been estimated that compensation for pain and suffering makes up nearly 50 per cent of the damages awarded in medical cases (ibid. 55).

[75] Ibid. 31.

The adversarial court system is not designed to produce such outcomes. Nevertheless, the introduction of a system of voluntary arbitration may not be easy. It must be asked how they should be financed, whether they should be available for all types of claims, whether plaintiffs should be free to choose between arbitration and a court hearing, and whether provision should be made for appeals.[76]

Another alternative would be the creation of an expert administrative tribunal to adjudicate on matters of medical malpractice. A proposal for such a reform was advanced by the American Medical Association.[77] The essential feature of the scheme was that it would remove negligence claims from the courts to a specialized administrative tribunal—a State Medical Practices Review Board—which would be a reconstituted medical licensing board with full-time members, a minority of whom would be drawn from the medical profession. A patient alleging negligence would file an informal claim, which would be reviewed by members of the agency and of the relevant specialty. The agency staff would take the initiative in calling for medical records and interviewing witnesses. If the claim was thought to be valid, a hearing examiner would conduct a hearing and determine whether the treatment had been negligent and, if so, award damages. The agency would provide the plaintiff with legal representation by staff lawyers, although the plaintiff would also be free to use his or her own lawyer. The decision of the hearing examiner would be subject to review by the Board.

An important feature of the proposal is that all settlements and awards would be reported to an investigative branch for comparison with other malpractice or disciplinary reports to determine if a pattern of substandard conduct exists. All the information received would be maintained in a clearinghouse accessible to credentialling agencies (such as hospitals) and to persons who conduct professional reviews. The Board would also be able to establish guidelines defining appropriate standards of care. Thus what was envisaged was an integrated system that would do more than respond to individual claims: the Board would play a supervisory role and establish procedures to allow the systematic review of performance.

Adopting such a system would have a number of advantages. It would offer a more accessible and informal tribunal that would handle cases more quickly and cheaply than a court. The onus would not be on the plaintiff to overcome the barriers erected by the existing system. The tribunal would

---

[76] See M. Jones, 'Arbitration for Medical Negligence Claims in the NHS' (1992) 8 Professional Negligence 142.

[77] American Medical Association: Report of the American Medical Association/Specialty Society Medical Liability Project, *A Proposed Alternative to the Civil Justice System for Resolving Medical Liability Disputes: A Fault-Based Administrative System* (Chicago, 1987). The discussion of the report's proposals is based on the analysis offered by P. C. Weiler, *Medical Malpractice on Trial* (Cambridge, Mass, 1991) 114–22.

have the special expertise necessary to evaluate complex medical evidence. It would not be subject to the criticism that it would look for reasons to make a sympathetic award of damages from the deep pocket of the insurer. There is also the argument that the tribunal's decisions—being part of a broader system of professional regulation—would offer sensible, consistent, and comprehensible guidance on the standard of care expected.

There would also be disadvantages. There are some who would be suspicious of a proposal designed to introduce procedures with which doctors will feel more comfortable. As will be seen below, the performance of medical disciplinary boards raises doubts about the effectiveness of self-regulation. Further, the suggested reform would meet stiff resistance from lawyers because it would remove or reduce patients' well-established right to obtain justice from the ordinary courts. Equally important, those who seek substantial change can argue that the scheme would leave many of the features of malpractice law untouched. The tribunal would need to determine questions of fault and causation.[78] Plaintiffs would have to prove a case to succeed. Doctors 'would still be required to hear their professional performance being impugned by witnesses and lawyers, only this time in front of a medical board with authority over their licence to practice'.[79] To some extent, therefore, the proposal to introduce an administrative tribunal can be criticized on the same ground as proposals to reform the operation of negligence law: altering one aspect of the system—even one as central as the forum in which decisions are made—'falls far short of addressing all the dissatisfactions of either doctors or patients with the present tort/fault regime'.[80]

No Fault Schemes

One of the major problems with the existing system is that success in a damages claim depends on proof that the practitioner's fault caused the harm. The obvious response is to develop a mechanism to provide compensation without requiring proof of negligence. Such a mechanism will offer assistance purely on the basis that the patient has financial needs caused by a medical condition.

A frequently cited example is New Zealand's no fault compensation

---

[78] The proposal did, however, include an interesting recommendation as to proof of causation. It was suggested that recovery of damages should be permitted if the defendant's negligence was a contributing factor in causing the harm. The aim was to allow the damages to be apportioned according to the defendant's degree of fault. For a discussion of this aspect, see C. G. Phillips and E. H. Esty, 'A Fault-Based Administrative Alternative for Resolving Medical Malpractice Claims: the AMA-Specialty Society Medical Liability Project's Proposal and its Relevance to the Crisis in Obstetrics', in V. P. Rostow and R. J. Bulger (eds.), *Medical Professional Liability and the Delivery of Obstetrical Care, Volume 2, An Interdisciplinary Review* (Washington, 1989) 136, 146, and 151.

[79] P. C. Weiler, *Medical Malpractice on Trial* (Cambridge, Mass, 1991) 123.

[80] Ibid. 122.

scheme.[81] This operates as an insurance scheme and so does not depend on litigation to establish entitlement. While the advantages of this approach are obvious, it is not free of problems. The New Zealand experience suggests that once a no fault scheme is established there will be pressure to narrow its scope in order to reduce costs. Further, there are legal difficulties. The legislation[82] uses terms such as 'personal injury', 'medical misadventure', 'medical error', and 'medical mishap'. Interpretation of these terms can produce difficulties. More important, a successful claim requires proof that 'personal injury' has been *caused* by a 'medical error' or 'medical mishap'. Thus claimants cannot always avoid the problems of proof of causation that have given rise to difficulties in common law negligence actions. There is also the question of the level of payments that the scheme offers. For those who can surmount the hurdles and bring a successful negligence action, the financial benefits of the tort system are obvious. The sums paid under no fault schemes are likely to be modest compared with those awarded as damages. If the no fault alternative to a damages action is judged on the basis of its potential to deliver large sums of money to claimants, it cannot compete.

It should not be thought, however, that these problems indicate that no fault compensation should be rejected on the ground that any affordable scheme would inevitably provide an inadequate level of compensation. A number of reviews of the operation of the law relating to medical malpractice have suggested that the development of a no fault scheme is a feasible option. This view has been expressed in Canadian[83] and English[84] studies. One of the conclusions of the Harvard Medical Practice Study's analysis of the operation of medical malpractice law in New York was that it would be possible to finance a no fault system provided it was limited to reimbursing seriously injured patients in respect of long-term financial losses. It was calculated that this could be done for approximately the same sum as that currently spent on medical malpractice liability in that State.[85]

There are alternative methods of providing compensation specifically for those who have suffered adverse obstetric outcomes. The birth of a child with a severely disabling condition such as cerebral palsy creates a particularly troubling problem. As has been noted, only a small minority of children born with such a condition can establish that it was the result of negligence; the great majority therefore cannot obtain damages. Damages claims brought on

---

[81] Another example is the Swedish patient insurance scheme.

[82] Accident Insurance Act 1998 (NZ).

[83] Liability and Compensation in Health Care, *Appendix A: Health Care Liability and Compensation Review — Working Paper* (Toronto, 1990) 298–303.

[84] British Medical Association, *No Fault Compensation Working Party Report* (London, 1987).

[85] P. C. Weiler *et al.*, *A Measure of Malpractice. Medical Injury, Malpractice Litigation, and Patient Compensation* (Cambridge, Mass, 1993) 145–6.

behalf of these children are frequently despairing attempts to obtain the financial support that the community fails to provide for its disabled children. Alternatives designed to make such actions unnecessary deserve special consideration.

One example is the Virginia Birth-Related Neurological Injury Compensation Act 1987.[86] It has been copied in Florida.[87] The purpose of the statute is to provide financial support for severely disabled children without the need for proof that their condition was caused by medical negligence. It was not, however, enacted solely to fulfil this aim. It has been suggested that it is 'no secret' that the inspiration for the legislation was political: 'Obstetricians feeling oppressed by malpractice litigation and insurance premiums had demanded relief.'[88] The Act applies to a child born with a 'birth-related neurological injury'. This is defined as:

[I]njury to the brain or spinal cord . . . caused by the deprivation of oxygen or mechanical injury occurring in the course of labor, delivery, or resuscitation in the immediate post-delivery period in a hospital which renders the infant permanently non-ambulatory, aphasic, incontinent, and in need of assistance in all phases of daily living.[89]

To compensate such a child, the Act created a scheme in which hospitals and doctors practising in the State participate by contributing to a fund. If providers of obstetric care choose to participate, the fund becomes the exclusive source of compensation following the birth of a disabled child. All rights to sue are waived unless the injuries were intentionally or wilfully caused. A successful claim on the fund results in compensation for expenses not covered by other private or public insurance funds. A claim can be made for medical and rehabilitation expenses, residential care and services, special equipment and facilities, and for income loss after the age of 18. No recovery is available for non-economic loss.

It is important to appreciate the limitations and difficulties inherent in the scheme. It provides compensation only if the injuries are of a specified kind ('to the brain or spinal cord') and only if they are caused 'by the deprivation of oxygen or mechanical injury' occurring during labour or delivery or

---

[86] Va Code Ann §§ 38.2–5000 to –5021 (Supp 1987). For description and discussion of the Act, see D. G. Duff, 'Compensation for Neurologically Impaired Infants: Medical No-Fault in Virginia' (1990) 27 Harvard Journal of Legislation 391; P. H. White, 'Innovative No-Fault Tort Reform for an Endangered Specialty' (1988) 74 Virginia Law Review 1487; R. R. Bovbjerg *et al.*, 'Obstetrics and Malpractice: Evidence on the Performance of a Selective No-Fault System' (1991) 265 *Journal of the American Medical Association* 2836.

[87] Fla Stat Ann §§ 766.301–766.316 (West 1988).

[88] P. C. Weiler, *Medical Malpractice on Trial* (Cambridge, Mass, 1991) 153–4. The Act has been described as 'a carefully crafted exercise in special interest legislation': D. G. Duff, 'Compensation for Neurologically Impaired Infants: Medical No-Fault in Virginia' (1990) 27 Harvard Journal of Legislation 391, 449.

[89] Va Code Ann § 38.2–5001 (Supp 1987).

immediately post partum. The Act applies only to live births and specifically excludes a disability 'caused by genetic or congenital abnormalities'.[90] Thus the application of the legislation might give rise to problems as to proof of causation: there might be a dispute as to the origin of a child's injuries. Further, because the scheme is funded primarily by participating doctors and hospitals, it applies only to a child delivered by these doctors in these hospitals. The narrowness of the coverage was deliberate: those who framed the Act had no desire to bring too many claims within the system. For present purposes, the most important feature of the scheme is that although it offers a means of avoiding disputes about the presence or absence of fault, it offers no escape from disputes as to causation. A child will receive compensation only if the cause of the injuries can be established. When there is uncertainty as to causation, the matter is resolved by the State's Industrial Commission, the agency responsible for adjudicating claims under the Workers' Compensation Act.

The Virginian scheme thus falls far short of providing for the compensation needs of all infant victims of cerebral palsy. The only way to meet these needs would be through a properly funded insurance scheme or a state social security system. These would obviate the need to examine questions relating to fault and causation. They would represent recognition of society's obligations to severely disabled children. The chances that the legislatures in the four countries studied in this book will squarely confront the problem are, however, not high. The potential of state social security systems is limited. Eligibility for its benefits will invariably be narrowly defined and the level of payments offered to those who suffer medical conditions is likely to be low. In view of the current political climate in the United States, Canada, England, and Australia, it would be unrealistic to expect significant change in the immediate future: the tendency is for governments to withdraw from the field of welfare provision. In none of these countries is there a strong state commitment to the provision of support for the disadvantaged. Occasionally, however, schemes are introduced offering a response directed simply at meeting the needs of disabled children. In England, following the thalidomide tragedy, the Government set up the Family Fund to help families with handicapped children.[91]

A major shortcoming of no fault schemes is that by distributing the cost of compensating the victims of medical injuries, they do not hold individuals accountable and thus might eliminate an important incentive to maintain high standards of care. By abandoning the 'morality play of tort litigation',[92]

---

[90] Va Code Ann § 38.2–5014 (Supp 1987).

[91] Royal Commission on Civil Liability and Compensation for Personal Injury, *Report, Volume 1* (London, 1978) paras 1509–13.

[92] P. C. Weiler, *Medical Malpractice on Trial* (Cambridge, Mass, 1991) 149.

no fault schemes do not provide for the censure of a negligent practitioner. The design of the Virginia and Florida programmes, for example, has been criticized on the ground that no attention was paid to prevention of negligence.[93] This is an important consideration. While questions can be raised about the capacity of negligence law to promote the maintenance of health care standards, its ability to achieve this goal should not be entirely discounted: it would be difficult for proponents of no fault insurance to persuade the community that it should dispense with the contribution that malpractice litigation can make to preventing medical injuries.[94]

This prompts the question whether the contribution that tort law makes to setting medical standards might be substantially reduced and alternative methods of regulating health care might be further developed. A number of approaches can be considered, including complaints and disciplinary procedures, and procedures designed to monitor and maintain professional standards.

Regulation by Professional Bodies

Procedures for dealing with complaints can be provided by tribunals other than courts. These procedures must be efficient and credible. To be efficient they must be simple and accessible. To be credible they must be seen to be genuinely independent. They must also avoid creating a culture of complaint and so producing an environment in which professionals are reluctant to practise.

The role of complaints procedures in monitoring professional standards is limited in comparison with the role that could be played by medical boards or their equivalents. Boards are responsible for administering practitioners' registration or licensing and disciplinary processes. They can enforce appropriate standards of practice by setting requirements for admission to a specialty and by imposing sanctions such as fines, suspension, or revocation of a practitioner's registration or licence. When the latter powers are used, the focus is not only on individual complaints, but also on the overall standard of care provided by a practitioner 'manifested not simply in a particular incident but also in a broader pattern of behavior that may indicate a serious risk for future patients'.[95]

While the powers wielded by a medical board can operate as a powerful deterrent to sub-standard practices, United States and English research suggests that in practice the potential of self-regulation is difficult to realize. Most disciplinary proceedings conducted by boards in the United States and by the General Medical Council in England have dealt with behaviour such

---

[93] Ibid. 153.
[94] P. C. Weiler *et al.*, *A Measure of Malpractice. Medical Injury, Malpractice Litigation, and Patient Compensation* (Cambridge, Mass, 1993) 144.
[95] P. C. Weiler, *Medical Malpractice on Trial* (Cambridge, Mass, 1991) 107.

as improper drug prescription, alcohol or drug abuse, or sexual misconduct with patients, rather than with substandard practices.[96] Further, 'there is notorious underreporting of incompetent practice by [doctors'] professional peers'. Even if those in charge of a hospital or clinic learn of the danger posed by one of their colleagues and are willing to take action 'their natural inclination is simply to ease the offending doctor out of the institution rather than go public with complaints to the authorities'.[97] There is also the possibility of bias by boards staffed wholly or predominantly by doctors; such boards have been described as being 'disinclined to judge their colleagues sufficiently incompetent to lose the right to practice entirely'.[98] Finally, there is evidence that medical boards are not very successful in setting broad standards of practice: 'The focus is on identifying and eliminating a tiny number of especially poor doctors rather than on trying to enhance the quality of care provided by the vast majority of typical doctors.'[99]

It is necessary for this focus to change if medical boards are to make a significant contribution to the monitoring of standards of care. The aim should be quality control pursued by audit procedures designed to ensure routine reviews of outcomes. These procedures can take a number of forms: incident reporting, regular meetings to monitor performance (for example, hospital meetings to consider all cases of perinatal morbidity and mortality), and epidemiological studies. The aim should be to identify situations in which substandard practices have harmed patients and to generate changes designed to avoid or minimize the repetition of these practices. In addition, educational programmes—particularly those that are compulsory if practitioners are to continue to be accredited—have a part to play.

One feature of reforms designed to promote quality control rather than the censure of individual practitioners should be emphasized. Preoccupation with the identification of individual fault might prove to be an inefficient means of promoting improved standards of care. In many situations it might be more productive to focus on the *system* that produced the harm to the patient.[100] This would involve an examination of organizational failures, an approach having particular relevance to the management of childbirth. The delivery of a child may involve nurses, midwives, and junior and senior doctors (including anaesthetists). A procedure designed to recognize this might

---

[96] P. C. Weiler, *Medical Malpractice on Trial* (Cambridge, Mass, 1991) 108 and K. Walshe, 'Medical Accidents in the UK: a Wasted Opportunity for Improvement?', in M. M. Rosenthal *et al.* (eds.), *Medical Mishaps: Pieces of the Puzzle* (Buckingham, 1999) 59, 71.

[97] P. C. Weiler, *Medical Malpractice on Trial* (Cambridge, Mass, 1991) 108.

[98] Ibid. 109.   [99] Ibid. 121.

[100] This argument can be taken further: one possible reform of the system would be entirely to replace individual liability with organizational liability. Under this approach, it is the hospital, not the individual doctor or midwife, which should be sued for any obstetric misadventure. For a discussion of organizational liability, see P. C. Weiler, *Medical Malpractice on Trial* (Cambridge, Mass, 1991) 122–32.

be more successful in contributing to the overall improvement of standards of care. For example, the cause of an adverse outcome might be found to lie not in a junior doctor's failure to display the required level of competence, but in a consultant's failure to exercise supervision of a doctor who has been continuously on duty for twenty hours. The hospital administration could also be implicated for allowing such hours to be worked and not ensuring that the consultants provided the necessary support.

Finally, the need for health care professionals further to develop systems of self-regulation must be stressed. It is important for practitioners to be seen to play an active role in monitoring standards and taking action when appropriate care is not provided. Procedures for self-regulation have not always functioned as well as they should. If professionals are lethargic and inclined to close ranks, they cannot complain if the task of standard setting is dominated by courts hearing damages claims. The changing climate in which doctors and midwives now practise—a climate in which there is a demand for increased opportunities to seek redress—makes it imperative for them to develop credible and effective responses.

Redesigning the System

Society cannot expect one legal mechanism to provide satisfactory solutions when there has been an adverse obstetric outcome. Responding to such an outcome requires the pursuit of a number of objectives: enforcing standards of care, imposing accountability, censuring substandard performance, and providing compensation. Any attempt to achieve these aims demands the adoption of a combination of strategies and the identification of the functions that a particular strategy can most effectively perform. The task of identifying these functions involves a search for answers to difficult questions about the interrelationships between the various options.

In view of the emphasis throughout this book on negligence law, it is the operation of this body of law that must be taken as the starting-point. Its deficiencies in compensating the victims of medical malpractice are indisputable. Questions can also be asked about its efficacy in maintaining standards of care: 'It would be better if legal incentives to reduce the dangers of medical treatment were generated by a regime that did somewhat less damage to the therapeutic goals of the physician–patient relationship.'[101] Nevertheless, in spite of its failings, it would be difficult to sustain the argument that negligence law should no longer be used to deal with medical malpractice. Instead, tort law should be relegated to a secondary role and supplemented by a range of initiatives designed to provide solutions to specific problems to which it can offer only clumsy and inadequate solutions. In pursuing this

---

[101] Ibid. 114.

strategy, however, it is necessary to be aware of the danger of erecting unwarranted obstacles to patients who have suffered harm. Rights should not be taken away without providing appropriate alternative remedies. It must also be appreciated that alternative methods cannot fulfil all the functions presently performed by damages claims.

In the fields of obstetrics and midwifery, the supplementary initiatives to be pursued should reflect a recognition of the need to respond to a number of problems. The most obvious is that presented by the seriously disabled child. Whether it is the concerns of the child, his or her parents, or the doctor or midwife that are uppermost, it is clear that steps must be taken to ensure that substantial financial support is provided regardless of fault and regardless of the cause of the child's condition. This could be done by creating an insurance fund that avoids the weaknesses of the Virginian scheme or by political action that results in the state accepting responsibility for the child by way of the social security system. Whether the notion of no fault compensation should be extended beyond this category of children should also be considered. The question to be resolved is 'how should an island of no-fault be situated in the broader sea of tort liability?'[102]

In addition to experimenting with no fault schemes, a redesigned system should reflect an appreciation of the fact that effective regulation of the standards of antenatal and perinatal care might be more likely to be achieved by audit and quality control programmes that address organizational factors. Such programmes would largely replace systems preoccupied with singling individuals out for blame and, it is hoped, promote high standards of care. Procedures designed to monitor patterns of practice are more likely to be efficient than those that respond idiosyncratically to individual incidents. Effective regulation of health care standards is unlikely to occur if the problem is viewed as 'holding to account a few bad apples'.[103] Finally, whatever supplementary schemes are ultimately adopted, it is important for health care professionals to assume greater responsibility for the development of vigorous and credible methods of monitoring and maintaining standards of care.

[102] P. C. Weiler, *Medical Malpractice on Trial* (Cambridge, Mass, 1991) 158.
[103] Ibid. 149.

14

Conclusion: The Role of the Law

This book has examined legal intervention during pregnancy and after child-birth. Intervention before birth can be undertaken in an attempt to protect the fetus against harmful conduct. After birth, it can take the form of a damages claim if negligence has caused an adverse outcome. Action of the first kind is designed to promote the safe delivery of a healthy child. Action of the second kind, while not directly promoting this aim, can indirectly protect maternal and fetal welfare by seeking to deter the repetition of similar negligent conduct. It also has the aim of providing compensation for those affected by the negligence.

This chapter offers concluding comments on the role of the law in fulfilling these varied objectives. In doing so, it considers the concepts and techniques on which the law relies. In addition, it returns to the legal problems posed by the relationship between a pregnant woman and her fetus and to the implications of recognizing the woman's autonomy.

INTERVENTION DURING PREGNANCY

As was shown in Chapter 2, criminal and child protection proceedings can be taken to protect fetuses, while the same purpose can be pursued in actions aimed at authorizing the non-consensual medical treatment of pregnant women. These procedures have no part to play in facilitating the safe delivery of healthy children. The law should not be used to coerce or restrict a pregnant woman in an attempt to protect her fetus. Its methods are clumsy, intrusive, and, at times, counter-productive. This conclusion is generally consistent with the approach recently adopted by the courts in the United States, Canada, and England. While actions involving pregnant women who have taken illicit drugs or declined medical treatment have occasionally succeeded, they are unlikely to do so in future if the principles articulated in cases such as *State of Ohio v Gray, Winnipeg Child and Family Services (Northwest Area) v G, Re Baby Boy Doe*, and *St George's Healthcare NHS v S* are applied.[1] Decisions such as these have accepted that a pregnant woman should be free to engage in conduct and to make choices that may harm her fetus.

In reaching this conclusion, the courts have recognized that the law should respect maternal autonomy. This should not, however, be taken as indicating

---

[1] These cases are discussed in Chapter 2.

that the exercise of autonomy during pregnancy is unproblematic. The conduct of a pregnant woman cannot be regarded as affecting her alone. It is impossible to ignore the fact that her actions and decisions have the capacity to affect another human being: the child that the fetus will become. With regard to potential harm to the fetus, a distinction can be made between conduct such as illicit drug taking and a decision to decline medical intervention. It would be difficult to argue that taking illicit drugs during pregnancy is behaviour that the law should respect as a manifestation of the right to self-determination. Rather, society should view such conduct with sadness, while recognizing that it is inappropriate to take coercive legal action in an attempt to prevent it. When the relevant conduct is a decision to decline medical intervention, arguments resting on the importance of respecting maternal autonomy are stronger. At issue here is the right to bodily integrity, a right the law can properly proclaim.

The current law's adoption of principles inimical to coercive intervention to protect a fetus against maternal conduct will not remove all uncertainty as to the appropriateness of legal intervention. The recent changes in the law do not mean that legal action against a pregnant woman will inevitably fail. There might be a wide gulf between the formal law and day-to-day practices: there will always be the possibility that intervention will occur in circumstances in which there will be no scrutiny by a court. More important, even when a court accepts that the relevant principles are those established in the more recent decisions, intervention to protect a fetus may still be authorized. This is particularly likely when a doctor wishes to perform a caesarean section and the woman has declined to consent. The difficulty lies in the fact that while cases such as *Re Baby Boy Doe* and *St George's Healthcare NHS v S* have expressly ruled that the wishes of a competent woman must be respected, doubts may be raised about a woman's competence in order to sanction intervention to protect the fetus. When an emergency arises at the time of a delivery, such doubts can be readily produced. It is always open to a court to accept the argument that because she is in the throes of labour a woman lacks the competence to reach a considered decision. The outcome would be that although lip-service would be paid to the need to recognize a woman's right to bodily integrity, the result desired by those who wish to protect the fetus would be reached.

There may therefore be situations in which analysis in terms of formal legal principles will be insufficient. Further, the possible effect of changes in the way the law views the fetus must also constantly be borne in mind. In Chapter 8, I argued that a distinction can and should be made between the law's response to maternal conduct that harms a fetus and similar conduct by a third party. This argument was based on the view that account must be taken of the relationship between a pregnant woman and her fetus. This relationship justifies conferring immunity on a woman whose conduct threatens or has harmed her fetus. A different result can be reached, for example, in the case of a third party who attacks a pregnant woman and injures or destroys her fetus. This person can appropriately be punished for the harm caused to the fetus. Some courts and legislatures in the United States, England, and Australia have accepted that the criminal law can be properly used to achieve this end.[2] The way they have reached this conclusion can be seen as requiring recognition of the distinctiveness of the fetus. This rings warning bells for those concerned about the autonomy of a pregnant woman. The fear is that the law will inexorably develop on the basis that if a fetus is protected from harm in one context, it must be protected from *all* harm, including that threatened or inflicted by the mother.[3] As has been said of statutes passed with the narrow purpose of safeguarding fetuses from attack, the danger is that these Acts 'might serve as a wedge, opening the door to legislation that protects fetuses at the expense of women's rights of privacy and self-determination'.[4]

While I have argued that such concerns should not prevent the law from protecting the fetus in some situations, the views expressed by those who believe otherwise should not be ignored. My conclusion that the law has no part to play in coercing or restricting a pregnant woman in an attempt to protect her fetus is not offered as a confident assertion that in future the courts will inevitably reject attempts to use the law in this way. Difficulties will continue to arise, both from the application of the newly emerging principles and from the law's changing perceptions of the legal status of the fetus.

THE LAW'S RESPONSE WHEN SOMETHING GOES WRONG

In contrast with the view that, at best, the law has a limited function to fulfil before a child is born, a different conclusion emerges from analysis of the law's role in responding to harm caused by negligent antenatal or perinatal care. Here the law's role is well established. Future developments in the field of childbirth and the law are likely to be driven by the way that the law of negligence is interpreted in cases involving adverse obstetric outcomes.

The Nature of Obstetric Malpractice Claims

In Chapters 10 and 13, I suggested that on both theoretical and practical grounds there are reasons for disquiet as to the capacity of the law of medical

---

[2] See above 139–43.
[3] S. Fovargue and J. Miola, 'Policing Pregnancy: Implications of the Attorney-General's Reference (No 3 of 1994)' [1998] Medical Law Review 265, 288.
[4] B. Steinbock, *Life before Birth: the Moral and Legal Status of Embryos and Fetuses* (New York, 1992) 111.

malpractice to deal satisfactorily with claims arising in the context of child-birth. Questions can be raised about the system's ability to ensure the just allocation of responsibility, to enforce appropriate standards of care, or to provide adequate compensation for those who have suffered harm.

It should come as no surprise that the law is often unable to provide satis-fying solutions to the problems posed by damages claims resulting from obstetric misadventures. These problems involve matters as complex as any arising in the course of human life. When a child is expected, the implications for the parents-to-be are far-reaching. Their hopes and aspirations will be high. If something goes wrong, their sense of loss and disappointment will be acute. For some parents, in contrast, the birth will not be welcomed and they will face an unwanted burden. Whether wanted or unwanted, the birth of a child with a major disability will be a devastating blow. It will dominate the rest of the parents' lives and have disturbing effects on other members of the family. In such a case, it is questionable whether culpability can be properly assigned and a monetary value put on the harm suffered by the child and the parents. Yet lawyers tend to assume that the law of negligence can perform these tasks in a principled manner. The comment made by a court dealing with an action arising from the unwanted birth of a normal child has broader relevance: 'Litigation cannot answer every question; every question cannot be answered in terms of dollars and cents.'[5]

An additional consideration is the extent to which the courts' sympathy for plaintiffs results, if not in the abandonment of basic principles, at least in their distorted application. This is understandable, in view of the magnitude of the burdens that obstetric misadventures impose on children and parents. Courts will occasionally be affected by the belief that wherever possible, financial support should be given to the victims of these misadventures. In a case arising from the birth of a disabled child, this belief will sometimes be combined with the view that recognition of a claim will avoid casting a bur-den on taxpayers who would otherwise have to contribute to the child's upkeep.[6] When responding to such considerations, judges and juries may pay insufficient attention to the need for careful proof of all the elements of a damages claim. In the opinion of an Illinois judge, 'the traditional legal con-cepts of duty and foreseeability have increasingly come to be seen as mere catchwords to be manipulated according to the results one wishes to reach'.[7]

---

[5] *Wilbur v Kerr* Ark, 628 SW 2d 568, 571 (1982), adopted in *McKernan v Aasheim* 687 P 2d 850, 856 (Wash, 1984).
[6] See *Harbeson v Parke-Davis Inc* Wash 656 P 2d 483, 495 (1983), in which the court, rather than letting the expenses of a disabled child's continuing medical care and training fall on the parents or the state, preferred to place the burden on 'the party whose negligence was in fact a proximate cause of the child's need for such medical care and training'. See also *Day v Nation-wide Mutual Insurance Co* Fla App, 328 So 2d 560, 562 (1976).
[7] *Renslow v Mennonite Hospital* 367 NE 2d 1250, 1263 (1977).

This comment was made in the course of a dissenting judgment in a case in which the majority had allowed a child to bring an action for pre-conception negligence. Although conceding the 'philanthropic appeal' of this outcome, the judge expressed fear that the decision would place an intolerable burden on insurance companies and therefore on the public:

My deepest concern with the majority decision is that it is symptomatic of the increasing tendency of the courts to expand the traditional limits of tort law with little regard for the resultant social consequences. . . . [T]he idea has developed that the damages suffered by innocent persons should be spread over a broad base either through insurance or as a cost of doing business. An ever-broadening concept of duty has evolved to accommodate this theory, bringing more persons under the protective umbrella. Once under this umbrella, sympathetic juries and an increasingly efficient plaintiff's [*sic*] bar have managed to inflate the size of verdicts. . . . We have painfully learned that the 'spread the risk' theory of tort law depends upon the 'deep pockets' of the general public.[8]

Thus to his doubts about the theoretical justification for the damages award, he added practical concerns about the effect of sympathetic verdicts prompted by an awareness of the availability of a 'deep pocket'.

The analysis can be broadened to take account of the context in which doctors and midwives practise, and hence the context in which the courts must apply the law of negligence. This is changing. While pregnancy and childbirth are natural processes, the capacity of the medical profession to influence their course has greatly increased in recent years. New knowledge and the availability of sophisticated technology have created an environment in which it is accepted that society has the power to control reproduction. This can lead to expectations of perfection. The trouble-free delivery of a perfect child is increasingly accepted as the norm. In the past, parents who had experienced a stillbirth or the birth of a disabled child would have regarded their disappointment as one of the vicissitudes of life, the product of chance or fate. Today such events are much more likely to be viewed as having been avoidable. If something goes wrong, it will be assumed that the cause can be discovered. If a cause can be found, someone should be answerable. Someone must be to blame.

It is interesting to speculate on how these changes have affected and will continue to affect the way that courts respond to claims arising from obstetric misadventures. The pressure on doctors and midwives to meet increasingly high standards is likely to mount: as doctors and midwives acquire greater knowledge of genetics and of the nature of pregnancy and childbirth, they must expect courts to take the view that access to that knowledge creates higher expectations. Those who practise obstetrics and midwifery are both

---

[8] Ibid. 1265. See also *Amadio v Levin* 501 A 2d 1085, 1101 (Pa, 1985), where a dissenting judge expressed concern about the pervasiveness of the concept of a 'deep pocket'.

the beneficiaries and the prisoners of the phenomenal rate of increase of knowledge and advances in technology in the field. The more practitioners can do, the more they are expected to do. The implications for the application of negligence law are obvious. The higher the expectations, the greater the opportunities for the perception of error and hence for damages claims. This is particularly clear in actions arising from unwanted births. The more willing parents are to assert that they have a right to avoid the burden of caring for a child whose abnormalities were foreseeable, the more vulnerable do doctors become.

Some courts have been troubled by the impact on the legal system of developments exposing health care professionals to ever-increasing liability. In 1980, a judge of the Supreme Court of New Hampshire drew attention to 'the never-ending effort to widen more and more the circle of liability which surrounds us'. He added: '[T]he pressure never ends. When a new line is drawn, the pressure shifts to form a new and wider circle. . . . If life is not to become intolerable, there must be some boundaries to the zone of liability. . . . It is the policy of the law which must establish a reasonable limitation on liability.'[9] The question is whether the law can satisfactorily set such boundaries and draw distinctions between situations in which culpability can be fairly assigned and damages assessed and those in which liability should not be imposed.

The foregoing analysis might prompt two responses. One is that while obstetric misadventures might occasionally result in aberrant judgments—whether in favour of plaintiffs or defendants—the legal system is fundamentally sound and can accommodate both actions of the kind that have already come before the courts and those that changes in the medical and social climate will in future bring before them. On this view, society can rely on the courts to distinguish between harms that are compensable and those that are not and to assign culpability in a fair manner. The other view is that an examination of the operation of negligence law in this field raises too many unanswered questions and that society must recognize that this body of law is not always well equipped to enforce appropriate standards of care or to do justice when there has been an adverse outcome. This is to assert that the nature of pregnancy and childbirth are such that it is often not clear whether a doctor or midwife should be held liable for failing to facilitate a successful outcome.

The evidence offered in this book supports the latter conclusion. When there is an adverse obstetric outcome, it is difficult to argue that the law of negligence can be relied on to provide a framework within which culpability can be fairly assessed and just compensation provided.

---

[9] *Wallace v Wallace* NH, 421 A 2d 134, 136 (1980).

The Challenge to Medicalization

Further doubts as to the operation of negligence law arise from the changes in the social climate in which doctors and midwives now practise. These changes—which are a manifestation of the increased recognition given to maternal autonomy—have expressed themselves in the form of a challenge to the 'medicalization' of childbirth. This is an expression of a view emphasizing the naturalness of the process and hence asserting the undesirability of medical intervention. To adopt this view is to urge the need for women to have greater control over their antenatal and perinatal care. This alters the relationship between a pregnant woman and the practitioner who cares for her. Instead of deference to professional opinion there is a demand for a greater opportunity to participate in decision-making; this demand sometimes takes the form of support for more 'woman centred' maternity services.[10] The possible effect of these changed attitudes on the operation of the law of negligence must be noted. The more the emphasis is placed on the importance of the woman determining the course of her pregnancy and delivery, the less the opportunity to blame a doctor or midwife for an adverse outcome. Yet there is a possible paradox here. Some of those who distrust doctors and are suspicious of their claims to expertise may have absorbed the high expectations to which I have referred. When these expectations are disappointed, it is not clear whether supporters of natural childbirth will accept an adverse outcome as one of life's vicissitudes or whether they will view it as avoidable and seek damages.

The extent to which changes in attitudes to childbirth will affect the way that courts apply negligence law is therefore difficult to determine. The law must be prepared to respond to the emergence of a school of thought characterized by an emphasis on the importance of maternal autonomy and a consequent suspicion of medical expertise. It may do so by acknowledging that the critics of 'medicalization' have to some extent undermined the basis on which a damages claim can be brought following an adverse obstetric outcome. Alternatively, the law might respond by accepting that a corollary of respect for maternal autonomy is a recognition that this autonomy can be properly exercised only if women are given full information as to the risks of childbirth. This would be consistent with recent developments in medical malpractice law. These have placed increased emphasis on a practitioner's duty to avoid paternalism and to provide information on the basis of which the woman can make decisions. The authentic exercise of autonomy depends on the provision of this information.

Thus the changes brought about by the law's increased willingness to recognize maternal autonomy have implications for the operation of the law

[10] Department of Health, *Changing Childbirth: Part 1: Report of the Expert Maternity Group* (London, 1993) 5.

of negligence. The legal system must accommodate the campaign for greater maternal control over antenatal and perinatal care, while at the same time determining whether—and if so, how—to offer the woman and her child the protection normally given by the law of medical malpractice.

The difficulties do not end with the identification of these problems. The analysis so far has equated the exercise of autonomy with the assertion of the power of control. In the context of childbirth, however, this approach may be open to question. In Chapter 9, I drew attention to the need to appreciate the interdependence of a woman and her fetus. This was stressed in order to avoid adopting a model of pregnancy postulating the existence of two entities in potential conflict. If the concept of interdependence can be invoked to cast doubt on the assumption of maternal/fetal conflict, it can also be invoked to question the appropriateness of speaking of maternal control. If the relationship between a pregnant woman and those who care for her is characterized as one that she must control, that relationship is likely to suffer in just the same way as if the doctor or midwife is intent on establishing control. The woman is dependent on her care giver, just as the care giver is dependent on the woman. The fetus—and hence the child—is dependent on both. To recognize the significance of this interdependence is to recognize that a successful outcome of a pregnancy will not be achieved if this outcome is viewed as requiring the resolution of a conflict or the assertion of control. Rather, it requires the establishment of a partnership.

On one view, it is appropriate for the law to promote this aim: to accept that the law imposes on a practitioner an obligation to provide information is to acknowledge that the aim should be the facilitation of shared decision-making. The achievement of this goal will not always be easy. Indeed, the difficulties may sometimes be insurmountable. Rhoden, a critic of the 'medicalization' of childbirth, has stated that 'the prognosis for shared decision-making in obstetrics is grim'.[11] In her view, 'the barriers to achieving . . . empathy in obstetrics are higher than usual'.[12] Her argument is that the medical culture in the United States promotes the view that in any given situation there is only one course of action that is correct. Doctors' training equips them to intervene during childbirth in order to minimize risk: '[M]any obstetricians are not fully aware that they are trained to react to uncertainty in a particular manner: they may believe that their response is the only possible response or, because uncertainty makes them so uncomfortable, may fail to take it fully into account.'[13] If doctors do not acknowledge uncertainty, women in labour are unlikely to be told that choices can sometimes be made. The result will be that the possibility of shared decision-making will simply

---

[11] N. K. Rhoden, 'Informed Consent in Obstetrics: Some Special Problems' (1987) 9 Western New England Law Review 67, 68.
[12] Ibid. 77.   [13] Ibid. 84.

not arise. For their part, the women are in a vulnerable situation. They will normally want what is best for their children. 'Women are often told nothing more than that a particular procedure is necessary for their baby's health. Given the circumstances it is no wonder that the recommended procedure is almost always performed.'[14]

This is to view the 'medicalization' of childbirth as inevitably preventing women from playing a part in the decision-making process. This may or may not be unduly pessimistic. For present purposes, the important point is that this analysis recognizes that the aim should be the promotion of a partnership between a woman and her doctor. Yet it also impliedly concedes the value of medical expertise. If the aim is a partnership, not only will doctors have to listen to pregnant women, but women must also take account of the views of their doctors. This is simply to observe that any genuine partnership must accommodate different views on the proper management of childbirth. There can be no partnership if the assumption is that one view must always prevail.

The significance of this is sometimes overlooked by the more radical critics of the 'medicalization' of childbirth. Some of these critics rest their analyses on a denigration of medical expertise. An example of a challenge to medical expertise was provided in a report by a United Kingdom committee on maternity services. This cited evidence hinting that doctors who advise of risks tend to give biased information.[15] Later this was explained on the basis that doctors are 'reared . . . on a diet of abnormality'.[16] Speaking of the Royal College of Obstetricians and Gynaecologists (the body responsible for the training of specialists), the committee claimed that the College's presumption in favour of a medical model of care 'would inevitably continue to compromise the degree of even-handedness that was likely to be introduced by many obstetricians' into the provision of information as to risks.[17] The committee also stated that it had received evidence suggesting that 'there is an inherent bias in the education and culture of the obstetric specialty which pushes it in the direction of a pathological view of pregnant women'.[18]

This view embodies a perception of childbirth as a natural process that in the great majority of cases results in a normal and uncomplicated outcome; it is therefore argued that risks should not be the principal concern of those who assist at deliveries.[19] It is beyond the scope of this book to consider the

---

[14] Ibid. 76.
[15] House of Commons, Health Committee, Second Report, *Maternity Services, Volume 1* (London, 1992) para 65.
[16] Ibid. para 77.   [17] Ibid. para 183.   [18] Ibid. para 368.
[19] On this view, it is interesting to note that the committee quoted the comment that society is 'hung up' on mortality as an outcome: ibid. para 30. See also Department of Health, *Changing Childbirth: Part 1: Report of the Expert Maternity Group* (London, 1993) 19, where concern was expressed about 'the possible over-surveillance' of women during the antenatal period.

correctness of this view. My purpose is to draw attention to the possible legal implications of its adoption. At issue is a fundamental question relating to the management of pregnancy and childbirth. How active should doctors and midwives be? Should a nation's system of maternity care be driven by a desire to avoid intervention? This is a question on which those who practise in the field express opposing views. The debate is one that lawyers cannot ignore, for it has implications for the future operation of medical malpractice law. To answer the question about how active a practitioner should be is to define obligations, the breach of which may result in legal liability. It is also the first step to recognizing that at the heart of many obstetric malpractice actions is the problem of the extent to which doctors and midwives should be held liable for the outcome of a natural process.

Thus the difficulties multiply. Increased recognition of maternal autonomy might reduce the circumstances in which a practitioner can be sued in respect of an adverse obstetric outcome. Alternatively, reliance on what can loosely be described as the doctrine of 'informed consent' could lead to the proliferation of actions alleging non-disclosure: the allegation would be that although the woman exercised her power to make decisions, these decisions were reached on the basis of inadequate information. Such a development would underline the fact that those who practise in the fields of obstetrics and midwifery cannot transfer responsibility to the women for whom they care and thus cannot remove themselves from the operation of negligence law. Yet if Rhoden's analysis of doctors' practices is accepted, it is unrealistic to rely on a body of law resting on the assumption that the information necessary to facilitate informed decision-making will be provided. Even more challenging to the advocate of the need for 'informed consent' is the view rejecting the validity and relevance of medical information as to risks. This is to deny that doctors possess expertise giving them access to information that they are obliged to share with pregnant women. To adopt this perspective is to call into question the understanding of childbirth previously adopted by the law of negligence.

The range of matters to be taken into account by those concerned about the operation of the law of negligence in the fields of obstetrics and midwifery is therefore broad. When there has been an adverse obstetric outcome, the application of the concepts and principles employed in this area of law is sometimes at best difficult and at worst unconvincing. In some cases, a satisfactory resolution of the problems of assigning liability and awarding appropriate compensation cannot be achieved. Further, in the light of technological advances, it is likely that the law will impose ever-increasing burdens on those who practise obstetrics and midwifery. In addition, there are the questions that changed attitudes and expectations raise about the role of the law of negligence.

RECOGNIZING THE LIMITS OF THE LAW

The principal lesson to be learned from the analysis offered in this book is the need to question assumptions about the contribution that the law can make to the prevention of adverse obstetric outcomes and to the resolution of claims arising from them. The law should not play a part in coercing or restraining pregnant women. Its capacity to resolve the problems posed by obstetric misadventures is limited. Society should minimize the role of the law of negligence in the field of obstetrics and midwifery. This conclusion is the product not only of reservations about the applicability of the principles of tort law, but also of concerns raised by an appreciation of the realities of the rough and tumble of medical malpractice litigation. The deficiencies of the law of negligence are such as to raise serious doubts about its ability to respond in a sensitive, just, and effective manner to a significant proportion of the cases in which there has been an adverse obstetrical outcome. Alternatives should be sought. What is required is a reassessment of the functions that the law can appropriately perform and an identification of the legal mechanisms best suited to performing them. In particular, it must be accepted that mechanisms that will provide adequate financial compensation for an adverse outcome will not offer the most satisfactory means of promoting high standards of antenatal and perinatal care or of ensuring that those who fail to provide it will be held accountable. A combination of strategies must replace over-reliance on the law of negligence.

It is necessary, however, to go further. The task must not be simply to develop new and more effective legal mechanisms. Rather, it must be accepted that many of the problems discussed in this book cannot be wholly resolved by resort to the law. Legal concepts and techniques can impede the search for appropriate solutions to the problems with which this book deals. The law tends to respond to conduct such as illicit drug taking during pregnancy or a decision to decline medical intervention by thinking in terms of a conflict between the pregnant woman and her fetus. Equally, a damages claim takes the form of an adversarial conflict. This is a framework with which lawyers feel comfortable. Much of the business of the law is the resolution of conflict and this task is usually undertaken by identifying adversaries, weighing their interests, and deciding which set of interests should prevail. This process regularly entails reliance on concepts such as 'rights', 'autonomy', 'accountability', and 'deterrence'. Use of such terminology frequently produces inappropriate responses.

A society wishing to promote the shared needs of the woman and her fetus, and so to facilitate the safe delivery of a healthy child, will find it more productive to focus on educational programmes. This approach is more likely than the threat of legal action to lead the woman to accept that she shares responsibility for the outcome of her pregnancy with those who care for her.

When the issue is the desirability of medical intervention, the creation of an environment in which to communicate information as to the risks the woman is facing may sometimes be difficult. For many doctors, it is not always easy to accept that they and the pregnant woman are in a partnership and that they have an obligation to assist her in making decisions. They may not take sufficiently seriously their obligation to respect her autonomy. The doctor who was reported as telling a patient's husband, 'I am the doctor, you're not, and I'm the one who decides whether or not she gets a c-section, not you!'[20] may represent an extreme example of a failure to engage in dialogue. Nevertheless, there are numerous occasions on which doctors do not communicate well with their patients and discourage questioning of the course they wish to take. Equally, when doctors make a genuine effort to communicate, there are some women who are unwilling to accept that information as to risks should be considered in an open-minded manner. I have already referred to the assumption, made by some groups, that doctors tend to give biased information as to the risks of childbirth. There is a fine line between healthy scepticism and prejudice. An atmosphere in which prejudice prevails is inimical to the creation of the necessary partnership between pregnant women and those who care for them. Those who denigrate all forms of perinatal intervention do women a disservice if they create a climate in which evidence of the risks posed by childbirth is dismissed as medical propaganda.

While the law does have a legitimate role to play if something goes wrong, its limitations must also be acknowledged. This is so regardless of the effort devoted to reforming the law of negligence and to developing alternative procedures such as are discussed in Chapter 13. Some of the cases discussed in this book give rise to extraordinarily difficult questions. Is the unwanted birth of a normal child a harm to the parents and, if so, should society provide them with assistance not offered to other parents who willingly care for a large family? Can society quantify the harm suffered by the parents who must face the burden of bringing up a severely disabled child? Should society take seriously such a child's complaint that someone should be held responsible for allowing him or her to be born? In view of the uncertainty surrounding the causes of cerebral palsy, should society abandon all attempts to identify those cases in which a doctor or midwife can be blamed for the child's condition? To what extent can culpability be fairly assigned in respect of the outcome of a natural process? These are not questions of the kind that the law can answer.

Thus there is a need for scepticism about the role of the law in responding to problems relating to pregnancy and childbirth. Its techniques and

---

[20] *Bankert by Bankert v United States* 937 F Supp 1169, 1177 (D Md, 1996). In this case the woman and her husband had requested the performance of a caesarean section. Although the evidence that this statement had been made was 'highly disputed', the court accepted that the doctor had used words to this effect.

remedies cannot always be employed to resolve these problems. Whenever there is a call for legal intervention in this context, it must be asked whether the matter is one that is susceptible to a legal solution. The less effort that society expends on the search for such a solution, the more it can devote to positive means of promoting the welfare of parents and their children.

Glossary of Medical Terms

* Indicates that this word is explained elsewhere in this glossary

abruptio placentae	partial or complete separation of the placenta before birth
alpha-feto-protein	a glycoprotein. The AFP-levels in the amniotic fluid are raised in open neural tube* defects
amniocentesis	aspiration of fluid from the amniotic sac*
amniotic embolism	plug of amniotic fluid dislodged into the blood circulation and causing obstruction of the blood flow
amniotic fluid	fluid secreted by the amnion
amniotic sac	sac of fluid secreted by the amnion, the inner layer of the fetal membranes
angiogram	an X-ray of a blood vessel
antenatal	occurring or formed before birth
antepartum haemorrhage	large blood loss occurring before birth
antibody screening	blood test to determine the presence of antibodies to the patient's blood group or disease factors
apnoea	transient cessation of breathing
arthrogryposis	persistent flexure or contracture of a joint
atresia	absence or closure of a normal body orifice or passage
brachial plexus	network of nerves supplying the arm and upper trunk
bradycardia	slowing of the heart rate
breech presentation	the fetal position in which the buttocks and/or lower extremities form the presenting part*
breech extraction	assistance is given to deliver the buttocks by applying traction to the baby before the spontaneous delivery of any part of the baby
caesarean section	incision through the abdominal and uterine walls for delivery of a fetus
cardiotocograph	continuous simultaneous recording of fetal heart rate and uterine contractions
cephalic	head

cerebral palsy	persisting motor disorder
cervical cerclage	encircling the cervix* with a suture to maintain its closure during the pregnancy
cervix	the lower, neck, part of the uterus
chorionic villous sampling	removal of cells from the chorionic (outer) layer of the placenta to allow examination of the cells, biochemically and genetically, for prenatal diagnosis of chromosomal and other anomalies
clavicle	collar bone
cleft lip	uni- or bi-lateral failure of fusion of the lip, harelip
cleft palate	uni- or bi-lateral failure of fusion of the palate
congenital	referring to conditions that are present at birth, regardless of their causation
congenital rubella syndrome	malformations which are present at birth due to infection of the mother with rubella (german measles) during the early months of pregnancy. Commonly: heart malformations, eye and hearing defects
congenital varicella syndrome	malformations which are present at birth due to infection of the mother with varicella (chicken-pox) during pregnancy
cord prolapse	a complication in which, after rupture of the membranes, a loop of umbilical cord is found in front of the presenting part
cystic fibrosis of the pancreas	generalized hereditary disorder characterized by signs of chronic lung and pancreatic disease
D and C	dilatation and curettage. A minor procedure involving dilatation of the cervix* and sampling of the contents of the uterus
deep venous thrombosis	blood clot formation in the deep veins of the legs
diabetes (mellitus)	metabolic disorder producing high blood sugar levels
diaphragmatic hernia	hole in the membrane separating the chest and abdominal cavities
disproportion	disparity between the maternal pelvis and the fetal head

Down syndrome

Trisomy 21 or 'mongolism'. Typically: mental retardation, skin fold around the eyes suggesting slanted eyes, depressed nose, single crease in palm of hand, muscle hypotonia

eclampsia

convulsions in the course of severe pre-eclampsia*

ectodermal dysplasia

rare hereditary condition marked by a smooth glossy skin, absent sweat glands and defective hair formation; may also include prominent eye-brows and mental retardation

ectopic pregnancy

extra-uterine pregnancy

Erb palsy

upper brachial* plexus palsy resulting in raising, turning out, and flexion of the arm

facial nerve palsy

Bell palsy: peripheral facial paralysis resulting in characteristic distortion of the face

fetal alcohol syndrome

fetal disorder, caused by alcohol consumption by the mother during the pre-natal period, characterized by intra-uterine and postnatal growth retardation and mental retardation

fetal distress

collective term for states of fetal jeopardy, commonly used in labour in the presence of meconium* stained amniotic fluid, deviations of the fetal heart rate, or fetal acidosis

fetal hydantoin syndrome

syndrome of congenital abnormalities caused by maternal ingestion of the anti-convulsant hydantoin (phenytoin) which may manifest as craniofacial abnormalities, small fingers, growth and mental retardation.

fistula

an abnormal passage or communication, usually between two internal organs, or leading from an internal organ to the surface of the body

footling breech presentation

one or both feet precede the buttocks

forceps

instrument used for the assisted delivery of a baby, consisting of two blades which can be applied around the fetal skull, allowing traction on the skull

gastroschisis	congenital opening of the abdominal cavity
gestational diabetes	diabetes* appearing during pregnancy
glaucoma	condition of the eye characterized by increased intra-ocular pressure
glucose loading test	screening test for diabetes*
glucose tolerance test	definitive test for the diagnosis of diabetes*
group B streptococci	micro-organisms commonly found in the genital tract
haemolytic disease of the newborn	disorder resulting from the increased breakdown of red blood cells commonly caused by rhesus sensitization*
haemophilia	hereditary bleeding disorder
haemorrhage	copious blood loss
hepatitis	inflammation of the liver which may be caused by infection, drugs, or metabolic disorders
HIV	human immunodeficiency virus
hirsutism	abnormal hairiness
HPV	human papilloma (wart) virus
hydrancephaly	complete or almost complete absence of the cerebral hemispheres (brain tissue), the space they normally occupy being filled with fluid
hydrocephaly	condition characterized by abnormal accumulation of fluid in the cranial vault, accompanied by enlargement of the head and atrophy of the brain
hyperbilirubinemia	excess bilirubin, a breakdown product of blood, in the bloodstream. Excess levels may cause kernicterus*
hypertension	raised blood pressure
hypoxia	lack of oxygen
hysterectomy	removal of the uterus
imperforate anus	congenitally closed anus
induction of labour	artificial stimulation of the onset of labour by mechanical procedures or drug administration
intracranial haemorrhage	bleeding inside the head
intrapartum	during labour
intraventricular haemorrhage	bleeding into the ventricles of the brain

JLP	juvenile laryngeal papillomatosis, benign tumours on an infant's vocal cords
kernicterus	condition with severe neural symptoms including mental retardation and deafness, associated with hyperbilirubinaemia*
Kielland forceps	type of obstetrical forceps, commonly used to rotate and deliver the fetal head
laminectomy	excision of part of a spinal vertebrum
macrosomic	enlarged body
malpresentation	fetal presentation other than by the head
meconium	fetal faeces
meningitis	inflammation of the membranes covering the brain
meningomyelocoele	protrusion of a part of the spinal cord through a defect in the spinal column
miscarriage	abortion, termination of a pregnancy before viability
multicystic-leuco-encephalo-malacia	cystic softening of the brain
necrotizing enterocolitis	severe inflammation of the bowel
neonatal	pertaining to the first four weeks after birth
neural tube	spinal cord
nuchal scanning	ultrasonic scanning of the fetal neck used as a screening test for chromosomal abnormalities
obstructed labour	non-progressive labour with failure of descent of the presenting part
occipital presentation	the head of the fetus is acutely flexed and the back of the head delivers first
occipito anterior	the back of the head is directed anteriorly
occipito posterior	the back of the head is directed posteriorly
oedema	accumulation of fluid in the tissues
oestriol estimation	measurement of a hormone produced during pregnancy, formerly used as a measure of fetal wellbeing
oligohydramnios	reduction of the volume of amniotic fluid*
perinatal	period of time shortly before birth until the seventh day of life
perinatal death	stillbirth or death within the first seven days of life

placenta	the afterbirth; intra-uterine organ which establishes communication between the mother and child
placenta praevia	atypical localization of the placenta in the lower part of the uterus
pre-eclampsia	pregnancy-induced hypertension: characterized by hypertension*, proteinuria*, and generalized oedema*
polycystic kidneys	kidneys containing multiple cysts
polyhydramnios	abnormally increased volume of amniotic fluid*
post partum haemorrhage	excessive bleeding after the birth of the baby
progestogen	female hormone
proteinuria	protein in the urine
pulmonary embolism	clot of blood or other fluid lodging in the lungs
quickening	fetal movements become obvious to the mother
respiratory distress syndrome	acute breathing difficulties in the newborn, usually due to prematurity
retrolental fibroplasia	an eye disorder leading to blindness with formation of vascular fibrous tissue behind the lens, most commonly seen in premature infants given high doses of oxygen
retained placenta	delayed expulsion of the placenta, usually defined as greater than 15 minutes after delivery of the child
rhesus antibodies	antibodies to the rhesus antigens in the blood type
rhesus sensitized	the mother has developed rhesus antibodies which can act against a rhesus positive fetus
rubella	German Measles: viral infection, commonly presenting with mild rash
rupturing membranes	artificially breaking the bag of membranes surrounding the fetus
sepsis	infection
shoulder dystocia	fetal shoulder remains caught above the pelvic brim after delivery of the head
sickle cell anaemia	hereditary, genetically determined haemolytic anaemia

spastic quadriplegia	stiff paralysis of all four limbs
spina bifida	developmental anomaly characterized by a defect in the bones around the spinal cord
stillbirth	the birth of a dead child
subdural haematoma	blood clot beneath the dural covering of the brain
suprapubic pressure	pressure applied above the pubic arch. This pressure may be used to help deliver the fetal shoulders
sympathetic ophthalmia	granulomatous lesion of the eye characteristically involving both eyes
syphilis	a contagious venereal disease
Tay Sachs disease	hereditary disease causing blindness and mental retardation
toxaemia	pre-eclampsia*
toxoplasmosis	parasitic disease which may cause fetal abnormalities
transverse lie	the fetus lies transversely in the uterus
triple test	screening test for Down syndrome*
trisomy	the presence of an additional chromosome
trisomy 21	Down syndrome*
twin-to-twin transfusion syndrome	intra-uterine blood transfusion from one fetus to the other resulting in excess blood in one fetus and anaemia in the other
ultrasound	diagnostic procedure with the use of ultrasound waves. Obstetric ultrasounds may be performed either by the abdominal or vaginal route
vacuum suction (extraction)	method of delivery of the fetal skull by the application of a cup to the skull, the creation of a vacuum within the cup and traction to the cup
varicella	chicken-pox
ventriculomegaly	enlargement of the ventricles of the brain
vertex	the top of the head

Glossary of Legal Terms

administrator
person responsible for administering the estate of a deceased person

appellate
an appellate court is one that hears an appeal

balance of probabilities
proof of an event on the balance of probabilities requires proof that it was more likely than not that it occurred

battery
inflicting unlawful personal violence on another

cause of action
basis on which a legal action is brought. For example, negligence is the cause of action when injury has resulted from the breach of a duty of care

child protection
child protection proceedings are proceedings in which an abused or neglected child is brought before a children's, juvenile, or family court in order to determine whether action should be taken to protect the child, perhaps by removing him or her from home

chose in action
a chose is a thing and a chose in action is a future entitlement

cognizable
recognizable. A legally cognizable injury is one that the law will recognize for the purposes of a damages claim

common law
term having many meanings. For the purposes of this book the most important is the body of law emerging from judicial decisions, as opposed to that embodied in legislation

consortium
right of a husband or wife to the affection and companionship of the other

contributory negligence
carelessness by a plaintiff which has contributed to the harm which he or she has suffered as a result of a defendant's negligence. If a defendant can show such carelessness, the damages payable might be reduced

damages
sum of money granted to a plaintiff as compensation. Damages can take the form of special damages and general damages. Special damages are those that are capable of calculation, such as medical expenses. General damages are

	those that can only be estimated, such as compensation for pain and suffering and loss of enjoyment of life
decedent	deceased person
declaration	order by a court declaring a person's rights. A court making such an order can be described as making a declaratory judgment or giving declaratory relief
defendant	person against whom a legal claim is brought
dissenting	of a judge or judgment. A dissenting judgment is one that disagrees in whole or in part with the judgment of the majority. It thus does not represent the law as expressed by the majority
en ventre sa mere	in the mother's uterus
felony	a serious crime
feticide	killing a fetus
homicide	killing a human being
injunction	court order restraining or compelling a particular action
joint liability	two or more persons whose negligence has injured another can be jointly liable to pay damages
locus standi	legal standing: a person's right to appear before and be heard by a court or other tribunal
manslaughter	unlawful killing of a human being, not amounting to murder
majority	of judges or a judgment. A judgment by a majority of judges in a case represents the statement of law for which the case stands as an authority
mens rea	guilty mind. The mental state required to establish criminal guilt (such as intention or recklessness in murder)
mitigation of damages	reduction of damages. A plaintiff who sues for damages has a duty to mitigate his or her losses
parens patriae	parent of the nation. A term originally used to describe the role of the sovereign, but now applied to the role assumed by a court to provide protection to a vulnerable person such as a child
plaintiff	person bringing a legal claim against another
qua	as, in the capacity of
solatium	award of money as a solace for hurt feelings

tort	a wrong. The term is generally used to describe a wrong (such as defamation, assault, trespass, or negligence) in respect of which damages can be sought. It is also used to describe the branch of the law dealing with such wrongs. The adjective is tortious, as in tortious acts and tortious liability
tortfeasor	one guilty of a tort
trial court	court which initially tries an action, as opposed to an appellate court
vel non	or not
vicarious liability	liability of one person for the acts or omissions of another
ward/wardship	a child who is made a ward of court is brought under the protection of the court

Index